THEORIES OF DEVIANCE

THEORIES OF DEVIANCE

Fourth Edition

Edited by
STUART H. TRAUB AND CRAIG B. LITTLE
State University College at Cortland
Cortland, New York

F.E. Peacock Publishers, Inc.
Itasca, Illinois

Contents

Preface to the Fourth Edition

Our objective in presenting the fourth edition of *Theories of Deviance* is to expose students to theoretical foundation statements from diverse perspectives within sociology. We believe that a large part of the writing and research concerning deviance emanates from a relatively small number of key passages, which ought to be read in the original. We also see substantial value in offering students a varied, as opposed to uniform, theoretical background for the study of deviance. We believe that examination of seminal contributions heightens critical insight and appreciation for the complexities of theory construction, and the selections in the first seven chapters represent what we see as the mainstream approaches in the sociology of deviance. In this edition we also consider some more recent approaches in a new final chapter entitled "New Directions in Deviance Theory."

Because these principles continue to be important to us in our own teaching and in the organization of this edition, many of the readings in prior editions also appear in the fourth. Analysis and Critique sections at the end of each chapter have also been retained to extend the scope and flexibility of the text as a teaching tool. These theoretical critiques expose students to the scholarly debate that is central to the theoretical development of any field, and they tie the perspectives together and help demonstrate the cumulative development of theories of deviance. We have also retained the essay on social structure and anomie from Robert Merton's *Social Theory and Social Structure* (Macmillan, 1968), rather than the more frequently reprinted article of the same title from the *American Sociological Review* (October 1938). In this case, we believe that students can acquire a fuller understanding of anomie theory by reading Merton's more complete formulation of it.

This edition does differ from the third edition in important ways, however. Chapter 8 on new directions includes selections on biology and deviance, the medicalization of deviance, rational choice and routine activity theories, and a feminist analysis of deviance theory. There is also a new selection on a theory of family violence in Chapter V. Selections from Chapters VII and VIII in the third edition have been combined in a new chapter under the title "Politics and Class in the Study of Deviance." The Introduction to the text and the chapter introductions have all been revised and expanded.

While there is considerable theoretical breadth in the readings selected for the fourth edition of *Theories of Deviance*, we do not think this will confuse students with disorganized eclecticism. The flow of the text follows the development of the sociology of deviance from 19th-century functionalism to the societal reaction school, and the last chapter is devoted to what we perceive to be emerging issues in the literature. In selecting the readings, we have sought to provide students with an opportunity to recognize cross-fertilization, compatibility, and counterpoint among the theorists whose works are represented.

We gratefully acknowledge the authors and publishers who have granted permission for their works to appear in this text. We continue to be indebted to Richard A. Dodder, Richard J. Gelles, and Arnold S. Linsky for their insightful reaction to the selections and chapter introductions in the first edition. In addition, we extend our appreciation to Barry Cohen, Robert G. Dunn, and James D. Orcutt for their reactions and suggestions concerning the second edition. This edition benefited from the comments of Phil Brown, Joseph Harry, Ronald Kramer, and Richard O'Toole. Once again, we express our gratitude to Ted Peacock, publisher, and Gloria Reardon, editor, of F. E. Peacock Publishers for making this latest enterprise a pleasant one for us. Thanks also to Lisa Smith for her assistance in securing author and publisher permissions, as well as to Gilda Haines for carefully typing the manuscript.

Finally, as we have noted in the preceding editions of this text, the order of our names on the cover was decided by a flip of the coin and does not imply that either of us contributed more than the other. Thus, we share equally the responsibility for its success and its shortcomings.

Stuart H. Traub
Craig B. Little

Introduction

Explaining why some members of a society deviate from its commonly accepted rules, or norms, seems always to have fascinated students of society. Plato apparently wrote *The Republic* to explain the aberrant behavior of many Athenians, which he interpreted as symptomatic of an underlying social pathology.[1] From this early utopian treatise to Auguste Comte's call for a separate science of society, and continuing to the present, social philosophers often have been concerned with investigating the relationship between social order and disorganization, social control and individual liberty, and conformity and deviance.

In this text we have not reached back into the earliest foundations of theories of deviance for our selections. We readily acknowledge that our starting point is somewhat arbitrary. Nevertheless, we want to make it clear that concern for deviance is not an exclusively modern phenomenon, and theories to explain it are not entirely contemporary developments. As American sociologists, we are mainly interested in the origins and themes found in American sociological theories of deviance.[2] In Chapters I–VII we sketch broadly the evolution of the theories we have chosen to present and define the relationships among them. In Chapter VIII, we introduce several more recent, emergent theories or approaches.

The French sociologist Emile Durkheim (1858 1917) has surely had a more profound impact on American sociological theorizing about deviance than any other classical European theorist. It was Durkheim who most dramatically gave sociology its raison d'etre by arguing that social facts such as crime rates or suicide rates can be explained adequately only by analyzing uniquely social conditions such as the breakdown in the norms that operate throughout a society. Durkheim's approach was radically sociological because it required

1

the theorist to remain at the societal level of analysis for explanations of social phenomena, rather than searching for presumed psychological or biological causes.

Durkheim was clearly opposed to the analytical individualism of his contemporaries, such as the Italian criminologist Cesare Lombroso (1836–1909). Lombroso, generally acknowledged as the founding father of modern criminology, is best known for his biological theory of atavism, which states that criminals are evolutionary throwbacks to earlier stages of physiological development. This aspect of Lombroso's theory is an attempt to explain deviant behavior at the individual level of analysis by reference to the most rudimentary biological determinism, wherein social environmental factors are all but ignored. Durkheim, to the contrary, argued that the existence of crime in a society could be explained without searching for pathology-producing anomalies in the individual's physical makeup or psyche. Crime, according to Durkheim, actually helps to maintain a society as a healthy, surviving entity. Thus crime can be accounted for in terms of the functions it performs or the positive contributions it makes to the adaptation and survival of the society. As used in Chapter I, therefore, the term *functionalist* refers to the theory of Durkheim and those who have built upon it.

David Matza has remarked that the principal legacy of the functionalists was to establish and extend "appreciation" for deviance as a natural product of human collectivities.[3] In doing this, functionalism contributed to the elimination of the initial assumption that deviance is a pathological trait of the individual or society that must be "cured." However, this contribution was not directly introduced into American sociology until many years after it was developed. Durkheim did most of his writing during the late 1800s, but it did not have a significant impact on American sociology until Talcott Parsons directed attention to its importance to the functionalist approach in the mid-1900s.

When the earliest American sociologists, members of the Department of Sociology at the University of Chicago, studied social problems and deviance in the 1920s and 1930s, they organized most of their work around the idea of social pathology. The Chicago School, as it became known, included theorists such as W. I. Thomas, Robert E. Park, Ernest Burgess, Clifford R. Shaw, Henry D. McKay, Robert E. L. Faris, and H. Warren Dunham, who were reacting to the rapidly increasing heterogeneity or diversity of American society during the first third of the 20th century. For these writers, social ills such as juvenile delinquency, suicide, and mental illness were essentially urban problems that could best be understood through a detailed analysis of the urban setting. Their ecological studies of Chicago neighborhoods established that differential rates of deviance could be found in various areas of the city, and, further, that the areas with high rates of deviance were socially disorganized.

Social disorganization theory, which is considered in Chapter II, proposed that rapid immigration, industrialization, and urban growth were tending to disrupt or inhibit stable, well-organized patterns of life guided by mutually agreed-upon rules of conduct. As the rules disintegrated during periods of rapid social change, standards to regulate people's behavior and relationships were weakened or disappeared. The resulting social disorganization in areas that were also characterized by other problems such as transient populations, speculative real estate practices, and high rates of disease created fertile ground for social pathologies.

The functionalist and social disorganization perspectives converged in American sociology, if somewhat indirectly, in Robert K. Merton's anomie theory, which is discussed in Chapter III. The idea of anomie was first proposed by Durkheim, who conceptualized it as a condition of "normlessness" in a society. Not unlike the Chicago theorists, Durkheim suggested that as social rules become less binding due to decreasing consensus in a complex society, people feel less constrained by social norms. As a consequence, evidence of deviance such as crime and suicide is bound to increase. This social condition was called anomie, or normlessness, by Durkheim, while the Chicagoans spoke of it as social disorganization. Both hypothesized that increasing rates of deviance are the result of structural conditions in society.

Merton was even more explicit in specifying the societal sources of the breakdown in consensus about norms and the conditions under which different types of deviance are most likely to emerge. His argument was that when virtually all people in a society are taught to seek culturally prescribed goals (such as occupational success and money) that everyone cannot attain because some do not have access to the legitimate means by which these goals can be secured, the result will be higher rates of deviance. A prediction derived from Merton's theory is that deviance will be more prevalent in the lower socioeconomic classes than in the higher classes because people in the lower classes are less likely to have available to them the legitimate means to success. Therefore, they will be under more strain to use illegitimate means to attain the culturally prescribed ends.

Every sociologist was not satisfied with this sort of reasoning, however. One who reacted strongly to it was Edwin H. Sutherland, who offered as an alternative to Merton's analysis his theory of differential association, presented in Chapter IV. Sutherland raised two important points about anomie theory. First was the question of how it explains crime outside the lower class (generally, white-collar crime). Middle- and upper-class people presumably have access to the legitimate means to success, yet there is evidence of a great deal of white-collar crime. The problem then is how to explain crime among those who do have access to legitimate means of success. Second, Sutherland's standard of an adequate theory was that it must apply to every single case it is supposed to explain. The method of theory construction he used was analytic induction, which amounts to stating a hypothesis or series of hypotheses about a phenomenon such as crime. If a single case of crime, for example, fails to correspond to a hypothesis about crime, the theorist must redefine that case as something other than a crime. If this is not possible, the hypothesis must be modified to include the case.

Sutherland's theory of differential association states that individuals learn criminal techniques and motives in association with others, in exactly the same ways they learn noncriminal behavior and motives. The primary condition for criminal behavior, therefore, is association with others whose definitions are favorable to violation of the law. Sutherland's theory is a very general one which is intended to explain criminal behavior in any social class. In contrast to Merton's anomie theory, which deals with rates of deviant behavior under specified circumstances, differential association theory distinctly focuses on the interactive (learning) aspects of becoming deviant. The other theorists discussed in Chapter IV also draw attention to how, under certain conditions, people go through a process of learning, rationalizing, and decision making that makes deviant behavior possible.

In control theory, presented in Chapter V, attention was shifted from exclusive concern with the processes involved in becoming deviant to factors considered important in maintaining conformity. The focal point in understanding deviance clearly then is explaining why the majority of people do not deviate. Control theorists pointed out that while individuals are motivated to violate norms, most people are contained or controlled by various forces from acting upon these impulses. Rather than explaining deviance in terms of interactional patterns, as sociological learning theory proposed, they viewed deviance as an outcome of inadequate socialization. Most individuals conform because internal and external controls are strong, routes to goal achievement are not restricted, and there is a high degree of social integration, as evidenced by the individual's attachment to others and the normative structure of society. Deviance results where these controlling mechanisms break down or deteriorate.

A number of theorists, also identified with the University of Chicago tradition, have continued the emphasis on interactive processes as well as the effects of control agents on deviance production, but they have focused on the consequences for the individual of being tagged with the label *deviant*. What happens, for example, when a young person who engages in a prank or minor crime is arrested and officially declared a juvenile delinquent by the courts? The consensus of the labeling theorists presented in Chapter VI is that a person who is officially labeled a deviant:

1. May be more inclined to see himself or herself as an outcast and act accordingly.
2. May be blocked from the opportunity to take on nondeviant roles due to an unsavory reputation.
3. Because of 1 and 2, may be more likely to seek the moral and physical support of others who have been similarly stigmatized with a deviant label.

As a result, subcultural communities of deviants are formed.

Labeling theory concentrates on the results of interaction between the alleged deviant and those in the society who seek to sanction such an individual. The theory clearly suggests that social control agents, rather than reducing or "correcting" the behavior they are reacting to, may in fact be perpetuating this behavior and solidifying the labeled person's self-image as deviant. At the same time, these agents are creating conditions under which deviant subcultures flourish at the group level by establishing the need of those so labeled for physical and moral support from others.

One effect of labeling theory has been to shift attention away from the individual deviant and toward those persons and groups in society with the power to designate certain individuals or actions as deviant. This is also the emphasis in Chapter VII, "Politics and Class in the Study of Deviance." Several theorists concerned with the conflict and political aspects of deviance offer a response to the question of how certain types of behavior come to be defined as "deviant" in the first place. An essential assumption is that, as Durkheim carefully noted in his functionalist argument, no behavior is *inherently* deviant. Rather, conformity and deviance are established by adherence to or disregard for the standards adopted by a particular group, community, or society. A behavior is officially classified as deviant when it harms or offends those with enough political power to pass a law against it, or when labeling that behavior as deviant appears to serve their interests. Joseph F. Gusfield (Reading 26) argues that the ability of members of an interest group to define as deviant the behavior commonly associated with members of some outgroup itself significantly enhances their own power, prestige, and status.

The other theorists represented in Chapter VII not only expand upon these views, they offer critical reactions to all of the theories presented in the preceding chapters. These theorists contend that too often in the past, theorizing about deviance concentrated on a "dramatic deviant," without examining carefully the role of advanced capitalism in the production of deviance and deviant populations. The selections by Richard Quinney, Alexander Liazos, and Steven Spitzer represent recent attempts to redress this class bias in deviance theories by explicitly taking into account the role of the state and the political-economic elite in the creation of deviance and the formulation and application of criminal law.

From one viewpoint, theories of deviance that emphasize politics and class appear to be an outright rejection of their predecessors. However, it is important to note the debt these critics owe to the targets of their sometimes harsh words. Durkheim insisted on the need to look further than the biological or psychological constitution of the individual for explanations of deviance. The American social pathologists who looked for causes in social disorganization also sought to understand deviance at the societal level of analysis. While C. Wright Mills (Reading 8) condemned the middle-class ideology of social pathologists for placing too much blame on the individual, even he would probably have agreed with Matza's conclusion that both Durkheim and the Chicagoans made a major breakthrough in their search for societal causes of deviance.[5]

We have suggested that functionalism and social disorganization theory seemed to merge in Merton's extension of Durkheim's anomie theory. In Merton's "Social Structure and Anomie" (Reading 10), the explanation of deviance remains very much at the societal level, with the imbalance between cultural goals and institutionalized means described as the key causal factor. Sutherland's alternative to Merton's approach was the theory of differential association (Reading 13), which proposed an explanation of crime at the interactional level of analysis. A somewhat different view was expressed by control theorists, who sought to explain deviance as a failure of adequate socialization to conform rather than as the outcome of socialization in deviant subcultures and the acceptance of nonconforming values. The labeling perspective on deviance emerged from a concern about the consequences of being labeled for the individual. Theorists in the political-economic tradition have emphasized instead the dynamics behind the labeling of certain behaviors as deviant. The common thread linking all of these theories is a movement toward an understanding of deviance as more than simply the bizarre, idiosyncratic, pathological behavior of individuals that, like illness or disease, must be treated and cured.

Chapter VIII, "New Directions in Deviance Theory," presents some recent developments in the field. The first selection reviews contemporary biological perspectives on deviance, reflecting the reemergence of an approach that was influential in the earlier part of the 20th century. Today, however, the study of biological determinants of antisocial behavior goes far beyond genetic explanations to include biochemistry, psychophysiology, and psychopharmacology. The results of such work are being treated cautiously by responsible researchers who are careful to give recognition to the likely interactions among biological, psychological, and sociological factors.

Increased attention to the biology of crime, no matter how prudent, inevitably nudges theories of deviance and their associated social policies toward the medical domain, however. To the extent that deviance is conceptualized as an illness, the medical establishment becomes the arena for its control. The "medicalization of deviance" has been a major theme in the orchestration of social control during the latter half of this century. A medical explanation of deviance necessarily assumes a lack of responsibility on the part of the aberrant individual for his or her behavior. Those who are sick or biologically "flawed" can hardly be held accountable for behavior that flows from their "pathology." In sharp contrast to biological approaches, the "rational choice" perspective assumes that deviants make calculated decisions about how they act, and the most effective deterrents to deviance are those that are designed to minimize opportunities to deviate.

The underlying differences between the biological and rational-choice approaches date back more than 100 years. Positivists sought explanations for behavior that employ factors such as genetic constitution over which the individual has no control. Classical theorists sought explanations that emphasize humans' capacities to make conscious choices about how they behave. The unresolved debate between positivist and classical theorists continues today: How much deviance is *determined by* factors or forces over which the individual has no control? And how much is a result of individuals exercising *free will* in a rational calculation to commit deviant acts?

Contemporary theories of deviance are also being shaped by feminist theorists. In this perspective, established male-oriented deviance theories are critiqued, and distinctly sociological concerns that particularly affect the lives of women and children, such as poverty, racism, child abuse, patriarchal domination, and other forms of sexism, are reintroduced as central to an understanding of deviance in American society.

NOTES

1. Robert Nisbet, *The Social Philosophers* (New York: Thomas Y. Crowell Co., 1973), pp. 105–117.
2. Throughout this book we use the term *theory* in its broadest sense. For our purposes, a theory is a proposed explanation of an event or phenomenon.
3. David Matza, *Becoming Deviant* (Englewood Cliffs, N.J.: Prentice-Hall, 1969), pp. 31–37.
4. Talcott Parsons, *The Structure of Social Action* (New York: McGraw-Hill Book Co., 1937).
5. Matza, *Becoming Deviant*, pp. 31–32.

I

Functionalism

To say that something fulfills a function usually means that it serves some useful purpose or need. The function of the circulatory system in higher animals, for example, is to satisfy the body's needs for nourishment, oxygen, and the removal of waste (among other things). It seems reasonable to assume that in the ever-evolving biological world, most organs or systems that are developed and retained by any particular species exist because they satisfy some need; that is, they serve some function. If they were not functional, they would not persist. This sort of reasoning found expression in Darwin's theory of natural selection in biology and is the foundation of the functional perspective on deviance in sociology.

The major hypothesis in sociological functionalism is that recurrent social processes serve the function of maintaining a social system. With the larger whole (for example, a society or social group) as the unit of analysis, a social pattern is studied in terms of its functions or the positive part it plays in the adaptation and persistence of the system. As in Darwin's biological model, in sociology functionalism posits that established social institutions or patterns of behavior would cease to exist if they did not serve some positive function. All social activities therefore are studied with an eye to how they contribute to the maintenance and continuity of the society or group. For the functionalist, recurrent patterns of both conventional and deviant behavior exist and survive in groups and societies because each serves some useful purpose or need.

Reading 1 is from Emile Durkheim's classic book *The Rules of Sociological Method*, originally published in 1895. Durkheim begins by observing that crime and criminals are present in all societies. Therefore, he reasons, crime must serve some social function; otherwise, it would not universally exist. The members of various societies may choose very different types of behavior to label as crime, but because every society contains criminals, crime must be functional for all societies.

According to Durkheim, crime contributes to the maintenance of a society by providing its members with targets for collective moral outrage, and this creates greater cohesion in the society. Further, when the criminal is tried and punished, crime provides a dramatic opportunity to publicize the rules of the society to all of its members. But criminal activity can also be a catalyst for positive social change. For example, American civil rights demonstrators in the middle of the 20th century frequently broke the existing segregation laws as a form of protest. In the eyes of the law at that time, those activists were criminals, but their law-breaking paved the way for a more just, defensible legal order. For Durkheim, the criminal or deviant should be regarded not as an unsociable being or a parasite but as one who plays a definite and necessary social role. Durkheim's apparent homage to the criminal anticipates what David Matza has called the "appreciation" of deviance and deviants.[1] Rather than viewing deviance as a pathology to be cured, the sociologist is encouraged to search for ways that nonconforming behavior contributes to the maintenance of the social group.

Reading 2, "The Sociology of Prostitution," by Kingsley Davis, closely follows Durkheim's functionalist reasoning in response to an initial question: "Why is it that a practice so thoroughly disapproved ...can yet flourish so universally?" He begins by observing that to maintain order in most societies it is necessary to link sexuality to social ends such as bearing and rearing children. In this way the "morally legitimate" practice of sex is restricted to the family. However, since sexual behavior in males is not inherently limited by any social arrangement, prostitution is a functional institution because it provides them with an opportunity for impersonal, transitory sex outside the family.[2] This reasoning leads to the conclusion that prostitution functions as a safety valve for the short-term gratification of sexual desires without the elaborate, intense social commitment of marriage. According to Davis's functionalist analysis, the family and prostitution are complementary institutions.

In Reading 3, "On the Sociology of Deviance," Kai T. Erikson discusses the functions of deviance in the community. He describes communities as "boundary maintaining"; following Durkheim's lead, he argues that deviants are necessary in a community to help identify the normative boundaries (rules) for its members. In this way the deviant actually contributes to community stability. Erikson describes a social scheme in which the deviant would appear as a natural product of group differentiation. He is not a bit of debris spun out by faulty social machinery, but a relevant figure in the community's overall division of labor. He implies, however, that the deviant cannot alone create or maintain a community's normative boundaries. Identification and maintenance of normative boundaries result from interactions (often dramatic, such as those in trials or executions) between deviants on the one hand and the community's agents of social control (police, judges, psychiatrists, educators, religious leaders and the like) on the other.

The functionalist argument introduced by Durkheim was one of the earliest contributions to a sociology of deviant behavior, and it has continued to have considerable impact on the development of deviance theory up to the present. At the same time, it has been subject to a broad range of criticisms, such as those offered by Melvin Tumin in Reading 4, the Analysis and Critique section for this chapter. While functionalists now seem to recognize that any institution or behavior can have eufunctions (positive consequences) and dysfunctions (negative consequences), there is no way to decide definitively the total, overall impact of behavior such as crime. Indeed, one is always forced back to the question: For what or for whom is a given institution or activity functional? Crime is after all at the same time eufunctional for the criminal and dysfunctional for the victim.

Tumin also notes that functional analysis is usually ahistorical. That is, it rarely examines the effects of an institution or pattern of behavior over time. And finally, although functional analysts claim to take a neutral, value-free, scientific approach, there seems to be an underlying bias in their work that implicitly brands some social problems (such as prostitution) as "good," by emphasizing their positive functions, and others (such as poverty and racism) as "bad," by emphasizing their negative functions.

NOTES

1. David Matza, *Becoming Deviant* (Englewood Cliffs, N.J.: Prentice-Hall, 1969), pp. 30–37.
2. A careful reader will immediately note a sexist bias in the Davis piece which implies that only *men* might need to have available an institution such as prostitution to satisfy their sexual appetites outside marriage. Thus an apparently value-free, neutral theoretical analysis may have behind it the hidden agenda of justifying existing social arrangements —a position Melvin Tumin alludes to in the Analysis and Critique selection for this chapter (Reading 4).

1   The Normal and the Pathological
EMILE DURKHEIM

Crime is present not only in the majority of societies of one particular species but in all societies of all types. There is no society that is not confronted with the problem of criminality. Its form changes; the acts thus characterized are not the same everywhere; but, everywhere and always, there have been men who have behaved in such a way as to draw upon themselves penal repression. If, in proportion as societies pass from the lower to the higher types, the rate of criminality, i.e., the relation between the yearly number of crimes and the population, tended to decline, it might be believed that crime, while still normal, is tending to lose this character of normality. But we have no reason to believe that such a regression is substantiated. Many facts would seem rather to indicate a movement in the opposite direction. From the beginning of the [nineteenth] century, statistics enable us to follow the course of criminality. It has everywhere increased. In France the increase is nearly 300 per cent. There is, then, no phenomenon that presents more indisputably all the symptoms of normality, since it appears closely connected with the conditions of all collective life. To make of crime a form of social morbidity would be to admit that morbidity is not something accidental, but, on the contrary, that in certain cases it grows out of the fundamental constitution of the living organism; it would result in wiping out all distinction between the physiological and the pathological. No doubt it is possible that crime itself will have abnormal forms, as, for example, when its rate is unusually high. This excess is, indeed, undoubtedly morbid in nature. What is normal, simply, is the existence of criminality, provided that it attains and does not exceed, for each social type, a certain level, which it is perhaps not impossible to fix in conformity with the preceding rules.[1]

Here we are, then, in the presence of a conclusion in appearance quite paradoxical. Let us make no mistake. To classify crime among the phenomena of normal sociology is not to say merely that it is an inevitable, although regrettable phenomenon, due to the incorrigible wickedness of men; it is to affirm that it is a factor in public health, an integral part of all healthy societies. This result is, at first glance, surprising enough to have puzzled even ourselves for a long time. Once this first surprise has been overcome, however, it is not difficult to find reasons explaining this normality and at the same time confirming it.

In the first place crime is normal because a society exempt from it is utterly impossible. Crime, we have shown elsewhere, consists of an act that offends certain very strong collective sentiments. In a society in which criminal acts are no longer committed, the sentiments they offend would have to be found without exception in all individual consciousnesses, and they must be found to exist with the same degree as sentiments contrary to them. Assuming that this condition could actually be realized, crime would not thereby disappear; it would only change its form, for the very cause which would thus dry up the sources of criminality would immediately open up new ones.

Indeed, for the collective sentiments which are protected by the penal law of a people at a specified moment of its history to take possession of the public conscience or for them to acquire a stronger hold where they have an insufficient grip, they must acquire an intensity greater than that which they had hitherto had. The community as a whole must experience them more vividly, for it can acquire from no other source the greater force necessary to control these individuals who formerly were the most refractory. For murderers to disappear, the horror of bloodshed must become greater in those social strata from which murderers are recruited; but, first it must become greater throughout the entire society. Moreover, the very absence of crime would directly contribute to produce this horror; because any sentiment seems much more respectable when it is always and uniformly respected.

One easily overlooks the consideration that these strong states of the common consciousness cannot be thus reinforced without reinforcing at the same time the more feeble states, whose violation previously gave birth to mere infraction of convention—since the weaker ones are only the prolongation, the attenuated form, of the stronger. Thus robbery and simple bad taste injure the same single altruistic sentiment, the respect for that which is another's. However, this same sentiment is less grievously offended by bad taste than by robbery; and since, in addition, the average consciousness has not sufficient intensity to react keenly to the bad taste, it is treated with greater tolerance. That is why the person guilty of bad taste is merely blamed, whereas the thief is punished. But, if this sentiment grows stronger, to the point of silencing in all consciousnesses the inclination which disposes man to steal, he will become more sensitive to the offenses which, until then, touched him but lightly. He will react against them, then, with more energy; they will be the object of greater opprobrium, which will transform certain of them from the simple moral faults that they were and give them the quality of crimes. For example, improper contracts, or contracts improperly executed, which only incur public blame or civil damages, will become offenses in law.

Imagine a society of saints, a perfect cloister of exemplary individuals. Crimes, properly so called, will there be unknown; but faults which appear venial to the layman will create there the same scandal that the ordinary offense does in ordinary consciousnesses. If, then, this society has the power to judge and punish, it will define these acts as criminal and will treat them as such. For the same reason, the perfect and upright man judges his smallest failings with a severity that the majority reserve for acts more truly in the nature of an offense. Formerly, acts of violence against persons were more frequent than they are today, because respect for individual dignity was less strong. As this has increased, these crimes have become more rare; and also, many acts violating this sentiment have been introduced into the penal law which were not included there in primitive times.[2]

In order to exhaust all the hypotheses logically possible, it will perhaps be asked why this unanimity does not extend to all collective sentiments without exception. Why should not even the most feeble sentiment gather enough energy to prevent all dissent? The moral consciousness of the society would be present in its entirety in all the individuals, with a vitality sufficient to prevent all acts offending it— the purely conventional faults as well as the crimes. But a uniformity so universal and absolute is utterly impossible; for the immediate physical milieu in which each one of us is placed, the hereditary antecedents, and the social influences vary from one individual to the next, and consequently diversify consciousnesses. It is impossible for all to be alike, if only because each one has his own organism and that these organisms occupy different areas in space. That is why, even among the lower peoples, where individual originality is very little developed, it nevertheless does exist.

Thus, since there cannot be a society in which the individuals do not differ more or less from the collective type, it is also inevitable that, among these divergences, there are some with a criminal character. What confers this character upon them is not the intrinsic quality of a given act but that definition which the collective conscience lends them. If the collective conscience is stronger, if it has enough authority practically to suppress these divergences, it will also be more sensitive, more exacting; and, reacting against the slightest deviations with the energy it otherwise displays only against more considerable infractions, it will attribute to them the same gravity as formerly to crimes. In other words, it will designate them as criminal.

Crime is, then, necessary; it is bound up with fundamental conditions of all social life, and by that very fact it is useful, because these conditions of which it is a part are themselves indispensable to the normal evolution of morality and law.

Indeed, it is no longer possible today to dispute the fact that law and morality vary from one social type to the next, nor that they change within the same type if the conditions of life are modified. But, in order that these transformations may be possible, the collective sentiments at the basis of morality must not be hostile to change, and consequently must have but moderate energy. If they were too strong, they would no longer be plastic. Every pattern is an obstacle to new patterns, to the extent that the first pattern is inflexible. The better a structure is articulated, the more it offers a healthy resistance to all modification; and this is equally true of functional, as of anatomical, organization. If there were no crimes, this condition could not have been fulfilled; for such a hypothesis presupposes that collective sentiments have arrived at a degree of intensity unexampled in history. Nothing is good indefinitely and to an unlimited extent. The authority which the moral conscience enjoys must not be excessive; otherwise no one would dare criticize it, and it would too easily congeal into an immutable form. To make progress, individual originality must be able to express itself. In order that the originality of the idealist whose dreams transcend his century may find expression, it is necessary that the originality of the criminal, who is below the level of his time, shall also be possible. One does not occur without the other.

Nor is this all. Aside from this indirect utilty, it happens that crime itself plays a useful role in this evolution. Crime implies not only that the way remains open to necessary changes but that in certain cases it directly prepares these changes. Where crime exists, collective sentiments are sufficiently flexible to take on a new form, and crime sometimes helps to determine the form they will take. How many times, indeed, it is only an anticipation of future morality—a step toward what will be! According to Athenian law, Socrates was a criminal, and his condemnation was no more than just. However, his crime, namely, the independence of his thought, rendered a service not only to humanity but to his country. It served to prepare a new morality and faith which the Athenians needed, since the traditions by which they had lived until then were no longer in harmony with the current conditions of life. Nor is the case of Socrates unique; it is reproduced periodically in history. It would never have been possible to establish the freedom of thought we now enjoy if the regulations prohibiting it had not been violated before being solemnly abrogated.

At that time, however, the violation was a crime, since it was an offense against sentiments still very keen in the average conscience. And yet this crime was useful as a prelude to reforms which daily became more necessary. Liberal philosophy had as its precursors the heretics of all kinds who were justly punished by secular authorities during the entire course of the Middle Ages and until the eve of modern times.

From this point of view the fundamental facts of criminality present themselves to us in an entirely new light. Contrary to current ideas, the criminal no longer seems a totally unsociable being, a sort of parasitic element, a strange and unassimilable body, introduced into the midst of society.[3] On the contrary, he plays a definite role in social life. Crime, for its part, must no longer be conceived as an evil that cannot be too much suppressed. There is no occasion for self-congratulation when the crime rate drops noticeably below the average level, for we may be certain that this apparent progress is associated with some social disorder. Thus, the number of assault cases never falls so low as in times of want.[4] With the drop in the crime rate, and as a reaction to it, comes a revision, or the need of a revision in the theory of punishment. If, indeed, crime is a disease, its punishment is its remedy and cannot be otherwise conceived; thus, all the discussions it arouses bear on the point of determining what the punishment must be in order to fulfil this role of remedy. If crime is not pathological at all, the object of punishment cannot be to cure it, and its true function must be sought elsewhere.

NOTES

1. From the fact that crime is a phenomenon of normal sociology, it does not follow that the criminal is an individual normally constituted from the biological and psychological points of view. The two questions are independent of each other. This independence will be better understood when we have shown, later on, the difference between psychological and sociological facts.
2. Calumny, insults, slander, fraud, etc.
3. We have ourselves committed the error of speaking thus of the criminal, because of a failure to apply our rule (*Division du travail social*, pp. 395–96).
4. Although crime is a fact of normal sociology, it does not follow that we must not abhor it. Pain itself has nothing desirable about it; the individual dislikes it as society does crime, and yet it is a function of normal physiology. Not only is it necessarily derived from the very constitution of every living organism, but it plays a useful role in life,

for which reason it cannot be replaced. It would, then, be a singular distortion of our thought to present it as an apology for crime. We would not even think of protesting against such an interpretation, did we not know to what strange accusations and misunderstandings one exposes oneself when one undertakes to study moral facts objectively and to speak of them in a different language from that of the layman.

2   *The Sociology of Prostitution*
KINGSLEY DAVIS

I

To the theoretical even more than to the applied sociologist, prostitution sets a profound problem: Why is it that a practice so thoroughly disapproved, so widely outlawed in Western civilization, can yet flourish so universally? Social theorists, in depicting the power of collective representations and the mores as determinants of human conduct, have at times implied that institutions are maintained only by *favorable* attitudes and sentiments. But prostitution is a veritable institution, thriving even when its name is so low in public opinion as to be synonymous with "the social evil." How, then, can we explain its vitality?

A genuine explanation must transcend the facile generalizations both of those who believe that prostitution can be immediately abolished, and of those who think vaguely that human nature and the lessons of history guarantee its immortality. In what follows I have tried to give a sociological analysis—to describe the main features of the interrelational system binding prostitution to other institutions (particularly those involving sexual relations). Such an analysis, though brief and tentative, seems to carry us a long way toward explaining not only the heedless vitality of commercial promiscuity, but also the extreme disrepute in which it and its personnel are held.[1]

II

Human sexuality, as Zuckerman and others have demonstrated, bears a striking resemblance to the sexual behavior of monkeys and apes.[2] This resemblance rests upon two orders of facts—the first physiological, the second sociological.

Due to her physical nature, the primate female, as distinct from her lower mammalian sisters, is always sexually responsive. She experiences a regular menstrual cycle but has no period of anoestrus (com-

Reprinted from Kingsley Davis, "The Sociology of Prostitution," *American Sociological Review*, vol. 2 (1937), pp. 744–755.

plete unresponsiveness to sexual stimuli), whereas among most mammals below the primates the female does have, instead of a menstrual cycle, a period of anoestrus alternating with a period of oestrus (heat). This difference has a fundamental effect upon the nature of primate (including human) society. *It introduces sex as a permanent element in social life and insures constant association of the two sexes.*[3]

Moreover, the primates possess a more complex sensori-motor equipment than the lower mammals, and have a longer period of infancy. These possessions, plus their continuous sexuality, facilitate more extensive *conditioning* of the sexual response, with the result that among the primates sexual behavior is not simply automatic, but is associated with numerous stimuli that are themselves non-sexual. Whereas among lower mammals the sexual responses can scarcely be conditioned at all, *the primates may be said to prostitute their sex by introducing sexual stimuli into intrinsically non-sexual situations.*[4] In other words, the sexual responses of apes and monkeys may have no connection with sexual appetite, being used, instead, as a means of obtaining material advantages.

What leads to this sexual conditioning? Here we turn from physical to social facts. Reproductive physiology and neural complexity permit the conditioning, but sociological forces alone compel it. Zuckerman points out that monkeys and apes live in a society characterized by a system of dominance.[5] Every ape or monkey enjoys within his social group a precarious position determined by the interrelation of his own dominant characteristics with those of his fellows. The degree of his dominance determines how his bodily appetites will be satisfied— amount of food, number of females, and degree of safety he will enjoy. Primates, both male and female, adapt themselves to such a hostile social system partly through sexual reactions. Since they are always to some extent sexually excitable and the stimuli capable of releasing this sexuality [are] enormously varied, it is easy for their sexual behavior to become adjusted to the rigors of a social life based upon dominance. Hence all situations which evoke sexual prostitution are alike in so far as they allow an animal some advantage that it would otherwise be denied. For example, if a weaker animal secures food and a stronger one comes to take it away from him, the weaker animal immediately presents himself sexually, no matter whether his sex be the same or different. If he thus diverts the dominant animal's attention, he can swallow his food.[6] In such cases it is by means of his sex reactions that a monkey obtains advantages to which he is not entitled by his position in the scale of dominance.

These facts are mentioned for the purpose of bringing out the basic principle in prostitution—namely, the use of sexual stimulation in a system of dominance to attain non-sexual ends. They are not mentioned for the purpose of drawing an analogy between animal and human society or speculating as to the origin of human institutions. Zuckerman himself has adequately warned us against this error.[7] Yet "the socio-sexual activities of sub-human primates are much further removed from those of the lower mammal than from those of man."[8] Among both man and the apes the same physiological and sociological factors appear to be present, at least to the degree that among both can be found the fundamental trait of prostitution.

III

We cannot, however, define human prostitution simply as the use of sexual responses for an ulterior purpose. This would include a great portion of all social behavior, especially that of women. It would include marriage, for example, wherein women trade their sexual favors for an economic and social status supplied by men.[9] It would include the employment of pretty girls in stores, cafes, charity drives, advertisements. It would include all the feminine arts that women use in pursuing ends that require men as intermediaries, arts that permeate daily life, and, while not generally involving actual intercourse, contain and utilize erotic stimulation.

But looking at the subject in this way reveals one thing. The basic element in what we actually call prostitution—the employment of sex for non-sexual ends within a competitive-authoritative system— characterizes not simply prostitution itself but all of our institutions in which sex is involved, notably courtship and wedlock. Prostitution therefore resembles, from one point of view, behavior found in our most respectable institutions. It is one end of a long sequence or gradation of essentially similar phenomena that stretches at the other end to such approved patterns as engagement and marriage. What, then, is the difference between prostitution and these other institutions involving sex?

The difference rests at bottom upon the functional relation between society and sexual institutions. It is through these institutions that erotic gratification is made dependent on, and subservient to, certain cooperative performances inherently necessary to societal continuity. The sexual institutions are distinguished by the fact that although they all provide gratification, they do not all tie it to the same social functions.[10] This explains why they are differently evaluated in the eyes of the mores.

The institutional control of sex follows three correlative lines. First, it permits, encourages, or forces various degrees of sexual intimacy within specific customary relations, such as courtship, concubinage, and marriage. Second, to bolster this positive control, it discourages sexual intimacy in all other situations, e.g., when the persons are not potential mates or when they are already mated to other persons.[11] Finally, in what is really a peculiar category of the negative rules, it absolutely prohibits sexual relations in certain specified situations. This last form of control refers almost exclusively to incest taboos, which reinforce the first-named (positive) control by banishing the disruptive forces of sexual competition from the family group.

These lines of control are present no matter what the specific kind of institutional system. There may be monogamy, polygyny, or concubinage; wife exchange or religious prostitution; premarital chastity or unchastity. The important point is not the particular kind of concrete institution, but the fact that without the positive and negative norms there could be no institutions at all. Since social functions can be performed only through institutional patterns, the controls are indispensable to the continuance of a given social system.

Of the numerous functions which sexual institutions subserve, the most vital relate to the physical and social reproduction of the next generation. If we ask, then, which sexual institutions in a society receive the greatest support from law and mores, we must point to those which facilitate the task of procreating and socializing the young. It follows that sanctioned sexual relations are generally those within these (or auxiliary) institutions, while unsanctioned relations are those outside them.

Marriage and its subsidiary patterns constitute the chief cultural arrangement through which erotic expression is held to reproduction. It is accordingly the most respectable sexual institution, with the others diminishing in respectability as they stand further away from wedlock. Even the secondary forms of erotic behavior—flirtation, coquetry, petting, etc.—have their legitimate and their illegitimate settings. Their legitimate aspects may be subsumed under courtship, leading to marriage; but if indulged in for themselves, with no intention of matrimony, they are devoid of the primary function and tend to be disapproved. If practised by persons married to others, they are inimical to reproductive relations already established and are more seriously condemned. If practised by close relatives within the primary family, they represent a threat to the very structure of the reproductive institution itself, and are stringently tabooed. These attitudes are much more rigid with regard to actual intercourse, not solely because coitus is the essence of the sexual but because it has come to symbolize the *gemeinschaft* type of relation present in the family. With this in mind we can add that when coitus is practised for money its social function is indeterminate, secondary, and extrinsic. The buyer clearly has pleasure and not reproduction in mind. The seller may use the money for any purpose. Hence unless the money is earmarked for some legitimate end (such as the support of a family, a church, or a state), the sexual relation between the buyer and seller is illegitimate, ephemeral, and condemned. It is pure commercial prostitution.

Of course many sexual institutions besides courtship and marriage receive, in various cultures and to varying degrees, the sanction of society. These generally range themselves between marriage and commercial prostitution in the scale of social approval. They include concubinage, wife exchange, and forms of sanctified prostitution.[12] Religious prostitution, for example, not only differs from wedlock, but also from commercial prostitution; the money that passes is earmarked for the maintenance of the church, the woman is a religious ministrant, and the act of intercourse is sacred.[13] Similar considerations apply to that type of prostitution in which the girl obtains a dowry for her subsequent marriage. Whenever the money earned by prostitution is spent for a sanctified purpose, prostitution is in higher esteem than when it is purely commercial. If, for instance, prostitution receives more approval in Japan than in America, it is significant that in the former country most of the *joro* enter the life because their family needs money; their conduct thereby subserves the most sacred of all Japanese sentiments—filial piety.[14] The regulation of prostitution by governments and churches in such a way that at least some of the proceeds go towards their maintenance is control of sex behavior at a second remove. By earmarking a part of the money, the bought intercourse is made to serve a social function; but *this function is not intrinsically related to coitus in the same way as the procreative function of the family.*

In commercial prostitution both parties use sex for an end not socially functional, the one for pleasure, the other for money. To tie intercourse to sheer physical pleasure is to divorce it both from reproduction and from the sentimental primary type of relation which it symbolizes. To tie it to money, the most impersonal and atomistic type of reward possible, with no stipulation as to the use of this medium, does the same thing. Pure prostitution is promiscuous, impersonal. The sexual response of the prostitute does not hinge upon the personality of the other party, but upon the reward. The response of the customer likewise does not depend upon the particular identity of the prostitute, but upon the bodily gratification. On both sides the relationship is merely a means to a private end, a contractual rather than a personal association.

These features sharply distinguish prostitution from the procreative sexual institutions. Within a group organized for bearing and rearing children bonds tend to arise that are cemented by the condition of relative permanence and the sentiment of personal feeling, for the task requires long, close, and sympathetic association. Prostitution, in which the seller takes any buyer at the price, necessarily represents an opposite kind of erotic association. It is distinguished by the elements of hire, promiscuity, and emotional indifference—all of which are incompatible with primary or *gemeinschaft* association.

The sexual appetite, like every other, is tied to socially necessary functions. The function it most logically and naturally relates to is procreation. The nature of procreation and socialization is such that their performance requires institutionalized primary-group living. Hence the family receives the highest estimation of all sexual institutions in society, the others receiving lower esteem as they are remoter from its *gemeinschaft* character and reproductive purpose. Commercial prostitution stands at the lowest extreme; it shares with other sexual institutions a basic feature, namely the employment of sex for an ulterior end in a system of differential advantages, but it differs from them in being mercenary, promiscuous, and emotionally indifferent. From *both* these facts, however, it derives its remarkable vitality.

IV

Since prostitution is a contractual relation in which services are traded (usually in terms of an exchange medium) and sex is placed in an economic context,[15] it is strange that modern writers have made so much of the fact that the "social evil" has economic causes.[16] One might as well say, with equal perspicacity, that retail merchandising has economic causes. Prostitution embraces an economic relation, and is naturally connected with the entire system of economic forces. But to jump from this truism to the conclusion that prostitution can be abolished by eliminating its economic causes is erroneous. Economic causes seldom act alone, and hence their removal is seldom a panacea.

The causal ramifications of commercial coitus extend beyond the economic sphere. At least three separable but related problems must be recognized: (1) the causes of the existence of prostitution; (2) the causes of the *rate* or *amount* of prostitution; and (3) the causes of *any particular individual's entrance into, or patronage of,* prostitution. The existence of prostitution seems related both to the physiological nature of man and to the inherent character of society, both of which include more than the sheer economic element. These basic factors, constantly operative, account for the ubiquity of prostitution, but not for the variations in its rate. This second problem must be dealt with in terms of the specific institutional configuration existing at the time, in which economic factors are highly but not exclusively important. Finally, any particular person's connection with prostitution is a result of his or her own unique life-history, into which an infinite variety of strands, some economic and some not economic, are woven. The factors in (1) and (2) are operative in the individual's life, but are never sufficient in themselves to explain his or her behavior.

These issues are generally confused by those who believe that by removing alleged economic causes one can abolish prostitution. Let us follow their arguments further, considering first the removal of economic causes within the capitalist system, and second the removal of them in a non-capitalist system.

1. A frequent proposal for abolition under capitalism is that the salaries of working girls be raised. This proposal, which ignores the demand side, assumes that girls enter prostitution through economic necessity—a parodoxical assumption, for if it is true it indicates that prostitution must have other than economic causes and remedies, while if it is untrue this particular proposal is fallacious.

Why should a girl enter prostitution *only* through economic necessity? Is the occupation so arduous? On the contrary, we often speak as if harlots "would rather prostitute themselves than work."[17] It is even true that some women enjoy the intercourse they sell. From a purely economic point of view prostitution comes perilously near the situation of getting something for nothing. The woman may suffer no loss at all, yet receive a generous reward, resembling the artist who, though paid for his work, loves it so well that he would paint anyway. Purely from the angle of economic return, the hard question is not why so many women become prostitutes, but why so few of them do. The harlot's return is not primarily a reward for abstinence, labor, or rent. It is primarily a reward for loss of social standing. She loses social esteem because our moral system condemns the commercialization of intercourse. If, then, she refuses to enter the profession until forced by sheer want, the basic cause of her hesitation is not economic but moral. Only when the moral condition is assumed, do wages or economic want take on any importance. Prostitution, therefore, is not purely a matter of economic factors alone.

We have taken for granted that in the face of moral condemnation, only starvation wages can drive girls into prostitution. Actually this is only partly true. But even if it were, the proposal to eliminate prostitution by raising wages would not work. In a competitive system, as soon as the salaries of working girls are increased, the supply of prostitutes diminishes. The resulting scarcity increases the effective demand, in the form of price, which rises as the supply diminishes. (The demand rests upon a constant imperative need, not always conveniently satisfiable by substitutes.) With the rise in price, working girls even with good salaries will be tempted into the profession. Moreover, it will be possible for more women to live on the proceeds of prostitution alone—without performing arduous labor in store or restaurant. The net result will be as much prostitution as before, and in terms of actual money invested and changing hands, there may be more.[18] The facts seem to bear out these theoretical propositions, for apparently prostitution does not increase greatly with low wages for women nor decrease with high, although other factors, such as the correlation between men's wages and women's wages, must be considered in working out the relationship.[19]

Finally, this proposal does not touch the demand for prostitution. To touch demand requires more than economic changes; for even less than the woman who sells herself, is the man who buys guided by economic motives. His motivation, as we shall see later, springs from bio-social forces for which the economic are simply instrumental.

2. In her book, *Red Virtue*, Ella Winter has a chapter entitled "Ending Prostitution," at the head of which stands a quotation from a Soviet physician: "Soviet life does not permit of prostitution." Widely accepted and frequently repeated, this belief is taken for granted as one of the main values of a communist as against a capitalist system.

There can be little doubt, I think, that in Soviet cities prostitution has diminished in the last few years, but there can be grave doubt that it has been ended or that the diminution has resulted solely from the abolition of private property. Not only did prostitution exist before capitalism arose, but capitalist countries themselves have frequently tried to stop private ownership of prostitutes for purposes of profit. They have consistently legislated against third parties—pimps, real estate owners, bookers—only to find that none of these measures succeed.[20] In short, capitalism, like communism, has tried in the case of prostitution to negate the basic capitalistic principle.

Doubtless it is harder to eliminate the business aspect of prostitution (organized syndicates operated by third parties) in a capitalist system where business prevails anyway, than it is in a communist system where all business is frowned upon. In the latter, profit-making organizations possess high visibility, are easily hunted down. But this does not mean that unorganized prostitution, in which seller, manager, and worker are all rolled into the same person, cannot thrive.

Payment for prostitution need not be in terms of money. It may be in terms of privilege, power, food, clothing, almost any form of exchangeable value. These exchangeable commodities (and some medium of exchange) must exist in any complex society, no matter what the system of political control, because the specialized producers must mutually exchange their surpluses. At the same time there is, in any society, a system of privilege, authority, and dominance. Some have rights, belongings, and talents that others lack. Soviet Russia may have abolished the capitalistic alignment of classes, but it has not abolished social class; the class principle is inherent in the nature of social organization.[21] In the Soviet system, as in any other social structure, there lies the eternal possibility and the eternal incentive to trade sexual favor for non-sexual advantage. This becomes clearer after analyzing the demand side of prostitution.

V

When outlawed, prostitution falls into one peculiar category of crime—a type exceedingly hard to deal with—in which one of the willful parties is the ordinary law-abiding citizen. This kind of crime, of which bootlegging is the archetype, is supported by the money and behavior of a sizeable portion of the citizenry, because in it the citizen receives a service. Though the service is illegitimate, the citizen cannot be held guilty, for it is both impossible and inadvisable to punish half the populace for a crime. Each citizen participates in vital institutional relationships—family, business, church, and state. To disrupt all of these by throwing him in jail for a mere vice would be, on a large scale, to disrupt society.[22] But the eagerness of otherwise decent citizens to receive the illicit service attests powerful forces behind the demand element.

On the one hand, the demand is the result of a simple biological appetite. When all other sources of gratification fail, due to defects of person or circumstance, prostitution can be relied upon to furnish relief. None of the exacting requirements of sex attraction and courtship are necessary. All that is needed is the cash, and this can be obtained in a thousand ways. Prostitution is the most malleable, the most uninvolved form of physical release.

But in addition to the sheer desire for sexual satisfaction, there is the desire for satisfaction in a particular (often an unsanctioned) way.

> The common and ignorant assumption that prostitution exists to satisfy the gross sensuality of the young unmarried man, and that if he is taught to bridle gross sexual impulse or induced to marry early the prostitute must be idle, is altogether incorrect....The prostitute is something more than a channel to drain off superfluous sexual energy, and her attraction by no means ceases when men are married, for a large number of men who visit prostitutes, if not the majority, are married. And alike whether they are married or unmarried the motive is not one of uncomplicated lust.[23]

The craving for variety, for perverse gratification, for mysterious and provocative surroundings, for intercourse free from entangling cares and civilized pretense, all play their part.

Prostitution, again by its very nature, is aptly suited to satisfy this second side of demand. The family, an institution of status rather than contract, limits the variety, amount, and nature of a person's satisfactions. But since with the prostitute the person is paying for the privilege, he is in a position to demand almost anything he wants. The sole limitation on his satisfactions is not morality or convention, but his ability to pay the price. This is an advantage which commercial recreation generally has over kinds handled by other institutional channels.

There is no reason to believe that a change in the economic system will eliminate either side of demand. In any system the effective demand as expressed by price will vary with current economic and moral forces, but the underlying desire both for sheer gratification and for gratification in particular ways will remain impregnable.

VI

We can imagine a social system in which the motive for prostitution would be completely absent, but we cannot imagine that the system could ever come to pass. It would be a regime of absolute sexual freedom, wherein intercourse were practised solely for the pleasure of it, by both parties. This would entail at least two conditions: *First*, there could be no institutional control of sexual expression. Marriage, with its concomitants of engagement, jealousy, divorce, and legitimacy, could not exist. Such an institution builds upon and limits the sexual urge, making sex expression contingent upon non-sexual factors, and thereby paving the way for intercourse against one's physical inclination. *Second*, all sexual desire would have to be mutually complementary. One person could not be erotically attracted to a non-responsive person, because such a situation would inevitably involve frustration and give a motive for using force, fraud, authority, or money to induce the unwilling person to co-operate.

Neither of these conditions can in the nature of things come to pass. As we have seen, every society attempts to control, and for its own survival must control, the sexual impulse in the interest of social order, procreation, and socialization. Moreover, all men are not born handsome nor all women beautiful. Instead there is a perfect gradation from extremely attractive to extremely unattractive, with an unfavorable balance of the old and ugly. This being the case, the persons at the wrong end of the scale must, and inevitably will, use extraneous means to obtain gratification.[24]

While neither the scale of attractiveness nor the institutionalization of sex are likely to disappear, it is possible that the *particular form of institutionalization* may change. The change may be in the direction of greater sex freedom. Such a change must inevitably affect prostitution, because the greater the proportion of free, mutually pleasurable intercourse, the lesser is the demand for prostitution. This, it seems, is the true explanation of the diminution of prostitution in Soviet Russia.[25]

The conclusion that free intercourse for pleasure and friendship rather than for profit is the greatest enemy of prostitution emerges logically from our statement that a basic trait of prostitution is the use of sex for an ulterior purpose. Should one wish to abolish commercial coitus, one would have to eliminate this trait. This proposition, however, is unacceptable to moralists, because, as we saw, the underlying trait of prostitution is also a fundamental feature of reputable sexual institutions, and intercourse for sheer pleasure is as inimical to our sacred institutions as it is to the profane one of mercenary love. Though Lecky's suggestion that harlotry sustains the family is perhaps indefensible, it seems true that prostitution is not so great a danger to the family as complete liberty.

Where the family is strong, there tends to be a well-defined system of prostitution and the social regime is one of status. Women are either part of the family system, or they are definitely not a part of it. In the latter case they are prostitutes, members of a caste set apart. There are few intermediate groups, and there is little mobility. This enables the two opposite types of institutions to function side by side without confusion; they are each staffed by a different personnel, humanly as well as functionally distinct. But where familial controls are weak, the system of prostitution tends to be poorly defined. Not only is it more nearly permissible to satisfy one's desire outside the family, but also it is easier to find a respectable member of society willing to act as partner. This is why a decline of the family and a decline of prostitution are both associated with a rise of sex freedom. Women, released from close family supervision, are freer to seek gratification outside it. The more such women, the easier it is for men to find in intimate relations with them the satisfactions formerly supplied by harlots. This is why the unrestricted indulgence in sex for the fun of it by both sexes is the greatest enemy, not only of the family, but also of prostitution.

Not only in Soviet Russia has pleasurable sex freedom invaded and reduced prostitution, but also in America and England, where "amateur competition" is reputedly ruining the business of streetwalkers and call girls.[26] This indicates that independently of communism or capitalism, due to factors more profound than mere economic organization, sex freedom can arise and, having arisen, can contribute to the decline of prostitution. Its rise seems correlated with the growth of individualization in an increasingly complex society where specialization, urbanism, and anonymity prevail—factors which are also inimical to reproductive institutions of the familial type.

But even if present trends continue, there is no likelihood that sex freedom will ever displace prostitution. Not only will there always be a set of reproductive institutions which place a check upon sexual liberty, a system of social dominance which gives a motive for selling sexual favors, and a scale of attractiveness which creates the need for buying these favors, but prostitution is, in the last analysis, economical. Enabling a small number of women to take care of the needs of a large number of men, it is the most convenient sexual outlet for an army, and for the legions of strangers, perverts, and physically repulsive in our midst. It performs a function, apparently, which no other institution fully performs.

NOTES

1. Disapproval of purely commercial (i.e., non-religious, non-familial) prostitution is extraordinarily widespread. Though the distinction is seldom made, disapproval of the prostitute is one thing and disapproval of the institution another. In Mongolian China, for example, prostitution was viewed with no serious disfavor, but the prostitute was treated with contempt. H. Ellis, *Studies in the Psychology of Sex*, vol. 6, p. 236.

2. S. Zuckerman, *The Social Life of Monkeys and Apes*, New York: Harcourt, Brace, 1932; G. V. Hamilton, "A Study of Sexual Tendencies in Monkeys and Baboons," *Journal of Animal Behavior*, 4, 1914, 295–318; H. C. Bingham, "Sex Development in Apes," *Comparative Psychology Monographs*, 5, 1928, 1–161.

3. Zuckerman, *op. cit.*, especially chaps. iii, iv, vi, viii, ix.

4. *Ibid.*, p. 152. Zuckerman repeatedly uses the term prostitution to describe this behavior, as do others.

5. *Op. cit.*, pp. 312–314. The generalized picture given in these few paragraphs of course does not apply in detail to all genera of infra-human primates, nor does it do full justice to Zuckerman's qualifications.

6. *Ibid.*, pp. 240–242.

7. *Ibid.*, chap. ii. It is worth noting that while Westermarck and his followers have used the anecdotal literature on anthropoid life to bolster their theory of universal monogamy in human society, it is just as logical to argue from the scientific literature on the same subject that

prostitution is equally rooted in primate nature and hence equally universal in human life.

8. Zuckerman, *op. cit.*, p. 313.

9. She also contributes other services, though these are sometimes difficult to see in our middle-class society.

10. Any institution appeals to *several* motives and performs *several* functions. Strictly speaking, therefore, there are no purely sexual institutions. Wedlock is not simply sexual, not simply procreative, not simply economic. It is all three. This linking of the sexual impulse to other things is not haphazard, but shows a high degree of structural and functional articulation, demonstrable on two different but interdependent levels: the life organization of persons, and the institutional organization of society. Sex, like other elements in human nature, is drawn into the integration, and is thus controlled.

11. For the emotional attitudes maintaining these norms see K. Davis, "Jealousy and Sexual Property," *Social Forces*, 14, March 1936, 395–405.

12. Concubinage evidently stands part way between prostitution and marriage. It resembles marriage in that it is relatively permanent, partly reproductive, and implies a *gemeinschaft* bond; but it resembles prostitution in that the woman more definitely and exclusively exists for the sexual pleasure of the master, and her social position is inferior to that of the wife. E. Westermarck, *History of Human Marriage*, 5th ed., New York: Allerton Book Co., 1922; D. Kulp, *Country Life in South China*, Columbia University Press, 1925, chap. vi; Pearl Buck's novel, *The Good Earth*. Wife exchange differs from marriage in that its social function appears to be not propagation, but the cementing of solidarity within a group. W. Bogoras, *The Chukchee*, American Museum of Natural History Memoirs, 7, 602–607.

13. G. May, "Prostitution," *Encyclopedia of Social Science*; Westermarck, *op. cit.*, vol. 1, pp. 219 *et seq.*

14. A. M. Bacon, *Japanese Girls and Women*, Boston: Houghton Mifflin Co., 1902, pp. 175–178; D. C. McMurtrie, "Prostitution in Japan," *New York Medical Journal*, February 8, 1913.

15. Yet no economist has written a treatise on it in the same way that economists write treatises on banking and the coal industry. See L. Robbins, *An Essay on the Nature and Significance of Economic Science* (rev. ed., 1935), 28.

16. *Encyclopaedia Sexualis*, article on "Prostitution," p. 667.

17. W. L. George's novel, *Bed of Roses*, vividly contrasts the hard life of the working girl with the easy life of the prostitute.

18. Another difficulty is that the wages of prostitution are already far above the wages of ordinary women's work. "No practicable rise in the rate of wages paid to women in ordinary industries can possibly compete with the wages which fairly attractive women of quite

ordinary ability can earn by prostitution" (Ellis, *op. cit.*, p. 263). The discrepancy between the wages of ordinary work and the wages of prostitution results from the fact, as indicated above, that the latter is morally tabooed. This increases the wage differential until there is *every economic* incentive for entering.

19. The wages of one class cannot be arbitrarily raised without affecting those of all other earners. Under competition women's wages could scarcely be raised without also raising men's. Men would then have more to spend on prostitution. A. Depres, *La prostitution en France* (1883), concluded that as wealth and prosperity increased, so did prostitution.

20. See M. L. Ernst's chapter in *The Sex Life of the Unmarried Adult*, ed. by Ira S. Wile, Vanguard Press, 1934, especially pp. 230–231. Also, Flexner, *op. cit.*, chap iv.

21. By social class is meant the differential sharing of the values (educational, artistic, recreational, political as well as economic) of the community by different segments of the population. The Party in Russia forms one class, enjoying privileges and responsibilities not shared by the rest of the people. The same is true of the skilled as against the unskilled workers.

22. "The professional prostitute, being a social outcast, may be periodically punished without disturbing the usual course of society; no one misses her while she is serving out her turn—no one, at least, about whom society has any concern. The man, however, is something more than partner in an immoral act: he discharges important social and business relations...He cannot be imprisoned without deranging society." Flexner, *op. cit.*, p. 108.

23. Ellis, *op. cit.*, pp. 295–296. The author describes in detail the various motives involved.

24. The question, why are women more frequently prostitutes than men (and why is male prostitution usually homosexual), leads to interesting conclusions. Men have authority and economic means in greater amount than women. They are, therefore, in a more favorable position to offer inducements, and this inequality characterizes not only prostitution but all relations in which sex is used for ulterior ends. But why the inequality? Women are perhaps physically weaker, and they are naturally connected more closely with procreation and socialization. The latter constitute their main functions. Hence women must depend upon sex for their social position much more than men do. A man who relies on sex for his status has at best an inferior station, while in many ways the very best that a woman can do is through use of her sexual charms.

Out of the female population there are relatively few who are young and pretty. These are in great demand by the *entire* male population, who use every inducement, sanctioned and otherwise.

Most of the women are taken by the inducement of a definite social status—marriage. They are thereby withdrawn from competition. But the remainder are in a very favorable position so far as profiting by their attractiveness is concerned. They can, therefore, make much more if they enter an occupation in which their sexual appeal is the intrinsic quality desired. One such occupation is prostitution.

25. Communist theory has generally condemned the private family. At the same time Russia emancipated women, making them less dependent upon their sexual qualities, more dependent upon their citizenship and productiveness. Both the incentive for them to settle in a permanent marital relation and the incentive to indulge in prostitution were therefore lessened.

26. G. M. Hall, *op. cit.*, p. 168. "Prostitution," *Encyclopaedia Sexualis*, p. 665. J. K. Folsom, *The Family*, New York: Wiley, 1934, chap. xiii.

3 *On the Sociology of Deviance*
KAI T. ERIKSON

Human actors are sorted into various kinds of collectivity, ranging from relatively small units such as the nuclear family to relatively large ones such as a nation or culture. One of the most stubborn difficulties in the study of deviation is that the problem is defined differently at each one of these levels: behavior that is considered unseemly within the context of a single family may be entirely acceptable to the community in general, while behavior that attracts severe censure from the members of the community may go altogether unnoticed elsewhere in the culture. People in society, then, must learn to deal separately with deviance at each one of these levels and to distinguish among them in his own daily activity. A man may disinherit his son for conduct that violates old family traditions or ostracize a neighbor for conduct that violates some local custom, but he is not expected to employ either of these standards when he serves as a juror in a court of law. In each of the three situations he is required to use a different set of criteria to decide whether or not the behavior in question exceeds tolerable limits.

In the next few pages we shall be talking about deviant behavior in social units called "communities," but the use of this term does not mean that the argument applies only at that level of organization. In theory, at least, the argument being made here should fit all kinds of human collectivity—families as well as whole cultures, small groups as well as nations—and the term "community" is only being used in this context because it seems particularly convenient.[1]

The people of a community spend most of their lives in close contact with one another, sharing a common sphere of experience which makes them feel that they belong to a special "kind" and live in a special "place." In the formal language of sociology, this means that communities are boundary maintaining: each has a specific territory in the world as a whole, not only in the sense that it occupies a defined region of geographical space but also in the sense that it takes over a particular niche in what might be called cultural space and develops its own "ethos" or "way" within that compass. Both of these dimensions of group space, the geographical and the cultural, set the community apart as a special place and provide an important point of reference for its members.

When one describes any system as boundary maintaining, one is saying that it controls the fluctuation of its constituent parts so that the whole retains a limited range of activity, a given pattern of constancy and stability, within the larger environment. A human community can be said to maintain boundaries, then, in the sense that its members tend to confine themselves to a particular radius of activity and to regard any conduct which drifts outside that radius as somehow inappropriate or immoral. Thus the group retains a kind of cultural integrity, a voluntary restriction on its own potential for expansion, beyond that which is strictly required for accommodation to the environment. Human behavior can vary over an enormous range, but each community draws a symbolic set of parentheses around a certain segment of that range and limits its own activities within that narrower zone. These parentheses, so to speak, are the community's boundaries.

Now people who live together in communities cannot relate to one another in any coherent way or even acquire a sense of their own stature as group members unless they learn something about the boundaries of the territory they occupy in social space, if only because they need to sense what lies beyond the margins of the group before they can appreciate the special quality of the experience which takes place within it. Yet how do people learn about the boundaries of their community? And how do they convey this information to the generations which replace them?

To begin with, the only material found in a society for marking boundaries is the behavior of its members—or rather, the networks of interaction which link these members together in regular social relations. And the interactions which do the most effective job of locating and publicizing the group's outer edges would seem to be those which take place between deviant persons on the one side and official agents of the community on the other. The deviant is a person whose activities have moved outside the margins of the group, and when the community calls him to account for that vagrancy it is making a statement about the nature and placement of its boundaries. It is declaring how much variability and diversity can be tolerated within the group before it begins to lose its distinctive shape, its unique identity. Now there may be other moments in the life of the group which perform a similar service: wars, for instance, can publicize a group's boundaries by drawing attention to the line separating the group from an adversary, and certain kinds of religious ritual, dance ceremony, and other traditional pageantry can dramatize the difference between "we" and "they" by portraying a symbolic encounter between the two. But on the whole, members of a community inform one another about the placement of their boundaries by participating in the confrontations which occur when persons who venture out to the edges of the group are met by policing agents whose special business it is to guard the cultural integrity of the community. Whether these confrontations take the form of criminal trials, excommunication hearings, courts-martial, or even psychiatric case conferences, they act as boundary-maintaining devices in the sense that they demonstrate to whatever audience is concerned where the line is drawn between behavior that belongs in the special universe of the group and behavior that does not. In general, this kind of information is not easily relayed by the straightforward use of language. Most readers of this paragraph, for instance, have a fairly clear idea of the line separating theft from more legitimate forms of commerce, but few of them have ever seen a published statute describing these differences. More likely than not, our information on the subject has been drawn from publicized instances in which the relevant laws were applied—and for that matter, the law itself is largely a collection of past cases and decisions, a synthesis of the various confrontations which have occurred in the life of the legal order.

It may be important to note in this connection that confrontations between deviant offenders and the agents of control have always attracted a good deal of public attention. In our own past, the trial and punishment of offenders were staged in the market place and afforded the crowd a chance to participate in a direct, active way. Today, of course, we no longer parade deviants in the town square or expose them to the carnival atmosphere of a Tyburn, but it is interesting that the "reform" which brought about this change in penal practice coincided almost exactly with the development of newspapers as a medium of mass information. Perhaps this is no more than an accident of history, but it is nonetheless true that newspapers (and now radio and television) offer much the same kind of entertainment as public hangings or a Sunday visit to the local gaol. A considerable portion of what we call "news" is devoted to reports about deviant behavior and its consequences, and it is no simple matter to explain why these items should be considered newsworthy or why they should command the extraordinary attention they do. Perhaps they appeal to a number of psychological perversities among the mass audience, as commentators have suggested, but at the same time they constitute one of our main sources of information about the normative outlines of society. In a figurative sense, at least, morality and immorality meet at the public scaffold, and it is during this meeting that the line between them is drawn.

Boundaries are never a fixed property of any community. They are always shifting as the people of the group find new ways to define the outer limits of their universe, new ways to position themselves on the larger cultural map. Sometimes changes occur within the structure of the group which require its members to make a new survey of their territory—a change of leadership, a shift of mood. Sometimes changes occur in the surrounding environment, altering the background against which the people of the group have measured their own uniqueness. And always, new generations are moving in to take their turn guarding old institutions and need to be informed about the contours of the world they are inheriting. Thus single encounters between the deviant and his community are only fragments of an ongoing social process. Like an article of common law, boundaries remain a meaningful point of reference only so long as they are repeatedly tested by persons on the fringes of the group and repeatedly defended by persons chosen to represent the group's inner morality. Each time the community moves to censure some act of deviation, then, and convenes a formal ceremony to deal with the responsible offender, it sharpens the authority of the violated norm and restates where the boundaries of the group are located.

For these reasons, deviant behavior is not a simple kind of leakage which occurs when the machinery of society is in poor working order, but may be, in controlled quantities, an important condition for preserving the stability of social life. Deviant forms of behavior, by marking the outer edges of group life, give the inner structure its special character and thus supply the framework within which the people of the group develop an orderly sense of their own cultural identity. Perhaps this is what Aldous Huxley had in mind when he wrote:

Now tidiness is undeniably good—but a good of which it is easily possible to have too much and at too high a price.... The good life can only be lived in a society in which tidiness is preached and practised, but not too fanatically, and where efficiency is always haloed, as it were, by a tolerated margin of mess.[2]

This raises a delicate theoretical issue. If we grant that human groups often derive benefit from deviant behavior, can we then assume that they are organized in such a way as to promote this resource? Can we assume, in other words, that forces operate in the social structure to recruit offenders and to commit them to long periods of service in the deviant ranks? This is not a question which can be answered with our present store of empirical data, but one observation can be made which gives the question an interesting perspective—namely, that deviant forms of conduct often seem to derive nourishment from the very agencies devised to inhibit them. Indeed, the agencies built by society for preventing deviance are often so poorly equipped for the task that we might well ask why this is regarded as their "real" function in the first place.

It is by now a thoroughly familiar argument that many of the institutions designed to discourage deviant behavior actually operate in such a way as to perpetuate it. For one thing, prisons, hospitals, and other similar agencies provide aid and shelter to large numbers of deviant persons, sometimes giving them a certain advantage in the competition for social resources. But beyond this, such institutions gather marginal people into tightly segregated groups, give them an opportunity to teach one another the skills and attitudes of a deviant career, and even provoke them into using these skills by reinforcing their sense of alienation from the rest of society.[3] Nor is this observation a modern one:

The misery suffered in gaols is not half their evil; they are filled with every sort of corruption that poverty and wickedness can generate; with all the shameless and profligate enormities that can be produced by the impudence of ignominy, the range of want, and the malignity of dispair. In a prison the check of the public eye is removed; and the power of the law is spent. There are few fears, there are no blushes. The lewd inflame the more modest; the audacious harden the timid. Everyone fortifies himself as he can against his own remaining sensibility; endeavoring to practice on others the arts that are practised on himself; and to gain the applause of his worst associates by imitating their manners.[4]

These lines, written almost two centuries ago, are a harsh indictment of prisons, but many of the conditions they describe continue to be reported in even the most modern studies of prison life. Looking at the matter from a long-range historical perspective, it is fair to conclude that prisons have done a conspicuously poor job of reforming the convicts placed in their custody; but the very consistency of this failure may have a peculiar logic of its own. Perhaps we find it difficult to change the worst of our penal practices because we *expect* the prison to harden the inmate's commitment to deviant forms of behavior and draw him more deeply into the deviant ranks. On the whole, we are a people who do not really expect deviants to change very much as they are processed through the control agencies we provide for them, and we are often reluctant to devote much of the community's resources to the job of rehabilitation. In this sense, the prison which graduates long rows of accomplished criminals (or, for that matter, the state asylum which stores its most severe cases away in some back ward) may do serious violence to the aims of its founders, but it does very little violence to the expectations of the population it serves.

These expectations, moveover, are found in every corner of society and constitute an important part of the climate in which we deal with deviant forms of behavior.

To begin with, the community's decision to bring deviant sanctions against one of its members is not a simple act of censure. It is an intricate rite of transition, at once moving the individual out of his ordinary place in society and transferring him into a special deviant position.[5] The ceremonies which mark this change of status, generally, have a number of related phases. They supply a formal stage on which the deviant and his community can confront one another (as in the criminal trial); they make an announcement about the nature of his deviancy (a verdict or diagnosis, for example); and they place him in a particular role which is thought to neutralize the harmful effects of his misconduct (like the role of prisoner or patient). These commitment ceremonies tend to be occasions of wide public interest and ordinarily take place in a highly dramatic setting.[6] Perhaps the most obvious example of a commitment ceremony is the criminal trial, with its elaborate formality and exaggerated ritual, but more modest equivalents can be found wherever procedures are set up to judge whether or not someone is legitimately deviant.

Now an important feature of these ceremonies in our own culture is that they are almost irreversible. Most provisional roles conferred by society—those of the student or conscripted soldier, for example—include some kind of terminal ceremony to mark the individual's movement back out of the role once its temporary advantages have been exhausted. But the roles allotted the deviant seldom make allowance for this type of passage. He is ushered into the deviant position by a decisive and often dramatic ceremony, yet is retired from it with scarcely a word of public notice. And as a result, the deviant often returns home with no proper license to resume a normal life in the community. Nothing has happened to cancel out the stigmas imposed upon him by earlier commitment ceremonies; nothing has happened to revoke the verdict or diagnosis pronounced upon him at that time. It should not be surprising, then, that the people of the community are apt to greet the returning deviant with a considerable degree of apprehension and distrust, for in a very real sense they are not at all sure who he is.

A circularity is thus set into motion which has all the earmarks of a "self-fulfilling prophesy," to use Merton's fine phrase. On the one hand, it seems quite obvious that the community's apprehensions help reduce whatever chances the deviant might otherwise have had for a successful return home. Yet at the same time, everyday experience seems to show that these suspicions are wholly reasonable, for it is a well-known and highly publicized fact that many if not most ex-convicts return to crime after leaving prison and that large numbers of mental patients require further treatment after an initial hospitalization. The common feeling that deviant persons never really change, then, may derive from a faulty premise; but the feeling is expressed so frequently and with such conviction that it eventually creates the facts which later "prove" it to be correct. If the returning deviant encounters this circularity often enough, it is quite understandable that he, too, may begin to wonder whether he has fully graduated from the deviant role, and he may respond to the uncertainty by resuming some kind of deviant activity. In many respects, this may be the only way for the individual and his community to agree what kind of person he is.

Moreover this prophesy is found in the official policies of even the most responsible agencies of control. Police departments could not operate with any real effectiveness if they did not regard ex-convicts as a ready pool of suspects to be tapped in the event of trouble, and psychiatric clinics could not do a successful job in the community if they were not always alert to the possibility of former patients suffering relapses. Thus the prophesy gains currency at many levels within the social order, not only in the poorly informed attitudes of the community at large, but in the best informed theories of most control agencies as well.

In one form or another this problem has been recognized in the West for many hundreds of years, and this simple fact has a curious implication. For if our culture has supported a steady flow of deviation throughout long periods of historical change, the rules which apply to any kind of evolutionary thinking would suggest that strong forces must be at work to keep the flow intact—and this because it contributes in some important way to the survival of the culture as a whole. This does not furnish us with sufficient warrant to declare that deviance is "functional" (in any of the many senses of that term), but it should certainly make us wary of the assumption so often made in sociological circles that any well-structured society is somehow designed to prevent deviant behavior from occurring.[7]

It might be then argued that we need new metaphors to carry our thinking about deviance onto a different plane. On the whole, American sociologists have devoted most of their attention to those forces in society which seem to assert a centralizing influence on human behavior, gathering people together into tight clusters called "groups" and bringing them under the jurisdiction of governing principles called "norms" or "standards." The questions which sociologists have traditionally asked of their data, then, are addressed to the uniformities rather than the divergencies of social life: how is it that people learn to think in similar ways, to accept the same group moralities, to move by the same rhythms of behavior, to see life with the same eyes? How is it, in short, that cultures accomplish the incredible alchemy of making unity out of diversity, harmony out of conflict, order out of confusion? Somehow we often act as if the differences between people can be taken for granted, being too natural to require comment, but that the symmetry which human groups manage to achieve must be explained by referring to the molding influence of the social structure.

But variety, too, is a product of the social structure. It is certainly remarkable that members of a culture come to look so much alike; but it is also remarkable that out of all this sameness a people can develop a complex division of labor, move off into diverging career lines, scatter across the surface of the territory they share in common, and create so many differences of temper, ideology, fashion, and mood. Perhaps we can conclude, then, that two separate yet often competing currents are found in any society: those forces which promote a high degree of conformity among the people of the community so that they know what to expect from one another, and those forces which encourage a certain degree of diversity so that people can be deployed across the range of group space to survey its potential, measure its capacity, and, in the case of those we call deviants, patrol its boundaries. In such a scheme, the deviant would appear as a natural product of group differentiation. He is not a bit of debris spun out by faulty social machinery, but a relevant figure in the community's overall division of labor.

NOTES

1. In fact, the first statement of the general notion presented here was concerned with the study of small groups. See Robert A. Dentler and Kai T. Erikson, "The Functions of Deviance in Groups," *Social Problems*, VII (Fall 1959), pp.98–107.
2. Aldous Huxley, *Prisons: The "Carceri" Etchings by Piranesi* (London: The Trianon Press, 1949), p. 13.
3. For a good description of this process in the modern prison, see Gresham Sykes, *The Society of Captives* (Princeton, N.J.: Princeton University Press, 1958). For discussions of similar problems in two different kinds of mental hospital, see Erving Goffman, *Asylums* (New York: Bobbs-Merrill, 1962) and Kai T. Erikson, "Patient Role and Social Uncertainty: A Dilemma of the Mentally Ill," *Psychiatry*, XX (August 1957), pp. 263–274.
4. Written by "a celebrated" but not otherwise identified author (perhaps Henry Fielding) and quoted in John Howard, *The State of the Prisons*, London, 1777 (London: J. M. Dent and Sons, 1929), p. 10.
5. The classic description of this process as it applies to the medical patient is found in Talcott Parsons, *The Social System* (Glencoe, Ill.: The Free Press, 1951).
6. See Harold Garfinkel, "Successful Degradation Ceremonies," *American Journal of Sociology*, LXI (January 1956), pp. 420–424.
7. Albert K. Cohen, for example, speaking for a dominant strain in sociological thinking, takes the question quite for granted: "It would seem that the control of deviant behavior is, by definition, a cultural goal." See "The Study of Social Disorganization and Deviant Behavior" in Merton, et al., *Sociology Today* (New York: Basic Books, 1959), p. 465.

Analysis and Critique

4 The Functionalist Approach to Social Problems
MELVIN TUMIN

It has been the steady fate of twentieth century sociology to be deeply involved in matters of the highest relevance for policy, and often intentionally so. Our most recent involvements, however, have been matters of mixed blessings. For, while we have been handsomely sup-

Reprinted from Melvin Tumin, "The Functionalist Approach to Social Problems," *Social Problems*, vol. 12, no. 4 (Spring 1965), pp 379–388. By permission of the author and the Society for the Study of Social Problems.

ported in important and useful works, we have not altogether avoided some of the less benign features of affluence. One cannot easily shrug off, for instance, the moral and aesthetic pinch one feels at the fact that we prosper anew with each fresh wave of crime, delinquency, divorce, mental illness, and poverty.

It is surely not visionary to predict that in the next several decades the services of sociologists will be sought with even greater frequency by all kinds of governmental and private agencies. If portents are not altogether misleading, the next twenty years are likely to be known as the sociological decades. It may be more difficult to recruit sociologists to work for one rather than another administration. I am confident, however, that we shall find some satisfactory rationale for continuing to apply for and accept governmental funds for research on the problems of interest to us, and I have no less confidence that such funds will be available in fairly satisfactory amounts, no matter who is in the White House.

If these allegations prove true, it follows that an increasing number of sociologists will self-consciously orient their scientific work on the basis of significant value commitments. It is equally probable, however, that in the next two decades we shall also witness the most profound refinement and elaboration of scientific method in sociology. The number of sociologists able to employ sophisticated devices for analysis and measurement of social phenomena in scientifically rigorous ways is likely to reach an all-time high, both absolutely and proportionately.

While it may at first strike us as disturbing that sociology should be approaching a period when it will become both more satisfactorily scientific and more consequentially political than it has ever been before, it is a happy coincidence that our dominant approach to social phenomena—namely, functional analysis—is in some ways ideally suited for just such a period. For a functionalist approach permits the investigator to take certain ends or interests or system-states as given, and to analyze the consequences—supportive and destructive—of any given set of practices for those ends, interests, or system-states. In the process, one may, without apparent penalty, narrow one's focus of attention so that only certain lines of consequence for certain actors are highlighted while others are ignored. This has the dual result of permitting scientific work to generate certain apparent value implications without really doing so, and, simultaneously, to carry real value implications without apparently doing so.

This two-sided role of functionalist science *vis-à-vis* social values is an important feature in view of the fact that there has developed among sociologists in recent years a substantial consensus around certain quite explicit value commitments. The functionalist approach has made the growth of these value commitments comfortably possible without impeding the concomitant development of rigor in the scientific procedures.

Now, functional analysis has come in for a good deal of scrutiny in the last ten years in the sociological journals. Some have contended it is a specific and unique form of sociological analysis, while others have insisted it is coterminous with all of sociological analysis. Some, too, have claimed that functionalism is essentially teleological and mystical, while others have denied these allegations and have shown how functional analysis can be free of any such teleologies and can be scientifically rigorous. Other students have alleged that functional analysis is really a form of causal analysis, while their opponents have insisted that it is very difficult to go from a functionalist proposition to a causal proposition, unless one adds certain assumptions about human motives or evolutionary selection. Still other sociologists have tried to show how functional analysis is essentially conservative or reactionary in its political orientation, while their adversaries have denied that it has any inherent political orientation at all. Finally, significant disputes have arisen as to whether functional analysis can be used to deal with problems of social change or whether such analysis limits the sociologist alone to studying structure, statics, and the *status quo*.

You will all recognize these as references to matters raised explicitly or implicitly by such sociologists as Kingsley Davis, Wilbert Moore, Talcott Parsons, Robert Merton, Dennis Wrong, Ronald Dore, Harry Bredemeier, Walter Buckley, Francesca Cancion, and others; and I am sure all here will know of the contributions of the distinguished philosophers Carl Hempel and Ernest Nagel to these questions regarding functionalism.

If, as Kingsley Davis suggested, it was shrewd of Merton to show how the existence of contradictory claims regarding the political orientation of functionalism justified our concluding that it was neither conservative nor liberal, I am hard pressed to know what would be the shrewd conclusion to draw from all these opposing claims pro and con functionalism. The interesting thing is that, like schools of philosophy, they all sound right when one reads them, but they all sound wrong when one reads their critics.

There are two features of functionalist method, however, that have not received as much attention as they merit in these recent debates. The first is a set of difficulties for sociology as a science which functional analysis presents; the second is the variability of the values to which most of us have become committed. I want to look at each of these in turn.

Functionalism becomes most interesting—to sociologist and layman alike—when it is used as a means for determining the extent to which a given event or custom (or attitude, or practice, or law, or whatever) helps to maintain a system intact or works against the maintenance of the system, however that system may be defined. It seems to hold the highest promise when so conceived—a promise of scientific rigor and neutrality. Nothing need be said about the desirability or undesirability of the system; indeed, nothing *may* be said if functionalism, so conceived, is to be scientifically neutral.

The disturbing thing about functionalism, and maybe about all sociological analysis, is that there is one crucial thing we don't yet know how to do: devise a sensible, scientifically neutral arithmetic by which we can add up the so-called eufunctions and dysfunctions of any given set of practices and arrive at some meaningful over-all number or symbol which would specify the net extent to which the system under question was being maintained or destroyed. We can and do make a series of sequential but essentially unconnected statements about the consequences of actions—and some *have* to be "eufunctional" and some *have* to be "dysfunctional"; there is no way out of that. But an over-all summation of such mixed partial effects is out of our reach now—and may be inherently impossible.

Take, as an example, crime. The dysfunctions—their targets and their relative "amounts"—are roughly determinable. And while Durkheimian sophistication is often required to spell out and make convincing the eufunction of crime, simple observation of the persisting recidivism in the normal crime careers of some of our fellow citizens reveals an imposing array of the eufunctions of crime for criminals. Even for those who are caught and punished, crime may be eufunctional, and often is.

Other examples readily come to mind. Every young sociologist learns, for instance, what attention he can command by being sophisticated about the positive functions of prostitution, adultery, premarital sexual intercourse, divorce, and related practices. The interesting thing, of course, is that these claims for the positive functions of practices that are generally morally condemned are absolutely correct, if sensibly specified and limited.

But, on balance, what can one say about the total impact—eupacts and dyspacts (why not coin some terms while we're about it?)—of such practices. On the net balance, are they supportive or destructive of that system; and of which system? And how could one test the truth of any such claim? Notice, for instance, that no single institutional arrangement has enjoyed so much published disputation regarding its positive and negative functions as the phenomenon of social inequality. A number of us have variously taken turns reminding our antagonists of either eufunctions or dysfunctions they have overlooked. But in the end we come out where we started, namely, with a preference—supported by data, of course, but data that have been weighted and added according to our preferences. And there are no rules to determine which is the better or more correct method of toting up the diverse effects.

Now we can look at a second shortcoming of so-called functional analysis. We have just assumed it is possible, sometimes easily, sometimes with greater difficulty, to identify separate lines of consequences of various practices as either eupactful or dyspactful for a system which is taken as a given. But that assumption needs to be examined more carefully, for there is, I think, an inherent tendency in functional analysis to close down one's observations too quickly. Let me give an example. Suppose we are analyzing the structure and function of a gang of delinquent boys. We find they have dramatic initiation ceremonies. With our newly acquired sophistication about such matters, we see that these ceremonies help to smooth the integration of new members into the group, solidify consensus, reawaken flagging commitments of old members, and generally distribute higher morale throughout the membership. Naturally, we would be led to assert that these ceremonies are eufunctional for the continuity and vigorous conduct of the gang and its affairs. Since we have taken the gang as the system, and, therefore, as our "given," we tend, naturally, not to go much further in the analysis. But suppose this reinvigoration of the group leads it to excesses of delinquent behavior into which it would not have been tempted if it had not been so reinvigorated, and suppose these excesses provide just that margin of outrage to the norm-minded community needed to incite a serious crackdown. What, then, of the so-called eufunctions of the initiation ceremonies, if in heightening group morale and consensus and unity they lead the group to engage in self-defeating and destroying actions? My point is that we do not often go on to look at the longer and larger and delayed consequences of actions, and we do not do so for two reasons: (1) The rules of functional analysis are pretty rigorously insistent that we delimit and specify the system to whose support or destruction we are referring our analysis. (2) Typically, moreover, we have *not* designed studies to watch the changing impact over time of various occurrences, events, and practices. Our analysis is not geared to historical waiting and depth. And so we often speak too easily and too quickly. For instance, is the emergence of a fairly rock-ribbed conservative trend in politics, such as is exemplified by Goldwater, positively or negatively functional for American democracy? Suppose there is backlash against the backlash in the near future, and a reinvigoration of liberalism? Suppose this in turn generates a third party force? Suppose this leads to a real fractionating of political power, with strategic minorities coming to play even more dominant roles? How, then, will we assess the long range effects of the Goldwater party?

Examples such as these point up a painful dilemma. The strength of functional analysis presumably lies in its ability to do skilled dissection and analysis of the ways in which social actions interplay in a network of interdependence within a given system, and thus presumably clarify in some as yet unnamed way "why" the practices are present. In short, there is some presumed *unique* strength in the *ahistoricity* of the analytic method. But now we find that it is precisely this ahistoricity which makes our analyses often of such dubious value. And even worse, it is future history rather than past history that we seem to need to control. And how do we do that?

Let me briefly mention two other problems presented by functional analysis. The first of these can be stated simply as follows: using functional analysis, sociologists have no way of making relevant, competent scientific statements about any *system* taken as a *whole*. If we are in trouble, as we are, because we cannot sensibly add up the diversities of eupacts and dyspacts of various substructures within any given system, we are in even worse trouble when it comes to assessing a system as a whole. We simply have not developed a method or language adequate to total system comparison. Our only "out" is to take the system which we first used as a "given" and place it in a context of a larger system of which it is a sub-unit and ask questions about its positive and negative contributions to that larger system. Thus, we do reasonably well in considering, functionally, the sub-units of national state aggregates; but when we get to the level of nation-state aggregation, or go on to multi-national systems, we are simply unable to say things that couldn't just as well be said by anybody else. One has only to listen to the usual comparisons of, say, America with England or France to realize that one might just as well hold these conversations with untrained fellow tourists in the bar of the S.S. Rotterdam.

I believe the difficulty just stated is inherent in functional analysis taken in its best and most generous terms.

The second difficulty has to do with the internal pressure of functionalism to find a rationale for all things. Of course, all things have reasons for coming into being and other reasons for persisting. But to say this is to say nothing. For it is clear that some social events are much more deterministically generated by a given system, while others can be seen as system-bound and determined only in the loosest sense. I am trying to suggest that a great deal of what we do in any given day simply is irrelevant and unnecessary from the point of view of system maintenance. It is a frill or a fringe benefit, or deficit of the system; it is garbage or junk from the point of view of system-requirements. It may be esthetically gratifying, or neurotically compulsive, or luxuriously enjoyable; but those are very different kinds of reasons for the existence of practices than the reasons we might offer for the existence of a division of labor. Functionalism—and maybe that means sociology in general as presently practiced, in whatever version—is inadequate to this problem. Either we must learn to ignore the junk and garbage and frills and fringes; or we must find a meaningful place for them in our system of analysis, especially if they are features by which we are often most dramatically characterised, such as the state of our creative arts. At the moment, all we can do is be uneasy about these things because we neither ignore them nor find a place for them.

I now want to turn from this first set of problems presented by functional analysis and consider a second set of problems to which only sparse attention has been paid in recent discussions of functionalism. These problems concern the relationships between functional analysis as a method, on the one hand, and our variable value commitments, on the other, specifically, our variable attitudes toward different "social problems." Here one must be avowedly more impressionistic.

Why is it, one must ask, that while we, i.e., practicing sociologists, seem to be almost uniformly against poverty, mental illness, and racial discrimination, we are somewhat less than uniformly against war, and in some important senses, we are *for* such things as divorce, adultery, prostitution, crime, delinquency, and interracial disorders.

When I say we are "for" or "against" any of these, I mean several things.

First, sociologists who work and report on problems of poverty, mental illness, and racial discrimination couldn't be clearer about their implied condemnation of these phenomena. These are social abominations to be done away with as quickly as possible.

By contrast, the sociological profession as a whole is much more ambivalent about war, and some sociologists have even made reputations as cold-war warriors, counselling very important persons lodged in the highest reaches of the Establishment. The implication here is also clear: war is sometimes good, or at least necessary.

By further contrast, sociological analyses of such matters as divorce, delinquency, crime, prostitution, and adultery often show either a cool detachment and implied lack of concern about the problematic aspects of these phenomena ordinarily attributed to them by the laymen of our society; or sociologists tend to display an almost whimsical kind of affection, guided by a thoroughly sympathetic understanding of how people could get involved in these normally disapproved patterns of behavior. Sometimes the attitude is not only "Well, what could you expect, given the situation of these people and the structure of society," but also includes a kind of militant applause for these types of reactions to the implied malfunctioning of the society.

A second indication of variable attitudes toward social problems is revealed in the informal judgments we tend to make about the expectability of the incidences and rates of these problematic phenomena. We write as if there were no good grounds on which to expect *any* poverty or racial discrimination—there are no ineluctable cultural compulsions in these directions, we imply. By contrast, we are somewhat tentatively expectant of a discernible incidence of mental disorder; and we tend to see recurring wars as quite expectable. And when it comes to divorce, adultery, delinquency, crime, prostitution, and racial protests, we often imply that, sociologically speaking, we are a lucky society to experience only as little of these matters as we do. We often add wisely that there is probably a lot more of these things than is ever recorded—except divorce, of course, and here we count "unhappy marriage" as the equivalent of divorce.

Third, and most relevantly here, we reveal our variable attitudes toward a range of social problems by the kinds of so-called functional analyses we do of these problems. Mental illness, racial discrimination, and poverty have no positive functions for anyone, judging by most sociological writings; or, if they do, then clearly the persons or interest blocs who do profit from these problems are villainous. Above all, no good can be identified for the system as a whole. By contrast, some wars are often seen at least as better than some peaceful alternatives; and in considering such phenomena as delinquency, divorce, adultery, prostitution, and crime, we have become very adroit at identifying positive functions for actors, interest blocs, and the society as a whole.

In sum, our so-called scientific analyses tend often to lean heavily on the side of negative functions in the case of some problem phenomena; range around a balance of positive and negative functions in the case of other phenomena; and lean heavily toward the other pole of positive functions in the case of still other problems.

Why should this be so? There is little, if anything, in the scientific findings *per se* that would suggest that these variable one-sidednesses in our analyses are justified. That all of these phenomena have both positive and negative functions is quite clear. There is no difficulty, for instance, in spelling out certain benign consequences of poverty, especially if one is indifferent to his moral standing in the community. One could, for example, mention the positive functions for wealthy people of the poverty of others; or the availability of cheap services and labor; or the disparate power quotients that some can enjoy; or the feelings of well-being that do-gooders and philanthropists can secure; or the political strength of party programs that pay attention to poverty; or the smug euphoria that reports of our poverty bring to Americanophobic Europeans.

So, too, one can even talk about the positive functions for the *system as a whole* of a quotient of poverty that can function as a rallying point for general social conscience and can energize ameliorative concern that might otherwise lie dormant. It does not take much imagination to do this kind of thing. Ever since Durkheim showed us how some crime is positively functional for the rest of society, it has not taken much sensitivity or cleverness to extrapolate to other phenomena and do the same thing.

Since, then, we can identify both positive and negative consequences or functions for all the social problems we face, the only possible justification for favoring some problems above others would lie in the net *balance* of positive and negative consequences. But we have shown earlier that we have no techniques available to us for adding up the pluses and minuses and coming out with some meaningful overall calculation or quotient of net effect. We have no way, in short, of saying whether, on balance, the society is threatened more by the totality of mental illness and its consequences than by the totality of delinquency and its consequences. If we cannot do so, then we cannot scientifically justify our tendency to stress the negative aspects of some phenomena and the positive aspects of others.

So, it is not in the scientific findings themselves that we will discover why our biases are so variously distributed. Nor will we find the reason in the relative difficulty and ease of analysis of these problems. They are all relatively equally susceptible to clever or banal, mediocre or insightful analyses.

Nor can one find in the historical span of the problems any good grounds for feeling so differently about them. Poverty has been with us for as long as prostitution and adultery; and while it may be true that it required official certification by a presidential office to establish poverty as a legitimate focus of interest and attention, that would only account for the novelty of the interest and not the type of interest expressed.

I want to offer a number of hypotheses as to why some problems seem more baleful than others. We have spoken of the senselessness and needlessness of certain problems. Poverty doesn't make any sense; mental illness doesn't; racial discrimination doesn't—not by any tolerable moral standards accepted in our community. There are no good grounds for poverty, especially when there is so much wealth. Mental illness may serve many positive functions ancillary to the main body of identified negative functions, but there is no acceptable ground for putting up with it. This is, I think, how the public conscience runs among sociologists.

But this conscience needs accounting for.

The reason our analyses run the way they do, I think, has to do with a part of functional analysis once again—namely, the doctrine of functional equivalents. Simply, I mean that the possible functional equivalents of the disapproved phenomena either are nonexistent or are even more repulsive than the actual problems themselves, while, by contrast, the functional equivalents of the more approved phenomena are themselves either as tolerable and acceptable as the phenomena, or even morally praiseworthy.

What, for instance, is the functional equivalent of mental disorder? If we pretend to know that mental illness functions to help the victim to get out of an intolerable situation, then some other forms of escape are the functional equivalents; and we don't approve of these escapes any more than we do of the illness itself.

One has to be careful, of course, with the doctrine of functional equivalents. For one must always ask: functionally equivalent for whom? It is one thing to ask what could serve the same functions for poverty-stricken people as poverty—and that would be an idiotic question—but it is not idiotic to ask what could substitute for poverty in the total culture that would have the same effects on the culture as poverty. For here one can think of such things as rigorous caste structures; or other forms of extreme status deprivations; or totalitarian power structures that would yield many of the same functions. As I noted before, these functional equivalents are even less tolerable than the actual manifestations.

By contrast, the functional equivalents of the more approved problems often have very strong positive connotations. Thus, one equivalent of delinquency is the expression of independence of adult norms and stuffiness. So, too, prostitution can be seen, and often is seen, as a symbolic rejection of intolerable sexual standards of the bourgeoisie, and an implicit denunciation of commercialized sale of sex hiding under the guise of marriage. Or, divorce and adultery are simply evil-sounding terms for expressions of spirit that rise above the ordinary limitations of unjustified normative restraints. These may be hyperbolic ways of stating these matters—but the essential truth, or claim for it at least, is evidently there and quite plain to be seen.

In effect, then, I am contending we like some problems more than others because we don't think they are really problems. And we don't think they are really problems because we see them as indirect expressions of laudable human spirit and verve and honesty or straightforwardness breaking through the hypocritical bounds of our ordinary norms. For these reasons, I suggest, we tacitly applaud some of these problems by insisting on revealing a large proportion of positive functions these actions serve for a number of actors with whom we identify, and tacitly deny importance to the negative functions they play for other actors with whom we have not very much sympathy, or for the system as a whole, which we hold blameworthy in the first place.

A second source of our variable attitudes toward problems is also connected intimately with functional analysis. I suggest that most of us have been pressed against our own political inclinations to play the role of neutral social scientist, committed to withholding value judgments in those roles. Functional analysis does not make possible an over-all critical evaluation of our society. But our own inner selves will out, whether we like it or not. And so we employ functional analysis in such a way as to permit ourselves to be both sociologists and concerned citizens. What, in fact, we do is deliver ourselves of our over-all evaluations of our society by emphasizing the positive aspects of certain phenomena and the negative aspects of others. Our cultivated but repressed tendencies toward informed muckraking, our views of ourselves as conscientious citizens, which our neutral sociological roles do not permit us to indulge: these are given expression by the way in which we slant our work. So we give short shrift to poverty, mental illness, and racial discrimination; we are sophisticatedly ambivalent about war; and we portray our sympathies for the downtrodden in our analyses of crime and delinquency. In our own minds, we add up all these un-addible things and see ourselves as giving public vent to our condemnation of our society's malfunctionings. In short, we let people know where we stand on our society as a system and not simply what we know about it.

A third reason why we bias our functional analyses has to do with the process of identification. The victims of mental illness, poverty, and racial discrimination are not the least bit appealing, at least not by any sort of ordinary standards. It takes quite an effort, I suggest, for most people really to identify with the poor, the Negro, or the mentally sick in our society. Understand them, yes; and sympathize, yes; and want to help, yes; but *identify?* No. For that means actively thinking of ourselves as poor or Negro or mad. And not many of us are built to be able to take on those nightmares.

One might even suggest that the victims of these social outrages generate in us a certain amount of moral despisal which we recognize as cruelty, and about which we feel guilty; we handle our guilt by converting it into professed outrage at the society which throws up such victims.

By contrast, the actors in delinquency, crime, adultery, and divorce often tend to command our positive sympathies because, I suggest, they are doing things many of us would like to be able to do. Mitty-like, we dream about doing them, but never manage to get to them. And while it is probably rare for a male sociologist to dream affectionately about being a prostitute, or to wish he could be one, the kind of total situation in which the relative sexual freedom of the prostitute would be the prevailing norm is surely one about which many of us must often fantasize. Even the more pleasant aspects of taking drugs and of intoxication are probably quite within our scope of positive identification.

A fourth dynamic that may shape our attitudes toward social problems lies in the distinction between cause and symptom. As sociologists, we tend to see crime and delinquency and such other phenomena as symptoms of deep-lying disorders of the social system—of poverty, for instance. We are reluctant to condemn such symptomatic behaviors, especially if we see them as naturally arising out of the basic disorders over which the "deviant" actors or victims have little or no control. In some senses, indeed, we tend to impute certain "healthy" attributes to these symptomatic reactions to inadequacies and inequities in the social system. In much the same way we invest racial demonstrations with positive functionality, seeing such demonstrations as natural reactions to racial discrimination and as "healthier" modes of reaction than the historically traditional subservience of the "oppressed" groups. (We recognize that this line of reasoning will not apply to the attitudes we express toward mental illness, but that is no reason not to consider its relevance for the other phenomena just discussed.)

A fifth and final possible source of our variable attitudes toward social problems has to do with our judgment of the relative importance of the various problems. I suggest that we are relatively offhanded about crime and delinquency and prostitution and divorce, partly because we believe that they don't really matter very much— that they really don't disturb any important social values and don't really gum up the social works to any significant degree. This attitude is perhaps most obvious in the case of divorce, which we rarely deplore because we feel it is not only natural and expectable but a rather good institution, all things considered. Our tendency to press for far more liberal divorce laws is evidence in point. Our informal and perhaps unjustified sneers at marriage counseling also testify to our endorsement of the importance of the freedom to divorce.

If there is any credence to be given to these five suggested reasons for variable attitudes toward problems, then it is clear our functional analyses, attuned to these desires and preferences, are slanted in most unscientific ways. While some of our biasing sentiments match those of the rest of the community, by and large, as sociologists we tend to be less "square" about these matters than most other segments of the community. We stand in between the morally disapproving sections of the community, on the one hand, and the actual participants in the problems themselves, on the other.

I have indicated the intimate connection between so-called scientific sociology and a range of non- or unscientific elements that guide and condition that activity in important ways. I wish further to suggest, finally, that this kind of close interplay of values and science, or of sentiment and science, is probably most difficult to avoid. Perhaps it is altogether unavoidable, so long as functional analysis is our dominant mode of approach to social problems. Whether we *should avoid* these unscientific predilections and prefigurings of our scientific activity is quite another question. But it is interesting to note that a major function of funtionalism for sociologists is that it minimizes role strain for them as they seek simultaneously to play the parts of both concerned citizens and neutral, value-free scientists. In an era when both these roles have high salience for a group of professionals, a general approach which reduces the potentially great role strain is not without virtue.

CHAPTER II

Social Disorganization

Around the turn of the 19th century, two major events took place in the development of the sociology of deviance. The first was the creation in 1892, at the University of Chicago, of the first sociology department in the United States. The faculty of this department freed themselves from the moral focus that had characterized earlier explanations of deviance and created a new, distinctly American social science. The second development was the emergence of the Chicago School of theorists in the early part of the 20th century. The work of these sociologists provided coherence to theory, research, and the development of a substantial body of knowledge that came to influence numerous other theoretical developments and research paradigms within the field of sociology in general and the study of deviance in particular.

One of the distinctive features of the Chicago School was its attentiveness to documenting various aspects of social life in its immediate geographical environment, the city of Chicago. Borrowing somewhat loosely from biology, the Chicagoans developed an ecological model of urban life and used it to study extensively the growth of the city, the various social territories in it, the life-styles of its inhabitants, and the effects of social change on organization, disorganization, and reorganization within the city. The ecological perspective offered a framework within which these sociologists could study the social order of the city in terms of selection, competition, change, cooperation, and symbiosis. They concluded that these natural processes were affecting and disrupting the mechanisms of social control, with the result that social disorganization and deviance were increasing.

This social disorganization theory concentrated on the political, economic, and social changes that were sweeping the country at the time, affecting virtually all aspects of American life. It emphasized the problems of the heterogeneous, rapidly changing nature of the society of the United States, in contrast to the established European orientation of the functionalists. While the changes themselves were generally viewed as progressive, their concurrent effects, such as increases in the rates of crime, delinquency, suicide, and mental illness, were seen as negative. A noticeable weakening in the organization of social life seemed to follow from the rapid increases in industrialization, urbanization, immigration, and internal migration.

Social disorganization theorists hypothesized a relationship between this increasing social complexity and higher rates of deviance, particularly in the large urban areas of America. They took note of the apparent predominance of deviance in certain city areas or zones that were characterized by numerous large immigrant groups, extreme poverty, transient residents, deteriorated housing, and a general lack of stable community institutions. On the assumption that such factors contribute to instability, an absence of close interpersonal relationships, and a breakdown in effective social control of behavior, they concluded that these zones could be expected to be disproportionately characterized by social disorganization. In the cities they studied, the social disorder of the central-city areas appeared to possess distinct characteristics that created the conditions conducive to continuously high rates of deviance, irrespective of the composition of the populations residing in them.

Like the functionalists, disorganization theorists accepted the basic proposition that a society is a complex whole whose parts (i.e., institutions, associations) are interdependent and maintain some sort of equilibrium. Their writings emphasize the harmony that can unify a society; normally, people are presumed to agree with one another about values and norms, so high degrees of behavioral regularity and social organization can be expected. Put another way, social organization (social order) exists when behavioral regularity and internal cohesion bind the individuals and institutions in a society closely together. This cohesion consists largely of consensus about goals worth striving for (values) and how or how not to behave (norms). When consensus concerning values and norms is upset and traditional rules no longer appear to apply, conflict, social disorganization, and the volume of deviance are all apt to increase.

The first reading in this chapter (Reading 5) is from *The Polish Peasant in Europe and America*, by W. I. Thomas and Florian Znaniecki. These authors stress that social disorganization develops whenever a society or social group is exposed to new ideas and customs that are not effectively incorporated into the "host" social order. They view disorganization as common to all societies in periods of rapid change and especially when massive immigration occurs, as it did in the United States during the early part of this century.

Thomas and Znaniecki attempt to explain the processes that led to the erosion of primary (face-to-face) relationships within both immigrant groups and the society to which these groups were emigrating. They define social disorganization in terms of the decreasing effectiveness of existing social rules in controlling the behavior of individuals. In a group or a society whose composition is quickly changing, the members often develop new attitudes which free them to engage in activities that do not comply with the established rules, and this weakens the social order. For Thomas and Znaniecki, then, it is during periods of sociocultural change that social disorganization is apt to be most widespread and intense.

Robert Park maintains in Reading 6 that as a society becomes more heterogeneous, primary relationships are subject to strain, which in turn leads to a decrease in traditional social control mechanisms. This reading is a section from *The City*, by Park, Ernest W. Burgess, and Roderick D. McKenzie, that was authored by Park in 1925. At that time, rapid social change was taking place due to urbanization, industrialization, and mobility of the population. According to Park, the change accompanying the movement from village communities to cities was disrupting routine ways of living and traditional methods of regulating behavior, resulting in social disorganization.

Reading 7, by Robert E. L. Faris and H. Warren Dunham, also deals with the effects of social change on social order in urban areas. This excerpt from their book *Mental Disorders in Urban Areas* is concerned with how the degree of social disorganization was related to the amount and types of deviant behavior found in various sections of Chicago during the 1920s and 1930s. Each area of the city was analyzed on the basis of a number of indicators to measure the extent of its social disorganization. Faris and Dunham reported that mental disorders (especially schizophrenia), like many other types of deviance, were comparatively more prevalent in highly disorganized areas of the city.

C. Wright Mills criticizes the assumptions he sees as inherent in the writings of social disorganization theorists in Reading 8, the Analysis and Critique section for this chapter. Mills notes that what he calls the "social pathologists" share an essentially similar view of deviant behavior which reflects their relatively homogeneous middle-class, rural backgrounds. The orientation of these theorists toward deviance also was shaped by an ideology which places the blame on individuals for their transgressions from generally accepted societal norms. thus, in Mills's view, the social pathologists see individual deviance as peculiar behavior attributable to inadequate socialization, rather than a phenomenon inextricably bound to the social structure of American society. By accepting and legitimizing the status quo, these writers ignore a broader theoretical framework which would include social, historical, and political forces in an analysis of deviance. Furthermore, by denigrating the individual deviant, the social pathologists fail to take into account the roles played by special-interest and power groups in the formulation of definitions of deviance and the application of sanctions with reference to who and what is deviant.

Mills's focus on the reliance on middle-class norms in disorganization theory has been the basis for three pertinent criticisms of this theory. One is the attempt of disorganization theorists to explain deviance in the lower class to the virtual exclusion of the middle and upper classes. The lower class was assumed to have higher rates of deviance because its members were located in the most disorganized areas of the city. Thus, by circular reasoning, the lower class was most deviant because it was the most disorganized, and it was, at the same time, the most disorganized because it contained the most deviants. Another criticism of the theory concerns its emphasis on "official" statistics of pathological behavior. In relying almost exclusively on official rates of deviance—for example, admissions to mental hospitals, criminal justice agency data on crime and delinquency, and so on—disorganization theorists overlooked the fact that these data might actually be a reflection of factors related to social control or social class practices (see Chapters V and VII), rather than ecological processes. The third criticism is that disorganization theorists appear to have been biased in favor of prevailing middle-class values and norms in their production of a consensus model of society wherein disorganization is viewed as dysfunctional. Any divergence from these orientations was viewed as dysfunctional and upsetting to the established harmony in society. Little attention was paid to the fact that social change, while it may disrupt the existing consensus, may at the same time increase social solidarity. That is, all social change does not necessarily lead to social disorganization.

5 *The Concept of Social Disorganization*
W. I. THOMAS and FLORIAN ZNANIECKI

The concept of social disorganization as we shall use it...refers primarily to institutions and only secondarily to men. Just as group-organization embodied in socially systematized schemes of behavior

Reprinted by permission from *The Polish Peasant in Europe and America*, by W. I. Thomas and Florian Znaniecki, Vol. IV (Chicago: The University of Chicago Press, 1918).

imposed as rules upon individuals never exactly coincides with individual life-organization consisting in personally systematized schemes of behavior, so social disorganization never exactly corresponds to individual disorganization. Even if we imagined a group lacking all internal differentiation, *i.e.*, a group in which every member would accept all the socially sanctioned and none but the socially sanctioned rules of behavior as schemes of his own conduct, still every member would systematize these schemes differently in his personal evolution, would make a different life-organization out of them, because neither his temperament nor his life-history would be exactly the same as those of other members. As a matter of fact, such a uniform group is a pure fiction; even in the least differentiated groups we find socially sanctioned rules of behavior which explicitly apply only to certain classes of individuals and are not supposed to be used by others in organizing their conduct, and we find individuals who in organizing their conduct use some personal schemes of their own invention besides the traditionally sanctioned social rules. Moreover, the progress of social differentiation is accompanied by a growth of special institutions, consisting essentially in a systematic organization of a certain number of socially selected schemes for the permanent achievement of certain results. This institutional organization and the life-organization of any of the individuals through whose activity the institution is socially realized partly overlap, but one individual cannot fully realize in his life the whole systematic organization of the institution since the latter always implies the collaboration of many, and on the other hand each individual has many interests which have to be organized outside of this particular institution.

◄○►

These points must be kept in mind if we are to understand the question of social disorganization. We can define the latter briefly as a *decrease of the influence of existing social rules of behavior upon individual members of the group*. This decrease may present innumerable degrees, ranging from a single break of some particular rule by one individual up to a general decay of all the institutions of the group. Now, social disorganization in this sense has no unequivocal connection whatever with individual disorganization, which consists in a decrease of the individual's ability to organize his whole life for the efficient, progressive and continuous realization of his fundamental interests. An individual who breaks some or even most of the social rules prevailing in his group may indeed do this because he is losing the minimum capacity of life-organization required by social conformism; but he may also reject the schemes of behavior imposed by his milieu because they hinder him in reaching a more efficient and more comprehensive life-organization. On the other hand also, the social organization of a group may be very permanent and strong in the sense that no opposition is manifested to the existing rules and institutions; and yet, this lack of opposition may be simply the result of the narrowness of the interests of the group-members and may be accompanied by a very rudimentary, mechanical and inefficient life-organization of each member individually. Of course, a strong group organization may be also the product of a conscious moral effort of its members and thus correspond to a very high degree of life-organization of each of them individually. It is therefore impossible to conclude from social as to individual organization or disorganization, or vice versa. In other words, social organization is not coextensive with individual morality, nor does social disorganization correspond to individual demoralization.

Social disorganization is not an exceptional phenomenon limited to certain periods or certain societies; some of it is found always and everywhere, since always and everywhere there are individual cases of breaking social rules, cases which exercise some disorganizing influence on group institutions and, if not counteracted, are apt to multiply and to lead to a complete decay of the latter. But during periods of social stability this continuous incipient disorganization is continuously neutralized by such activities of the group as reinforce with the help of social sanctions the power of existing rules. The stability of group institutions is thus simply a dynamic equilibrium of processes of disorganization and *reorganization*. This equilibrium is disturbed when processes of disorganization can no longer be checked by any attempts to reinforce the existing rules. A period of prevalent disorganization follows, which may lead to a complete dissolution of the group. More usually, however, it is counteracted and stopped before it reaches this limit by a new process of reorganization which in this case does not consist in a mere reinforcement of the decaying organization, but in a production of new schemes of behavior and new institutions better adapted to the changed demands of the group; we call this production of new schemes and institutions *social reconstruction*. Social reconstruction is possible only because and in so far as, during the period of social disorganization a part at least of the members of the group have not become individually disorganized, but, on the contrary, have been working toward a new and more efficient personal life-organization and have expressed a part at least of the constructive tendencies implied in their individual activities in an effort to produce new social institutions.

◄o►

As long as we are concerned with disorganization alone, leaving provisionally aside the following process of reconstruction, the phenomenon which we want to explain is evidently the appearance of such attitudes as impair the efficiency of existing rules of behavior and thus lead to the decay of social institutions. Every social rule is the expression of a definite combination of certain attitudes; if instead of these attitudes some others appear, the influence of the rule is disturbed. There may be thus several different ways in which a rule can lose its efficiency, and still more numerous ways in which an institution, which always involves several regulating schemes, can fall into decay. The causal explanation of any particular case of social disorganization demands thus that we find, first of all, what are the particular attitudes whose appearance manifests itself socially in the loss of influence of the existing social rules, and then try to determine the causes of these attitudes. Our tendency should be, of course, to analyze the apparent diversity and complexity of particular social processes into a limited number of more or less general causal facts, and this tendency can be realized in the study of disorganization if we find that the decay of *different rules* existing in a given society is the objective manifestation of *similar attitudes*, that, in other words, many given, apparently different phenomena of disorganization can be causally explained in the same way. We cannot reach any laws of social disorganization, *i. e.,* we cannot find causes which always and everywhere produce social disorganization; we can only hope to determine laws of socio-psychological becoming, *i. e.,* find causes which always and everywhere produce certain definite attitudes, and these causes will explain also social disorganization in all those cases in which it will be found that the attitudes produced by them are the real background of social disorganization, that the decay of given rules or institutions is merely the objective, superficial manifestation of the appearance of these attitudes. Our task is the same as that of the physicist or chemist who does not attempt to find laws of the multiform changes which happen in the sensual appearance of our material environment, but searches for laws of the more fundamental and general processes which are supposed to underlie those directly observable changes, and explains the latter causally only in so far as it can be shown that they are the superficial manifestations of certain deeper, causally explicable effects.

6 *Social Change and Social Disorganization*
ROBERT E. PARK

In the family and in the neighborhood such organization as exists is based upon custom and tradition, and is fixed in what Sumner calls the folkways and the mores. At this stage, society is a purely natural product; a product of the spontaneous and unreflective responses of individuals living together in intimate, personal, and face-to-face relations. Under such circumstances conscious efforts to discipline the individual and enforce the social code are directed merely by intuition and common sense.

In the larger social unit, the community, where social relations are more formal and less intimate, the situation is different. It is in the community, rather than in the family or the neighborhood, that formal organizations like the church, the school, and the courts come into existence and get their separate functions defined. With the advent of these institutions, and through their mediation, the community is able to supplement, and to some extent supplant, the family and the neighborhood as a means for the discipline and control of the individual. However, neither the orphan asylum nor any other agency has thus far succeeded in providing a wholly satisfactory substitute for the home. The evidence of this is that they have no alumni association. They create no memories and traditions that those who graduate from them are disposed to cherish and keep alive.

It is in this community with its various organizations and its rational, rather than traditional, schemes of control, and not elsewhere, that we have delinquency. Delinquency is, in fact, in some sense the measure of the failure of our community organizations to function.

Historically, the background of American life has been the village community. Until a few years ago the typical American was, and perhaps still is, an inhabitant of a middle western village; such a village, perhaps, as Sinclair Lewis describes in *Main Street*. And still, today, the most characteristic trait of Homo Americanus is an inveterate individualism which may, to be sure, have been temperamental, but in that case temperament has certainly been considerably reinforced by the conditions of life on the frontier.

But with the growth of great cities, with the vast division of labor which has come in with machine industry, and with movement and change that have come about with the multiplication of the means of transportation and communication, the old forms of social control represented by the family, the neighborhood, and the local community have been undermined and their influence greatly diminished.

This process by which the authority and influence of an earlier culture and system of social control is undermined and eventually destroyed is described by Thomas—looking at it from the side of the individual—as a process of "individualization." But looking at it from the point of view of society and the community it is social disorganization.

We are living in such a period of individualization and social disorganization. Everything is in a state of agitation—everything seems to be undergoing a change. Society is, apparently, not much more than a congeries and constellation of social atoms. Habits can be formed only in a relatively stable environment, even if that stability consists merely—as, in fact, it invariably does, since there is nothing in the universe that is absolutely static—in a relatively constant form of change. Any form of change that brings any measurable alteration in the routine of social life tends to break up habits; and in breaking up the habits upon which the existing social organization rests, destroys that organization itcslf. Every new device that affects social life and the social routine is to that extent a disorganizing influence. Every new discovery, every new invention, every new idea, is disturbing. Even news has become at times so dangerous that governments have felt it wise to suppress its publication.

It is probable that the most deadly and the most demoralizing single instrumentality of present-day civilization is the automobile. The automobile bandit, operating in our great cities, is much more successful and more dangerous than the romantic stage robber of fifty years ago. The connection of the automobile with vice is notorious. "The automobile is connected with more seductions than happen otherwise in cities altogether."[1]

The newspaper and thc motion picture show, while not so deadly, are almost as demoralizing. If I were to attempt to enumerate all the social forces that have contributed to the disorganization of modern society I should probably be compelled to make a catalogue of everything that has introduced any new and striking change into the otherwise dull routine of our daily life. Apparently anything that makes life interesting is dangerous to the existing order.

The mere movement of the population from one part of the country to another—the present migration of the Negroes northward, for example—is a disturbing influence. Such a movement may assume, from the point of vicw of the migrants themselves, the character of an emancipation, opening to them new economic and cultural opportunities, but it is none the less disorganizing to the communities they have left behind and to the communities into which they are now moving. It is at the same time demoralizing to the migrating people themselves, and particularly, I might add, to the younger generation.

The enormous amount of delinquency, juvenile and adult, that exists today in the Negro communities in northern cities is due in part, though not entirely, to the fact that migrants are not able to accommodate themselves at once to a new and relatively strange environment. The same thing may be said of the immigrants from Europe, or of the younger generation of women who are just now entering in such large numbers into the newer occupations and the freer life which the great cities offer them.

"Progress," as I once heard William James remark, "is a terrible thing." It is a terrible thing in so far as it breaks up the routine upon which an existing social order rests, and thus destroys the cultural and the economic values, i.e., the habits of thrift, of skill, of industry, as well as the personal hopes, ambitions, and life-programs which are the content of that social order.

Our great cities, as those who have studied them have learned, are full of junk, much of it human, i.e., men and women who, for some reason or other, have fallen out of line in the march of industrial progress and have been scrapped by the industrial organization of which they were once a part.

A recent study by Nels Anderson of what he calls "Hobohemia," an area in Chicago just outside the "Loop," that is to say, the downtown business area, which is almost wholly inhabited by homeless men, is a study of such a human junk heap. In fact, the slum areas that invariably grow up just on the edge of the business areas of great cities, areas of deteriorated houses, of poverty, vice, and crime, are areas of social junk.

I might add, because of its immediate connection with the problems and interests of this association, that recent studies made in Chicago of boys' gangs seem to show that there are no playgrounds in the city in which a boy can find so much adventure, no place where he can find so much that may be called "real sport," as in these areas of general deterioration which we call the slums.

In order to meet and deal with the problems that have been created by the rapid changes of modern life, new organizations and agencies have sprung into existence. The older social agencies, the church, the school, and the courts, have not always been able to meet the problems which new conditions of life have created. The school, the church, and the courts have come down to us with their aims and methods defined under the influence of an older tradition. New agencies have been necessary to meet the new conditions. Among these new agencies are the juvenile courts, juvenile protective associations, parent-teachers' associations, Boy Scouts, Young Men's Christian Associations settlements, boys' clubs of various sorts, and I presume, playgrounds and playground associations. These agencies have taken over to some extent the work which neither the home, the neighborhood, nor the other older communal institutions were able to carry on adequately.

These new institutions, perhaps because they are not to the same extent hampered by our earlier traditions, are frankly experimental and are trying to work out a rational technique for dealing with social problems, based not on sentiment and tradition, but on science.

Largely on the basis of the experiments which these new agencies are making, a new social science is coming into existence. Under the impetus which the social agencies have given to social investigation and social research, sociology is ceasing to be a mere philosophy and is assuming more and more the character of an empirical, if not an exact, science.

As to the present condition of our science and of the devices that we have invented for controlling conduct and social life, I can only repeat what I said at the very outset of our paper: "The thing of which we still know least is the business of carrying on an associated existence."

NOTES

1. W. I. Thomas, *The Unadjusted Girl—with Cases and Standpoint for Behavior Analysis*, Criminal Science Monograph No. 4, Boston, 1923, p. 71.

7 *Natural Areas of the City*
ROBERT E. L. FARIS and H. WARREN DUNHAM

A relationship between urbanism and social disorganization has long been recognized and demonstrated. Crude rural-urban comparisons of rates of dependency, crime, divorce and desertion, suicide, and vice have shown these problems to be more severe in the cities, especially the large rapidly expanding industrial cities. But as the study of urban sociology advanced, even more striking comparisons between

Reprinted from Robert E. L. Faris and H. Warren Dunham, *Mental Disorders in Urban Areas* (Chicago: University of Chicago Press, 1965), pp. 1–10, 19–21. By permission of Vera S. Dunham.

the different sections of a city were discovered. Some parts were found to be as stable and peaceful as any well-organized rural neighborhood while other parts were found to be in the extreme stages of social disorganization. Extreme disorganization is confined to certain areas and is not characteristic of all sections of the city.

Out of the interaction of social and economic forces that cause city growth a pattern is formed in these large expanding American cities which is the same for all the cities, with local variations due to topographical and other differences. This pattern is not planned or intended, and to a certain extent resists control by planning. The understanding of this order is necessary to the understanding of the social disorganization that characterizes urban life.

THE NATURAL AREAS DEPICTED AS CIRCULAR ZONES

The most striking characteristics of this urban pattern, as described by Professor Burgess,[1] may be represented by a system of concentric zones, shown in Chart I. Zone I, at the center, is the central business district. The space is occupied by stores, business offices, places of amusement, light industry, and other business establishments. There are few residents in this area, except for transients inhabiting the large hotels, and the homeless men of the "hobohemia" section which is usually located on the fringe of the business district.

Zone II is called the zone in transition. This designation refers to the fact that the expanding industrial region encroaches on the inner edge. Land values are high because of the expectation of sale for industrial purposes, and since residential buildings are not expected to occupy the land permanently, they are not kept in an improved state. Therefore, residential buildings are in a deteriorated state and rents are low. These slums are inhabited largely by unskilled laborers and their families. All the settlements of foreign populations as well as the rooming-house areas are located in this zone.

Zone III, the zone of workingmen's homes, is inhabited by a somewhat more stable population with a higher percentage of skilled laborers and fewer foreign-born and unskilled. It is intermediate in many respects between the slum areas and the residential areas. In it is located the "Deutschlands," or second immigrant settlement colonies, representing the second generation of those families who have migrated from Zone II.

Zones IV and V, the apartment-house and commuters' zones, are inhabited principally by upper-middle-class families. A high percent-

CHART 1 NATURAL AREAS AND URBAN ZONES

URBAN AREAS

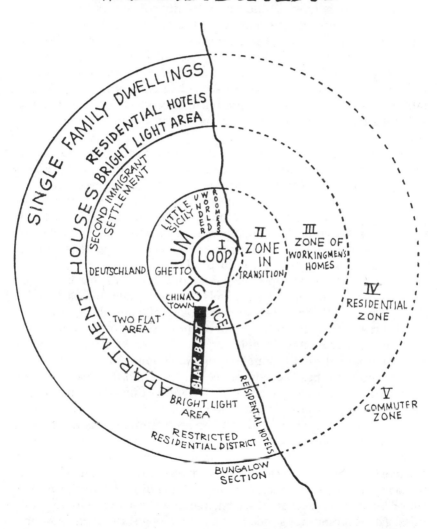

From R. E. Park and E. W. Burgess, *The City* (Chicago: University of Chicago Press, 1925).

age own their homes and reside for long periods at the same address. In these areas stability is the rule and social disorganization exceptional or absent.

The characteristics of the populations in these zones appear to be produced by the nature of the life within the zones rather than the reverse. This is shown by the striking fact that the zones retain all their characteristics as different populations flow through them. The large part of the population migration into the city consists of the influx of unskilled labor into the second zone, the zone in transition. These new arrivals displace the populations already there, forcing them to move farther out into the next zone. In general, the flow of population in the city is of this character, from the inner zones toward the outer ones. Each zone, however, retains its characteristics whether its inhabitants be native-born white, foreign-born, or Negro. Also each racial or national group changes its character as it moves from one zone to the next.

Within this system of zones, there is further sifting and sorting of economic and social institutions and of populations. In the competition for land values at the center of the city, each type of business finds the place in which it can survive. The finding of the place is not infrequently by trial and error, those locating the wrong place failing. There emerge from this competition financial sections, retail department store sections, theater sections, sections for physicians' and dentists' offices, for specialized shops, for light industry, for warehouses, etc.

Similarly, there are specialized regions for homeless men, for rooming-houses, for apartment hotels, and for single homes. The location of each of these is determined ecologically and the characteristics also result from the interaction of unplanned forces. They maintain their characteristics in spite of the flow of various racial and national groups through them and invariably impress their effects on each of these groups. These have been called "natural areas" by Professor Park,[2] because they result from the interactions of natural forces and are not the result of human intentions.

Fortunately, the city of Chicago has been studied somewhat more intensively than most cities of its size. Certain of these areas are significant in relation to social disorganization. It is possible to define and describe these areas with certain kinds of objective data. The major divisions of the city can be seen in Map I. Extending outward from the central business district are the principal industrial and railroad properties. The rooming-house sections extend along three arms radiating from the center to the north, west, and south. The slum areas are roughly defined by the regions containing over 50 per cent foreign-born and native-born of foreign parentage and over 50 per cent Negro.

MAP 1 Types of Cultural and Economic Areas

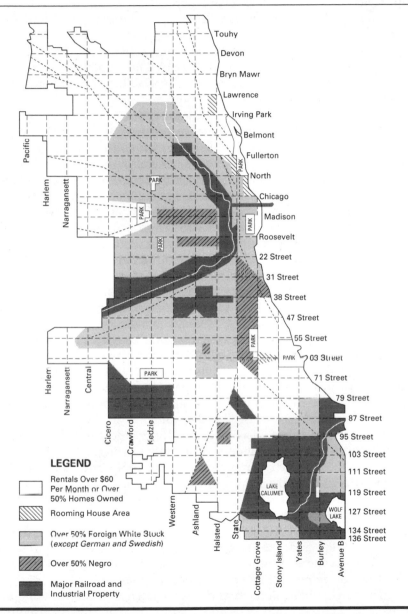

Adapted from Robert E. L. Faris and H. Warren Dunham, *Mental Disorders in Urban Areas*, copyright © 1965 by the University of Chicago. Original map adapted from maps prepared by the Social Science Research Committee, the University of Chicago.

Beyond these areas is the residential section. In the Lake Calumet section at the southeastern corner of the city is another industrial region inhabited by a foreign-born population.

Too small to be shown on this map are the areas of homeless men—the "hobohemia" areas.[3] These are located on three main radial streets and are just outside the central business district. Their inhabitants are the most unstable in the the city. The mobility and anonymity of their existence produces a lack of sociability and in many cases deterioration of the personality. Although spending their time in the most crowded parts of the city, these homeless men are actually extremely isolated. For the most part they represent persons unable to obtain an economic foothold in society, and so they maintain themselves by occasional labor, by petty thievery, by begging, and by receiving charity. As they have no opportunity for normal married life, their sexual activities are limited to relations with the lowest type of prostitutes and to homosexuals. The rate of venereal infection is high among these men. Chronic alcoholism is also a common characteristic of the members of this group. Their lives are without goal or plan, and they drift aimlessly and alone, always farther from the conventional and normal ways of living.

Another area of importance is the rooming-house area. This is usually located along main arteries of transportation and a little farther from the center of the city. In Chicago there are several rooming-house sections, the three largest consisting of arms radiating to the north, west, and south, just beyond the hobohemia areas, each extending for something over two miles in length and from a half-mile to over a mile in width. The populations of these areas are principally young, unmarried white-collar workers, who are employed in the central business district during the day and live in low-priced rented rooms within walking distance or a short ride from their work.[4] Within the area the population is constantly shifting, turning over entirely about once each four months. Anonymity and isolation also characterize the social relations in this area; no one knows his neighbors and no one cares what they might think or say. Consequently the social control of primary group relations is absent, and the result is a breakdown of standards of personal behavior and a drifting into unconventionality and into dissipations and excesses of various sorts. The rates of venereal diseases and of alcoholism are high in this area, and the suicide rate is higher than for any other area of the city.[5]

The foreign-born slum areas occupy a large zone surrounding the central business and industrial area. Within this zone there are a number of segregated ethnic communities, such as the Italian, Polish, Jewish, Russian, and Mexican districts. The newly arrived immigrants of any nationality settle in these communities with their fellow-countrymen. In these groups the language, customs, and many institutions of their former culture are at least partly preserved. In some of the most successfully isolated of these, such as the Russian-Jewish "ghetto," the Old-World cultures are preserved almost intact. Where this is the case, there may be a very successful social control and little social disorganization, especially in the first generation. But as soon as the isolation of these first-settlement communities begins to break down, the disorganization is severe. Extreme poverty is the rule; high rates of juvenile delinquency, family disorganization, and alcoholism reflect the various stresses in the lives of these populations.

Two distinct types of disorganizing factors can be seen in the foreign-born slum areas. The first is the isolation of the older generation, the foreign-born who speak English with difficulty or not at all and who are never quite able to become assimilated to the point of establishing intimate friendships with anyone other than their native countrymen. Within the segregated ethnic communities these persons are well adapted to their surroundings, but as soon as they move away or are deserted by their neighbors, they suffer from social isolation.[6] The second type of disorganizing factor operates among the members of the second and third generations. The very high delinquency rate among the second-generation children has been shown by Shaw.[7] This disorganization can be shown to develop from the nature of the child's social situation. Also growing out of the peculiar social situation of the second generation is the mental conflict of the person who is in process of transition between two cultures—the culture of his ancestors and the culture of the new world in which he lives. As he attends American schools and plays with children of other than his own nationality, the child soon finds himself separated from the world of his parents. He loses respect for their customs and traditions and in many cases becomes ashamed of his own nationality, while at the same time he often fails to gain complete acceptance into the American group of his own generation. This is particularly true if he is distinguished by color or by features which betray his racial or national origin. This person is then a "man without a culture," for though he participates to some extent in two cultures, he rejects the one and is not entirely accepted by the other.[8]

The Negro areas are, in general, similar in character to the foreign-born slum areas. The principal Negro district in Chicago extends for several miles southward from the business district. Two smaller Negro districts are located on the Near West Side, as well as one on the Near North Side. In the larger area on the South Side, the social disorganization is extreme only at the part nearest the business district.[9] In the parts farther to the south live the Negroes who have resided longer in the city and who have become more successful economically. These communities have much the same character as the nearby apartment-house areas inhabited by native-born whites.

For some miles along the Lake Front in Chicago a long strip of apartment-hotel districts has grown up. These districts occupy a very pleasant and favorable location and attract residents who are able to pay high rentals. The rates of various indices of social disorganization are in general low in these sections.

The outlying residential districts of middle-class and upper-middle-class native-born white population live in apartments, two-flat homes, and single homes. In these districts, and especially the single home areas in which there is a large percentage of homes owned by the inhabitants, the population is stable and there is little or no social disorganization in comparison with those areas near the center of the city.

—◄o►—

Not only are such statistical facts as population composition, literacy, dependency rates, and disease rates known to vary greatly in the different sections of the city, but also mental life and behavior. In one of the most conclusive of these studies, the study of juvenile delinquency by Clifford R. Shaw and his associates,[10] sufficient control was obtained to establish with reasonable certainty that the high rates of delinquency were products not of the biological inferiority of the population stocks that inhabit the slum areas, nor of any racial or national peculiarity, but rather of the nature of the social life in the areas themselves. The delinquency rates remained constantly high in certain urban areas which were inhabited by as many as six different national groups in succession. Each nationality suffered from the same disorganization in these areas and each nationality alike improved after moving away from the deteriorated areas.

As has been shown, the natural areas which have been defined above can be identified by the use of certain mathematical indices for different types of social phenomena. Such indices as the percentage of foreign-born, the percentage of homes owned, the sex ratio, the median rentals paid, the density of population, the rate of mobility, the educational rate, the percentage of rooming-houses and hotels, and the percentage of condemned buildings, roughly tend to identify these areas and to differentiate between them. These indices might be regarded as ones which measure the extent of social disorganization between the different communities and the natural areas of the city. Other types of objective data, representing such social problems as ju-

venile delinquency, illegitimacy, suicide, crime, and family disorganization, might be considered as indices representing effects or results
of certain types of social processes. As in the research of Clifford
Shaw which has been described above, the rates for these different social problems tend to fit rather closely into the ecological structure of
the city as described by Park, Burgess, and others. In other words, in
all of these social problems there is the concentration of high rates
close to the center of the city, with the rates declining in magnitude as
one travels in any direction toward the city's periphery. Shaw's study
of juvenile delinquency gives one of the most complete pictures of this
pattern. The other studies, in general, show the same pattern with
certain variations which develop because of the location of certain ethnic groups in certain parts of the city.

The problem of mental disorder has been for the first time approached by the utilizing of this ecological technique. It is the attempt
to examine the spatial character of the relations between persons who
have different kinds of mental breakdowns. While this type of approach is used in this study, the authors wish to emphasize that they
regard it as having definite limitations in understanding the entire
problem of mental disorder. It can be looked upon as a purely cultural
approach and as such does not tend to conflict with any understanding of this problem which may come from biological, physiological, or
psychological approaches. However, in the light of these previous
studies of social problems utilizing this method it does seem particularly desirable to study the distribution of the different types of mental disorders.

NOTES

1. R. E. Park and E. W. Burgess, *The City* (Chicago: University of Chicago Press, 1925).

2. R. E. Park, "Sociology," in *Research in the Social Sciences*, ed. Wilson Gee (New York: Macmillan Co., 1929), pp. 28–29.

3. Nels Anderson, *The Hobo* (Chicago: University of Chicago Press, 1923).

4. H. W. Zorbaugh, *The Gold Coast and the Slum* (Chicago: University of Chicago Press, 1929).

5. R. S. Cavan, *Suicide* (Chicago: University of Chicago Press, 1928).

6. Louis Wirth, *The Ghetto* (Chicago: University of Chicago Press, 1928).

7. C. R. Shaw *et al.*, *Delinquency Areas* (Chicago: University of Chicago Press, 1929).

8. Everett Stonequist, *The Marginal Man* (New York: Charles Scribner's Sons, 1937).
9. E. Franklin Frazier, *The Negro Family in Chicago* (Chicago: University of Chicago Press, 1932).
10. C. R. Shaw and H. D. McKay, *Report on the Causes of Crime*, National Commission on Law Observance and Enforcement (Washington, D.C.: U.S. Government Printing Office, 1931).

Analysis and Critique

8 The Professional Ideology of Social Pathologists
C. WRIGHT MILLS

An analysis of textbooks in the field of social disorganization reveals a common style of thought which is open to social imputation. By grasping the social orientation of this general perspective we can understand why thinkers in this field should select and handle problems in the manner in which they have.

By virtue of the mechanism of sales and distribution, textbooks tend to embody a content agreed upon by the academic group using them. In some cases texts have been written only after an informal poll was taken of professional opinion as to what should be included, and other texts are consulted in the writing of a new one. Since one test of their success is wide adoption, the very spread of the public for which they are written tends to insure a textbook tolerance of the commonplace. Although the conceptual framework of a pathologist's textbook is not usually significantly different from that of such monographs as he may write, this essay is not concerned with the "complete thought" or with the "intentions" of individual authors; it is a study of a professional ideology variously exhibited in a set of textbooks.[1] Yet, because of its persistent importance in the development of American sociology and its supposed proximity to the social scene, "social pathology" seems an appropriate point of entry for the examination of the style of reflection and the social-historical basis of American sociology.

The level of abstraction which characterizes these texts is so low that often they seem to be empirically confused for lack of abstraction to knit them together.[2] They display bodies of meagerly connected facts, ranging from rape in rural districts to public housing, and intellectually sanction this low level of abstraction.[3] The "informational" character of social pathology is linked with a failure to consider total social structures. Collecting and dealing in a fragmentary way with scattered problems and facts of milieux, these books are not focused on larger stratifications or upon structured wholes. Such an omission may not be accounted for merely in terms of a general "theoretical weakness." Such structural analyses have been available; yet they have not been attended to or received into the tradition of this literature. American sociologists have often asserted an interest in the "correlation of the social sciences"; nevertheless, academic departmentalization may well have been instrumental in atomizing the problems which they have addressed.[4] Sociologists have always felt that "not many representatives of the older forms of social science are ready to admit that there is a function for sociology."[5] However, neither lack of theoretical ability nor restrictive channeling through departmentalization constitutes a full explanation of the low level of abstraction and the accompanying failure to consider larger problems of social structure.

If the members of an academic profession are recruited from similar social contexts and if their backgrounds and careers are relatively similar, there is a tendency for them to be uniformly set for some common perspective. The common conditions of their profession often seem more important in this connection than similarity of extraction. Within such a generally homogeneous group there tend to be fewer divergent points of view which would clash over the meaning of facts and thus give rise to interpretations on a more theoretical level.[6]

The relatively homogeneous extraction and similar careers of American pathologists is a possible factor in the low level of abstraction characterizing their work. All the authors considered[7] (except one, who was foreign born) were born in small towns, or on farms near small towns, three-fourths of which were in states not industrialized during the youth of the authors. The social circles and strata in which they have severally moved are quite homogeneous; all but five have participated in similar "reform" groups and "societies" of the professional and business classes. By virtue of their being college professors (all but three are known to have the Ph.D.), of the similar type of temporary positions (other than academic) which they have held, of the sameness of the "societies" to which they have belonged and of the social positions of the persons whom they have married, the assertion as regards general similarity of social extraction, career, and circles of contact seems justified.[8]

A further determinant of the level of abstraction and lack of explicit systematization (beyond which the mentality we are examining
does not easily or typically go) is the immediate purpose and the type
of public for which they have presumably written. They have been
teachers and their specific public has been college students: this has
influenced the content and direction of their intellectual endeavors.[9]
Teaching is a task which requires a type of systematization to which
the textbook answers. Most of the "systematic" or "theoretical" work
in "social pathology" has been performed by teachers in textbooks for
academic purposes.[10] The fact that sociology often won its academic
right to existence in opposition to other departments may have increased the necessity for *textbook* systematization. Such systematization occurs in a context of presentation and of justification rather than
within a context of discovery.[11] The textbook-writing and the academic
profession of the writers thus figure in the character and function of
systematic theory within the field.[12] Systematization of facts for the
purpose of making them accessible to collegiate minds is one thing;
systematization which is oriented toward crucial growing-points in a
research process is quite another. An attempt to systematize on the
level of the textbook makes for a taxonomic gathering of facts and a
systematization of them under concepts that have already been logically defined.[13] The research possibilities of concepts are not as important as is the putting of the accumulated factual details into some sort
of order.

But, even though the perspectives of these texts are usually not
explicit, the facts selected for treatment are not "random." One way to
grasp the perspective within which they do lie is to analyze the scope
and character of their problems. What, then, are the selecting and organizing principles to be extracted from the range and content of these
texts? What types of fact come within their field of attention?

The direction is definitely toward particular "practical
problems"—problems of "everyday life."[14] The ideal of practicality, of
not being "utopian," operated, in conjunction with other factors, as a
polemic against the "philosophy of history" brought into American
sociology by men trained in Germany; this polemic implemented the
drive to lower levels of abstraction. A view of isolated and immediate
problems as the "real" problems may well be characteristic of a society
rapidly growing and expanding, as America was in the nineteenth
century and, ideologically, in the early twentieth century. The depic-
tive mode of speech and the heavy journalistic "survey" are intellectual concomitants of an expanding society in which new routines are
rising and cities are being built.[15] Such an approach is then sanctioned
with canons of what constitutes real knowledge; the practice of the

detailed and complete empiricism of the survey is justified by an epistemology of gross description. These norms of adequate knowledge linger in an academic tradition to mold the work of its bearers. The emphasis upon fragmentary,[16] practical problems tends to atomize social objectives. The studies so informed are not integrated into designs comprehensive enough to serve collective action, granted the power and intent to realize such action.

One of the pervasive ways of defining "problems" or of detecting "disorganization" is in terms of *deviation from norms*. The "norms" so used are usually held to be the standards of "society." Later we shall see to what type of society they are oriented. In the absence of studies of specific norms themselves this mode of problematization shifts the responsibility of "taking a stand" away from the thinker and gives a "democratic" rationale to his work.[17] Rationally, it would seem that those who accept this approach to "disorganization" would immediately examine these norms themselves. It is significant that, given their interest in reforming society, which is usually avowed, these writers typically assume the norms which they use and often tacitly sanction them.[18] There are few attempts to explain deviations from norms in terms of the norms themselves, and no rigorous facing of the implications of the fact that social transformations would involve shifts *in them*.

The easy way to meet the question of why norms are violated is in terms of biological impulses which break through "societal restrictions." A paste-pot eclectic psychology provides a rationale for this facile analysis.[19] Thus, more comprehensive problematization is blocked by a biological theory of social deviation. And the "explanation" of deviations can be put in terms of a requirement for more "socialization." "Socialization" is either undefined, used as a moral epithet, or implies norms which are themselves without definition. The focus on "the facts" takes no cognizance of the normative structures within which they lie.

The texts tend either to be "apolitical"[20] or to aspire to a "democratic" opportunism.[21] When the political sphere is discussed, its pathological phases are usually stated in terms of "the antisocial," or of "corruption," etc.[22] In another form the political is tacitly identified with the proper functioning of the current and unexamined political order; it is especially likely to be identified with a legal process or the administration of laws.[23] If the "norms" were examined, the investigator would perhaps be carried to see total structures of norms and to relate these to distributions of power. Such a structural point of sight is not usually achieved. The level of abstraction does not rise to permit examination of these normative structures themselves, or of why they come to be transgressed, or of their political implications. Instead, this literature discusses many kinds of apparently unrelated "situations."

About the time W. I. Thomas stated the vocabulary of the situational approach, a social worker was finding it congenial and useful. In M. E. Richmond's influential *Social Diagnosis* (1917) we gain a clue as to why pathologists tend to slip past structure to focus on isolated situations, why there is a tendency for problems to be considered as problems of individuals,[24] and why sequences of situations were not seen as linked into structures:

> Social diagnosis... may be described as the attempt to make as exact a definition as possible of the situation and personality of a human being in some social need—of his situation and personality, that is, in relation to the other human beings upon whom he in any way depends or who depend upon him, and in relation also to the social institutions of his community.[25]

This kind of formulation has been widely applied to isolated "problems" addressed by sociologists.[26] And the "situational approach" has an affinity with other elements which characterize their general perspective.[27]

Present institutions train several types of persons—such as judges and social workers—to think in terms of "situations."[28] Their activities and mental outlook are set within the existent norms of society; in their professional work they tend to have an occupationally trained incapacity to rise above series of "cases." It is in part through such concepts as "situation" and through such methods as "the case approach"[29] that social pathologists have been intellectually tied to social work with its occupational position and political limitations. And, again, the similarity of origin and the probable lack of any continuous "class experience" of the group of thinkers decrease their chances to see social structures rather than a scatter of situations. The mediums of experience and orientation through which they respectively view society are too similar, too homogeneous, to permit the clash of diverse angles which, through controversy, might lead to the construction of a whole.

The paramount fact of immigration in American culture, with each wave of immigrants displacing the lower-class position of former waves and raising the position of the earlier immigrants, also tends to obscure structural and class position.[30] Thus, instead of positional issues, pathologists typically see problems in terms of an individual, such as an immigrant, "adjusting" to a milieu[31] or being "assimilated" or Americanized. Instead of problems of class structure involving immigration, the tendency has been to institute problems in terms of immigration involving the nationalist assimilation of individuals. The fact that some individuals have had opportunities to rise in the American hierarchy decreases the chance fully to see the ceilings of class. Under these conditions such structures are seen as fluctuating and unsubstantial and are likely to be explained not in terms of *class position* but in terms of *status attitudes.*[32]

Another element that tends to obviate an analytic view of structure is the emphasis upon the "processual" and "organic" character of society. In Cooley, whose influence on these books is decisive, one gets a highly formal, many-sided fluidity where "nothing is fixed or independent, everything is plastic and takes influence as well as gives it."[33] From the standpoint of political action, such a view may mean a reformism dealing with masses of detail and furthers a tendency to be apolitical. There can be no bases or points of entry for larger social action in a structureless flux. The view is buttressed epistemologically with an emotionalized animus against "particularism" and with the intense approval of the safe, if colorless, "multiple-factor" view of causation.[34] The liberal "multiple-factor" view does not lead to a conception of causation which would permit points of entry for broader types of action, especially political action.[35] No set of underlying structural shifts is given which might be open to manipulation, at key points, and which, like the fact of private property in a corporate economy, might be seen as efficacious in producing many "problems." If one fragmentalizes society into "factors," into elemental bits, naturally one will then need quite a few of them to account for something,[36] and one can never be sure they are all in. A formal emphasis upon "the whole" plus lack of total structural consideration plus a focus upon scattered situations does not make it easy to reform the status quo.

The "organic" orientation of liberalism has stressed all those social factors which tend to a harmonious balance of elements.[37] There is a minimization of chances for action in a social milieu where "there is always continuity with the past, and not only with any one element only of the past, but with the whole interacting organism of man."[38] In seeing everything social as continuous process, changes in pace and revolutionary dislocations are missed[39] or are taken as signs of the "pathological." The formality and the assumed unity implied by "the mores" also lower the chances to see social chasms and structural dislocations.

Typically, pathologists have not attempted to construct a structural whole. When, however, they do consider totalities, it is in terms of such concepts as "society," "the social order," or "the social organization," "the mores and institutions," and "American culture." Four things should be noted about their use of such terms: (*a*) The terms represent undifferentiated entities. Whatever they may indicate, it is systematically homogeneous. Uncritical use of such a term as "the" permits a writer the hidden assumption in politically crucial contexts of a homogeneous and harmonious whole.[40] The large texture of "the society" will take care of itself, it is somehow and in the long run harmonious, [41] it has a "strain toward consistency" running through it,[42] or, if not this, then only the co-operation of all is needed,[43] or perhaps even a right moral feeling is taken as a solution.[44] (*b*) In their formal emptiness these terms are commensurate with the low level of abstraction. Their *formality* facilitates the empirical concern with "everyday" problems of (community) milieu. (*c*) In addition to their "descriptive" use, such terms are used normatively. The "social" becomes a good term when it is used in ethical polemics against "individualism" or against such abstract moral qualities as "selfishness," lack of "altruism," or of "antisocial" sentiments.[45] "Social" is conceived as a "co-operative" "sharing" of something or as "conducive to the general welfare."[46] The late eighteenth-century use of "society" as against "state" by the rising bourgeoisie had already endowed "society" with a "democratic" tinge which this literature transmits. (*d*) There is a strong tendency for the term "society" to be practically assimilated to, or conceived largely in terms of, primary groups and small homogeneous communities. Such a conception typically characterizes the literature within our purview.[47] In explaining it, we come upon an element that is highly important in understanding the total perspective.

The basis of "stability," "order," or "solidarity" is not typically analyzed in these books, but a conception of such a basis is implicitly used and sanctioned,[48] for some normative conception of a socially "healthy" and stable organization is involved in the determination of "pathological" conditions. "Pathological" behavior is not discerned in a *structural* sense (i.e., as incommensurate with an existent structural type) or in a *statistical* sense (i.e., as deviations from central tendencies). This is evidenced by the regular assertion that pathological conditions *abound* in the city.[49] If they "*abound*" therein, they cannot be "abnormal" in the statistical sense and are not likely to prevail in the structural sense. It may be proposed that the norms in terms of which "pathological" conditions are detected are "humanitarian ideals." But we must then ask for the social orientation of such ideals.[50] In this literature the operating criteria of the pathological are typically *rural* in orientation and extraction.[51]

Most of the "problems" considered arise because of the urban deterioration of certain values which can live genuinely only in a relatively homogeneous and primary rural milieu. The "problems" discussed typically concern urban behavior. When "rural problems" are discussed, they are conceived as due to encroaching urbanization.[52] The notion of disorganization is quite often merely the absence of that *type* of organization associated with the stuff of primary-group communities having Christian and Jeffersonian legitimations.[53]

Cooley, the local colorist of American sociology, was the chief publicist of this conception of normal organization. He held "the great historical task of mankind" to be the more effective and wider organization of that moral order and pattern of virtues developed in primary groups and communities.[54] Cooley took the idealists' absolute[55] and gave it the characteristics of an organic village; all the world should be an enlarged, Christian-democratic version of a rural village. He practically assimilated "society" to this primary-group community, and he blessed it emotionally and conceptually.[56] "There is reflected here," says T. V. Smith of Cooley—and what he says will hold for the typical social pathologist—"what is highly common in our culture, an ideal of intimacy short of which we do not rest satisfied where other people are concerned. Social distance is a dire fate, achieved with difficulty and lamented as highly unideal, not to say as immoral, in our Christian traditions. It is not enough to have saints; we must have 'communion' of the saints. In order to have social relations, we must nuzzle one another."[57]

The aim to preserve rurally oriented values and stabilities is indicated by the implicit model which operates to detect urban disorganization; it is also shown by the stress upon *community* welfare. The community is taken as a major unit, and often it sets the scope of concern and problematization.[58] It is also within the framework of ideally democratic communities that proposed solutions are to be worked out.[59] It should be noted that sometimes, although not typically or exclusively, solutions are conceived as dependent upon abstract moral traits or democratic surrogates of them, such as a "unanimous public will."[60]

"Cultural lag" is considered by many pathologists to be the concept with which many scattered problems may be detected and systematized. Whereas the approach by deviation from norms is oriented "ideologically" toward a rural type of order and stability, the cultural-lag model is tacitly oriented in a "utopian"[61] and progressive manner toward changing some areas of the culture or certain institutions so as to "integrate" them with the state of progressive technology.[62] We must analyze the use made by pathologists of "lag" rather than abstract formulations of it.[63]

Even though all the situations called "lags" *exist* in the present, their functional realities are referred back, away from the present. Evaluations are thus translated into a time sequence; cultural lag is an assertion of unequal "progress." It tells us what changes are "called for," what changes "ought" to have come about and didn't. In terms of various spheres of society it says what progress is, tells us how much we have had, ought to have had, didn't have, and when and where we didn't have it. The imputation of "lag" is complicated by the historical judgement in whose guise it is advanced and by the programmatic content being shoved into pseudo-objective phrases, as, for example, "called for."

It is not enough to recognize that the stating of problems in terms of cultural lag involves evaluations, however disguised. One must find the general loci of this kind of evaluation and then explain why just this form of evaluation has been so readily accepted and widely used by pathologists. The model in which institutions lag behind technology and science involves a positive evaluation of natural science and of orderly progressive change. Loosely, it derives from a liberal continuation of the enlightenment with its full rationalism, its messianic and now politically naïve admiration of physical science as a kind of thinking and activity, and with its concept of time as progress. This notion of progress was carried into American colleges by the once prevalent Scottish moral philosophy. From after the Civil War through the first two or three decades of the twentieth century the expanding business and middle classes were taking over instruments of production, political power, and social prestige; and many of the academic men of the generation were recruited from these rising strata and/or actively mingled with them. Notions of progress are congenial to those who are rising in the scale of position and income.

Those sociologists who think in terms of this model have not typically focused upon the conditions and interest groups underlying variant "rates of change" in different spheres. One might say that in terms of the rates of change at which sectors of culture *could* move, it is technology that is "lagging," for the specific reason of the control of patents, etc., by intrenched interests.[64] In contrast to the pathologists' use, Veblen's use of "lag, leak, and friction" is a structural analysis of industry versus business enterprise.[65] He focused on where "the lag" seemed to pinch; he attempted to show how the trained incapacity of legitimate businessmen acting within entrepreneurial canons would result in a commercial sabotage of production and efficiency in order to augment profits within a system of price and ownership. He did not like this "unworkman-like result," and he detailed its mechanism. In the pathologists' usage the conception has lost this specific and structural anchorage: it has been generalized and applied to everything fragmentarily. This generalization occurs with the aid of such blanket terms as "adaptive culture" and "material culture."[66] There is no specific focus for a program of action embodied in the application of such terms.

Another model in terms of which disorganizations are instituted is that of "social change" itself.[67] This model is not handled in any one typical way, but usually it carries the implicit assumption that human beings are "adjusted" satisfactorily to any social condition that has existed for a long time and that, when some aspect of social life changes, it may lead to a social problem.[68] The notion is oriented ideologically and yet participates in assumptions similar to those of cultural lag, which, indeed, might be considered a variant of it. Such a scheme for problematization buttresses and is buttressed by the idea of continuous process, commented on above; but here the slow, "evolutionary" pace of change is taken explicitly as normal and organized,[69] whereas "discontinuity" is taken as problematic.[70] The orientation to "rural" types of organization should be recalled. In line with the stress on continuous process, the point where sanctioned order meets advisable change is not typically or structurally drawn.[71] A conception of "balance" is usual and sometimes is explicitly sanctioned.[72] The question, "Changes in what spheres induce disorganization?" is left open; the position taken is usually somewhere between extremes, both of which are held to be bad.[73] This comes out in the obvious fact that what a conservative calls *dis*organization, a radical might well call *re*organization. Without a construction of total social structures that are actually emerging, one remains caught between simple evaluations.

Besides deviation from norms, orientation to rural principles of stability, cultural lag, and social change, another conception in terms of which "problems" are typically discussed is that of adaptation or "adjustment" and their opposites.[74] The pathological or disorganized is the maladjusted. This concept, as well as that of the "normal," is usually left empty of concrete, social content,[75] or its content is, in effect, a propaganda for conformity to those norms and traits ideally associated with small-town, middle-class milieux.[76] When it is an individual who is thought to be maladjusted, the "social type" within which he is maladjusted is not stated. Social and moral elements are masked by a quasi-biological meaning of the term "adaptation"[77] with an entourage of apparently socially bare terms like "existence" and "survival," which seem still to draw prestige from the vogue of evolutionism.[78] Both the quasi-biological and the structureless character of the concept "adjustment" tend, by formalization, to universalize the term, thus again obscuring specific social content. Use of "adjustment" accepts the goals and the means of smaller community milieux.[79] At the most, writers using these terms suggest techniques or means believed to be less disruptive than others to attain the goals that are given. They do not typically consider whether or not certain groups or individuals caught in economically underprivileged situations can possibly obtain the current goals without drastic shifts in the basic institutions which channel and promote them. The idea of adjustment seems to be most directly applicable to a social scene in which, on the one hand, there is a society and, on the other, an individual immigrant.[80] The immigrant then "adjusts" to the new environment. The "immigrant problem" was early in the pathologist's center of focus, and the concepts used in stating it may have been carried over as the bases for a model of experience and formulations of other "problems." *The Polish Peasant* (1918), which has had a very strong influence on the books under consideration, was empirically focused upon an immigrant group.

In approaching the notion of adjustment, one may analyze the specific illustrations of maladjustment that are given and from these instances infer a type of social person who in this literature is evaluated as "adjusted." The ideally adjusted man of the social pathologists is "socialized." This term seems to operate ethically as the opposite of "selfish";[81] it implies that the adjusted man conforms to middle-class morality and motives and "participates" in the gradual progress of respectable institutions. If he is not a "joiner," he certainly gets around and into many community organizations.[82] If he is socialized, the individual thinks of others and is kindly toward them. He does not brood or mope about but is somewhat extrovert, eagerly participating in his community's institutions. His mother and father were not divorced, nor was his home ever broken. He is "successful"—at least in a modest way—since he is ambitious; but he does not speculate about matters too far above his means, lest he become "a fantasy thinker," and the little men don't scramble after the big money. The less abstract the traits and fulfilled "needs" of "the adjusted man" are, the more they gravitate toward the norms of independent middle-class persons verbally living out Protestant ideals in the small towns of America.[83]

NOTES

1. No attempt has been made to trace specific concepts to their intellectual origins. Only elements admitted into the more stable textbook formulations have come within my view: the aim is to grasp typical perspectives and key concepts. Hence, no one of the texts to be quoted exemplifies *all* the concepts analyzed; certain elements are not so visible in given texts as in others, and some elements are not evidenced in certain texts at all. In general, the documentary

quotations which follow in footnotes are from the later editions of the
following books: W. G. Beach and E. E. Walker, *American Social
Problems* (1934); J. H. S. Bossard, (*a*) *Social Change and Social Problems*
(1934), and (*b*) *Problems of Social Well-Being* (1927); C. H. Cooley, (*a*)
The Social Process (1918), (*b*) *Human Nature and the Social Order* (1902,
1922), (*c*) *Social Organization* (1909); Edward T. Devine, (*a*) *The Normal
Life* (1915, 1924), (*b*) *Progressive Social Action* (1933); R. C. Dexter, *Social
Adjustment* (1927); G. S. Dow, *Society and Its Problems* (1920, 1929); M.
A. Elliott and F. E. Merrill, *Social Disorganization* (1934, 1941); C. A.
Ellwood, (*a*) *The Social Problem, a Constructive Analysis* (1915, 1919); (*b*)
Sociology and Modern Social Problems (1910–35); H. P. Fairchild, *Outline of
Applied Sociology* (1916, 1921); M. P. Follett, (*a*) *The New State* (1918), (*b*)
Creative Experience (1924); James Ford, *Social Deviation* (1939); J. M.
Gillette and J. M. Reinhardt, *Current Social Problems* (1933, 1937); J. L.
Gillin, (*a*) *Poverty and Dependence* (1921, 1926, 1937), (*b*) *Social Pathology*
(1933, 1939); J. L. Gillin, C. G. Dittmer, and R. J. Colbert, *Social
Problems* (1928, 1932); E. C. Hayes, editor's introductions to text in the
"Lippincott Series"; W. J. Hayes and I. V. Shannon, *Visual Outline of
Introductory Sociology* (1935); G. B. Mangold, *Social Pathology* (1932,
1934); H. A. Miller, *Races, Nations, and Classes* (1924); H. W. Odum,
Man's Quest for Social Guidance: The Study of Social Problems (1927);
Maurice Parmelee, *Poverty and Social Progress* (1916); H. A. Phelps,
Contemporary Social Problems (1932, 1933, 1938); S. A. Queen and J. R.
Gruener, *Social Pathology* (1940); S. A. Queen, W. B. Bodenhafer, and
E. B. Harper, *Social Organization and Disorganization* (1935); C. M.
Rosenquist, *Social Problems* (1940); U. G. Weatherly, *Social Progress*
(1926).

2. See Read Bain, "The Concept of Complexity," *Social Forces*, VIII, 222
   and 369. K. Mannheim has called this type "isolating empiricism"
   ("German Sociology," *Politica*, February, 1934, p. 30).

3. H. P. Fairchild, p. vii: "Dealing with applied sociology [this book]
   devotes itself to facts rather than to theories." James H. S. Bossard (*a*),
   p. xi. "In [*Problems of Social Well-Being*] an effort was made to consider
   chiefly in a factual vein, certain elements which seemed of basic
   importance...." G. B. Mangold, p. viii: "The author has tried to
   select that which [of factual material] best illustrates problems and
   practical situations."

   The quotations in the footnotes are merely indications of what is
   usual. The imputations presented must be held against the reader's
   total experience with the literature under purview.

4. In Germany the academic division of specialties prior to the rise of
   sociology channeled sociological work into a formal emphasis. In
   America a somewhat comparable situation led to a fragmentalization
   of empirical attention and especially to a channeling of work into
   "practical problems."

5. A. W. Small, *American Journal of Sociology,* May, 1916, p. 785, citing an editorial in the *American Journal of Sociology,* 1907.

6. Such "homogeneity" is not, however, the only condition under which some common style of thought is taken on by a group of thinkers. Compare the formal conception of "points of coincidence" advanced by H. H. Gerth in *Die Sozielgeschichtliche Lage der burgerlichen Intelligenz uns die Wende des 18 Jahrhunderts* (diss., Frankfurt A.M.) (V.D.I.-Verlag, G.m.b.H. Berlin, N.W. 7). The entire question of the grounding of imputations in terms of social extraction and career-lines is an unfinished set of methodological issues. In this paper the major imputations advanced do *not* proceed upon career data as much as upon the social orientation implied by general perspectives and specific concepts, and by the selection of "problems."

7. Information concerning twenty-four of the thirty-two authors was full enough to be considered. Five of the eight not considered were junior authors collaborating with persons who are included.

8. The order of their respective experience has not been systematically considered. All career data on contemporary persons should be held tentatively: open to revision by knowledge not now publicly available.

9. See above. A. W. Small, p. 754: "...the mental experience of the teacher-explorer in the course of arriving at the present outlook of sociologists...has also been due to the fact that many of the advances in perception or expression have been in the course of attempts to meet students' minds at their precise point of outlook." See C. Wright Mills, "Language, Logic, and Culture," *American Sociological Review,* October, 1939, for mechanisms involved in such determinations of the thinker by his public.

10. This statement, as is widely recognized, holds in a measure for all American sociology. Cf., e.g., Pitirim Sorokin, "Some Contrasts in Contemporary European and American Sociology," *Social Forces,* September, 1929, pp. 57–58. "In America sociology has grown as a child nursed by the universities and colleges....American literature in sociology has been composed largely out of textbooks."

11. Cf. Hans Reichenbach, *Experience and Prediction,* chap. i. See P. Sorokin's comment, *op. cit.,* p. 59.

12. J. L. Gillin (*a*), p. v.: "My years of experience as a social worker and teacher have gone into the content and method of presentation." J. H. S. Bossard (*a*), p. 759: "In the preceding chapters, problems have been grouped on the basis of one underlying fact or condition. Obviously, this is an arbitrary procedure which can be justified only on the basis of pedagogical expedience"; p. xi: "The...is the method followed.... By way of defense, this seems simpler and pedagogically preferable"; p. xii: "The decision to omit them was made...second, because in an increasing number of colleges and universities, these particular fields are dealt with in separate courses."

13. Cf. Fritz Mauthner, *Aristotle*, for the pedagogic character of the taxonomic logic of Aristotle. H. P. Fairchild, pp. 6–7: "...the essential features of the scientific method...are three in number. First, the accumulation of facts.... Second, the arrangement or classification of these facts according to some predetermined logical basis of classification...." J. H. S. Bossard (*a*), p. 34: "It is the present contention that the scientific study of social problems which confines itself to mere description and classification serves a useful purpose."

14. M. A. Elliott, *American Sociological Review*, June, 1941, p. 317: "The only problems which need concern the sociologists' theories and research are the real, practical problems of everyday living." Queen and Gruener, p. 42: "[In contradistinction to scientific problems] social problems...pertain directly to everyday life....Their concern is usually 'practical,' and often personal." J. H. S. Bossard (*a*), p. 32: "Frankly, applied sociology is utilitarian. It is concerned with practical problems and purposes." Gillette and Reinhardt, p. 22: "The study of social problems constitutes the heart of sociology as a science.... Even so-called 'pure' sociology, or theoretical sociology, more and more devotes itself to these practical problems of society."

    On the other hand, such writers as Ellwood, rising to a *very* high level of abstraction, conceive *formally* of "the social problem." C. A. Ellwood (*a*), pp. 13–14: "Some of us, at least, are beginning to perceive that the social problem is now, what it has been in all ages, namely, *the problem of the relations of men to one another*. It is the problem of human living together, and cannot be confined to any statement in economic, eugenic or other one-sided terms...it is as broad as humanity and human nature.... Such a statement [in terms of one set of factors] obscures the real nature of the problem, and may lead to dangerous, one-sided attempts at its solution." In terms of social and intellectual orientation, both ways of conceiving of "social problems" are similar in that neither is of a sort usable in collective action which proceeds against, rather than well within, more or less tolerated channels.

15. See H. D. Lasswell, *Politics* (1936), p. 148; K. Mannheim, *op. cit.*, pp. 30–31; and *Ideology and Utopia*, pp. 228–29.

16. Gillin, Dittmer, and Colbert, p. 44: "There are hundreds of social problems, big and little." Queen and Gruener, p. 171: "We present here some of the problems of day by day living encountered by diabetics and cardiacs." J. H. S. Bossard (*a*), p. 33: "Certain particular social problems are coming to be reserved for applied sociology. Their selection has been determined less by logic or principle than by accident and historical development"; p. 44: "The more one deals with life's problems at first hand, the more one is impressed with their concreteness, their specificity, and their infinite variety." Gillette and Reinhardt, p. 14: "From almost any point of view there must be a large number of social problems today"; p. 15: "This book is a treatise

on a large number of social problems. It does not claim to consider them all. It repeatedly recognizes the plurality of problems in its treatment of the great problems."

17. C. M. Rosenquist, p. 19: "...popular recognition of any social condition or process as bad, followed by any attempt to eliminate or cure it, serves as a criterion for its inclusion in a study of social problems. The writer merely accepts the judgment of public opinion. This is the method to be followed in this book." E. T. Devine (*a*), in Note to the Second Edition: "The object of Social Economy is that each shall be able to live as nearly as possible a normal life according to the standard of the period and the community."

18. C. M. Rosenquist, p. 19: "Perhaps we may be on solid ground through a recognition of the capitalist system and its accompaniments as normal. We may then deal with its several parts, treating as problems those which do not function smoothly. This, it seems, is what the more reputable sociologist actually does." H. P. Fairchild, p. 59: "...some of the social conditions which are the natural and consistent outcome of an individualistic-capitalistic organization of industry, and hence are to be considered as normal in modern societies." Examination of discussions of such items as poverty in most of the texts confirms this assertion. J. L. Gillin (*a*), p. 495: "For serious depressions carefully planned unemployment relief schemes should be formulated before the depression is felt."

19. That is, an eclecticism that does not analyze in any adequate way the elements and theories which it seeks to combine. Cf. Reuter's critique, *American Journal of Sociology*, November, 1940, pp. 293–304.

20. E. C. Hayes in the Introduction to H. A. Miller, p. x: "Not political action, the inadequacy of which Professor Eldridge (*Political Action*) has shown, nor revolution, the pathological character of which Professor Sorokin has demonstrated, but social interaction, the causal efficiency of human relationships, is the predominant factor in securing both order and progress."

21. J. H. S. Bossard (*a*), pp. 14–15: "The constructive approach...may be summarized in one sentence: It is always possible to do something. ...Such an approach represents in welfare work that hopelessly incurable optimism which in political life we call democracy." Gillette and Reinhardt, pp. 16–17: "There are no certain rules to be followed step by step in the discovery of the solution. Our best recourse is to employ scientific methods rigidly at every step...because of uncertain factors always present, we can never be sure that our conclusions are more than approximations of the truth.... Since we cannot completely control their activities...our cures must be partial and approximate." One type of link between democratic ideology and social pathology is shown in the following quotation, wherein a condition that deviates from the former is called pathological; the quotation also indicates a typical shying away from all orders of

domination other than that type legitimated traditionally, which is left open: H. A. Miller, p. 32: "When certain...psycho-pathological conditions are found, we may postulate an abnormal relationship as a cause...the particular form of pathology which is involved in our problem may be called the *oppression psychosis*. Oppression is the domination of one group by another." G. V. Price, reviewing Queen and Gruener, *Social Forces*, May, 1941, p. 566: "Without using the word democracy in the doctrinal sense the authors have shown what its utilities are in reducing pathologies."

22. M. A. Elliott and F. E. Merrill, p. 28: "The pathological phases of the political process include such anti-social behavior as delinquency, crime, disorder, revolt, and revolution. Corrupt political activity is an important example of such malfunctioning."

23. Note the identification of "political action" with legislation: Gillin, Dittmer, and Colbert, p. 94: "It is an American practice to attempt to solve any and every sort of social problem through political action. As a result, our statute-books are loaded with 'dead-letter' laws that are not enforced simply because public opinion does not respect them, nor does it feel responsible for them."

24. J. L. Gillin (*a*), p. 23: "Experience shows that rehabilitation is possible only when each case of poverty or dependency is taken separately and its difficulties handled with strict regard for all the attendant circumstances.... It must be done in terms of the individual, for...it cannot be done *en masse*."

25. Richmond, p. 357; see also pp. 51 and 62.

26. J. H. S. Bossard (*a*), p. 3: "Social problems consist of (*a*) a social situation, (*b*) which are...." Gillette and Reinhardt, p. 13: "A social problem is a situation, confronting a group...."

27. J. H. S. Bossard (*a*), p. 57: "...the emphasis in our social thinking upon the situation as a unit of experience, as 'an aggregate of interactive and interdependent factors of personality and circumstance,' is in essence a recognition of the idea of the emergent.... Queen recognizes the implications of the situational approach very clearly in these words: 'For purposes of sociological analysis, a situation consists in relationships between persons viewed as a cross section of human experience, constantly changing.... Thus we make of the concept "situation" an intellectual tool'" (S. Queen, "Some Problems of the Situational Approach," *Social Forces*, June, 1931, p. 481).

28. See K. Mannheim, *Man and Society*, p. 305.

29. Queen, Bodenhafer, and Harper, p. viii: Editor's Note by S. Eldridge: "The present volume...features the case approach to social problems."

30. Note the lack of structure in the conception of "class": Gillette and Reinhardt, p. 177: "Viewing the matter historically, then, it appears

that the chief cause of rigid *class systems* of society with their attendant evils is the prolonged concentration of wealth in the hands of a relatively few persons."

31. See below, the concept of "adjustment."

32. Gillin, Dittmer, and Colbert, p. 59: "The most fundamental cause of class and group conflict is the attitude of superiority on the part of one class, or group, toward another."

33. *The Social Process*, pp. 44–45.

34. Eliott and Merrill, p. 38: "One of the most significant concepts in the understanding of social problems is the idea of multiple causation."

35. See above comments on political relevance. C. A. Ellwood (*b*) p. 324: "We may, perhaps, sum up this chapter by saying that it is evident that the cure of poverty is not to be sought merely in certain economic rearrangements, but in scientific control of the whole life process of human society. This means that in order to get rid of poverty, the defects in education in government, in religion and morality, in philanthropy, and even in physical heredity, must be got rid of. Of course, this can only be done when there is a scientific understanding of the conditions necessary for normal human social life."

36. J. L. Gillin (*a*), pp. 51–128: " . . . . the modern theory of the causes of poverty has passed beyond any one-sided explanation to a many-sided theory." The following conditions of poverty and dependence are discussed: poor natural resources, adverse climate, adverse weather, insect pests, disasters, illness and diseases, physical inheritance, mental inheritance, adverse surroundings of children, death or disability of the earner, unemployment, lack of proper wages, traditions, customs, habits, advertising and instalment buying, fluctuations between costs of living and income, inequitable distribution of wealth and income, family marital relations, political conditions, unwise philanthropy, etc. After these discussions, *family cases* are presented as " . . . . studies in causation."

37. Whereas many socialist theories have tended to overlook the elastic elements that do exist in a society. Cf. K. Mannheim, *Politica*, pp. 25–26.

38. C. H. Cooley (*a*), p. 46.

39. See Max Lerner, *It Is Later than You Think*, pp. 14–15; and *Encyclopaedia of the Social Sciences*, article "Social Process." See documentation and consequences below.

40. Gillin, Dittmer, and Colbert, p. 11: "All this group life is nicely woven into a system that we call society . . . . "

41. *Ibid.*, p. 15: "But the aim of society is ever directed to the task of bringing uniform advantages to all." C. A. Ellwood (*b*), p. 195: "Social organization may refer to any condition or relation of the elements of a social group; but by social order we mean a settled and harmonious

relation between the individuals or the parts of a society. The problem
of social order is then the problem of harmonious adaptation among
the individuals of the group...."

42. It is significant that it was Sumner, with his tacit belief in "natural"
order, who set forth the phrase and what it implies.

43. Gillin, Dittmer, and Colbert, p. 13: "Since a community is made up of
a number of neighborhoods, it is necessary that all cooperate in order
to secure better schools, improved....."

44. J. L. Gillin (a), p. 133: "Only as a passion for social righteousness
takes the place of an imperative desire for selfish advantage....will
society do away with the conditions that now depress some classes of
the population and exhalt others."

45. C. A. Ellwood (b), p. 84: "....increasing altruism is necessary for the
success of those more and more complex forms of cooperation which
characterize higher civilization and upon which it depends." G. B.
Mangold, p. 17: "Without the spirit of altruism society would be but a
sorry exhibition of the collective humanity that we believe has been
made in the image of God." Conversely, the "anti-social" is held to
include certain abstract, moral traits of individuals. Elliott and Merrill,
p. 43: "An analysis of the disorganization process suggests two types
of anti-social forces: (1) the consciously directed anti-social forces and
(2) the impersonal organic forces which are an outgrowth of the
formalism discussed above....to advance their own selfish ends.
These men are thoroughly aware of their anti-social attitudes. Social
values have no meaning for them..... There has often been no
socializing influence in the lives of those men..... Cooperation, or
'mutual aid,' the implicit counterpart of effective social
organization..... Vice areas....function because of human appetites,
because individual desires are more deeply rooted than any sense of
the social implications..... The prostitute exists only because she is a
means to man's sensual pleasure and satiety"; p. 44: "Sin, vice, crime,
corruption, all consciously directed anti-social forces, offer a
primrose....." G. B. Mangold, p. 59: "Unsocial habits lead to
poverty; particularly do they degrade poverty into dependency. Chief
among these vices is intemperance. Before the advent of prohibition it
was....." Queen, Bodenhafer, and Harper, p. 4: "When there
is....characterized by harmony, teamwork, understanding, approval,
and the like, we may speak of organization. When the opposite is true
and there is a....marked by tension, conflict, or drifting apart, we
may speak of disorganization."

46. Gillin, Dittmer, and Colbert, p. 5: " 'The word [social] means
conducive to the collective welfare, and thus becomes nearly
equivalent to moral' [Cooley, *Human Nature and the Social Order*,
p. 4]....it is this....meaning that comes closest to our interpretation.
....—'conducive to the collective welfare'—relationships, and products

of relationships that are believed to foster and promote *group life,* and to insure *group survival."*

47. J. L. Gillin (*b*), p. 313: "....personal relationships....are the most important ties in the social organization...." C. A. Ellwood (*b*), pp. 3–4: "The tendency in the best sociological thinking is to emphasize the importance, for the understanding of our social life, of 'primary' or face-to-face groups"; p. 77: "Primary groups....are of most interest sociologically, because they exhibit social life at its maximum intensity, and because they are the bearers of the most vital elements in social life, especially the traditions of civilization"; pp. 79–80: "The chief importance of primary groups in our social life, however, is that they....furnish the 'patterns' which we attempt to realize in our social life in general"; pp. 84–85: "All human history has, from one point of view, been a struggle to transfer altruism and solidarity of the family to successively larger and larger groups of men"; pp. 90–91: "Primary, or face-to-face groups are the key to the understanding of our social life....." Gillin, Dittmer, Colbert, p. 282: "....the home is probably our most fundamental social institution...."; p. 285: "Anything that endangers the stability of the family endangers society." J. H. S. Bossard (*a*), p. 555: "Family life is the focal point of virtually all of our social problems."

48. C. A. Ellwood (*b*), pp. 79–80: "The very ideal of social solidarity itself comes from the unity experienced in such [primary] groups." Elliott and Merrill, p. 581: "An ever-increasing number of persons living in the giant cities has become completely deracinated, cut off from all stable primary ties. They have lost not only their physical home, but often their spiritual home as well. Social disorganization breeds in these unattached masses of the urban proletariat. They furnish willing nuclei for robbery, brigandage, and revolution."

49. J. L. Gillin (*b*), p. 411: "In the city we have a greater degree of disorganization in the sense in which we use that term"; p. 410: "....in the simple and well-organized ties of country life...."; p. 409: "Recreation in the country is largely homemade..... In the city it is professional.... The patterns of behavior....are here again disorganized and new patterns have to be found." Gillette and Reinhardt, p. 116: "Cities exhibit all the social problems, save those peculiar to agricultural extractive pursuits." H. P. Fairchild, p. 304: "Since there are no *natural* facilities available to the majority of *denizens* of cities for the gratification of the desire for dancing, it inevitably follows that provision is made on a commercial basis" (my italics). C. M. Rosenquist, p. 47: "The controls which were effective in the small, settled farm community no longer suffice in....the city. To this fact may be traced many of the conditions we speak of as social problems....." W. G. Beach and E. E. Walker, pp. 102–3: "...men find their life interests and values in group membership and participation. The most influential groups are those which provide

intimate, face-to-face relationships, as the family, the playground, the club, the neighborhood, and the small community . . . . . Any wholesome and satisfying life must provide for a continuation of such small groups and institutional forms . . . . . One of the most elusive and challenging problems arising from the growth of cities is that of preventing the complete disorganization of essential social groups. In the rural community . . . . ." J. H. S. Bossard (*a*), p. 113: "The marked trend of population to the city and the rapid rise of large urban centers, together with their reflex upon the rural regions, constitute the basis of virtually every problem to be discussed in this volume."

50. This is what Waller does *not* do in his provocative discussion of "humanitarian" and "organizing mores" ("Social Problems and the Mores," *American Sociological Review,* December, 1936, pp. 922–33).

51. J. L. Gillin (*b*), p. 407: The home "developing as . . . . rural" is considered "disorganized" in the city; p. 409: "[In the city] it is only the rebel, unable and unwilling to adjust himself to machine and organization, who retains personal independence . . . . . The farmer, conscious that he lives by his own thinking . . . . responds to his environment with a feeling of independence—a normal response. The city worker has no keen perception of his dependence upon nature." Elliott and Merrill, p. 32: "However different their approach, the basic dilemma of civilization is the fundamental disparity of values and standards of universally accepted definitions of the situation."

52. C. A. Ellwood (*b*), p. 281: "The reflex of the city problem is the rural problem." J. L. Gillin (*b*), p. 429: "[Urbanization] which has modified the solidarity of the rural family . . . . ." W. J. Hayes and I. V. Shannon, p. 22: "Contacts . . . . emancipate individuals from control of primary groups . . . . this leads to setting up personal norms of behavior instead of conforming to group standards." (Implies no conception of *urban* types of norms.)

53. The intellectual consequences of the rural to urban drift are much wider than the perspectives noted in the literature of pathology. In more general American sociology the writings of a man like E. A. Ross are to be understood in terms of a reaction of those oriented to a farmer's democracy against the growth of big business, in its control of railroads, etc. Another division of American sociology in which America's rural past is *intellectually* evident is "rural sociology" itself. This field shows the positive side of the matter, for here the yearning for the values associated with rural simplicity and neighborliness is even more noticeable. In this literature a primary, rural heritage is taken as the source of "stability" and is conceived as the reservoir of "values." Such straddling concepts as "urban" function to limit recognition of the urban character of dominant contemporary social structures. In a historical sense we need not argue with these emphases: the underlying form of American democracy and religion, e.g., has drawn much from the dominance of a rural society. And a

rapid urbanization may well be only a veneer upon masses of rurally oriented personalities. But the kind of structural stability in America which grew from rural patterns is historical. In the world today the kind of stability that can—indeed, in part has—emerged from the hunger for those primary contacts historically associated with ties of blood and closeness to soil is a streamlined variety.

54. *Social Organization*, chap. v.

55. G. H. Mead, "Cooley's Contribution to American Social Thought," *American Journal of Sociology*, XXXV, 701: "Cooley was Emersonian in finding the individual self in an oversoul." Cf. G. W. F. Hegel, *Lectures of the Philosophy of History* (London: Geo. Bell & Sons, 1884), especially pp. 39–44.

56. Note the common association of urban "impersonality" and "formalism" with "disorganization." Elliott and Merrill, p. 16: "....lack of harmony between the various units of the social order is in a sense....exemplified by the impersonal nature of the social organization and the consequent process of social disorganization....[cf. C. H. Cooley, *Social Process*, pp. 3–29]"; p. 574: "There is a very close relationship between formalism and disorganization, although at first glance the two states appear to be opposite poles in the social process. They are in reality sequential steps in the same great movement of disorganization, which grows out of formalism....."

57. *Beyond Conscience*, p. 111.

58. C. A. Ellwood (*b*), p. 12: "All forms of association are of interest to the sociologist, though not all are of equal importance. The natural, genetic social groups, which we may call 'communities,' serve best to exhibit sociological problems. Through the study of such simple and primary groups as the family and the neighborhood group, for example, the problems of sociology can be much better attacked than through the study of society at large or association in general"; pp. 76–77: "....natural groupings, such as the family, the neighborhood, the city, the state or province, and the nation. They may be, and usually are, called *communities*, since they are composed of individuals who carry on all phases of a common life. Voluntary, purposive associations always exist within some community, whether large or small. Groups which we call 'communities' are, therefore, more embracing, more stable, less artificial and specialized than purely voluntary groups. For this reason communities are of more interest to the sociologist than specialized voluntary groups, and sociology is in a peculiar sense a study of the problems of community life." J. H. S. Bossard (*a*), pp. 49–50: "Acceptance of the community as a definite unit in social work and in social theory has become general during the past fifteen years. American participation in the World War was an important factor in bringing this about, first because the community constituted the basic expression of that democratic spirit which the

war engendered, and second, the community was seized upon by the various war-time activities and drives as the most effective unit for the mobilization of the spirit and resources of the nation."

59. Gillin, Dittmer, and Colbert, p. 15: " . . . . *social work*, which means, scientifically developing and adjusting human relations in a way that will secure normal life to individuals and communities and encourage individual and community progress"; p. 47: " . . . . it is important to keep in mind that the central problem is that of adjusting our social life and our social institutions, so that, as individuals and as communities, we may use and enjoy the largest measure of civilization possible, and promote further progress." M. P. Follett (*a*), Part III, has suggested that neighborhood groups be organized into political units. This would permit the expression of daily life and bring to the surface live needs that they may become the substance of politics. The neighborhood as a political unit would make possible friendly acquaintance; it would socialize people and would make for "the realization of oneness."

60. J. L. Gillin (*b*), p. 97: "The 'liquor problem' is as acute in the United States today as it ever was in the past, perhaps even more so"; p. 101: "The solution must spring from an aroused and unanimous public will."

61. Cf. K. Mannheim, *Ideology and Utopia*, for definitions of these terms.

62. However, "lag" and "norms" are not unrelated: Queen, Bodenhafer, and Harper, p. 437: "Much of the discussion of cultural lags in the family assumes some kind of normal pattern which is commonly believed to have permanent validity because of the functions performed."

63. See examples given in J. W. Woodard's "Critical Notes on the Cultural Lag Concept," *Social Forces,* March, 1934, p. 388.

64. See, e.g., B. J. Stern's article in *Annals of the American Academy of Political and Social Science,* November, 1938.

65. *The Engineers and the Price System; The Theory of Business Enterprise.*

66. J. H. S. Bossard (*a*), p. 5: " . . . . as Ogburn put it [W. F. Ogburn, *Social Change* (1922)] to the extent that the adaptive culture has not kept pace with the material culture, the amount of social ill-being has increased relatively."

67. J. L. Gillin (*b*), p. 416: "Social disorganization is a function of rapidly changing conditions in people's lives." W. J. Hayes and I. V. Shannon, p. 20: "Social disorganization is an abrupt break in the existing social arrangements or a serious alteration in the routine of group life causing maladjustment." H. W. Odum, p. 100: " . . . . if one reviews the general categories of social problems already listed in previous chapters, it must be clear that most of them or their present manifestations are due to or accentuated by the process of social change."

68. The point is made and acutely discussed by Rosenquist, pp. 8–10.

69. Gillin, Dittmer, and Colbert, p. 48: "Social life and its products require long periods of time to develop and ripen....." Gillette and Reinhardt, p. 13: "The larger proportion of social changes are small and simple, and resemble osmosis in the field of physics and organic life." This gradualism is related to the orientation to primary group relations and experiences and hence to the "sharing" conception of the social. E.g., Elliott and Merrill, p. 11: "Assimilation, on the other hand, is gradual and depends upon some degree of contact and communication, if there is to be any vital sharing of common experience (Cf. M. P. Follett, *Creative Experience*)....."

70. Gillette and Reinhardt, p. 30: "....the need for thought about discontinuity in industry or education and about our dependence on proper training to keep society stabilized and progressive should be emphasized"; p. 21: "The habitual, daily, routine, conventional activities of life fortunately make up the greater part of life, most of the time. Often, however, they are broken across by social breakdowns, disturbances, and dislocations and the appearance of troublesome classes of persons." C. A. Ellwood (*a*), p. 230: "....revolution is not a *normal* method of social change;....it marks the breakdown of the normal means of social development;....it is not inevitable, but may easily be avoided by plasticity in social institutions and in the mental attitudes of classes and individuals....."

71. The notion of temporal contingency, at times extended to the point of historical irrationality, plays into the processual, nonstructural characteristics of the perspective; notice also its commensurability with the apolitical and one-thing-at-a-time reformism. Elliott and Merrill, p. 3: "Life is dynamic. Life is ceaseless, bewildering change, and man, armed though he is with the experience of the past, can never be certain of the future. He must recognize that the immediate present is a constantly changing frame of reference and that future problems are a matter of chance for which the past offers no sure panacea."

72. E. C. Hayes' Editor's Introduction to U. G. Weatherly, p. xii: "Realization that progressive change is not likely to be less in the generation next to come....and determination....to promote progress, is the normal attitude for every person who is animated by generous loyalty and....." Weatherly, p. 138: "Both innovation and conservatism have their value, and the balance between them, which is an ideal attitude...."; p. 380: "Discipline and liberation are not two antagonistic processes; they are complementary parts of the same process, which is social equilibration. They illustrate the law of physics....stability is reached only by a balance of forces."

73. C. A. Ellwood (*a*), p. vii: "The aim of the book is to indicate the direction which our social thinking must take if we are to avoid revolution, on the one hand, and reactions, on the other."

74. H. P. Fairchild, p. 35: " . . . . it can be safely said that maladjustments are among the most numerous and important of all forms of abnormality, frequently being so extensive as to include entire social groups or classes."

75. Gillin, Dittmer, and Colbert, p. 530: "All social problems grow out of *the* social problem—the problem of the adjustment of man to his universe, and of the social universe to man. The maladjustments in these relationships give us all our social problems . . . . . " H. P. Fairchild, p. 16: "While the word 'normal' carries a fairly definite and, for the most part, accurate implication to the mind of any intelligent person, it is nevertheless extremely difficult to define in concrete terms . . . . . As commonly used to convey a definite idea, the word 'normal' means that which is in harmony with the general make-up and organization of the object under discussion—that which is consistent with other normal factors."

76. Elliott and Merrill, p. 17, correctly assert that in "Edward T. Devine's discussion of 'the normal life' the norm is the healthy and uneventful life cycle of the average middle-class man or woman. These persons are never subjected to the temptations of great wealth. Neither do they come in contact with poverty, crime, vice, and other unpleasantly sordid aspects of life. [*The Normal Life*, pp. 5–8.] His discussion is thus a consideration of the 'normal standards' for the several ages of the bourgeoisie . . . . . "

77. When it is so hidden; but note the heavily sentimental endowment the term may receive: R. C. Dexter, p. 408: " . . . . few of the present generation of little ones, and fewer still of the next, will never see the sun or the green grass because of the sins of their parents or the carelessness of their physician; and thanks to our increasing provision for free public education, more and more adapted to the needs of the individual child, thousands of boys and girls will become intelligent, responsible citizens, worthy of a free nation, instead of pawns for unscrupulous politicians. All this and much more is due to social adjustments, made by the unceasing effort and sacrifice of men and women who . . . . . "

78. J. L. Gillin (*b*), p. 4: "Social pathology . . . is the study of the social patterns and processes involved in man's failure to adjust himself and his institutions to the necessities of existence to the end that he may survive and satisfy the felt needs of his nature."

79. J. L. Gillin (*b*), p. 8: "An individual who does not approximate these [socially approved] standards is said to be *unadjusted*. If he does not concern himself with living up to them, he is said to be demoralized or disorganized." R. C. Dexter, p. 407: "In this book the term Social

Adjustment has been. . . . used as applying to. . . . the necessary task of smoothing-off the rough edges and softening the sledge-hammer blows of an indifferent social system. The term. . . . is practically synonymous with social adaptation—the fitting of man to his complete environment, physical and social alike. Until the present it has been the especially maladjusted individual or group who has received the service of 'straighteners.'" (Note *ideological* orientation of concept.)

80. H. P. Fairchild, p. 34: "The other form of incompetence, which may be called 'maladjustment,' does not imply any lack on the part of the individual himself. . . . . The man is all right, but he is not in the right place. Our immigrants furnish abundant examples of this form of incompetence. . . . . But the foreigner is not by any means the sole example of maladjustment. Our modern life, particularly our modern city life, teems with cases of this sort." J. H. S. Bossard (*a*), p. 110 (under "The Immigrant's Problem of Adjustment"): "To most persons, life consists in large measure of habitual responses to the demands of a fairly fixed environment. When man changes his environment, new and perhaps untried responses are called for. New adjustments must be made, as we say." J. L. Gillin (*b*), p. 10: "Social pathology. . . . arises out of the maladjustment between the individual and the social structure." Elliott and Merrill, p. 22: "Just as an effective social organization implies a harmony between individual and social interests, so a disorganized social order must involve a conflict between individual and social points of view."

81. Gillin, Dittmer, and Colbert, pp. 16–17: "By *socialization* we mean the directing of human motives toward giving to 'even the least' of the members of the social whole the benefits of cultural development. Socialization is thus practically the opposite to *aloofness, selfishness, greed, exploitation,* and *profiteering.* It causes the individual and the group to *feel* their *oneness* with the social whole. . . . . In brief, what society regards as *moral, i.e.,* good for the whole, becomes the aim of socialized individuals and groups. This being true, the improvement of society rests to a very large extent upon *moral progress.*"

82. See Queen and Gruener, *Social Pathology: Obstacles to Social Participation.* These authors would deny this mode of statement, but such verbal denials must be tested against what they have done and the framework they have actually employed in defining pathologies. Their criterion of the pathological is correctly indicated in the subtitle of their book. Elliott and Merrill, p. 580: "There are various criteria by which the degree of individual participation may be measured roughly. . . . whether or not he votes at elections. . . . the individual's ownership of real or personal property. . . . the degree of specific interest in community activities may be roughly measured by the number and character of the institutions to which the individual belongs, as well as the voluntary community activities in which he participates. Communities in which there is a high percentage of

individuals with a positive rating on the items listed above are logically those which are the most highly organized and efficient." (Note the character of the institutions, participation in which is defined as organized.)

83. See above documentation; notice the Protestant ethical accent on *utility* and what it will do for one, apparently irrespective of social fact: Gillin, Dittmer, and Colbert, p. 106: "People who are useful, no matter what happens to be their race or color, come to be liked and respected. Consequently, the central aim of a sound educational program should be to teach people to be useful. (Hart, Hornell, *The Science of Social Relations*, 1927, pp. 521–524.)" In the following, note the norm of competitiveness: Elliott and Merrill, pp. 29–30: "Often, however, the individual cannot or will not compete. We then have the following pathological manifestations: '. . . . the *dependent*. . . . who is unable to compete; the *defective*. . . . who is, if not unable, at least handicapped in his efforts to compete. The *criminal*, on the other hand, ... who is perhaps unable, but at any rate refuses, to compete according to the rules which society lays down.' (Park and Burgess, *Introduction to the Science of Sociology*, p. 560.)" Among the traits thought to characterize "the good life from the standpoint of the individual," Odum, pp. 50–51, cites: "patience," "specialized knowledge of some particular thing," "skill," "optimism," "love of work," "dynamic personality," "moderation," "trained will power," etc. Cf., in this connection, K. Davis, "Mental Hygiene and the Class Structure," *Psychiatry: Journal of the Biology and Pathology of Interpersonal Relations*, February, 1938, pp. 55–65.

CHAPTER **III**

Anomie

What happens to people when the limitations imposed on them by social life are relaxed or are no longer binding? Are they likely to be more content freed from the restraints and obligations of social life, or would happiness be impossible if they were unencumbered by social rules? And on the societal level, would freedom from regulation by norms increase or decrease social pathology? The readings in Chapter III explore these questions by considering the relationships among human desires, social structural conditions, and deviance.

The social disorganization theories discussed in Chapter II focused on the negative effects of social change on traditional ways of life, implying that freedom from normative restraints is likely to lead to higher rates of deviance. As a starting point, this chapter picks up on a similar theme. The idea underlying Emile Durkheim's concept of anomie is that during periods of sudden social change, the traditional rules of a society or group become less binding on the individual members, and the hypothesized result is increased deviance. This idea is extended by Robert K. Merton to the deviance-producing difficulties which arise in societies (such as that of the United States) that are characterized by considerable class or ethnic stratification.

The first reading in this chapter, Reading 9, is from Durkheim's *Suicide*. As one of sociology's earliest proponents, Durkheim was trying to demonstrate how even a highly individualistic phenomenon such as suicide can be explained in reference to social arrangements. Durkheim postulates that happiness depends on a balance between individual desires and the possibility of fulfilling them. Humans have socially induced appetites which are virtually insatiable; their needs and desires are ever-increasing and therefore limitless if unchecked. Unless they curb these desires and hold them to a level at which fulfillment is possible, they are bound to suffer permanent malaise. Durkheim compares this to inextinguishable thirst, which is "constantly renewed torture." He maintains that "To pursue a goal which is by definition unattainable is to condemn oneself to a state of perpetual unhappiness."

Since it is apparent that in order to escape the torment of unattainable aspirations, desires must be restrained, and since it is not in people's nature to apply such restraints voluntarily, Durkheim concludes that some external regulative force must be applied to establish limits. This constraining force is society, which alone has the necessary power "to stipulate law and to set the point beyond which passions must not go." People are therefore dependent on societal norms to curb their limitless desires and make their existence tolerable.

Under most conditions the normative restrictions are clear, and most people adhere to them. But when there is social upheaval, as during an economic crisis, they may find themselves in unfamiliar situations. The limits of the possible and the impossible may then become unknown. The resulting social condition is what Durkheim calls anomie, or a state of normlessness. He argues that as anomie increases in a society, malaise and despair will also increase, and so will indicators of pathology such as the suicide rate.

Durkheim also argues that modern, industrial societies can be expected to be far more afflicted with anomie and to have chronically higher suicide rates than less developed societies. This is because the recurrent highs and lows in the economic cycles of modern societies, coupled with their greater social mobility, continually subject their members to anomie. Less developed societies, being more economically stable and socially rigid (though often highly stratified), have more enduring normative patterns and therefore less anomie and lower suicide rates. To this day, data comparing the suicide rates of developed countries (relatively high) with those of developing countries (relatively low) are consistent with Durkheim's anomie theory.

Durkheim attempts in Reading 9 to explain varying rates of what historically has been regarded as a highly individualistic phenomenon, suicide, by reference to a social condition—anomie. In Reading 10, Merton also seeks to show how social structures can exert pressure on certain persons to engage in deviant behavior.[1] Like Durkheim, he uses the term *anomie* to denote normlessness in a society, but he extends Durkheim's explanation of its causes.

Merton argues that anomie arises in a society when there is an imbalance of emphasis on the importance of attaining culturally valued goals and the availability of legitimate, institutionalized means to reach these goals. The requisite conditions for anomie are present when members of some segments of society (e.g., the poor, certain racial or ethnic minorities) are constantly informed through the media and popular wisdom that monetary success and its material rewards are positively valued goals, while at the same time their experience tells them that the legitimate means for achieving these goals are relatively unavailable to them. As a result of this anomic condition within the society—the discrepancy between means and ends—these individuals may maintain their desires to achieve the culturally valued goals but reject the traditionally legitimate means for achieving them because these means are not readily accessible. Merton suggests a typology of five ways in which individuals occupying different positions in the social structure adapt to anomie; they may conform, or they may engage in one of four deviant adaptations. In Merton's terms, the first deviant adaptation is innovation, which includes what is more commonly called crime; the other deviant adaptations are ritualism, retreatism, and rebellion.

Thus, whereas Durkheim attributes anomie to a breakdown or deregulation of the norms in a society, so that they no longer effectively control behavior, Merton accounts for anomie in the disparity between culturally accepted goals and the legitimate institutionalized means available to achieve them. Further, Durkheim sees anomie as the outcome of crisis situations in society, especially as the result of chronic economic instability in modern countries. In contrast, Merton views anomie as the outgrowth of a rather constant discrepancy in American society between an overemphasis on success-oriented goals and a corresponding failure to provide equality of opportunity.

Merton's proposition that people in a society who do not find legitimate means to success available are likely to turn to illegitimate means is based on the assumption that illegitimate opportunities to reach success goals *will be available.* In Reading 11, Richard Cloward builds upon Merton's work by suggesting that such means may not be equally accessible, just as legitimate means are not. He argues that there are different *illegal,* as well as different legal, opportunity structures. As a consequence, when legitimate means to success goals are blocked, the likelihood that a person will, for example, "innovate" (e.g., commit crime) or "retreat" (e.g., take drugs), depends in large part on which opportunities are most readily available. Thus, taken together, Merton and Cloward draw attention to the role of both legitimate and illegitimate opportunity structures for the production and shaping of deviant behavior. Cloward's examination of variations in the availability of illegitimate means as an explanation for why certain people become deviant refers to Edwin Sutherland's work on the concept of differential association, which is the topic of Chapter IV.

The Analysis and Critique section in this chapter, by Albert K. Cohen (Reading 12), deals mostly with Merton's formulation of anomie theory and serves as a bridge to a number of the theories that follow. Cohen argues that although it claims to be sociological, Merton's approach is "in certain respects, atomistic and individualistic." The problem stems from its failure to account for social-psychological processes in the explanation of how a person becomes deviant. For example, the theory seems to assume that the dominant values in a society are internalized at about the same level by all its members. Cohen suggests it is more realistic to consider the comparisons that people make with one another as they settle on their individual levels of aspiration.

In addition, anomie theory treats the transition from conformity to deviance as though it were an abrupt change. More accurately, Cohen contends, deviance theory should recognize the processes a person goes through—the tentative, groping, false starts and unintended actions—which lead to a deviant role. These processes include the responses to deviance made by social control agents and "the process of progressive involvement in, commitment to, and movement among social roles" that an individual undergoes in establishing a deviant identity. Thus, while people may be subject to the socially induced strain of anomie, they may also be affected by role models, peer pressures, their self-image, their perceptions of other people's reactions to their behavior, and their power to defend the norms of their groups and their own behavior. Attemps to deal with such issues underlie the theories presented in subsequent chapters.

NOTE

1. Also see Robert K. Merton, "Social Structure and Anomie," *American Sociological Review* 3 (October 1938): 672.

9 *Anomic Suicide*
EMILE DURKHEIM

No living being can be happy or even exist unless his needs are sufficiently proportioned to his means. In other words, if his needs require more than can be granted, or even merely something of a different sort, they will be under continual friction and can only function painfully. Movements incapable of production without pain tend not to be reproduced. Unsatisfied tendencies atrophy, and as the impulse to live is merely the result of all the rest, it is bound to weaken as the others relax.

In the animal, at least in a normal condition, this equilibrium is established with automatic spontaneity because the animal depends on purely material conditions. All the organism needs is that the supplies of substance and energy constantly employed in the vital process should be periodically renewed by equivalent quantities; that replacement be equivalent to use. When the void created by existence in its own resources is filled, the animal, satisfied, asks nothing further. Its power of reflection is not sufficiently developed to imagine other ends than those implicit in its physical nature. On the other hand, as the work demanded of each organ itself depends on the general state of vital energy and the needs of organic equilibrium, use is regulated in turn by replacement and the balance is automatic. The limits of one are those of the other; both are fundamental to the constitution of the existence in question, which cannot exceed them.

This is not the case with man, because most of his needs are not dependent on his body or not to the same degree. Strictly speaking, we may consider that the quantity of material supplies necessary to the physical maintenance of a human life is subject to computation, though this be less exact than in the preceding case and a wider margin left for the free combinations of the will; for beyond the indispensable minimum which satisfies nature when instinctive, a more awakened reflection suggests better conditions, seemingly desirable ends craving fulfillment. Such appetites, however, admittedly sooner or later reach a limit which they cannot pass. But how determine the quantity of well-being, comfort or luxury legitimately to be craved by a human being? Nothing appears in man's organic nor in his psychological constitution which sets a limit to such tendencies. The functioning of individual life does not require them to cease at one point rather than at another; the proof being that they have constantly increased since the beginnings of history, receiving more and more complete satisfaction, yet with no weakening of average health. Above all, how establish their proper variation with different conditions of life, occupations, relative importance of services, etc.? In no society are they equally satisfied in the different stages of the social hierarchy. Yet human nature is substantially the same among all men, in its essential qualities. It is not human nature which can assign the variable limits necessary to our needs. They are thus unlimited so far as they depend on the individual alone. Irrespective of any external regulatory force, our capacity for feeling is in itself an insatiable and bottomless abyss.

But if nothing external can restrain this capacity, it can only be a source of torment to itself. Unlimited desires are insatiable by definition and insatiability is rightly considered a sign of morbidity. Being unlimited, they constantly and infinitely surpass the means at their command; they cannot be quenched. Inextinguishable thirst is constantly renewed torture. It has been claimed, indeed, that human activity naturally aspires beyond assignable limits and sets itself unattainable goals. But how can such an undetermined state be any more reconciled with the conditions of mental life than with the demands of physical life? All man's pleasure in acting, moving and exerting himself implies the sense that his efforts are not in vain and that by walking he has advanced. However, one does not advance when one walks toward no goal, or—which is the same thing—when his goal is infinity. Since the distance between us and it is always the same, whatever road we take, we might as well have made the motions without progress from the spot. Even our glances behind and our feeling of pride at the distance covered can cause only deceptive satisfaction, since the remaining distance is not proportionately reduced. To pursue a goal which is by definition unattainable is to condemn oneself to a state of perpetual unhappiness. Of course, man may hope contrary to all reason, and hope has its pleasures even when unreasonable. It may sustain him for a time; but it cannot survive the repeated disappointments of experience indefinitely. What more can the future offer him than the past, since he can never reach a tenable condition nor even approach the glimpsed ideal? Thus, the more one has, the more one wants, since satisfactions received only stimulate instead of filling needs. Shall action as such be considered agreeable? First, only on condition of blindness to its uselessness. Secondly, for this pleasure to be felt and to temper and half veil the accompanying painful unrest, such unending motion must at least always be easy and unhampered. If it is interfered with only restlessness is left, with the lack of ease which it, itself, entails. But it would be a miracle if no insurmountable obstacle were never encountered. Our thread of life on these conditions is pretty thin, breakable at any instant.

To achieve any other result, the passions first must be limited. Only then can they be harmonized with the faculties and satisfied. But since the individual has no way of limiting them, this must be done by some force exterior to him. A regulative force must play the same role for moral needs which the organism plays for physical needs. This means that the force can only be moral. The awakening of conscience interrupted the state of equilibrium of the animal's dormant existence; only conscience, therefore, can furnish the means to re-establish it. Physical restraint would be ineffective; hearts cannot be touched by physiochemical forces. So far as the appetites are not automatically restrained by physiological mechanisms, they can be halted only by a limit that they recognize as just. Men would never consent to restrict their desires if they felt justified in passing the assigned limit. But, for reasons given above, they cannot assign themselves this law of justice. So they must receive it from an authority which they respect, to which they yield spontaneously. Either directly and as a whole, or through the agency of one of its organs, society alone can play this moderating role; for it is the only moral power superior to the individual, the authority of which he accepts. It alone has the power necessary to stipulate law and to set the point beyond which the passions must not go. Finally, it alone can estimate the reward to be prospectively offered to every class of human functionary, in the name of the common interest.

As a matter of fact, at every moment of history there is an dim perception, in the moral consciousness of societies, of the respective value of different social services, the relative reward due to each, and the consequent degree of comfort appropriate on the average to workers in each occupation. The different functions are graded in public opinion and a certain coefficient of well-being assigned to each, according to its place in the hierarchy. According to accepted ideas, for example, a certain way of living is considered the upper limit to which a workman may aspire in his efforts to improve his existence, and there is another limit below which he is not willingly permitted to fall unless he has seriously demeaned himself. Both differ for city and country workers, for the domestic servant and the day-laborer, for the business clerk and the official, etc. Likewise the man of wealth is reproved if he lives the life of a poor man, but also if he seeks the refinements of luxury overmuch. Economists may protest in vain; public feeling will always be scandalized if an individual spends too much wealth for wholly superfluous use, and it even seems that this severity relaxes only in times of moral disturbance.[1] A genuine regimen exists, therefore, although not always legally formulated, which fixes with relative precision the maximum degree of ease of living to which each social class may legitimately aspire. However, there is nothing immutable about such a scale. It changes with the increase or decrease of collective revenue and the changes occurring in the moral ideas of society. Thus what appears luxury to one period no longer does so to another; and the well-being which for long periods was granted to a class only by exception and supererogation, finally appears strictly necessary and equitable.

Under this pressure, each in his sphere vaguely realizes the extreme limit set to his ambitions and aspires to nothing beyond. At least if he respects regulations and is docile to collective authority, that is, has a wholesome moral constitution, he feels that it is not well to ask more. Thus, an end and goal are set to the passions. Truly, there is nothing rigid nor absolute about such determination. The economic ideal assigned each class of citizens is itself confined to certain limits, within which the desires have free range. But it is not infinite. This relative limitation and the moderation it involves, make men contented with their lot while stimulating them moderately to improve it; and this average contentment causes the feeling of calm, active happiness, the pleasure in existing and living which characterizes health for societies as well as for individuals. Each person is then at least, generally speaking, in harmony with his condition, and desires only what he may legitimately hope for as the normal reward of his activity. Besides, this does not condemn man to a sort of immobility. He may seek to give beauty to his life; but his attempts in this direction may fail without causing him to despair. For, loving what he has and not fixing his desire solely on what he lacks, his wishes and hopes may fail of what he has happened to aspire to, without his being wholly destitute. He has the essentials. The equilibrium of his happiness is secure because it is defined, and a few mishaps cannot disconcert him.

But it would be of little use for everyone to recognize the justice of the hierarchy of functions established by public opinion, if he did not also consider the distribution of these functions just. The workman is not in harmony with his social position if he is not convinced that he has his desserts. If he feels justified in occupying another, what he has would not satisfy him. So it is not enough for the average level of needs for each social condition to be regulated by public opinion, but another, more precise rule, must fix the way in which these conditions are open to individuals. There is no society in which such regulation does not exist. It varies with times and places. Once it regarded birth as the almost exclusive principle of social classification; today it recognizes no other inherent inequality than hereditary fortune and merit. But in all these various forms its object is unchanged. It is also only possible, everywhere, as a restriction upon individuals imposed by superior authority, that is, by collective authority. For it can be established only by requiring of one or another group of men, usually of all, sacrifices and concessions in the name of the public interest.

Some, to be sure, have thought that this moral pressure would become unnecessary if men's economic circumstances were only no longer determined by heredity. If inheritance were abolished, the argument runs, if everyone began life with equal resources and if the competitive struggle were fought out on a basis of perfect equality, no one could think its results unjust. Each would instinctively feel that things are as they should be.

Truly, the nearer this ideal equality were approached, the less social restraint will be necessary. But it is only a matter of degree. One sort of heredity will always exist, that of natural talent. Intelligence, taste, scientific, artistic, literary or industrial ability, courage and manual dexterity are gifts received by each of us at birth, as the heir to wealth receives his capital or as the nobleman formerly received his title and function. A moral discipline will therefore still be required to make those less favored by nature accept the lesser advantages which they owe to the chance of birth. Shall it be demanded that all have an equal share and that no advantage be given those more useful and deserving? But then there would have to be a discipline far stronger to make these accept a treatment merely equal to that of the mediocre and incapable.

But like the one first mentioned, this discipline can be useful only if considered just by the peoples subject to it. When it is maintained only by custom and force, peace and harmony are illusory; the spirit of unrest and discontent are latent; appetites superficially restrained are ready to revolt. This happened in Rome and Greece when the faiths underlying the old organization of the patricians and plebeians were shaken, and in our modern societies when aristocratic prejudices began to lose their old ascendancy. But this state of upheaval is exceptional; it occurs only when society is passing through some abnormal crisis. In normal conditions the collective order is regarded as just by the great majority of persons. Therefore, when we say that an authority is necessary to impose this order on individuals, we certainly do not mean that violence is the only means of establishing it. Since this regulation is meant to restrain individual passions, it must come from a power which dominates individuals; but this power must also be obeyed through respect, not fear.

It is not true, then, that human activity can be released from all restraint. Nothing in the world can enjoy such a privilege. All existence being a part of the universe is relative to the remainder; its nature and method of manifestation accordingly depend not only on itself but on other beings, who consequently restrain and regulate it. Here there are only differences of degree and form between the mineral realm and the thinking person. Man's characteristic privilege is that the bond he accepts is not physical but moral; that is, social. He is governed not by a material environment brutally imposed on him, but by a conscience superior to his own, the superiority of which he feels.

Because the greater, better part of his existence transcends the body, he escapes the body's yoke, but is subject to that of society.

But when society is disturbed by some painful crisis or by beneficent but abrupt transitions, it is momentarily incapable of exercising this influence; thence come the sudden rises in the curve of suicides which we have pointed out above.

In the case of economic disasters, indeed, somethings like a declassification occurs which suddenly casts certain individuals into a lower state than their previous one. Then they must reduce their requirements, restrain their needs, learn greater self-control. All the advantages of social influence are lost so far as they are concerned; their moral education has to be recommenced. But society cannot adjust them instantaneously to this new life and teach them to practice the increased self-repression to which they are unaccustomed. So they are not adjusted to the condition forced on them, and its very prospect is intolerable; hence the suffering which detaches them from a reduced existence even before they have made trial of it.

It is the same if the source of the crisis is an abrupt growth of power and wealth. Then, truly, as the conditions of life are changed, the standard according to which needs were regulated can no longer remain the same; for it varies with social resources, since it largely determines the share of each class of producers. The scale is upset; but a new scale cannot be immediately improvised. Time is required for the public conscience to reclassify men and things. So long as the social forces thus freed have not regained equilibrium, their respective values are unknown and so all regulation is lacking for a time. The limits are unknown between the possible and the impossible, what is just and what is unjust, legitimate claims and hopes and those which are immoderate. Consequently, there is no restraint upon aspirations. If the disturbance is profound, it affects even the principles controlling the distribution of men among various occupations. Since the relations between various parts of society are necessarily modified, the ideas expressing these relations must change. Some particular class especially favored by the crisis is no longer resigned to its former lot, and, on the other hand, the example of its greater good fortune arouses all sorts of jealousy below and about it. Appetites, not being controlled by a public opinion, become disoriented, no longer recognize the limits proper to them. Besides, they are at the same time seized by a sort of natural erethism simply by the greater intensity of public life. With increased prosperity desires increase. At the very moment when traditional rules have lost their authority, the richer prize offered these appetites stimulates them and makes them more exigent and impatient of control. The state of de-regulation or anomy is thus further heightened by passions being less disciplined, precisely when they need more disciplining.

But then their very demands make fulfillment impossible. Overweening ambition always exceeds the results obtained, great as they may be, since there is no warning to pause here. Nothing gives satisfaction and all this agitation is uninterruptedly maintained without appeasement. Above all, since this race for an unattainable goal can give no other pleasure but that of the race itself, if it is one, once it is interrupted the participants are left empty-handed. At the same time the struggle grows more violent and painful, both from being less controlled and because competition is greater. All classes contend among themselves because no established classification any longer exists. Effort grows, just when it becomes less productive. How could the desire to live not be weakened under such conditions?

This explanation is confirmed by the remarkable immunity of poor countries. Poverty protects against suicide because it is a restraint in itself. No matter how one acts, desires have to depend upon resources to some extent; actual possessions are partly the criterion of those aspired to. So the less one has the less he is tempted to extend the range of his needs indefinitely. Lack of power, compelling moderation, accustoms men to it, while nothing excites envy if no one has superfluity. Wealth, on the other hand, by the power it bestows, deceives us into believing that we depend on ourselves only. Reducing the resistance we encounter from objects, it suggests the possibility of unlimited success against them. The less limited one feels, the more intolerable all limitation appears. Not without reason, therefore, have so many religions dwelt on the advantages and moral value of poverty. It is actually the best school for teaching self-restraint. Forcing us to constant self-discipline, it prepares us to accept collective discipline with equanimity, while wealth, exalting the individual, may always arouse the spirit of rebellion which is the very source of immorality. This, of course, is no reason why humanity should not improve its material condition. But though the moral danger involved in every growth of prosperity is not irremediable, it should not be forgotten.

If anomy never appeared except, as in the above instances, in intermittent spurts and acute crisis, it might cause the social suicide-rate to vary from time to time, but it would not be a regular, constant factor. In one sphere of social life, however—the sphere to trade and industry—it is actually in a chronic state.

For a whole century, economic progress has mainly consisted in freeing industrial relations from all regulation. Until very recently, it was the function of a whole system of moral forces to exert this discipline. First, the influence of religion was felt alike by workers and masters, the poor and the rich. It consoled the former and taught them contentment with their lot by informing them of the providential nature of the social order, that the share of each class was assigned by God himself, and by holding out the hope for just compensation in a world to come in return for the inequalities of this world. It governed the latter, recalling that worldly interests are not man's entire lot, that they must be subordinate to other and higher interests, and that they should therefore not be pursued without rule or measure. Temporal power, in turn, restrained the scope of economic functions by its supremacy over them and by the relatively subordinate role it assigned them. Finally, within the business world proper, the occupational groups by regulating salaries, the price of products and production itself, indirectly fixed the average level of income on which needs are partially based by the very force of circumstances. However, we do not mean to propose this organization as a model. Clearly it would be inadequate to existing societies without great changes. What we stress is its existence, the fact of its useful influence, and that nothing today has come to take its place.

Actually, religion has lost most of its power. And government, instead of regulating economic life, has become its tool and servant. The most opposite schools, orthodox economists and extreme socialists, unite to reduce government to the role of a more or less passive intermediary among the various social functions. The former wish to make it simply the guardian of individual contracts; the latter leave it the task of doing the collective bookkeeping, that is, of recording the demands of consumers, transmitting them to producers, inventorying the total revenue and distributing it according to a fixed formula. But both refuse it any power to subordinate other social organs to itself and to make them converge toward one dominant aim. On both sides nations are declared to have the single or chief purpose of achieving industrial prosperity; such is the implication of the dogma of economic materialism, the basis of both apparently opposed systems. And as these theories merely express the state of opinion, industry, instead of being still regarded as a means to an end transcending itself, has become the supreme end of individuals and societies alike. Thereupon the appetites thus excited have become freed of any limiting authority. By sanctifying them, so to speak, this apotheosis of well-being has placed them above all human law. Their restraint seems like a sort of sacrilege. For this reason, even the purely utilitarian regulation of them exercised by the industrial world itself through the medium of occupational groups has been unable to persist. Ultimately, this liberation of desires has been made worse by the very development of industry and the almost infinite extension of the market.

So long as the producer could gain his profits only in his immediate neighborhood, the restricted amount of possible gain could not much overexcite ambition. Now that he may assume to have almost the entire world as his customer, how could passions accept their former confinement in the face of such limitless prospects?

Such is the source of the excitement predominating in this part of society, and which has thence extended to the other parts. There, the state of crisis and anomy is constant and, so to speak, normal. From top to bottom of the ladder, greed is aroused without knowing where to find ultimate foothold. Nothing can calm it, since its goal is far beyond all it can attain. Reality seems valueless by comparison with the dreams of fevered imagination; reality is therefore abandoned, but so too is possibility abandoned when it in turn becomes reality. A thirst arises for novelties, unfamiliar pleasures, nameless sensations, all of which lose their savor once known. Henceforth one has no strength to endure the least reverse. The whole fever subsides and the sterility of all the tumult is apparent, and it is seen that all these new sensations in their infinite quantity cannot form a solid foundation of happiness to support one during days of trial. The wise man, knowing how to enjoy achieved results without having constantly to replace them with others, finds in them an attachment to life in the hour of difficulty. But the man who has always pinned all his hopes on the future and lived with his eyes fixed upon it, has nothing in the past as a comfort against the present's afflictions, for the past was nothing to him but a series of hastily experienced stages. What blinded him to himself was his expectation always to find further on the happiness he had so far missed. Now he is stopped in his tracks; from now on nothing remains behind or ahead of him to fix his gaze upon. Weariness alone, moreover, is enough to bring disillusionment, for he cannot in the end escape the futility of an endless pursuit.

We may even wonder if this moral state is not principally what makes economic catastrophes of our day so fertile in suicides. In societies where a man is subjected to a healthy discipline, he submits more readily to the blows of chance. The necessary effort for sustaining a little more discomfort costs him relatively little, since he is used to discomfort and constraint. But when every constraint is hateful in itself, how can closer constraint not seem intolerable? There is no tendency to resignation in the feverish impatience of men's lives. When there is no other aim but to outstrip constantly the point arrived at, how painful to be thrown back! Now this very lack of organization characterizing our economic condition throws the door wide to every sort of adventure. Since imagination is hungry for novelty, and ungoverned, it gropes at random. Setbacks necessarily increase with risks and thus crises multiply, just when they are becoming more destructive.

Yet these dispositions are so inbred that society has grown to accept them and is accustomed to think them normal. It is everlastingly repeated that it is man's nature to be eternally dissatisfied, constantly to advance, without relief or rest, toward an indefinite goal. The longing for infinity is daily represented as a mark of moral distinction, whereas it can only appear within unregulated consciences which elevate to a rule the lack of rule from which they suffer. The doctrine of the most ruthless and swift progress has become an article of faith. But other theories appear parallel with those praising the advantages of instability, which, generalizing the situation that gives them birth, declare life evil, claim that it is richer in grief than in pleasure and that it attracts men only by false claims. Since this disorder is greatest in the economic world, it has most victims there.

Industrial and commercial functions are really among the occupations which furnish the greatest number of suicides (see Table 1). Almost on a level with the liberal professions, they sometimes surpass them; they are especially more afflicted than agriculture, where the old regulative forces still make their appearance felt most and where the fever of business has least penetrated. Here is best recalled what was once the general constitution of the economic order. And the divergence would be yet greater if, among the suicides of industry, employers were distinguished from workmen, for the former are probably most stricken by the state of anomy. The enormous rate of those with independent means (720 per million) sufficiently shows that the possessors of most comfort suffer most. Everything that enforces subordination attenuates the effects of this state. At least the horizon of the lower classes is limited by those above them, and for this same reason their desires are more modest. Those who have only empty space above them are almost inevitably lost in it, if no force restrains them.

Anomy, therefore, is a regular and specific factor in suicide in our modern societies; one of the springs from which the annual contingent feeds. So we have here a new type to distinguish from the others. It differs from them in its dependence, not on the way in which individuals are attached to society, but on how it regulates them. Egoistic suicide results from man's no longer finding a basis for existence in life; altruistic suicide, because this basis for existence appears to man situated beyond life itself. The third sort of suicide, the existence of which has just been shown, results from man's activity's lacking regulation and his consequent sufferings. By virtue of its origin we shall assign this last variety the name of *anomic suicide*.

TABLE 1   SUICIDES PER MILLION PERSONS OF DIFFERENT
OCCUPATIONS

	TRADE	TRANS-PORTATION	INDUSTRY	AGRI-CULTURE	LIBERAL*PROFESSIONS
France (1878–87)†	440	—	340	240	300
Switzerland (1876)	664	1,514	577	304	558
Italy (1866–76)	277	152.6	80.4	26.7	618‡
Prussia (1883–90)	754	—	456	315	832
Bavaria (1884–91)	465	—	369	153	454
Belgium (1886–90)	421	—	160	160	100
Wurttemberg (1873–78)	273	—	190	206	—
Saxony (1878)	—	341.59§	—	71.17	—

*When statistics distinguish several different sorts of liberal occupations, we show as a specimen the one in which the suicide-rate is highest.

†From 1826 to 1880 economic functions seem less affected (see *Compte-rendu* of 1880); but were occupational statistics very accurate?

‡This figure is reached only by men of letters.

§Figure represents Trade, Transportation and Industry combined for Saxony. (Ed.)

Certainly, this and egoistic suicide have kindred ties. Both spring from society's insufficient presence in individuals. But the sphere of its absence is not the same in both cases. In egoistic suicide it is deficient in truly collective activity, thus depriving the latter of object and meaning. In anomic suicide, society's influence is lacking in the basically individual passions, thus leaving them without a check-rein. In spite of their relationship, therefore, the two types are independent of each other. We may offer society everything social in us, and still be unable to control our desires; one may live in an anomic state without being egoistic, and vice versa. These two sorts of suicide therefore do not draw their chief recruits from the same social environments; one has its principal field among intellectual careers, the world of thought—the other, the industrial or commercial world.

NOTE

1. Actually, this is a purely moral reprobation and can hardly be judicially implemented. We do not consider any reestablishment of sumptuary laws desirable or even possible.

10 *Social Structure and Anomie*
ROBERT K. MERTON

Until recently, and all the more so before then, one could speak of a marked tendency in psychological and sociological theory to attribute the faulty operation of social structures to failures of social control over man's imperious biological drives. The imagery of the relations between man and society implied by this doctrine is as clear as it is questionable. In the beginning, there are man's biological impulses which seek full expression. And then, there is the social order, essentially an apparatus for the management of impulses, for the social processing of tensions, for the "renunciation of instinctual gratifications," in the words of Freud. Nonconformity with the demands of a social structure is thus assumed to be anchored in original nature.[1] It is the biologically rooted impulses which from time to time break through social control. And by implication, conformity is the result of an utilitarian calculus or of unreasoned conditioning.

With the more recent advancement of social science, this set of conceptions has undergone basic modification. For one thing, it no longer appears so obvious that man is set against society in an unceasing war between biological impulse and social restraint. The image of man as an untamed bundle of impulses begins to look more like a caricature than a portrait. For another, sociological perspectives have increasingly entered into the analysis of behavior deviating from prescribed patterns of conduct. For whatever the role of biological impulses, there still remains the further question of why it is that the frequency of deviant behavior varies within different social structures and how it happens that the deviations have different shapes and patterns in different social structures. Today, as then, we have still much to learn about the processes through which social structures generate the circumstances in which infringement of social codes constitutes a "normal" (that is to say, an expectable) response.[2] This chapter is an essay seeking clarification of the problem.

The framework set out in this essay is designed to provide one systematic approach to the analysis of social and cultural sources of deviant behavior. Our primary aim is to discover how some *social structures exert a definite pressure upon certain persons in the society to engage in nonconforming rather than conforming conduct.* If we can locate groups peculiarly subject to such pressures, we should expect to find fairly high rates of deviant behavior in these groups, not because the human beings comprising them are compounded of distinctive biological tendencies but because they are responding normally to the social situation in which they find themselves. Our perspective is sociological. We look at variations in the *rates* of deviant behavior, not at its incidence.[3] Should our quest be at all successful, some forms of deviant behavior will be found to be as psychologically normal as conforming behavior, and the equation of deviation and psychological abnormality will be put in question.

PATTERNS OF CULTURAL GOALS AND INSTITUTIONAL NORMS

Among the several elements of social and cultural structures, two are of immediate importance. These are analytically separable although they merge in concrete situations. The first consists of culturally defined goals, purposes and interests, held out as legitimate objectives for all or for diversely located members of the society. The goals are more or less integrated—the degree is a question of empirical fact—and roughly ordered in some hierarchy of value. Involving various degrees of sentiment and significance, the prevailing goals comprise a frame of aspirational reference. They are the things "worth striving for." They are a basic, though not the exclusive, component of what Linton has called "designs for group living." And though some, not all, of these cultural goals are directly related to the biological drives of man, they are not determined by them.

A second element of the cultural structure defines, regulates and controls the acceptable modes of reaching out for these goals. Every social group invariably couples its cultural objectives with regulations, rooted in the mores or institutions, of allowable procedures for moving toward these objectives. These regulatory norms are not necessarily identical with technical or efficiency norms. Many procedures which from the standpoint of particular individuals would be most efficient in securing desired values—the exercise of force, fraud, power—are ruled out of the institutional area of permitted conduct. At times, the disallowed procedures include some which would be efficient for the group itself—e.g., historic taboos on vivisection, on medical experimentation, on the sociological analysis of "sacred" norms—since the criterion of acceptability is not technical efficiency but value-laden sentiments (supported by most members of the group or by those able to promote these sentiments through the composite use of power and propaganda). In all instances, the choice of expedients for striving toward cultural goals is limited by institutionalized norms.

Sociologists often speak of these controls as being "in the mores" or as operating through social institutions. Such elliptical statements are true enough, but they obscure the fact that culturally standardized practices are not all of a piece. They are subject to a wide gamut of control. They may represent definitely prescribed or preferential or permissive or proscribed patterns of behavior. In assessing the operation of social controls, these variations—roughly indicated by the terms *prescription, preference, permission* and *proscription*—must of course be taken into account.

To say, moreover, that cultural goals and institutionalized norms operate jointly to shape prevailing practices is not to say that they bear a constant relation to one another. The cultural emphasis placed upon certain goals varies independently of the degree of emphasis upon institutionalized means. There may develop a very heavy, at times a virtually exclusive, stress upon the value of particular goals, involving comparatively little concern with the institutionally prescribed means of striving toward these goals. The limiting case of this type is reached when the range of alternative procedures is governed only by technical rather than by institutional norms. Any and all procedures which promise attainment of the all-important goal would be permitted in this hypothetical polar case. This constitutes one type of malintegrated culture. A second polar type is found in groups where activities originally conceived as instrumental are transmuted into self-contained practices, lacking further objectives. The original purposes are forgotten and close adherence to institutionally prescribed conduct becomes a matter of ritual.[4] Sheer conformity becomes a central value. For a time, social stability is ensured—at the expense of flexibility. Since the range of alternative behaviors permitted by the culture is severely limited, there is little basis for adapting to new conditions. There develops a tradition-bound, 'sacred' society marked by neophobia. Between these extreme types are societies which maintain a rough balance between emphases upon cultural goals and institutionalized practices, and these constitute the integrated and relatively stable, though changing, societies.

An effective equilibrium between these two phases of the social structure is maintained so long as satisfactions accrue to individuals conforming to both cultural constraints, *viz.*, satisfactions from the achievement of goals and satisfactions emerging directly from the institutionally canalized modes of striving to attain them. It is reckoned in terms of the product and in terms of the process, in terms of the outcome and in terms of the activities. Thus continuing satisfactions must derive from sheer participation in a competitive order as well as from eclipsing one's competitors if the order itself is to be sustained. If concern shifts exclusively to the outcome of competition, then those who perennially suffer defeat may, understandably enough, work for a change in the rules of the game. The sacrifices occasionally—not, as Freud assumed, invariably—entailed by conformity to institutional norms must be compensated by socialized rewards. The distribution of statuses through competition must be so organized that positive incentives for adherence to status obligations are provided *for every position* within the distributive order. Otherwise, as will soon become plain, aberrant behavior ensues. It is, indeed, my central hypothesis that aberrant behavior may be regarded sociologically as a symptom of dissociation between culturally prescribed aspirations and socially structured avenues for realizing these aspirations.

Of the types of societies that result from independent variation of cultural goals and institutionalized means, we shall be primarily concerned with the first—a society in which there is an exceptionally strong emphasis upon specific goals without a corresponding emphasis upon institutional procedures. If it is not to be misunderstood, this statement must be elaborated. No society lacks norms governing conduct. But societies do differ in the degree to which the folkways, mores and institutional controls are effectively integrated with the goals which stand high in the hierarchy of cultural values. The culture may be such as to lead individuals to center their emotional convictions upon the complex of culturally acclaimed ends, with far less emotional support for prescribed methods of reaching out for these ends. With such differential emphases upon goals and institutional procedures, the latter may be so vitiated by the stress on goals as to have the behavior of many individuals limited only by considerations of technical expediency. In this context, the sole significant question becomes: Which of the available procedures is most efficient in netting the culturally approved value?[5] The technically most effective procedure, whether culturally legitimate or not, becomes typically preferred to institutionally prescribed conduct. As this process of attenuation continues, the society becomes unstable and there develops what Durkheim called "anomie" (or normlessness).[6]

The working of this process eventuating in anomie can be easily glimpsed in a series of familiar and instructive, though perhaps trivial, episodes. Thus, in competitive athletics, when the aim of victory is shorn of its institutional trappings and success becomes construed as "winning the game" rather than "winning under the rules of the game," a premium is implicitly set upon the use of illegitimate but technically efficient means. The star of the opposing football team is surreptitiously slugged; the wrestler incapacitates his opponent through ingenious but illicit techniques; university alumni covertly subsidize "students" whose talents are confined to the athletic field. The emphasis on the goal has so attenuated the satisfactions deriving from sheer participation in the competitive activity that only a successful outcome provides gratification. Through the same process, tension generated by the desire to win in a poker game is relieved by successfully dealing one's self four aces or, when the cult of success has truly flowered, by sagaciously shuffling the cards in a game of solitaire. The faint twinge of uneasiness in the last instance and the surreptitious nature of public delicts indicate clearly that the institutional rules of the game are *known* to those who evade them. But cultural (or idiosyncratic) exaggeration of the success-goal leads men to withdraw emotional support from the rules.[7]

This process is of course not restricted to the realm of competitive sport, which has simply provided us with microcosmic images of the social macrocosm. The process whereby exaltation of the end generates a literal *demoralization, i.e.,* a de-institutionalization, of the means occurs in many[8] groups where the two components of the social structure are not highly integrated.

Contemporary American culture appears to approximate the polar type in which great emphasis upon certain success-goals occurs without equivalent emphasis upon institutional means. It would of course be fanciful to assert that accumulated wealth stands alone as a symbol of success just as it would be fanciful to deny that Americans assign it a place high in their scale of values. In some large measure, money has been consecrated as a value in itself, over and above its expenditure for articles of consumption or its use for the enhancement of power. "Money" is peculiarly well adapted to become a symbol of prestige. As Simmel emphasized, money is highly abstract and impersonal. However acquired, fraudulently or institutionally, it can be used to purchase the same goods and services. The anonymity of an urban society, in conjunction with these peculiarities of money, permits wealth, the sources of which may be unknown to the community in which the plutocrat lives or, if known, to become purified in the course of time, to serve as a symbol of high status. Moreover, in the American Dream there is no final stopping point. The measure of "monetary success" is conveniently indefinite and relative. At each income level, as H. F. Clark found, Americans want just about twenty-five per cent more (but of course this "just a bit more" continues to operate once it is obtained). In this flux of shifting standards, there is no stable resting point, or rather, it is the point which manages always to be "just ahead." An observer of a community in which annual salaries in six figures are not uncommon, reports the anguished words of one victim of the American Dream: "In this town, I'm snubbed socially because I only get a thousand a week. That hurts."[9]

To say that the goal of monetary success is entrenched in American culture is only to say that Americans are bombarded on every side by precepts which affirm the right or, often, the duty of retaining the goal even in the face of repeated frustration. Prestigeful representatives of the society reinforce the cultural emphasis. The family, the school and the workplace—the major agencies shaping the personality structure and goal formation of Americans—join to provide the intensive disciplining required if an individual is to retain intact a goal that remains elusively beyond reach, if he is to be motivated by the promise of a gratification which is not redeemed. As we shall presently see, parents serve as a transmission belt for the values and goals of the groups of which they are a part—above all, of their social class or of the class with which they identify themselves. And the schools are of course the official agency for the passing on of the prevailing values, with a large proportion of the textbooks used in city schools implying or stating explicitly "that education leads to intelligence and consequently to job and money success."[10] Central to this process of disciplining people to maintain their unfulfilled aspirations are the cultural prototypes of success, the living documents testifying that the American Dream can be realized if one but has the requisite abilities. Consider in this connection the following excerpts from the business journal, *Nation's Business*, drawn from large amount of comparable materials found in mass communications setting forth the values of business class culture.

The Document (Nation's Business, Vol. 27, No. 8, p. 7)	*Its Sociological Implications*
'You have to be born to those jobs, buddy, or else have a good pull.'	Here is a heretical opinion, possibly born of continued frustration, which rejects the worth of retaining an apparently unrealizable goal and, moreover, questions the legitimacy of a social structure which provides differential access to this goal.

That's an old sedative to ambition.

The counter-attack, explicitly asserting the cultural value of retaining one's aspirations intact, of not losing "ambition."

Before listening to its seduction, ask these men:

A clear statement of the function to be served by the ensuing list of "successes." These men are living testimony that the social structure is such as to permit these aspirations to be achieved, *if one is worthy*. And correlatively, failure to reach these goals testifies only to one's own personal shortcomings. Aggression provoked by failure should therefore be directed inward and not outward, against oneself and not against a social structure which provides free and equal access to opportunity.

Elmer R. Jones, president of Wells-Fargo and Co., who began life as a poor boy and left school at the fifth grade to take his first job.

Success prototype I: *All* may properly have the *same* lofty ambitions, for however lowly the starting-point, true talent can reach the very heights. Aspirations must be retained intact.

Frank C. Ball, the Mason fruit jar king of America, who rode from Buffalo to Muncie, Indiana, in a boxcar along with his brother George's horse, to start a little business in Muncie that became the biggest of its kind.

Success prototype II: Whatever the present results of one's strivings, the future is large with promise; for the common man may yet become a king. Gratifications may seem forever deferred, but they will finally be realized as one's enterprise becomes "the biggest of its kind."

J. L. Bevan, president of the Illinois Central Railroad, who at twelve was a messenger boy in the freight office at New Orleans.

Success prototype III: If the secular trends of our economy seem to give little scope to small business, than one may rise within the giant bureaucracies of private enterprise. If one can no longer be a king in a realm of his own creation, he may at least become a president in one of the economic democracies. No matter what one's present station, messenger boy or clerk, one's gaze should be fixed at the top.

From divers sources there flows a continuing pressure to retain high ambition. The exhortational literature is immense, and one can choose only at the risk of seeming invidious. Consider only these: the Reverend Russell H. Conwell, with his *Acres of Diamonds* address heard and read by hundreds of thousands and his subsequent book, *The New Day*, or *Fresh Opportunities: A Book for Young Men*; Elbert Hubbard, who delivered the famous *Message to Garcia* at Chautauqua forums throughout the land; Orison Swett Marden, who, in a stream of books, first set forth *The Secret of Achievment*, praised by college presidents, than explained the process of *Pushing to the Front*, eulogized by President McKinley and finally, these democratic testimonials notwithstanding, mapped the road to make *Every Man a King*. The symbolism of a commoner rising to the estate of economic royalty is woven deep in the texture of the American culture pattern, finding what is perhaps its ultimate expression in the words of one who knew whereof he spoke, Andrew Carnegie: "Be a king in your dreams. Say to yourself, 'My place is at the top.'"[11]

Coupled with this positive emphasis upon the obligation to maintain lofty goals is a correlative emphasis upon the penalizing of those who draw in their ambitions. American are admonished "Not to be a quitter" for in the dictionary of American culture, as in the lexicon of youth, "there is no such word as 'fail.'" The cultural manifesto is clear: one must not quit, must not cease striving, must not lessen his goals, for "not failure, but low aim, is crime."

Thus the culture enjoins the acceptance of three cultural axioms: First, all should strive for the same lofty goals since these are open to all; second, present seeming failure is but a way-station to ultimate success; and third, genuine failure consists only in the lessening or withdrawal of ambition.

In rough psychological paraphrase, these axioms represent, first, a symbolic secondary reinforcement of incentive; second, curbing the threatened extinction of a response through an associated stimulus; third, increasing the motive-strength to evoke continued responses despite the continued absence of reward.

In sociological paraphrase, these axioms represent, first, the deflection of criticism of the social structure onto one's self among those so situated in the society that they do not have full and equal access to opportunity; second, the preservation of a structure of social power by having individuals in the lower social strata identify themselves, not with their compeers, but with those at the top (whom they will ultimately join); and third, providing pressures for conformity with the cultural dictates of unslackened ambition by the threat of less than full membership in the society for those who fail to conform.

It is in these terms and through these processes that contemporary American culture continues to be characterized by a heavy emphasis on wealth as a basic symbol of success, without a corresponding emphasis upon the legitimate avenues on which to march toward this goal. How do individuals living in this cultural context respond? And how do our observations bear upon the doctrine that deviant behavior typically derives from biological impulses breaking through the restraints imposed by culture? What, in short, are the consequences for the behavior of people variously situated in a social structure of a culture in which the emphasis on dominant success-goals has become increasingly separated from an equivalent emphasis on institutionalized procedures for seeking these goals?

TYPES OF INDIVIDUAL ADAPTATION

Turning from these culture patterns, we now examine types of adaptation by individuals within the culture-bearing society. Though our focus is still the cultural and social genesis of varying rates and types of deviant behavior, our perspective shifts from the plane of patterns of cultural values to the plane of types of adaptation to these values among those occupying different positions in the social structure.

We here consider five types of adaptation, as these are schematically set out in the following table, where (+) signifies "acceptance," (–) signifies "rejection," and (±) signifies "rejection of prevailing values and substitution of new values."

Examination of how the social structure operates to exert pressure upon individuals for one or another of these alternative modes of behavior must be prefaced by the observation that people may shift from one alternative to another as they engage in different spheres of social activities. These categories refer to role behavior in specific types of situations, not to personality. They are types of more or less enduring response, not types of personality organization. To consider these types of adaptation in several spheres of conduct would introduce a complexity unmanageable within the confines of this chapter. For this reason, we shall be primarily concerned with economic activity in the broad sense of "the production, exchange, distribution and consumption of goods and services" in our competitive society, where wealth has taken on a highly symbolic cast.

I. CONFORMITY

To the extent that a society is stable, adaptation type I—conformity to

A TYPOLOGY OF MODES OF INDIVIDUAL ADAPTATION[12]

MODES OF ADAPTATION	CULTURE GOALS	INSTITUTIONALIZED MEANS
I. Conformity	+	+
II. Innovation	+	−
III. Ritualism	−	+
IV. Retreatism	−	−
V. Rebellion[13]	±	±

both cultural goals and institutionalized means—is the most common and widely diffused. Were this not so, the stability and continuity of the society could not be maintained. The mesh of expectancies constituting every social order is sustained by the modal behavior of its members representing conformity to the established, though perhaps secularly changing, culture patterns. It is in fact, only because behavior is typically oriented toward the basic values of the society that we may speak of a human aggregate as comprising a society. Unless there is a deposit of values shared by interacting individuals, there exist social relations, if the disorderly interactions may be so called, but no society. It is thus that, at mid-century, one may refer to a Society of Nations primarily as a figure of speech or as an imagined objective, but not as a sociological reality.

Since our primary interest centers on the sources of *deviant* behavior, and since we have briefly examined the mechanisms making for conformity as the modal response in American society, little more need be said regarding this type of adaptation, at this point.

II. INNOVATION

Great cultural emphasis upon the success-goal invites this mode of adaptation through the use of institutionally proscribed but often effective means of attaining at least the simulacrum of success—wealth and power. This response occurs when the individual has assimilated the cultural emphasis upon the goal without equally internalizing the institutional norms governing ways and means for its attainment.

From the standpoint of psychology, great emotional investment in an objective may be expected to produce a readiness to take risks, and this attitude may be adopted by people in all social strata. From the standpoint of sociology, the question arises, which features of our social structure predispose toward this type of adaptation, thus producing greater frequencies of deviant behavior in one social stratum than in another?

On the top economic levels, the pressure toward innovation not infrequently erases the distinction between business-like strivings this side of the mores and sharp practices beyond the mores. As Veblen observed, "It is not easy in any given case—indeed it is at times impossible until the courts have spoken—to say whether it is an instance of praiseworthy salesmanship or a penitentiary offense." The history of the great American fortunes is threaded with strains toward institutionally dubious innovation as is attested by many tributes to the Robber Barons. The reluctant admiration often expressed privately, and not seldom publicly, of these "shrewd, smart and successful" men is a product of a cultural structure in which the sacrosanct goal virtually consecrates the means. This is no new phenomenon. Without assuming that Charles Dickens was a wholly accurate observer of the American scene and with full knowledge that he was anything but impartial, we cite his perceptive remarks on the American

> love of "smart" dealing; which gilds over many a swindle and gross breach of trust; many a defalcation, public and private; and enables many a knave to hold his head up with the best, who well deserves a halter. . . . The merits of a broken speculation, or a bankruptcy, or of a successful scoundrel, are not gauged by its or his observance of the golden rule, "Do as you would be done by," but are considered with reference to their smartness. . . . The following dialogue I have held a hundred times: "Is it not a very disgraceful circumstance that such a man as So-and-so should be acquiring a large property by the most infamous and odious means, and notwithstanding all the crimes of which he has been guilty, should be tolerated and abetted by your Citizens? He is a public nuisance, is he not?" "Yes, sir." "A convicted liar?" "Yes, sir." "He has been kicked and cuffed, and caned?" "Yes, sir." "And he is utterly dishonorable, debased, and profligate?" "Yes, sir." "In the name of wonder, then, what is his merit?" "Well, sir, he is a smart man."

In this caricature of conflicting cultural values, Dickens was of course only one of many wits who mercilessly probed the consequences of the heavy emphasis on financial success. Native wits continued where alien wits left off. Artemus Ward satirized the commonplaces of American life until they seemed strangely incongruous. The "crackerbox philosophers," Bill Arp and Petroleum Volcano [later Vesuvius] Nasby, put wit in the service of iconoclasm, breaking the images of public figures with unconcealed pleasure. Josh Billings and his alter ego, Uncle Esek, made plain what many could not freely acknowledge, when he observed that satisfaction is relative since "most of the happiness in this world konsists in possessing what others kant git." All were engaged in exhibiting the social functions of tendentious wit, as this was later to be analyzed by Freud, in his monograph on *Wit and Its Relation to the Unconscious,* using it as "a weapon of attack upon what is great, dignified and mighty, [upon] that which is shielded by internal hindrances or external circumstance against direct disparagement...." But perhaps most in point here was the deployment of wit by Ambrose Bierce in a form which made it evident that *wit* had not cut away from its etymological origins and still meant the power by which one knows, learns, or thinks. In his characteristically ironical and deep-seeing essay on "crime and its correctives," Bierce begins with the observation that "Sociologists have long been debating the theory that the impulse to commit crime is a disease, and the ayes appear to have it—the disease." After this prelude, he describes the ways in which the successful rogue achieves social legitimacy, and proceeds to anatomize the discrepancies between cultural values and social relations.

> The good American is, as a rule, pretty hard on roguery, but he atones for his austerity by an amiable toleration of rogues. His only requirement is that he must personally know the rogues. We all "denounce" thieves loudly enough if we have not the honor of their acquaintance. If we have, why, that is different—unless they have the actual odor of the slum or the prison about them. We may know them guilty, but we meet them, shake hands with them, drink with them and, if they happen to be wealthy, or otherwise great, invite them to our houses, and deem it an honor to frequent theirs. We do not "approve their methods"—let that be understood; and thereby they are sufficiently punished. The notion that a knave cares a pin what is thought of his ways by one who is civil and friendly to himself appears to have been invented by a humorist. On the vaudeville stage of Mars it would probably have made his fortune.
>
> [And again:] If social recognition were denied to rogues they would be fewer by many. Some would only the more diligently cover their tracks along the devious paths of unrighteousness, but others would do so much violence to their consciences as to renounce the disadvantages of rascality for those of an honest life. An unworthy person dreads nothing so much as the withholding of an honest hand, the slow, inevitable stroke of an ignoring eye.
>
> We have rich rogues because we have "respectable" persons who are not ashamed to take them by the hand, to be seen with them, to say that they know them. In such it is treachery to censure them; to cry out when robbed by them is to turn state's evidence.

One may smile upon a rascal (most of us do many times a day) if one does not know him to be a rascal, and has not said he is; but knowing him to be, or having said he is, to smile upon him is to be a hypocrite—just a plain hypocrite or a sycophantic hypocrite, according to the station in life of the rascal smiled upon. There are more plain hypocrites than sycophantic ones for there are more rascals of no consequence than rich and distinguished ones, though they get fewer smiles each. The American people will be plundered as long as the American character is what it is; as long as it is tolerant of successful knaves; as long as American ingenuity draws an imaginary distinction between a man's public character and his private—his commercial and his personal. In brief, the American people will be plundered as long as they deserve to be plundered. No human law can stop, none ought to stop it, for that would abrogate a higher and more salutary law: "As ye sow, ye shall reap."[14]

Living in the age in which the American robber barons flourished, Bierce could not easily fail to observe what became later known as "white-collar crime." Nevertheless, he was aware that not all of these large and dramatic departures from institutional norms in the top economic strata are known, and possibly fewer deviations among the lesser middle classes come to light. Sutherland has repeatedly documented the prevalence of "white-collar criminality" among business men. He notes, further, that many of these crimes were not prosecuted because they were not detected or, if detected, because of " the status of the business man, the trend away from punishment, and the relatively unorganized resentment of the public against white-collar criminals."[15] A study of some 1,700 prevalently middle-class individuals found that "off the record crimes" were common among wholly "respectable" members of society. Ninety-nine per cent of those questioned confessed to having committed one or more of 49 offenses under the penal law of the State of New York, each of these offenses being sufficiently serious to draw a maximum sentence of not less than one year. The mean number of offenses in adult years—this excludes all offenses committed before the age of sixteen—was 18 for men and 11 for women. Fully 64% of the men and 29% of the women acknowledged their guilt on one or more counts of felony which, under the laws of New York is ground for depriving them of all rights of citizenship. One keynote of these findings is expressed by a minister, referring to false statements he made about a commodity he sold, "I tried truth first, but it's not always successful." On the basis of these results, the authors modestly conclude that "the number of acts legally constituting crimes are far in excess of those officially reported. Unlawful behavior, far from being an abnormal social or psychological manifestation, is in truth a very common phenomenon."[16]

But whatever the differential rates of deviant behavior in the several social strata, and we know from many sources that the official crime statistics uniformly showing higher rates in the lower strata are far from complete or reliable, it appears from our analysis that the greatest presures toward deviation are exerted upon the lower strata. Cases in point permit us to detect the sociological mechanisms involved in producing these pressures. Several researches have shown that specialized areas of vice and crime constitute a "normal" response to a situation where the cultural emphasis upon pecuniary success has been absorbed, but where there is little access to conventional and legitimate means for becoming successful. The occupational opportunities of people in these areas are largely confined to manual labor and the lesser white-collar jobs. Given the American stigmatization of manual labor *which has been found to hold rather uniformly in all social classes,*[17] and the absence of realistic opportunities for advancement beyond this level, the result is a marked tendency toward deviant behavior. The status of unskilled labor and the consequent low income cannot readily compete *in terms of established standards of worth* with the promises of power and high income from organized vice, rackets and crime.[18]

For our purposes, these situations exhibit two salient features. First, incentives for success are provided by the established values of the culture *and* second, the avenues available for moving toward this goal are largely limited by the class structure to those of deviant behavior. It is the *combination* of the cultural emphasis and the social structure which produces intense pressure for deviation. Recourse to legitimate channels for "getting in the money" is limited by a class structure which is not fully open at each level to men of good capacity.[19] Despite our persisting open-class-ideology,[20] advance toward the success-goal is relatively rare and notably difficult for those armed with little formal education and few economic resources. The dominant pressure leads toward the gradual attenuation of legitmate, but by and large ineffectual, strivings and the increasing use of illegitimate, but more or less effective, expedients.

Of those located in the lower reaches of the social structure, the culture makes incompatible demands. On the one hand, they are asked to orient their conduct toward the prospect of large wealth—"Every man a king," said Marden and Carnegie and Long—and on the other, they are largely denied effective opportunities to do so institutionally. The consequence of this structural inconsistency is a high rate of deviant behavior. The equilibrium between culturally designated ends and means becomes highly unstable with progressive emphasis on attaining the prestige-laden ends by any means whatsoever.

Within this context, Al Capone represents the triumph of amoral intelligence over morally prescribed "failure," when the channels of vertical mobility are closed or narrowed *in a society which places a high premium on economic affluence and social ascent for* all *its members.*[21]

This last qualification is of central importance. It implies that other aspects of the social structure, besides the extreme emphasis on pecuniary success, must be considered if we are to understand the social sources of deviant behavior. A high frequency of deviant behavior is not generated merely by lack of opportunity or by this exaggerated pecuniary emphasis. A comparatively rigidified class structure, a caste order, may limit opportunities far beyond the point which obtains in American society today. It is when a system of cultural values extols, virtually above all else, certain *common* success-goals *for the population at large* while the social structure rigorously restricts or completely closes access to approved modes of reaching these goals *for a considerable part of the same population,* that deviant behavior ensues on a large scale. Otherwise said, our egalitarian ideology denies by implication the existence of non-competing individuals and groups in the pursuit of pecuniary success. Instead, the same body of success-symbols is held to apply for all. Goals are held to transcend class lines, not to be bounded by them, yet the actual social organization is such that there exist class differentials in accessibility of the goals. In this setting, a cardinal American virtue, "ambition," promotes a cardinal American vice, "deviant behavior."

This theoretical analysis may help explain the varying correlations between crime and poverty.[22] "Poverty" is not an isolated variable which operates in precisely the same fashion wherever found; it is only one in a complex of identifiably interdependent social and cultural variables. Poverty as such and consequent limitation of opportunity are not enough to produce a conspicuously high rate of criminal behavior. Even the notorious "poverty in the midst of plenty" will not necessarily lead to this result. But when poverty and associated disadvantages in competing for the culture values approved for *all* members of the society are linked with a cultural emphasis on pecuniary success as a dominant goal, high rates of criminal behavior are the normal outcome. Thus, crude (and not necessarily reliable) crime statistics suggest that poverty is less highly correlated with crime in southeastern Europe than in the United States. The economic life-chances of the poor in these European areas would seem to be even less promising than in this country, so that neither poverty nor its association with limited opportunity is sufficient to account for the varying correlations. However, when we consider the full configuration—poverty, limited opportunity and the assignment of cultural goals—there appears some basis for explaining the higher correlation between poverty and crime in our society than in others where rigidified class structure is coupled with *differential class symbols of success.*

The victims of this contradiction between the cultural emphasis on pecuniary ambition and the social bars to full opportunity are not always aware of the structural sources of their thwarted aspirations. To be sure, they are often aware of a discrepancy between individual worth and social rewards. But they do not necessarily see how this comes about. Those who do find its source in the social structure may become alienated from that structure and become ready candidates for Adaptation V (rebellion). But others, and this appears to include the great majority, may attribute their difficulties to more mystical and less sociological sources. For as the distinguished classicist and sociologist-in-spite-of himself, Gilbert Murray, has remarked in this general connection, "The best seed-ground for superstition is a society in which the fortunes of men seem to bear practically no relation to their merits and efforts. A stable and well-governed society does tend, speaking roughly, to ensure that the Virtuous and Industrious Apprentice shall succeed in life, while the Wicked and Idle Apprentice fails. And in such a society people tend to lay stress on the reasonable or visible chains of causation. But in [a society suffering from anomie]..., the ordinary virtues of diligence, honesty, and kindliness seem to be of little avail."[23] And in such a society people tend to put stress on mysticism: the workings of Fortune, Chance, Luck.

In point of fact, both the eminently "successful" and the eminently "unsuccessful" in our society not infrequently attribute the outcome to "luck." Thus, the prosperous man of business, Julius Rosenwald, declared that 95% of the great fortunes were "due to luck."[24] And a leading business journal, in an editorial explaining the social benefits of great individual wealth, finds it necessary to supplement wisdom with luck as the factors accounting for great fortunes: "When one man through wise investments—aided, we'll grant, by good luck in many cases—accumulates a few millions, he doesn't thereby take something from the rest of us."[25] In much the same fashion, the worker often explains economic status in terms of chance. "The worker sees all about him experienced and skilled men with no work to do. If he is in work, he feels lucky. If he is out of work, he is the victim of hard luck. *He can see little relation between worth and consequences.'*[26]

But these references to the workings of chance and luck serve distinctive functions according to whether they are made by those who have reached or those who have not reached the culturally emphasized goals. For the successful, it is in psychological terms, a disarming expression of modesty. It is far removed from any semblance of conceit to say, in effect, that one was lucky rather than altogether deserving of one's good fortune. In sociological terms, the doctrine of luck as expounded by the successful serves the dual function of explaining the frequent discrepancy between merit and reward while keeping immune from criticism a social structure which allows this discrepancy to become frequent. For if success is primarily a matter of luck, if it is just in the blind nature of things, if it bloweth where it listeth and thou canst not tell whence it cometh or whither it goeth, then surely it is beyond control and will occur in the same measure *whatever the social structure.*

For the unsuccessful and particularly for those among the unsuccessful who find little reward for their merit and their effort, the doctrine of luck serves the psychological function of enabling them to preserve their self-esteem in the face of failure. It may also entail the dysfunction of curbing motivation for sustained endeavor.[27] Sociologically, as implied by Bakke,[28] the doctrine may reflect a failure to comprehend the workings of the social and economic system, and may be dysfunctional inasmuch as it eliminates the rationale of working for structural changes making for greater equities in opportunity and reward.

This orientation toward chance and risk-taking, accentuated by the strain of frustrated aspirations, may help explain the marked interest in gambling—an institutionally proscribed or at best permitted rather than preferred or prescribed mode of activity—within certain social strata.[29]

Among those who do not apply the doctrine of luck to the gulf between merit, effort and reward there may develop an individuated and cynical attitude toward the social structure, best exemplified in the cultural cliché that "it's not what you know, but who you know, that counts."

In societies such as our own, then, the great cultural emphasis on pecuniary success for all and a social structure which unduly limits practical recourse to approved means for many set up a tension toward innovative practices which depart from institutional norms. But this form of adaptation presupposes that individuals have been imperfectly socialized so that they abandon institutional means while retaining the success-aspiration. Among those who have fully internalized the institutional values, however, a comparable situation is more likely to lead to an alternative response in which the goal is abandoned but conformity to the mores persists. This type of response calls for further examination.

III. RITUALISM

The ritualistic type of adaptation can be readily identified. It involves the abandoning or scaling down of the lofty cultural goals of great pecuniary success and rapid social mobility to the point where one's aspirations can be satisfied. But though one rejects the cultural obligation to attempt "to get ahead in the world," though one draws in one's horizons, one continues to abide almost compulsively by institutional norms.

It is something of a terminological quibble to ask whether this represents genuinely deviant behavior. Since the adaptation is, in effect, an internal decision and since the overt behavior is institutionally permitted, though not culturally preferred, it is not generally considered to represent a social problem. Intimates of individuals making this adaptation may pass judgment in terms of prevailing cultural emphases and may "feel sorry for them," they may, in the individual case, feel that "old Jonesy is certainly in a rut." Whether this is described as deviant behavior or no, it clearly represents a departure from the cultural model in which men are obliged to strive actively, preferably through institutionalized procedures, to move onward and upward in the social hierarchy.

We should expect this type of adaptation to be fairly frequent in a society which makes one's social status largely dependent upon one's achievements. For, as has so often been observed,[30] this ceaseless competitive struggle produces acute status anxiety. One device for allaying these anxieties is to lower one's level of aspiration—permanently. Fear produces inaction, or more accurately, routinized action.[31]

The syndrome of the social ritualist is both familiar and instructive. His implicit life-philosophy finds expression in a series of cultural clichés: "I'm not sticking *my* neck out," "I'm playing safe," "I'm satisfied with what I've got," "Don't aim high and you won't be disappointed." The theme threaded through these attitudes is that high ambitions invite frustration and danger whereas lower aspirations produce satisfaction and security. It is a response to a situation which appears threatening and excites distrust. It is the attitude implicit among workers who carefully regulate their output to a constant quota in an industrial organization where they have occasion to fear that they will "be noticed" by managerial personnel and "something will happen" if their output rises and falls.[32] It is the perspective of the frightened employee, the zealously conformist bureaucrat in the teller's cage of the private banking enterprise or in the front office of the public works enterprise.[33] It is, in short, the mode of adaptation of individually seeking a *private* escape from the dangers and frustrations which seem to them inherent in the competition for major cultural goals by abandoning these goals and clinging all the more closely to the safe routines and the institutional norms.

If we should expect *lower-class* Americans to exhibit Adaptation II—"innovation"—to the frustrations enjoined by the prevailing emphasis on large cultural goals and the fact of small social opportunities, we should expect *lower-middle class* Americans to be heavily represented among those making Adaptation III, "ritualism." For it is in the lower middle class that parents typically exert continuous pressure upon children to abide by the moral mandates of the society, and where the social climb upward is less likely to meet with success than among the upper middle class. The strong disciplining for conformity with mores reduces the likelihood of Adaptation II and promotes the likelihood of Adaptation III. The severe training leads many to carry a heavy burden of anxiety. The socialization patterns of the lower middle class thus promote the very character structure most predisposed toward ritualism,[34] and it is in this stratum, accordingly, that the adaptive pattern III should most often occur.[35]

But we should note again, as at the outset of this chapter, that we are here examining *modes of adaptation* to contradictions in the cultural and social structure: we are not focusing on character or personality types. Individuals caught up in these contradictions can and do move from one type of adaptation to another. Thus it may be conjectured that some ritualists, conforming meticulously to the institutional rules, are so steeped in the regulations that they become bureaucratic virtuosos, that they over-conform precisely because they are subject to guilt engendered by previous nonconformity with the rules (*i.e.*, Adaptation II). And the occasional passage from ritualistic adaptation to dramatic kinds of illicit adaptation is well-documented in clinical case-histories and often set forth in insightful fiction. Defiant outbreaks not infrequently follow upon prolonged periods of over-compliance.[36] But though the psychodynamic mechanisms of this type of adaptation have been fairly well identified and linked with patterns of discipline and socialization in the family, much sociological research is still required to explain why these patterns are presumably more frequent in certain social strata and groups than in others. Our own discussion has merely set out one analytical framework for sociological research focused on this problem.

IV. RETREATISM

Just as Adaptation I (conformity) remains the most frequent, Adaptation IV (the rejection of cultural goals and institutional means) is probably the least common. People who adapt (or maladapt) in this fashion are, strictly speaking, *in* the society but not *of* it. Sociologically, these constitute the true aliens. Not sharing the common frame of values, they can be included as members of the *society* (in distinction from the *population*) only in a fictional sense.

In this category fall some of the adaptive activities of psychotics, autists, pariahs, outcasts, vagrants, vagabonds, tramps, chronic drunkards and drug addicts.[37] They have relinquished culturally prescribed goals and their behavior does not accord with institutional norms. This is not to say that in some cases the source of their mode of adaptation is not the very social structure which they have in effect repudiated nor that their very existence within an area does not constitute a problem for members of the society.

From the standpoint of its sources in the social structure, this mode of adaptation is most likely to occur when *both* the culture goals and the institutional practices have been thoroughly assimilated by the individual and imbued with affect and high value, but accessible institutional avenues are not productive of success. There results a twofold conflict: the interiorized moral obligation for adopting institutional means conflicts with pressures to resort to illicit means (which may attain the goal) and the individual is shut off from means which are both legitimate and effective. The competitive order is maintained but the frustrated and handicapped individual who cannot cope with this order drops out. Defeatism, quietism and resignation are manifested in escape mechanisms which ultimately lead him to "escape" from the requirements of the society. It is thus an expedient which arises from continued failure to near the goal by legitimate measures and from an inability to use the illegitimate route because of internalized prohibition, *this process occurring while the supreme value of the success-goal has not yet been renounced.* The conflict is resolved by abandoning *both* precipitating elements, the goals and the means. The escape is complete, the conflict is eliminated and the individual is asocialized.

In public and ceremonial life, this type of deviant behavior is most heartily condemned by conventional representatives of the society. In contrast to the conformist, who keeps the wheels of society running, this deviant is a non-productive liability; in contrast to the innovator who is at least "smart" and actively striving, he sees no value in the success-goal which the culture prizes so highly; in contrast to the ritualist who conforms at least to the mores, he pays scant attention to the institutional practices.

Nor does the society lightly accept these repudiations of its values. To do so would be to put these values into question. Those who have abandoned the quest for success are relentlessly pursued to their haunts by a society insistent upon having all its members orient themselves to success-striving. Thus, in the heart of Chicago's Hobohemia are the book stalls filled with wares designed to revitalize dead aspirations.

> The Gold Coast Book Store is in the basement of an old residence, built back from the street, and now sandwiched between two business blocks. The space in front is filled with stalls, and striking placards and posters.
>
> These posters advertise such books as will arrest the attention of the down-and-out. One reads: "...Men in thousands pass this spot daily, but the majority of them are not financially successful. They are never more than two jumps ahead of the rent men. Instead of that, they should be more bold and daring," "Getting Ahead of the Game," before old age withers them and casts them on the junk heap of human wrecks. If you want to escape the evil fate—the fate of the vast majority of men—come in and get a copy of *The Law of Financial Success.* It will put some new ideas in your head, and put you on the highroad to success. 35 cents.
>
> There are always men loitering before its stalls. But they seldom buy. Success comes high, even at thirty-five cents, to the hobo.[38]

But if this deviant is condemned in real life, he may become a source of gratification in fantasy-life. Thus Kardiner has advanced the speculation that such figures in contemporary folklore and popular culture bolster "morale and self-esteem by the spectacle of man rejecting current ideals and expressing contempt for them." The prototype in the films is of course Charlie Chaplin's bum.

> He is Mr. Nobody and is very much aware of his own significance. He is always the butt of a crazy and bewildering world in which he has no place and from which he constantly runs away into a contented do-nothingness. *He is free from conflict because he has abandoned the quest for security and prestige, and is resigned to the lack of any claim to virtue or distinction.* [A precise characterological portrait of Adaptation IV.] He always becomes involved in the world by accident. There he encounters evil and aggression against the weak and helpless which he has no power to combat. Yet always, in spite of himself, he becomes the champion of the wronged and oppressed, not by virtue of his great organizing ability but by virtue of homely and insolent trickiness by which he seeks out the weakness of the wrongdoer. He always remains humble, poor, and lonely, but is contemptuous of the incomprehensible world and its values. He therefore represents the character of our time who is *perplexed by the dilemma either of being crushed in the struggle to achieve the socially approved goals of success*

and power (he achieve it only once—in *The Gold Rush*) *or of succumbing to a hopeless resignation and flight from them.* Charlie's bum is a great comfort in that he gloats in his ability to outwit the pernicious forces aligned against him if he chooses to do so and affords every man the satisfaction of feeling that the ultimate flight from social goals to loneliness is an act of *choice* and not a symptom of his defeat. Mickey Mouse is a continuation of the Chaplin saga.[39]

This fourth mode of adaptation, then, is that of the socially disinherited who if they have none of the rewards held out by society also have few of the frustrations attendant upon continuing to seek these rewards. It is, moreover, a privatized rather than a collective mode of adaptation. Although people exhibiting this deviant behavior may gravitate toward centers where they come into contact with other deviants and although they may come to share in the subculture of these deviant groups, their adaptations are largely private and isolated rather than unified under the aegis of a new cultural code. The type of collective adaptation remains to be considered.

V. REBELLION

This adaptation leads men outside the environing social structure to envisage and seek to bring into being a new, that is to say, a greatly modified social structure. It presupposes alienation from reigning goals and standards. These come to be regarded as purely arbitary. And the arbitrary is precisely that which can neither exact allegiance nor possess legitimacy, for it might as well be otherwise. In our society, organized movements for rebellion apparently aim to introduce a social structure in which the cultural standards of success would be sharply modified and provision would be made for a closer correspondence between merit, effort and reward.

But before examining "rebellion" as a mode of adaptation, we must distinguish it from a superficially similar but essentially different type, *ressentiment.* Introduced in a special technical sense, by Nietzsche, the concept of *ressentiment* was taken up and developed sociologically by Max Scheler.[40] This complex sentiment has three interlocking elements. First, diffuse feelings of hate, envy and hostility; second, a sense of being powerless to express these feelings actively against the person or social stratum evoking them; and third, a continual re-experiencing of this impotent hostility.[41] The essential point distinguishing *ressentiment* from rebellion is that the former does not involve a genuine change in values. *Ressentiment* involves a sour-grapes pattern which asserts merely that desired but unattainable objectives do not actually embody the prized values—after all, the fox in the fable does not say that he abandons all taste for sweet grapes; he says only that these particular grapes are not sweet. Rebellion, on the other hand, involves a genuine transvaluation, where the direct or vicarious experience of frustration leads to full denunciation of previously prized values—the rebellious fox simply renounces the prevailing taste for sweet grapes. In *ressentiment*, one condemns what one secretly craves; in rebellion, one condemns the craving itself. But though the two are distinct, organized rebellion may draw upon a vast reservoir of the resentful and discontented as institutional dislocations become acute.

When the institutional system is regarded as the barrier to the satisfaction of legitimized goals, the stage is set for rebellion as an adaptive response. To pass into organized political action, allegiance must not only be withdrawn from the prevailing social structure but must be transferred to new groups possessed of a new myth.[42] The dual function of the myth is to locate the source of large-scale frustrations in the social structure and to portray an alternative structure which would not, presumably, give rise to frustration of the deserving. It is a charter for action. In this context, the functions of the counter-myth of the conservatives—briefly sketched in an earlier section of this chapter—become further clarified: whatever the source of mass frustration, it is not to be found in the basic structure of the society. The conservative myth may thus assert that these frustrations are in the nature of things and would occur in *any* social system: "Periodic mass unemployment and business depressions can't be legislated out of existence; it's just like a person who feels good one day and bad the next."[43] Or, if not the doctrine of inevitability, then the doctrine of gradual and slight adjustment: "A few changes here and there, and we'll have things running as ship-shape as they can possibly be." Or, the doctrine which deflects hostility from the social structure onto the individual who is a "failure" since "every man really gets what's coming to him in this country."

The myths of rebellion and of conservatism both work toward a "monopoly of the imagination" seeking to define the situation in such terms as to move the frustrate toward or away from Adaptation V. It is above all the renegade who, though himself successful, renounces the prevailing values that becomes the target of greatest hostility among those in rebellion. For he not only puts the values in question, as does the outgroup, but he signifies that the unity of the group is broken.[44] Yet, as has so often been noted, it is typically members of a rising class rather than the most depressed strata who organize the resentful and the rebellious into a revolutionary group.

THE STRAIN TOWARD ANOMIE

The social structure we have examined produces a strain toward anomie and deviant behavior. The pressure of such a social order is upon outdoing one's competitors. So long as the sentiments supporting this competitive system are distributed throughout the entire range of activities and are not confined to the final result of "success," the choice of means will remain largely within the ambit of institutional control. When, however, the cultural emphasis shifts from the satisfactions deriving from competition itself to almost exclusive concern with the outcome, the resultant stress makes for the breakdown of the regulatory structure. With this attenuation of institutional controls, there occurs an approximation to the situation erroneously held by the utilitarian philosophers to be typical of society, a situation in which calculations of personal advantage and fear of punishment are the only regulating agencies.

This strain toward anomie does not operate evenly throughout the society. Some effort has been made in the present analysis to suggest the strata most vulnerable to the pressures for deviant behavior and to set forth some of the mechanisms operating to produce those pressures. For purposes of simplifying the problem, monetary success was taken as the major cultural goal, although there are, of course, alternative goals in the repository of common values. The realms of intellectual and artistic achievement, for example, provide alternative career patterns which may not entail large pecuniary rewards. To the extent that the cultural structure attaches prestige to these alternatives and the social structure permits access to them, the system is somewhat stabilized. Potential deviants may still conform in terms of these auxiliary sets of values.

But the central tendencies toward anomie remain, and it is to these that the analytical scheme here set forth calls particular attention.

THE ROLE OF THE FAMILY

A final word should be said drawing together the implications scattered throughout the foregoing discussion concerning the role played by the family in these patterns of deviant behavior.

It is the family, of course, which is a major transmission belt for the diffusion of cultural standards to the oncoming generation. But what has until lately been overlooked is that the family largely transmits that portion of the culture accessible to the social stratum and groups in which the parents find themselves. It is, therefore, a mechanism for disciplining the child in terms of the cultural goals and mores characteristic of this narrow range of groups. Nor is the socialization confined to direct training the disciplining. The process is, at least in part, inadvertent. Quite apart from direct admonitions, rewards and punishments, the child is exposed to social prototypes in the witnessed daily behavior and casual conversations of parents. Not infrequently, *children detect and incorporate cultural uniformities even when these remain implicit and have not been reduced to rules.*

Language patterns provide the most impressive evidence, readily observable in clinical fashion, that children, in the process of socialization, detect uniformities which have not been explicitly formulated for them by elders or contemporaries and which are not formulated by the children themselves. Persistent errors of language among children are most instructive. Thus, the child will spontaneously use such words as "mouses" or "moneys," *even though he has never heard such terms or been taught "the rule for forming plurals."* Or he will create such words as "falled," "runned," "singed," "hitted," though he has not been taught, at the age of three, "rules" of conjugation. Or, he will refer to a choice morsel as "gooder" than another less favored, or perhaps through a logical extension, he may describe it as "goodest" of all. Obviously, he has detected the implicit paradigms for the expression of plurality, for the conjugation of verbs, and the inflection of adjectives. The very nature of his error and misapplication of the paradigm testifies to this.[45]

It may be tentatively inferred, therefore, that he is also busily engaged in *detecting and acting upon the implicit paradigms of cultural evaluation, and categorization of people and things, and the formation of estimable goals* as well as assimilating the explicit cultural orientation set forth in an endless stream of commands, explanations and exhortations by parents. It would appear that in addition to the important researches of the depth psychologies on the socialization process, there is need for supplementary types of direct observation of culture diffusion within the family. It may well be that the child retains the implicit paradigm of cultural values detected in the day-by-day behavior of his parents even when this conflicts with their explicit advice and exhortations.

The projection of parental ambitions onto the child is also centrally relevant to the subject in hand. As is well known, many parents confronted with personal "failure" or limited "success" may mute their original goal-emphasis and may defer further efforts to reach the goal, attempting to reach it vicariously through their children. "The influence may come through the mother or the father. Often it is the case of a parent who hopes that the child will attain heights that he or she failed to attain."[46] In a recent research on the social organization of public housing developments, we have found among both Negroes and Whites on lower occupational levels, a substantial proportion having aspirations for a professional career for their children.[47] Should this finding be confirmed by further research it will have large bearing upon the problem in hand. For if compensatory projection of parental ambition onto children is widespread, then it is precisely those parents least able to provide free access to opportunity for their children—the "failures" and "frustrates"—who exert great pressure upon their children for high achievement. And this syndrome of lofty aspirations and limited realistic opportunities, as we have seen, is precisely the pattern which invites deviant behavior. This clearly points to the need for investigation focused upon occupational goal-formation in the several social strata if the inadvertent role of family disciplining in deviant behavior is to be understood from the perspectives of our analytical scheme.

CONCLUDING REMARKS

It should be apparent that the foregoing discussion is not pitched on a moralistic plane. Whatever the sentiments of the reader concerning the moral desirability of coordinating the goals-and-means phases of the social structure, it is clear that imperfect coordination of the two leads to anomie. In so far as one of the most general functions of social structure is to provide a basis for predictability and regularity of social behavior, it becomes increasingly limited in effectiveness as these elements of the social structure become dissociated. At the extreme, predictability is minimized and what may be properly called anomie or cultural chaos supervenes.

This essay on the structural sources of deviant behavior remains but a prelude. It has not included a detailed treatment of the structural elements which predispose toward one rather than another of the alternative responses open to individuals living in an ill-balanced social structure; it has largely neglected but not denied the relevance of the social-psychological processes determining the specific incidence of these responses; it has only briefly considered the social functions fulfilled by deviant behavior; it has not put the explanatory power of the

analytical scheme to full empirical test by determining group variations in deviant and conformist behavior; it has only touched upon rebellious behavior which seeks to refashion the social framework.

It is suggested that these and related problems may be advanta-
geously analyzed by use of this scheme.

NOTES

1. See, for example, S. Freud, *Civilization and Its Dicontents (passim,* and
    esp. at 63); Ernest Jones, *Social Aspects of Psychoanalysis* (London, 1924),
    28. If the Freudian notion is a variety of the "original sin" doctrine,
    then the interpretation advanced in this paper is a doctrine of
    "socially derived sin."

2. "Normal" in the sense of the psychologically expectable, if not
    culturally approved, response to determinate social conditions. This
    statement does not, of course, deny the role of biological and
    personality differences in fixing the *incidence* of deviant behavior. It is
    simply that *this* is not the problem considered here. It is in this same
    sense, I take it, that James S. Plant speaks of the "normal reaction of
    normal people to abnormal conditions." See his *Personality and the
    Cultural Pattern* (New York, 1937), 248.

3. The position taken here has been perceptively described by Edward
    Sapir. " . . . problems of social science differ from problems of
    individual behavior in degree of specificity, not in kind. Every
    statement about behavior which throws the emphasis, explicitly or
    implicitly, on the actual, integral experiences of defined personalities
    or types of personalities is a datum of psychology or psychiatry rather
    than of social science. Every statement about behavior which aims, not
    to be accurate about the behavior of an actual individual or individuals
    or about the expected behavior of a physically and psychologically
    defined type of individual, but which abstracts from such behavior in
    order to bring out in clear relief certain expectancies with regard to
    those aspects of individual behavior which various people share, as an
    interpersonal or 'social' pattern, is a datum, however crudely
    expressed, of social science." I have here chosen the second
    perspective; although I shall have occasion to speak of attitudes,
    values and function, it will be from the standpoint of how the social
    structure promotes or inhibits their appearance in specified types of
    situations. See Sapir. "Why cultural anthropology needs the
    psychiatrist," *Psychiatry,* 1938, 1, 7–12.

4. This ritualism may be associated with a mythology which rationalizes
    these practices so that they appear to retain their status as means, but
    the dominant pressure is toward strict ritualistic conformity,

irrespective of the mythology. Ritualism is thus most complete when such rationalizations are not even called forth.

5. In this connection, one sees the relevance of Elton Mayo's paraphrase of the title of Tawney's well-known book. "Actually the problem is *not that of the sickness of an acquisitive society; it is that of the acquisitiveness of a sick society.*" *Human Problems of an Industrialized Civilization,* 153. Mayo deals with the process through which wealth comes to be the basic symbol of social achievement and sees this as arising from a state of anomie. My major concern here is with the social consequences of a heavy emphasis upon monetary success as a goal in a society which has not adapted its structure to the implications of this emphasis. A complete analysis would require the simultaneous examination of both processes.

6. Durkheim's resurrection of the term "anomie" which, so far as I know, first appears in approximately the same sense in the late sixteenth century, might well become the object of an investigation by a student interested in the historical filiation of ideas. Like the term "climate of opinion" brought into academic and political popularity by A. N. Whitehead three centuries after it was coined by Joseph Glanvill, the word "anomie" (or anomy or anomia) has lately come into frequent use, once it was re-introduced by Durkheim. Why the resonance in contemporary society? For a magnificent model of the type of research required by questions of this order, see Leo Spitzer, *Milieu and Ambiance:* an essay in historical semantics," *Philosophy and Phenomenological Research,* 1942, 3, 1–42, 169–218.

7. It appears unlikely that cultural norms, once interiorized, are wholly eliminated. Whatever residuum persists will induce personality tensions and conflict, with some measure of ambivalence. A manifest rejection of the once-incorporated institutional norms will be coupled with some latent retention of their emotional correlates. Guilt feelings, a sense of sin, pangs of conscience are diverse terms referring to this unrelieved tension. Symbolic adherence to the nominally repudiated values or rationalizations for the rejection of these values constitute a more subtle expression of these tensions.

8. "Many," not all, unintegrated groups, for the reason mentioned earlier. In groups where the primary emphasis shifts to institutional means, the outcome is normally a type of ritualism rather than anomie.

9. Leo C. Rosten, *Hollywood* (New York), 1940, 40.

10. Malcolm S. MacLean, *Scholars, Workers and Gentlemen* (Harvard University Press, 1938), 29.

11. *Cf.* A. W. Griswold, *The American Cult of Success* (Yale University doctoral dissertation, 1933); R. O. Carlson, *"Personality Schools": A Sociological Analysis* (Columbia University Master's Essay, 1948).

12. There is no lack of typologies of alternative modes of response to frustrating conditions. Freud, in his *Civilization and Its Discontents* (p.

30 ff.) supplies one; derivative typologies, often differing in basic details, will be found in Karen Horney, *Neurotic Personality of Our Time* (New York, 1937); S. Rosenzweig, "The experimental measurement of types of reaction to frustration," in H. A. Murray *et al.*, *Explorations in Personality* (New York, 1938). 585–99; and in the work of John Dollard, Harold Lasswell, Abram Kardiner, Erich Fromm. But particularly in the strictly Freudian typology, the perspective is that of types of individual responses, quite apart from the place of the individual within the social structure. Despite her consistent concern with "culture," for example, Horney does not explore differences in the impact of this culture upon farmer, worker and businessman, upon lower-, middle-, and upper-class individuals, upon members of various ethnic and racial groups, *etc.* As a result, the role of "inconsistencies in culture" is *not* located in its differential impact upon diversely situated groups. Culture becomes a kind of blanket covering all members of the society equally, apart from their idiosyncratic differences of life-history. It is a primary assumption of our typology that these responses occur with different frequency within various sub-groups in our society precisely because members of these groups or strata are differentially subject to cultural stimulation and social restraints. This sociological orientation will be found in the writings of Dollard and, less systematically, in the work of Fromm, Kardiner and Lasswell. On the general point, see note 3 of this chapter.

13. This fifth alternative is on a plane clearly different from that of the others. It represents a transitional response seeking to *institutionalize* new goals and new procedures to be shared by other members of the society. It thus refers to efforts to *change* the existing cultural and social structure rather than to accommodate efforts *within* this structure.

14. The observations by Dickens are from his *American Notes* (in the edition, for example, published in Boston: Books, Inc., 1940), 218. A sociological analysis which would be the formal, albeit inevitably lesser, counterpart of Freud's psychological analysis of the functions of tendentious wit and of tendentious wits is long overdue. The doctoral dissertation by Jeannette Tandy, though not sociological in character, affords one point of departure: *Crackerbox Philosophers: American Humor and Satire* (New York: Columbia University Press, 1925). In Chapter V of *Intellectual America* (New York: Macmillan, 1941), appropriately entitled "The Intelligentsia," Oscar Cargill has some compact observations on the role of the nineteenth century masters of American wit, but this naturally has only a small place in this large book on the "march of American ideas." The essay by Bierce from which I have quoted at such length will be found in *The Collected Works of Ambrose Bierce* (New York and Washington: The Neale Publishing Company, 1912), volume XI, 187–198. For what it is worth, I must differ with the harsh and far from justified judgment of Cargill on

Bierce. It seems to be less a judgment than the expression of a prejudice which, in Bierce's own understanding of "prejudice," is only "a vagrant opinion without visible means of support."

15. E. H. Sutherland, "White collar criminality," *op. cit.;* "Crime and business," *Annals, American Academy of Political and Social Science*, 1941, 217, 112–118; "Is 'white collar crime' crime?", *American Sociological Review*, 1945, 10, 132–139; Marshall B. Clinard, *The Black Market: A Study of White Collar Crime* (New York: Rinehart & Co., 1952); Donald R. Cressey, *Other People's Money: A Study in the Social Psychology of Embezzlement* (Glencoe: The Free Press, 1953).

16. James S. Wallerstein and Clement J. Wyle, "Our law-abiding law-breakers," *Probation*, April, 1947.

17. National Opinion Research Center, *National Opinion on Occupations*, April, 1947. This research on the ranking and evaluation of ninety occupations by a nation-wide sample presents a series of important empirical data. Of great significance is their finding that, despite a slight tendency for people to rank their own and related occupations higher than do other groups, there is substantial agreement in ranking of occupations among all occupational strata. More researches of this kind are needed to map the cultural topography of contemporary societies. (See the comparative study of prestige accorded major occupations in six industrialized countries: Alex Inkeles and Peter H. Rossi, "National comparisons of occupational prestige," *American Journal of Sociology*, 1956, 61, 329–339.)

18. See Joseph D. Lohman, "The participant observer in community studies," *American Sociological Review*, 1937, 2, 890–98 and William F. Whyte, *Street Corner Society* (Chicago, 1943). Note Whyte's conclusions: "It is difficult for the Cornerville man to get onto the ladder [of success], even on the bottom rung....He is an Italian, and the Italians are looked upon by upper-class people as among the least desirable of the immigrant peoples...the society holds out attractive rewards in terms of money and material possessions to the 'successful' man. For most Cornerville people these rewards are available only through advancement in the world of rackets and politics." (273–74)

19. Numerous studies have found that the educational pyramid operates to keep a large proportion of unquestionably able but economically disadvantaged youth from obtaining higher formal education. This fact about our class structure has been noted with dismay, for example, by Vannevar Bush in his governmental report, *Science: The Endless Frontier.* Also, see W. L. Warner, R. J. Havighurst and M. B. Loeb, *Who Shall Be Educated?* (New York, 1944).

20. The shifting historical role of this ideology is a profitable subject for exploration.

21. The role of the Negro in this connection raises almost as many theoretical as practical questions. It has been reported that large segments of the Negro population have assimilated the dominant caste's values of pecuniary success and social advancement, but have "realistically adjusted" themselves to the "fact" that social ascent is presently confined almost entirely to movement within the caste. See Dollard, *Caste and Class in a Southern Town,* 66 ff.; Donald Young, *American Minority Peoples,* 581; Robert A. Warner, *New Haven Negroes* (New Haven, 1940), 234. See also the subsequent discussion in this chapter.

22. This analytical scheme may serve to resolve some of the apparent inconsistencies in the relation between crime and economic status mentioned by P.A. Sorokin. For example, he notes that "not everywhere nor always do the poor show a greater proportion of crime...many poorer countries have had less crime than the richer countries....The economic improvement in the second half of the nineteenth century, and the beginning of the twentieth, has not been followed by a decrease in crime." See his *Contemporary Sociological Theories* (New York, 1928), 560–61. The crucial point is, however, that low economic status plays a different dynamic role in different social and cultural structures, as is set out in the text. One should not, therefore, expect a linear correlation between crime and poverty.

23. Gilbert Murray, *Five Stages of Greek Religion* (New York, 1925), 164–5. Professor Murray's chapter on "The Failure of Nerve," from which I have taken this excerpt, must surely be ranked among the most civilized and perceptive sociological analyses in our time.

24. See the quotation from an interview cited in Gustavus Meyers, *History of the Great American Fortunes* (New York, 1937), 706.

25. *Nation's Business,* Vol. 27, No. 9, pp. 8–9.

26. E.W. Bakke, *The Unemployable Man* (New York, 1934), p. 14 (I have supplied the emphasis). Bakke hints at the structural sources making for a belief in luck among workers. "There is a measure of hopelessness in the situation when a man knows that *most of his good or ill fortune is out of his own control and depends on luck.''* (Emphasis supplied.) In so far as he is forced to accommodate himself to occasionally unpredictable decisions of management, the worker is subject to job insecurities and anxieties: another "seed-ground" for belief in destiny, fate, chance. It would be instructive to learn if such beliefs become lessened where workers' organizations reduce the probability that their occupational fate will be out of their own hands.

27. At its extreme, it may invite resignation and routinized activity (Adaptation III) or a fatalistic passivism (Adaptation IV), of which more presently.

28. Bakke, *op. cit.,* 14, where he suggests that "the worker knows less about the processes which cause him to succeed or have no chance to

succeed than business or professional people. There are more points, therefore, at which events appear to have their incidence in good or ill luck."

29. *Cf.* R.A. Warner, *New Haven Negroes* and Harold F. Gosnell, *Negro Politicians* (Chicago, 1935), 123–5, both of whom comment in this general connection on the great interests in 'playing the numbers" among less-advantaged Negroes.

30. See, for example, H. S. Sullivan, "Modern conceptions of psychiatry," *Psychiatry*, 1940, 3, 111–12; Margaret Mead, *And Keep Your Powder Dry* (New York, 1942), Chapter VII; Merton, Fiske and Curtis, *Mass Persuasion*, 59–60.

31. P. Janet, "The fear of action," *Journal of Abnormal Psychology*, 1921, 16, 150–60, and the extraordinary discussion by F. L. Wells, "Social maladjustments: adaptive regression," *op, cit.*, which bears closely on the type of adaptation examined here.

32. F. J. Roethlisberger and W. J. Dickson, *Management and the Worker*, Chapter 18 and 531 ff.; and on the more general theme, the typically perspicacious remarks of Gilbert Murray, *op. cit.*, 138–39.

33. See the three following chapters [in Merton's *Social Theory and Social Structure*].

34. See, for example, Allison Davis and John Dollard, *Children of Bondage* (Washington, 1940), Chapter 12 ("Child Training and Class"), which, though it deals with the lower- and lower-middle class patterns of socialization among Negroes in the Far South, appears applicable, with slight modification, to the white population as well. On this, see further M. C. Erickson, "Child-rearing and social status," *American Journal of Sociology*, 1946, 53, 190–92; Allison Davis and R. J. Havighurst, "Social class and color differences in child-rearing," *American Sociological Review*, 1946, 11, 698–710: "...the pivotal meaning *of social class* to students of human development is that it defines and systematizes different learning environments for children of different classes." "Generalizing from the evidence presented in the tables, we would say that middle-class children [the authors do not distinguish between lower-middle and upper-middle strata] are subjected earlier and more consistently to the influences which make a child an orderly, conscientious, responsible, and tame person. In the course of this training middle-class children probably suffer more frustration of their impulses."

35. This hypothesis still awaits empirical test. Beginnings in this direction have been made with the "level of aspiration" experiments which explore the determinants of goal-formation and modification in specific, experimentally devised activities. There is, however, a major obstacle, not yet surmounted, in drawing inferences from the laboratory situation, with its relatively slight ego-involvement with the casual task—pencil-and-paper mazes, ring-throwing, arithmetical

problems, *etc.*—which will be applicable to the strong emotional investment with success-goals in the routines of everyday life. Nor have these experiments, with their *ad hoc* group formations, been able to reproduce the acute social pressures obtaining in daily life. (What laboratory experiment reproduces, for example, the querulous nagging of a modern Xantippe: "The trouble with you is, you've got no ambition; a real man would go out and do things"? Among studies with a definite though limited relevance, see especially R. Gould, "Some sociological determinants of goal strivings," *Journal of Social Psychology,* 1941, 13, 461–73; L. Festinger, "Wish, expectation and group standards as factors influencing level of aspiration," *Journal of Abnormal and Social Psychology,* 1942, 37, 184–200. For a resume of researches, see Kurt Lewin *et al.*, "Level of Aspiration," in J. McV. Hunt, ed., *Personality and the Behavior Disorders* (New York, 1944), I, Chap. 10.

The conception of "success" as a ratio between aspiration and achievement pursued systematically in the level-of-aspiration experiments has, of course, a long history. Gilbert Murray (*op. cit.,* 138–9) notes the prevalence of this conception among the thinkers of fourth century Greece. And in *Sartor Resartus,* Carlyle observes that "happiness" (gratification) can be represented by a fraction in which the numerator represents achievement and the denominator, aspiration. Much the same notion is examined by William James (*The Principles of Psychology* [New York, 1902], I, 310). See also F. L. Wells, *op. cit.,* 879, and P. A. Sorokin, *Social and Cultural Dynamics* (New York, 1937), III, 161–164. The critical question is whether this familiar insight can be subjected to rigorous experimentation in which the contrived laboratory situation adequately reproduces the salient aspects of the real-life situation or whether disciplined observation of routines of behavior in everyday life will prove the more productive method of inquiry.

36. In her novel, *The Bitter Box* (New York, 1946), Eleanor Clark has portrayed this process with great sensitivity. The discussion by Erich Fromm, *Escape from Freedom* (New York, 1941), 185–206, may be cited, without implying acceptance of his concept of "spontaneity" and "man's inherent tendency toward self-development." For an example of a sound sociological formulation: "As long as we assume...that the anal character, as it is typical of the European lower middle class, is caused by certain early experiences in connection with defecation, we have hardly any data that lead us to understand why a specific class should have an anal social character. However, if we understand it as one form of relatedness to others, rooted in the character structure and resulting from the experiences with the outside world, we have a key for understanding why the whole mode of life of the lower middle class, its narrowness, isolation, and hostility, made for the development of this kind of character structure." (293–4) For an

example of a formulation stemming from a kind of latter-day benevolent anarchism here judged as dubious: "...there are also certain psychological qualities inherent in man that need to be satisfied.... The most important seems to be the tendency to grow, to develop and realize potentialities which man has developed in the course of history—as, for instance, the faculty of creative and critical thinking.... It also seems that this general tendency to grow—which is the psychological equivalent of the identical biological tendency —results in such specific tendencies as the desire for freedom and the hatred against oppression, since freedom is the fundamental condition for any growth." (287–88).

37. Obviously, this is an elliptical statement. These individuals may retain some orientation to the values of their own groupings within the larger society or, occasionally, to the values of the conventional society itself. They may, in other words, shift to other modes of adaptation. But Adaptation IV can be easily detected. Nels Anderson's account of the behavior and attitudes of the bum, for example, can readily be recast in terms of our analytical scheme. See *The Hobo* (Chicago, 1923), 93–98, *et passim*.

38. H.W. Zorbaugh, *The Gold Coast and the Slum* (Chicago, 1929), 108.

39. Abram Kardiner, *The Psychological Frontiers of Society* (New York, 1945), 369—70. (Emphases supplied.)

40. Max Scheler, *L'homme du ressentiment* (Paris, n. d.). This essay first appeared in 1912; revised and completed, it was included in Scheler's *Abhandlungen und Aufsätze*, appearing thereafter in his *Vom Umsturz der Werte* (1919). The last text was used for the French translation. It has had considerable influence in varied intellectual circles. For an excellent and well-balanced discussion of Scheler's essay, indicating some of its limitations and biasses, the respects in which it prefigured Nazi conceptions, its anti-democratic orientation and, withal , its occasionally brilliant insights, see V. J. McGill, "Scheler's theory of sympathy and love," *Philosophy and Phenomenological Research*, 1942, 2, 273–91. For another critical account which properly criticizes Scheler's view that social structure plays only a secondary role in *ressentiment*, see Svend Ranulf, *Moral Indignation and Middle-Class Psychology: A Sociological Study* (Copenhagen, 1938), 199–204.

41. Scheler, *op. cit.*, 55–56. No English word fully reproduces the complex of elements implied by the word *ressentiment*; its nearest approximation in German would appear to be *Groll*.

42. George S. Pettee, *The Process of Revolution* (New York, 1938), 8–24; see particularly his account of "monopoly of the imagination."

43. R. S. and H. M. Lynd, *Middletown in Transition* (New York, 1937), 408, for a series of cultural clichés exemplifying the conservative myth.

44. See the acute observations by Georg Simmel, *Soziologie* (Leipzig, 1908), 276–77.

45. W. Stern, *Psychology of Early Childhood* (New York, 1924), 166, notes the *fact* of such errors (*e.g.*, "drinked" for "drank"), but does not draw the inferences regarding the detection of implicit paradigms.
46. H.A. Murray *et al.*, *Explorations in Personality*, 307.
47. From a study of the social organization of planned communities by R. K. Merton, Patricia S. West and M. Jahoda, *Patterns of Social Life*.

11 *Illegitimate Means, Anomie, and Deviant Behavior*
RICHARD A. CLOWARD

This paper[1] represents an attempt to consolidate two major sociological traditions of thought about the problem of deviant behavior. The first, exemplified by the work of Emile Durkheim and Robert K. Merton, may be called the anomie tradition.[2] The second, illustrated principally by the studies of Clifford R. Shaw, Henry D. McKay, and Edwin H. Sutherland, may be called the "cultural transmission" and "differential association" tradition.[3] Despite some reciprocal borrowing of ideas, these intellectual traditions developed more or less independently. By seeking to consolidate them, a more adequate theory of deviant behavior may be constructed.

DIFFERENTIALS IN AVAILABILITY OF LEGITIMATE MEANS: THE THEORY OF ANOMIE

The theory of anomie has undergone two major phases of development. Durkheim first used the concept to explain deviant behavior. He focused on the way in which various social conditions lead to "overweening ambition," and how, in turn, unlimited aspirations ultimately produce a breakdown in regulatory norms. Robert K. Merton has systematized and extended the theory, directing attention to patterns of disjunction between culturally prescribed goals and socially organized access to them by *legitimate* means. In this paper, a third phase is outlined. An additional variable is incorporated in the developing scheme of anomie, namely, the concept of *differentials in access to success-goals by illegitimate means.*[4]

Reprinted from Richard A. Cloward, "Illegitimate Means, Anomie, and Deviant Behavior," *American Sociological Review*, vol. 24 (April 1959), pp. 164-176.

PHASE I: UNLIMITED ASPIRATIONS AND THE BREAKDOWN OF REGULATORY NORMS

In Durkheim's work, a basic distinction is made between "physical needs" and "moral needs." The importance of this distinction was heightened for Durkheim because he viewed physical needs as being regulated automatically by features of man's organic structure. Nothing in the organic structure, however, is capable of regulating social desires; as Durkheim put it, man's "capacity for feeling is in itself an insatiable and bottomless abyss."[5] If man is to function without "friction," "the passions must first be limited. . . . But since the individual has no way of limiting them, this must be done by some force exterior to him." Durkheim viewed the collective order as the external regulating force which defined and ordered the goals to which men should orient their behavior. If the collective order is disrupted or disturbed, however, men's aspirations may then rise, exceeding all possibilities of fulfillment. Under these conditions, "de-regulation or anomy" ensues: "At the very moment when traditional rules have lost their authority, the richer prize offered these appetites stimulates them and makes them more exigent and impatient of control. The state of deregulation or anomy is thus further heightened by passions being less disciplined precisely when they need more disciplining." Finally, pressures toward deviant behavior were said to develop when man's aspirations no longer matched the possibilities of fulfillment.

Durkheim therefore turned to the question of *when* the regulatory functions of the collective order break down. Several such states were identified, including sudden depression, sudden prosperity, and rapid technological change. His object was to show how, under these conditions, men are led to aspire to goals extremely difficult if not impossible to attain. As Durkheim saw it, sudden depression results in deviant behavior because "something like a declassification occurs which suddenly casts certain individuals into a lower state than their previous one. Then they must reduce their requirements, restrain their needs, learn greater self-control. . . . But society cannot adjust them instantaneously to this new life and teach them to practice the increased self-repression to which they are unaccustomed. So they are not adjusted to the condition forced on them, and its very prospect is intolerable; hence the suffering which detaches them from a reduced existence even before they have made trial of it." Prosperity, according to Durkheim, could have much the same effect as depression, particularly if upward changes in economic conditions are abrupt. The very abruptness of these changes presumably heightens aspirations beyond possibility of fulfillment, and this too puts a strain on the regulatory apparatus of the society.

According to Durkheim, "the sphere of trade and industry...is actually in a chronic state [of anomie]." Rapid technological developments and the existence of vast, unexploited markets excite the imagination with the seemingly limitless possibilities for the accumulation of wealth. As Durkheim said of the producer of goods, "now that he may assume to have almost the entire would as his customer, how could passions accept their former confinement in the face of such limitless prospects?" Continuing, Durkheim states that "such is the source of excitement predominating in this part of society....Here the state of crisis and anomie [are] constant and, so to speak, normal. From top to bottom of the ladder, greed is aroused without knowing where to find ultimate foothold. Nothing can calm it, since its goal is far beyond all it can attain."

In developing the theory, Durkheim characterized goals in the industrial society, and specified the way in which unlimited aspirations are induced. He spoke of "dispositions...so inbred that society has grown to accept them and is accustomed to think them normal," and he portrayed these "inbred dispositions": "It is everlastingly repeated that it is man's nature to be eternally dissatisfied, constantly to advance, without relief or rest, toward an indefinite goal. The longing for infinity is daily represented as a mark of moral distinction...." And it was precisely these pressures to strive for "infinite" or "receding" goals, in Durkheim's view, that generate a breakdown in regulatory norms, for "when there is no other aim but to outstrip constantly the point arrived at, how painful to be thrown back!"

Phase II: Disjunction Between Cultural Goals and Socially Structured Opportunity

Durkheim's description of the emergence of "overweening ambition" and the subsequent breakdown of regulatory norms constitutes one of the links between his work and the later development of the theory by Robert K. Merton. In his classic essay, "Social Structure and Anomie," Merton suggests that goals and norms may vary independently of each other, and that this sometimes leads to malintegrated states. In his view, two polar types of disjunction may occur: "There may develop a very heavy, at times a virtually exclusive, stress upon the value of particular goals, involving comparatively little concern with the institutionally prescribed means of striving toward these goals....This constitutes one type of malintegrated culture."[6] On the other hand, "A second polar type is found where activities originally conceived as instrumental are transmuted into self-contained practices, lacking further objectives. . . . Sheer conformity becomes a central value." Merton notes that "between these extreme types are societies which maintain a rough balance between emphases upon cultural goals and institutionalized practices, and these constitute the integrated and relatively stable, though changing societies."

Having identified patterns of disjunction between goals and norms, Merton is enabled to define anomie more precisely: "Anomie [may be] conceived as a breakdown in the cultural structure, occurring particularly when there is an acute disjunction between cultural norms and goals and the socially structured capacities of members of the group to act in accord with them."

Of the two kinds of malintegrated societies, Merton is primarily interested in the one in which "there is an exceptionally strong emphasis upon specific goals without a corresponding emphasis upon institutional procedures." He states that attentuation between goals and norms, leading to anomie or "normlessness," comes about because men in such societies internalize an emphasis on common success-goals under conditions of varying access to them. The essence of this hypothesis is captured in the following excerpt: "It is only when a system of cultural values extols, virtually above all else, certain *common* success-goals for the population at large while the social structure rigorously restricts or completely closes access to approved modes of reaching these goals *for a considerable part of the same population,* that deviant behavior ensues on a large scale." The focus, in short, is on the way in which the social structure puts a strain upon the cultural structure. Here one may point to diverse structural differentials in access to culturally approved goals by legitimate means, for example, differentials of age, sex, ethnic status, and social class. Pressures for anomie or normlessness vary from one social position to another, depending on the nature of these differentials.

In summary, Merton extends the theory of anomie in two principal ways. He explicitly identifies types of anomic or malintegrated societies by focussing upon the relationship between cultural goals and norms. And, by directing attention to patterned differentials in the access to success-goals by legitimate means, he shows how the social structure exerts a strain upon the cultural structure, leading in turn to anomie or normlessness.

PHASE III: THE CONCEPT OF ILLEGITIMATE MEANS

Once processes generating differentials in pressures are identified, there is then the question of how these pressures are resolved, or how men respond to them. In this connection, Merton enumerates five basic categories of behavior or role adaptations which are likely to emerge: conformity, innovation, ritualism, retreatism, and rebellion. These adaptations differ depending on the individual's acceptance or rejection of cultural goals, and depending on his adherence to or violation of institutional norms. Furthermore, Merton sees the distribution of these adaptations principally as the consequence of two variables: the relative extent of pressure, and values, particularly "internalized prohibitions," governing the use of various illegitimate means.

It is a familiar sociological idea that values serve to order the choices of deviant (as well as conforming) adaptations which develop under conditions of stress. Comparative studies of ethnic groups, for example, have shown that some tend to engage in distinctive forms of deviance; thus Jews exhibit low rates of alcoholism and alcoholic psychoses.[7] Various investigators have suggested that the emphasis on rationality, fear of expressing aggression, and other alleged components of the "Jewish" value system constrain modes of deviance which involve "loss of control" over behavior.[8] In contrast, the Irish show a much higher rate of alcoholic deviance because, it has been argued, their cultural emphasis on masculinity encourages the excessive use of alcohol under conditions of strain.[9]

Merton suggests that differing rates of ritualistic and innovating behavior in the middle and lower classes result from differential emphases in socialization. The "rule-oriented" accent in middle-class socialization presumably disposes persons to handle stress by engaging in ritualistic rather than innovating behavior. The lower-class person, contrastingly, having internalized less stringent norms, can violate conventions with less guilt and anxiety.[10] Values, in other words, exercise a canalizing influence, limiting the choice of deviant adaptations for persons variously distributed throughout the social system.

Apart from both socially patterned pressures, which give rise to deviance, and from values, which determine choices of adaptations, a further variable should be taken into account: namely, *differentials in availability of illegitimate means*. For example, the notion that innovating behavior may result from unfulfilled aspirations and imperfect socialization with respect to conventional norms implies that illegitimate means are freely available—as if the individual, having decided that "you can't make it legitimately," then simply turns to illegitimate means which are readily at hand whatever his position in the social structure. However, these means may not be available. As noted above, the anomie theory assumes that conventional means are differentially distributed, that some individuals, because of their social position, enjoy certain advantages which are denied to others. Note, for example, variations in the degree to which members of various classes are fully exposed to and thus acquire the values, education, and skills which facilitate upward mobility. It should not be startling, therefore, to find similar variations in the availability of illegitimate means.

Several sociologists have alluded to such variations without explicitly incorporating this variable in a theory of deviant behavior. Sutherland, for example, writes that "an inclination to steal is not a sufficient explanation of the genesis of the professional thief."[11] Moreover, "the person must be appreciated by the professional thieves. He must be appraised as having an adequate equipment of wits, front, talking-ability, honesty, reliability, nerve and determination." In short, "a person can be a professional thief only if he is recognized and received as such by other professional thieves." But recognition is not freely accorded: "Selection and tutelage are the two necessary elements in the process of acquiring recognition as a professional thief....A person cannot acquire recognition as a professional thief until he has had tutelage in professional theft, *and tutelage is given only to a few persons selected from the total population.*" Furthermore, the aspirant is judged by high standards of performance, for only "a very small percentage of those who start on this process ever reach the stage of professional theft." The burden of these remarks—dealing with the processes of selection, induction, and assumption of full status in the criminal group—is that motivations or pressures toward deviance do not fully account for deviant behavior. The "self-made" thief—lacking knowledge of the ways of securing immunity from prosecution and similar techniques of defense—"would quickly land in prison." Sutherland is in effect pointing to differentials in access to the role of professional thief. Although the criteria of selection are not altogether clear from his analysis, definite evaluative standards do appear to exist; depending on their content, certain categories of individuals would be placed at a disadvantage and others would be favored.

The availability of illegitimate means, then, is controlled by various criteria in the same manner that has long been ascribed to conventional means. Both systems of opportunity are (1) limited, rather than infinitely available, and (2) differentially available depending on the location of persons in the social structure.

When we employ the term "means," whether legitimate or illegitimate, at least two things are implied: first, that there are appropriate learning environments for the acquisition of the values and skills associated with the performance of a particular role; and second, that the individual has opportunities to discharge the role once he has been prepared. The term subsumes, therefore, both *learning structures* and *opportunity structures.*

A case in point is recruitment and preparation for careers in the rackets. There are fertile criminal learning environments for the young in neighborhoods where the rackets flourish as stable, indigenous institutions. Because these environments afford integration of offenders of different ages, the young are exposed to "differential associations" which facilitate the acquisition of criminal values and skills. Yet preparation for the role may not insure that the individual will ever discharge it. For one thing, more youngsters may be recruited into these patterns of differential association than can possibly be absorbed, following their "training," by the adult criminal structure. There may be a surplus of contenders for these elite positions, leading in turn to the necessity for criteria and mechanisms of selection. Hence a certain proportion of those who aspire may not be permitted to engage in the behavior for which they have been prepared.

This illustration is similar in every respect, save for the route followed, to the case of those who seek careers in the sphere of legitimate business. Here, again, is the initial problem of securing access to appropriate learning environments, such as colleges and postgraduate schools of business. Having acquired the values and skills needed for a business career, graduates then face the problem of whether or not they can successfully discharge the roles for which they have been prepared. Formal training itself is not sufficient for occupational success, for many forces intervene to determine who shall succeed and fail in the competitive world of business and industry—as throughout the entire conventional occupational structure.

This distinction between learning structures and opportunity structures was suggested some years ago by Sutherland. In 1944, he circulated an unpublished paper which briefly discusses the proposition that "criminal behavior is partially a function of opportunities to commit specific classes of crimes, such as embezzlement, bank burglary, or illicit heterosexual intercourse."[12] He did not, however, take up the problem of differentials in opportunity as a concept to be systematically incorporated in a theory of deviant behavior. Instead, he held that "opportunity" is a necessary but not sufficient explanation of the commission of criminal acts, "since some persons who have opportunities to embezzle, become intoxicated, engage in illicit heterosexual intercourse or to commit other crimes do not do so." He also noted that the differential association theory did not constitute a full explanation of criminal activity, for, notwithstanding differential association, "it is axiomatic that persons who commit a specific crime must have the opportunity to commit that crime." He therefore concluded that "while opportunity may be partially a function of association with criminal patterns and of the specialized techniques thus acquired, *it is not determined entirely in that manner*, and consequently differential association is not the sufficient cause of criminal behavior." (emphasis not in original)

In Sutherland's statements, two meanings are attributed to the term "opportunity." As suggested above, it may be useful to separate these for analytical purposes. In the first sense, Sutherland appears to be saying that opportunity consists in part of learning structures. The principal components of his theory of differential association are that "criminal behavior is learned," and, furthermore, that "criminal behavior is learned in interaction with other persons in a process of communication." But he also uses the term to describe situations conducive to carrying out criminal roles. Thus, for Sutherland, the commission of a criminal act would seem to depend upon the existence of two conditions: differential associations favoring the acquisition of criminal values and skills, and conditions encouraging participation in criminal activity.

This distinction heightens the importance of identifying and questioning the common assumption that illegitimate means are freely available. We can now ask (1) whether there are socially structured differentials in access to illegitimate learning environments, and (2) whether there are differentials limiting the fulfillment of illegitimate roles. If differentials exist and can be identified, we may then inquire about their consequences for the behavior of persons in different parts of the social structure. Before pursuing this question, however, we turn to a fuller discussion of the theoretical tradition established by Shaw, McKay, and Sutherland.

DIFFERENTIALS IN AVAILABILITY OF ILLEGITIMATE MEANS: THE SUBCULTURE TRADITION

The concept of differentials in availability of illegitimate means is implicit in one of the major streams of American criminological theory. In this tradition, attention is focussed on the processes by which persons are recruited into criminal learning environments and ultimately inducted into criminal roles. The problems here are to account for the acquisition of criminal roles and to describe the social organization of criminal activities. When the theoretical propositions contained in this tradition are reanalyzed, it becomes clear that one underlying conception is that of variations in access to success-goals by illegitimate means. Furthermore, this implicit concept may be shown to be one of the bases upon which the tradition was constructed.

In their studies of the ecology of deviant behavior in the urban environment, Shaw and McKay found that delinquency and crime tended to be confined to delimited areas and, furthermore, that such behavior persisted despite demographic changes in these areas. Hence they came to speak of "criminal tradition," of the "cultural transmission" of criminal values.[13] As a result of their observations of slum life, they concluded that *particular importance must be assigned to the integration of different age-levels of offenders.* Thus:

> Stealing in the neighborhood was a common practice among the children and approved by the parents. Whenever the boys got together they talked about robbing and made more plans for stealing. I hardly knew any boys who did not go robbing. The little fellows went in for petty stealing, breaking into freight cars, and stealing junk. The older guys did big jobs like stick-up, burglary, and stealing autos. The little fellows admired the "big shots" and longed for the day when they could get into the big racket. Fellows who had "done time" were the big shots and looked up to and gave the little fellow tips on how to get by and pull off big jobs.[14]

In other words, access to criminal roles depends upon stable associations with others from whom the necessary values and skills may be learned. Shaw and McKay were describing deviant learning structures—that is, alternative routes by which people seek access to the goals which society holds to be worthwhile. They might also have pointed out that, in areas where such learning structures are unavailable, it is probably difficult for many individuals to secure access to stable criminal careers, even though motivated to do so.[15]

The concept of illegitimate means and the socially structured conditions of access to them were not explicitly recognized in the work of Shaw and McKay because, probably, they were disposed to view slum areas as "disorganized." Although they consistently referred to illegitimate activities as being organized, they nevertheless often depicted high-rate delinquency areas as disorganized because the values transmitted were criminal rather than conventional. Hence their work includes statements which we now perceive to be internally inconsistent, such as the following:

> This community situation [in which Sidney was reared] was not only disorganized and thus ineffective as a unit of control, but it was characterized by a high rate of juvenile delinquency and adult crime, not to mention the widespread political corruption which had long existed in the area. Various forms of stealing and many organized delinquent and criminal gangs were prevalent in the area. These groups exercised a powerful influence and tended to created a com-

munity spirit which not only tolerated but actually fostered delinquent and criminal practices.[16]

Sutherland was among the first to perceive that the concept of social disorganization tended to obscure the stable patterns of interaction among carriers of criminal values. Like Shaw and McKay, he had been influenced by the observation that lower-class areas were organized in terms of both conventional and criminal values, but he was also impressed that these alternative value systems were supported by patterned systems of social relations. He expressly recognized that crime, far from being a random, unorganized activity, was typically an intricate and stable system of human arrangements. He therefore rejected the concept of "social disorganization" and substituted the concept of "differential group organization."

> The third concept, social disorganization, was borrowed from Shaw and McKay. I had used it but had not been satisfied with it because the organization of the delinquent group, which is often very complex, is social disorganization only from an ethical or some other particularistic point of view. At the suggestion of Albert K. Cohen, this concept has been changed to differential group organization, with organization for criminal activities on one side and organization against criminal activities on the other.[17]

Having freed observation of the urban slum from conventional evaluations, Sutherland was able to focus more clearly on the way in which its social structure constitutes a "learning environment" for the acquisition of deviant values and skills. In the development of the theory of "differential association" and "differential group organization," he came close to stating explicitly the concept of differentials in access to illegitimate means. But Sutherland was essentially interested in learning processes, and thus he did not ask how such access varies in different parts of the social structure, nor did he inquire about the consequences for behavior of variations in the accessibility of these means.[18]

William F. Whyte, in his classic study of an urban slum, advanced the empirical description of the structure and organization of illegitimate means a step beyond that of Sutherland. Like Sutherland, Whyte rejected the earlier view of the slum as disorganized:

> It is customary for the sociologist to study the slum district in terms of "social disorganization" and to neglect to see that an area such as Cornerville has a complex and well-established organization of its own....I found that in every group there was a hierarchical structure of social relations binding the individuals to one another. Where the group was formally organized into a political club, this was immediately apparent, but for informal groups it was no less true.[19]

Whyte's contribution to our understanding of the organization of illegitimate means in the slum consists primarily in showing that individuals who participate in stable illicit enterprise do not constitute a separate or isolated segment of the community. Rather, these persons are closely integrated with the occupants of conventional roles. In describing the relationship between racketeers and politicians, for example, he notes that "the rackets and political organizations extend from the bottom to the top of Cornerville society, mesh with one another, and integrate a large part of the life of the district. They provide a general framework for the understanding of the actions of both 'little guys' and 'big shots,'"[20] Whyte's view of the slum differs somewhat from that conveyed by the term "differential group organization." He does not emphasize the idea that the slum is composed of two different systems, conventional and deviant, but rather the way in which the occupants of these various roles are integrated in a single, stable structure which organizes and patterns the life of the community.

The description of the organization of illegitimate means in slums is further developed by Solomon Kobrin in his article, "The Conflict of Values in Delinquency Areas."[21] Kobrin suggests that urban slum areas vary in the degree to which the carriers of deviant and conventional values are integrated with one another. Hence he points the way to the development of a "typology of delinquency areas based on variations in the relationship between these two systems," depicting the "polar types" on such a continuum. The first type resembles the integrated areas described in preceding paragraphs. Here, claims Kobrin, there is not merely structural integration between carriers of the two value systems, but reciprocal participation by each in the value system of the other. Thus:

> Leaders of [illegal] enterprises frequently maintain membership in such conventional institutions of their local communities as churches, fraternal and mutual benefit societies and political parties. . . . Within this framework the influence of each of the two value systems is reciprocal, the leaders of illegal enterprise participating in the primary orientation of the conventional elements in the population, and the latter, through their participation in a local power structure sustained in large part by illicit activity, participating perforce in the alternate, criminal value system.

Kobrin also notes that in some urban slums there is a tendency for the relationships between carriers of deviant and conventional values to break down. Such areas constitute the second polar type. Because of disorganizing forces such as "drastic change in the class, ethnic, or racial characteristics of its population," Kobrin suggests that "the bearers of the conventional culture and its value system are without the customary institutional machinery and therefore in effect partially de-mobilized with reference to the diffusion of their value system." At the same time, the criminal "value system remains implicit" since this type of area is "characterized principally by the absence of systematic and organized adult activity in violation of the law, despite the fact that many adults in these areas commit violations." Since both value systems remain implicit, the possibilities for effective integration are precluded.

The importance of these observations may be seen if we ask how accessibility of illegal means varies with the relative integration of con-ventional and criminal values from one type of area to another. In this connection, Kobrin points out that the "integrated" area apparently constitutes a "training ground" for the acquisition of criminal values and skills.

> The stable position of illicit enterprise in the adult society of the com-munity is reflected in the character of delinquent conduct on the part of children. While delinquency in all high rate areas is intrinsically disorderly in that it is unrelated to official programs for the education of the young, in the [integrated community] boys may more or less realistically recognize the potentialities for personal progress in local society through access to delinquency. In a general way, therefore, delinquent activity in these areas constitutes a training ground for the acquisition of skill in the use of violence, concealment of offense, evasion of detection and arrest, and the purchase of immunity from punishment. Those who come to excel in these respects are fre-quently noted and valued by adult leaders in the rackets who are confronted, as are the leaders of all income-producing enterprises, with problems of the recruitment of competent personnel.

With respect to the contrasting or "unintegrated area," Kobrin makes no mention of the extent to which learning structures and op-portunities for criminal careers are available. Yet his portrayal of such areas as lacking in the articulation of either conventional or criminal values suggests that the appropriate learning structures—principally the integration of offenders of different age levels—are not available. Furthermore, his depiction of adult violative activity as "unorgan-ized" suggests that the illegal opportunity structure is severely lim-ited. Even if youngsters were able to secure adequate preparation for criminal roles, the problem would appear to be that the social struc-ture of such neighborhoods provides few opportunities for stable, criminal careers. For Kobrin's analysis—as well as those of Whyte and others before him—leads to the conclusion that illegal opportunity structures tend to emerge in lower-class areas only when stable pat-terns of accommodation and integration arise between the carriers of conventional and deviant values. Where these values remain unorganized and implicit, or where their carriers are in open conflict, opportunities for stable criminal role performance are more or less limited.[22]

Other factors may be cited which affect access to criminal roles. For example, there is a good deal of anecdotal evidence which reveals that access to the upper echelons of organized racketeering is controlled, at lease in part, by ethnicity. Some ethnic groups are found disproportionately in the upper ranks and others disproportionately in the lower. From an historical perspective, as Bell has shown, this realm has been successively dominated by Irish, East-European Jews, and more recently, by Italians.[23] Various other ethnic groups have been virtually excluded or at least relegated to lower-echelon positions. Despite the fact that many rackets (especially "policy") have flourished in predominantly Negro neighborhoods, there have been but one or two Negroes who have been known to rise to the top in syndicated crime. As in the conventional world, Negroes are relegated to the more menial tasks. Moreover, access to elite positions in the rackets may be governed in part by kinship criteria, for various accounts of the blood relations among top racketeers indicate that nepotism is the general rule.[24] It has also been noted that kinship criteria sometimes govern access to stable criminal roles, as in the case of the pickpocket.[25] And there are, of course, deep-rooted sex differentials in access to illegal means. Although women are often employed in criminal vocations—for example, thievery, confidence games, and extortion—and must be employed in others—such as prostitution—nevertheless females are excluded from many criminal activities.[26]

Of the various criteria governing access to illegitimate means, class differentials may be among the most important. The differentials noted in the preceding paragraph—age, sex, ethnicity, kinship, and the like—all pertain to criminal activity historically associated with the lower class. Most middle- or upper-class persons—even when interested in following "lower-class" criminal careers—would no doubt have difficulty in fulfilling this ambition because of inappropriate preparation. The prerequisite attitudes and skills are more easily acquired if the individual is a member of the lower class; most middle- and upper-class persons could not easily unlearn their own class culture in order to learn a new one. By the same token, access to many "white collar" criminal roles is closed to lower-class persons. Some occupations afford abundant opportunities to engage in illegitimate activity; others offer virtually none. The businessman, for example, not only has at his disposal the means to do so, but, as some studies have shown, he is under persistent pressure to employ illegitimate means, if only to maintain a competitive advantage in the market place. But for those in many other occupations, white collar modes of criminal activity are simply not an alternative.[27]

SOME IMPLICATIONS OF A CONSOLIDATED APPROACH TO DEVIANT BEHAVIOR

It is now possible to consolidate the two sociological traditions described above. Our analysis makes it clear that these traditions are oriented to different aspects of the same problem: differentials in access to opportunity. One tradition focusses on legitimate opportunity, the other on illegitimate. By incorporating the concept of differentials in access to *illegitimate* means, the theory of anomie may be extended to include seemingly unrelated studies and theories of deviant behavior which form a part of the literature of American criminology. In this final section, we try to show how a consolidated approach might advance the understanding of both rates and types of deviant conduct. The discussion centers on the conditions of access to *both* systems of means, legitimate and illegitimate.

THE DISTRIBUTION OF CRIMINAL BEHAVIOR

One problem which has plagued the criminologist is the absence of adequate data on social differentials in criminal activity. Many have held that the highest crime rates are to be found in the lower social strata. Others have suggested that rates in the middle and upper classes may be much higher than is ordinarily thought. The question of the social distribution of crime remains problematic.

In the absence of adequate data, the theorist has sometimes attacked this problem by assessing the extent of pressures toward normative departures in various parts of the social structure. For example, Merton remarks that his "primary aim is to discover how some social structures exert a definite pressure upon certain persons in the society to engage in non-conforming rather than conforming conduct."[28] Having identified structural features which might be expected to generate deviance, Merton suggests the presence of a correlation between "pressures toward deviation" and "rate of deviance."

> But whatever the differential rates of deviant behavior in the several social strata, and we know from many sources that the official crime statistics uniformly showing higher rates in the lower strata are far from complete or reliable, *it appears from our analysis that the greater pressures toward deviation are exerted upon the lower strata*. . . . Of social structure, the culture makes incompatible demands. On the one

hand they are asked to orient their behavior toward the prospect of large wealth . . . and on the other, they are largely denied effective opportunities to do so institutionally. *The consequence of this structural inconsistency is a high rate of deviant behavior.*[29]

Because the paucity and unreliability of existing criminal statistics, there is as yet no way knowing whether or not Merton's hypothesis is correct. Until comparative studies of crime rates are available the hypothesized correlation cannot be tested.

From a theoretical perspective, however, questions may be raised about this correlation. Would we expect, to raise the principal query, the correlation to be fixed or to vary depending on the distribution of access to illegitimate means? The three possibilities are (1) that access is distributed uniformly throughout the class structure, (2) that access varies inversely with class position, and (3) that access varies directly with class position. Specification of these possibilities permits a more precise statement of the conditions under which crime rates would be expected to vary.

If access to illegitimate means is *uniformly distributed* throughout the class structure, then the proposed correlation would probably hold—higher rates of innovating behavior would be expected in the lower class than elsewhere. Lower-class persons apparently experience greater pressure toward deviance and are less restrained by internalized prohibitions from employing illegitimate means. Assuming uniform access to such means, it would therefore be reasonable to predict higher rates of innovating behavior in the lower social strata.

If access to illegitimate means varies *inversely* with class position, then the correlation would not only hold, but might even be strengthened. For pressures toward deviance, including socialization that does not altogether discourage the use of illegitimate means, would coincide with the availability of such means.

Finally, if access varies *directly* with class position, comparative rates of illegitimate activity become difficult to forecast. The higher the class position, the less the pressure to employ illegitimate means; furthermore, internalized prohibitions are apparently more effective in higher positions. If, at the same time, opportunities to use illegitimate methods are more abundant, then these factors would be in opposition. Until the precise effects of these several variables can be more adequately measured, rates cannot be safely forecast.

The concept of differentials in availability of illegitimate means may also help to clarify questions about varying crime rates among ethnic, age, religious, and sex groups, and other social divisions. This concept, then, can be systematically employed in the effort to further

our understanding of the distribution of illegitimate behavior in the
social structure.

MODES OF ADAPTATION: THE CASE OF RETREATISM

By taking into account the conditions of access to legitimate *and* illegitimate means, we can further specify the circumstances under which
various modes of deviant behavior arise. This may be illustrated by
the case of retreatism.[30]

As defined by Merton, retreatist adaptations include such categories of behavior as alcoholism, drug addiction, and psychotic withdrawal. These adaptations entail "escape" from the frustrations of unfulfilled aspirations by withdrawal from conventional social
relationships. The processes leading to retreatism are described by
Merton as follows: "[Retreatism] arises from continued failure to near
the goal by legitimate measures and from an inability to use the illegitimate route because of internalized prohibitions, *this process occurring
while the supreme value of the success-goal has not yet been renounced.* The
conflict is resolved by abandoning *both* precipitating elements, the
goals and means. The escape is complete, the conflict is eliminated
and the individual is asocialized."[31]

In this view, a crucial element encouraging retreatism is internalized constraint concerning the use of illegitimate means. But this element need not be present. Merton apparently assumed that such prohibitions are essential because, in their absence, the logic of his
scheme would compel him to predict that innovating behavior would
result. But the assumption that the individual uninhibited in the use
of illegitimate means becomes an innovator presupposes that successful innovation is only a matter of motivation. Once the concept of differentials in access to illegitimate means is introduced, however, it becomes clear that retreatism is possible even in the absence of
internalized prohibitions. For we may now ask how individuals respond when they fail in the use of *both* legitimate and illegitimate
means. If illegitimate means are unavailable, if efforts at innovation
fail, then retreatist adaptations may still be the consequence, and the
"escape" mechanisms chosen by the defeated individual may perhaps
be all the more deviant because of his "double failure."

This does not mean that retreatist adaptations cannot arise precisely as Merton suggests: namely, that the conversion from conformity to retreatism takes place in one step, without intervening adaptations. But this is only one route to retreatism. The conversion may at
times entail intervening stages and intervening adaptations, particu-

larly of an innovating type. This possibility helps to account for the fact that certain categories of individuals cited as retreatists—for example, hobos—often show extensive histories of arrests and convictions for various illegal acts. It also helps to explain retreatist adaptations among individuals who have not necessarily internalized strong restraints on the use of illegitimate means. In short, retreatist adaptations may arise with considerable frequency among those who are failures in both worlds, conventional and illegitimate alike.[32]

Future research on retreatist behavior might well examine the interval between conformity and retreatism. To what extent does the individual entertain the possibility of resorting to illegitimate means, and to what extent does he actually seek to mobilize such means? If the individual turns to innovating devices, the question of whether or not he becomes a retreatist may then depend upon the relative accessibility of illegitimate means. For although the frustrated conformist seeks a solution to status discontent by adopting such methods, there is the further problem of whether or not he possesses appropriate skills and has opportunities for their use. We suggest therefore that data be gathered on preliminary responses to status discontent—and on the individual's perceptions of the efficacy of employing illegitimate means, the content of his skills, and the objective situation of illegitimate opportunity available to him.

Respecification of the processes leading to retreatism may also help to resolve difficulties entailed in ascertaining rates of retreatism in different parts of the social structure. Although Merton does not indicate explicitly where this adaptation might be expected to arise, he specifies some of the social conditions which encourage high rates of retreatism. Thus the latter is apt to mark the behavior of downwardly mobile persons, who experience a sudden breakdown in establishing social relations, and such individuals as the retired, who have lost major social roles.[33]

The long-standing difficulties in forecasting differential rates of retreatism may perhaps be attributed to the assumption that retreatists have fully internalized values prohibiting the use of illegitimate means. That this prohibition especially characterizes socialization in the middle and upper classes probably calls for the prediction that retreatism occurs primarily in those classes—and that the hobohemias, "drug cultures," and the ranks of the alcoholics are populated primarily by individuals from the upper reaches of society. It would appear from various accounts of hobohemia and skid row, however, that many of these persons are the products of slum life, and, furthermore, that their behavior is not necessarily controlled by values which preclude resort to illegitimate means. But once it is recognized that retreatism may arise in response to limitations on both systems of means, the difficulty of locating this adaptation is lessened, if not resolved. Thus retreatist behavior may vary with the particular process by which it is generated. The process described by Merton may be somewhat more characteristic of higher positions in the social structure where rule-oriented socialization is typical, while in the lower strata retreatism may tend more often to be the consequence of unsuccessful attempts at innovation.

SUMMARY

This paper attempts to identify and to define the concept of differential opportunity structures. It has been suggested that this concept helps to extend the developing theory of social structure and anomie. Furthermore, by linking propositions regarding the accessibility of *both* legitimate and illegitimate opportunity structures, a basis is provided for consolidating various major traditions of sociological thought on nonconformity. The concept of differential systems of opportunity and of variations in access to them, it is hoped, will suggest new possibilities for research on the relationship between social structure and deviant behavior.

NOTES

1. This paper is based on research conducted in a penal setting. For a more detailed statement see Richard A. Cloward, *Social Control and Anomie: A Study of a Prison Community* (to be published by The Free Press).

2. See especially Emile Durkheim, *Suicide,* translated by J. A. Spaulding and George Simpson, Glencoe, Ill.: Free Press, 1951; and Robert K. Merton, *Social Theory and Social Structure,* Glencoe, Ill.: Free Press, 1957, Chapters 4 and 5.

3. See especially the following: Clifford R. Shaw, *The Jack-Roller,* Chicago: The University of Chicago Press, 1930; Clifford R. Shaw, *The Natural History of a Delinquent Career,* Chicago: The University of Chicago Press, 1931; Clifford R. Shaw et al., *Delinquency Areas,* Chicago: The University of Chicago Press, 1940; Clifford R. Shaw and Henry D. McKay, *Juvenile Delinquency and Urban Areas,* Chicago: The University of Chicago Press, 1942; Edwin H. Sutherland, editor, *The Professional Thief,* Chicago: The University of Chicago Press, 1937; Edwin H. Sutherland, *Principles of Criminology,* 4th edition, Philadelphia: Lippincott, 1947; Edwin H. Sutherland, *White Collar Crime,* New York: Dryden, 1949.

4. "Illegitimate means" are those proscribed by the mores. The concept therefore includes "illegal means" as a special case but is not coterminous with illegal behavior, which refers only to the violation of legal norms. In several parts of this paper, I refer to particular forms of deviant behavior which entail violation of the law and there use the more restricted term, "illegal means." But the more general concept of illegitimate means is needed to cover the wider gamut of deviant behavior and to relate the theories under review here to the evolving theory of "legitimacy" in sociology.

5. All of the excerpts in this section are from Durkheim, *op. cit.*, pp. 247–257.

6. For this excerpt and those which follow immediately, see Merton, *op. cit.*, pp. 131–194.

7. See, e.g., Seldon D. Bacon, "Social Settings Conducive to Alcoholism—A Sociological Approach to a Medical Problem," *Journal of the American Medical Association*, 16 (May, 1957), pp. 177–181; Robert F. Bales, "Cultural Differences in Rates of Alcoholism," *Quarterly Journal of Studies on Alcohol*, 16 (March, 1946), pp. 480–499; Jerome H. Skolnick, "A Study of the Relation of Ethnic Background to Arrests for Inebriety," *Quarterly Journal of Studies on Alcohol*, 15 (December, 1954), pp. 451–474.

8. See Isidor T. Thorner, "Ascetic Protestantism and Alcoholism," *Psychiatry*, 16 (May, 1953), pp. 167–176; and Nathan Glazer, "Why Jews Stay Sober," *Commentary*, 13 (February, 1952), pp. 181–186.

9. See Bales, *op. cit.*

10. Merton, *op. cit., p. 151.*

11. For this excerpt and those which follow immediately, see Sutherland, *The Professional Thief*, pp. 211–213.

12. For this excerpt and those which follow immediately, see Albert Cohen, Alfred Lindesmith and Karl Schuessler, editors, *The Sutherland Papers*, Bloomington: Indiana University Press, 1956, pp. 31–35.

13. See especially *Delinquency Areas*, Chapter 16.

14. Shaw, *The Jack-Roller*, p. 54.

15. We are referring here, and throughout the paper, to stable criminal roles to which persons may orient themselves on a career basis, as in the case of racketeers, professional thieves and the like. The point is that access to stable roles depends in the first instance upon the availability of learning structures. As Frank Tannenbaum says, "it must be insisted on that unless there were older criminals in the neighborhood who provided a moral judgment in favor of the delinquent and to whom the delinquents could look for commendation, the careers of the younger ones could not develop at all." *Crime and the Community*, New York: Ginn, 1938, p. 60.

16. Shaw, *The Natural History of a Delinquent Career*, p. 229.

17. Cohen, Lindesmith and Schuessler, *op. cit.*, p. 21.

18. It is interesting to note that the concept of differentials in access to *legitimate* means did not attain explicit recognition in Sutherland's work, nor in the work of many others in the "subculture" tradition. This attests to the independent development of the two traditions being discussed. Thus the ninth proposition in the differential association theory is stated as follows:

    (9) *Though criminal behavior is an expression of general needs and values, it is not explained by those general needs and values since noncriminal behavior is an expression of the same needs and values.* Thieves generally steal in order to secure money, but likewise honest laborers work in order to secure money. The attempts by many scholars to explain criminal behavior by general drives and values, such as the happiness principle, striving for social status, the money motive, or frustration, have been and must continue to be futile since they explain lawful behavior as completely as they explain criminal behavior.

    Of course, it is perfectly true that "striving for status," the "money motive" and similar modes of socially approved goal-oriented behavior do not as such account for both deviant and conformist behavior. But if goal-oriented behavior occurs under conditions of socially structured obstacles to fulfillment by legitimate means, the resulting pressures might then lead to deviance. In other words, Sutherland appears to assume that the distribution of access to success-goals by legitimate means is uniform rather than variable, irrespective of location in the social structure. See his *Principle of Criminology*, 4th edition, pp. 7–8.

19. William F. Whyte, *Street Corner Society* (original edition, 1943). Chicago: The University of Chicago Press, 1955, p. viii.

20. *Ibid.*, p. xviii.

21. *American Sociological Review*, 16 (October, 1951), pp. 657–658, which includes the excerpts which follow immediately.

22. The excellent work by Albert K. Cohen has been omitted from this discussion because it is dealt with in a second article, "Types of Delinquent Subcultures," prepared jointly with Lloyd E. Ohlin (mimeographed, December, 1958, New York School of Social Work, Columbia University). It may be noted that although Cohen does not explicitly affirm continuity with either the Durkheim-Merton or the Shaw-McKay-Sutherland traditions, we believe that he clearly belongs in the former. He does not deal with what appears to be the essence of the Shaw-McKay-Sutherland tradition, namely, the crucial social functions performed by the integration of offenders of differing age-levels and the integration of adult carriers of criminal and conventional values. Rather, he is concerned primarily with the way in which discrepancies between status aspirations and possibilities for

achievement generate pressures for delinquent behavior. The latter notion is a central feature in the anomie tradition.

23. Daniel Bell, "Crime as an American Way of Life," *The Antioch Review* (Summer, 1953), pp. 131–154.

24. For a discussion of kinship relationships among top racketeers, see Stanley Frank, "The Rap Gangsters Fear Most," *The Saturday Evening Post* (August 9, 1958), pp. 26 ff. This article is based on a review of the files of the United States Immigration and Naturalization Service.

25. See David W. Maurer, *Whiz Mob: A Correlation of the Technical Argot of Pickpockets with Their Behavior Pattern*, Publication of the American Dialect Society, No. 24, 1955.

26. For a discussion of racial, nationality, and sex differentials governing access to a stable criminal role, see *ibid.*, Chapter 6.

27. Training in conventional, specialized occupational skills is often a prerequisite for the commission of white collar crimes, since the individual must have these skills in hand before he can secure a position entailing "trust." As Cressey says, "it may be observed that persons trained to carry on the routine duties of a position of trust have at the same time been trained in whatever skills are necessary for the violation of that position, and the technical skill necessary to trust violation is simply the technical skill necessary to holding the position in the first place." (Donald R. Cressey, *Other People's Money*, Glencoe, Ill.: Free Press, 1953, pp. 81–82.) Thus skills required in certain crimes need not be learned in association with criminals; they can be acquired through conventional learning.

28. Merton, *op., cit.*, p. 132.

29. *Ibid.*, pp. 144–145.

30. Retreatist behavior is but one of many types of deviant adaptations which might be re-analyzed in terms of this consolidated theoretical approach. In subsequent papers, being prepared jointly with Lloyd E. Ohlin, other cases of deviant behavior—e.g., collective disturbances in prisons and subcultural adaptations among juvenile delinquents—will be examined. In this connection, see footnote 22.

31. Merton, *op. cit.*, pp. 153–154.

32. The processes of "double failure" being specified here may be of value in reanalyzing the correlation between alcoholism and petty crime. Investigation of the *careers* of petty criminals who are alcoholic may reveal that after being actively oriented toward stable criminal careers they then lost out in the competitive struggle. See, e.g., Irwin Deutscher, "The Petty Offender: A Sociological Alien," *The Journal of Criminal Law, Criminology and Police Science*, 44 (January-February, 1954), pp. 592–595; Albert D. Ullman et al., "Some Social Characteristics of Misdemeanants," *The Journal of Criminal Law, Criminology and Police Science*, 48 (May–June, 1957), pp. 44–53.

33. Merton, *op. cit.*, pp. 188–189.

Analysis and Critique

12 The Sociology of the Deviant Act: Anomie Theory and Beyond
ALBERT K. COHEN

My concern in this paper is to move toward a general theory of deviant behavior. Taking "Social Structure and Anomie"[1] as a point of departure, I shall note some of the imperfections and gaps in the theory as originally stated, how some of these have been rectified, some theoretical openings for further exploration, and some problems of relating anomie theory to other traditions in the sociology of deviance. It is not important, for my purposes, how broadly or narrowly Merton himself conceived the range of applicability of his anomie theory. Whatever the intention or vision of the author of a theory, it is the task of a discipline to explore the implications of a theoretical insight, in all directions. Many of the points I shall make are, indeed, to be found in Merton's work. In many instances, however, they either appear as leads, suggestions, or *obiter dicta*, and are left undeveloped, or they appear in some other context and no effort is made systematically to link them with anomie theory.[2]

THE ANOMIE THEORY OF DEVIANT BEHAVIOR

Merton's theory has the reputation of being the pre-eminently *sociological* theory of deviant behavior. Its concern is to account for the distribution of deviant behavior among the positions in a social system and for differences in the distribution and rates of deviant behavior among systems. It tries to account for these things as functions of system properties—*i.e.*, the ways in which cultural goals and opportunities for realizing them within the limits of the institutional norms are distributed. The emphasis, in short, is on certain aspects of the culture (goals and norms) and of the social structure (opportunities, or access

Reprinted with permission from Albert K. Cohen, "The Sociology of the Deviant Act: Anomie Theory and Beyond," *American Sociological Review*, vol. 30 (February 1965), pp. 5–15.

This is a revised version of a paper read at the annual meeting of the American Sociological Association, August 1963.

to means). The theory *is*, then, radically sociological. And yet, as far as the formal and explicit structure of Merton's first formulation is concerned, it is, in certain respects, atomistic and individualistic. Within the framework of goals, norms, and opportunities, the process of deviance was conceptualized as though each individual—or better, role incumbent—were in a box by himself. He has internalized goals and normative, regulatory rules; he assesses the opportunity structure; he experiences strain; and he selects one or another mode of adaptation. The bearing of others' experience—their strains, their conformity and deviance, their success and failure—on ego's strain and consequent adaptations is comparatively neglected.

Consider first the concept of strain itself. It is a function of the degree of disjunction between goals and means, or of the sufficiency of means to the attainment of goals. But how imperious must the goals be, how uncertain their attainment, how incomplete their fulfillment, to generate strain? The relation between goals as components of that abstraction, culture, and the concrete goals of concrete role incumbents, is by no means clear and simple. One thing that is clear is that the level of goal attainment that will seem just and reasonable to concrete actors, and therefore the sufficiency of available means, will be relative to the attainments of others who serve as reference objects. Level of aspiration is not a fixed quantum, taken from the culture and swallowed whole, to lodge unchanged within our psyches. The sense of proportionality between effort and reward is not determined by the objective returns of effort alone. From the standpoint of the role sector whose rates of deviance are in question, the mapping of reference group orientations, the availability *to others* of access to means, and the actual distribution of rewards are aspects of the social structure important for the determination of strain.[3]

Once we take explicit cognizance of these processes of comparison, a number of other problems unfold themselves. For example, others, whom we define as legitimate objects of comparison, may be more successful than we are by adhering to legitimate means. They not only do better than we do, but they do so "fair and square." On the other hand, they may do as well as we or even better by cutting corners, cheating, using illegitimate means. Do these two different situations have different consequences for the sense of strain, for attitudes toward oneself, for subsequent adaptations? In general, what strains does deviance on the part of others create for the virtuous? In the most obvious case ego is the direct victim of alter's deviance. Or ego's interests may be adversely but indirectly affected by the chicanery of a competitor—unfair trade practices in business, unethical advertising in medicine, cheating in examinations when the instructor grades on a curve. But there is a less obvious case, the one which, according to Ranulf,[4] gives rise to disinterested moral indignation. The dedicated pursuit of culturally approved goals, the eschewing of interdicted but tantalizing goals, the adherence to normatively sanctioned means—these imply a certain self restraint, effort, discipline, inhibition. What is the effect of the spectacle of others who, through their activities do not manifestly damage our own interests, are morally undisciplined, who give themselves up to idleness, self-indulgence, or forbidden vices? What effect does the propinquity of the wicked have on the peace of mind of the virtuous?

In several ways, the virtuous can make capital out of this situation, can convert a situation with a potential for strain to a source of satisfaction. One can become even more virtuous letting his reputation hinge on his righteousness, *building his self out of invidious comparison to the morally weak*. Since others' wickedness sets off the jewel of one's own virtue, and one's claim to virtue is at the core of his public identity, one may actually develop a stake in the existence of deviant others, and be threatened should they pretend to moral excellence. In short, another's virtue may become a source of strain! One may also join with others in righteous puritanical wrath to mete out punishment to the deviants, not so much to stamp out their deviant behavior, as to reaffirm the central importance of conformity as the basis for judging men and to reassure himself and others of his attachment to goodness. One may even make a virtue of tolerance and indulgence of others' moral deficiencies, thereby implicitly calling attention to one's own special strength of character. If the weakness of others is only human, then there is something more than human about one's own strength. On the other hand, one might join the profligate.

What I have said here is relevant to social control, but my concern at present is not with social control but with some of the ways in which deviance of others may aggravate or lighten the burdens of conformity and hence the strain that is so central to anomic theory.

The student of Merton will recognize that some of these points are suggested or even developed at some length here and there in Merton's own writing. Merton is, of course, one of the chief architects of reference group theory, and in his chapter on "Continuities in the Theory of Reference Groups and Social Structure," he has a section entitled "Nonconformity as a Type of Reference Group Behavior."[5] There he recognizes the problems that one actor's deviance creates for others, and he explicitly calls attention to Ranulf's treatment of disinterested moral indignation as a way of dealing with this problem.[6] In

"Continuities in the Theory of Social Structure and Anomie," he describes how the deviance of some increases the others' vulnerability to deviance.[7] In short, my characterization of the earliest version of "Social Structure and Anomie" as "atomistic and individualistic" would be a gross misrepresentation if it were applied to the total corpus of Merton's writing on deviance. He has not, however, developed the role of comparison processes in the determination of strain or considered it explicitly in the context of anomie theory. And in general, Merton does not identify the complexities and subtleties of the concept strain as a problem area in their own right.

Finally, in connection with the concept strain, attention should be called to Smelser's treatment of the subject in his *Theory of Collective Behavior*.[8] Although Smelser does not deal with this as it bears on a theory of deviance, it is important here for two reasons. First, it is, to my knowledge, the only attempt in the literature to generate a systematic classification of types of strain, of which Merton's disjunction between goals and means is only one. The second reason is Smelser's emphasis that to account for collective behavior, one must *start with* strain, but one's theory must also specify a hierarchy of constraints, each of which further narrows the range of possible responses to strain, and the last of which rules out all alternatives but collective behavior. If the "value-added" method is sound for a theory of collective behavior, it may also be useful for a theory of deviance, starting from the concept strain, and constructed on the same model.

Now, *given strain*, what will a person do about it? In general, Merton's chief concern has been with the structural factors that account for variations in strain. On the matter of choice of solution, as on other matters, he has some perceptive observations,[9] but it has remained for others to develop these systematically. In particular, in the original version of his theory each person seems to work out his solution by himself, as though it did not matter what other people were doing. Perhaps Merton assumed such intervening variables as deviant role models, without going into the mechanics of them. But it is one thing to assume that such variables are operating; it is quite another to treat them explicitly in a way that is integrated with the more general theory. Those who continue the anomie tradition, however—most notably Merton's student, Cloward—have done much to fill this gap. Cloward, with Ohlin,[10] has accomplished this in large part by linking anomie theory with another and older theoretical tradition, associated with Sutherland, Shaw and McKay, and Kobrin—the "cultural transmission" and "differential association" tradition of the "Chicago school." Cloward and Ohlin also link anomie theory to a more recent theoretical development, the general theory of subcultures, and especially the aspect of the theory that is concerned with the emergence and development of new subcultural forms.[11] What these other theories have in common is an insistence that deviant as well as non-deviant action is typically not contrived within the solitary individual psyche, but is part of a collaborative *social* activity, in which the things that other people say and do give meaning, value, and effect to one's own behavior.

The incorporation of this recognition into anomie theory is the principal significance of Cloward's notion of illegitimate opportunity structures. These opportunity structures are going social concerns in the individual's milieu, which provide opportunities to learn and to perform deviant actions and lend moral support to the deviant when he breaks with conventional norms and goals.

This is the explicit link with the cultural transmission–differential association tradition. The argument is carried a step farther with the recognition that, even in the absence of an already established deviant culture and social organization, a number of individuals with like problems and in effective communication with one another may join together to do what no one can do alone. They may provide one another with reference objects, collectively contrive a subculture to replace or neutralize the conventional culture, and support and shield one another in their deviance. This is the explicit link to the newer theory of subcultures.[12]

There is one more step in this direction that has not been so explicitly taken. Those who join hands in deviant enterprises need not be people with like problems, nor need their deviance be of the same sort. Within the framework of anomie theory, we may think of these people as individuals with quite variant problems or strains which lend themselves to a common solution, but a common solution in which each participates in different ways. I have in mind the brothel keeper and the crooked policeman, the black marketeer and his customer, the desperate student and the term paper merchant, the bookie and the wire services. These do not necessarily constitute solidary collectivities, like delinquent gangs, but they are structures of action with a division of labor through which each, by his deviance, serve the interests of the others. Theirs is an "organic solidarity," in contrast to the "mechanical solidarity" of Cloward and Ohlin's gangs. Some of Merton's own writing on functionalism—for example, his discussion of the exchange of services involved in political corruption—is extremely relevant here, but it is not explicitly integrated into his anomie theory.[13]

THE ASSUMPTION OF DISCONTINUITY

To say that anomie theory suffers from the assumption of discontinuity is to imply that it treats the deviant act as though it were an abrupt change of state, a leap from a state of strain or anomie to a state of deviance. Although this overstates the weakness in Merton's theory the expression, "the assumption of discontinuity," does have the heuristic value of drawing attention to an important difference in emphasis between anomie theory and other traditions in American sociology, and to the direction of movement in anomie theory itself. Human action, deviant or otherwise, is something that typically develops and grows in a tentative, groping, advancing, backtracking, sounding-out process. People taste and feel their way along. They begin an act and do not complete it. They start doing one thing and end up by doing another. They extricate themselves from progressive involvement or become further involved to the point of commitment. These processes of progressive involvement and disinvolvement are important enough to deserve explicit recognition and treatment in their own right. They are themselves subject to normative regulation and structural constraint in complex ways about which we have much to learn. Until recently, however, the dominant bias in American sociology has been toward formulating theory in terms of variables that describe initial states, on the one hand, and outcomes, on the other, rather than in terms of processes whereby acts and complex structures of action are built, elaborated and transformed. Notable exceptions are interaction process analysis,[14] the brand of action theory represented by Herbert Blumer,[15] and the descriptions of deviance by Talcott Parsons[16] and by Howard Becker.[17] Anomie theory has taken increasing cognizance of such processes. Cloward and Merton both point out, for example, that behavior may move through "patterned sequences of deviant roles" and from "one type of adaptation to another."[18] But this hardly does justice to the microsociology of the deviant act. It suggests a series of discontinuous leaps from one deviant state to another almost as much as it does the kind of process I have in mind.

RESPONSES TO DEVIANCE

Very closely related to the foregoing point is the conception of the development of the act as a feedback, or, in more traditional language, interaction process. The history of a deviant act is a history of an interaction process. The antecedents of the act are an unfolding sequence of acts contributed by a set of actors. A makes a move, possibly in a deviant direction; B responds; A responds to B's responses, etc. In the course of this interaction, movement in a deviant direction may become more explicit, elaborated, definitive—or it may not. Although the act may be socially ascribed to only one of them, both ego and alter help to shape it. The starting point of anomie theory was the question, "*Given* the social structure, or ego's milieu, what will ego do?" The milieu was taken as more-or-less given, an independent variable whose value is fixed, and ego's behavior as an adaptation, or perhaps a series of adaptations, to that milieu. Anomie theory has come increasingly to recognize the effects of deviance upon the very variables that determine deviance. But if we are interested in a general theory of deviant behavior we must explore much more systematically ways of conceptualizing the *interaction* between deviance and milieu.[19] I suggest the following such lines of exploration.

If ego's behavior can be conceptualized in terms of acceptance and rejection of goals and means, the same can be done with alter's responses. Responses to deviance can no more be left normatively unregulated than deviance itself. Whose business it is to intervene, at what point, and what he may or may not do is defined by a normatively established division of labor. In short, for any given role—parent, priest, psychiatrist, neighbor, policeman, judge—the norms prescribe, with varying degrees of definiteness, *what* they are supposed to do and *how* they are supposed to do it when other persons, in specified roles, misbehave. The culture prescribes goals and regulates the choice of means. Members of ego's role set can stray from cultural prescriptions in all the ways that ego can. They may overemphasize the goals and neglect the normative restrictions, they may adhere ritualistically to the normatively approved means and neglect the goals, and so forth. I have spelled out the five possibilities on alter's side more fully elsewhere.[20] The theoretical value of applying Merton's modes of adaptation to responses to deviant acts is not fully clear; yet it seems worthy of exploration for at least two reasons.

First, *one* determinant of ego's response to alter's attempts at control, and of the responses of third parties whom ego or alter might call to their aid, is certainly the perceived legitimacy of alter's behavior. Whether ego yields or resists, plays the part of the good loser or the abused victim, takes his medicine or is driven to aggravated deviance, depends in part on whether alter has the right to do what he does, whether the response is proportional to the offense, and so on.

Normative rules also regulate the deviant's response to the intervention of control agents. How the control agent responds to the deviant, after the first confrontation, depends on his perception of the legitimacy of the deviant's response *to him*, and not only on the nature

TABLE 1 Responses of the Opportunity Structure to Ego's
Deviance

	Legitimate Opportunities	Illegitimate Opportunities
Open up	I	II
Close off	III	IV

of the original deviant act. For example, this perceived legitimacy
plays an important part in police dispositions of cases coming to their
attention.

This approach also directs attention to strain in alter's role, the adequacy of *his* resources relative to the responsibilities with which he is
charged by virtue of his role, and the illegitimate opportunities available to *him*. A familiar example would be the normative restrictions on
the means police may consider effective to do the job with which they
are charged, and variations in the availability to them of various illegitimate means to the same end.

The disjunction between goals and means and the choice of adaptations depend on the opportunity structure. The opportunity structure consists in or is the result of the actions of other people. These in
turn are in part reactions to ego's behavior and may undergo change
in response to that behavior. The development of ego's action can,
therefore, be conceptualized as a series of responses, on the part of
ego, to a series of changes in the opportunity structure resulting from
ego's actions. More specifically, alter's responses may open up, close
off, or leave unaffected legitimate opportunities for ego, and they may
do the same to illegitimate opportunities. The following simplified table [Table 1] reduces the possibilities to four.

I. Open up Legitimate Opportunities

Special efforts may be made to find employment opportunities for delinquents and criminals. On an individual basis this has long been one
of the chief tasks of probation officers. On a mass basis it has become
more and more prominent in community-wide efforts to reduce delinquency rates.

Black markets may sometimes be reduced by making more of the
product available in the legal market or by reducing the pressure on
the legal supply through rationing.

Several years ago the Indiana University faculty had a high rate of violation of campus parking regulations, in part because of the disjunction between the demand for parking spaces and the supply. The virtuous left early for work and hunted wearily for legitimate parking spaces. The contemptuous parked anywhere and sneered at tickets. One response to this situation was to create new parking lots and to expand old ones. Since the new parking spaces were available to all, and not only to the former violators, this provides a clear instance where the virtuous—or perhaps the timid—as well as the deviants themselves are the beneficiaries of deviance.[21]

II. Open up Illegitimate Opportunities

Alter, instead of fighting ego, may facilitate his deviance by joining him in some sort of collusive illicit arrangement from which both profit. The racketeer and the law enforcement officer, the convict and the guard, the highway speeder and the traffic policeman, may arrive at an understanding to reduce the cost of deviance.

Alter, whether he be a discouraged parent, a law enforcement official, or a dean of students, may simply give up efforts systematically to enforce a rule and limit himself to sporadic, token gestures.

An important element in Cloward and Ohlin's theory of delinquent subcultures is that those who run the criminal syndicates are ever alert for promising employees, and that a certain number of those who demonstrate proficiency in the more juvenile forms of crime will be given jobs in the criminal organization.

III. Closing off Legitimate Opportunities

The example that comes most readily to mind is what Tannenbaum calls the "dramatization of evil."[22] A deviant act, if undetected or ignored, might not be repeated. On the other hand, others might react to it by publicly defining the actor as a delinquent, a fallen woman, a criminal. These definitions ascribe to him a social role, change his public image, and activate a set of appropriate responses. These responses may include exclusion from avenues of legitimate opportunity formerly open to him, and thus enhance the relative attractiveness of the illegitimate.

IV. Closing off Illegitimate Opportunities

This is what we usually think of first when we think about "social control." It includes increasing surveillance, locking the door, increasing the certainty and severity of punishment, cutting off access to necessary supplies, knocking out the fix. These measures may or may not achieve the intended effect. On the one hand, they make deviance more difficult. On the other hand, they may stimulate the deviant, or the deviant coalition, to ingenuity in devising new means to circumvent the new restrictions.

The table is a way of conceptualizing alter's actions. The same alter might respond simultaneously in different cells of the table, as may different alters, and these responses might reinforce or counteract one another. Responses might fall in different cells at different stages of the interaction process. In any case, as soon as we conceive of the opportunity structure as a dependent as well as an independent variable, this way of thinking suggests itself as a logical extension of the anomie schema.

Parsons' paradigm of social control is in his opinion applicable not only to deviance, but also to therapy and rehabilitative processes in general. According to this paradigm, the key elements in alter's behavior are support, permissiveness, denial of reciprocity, and rewards, judiciously balanced, and strategically timed and geared to the development of ego's behavior.[23] To exploit the possibilities of this and other paradigms of control, one must define more precisely these categories of alter's behavior, develop relevant ways of coding ego's responses to alter's responses, and investigate both theoretically and empirically the structure of extended interaction processes conceptualized in these terms.

Finally, the interaction process may be analyzed from the standpoint of its consequences for stability or change in the normative structure itself. Every act of deviance can be thought of as a pressure on the normative structure, a test of its limits, an exploration of its meaning, a challenge to its validity. Responses to deviance may reaffirm or shore up the normative structure; they may be ritual dramatizations of the seriousness with which the community takes violations of its norms. Or deviance may prompt reexamination of the boundaries of the normatively permissible, resulting in either explicit reformulation of the rule or implicit changes in its meaning, so that the deviant becomes redefined as nondeviant, or the nondeviant as deviant. Thus deviance may be reduced or increased by changes in the norms.[24] These processes go on within the household, courts of law, administrative agencies, and legislative chambers, but also in the mass media, the streets, and the other forums in which "public opinion" is shaped. Although these processes may be punctuated by dramatic, definitive events, like the passage of a new law or the promulgation of a new set of regulations on allowable income tax deductions, the pressure of deviance on the normative structure and the responses of the normative structure to deviance constitute continuing, uninterrupted, interaction processes. One goal of deviance theory is to determine under what conditions feedback circuits promote change and under what conditions they inhibit change in the normative structure.

In this connection, one of Merton's most perceptive and fruitful distinctions is that between the "nonconformist" and other types of deviant.[25] Whereas the criminal and others typically *violate* the norms in pursuit of their own ends, but in no sense seek to *change* those norms (though such change might very well be an unanticipated consequence of their cumulative deviance), the nonconformist's objective is precisely to change the normative system itself. This distinction suggests, in turn, the concept of the "test case" (which need not be limited to the context of legal norms and the formal judicial system)—*i.e.*, the act openly committed, with the intention of forcing a clarification or redefinition of the norms. What we must not overlook, however, is that *any* deviant act, whatever its intention, may, in a sense, function as a test case.

DEVIANCE AND SOCIAL IDENTITY

There is another piece of unfinished business before anomie theory, and that is to establish a more complete and successful union with role theory and theory of the self. The starting point of Merton's theory is the means-ends schema. His *dramatis personae* are cultural goals, institutional norms, and the situation of action, consisting of means and conditions. The disjunction between goals and means provides the motive force behind action. Deviance is an effort to reduce this disjunction and re-establish an equilibrium between goals and means. It issues from tension; it is an attempt to reduce tension. Roles figure in this theory as a locational grid. They are the positions in the social structure among which goals, norms and means are distributed, where such disjunctions are located and such adaptations carried out.

Another starting point for a theory of deviant behavior grows out of the social theory of George Herbert Mead. This starting point is the actor engaged in an ongoing process of finding, building, testing, validating, and expressing a self. The self is linked to roles, but not primarily in a locational sense. Roles enter, in a very integral and dynamic way, into the very structure of the self. They are part of the categorical system of a society, the socially recognized and meaningful categories of persons. They are the kinds of people it is possible to be in that society. The self is constructed of these possibilities. One establishes a self by successfully claiming membership in such categories.[26]

To validate such a claim one must know the social meaning of membership in such roles: the criteria by which they are assigned, the qualities or behavior that function as signs of membership, the characteristics that measure adequacy in the roles. These meanings must be learned. To some degree, this learning may be accomplished before one has identified or even toyed with the roles. Such learning Merton has called anticipatory socialization. To some degree, however, it continues even after one has become more or less committed to a role, in the process of presenting one's self, experiencing and reading the feedback, and correcting one's notion of what it is to be that kind of person. An actor learns that the behavior signifying membership in a particular role includes the kinds of clothes he wears, his posture and gait, his likes and dislikes, what he talks about and the opinions he expresses—everything that goes into what we call the style of life. Such aspects of behavior are difficult to conceptualize as either goals or means; in terms of their relation to the role, at least, their function is better described as expressive or symbolic. But the same can be said even of the goals one pursues and the means one employs; they too may communicate and confirm an identity.

Now, *given* a role, and *given* the orientations to goals and to means that have been assumed because they are part of the social definition of that role, there may be a disjunction between goals and means. Much of what we call deviant behavior arises as a way of dealing with this disjunction. As anomie theory has been formally stated, this is where it seems to apply. But much deviant behavior cannot readily be formulated in these terms at all. Some of it, for example, is directly expressive of the roles. A tough and bellicose posture, the use of obscene language, participation in illicit sexual activity, the immoderate consumption of alcohol, the deliberate flouting of legality and authority, a generalized disrespect for the sacred symbols of the "square" world, a taste for marijuana, even suicide—all of these may have the primary function of affirming, in the language of gesture and deed, that one is a certain kind of person. The message-symbol relationship, or that of claim and evidence, seems to fit this behavior better than the ends-means relationship.

Sexual seduction, for example, may be thought of as illicit means to the achievement of a goal. The point is, however, that the seduction need not be an adaptation to the insufficiency of other means, a response to disjunction. One may cultivate the art of seduction because this sort of expertise is directly significant of a coveted role. Indeed, the very value and meaning of the prize are conferred by the means employed. One could, of course, say that the expertise is itself the goal, but then it is still a goal that expresses and testifies to a role. Finally, one could say that the goal of the act is to validate the role, and all these kinds of behavior are means to this end. I think this statement is plausible and can be defended. If it *is* the intent of anomie theory, then the language of tension reduction does not seem to fit very well. The relation I have in mind, between deviant act and social role, is like the relation between pipe and elbow patches and the professorial role. Like the professor's behavior, it is not necessarily a *pis aller*, a means that one has hit on after others have failed. It commends itself, it is gratifying, because it seems so right—not in a moral sense, but in the sense that it fits so well with the image one would like to have of oneself.

One important implication of this view is that it shifts the focus of theory and research from the disjunction and its resolution to the process of progressive involvement in, commitment to, and movement among social roles, and the processes whereby one learns the behavior that is significant of the roles. One may, like the child acquiring his sex identity, come to accept and identify with a role before he is quite clear what it means to be that sort of person, how one goes about being one. But once one has established the identity, he has an interest in learning these things and making use of that learning. Thus Howard Becker's dance band musicians arrive at that estate by various routes. For many of them, however, it is only as this identity is crystallizing that they fully learn what being a musician means within the world of musicians. They discover, so to speak, what they are, and what they are turns out to be highly unconventional people.[27] We seek roles for various reasons, some of them having little to do with tension reduction, and having found the role, come into unanticipated legacies of deviant behavior.

The same processes operate in movement in the other direction, toward restoration to conformity. They are most dramatically illustrated in religious conversion. As the sinner is born again, with a new identity fashioned out of new roles, whole bundles of behavior, not all of them deviant, are cast aside, and new bundles are picked up. Relatively little may be learned by examining, one at a time, the items these bundles contain, the sense in which they constitute means to ends, and their adequacy to their respective goals. The decisive event is the transformation of self and social identity. At that moment a wholesale transformation of behavior is determined.

Anomie theory is, perhaps, concerned with *one* structural source of deviance, while the ideas just presented are concerned with another. Neither one need to be more faithful to reality than the other, and the defense of one need not be a challenge to the other. But those who are interested in the development of a general theory of deviance can hardly let matters stand at that. Is it possible to make any general statements about the kinds of deviance that may be attributed to anomie and the kinds that may be attributed to role validation through behavior culturally significant of membership in the role? Or may two instances of *any* sort of deviant behavior, identical in their manifest or "phenotypic" content, differ in their sources of "genotypic" structure?

Ultimately, however, we must investigate the possible ways in which the two kinds or sources of deviance interact or interpenetrate. For example, does role symbolism function as a structural constraint on the choice of means, and instrumental or means-ends considerations as a structural constraint on the choice of expressive symbolism? Does behavior that originates as a characteristic adaptation to the anomie associated with a particular role, come in time to signify membership in that role and thereby to exercise a secondary or even independent attraction or repulsion, depending on one's orientation toward the role itself? Finally, is it possible that in any instance of deviant behavior, or, for that matter, *any* behavior, both processes are intertwined in ways that cannot be adequately described in terms of presently available modes of conceptualization? I suggest that we must bring the two schemes into more direct and explicit confrontation and try to evolve a formulation that will fuse and harness the power of both.

NOTES

1. Robert K. Merton, "Social Structure and Anomie," *American Sociological Review*, 3 (October, 1938), pp. 672–682, *Social Theory and Social Structure*, Glencoe, Ill.: The Free Press, 1957, Chs. 4 and 5, and "Conformity, Deviation, and Opportunity-Structures," *American Sociological Review*, 24 (April, 1959), pp. 177–189; Richard A. Cloward, "Illegitimate Means, Anomie, and Deviant Behavior," *American Sociological Review*, 24 (April, 1959), pp. 164–176; and Robert Dubin, "Deviant Behavior and Social Structure: Continuities in Social Theory," *American Sociological Review*, 24 (April, 1959), pp. 147–164.

2. I am not here concerned with empirical applications and tests of anomie theory, on which there is now a large literature. In view of the sustained interest in anomie theory, its enormous influence, and its numerous applications, however, it is worth noting and wondering at the relatively slow and fitful growth of the substantive theory itself. It is of some interest also that, with respect to both substantive theory and its applications, there has been little follow-up of Merton's own

leads relative to the implications of anomie theory for intersocietal differences in deviance behavior. Almost all of the work has been on variations in deviance within American society.

3. See, for example, how Henry and Short explicitly incorporate reference group theory and relative deprivation into their theory of suicide. Andrew Henry and James F. Short, Jr., *Suicide and Homicide*, Glencoe, Ill.: The Free Press, 1954, pp. 56–59.

4. Svend Ranulf, *Moral Indignation and Middle-Class Psychology: A Sociological Study*, Copenhagen: Levin and Munksgaard, 1938.

5. *Social Theory and Social Structure, op. cit.*, pp. 357–368.

6. *Ibid.*, pp. 361-362.

7. *Ibid.*, pp. 179-181.

8. Neil J. Smelser, *Theory of Collective Behavior*, New York: The Free Press of Glencoe, 1963, esp. Ch. 3.

9. *Social Theory and Social Structure, op. cit.*, p. 151.

10. Cloward, *op. cit.*, and Richard E. Ohlin, *Delinquency and Opportunity, A Theory of Delinquent Gangs*, Glencoe, Ill.: The Free Press, 1960.

11. *Ibid.*

12. Albert K. Cohen, *Delinquent Boys, The Culture of the Gang*, Glencoe, Ill.: The Free Press, Ch. 3, and Merton, *Social Theory and Social Structure, op. cit.*, p. 179.

13. *Social Theory and Social Structure, op. cit.*, pp. 71-82.

14. Robert F. Bales, *Interaction Process Analysis: A Method for the Study of Small Groups*, Cambridge: Addison-Wesley, 1950.

15. Herbert Blumer, "Society as Symbolic Interaction," in Arnold M. Rose (ed.), *Human Behavior and Social Processes*, Boston: Houghton, Mifflin, 1962, pp. 179–192.

16. Talcott Parsons, *The Social System*, Glencoe, Ill.: The Free Press, 1951, Ch. 7.

17. Howard S. Becker, *Outsiders: Studies in the Sociology of Deviance*, New York: The Free Press of Glencoe, 1963, esp. Ch. 2

18. Merton, *Social Theory and Social Structure, op. cit.*, p. 152; Cloward, *op.cit.*, p. 175; Cloward and Ohlin, *op. cit.*, pp. 179–184; Merton, "Conformity, Deviation, and Opportunity-Structures," *op. cit.*, p.188.

19. Dubin, *op.cit.*, esp. p. 151, and Merton's remarks on "typology of responses to deviant behavior, " in his "Conformity, Deviation, and Opportunity-Structures," *op. cit.*, pp. 185–186.

20. Albert K. Cohen, "The Study of Social Disorganization and Deviant Behavior," in Robert K. Merton, Leonard Broom, and Leonard S. Cottrell, Jr. (eds.), *Sociology Today*, New York: Basic Books, 1959, pp. 464-465.

21. William J. Chambliss, *The Deterrent Influence of Punishment: A Study of the Violation of Parking Regulations*, M.A. thesis (sociology), Indiana University, 1960.

22. Frank Tannenbaum, *Crime and the Community,* New York: Ginn, 1938, Ch. 7.

23. *Op. cit.,* pp. 297-325.

24. Theodore M. Mills, "Equilibrium and the Processes of Deviance and Control," *American Sociological Review,* 24 (October, 1959), pp. 671-679.

25. Merton, *Social Theory and Social Structure, op. cit.,* pp. 360–368; Robert K. Merton and Robert A. Nisbet, *Contemporary Social Problems,* New York: Harcourt, Brace, 1961, pp. 725–728.

26. George Herbert Mead, *Mind, Self, and Society,* Chicago: University of Chicago Press, 1934; Erving Goffman, *The Presentation of Self in Everyday Life,* New York: Doubleday Anchor, 1959, and *Stigma, Notes on the Management of Spoiled Identity*, Englewood Cliffs: Prentice-Hall, 1963.

27. Howard S. Becker, *op. cit.,* Ch. 5.

CHAPTER IV

Differential Association
and Neutralization

The theoretical approaches discussed in the preceding chapters—functionalism, social disorganization, and anomie—all concentrate on the relationship between social structure and deviance. They examine structural conditions in a society that are conducive to the development and perpetuation of deviant behavior. None of these approaches, however, adequately specifies the processes by which situations conducive to deviance are actually translated into action by individuals. The theory presented in this chapter represents an attempt to explicate the links between social structural conditions and individuals' deviant behavior. Differential association and neutralization theory share the basic viewpoint that deviant behavior is learned in much the same way that conforming behavior is. While the processes involved in learning any behavior pattern are essentially the same, the content and direction of the learning differ as individuals respond to the varying pressures and constraints of their environment.

As an explanation of the processes by which people learn to behave in violation of conventional norms, Edwin H. Sutherland's theory of differential association has had an impact on sociology in general and the study of deviance in particular that has been at least as great as that of social disorganization and anomie theories. In noting the effects of social structure on behavior, Sutherland acknowledged the importance of what he called differential social organization and differential association. His focus, however, was less on social structure and more on the interactional processes or associations that are involved in transmitting and learning any behavior, deviant or conforming.

Sutherland challenged the prevailing determinism of disorganization and anomie theories and the concept of lower-class deviance, instead basing his ideas on the notion that high rates of deviance (crime, for instance) are due to factors related to the differential organization of various geographical areas. Deviant behavior therefore is not simply a reaction to defects within the society (i.e., disorganization), social or personal pathologies, or underlying social ills such as broken homes. Rather, deviant behavior and high rates of deviance are normal expressions of the social organization of subcultures within "deviant areas" of the city. Specifically, deviant behavior is the product of the social life of subcultural groups, the conflicting definitions of deviance to which they are exposed, and various psychological processes that produce in them an "excess of definitions favorable to violation of the law over definitions unfavorable to violation of the law." This is the principle of differential association specified by Sutherland and his co-author, Donald Cressey, in Reading 13.

Sutherland hypothesized that people acquire criminal behavior patterns through the same process by which they acquire conventional behavior patterns: "Criminal behavior is human behavior, and has much in common with noncriminal behavior." It must be explained within the same general framework used to explain other human behavior, but using specific conditions and processes to explain crime. In Sutherland's learning approach to the study of criminal behavior, crime is seen as related to people's associations over time; criminal acts occur when situations are appropriate for their execution, as defined by the individuals who commit them. Through their associations with others, individuals learn values, norms, motivations, rationalizations, techniques, and definitions that may be either favorable or unfavorable to violation of the law. They then define the situations they are presented with as being either favorable or not favorable to law violation, depending on a person-situation complex involving inclinations and abilities acquired in interaction with others. Individuals learn criminal behavior patterns and are more likely to engage in criminal activity when an opportunity presents itself if they have been exposed to criminal definitions for a longer period of time, earlier in life, with more intensity, and more frequently than they have been exposed to anticriminal definitions.

Donald Cressey develops these ideas in Reading 14, attempting to specify further the content of what is learned. In this brief excerpt from *Other People's Money* he analyzes how embezzlers can commit crimes without suffering self-incrimination or feelings of guilt. He also suggests that "violation of trust" is learned not necessarily through *direct* association with others but rather through any number of indirect influences within the larger society. Cressey describes how rationalizations, coupled with a nonshareable problem, precede action and allow individuals to behave in ways they might otherwise find unacceptable. More important, he shows that rationalizations are learned and are part of the cultural fabric of groups and societies.

In extending this basic premise, Gresham M. Sykes and David Matza's "Techniques of Neutralization: A Theory of Delinquency" (Reading 15) deals with the content of what is both learned and rationalized. In an extension of the fourth statement of Sutherland's theory, specifically in reference to rationalizations (see Reading 13), Sykes and Matza focus on how a person who deviates copes with the problem of his or her norm violation. These authors oppose arguments that delinquent behavior springs from an all-pervasive deviant value-norm system. Rather, they maintain that individuals seek to rationalize or neutralize the guilt associated with deviance through a series of defenses that place it in a favorable light.

Sykes and Matza suggest that delinquents are essentially committed to the society's accepted values and norms, and engaging in delinquent activity causes shame which must be neutralized if the delinquency is to persist. They learn various verbal justifications or techniques of neutralization for deviant behavior that serve to protect their self-image and allow them to engage in delinquent behavior without experiencing cognitive dissonance. Sykes and Matza believe that these techniques are a crucial part of Sutherland's "definitions favorable to the violation of law." They assert that delinquents essentially "neutralize" the importance of dominant cultural values, which enables them to view their delinquent acts as acceptable, if not right.

In the Analysis and Critique section in this chapter (Reading 16), Donald Cressey examines criticisms advanced against Sutherland's theory of differential association, including:

1. It apparently overemphasizes *personal* associations (as opposed to secondary ones like movies or the news media) in the learning of criminal behavior.
2. It does not apply to some forms of criminal behavior, such as impulsive violence.
3. It does not appear to account for why a person associates with certain types of people in the first place.

Even more important, critics have noted the failure of the theory to explain exactly what processes are involved in learning criminal behavior (as well as conforming behavior). They have pointed to the difficulty involved in defining some of the major terms so the theory can be empirically validated. While some sociologists have attempted to test empirically the general notions of the theory, the findings have been relatively inconsistent. Indeed, inconclusive empirical support has resulted in numerous attempts to revise and modify the theory of differential association.

In his defense of Sutherland's theory, Cressey summarizes the main issues in the debate concerning whether differential association is an adequate explanation of crime and the processes by which an individual comes to engage in criminal behavior. Basing his remarks on his own interpretation of the theory as well as Sutherland's extensive writings, Cressey argues that many of the criticisms are invalid because they are due to Sutherland's failure to elaborate clearly the nine statements or propositions that constitute the theory, or to others' errors in interpreting the intended meaning of the theory. Moreover, many of the criticisms are not based on research and thus are actually proposals for more research in this area.

The crux of Cressey's argument is that the theory of differential association answers the need for an integrated theory of crime and criminality. He points out that, much like Darwin's theory in biology, Sutherland's theory is an attempt to organize and make sense of the gross rates of crime in society and then to relate individual deviation to the factors accounting for varying high and low crime rates. In these terms, differential theory helps make sense of the known facts about variations in crime rates, and it indicates the general processes that are important in developing "efficient theory of individual criminal conduct."

13 *The Theory of Differential Association*
EDWIN H. SUTHERLAND and
DONALD R. CRESSEY

THE PROBLEM FOR CRIMINOLOGICAL THEORY

If criminology is to be scientific, the heterogeneous collection of multiple factors known to be associated with crime and criminality must be organized and integrated by means of explanatory theory which has the same characteristics as the scientific theory in other fields of study.

Reprinted from Edwin H. Sutherland and Donald R. Cressey, *Criminology,* 10th edition (New York: Harper & Row Publishing, 1978), pp. 77–83. Copyright © 1978 by Donald R. Cressey Estate.

That is, the conditions which are said to cause crime should be present when crime is present, and they should be absent when crime is absent. Such a theory or body of theory would stimulate, simplify, and give direction to criminological research, and it would provide a framework for understanding the significance of much of the knowledge acquired about crime and criminality in the past. Furthermore, it would be useful in minimizing crime rates, provided it could be "applied" in much the same way that the engineer "applies" the scientific theories of the physicist.

There are two complementary procedures which may be used to put order into criminological knowledge. The first is logical abstraction. Blacks, males, urban-dwellers, and young adults all have comparatively high crime rates. What do they have in common that results in these high crime rates? Research studies have shown that criminal behavior is associated, in greater or lesser degree, with such social and personal pathologies as poverty, bad housing, slum-residence, lack of recreational facilities, inadequate and demoralized families, mental retardation, emotional instability, and other traits and conditions. What do these conditions have in common which apparently produces excessive criminality? Research studies have also demonstrated that many persons with those pathological traits and conditions do not commit crimes and that persons in the upper socioeconomic class frequently violate the law, although they are not in poverty, do not lack recreational facilities, and are not mentally retarded or emotionally unstable. Obviously, it is not the conditions or traits themselves which cause crime, for the conditions are sometimes present when criminality does not occur, and they also are sometimes absent when criminality does occur. A generalization about crime and criminal behavior can be reached by logically abstracting the conditions and processes which are common to the rich and the poor, the males and the females, the blacks and the whites, the urban- and the rural-dwellers, the young adults and the old adults, and the emotionally stable and the emotionally unstable who commit crimes.

In developing such generalizations, criminal behavior must be precisely defined and carefully distinguished from noncriminal behavior. Criminal behavior is human behavior, and has much in common with noncriminal behavior. An explanation of criminal behavior should be consistent with a general theory of other human behavior, but the conditions and processes said to produce crime and criminality should be specific. Many things which are necessary for behavior are not important to criminality. Respiration, for instance, is necessary for any behavior, but the respiratory process cannot be used in an explanation of criminal behavior, for it does not differentiate criminal behavior from noncriminal behavior.

The second procedure for putting order into criminological knowledge is differentiation of levels of analysis. The explanation or generalization must be limited, largely in terms of chronology, and in this way held at a particular level. For example, when Renaissance physicists stated the law of falling bodies, they were not concerned with the reasons why a body began to fall except as this might affect the initial momentum. Galileo did not study the "traits" of falling objects themselves, as Aristotle might have done. Instead, he noted the relationship of the body to its environment while it was falling freely or rolling down an inclined plane, and it made no difference to his generalization whether a body began to fall because it was dropped from the hand of an experimenter or because it rolled off the ledge of a bridge due to vibration caused by a passing vehicle. Also, a round object would roll off the bridge more readily than a square object, but this fact was not significant for the law of falling bodies. Such facts were considered as existing on a different level of explanation and were irrelevant to the problem of explaining the behavior of falling bodies.

Much of the confusion regarding crime and criminal behavior stems from a failure to define and hold constant the level at which they are explained. By analogy, many criminologists and others concerned with understanding and defining crime would attribute some degree of causal power to the "roundness" of the object in the above illustration. However, consideration of time sequences among the conditions associated with crime and criminality may lead to simplicity of statement. In the heterogeneous collection of factors associated with crime and criminal behavior, one factor often occurs prior to another (in much the way that "roundness" occurs prior to "vibration," and "vibration" occurs prior to "rolling off a bridge"), but a theoretical statement can be made without referring to those early factors. By holding the analysis at one level, the early factors are combined with or differentiated from later factors or conditions, thus reducing the number of variables which must be considered in a theory.

A motion picture made several years ago showed two boys engaged in a minor theft; they ran when they were discovered; one boy had longer legs, escaped, and became a priest; the other had shorter legs, was caught, committed to a reformatory, and became a gangster. In this comparison, the boy who became a criminal was differentiated from the one who did not become a criminal by the length of his legs. But "length of legs" need not be considered in a criminological theory because it is obvious that this condition does not determine criminality and has no necessary relation to criminality. In the illustration, the differential in the length of the boys' legs apparently was significant to subsequent criminality or noncriminality only to the degree that it determined the subsequent experiences and associations of the two boys. It is in these experiences and associations, then, that the mechanisms and processes which are important to criminality or noncriminality are to be found.

TWO TYPES OF EXPLANATIONS OF CRIMINAL BEHAVIOR

Scientific explanations of criminal behavior may be stated either in terms of the processes which are operating at the moment of the occurrence of crime or in terms of the processes operating in the earlier history of the criminal. In the first case, the explanation may be called "mechanistic," "situational," or "dynamic"; in the second, "historical" or "developmental." Both types of explanation are desirable. The mechanistic type of explanation has been favored by physical and biological scientists, and it probably could be the more efficient type of explanation of criminal behavior. As Gibbons said:

> In many cases, criminality may be a response to nothing more temporal than the provocations and attractions bound up in the immediate circumstances. It may be that, in some kinds of lawbreaking, understanding of the behavior may require detailed attention to the concatenation of events immediately preceding it. Little or nothing may be added to this understanding from a close scrutiny of the early development of the person.[1]

However, criminological explanations of the mechanistic type have thus far been notably unsuccessful, perhaps largely because they have been formulated in connection with an attempt to isolate personal and social pathologies among criminals. Work from this point of view has, at least, resulted in the conclusion that the immediate determinants of criminal behavior lie in the person-situation complex.

The objective situation is important to criminality largely to the extent that it provides an opportunity for a criminal act. A thief may steal from a fruit stand when the owner is not in sight but refrain when the owner is in sight; a bank burglar may attack a bank which is poorly protected but refrain from attacking a well-protected bank. A corporation which manufactures automobiles seldom violates the pure food and drug laws, but a meat-packing corporation might violate these laws with great frequency. But in another sense, a psychological or sociological sense, the situation is not exclusive of the person, for the situation which is important is the situation as defined by the person who is involved. That is, some persons define a situation in which a fruit-stand owner is out of sight as a "crime-committing" situation, while others do not so define it. Furthermore, the events in the person-situation complex at the time a crime occurs cannot be separated from the prior life experiences of the criminal. This means that the situation is defined by the person in terms of the inclinations and abilities which he or she has acquired. For example, while a person could define a situation in such a manner that criminal behavior would be the inevitable result, past experiences would, for the most part, determine the way in which he or she defined the situation. An explanation of criminal behavior made in terms of these past experiences is a historical or developmental explanation.

The following paragraphs state such a developmental theory of criminal behavior on the assumption that a criminal act occurs when a situation appropriate for it, as defined by the person, is present. The theory should be regarded as tentative, and it should be tested by the factual information presented in the later chapters and by all other factual information and theories which are applicable.

DEVELOPMENTAL EXPLANATION OF CRIMINAL BEHAVIOR

The following statements refer to the process by which a particular person comes to engage in criminal behavior:

1. *Criminal behavior is learned.* Negatively, this means that criminal behavior is not inherited, as such; also, the person who is not already trained in crime does not invent criminal behavior, just as a person does not make mechanical inventions unless he has had training in mechanics.

2. *Criminal behavior is learned in interaction with other persons in a process of communication.* This communication is verbal in many respects but includes also "the communication of gestures."

3. *The principal part of the learning of criminal behavior occurs within intimate personal groups.* Negatively, this means that the impersonal agencies of communication, such as movies and newspapers, play a relatively unimportant part in the genesis of criminal behavior.

4. *When criminal behavior is learned, the learning includes (a) techniques of committing the crime, which are sometimes very complicated, sometimes very simple; (b) the specific direction of motives, drives, rationalizations, and attitudes.*

5. *The specific direction of motives and drives is learned from definitions of the the legal codes as favorable or unfavorable.* In some societies an individual is surrounded by persons who invariably define the legal codes as rules to be observed, while in others he is surrounded by persons whose definitions are favorable to the violation of the legal codes. In our American society these definitions are almost always mixed, with the consequence that we have culture conflict in relation to the legal codes.

6. *A person becomes delinquent because of an excess of definitions favorable to violation of law over definitions unfavorable to violation of law.* This is the principle of differential association. It refers to both criminal and anticriminal associations and has to do with counteracting forces. When persons become criminal, they do so because of contact with criminal patterns and also because of isolation from anticriminal patterns. Any person inevitably assimilates the surrounding culture unless other patterns are in conflict; a southerner does not pronounce *r* because other southerners do not pronounce *r*. Negatively, this proposition of differential association means that associations which are neutral so far as crime is concerned have little or no effect on the genesis of criminal behavior. Much of the experience of a person is neutral in this sense, for instance, learning to brush one's teeth. This behavior has no negative or positive effect on criminal behavior except as it may be related to associations which are concerned with the legal codes. This neutral behavior is important especially as an occupier of the time of a child so that he or she is not in contact with criminal behavior during the time the child is so engaged in the neutral behavior.

7. *Differential associations may vary in frequency, duration, priority, and intensity.* This means that associations with criminal behavior and also associations with anticriminal behavior vary in those respects. Frequency and duration as modalities of associations are obvious and need no explanation. Priority is assumed to be important in the sense that lawful behavior developed in early childhood may persist throughout life, and also that delinquent behavior developed in early childhood may persist throughout life. This tendency, however, has not been adequately demonstrated, and priority seems to be important principally through its selective influence. Intensity is not precisely defined, but it has to do with such things as the prestige of the source of a criminal or anticriminal pattern and with emotional reactions related to the associations. In a precise description of the criminal behavior of a person, these modalities would be rated in quantitative form and a mathematical ratio would be reached. A formula in this sense has not been developed, and the development of such a formula would be extremely difficult.

8.   *The process of learning criminal behavior by association with criminal and anticriminal patterns involves all of the mechanisms that are involved in any other learning.* Negatively, this means that the learning of criminal behavior is not restricted to the process of imitation. A person who is seduced, for instance, learns criminal behavior by association, but this process would not ordinarily be described as imitation.

9.   *While criminal behavior is an expression of general needs and values, it is not explained by those general needs and values, since noncriminal behavior is an expression of the same needs and values.* Thieves generally steal in order to secure money, but likewise honest laborers work in order to secure money. The attempts by many scholars to explain criminal behavior by general drives and values, such as the happiness principle, striving for social status, the money motive, or frustration, have been, and must continue to be, futile, since they explain lawful behavior as completely as they explain criminal behavior. They are similar to respiration, which is necessary for any behavior, but which does not differentiate criminal from noncriminal behavior.

It is not necessary, at this level of explanation, to explain why persons have the associations they have; this certainly involves a complex of many things. In an area where the delinquency rate is high, a boy who is sociable, gregarious, active, and athletic is very likely to come in contact with the other boys in the neighborhood, learn delinquent behavior patterns from them, and become a criminal; in the same neighborhood the psychopathic boy who is isolated, introverted, and inert may remain at home, not become acquainted with the other boys in the neighborhood, and not become delinquent. In another situation, the sociable, athletic, aggressive boy may become a member of a scout troop and not become involved in delinquent behavior. The person's associations are determined in a general context of social organization. A child is ordinarily reared in a family; the place of residence of the family is determined largely by family income; and the delinquency rate is in many respects related to the rental value of the houses. Many other aspects of social organization affect the associations of a person.

The preceding explanation of criminal behavior purports to explain the criminal and noncriminal behavior of individual persons. As indicated earlier, it is possible to state sociological theories of criminal behavior which explain the criminality of a community, nation, or other group. The problem, when thus stated, is to account for variations in crime rates, which involves a comparison of the crime rates of various groups or the crime rates of a particular group at different times. The explanation of a crime rate must be consistent with the explanation of the criminal behavior of the person, since the crime rate is a summary statement of the number of persons in the group who commit crimes and the frequency with which they commit crimes. One of the best explanations of crime rates from this point of view is that a high crime rate is due to social disorganization. The term *social disorganization* is not entirely satisfactory, and it seems preferable to substitute for it the term *differential social organization*. The postulate on which this theory is based, regardless of the name, is that crime is rooted in the social organization and is an expression of that social organization. A group may be organized for criminal behavior or organized against criminal behavior. Most communities are organized for both criminal and anticriminal behavior, and, in that sense, the crime rate is an expression of the differential group organization. Differential group organization as an explanation of variations in crime rates is consistent with the differential association theory of the processes by which persons become criminals.

NOTE

1. Don C. Gibbons, "Observations on the Study of Crime Causation," *American Journal of Sociology*, 77:262-78, 1971.

14 *Other People's Money*
DONALD R. CRESSEY

THE VIOLATORS' VOCABULARIES OF ADJUSTMENT

After a trusted person has defined a problem as non-shareable, the total pertinent situation consists of a problem which must be solved by an independent, secret, and relatively safe means by virtue of general and technical information about trust violation. In this situation the potential trust violator identifies the possibilities for resolving the problem by violating his position of trust and defines the relationship between the non-shareable problem and the illegal solution in language which enables him to look upon trust violation (a) as essentially non-criminal, (b) as justified, or (c) as a part of a general irresponsibility for which he is not completely accountable. The total identifying and defining process was considered in the last chapter as being equal to perception of the objective fact that the position of trust offers an opportunity for solving the problem. The term "rationalization" has been applied to the last phase, and it is with this process that we are concerned in this chapter.

We began using the "rationalization" terminology when it was discovered that the application of certain key verbalizations to his conduct enables the trusted person to "adjust" his conceptions of himself as a trusted person with his conceptions of himself as a user of entrusted funds for solving a non-shareable problem, but the use of the term in this way is not in keeping with popular usage or with usage by some sociologists, psychologists, and psychiatrists. An ordinary definition of the term indicates that rationalization takes place *after* the specific behavioral item in question has occurred. One buys an automobile and then "rationalizes" that he needs it because his health is poor. The notion here is that of an *ex post facto* justification for behavior which "has really been prompted by deeply hidden motives and unconscious tendencies."[1] But the term is also used to refer to a process of finding some logical excuse for questionable behavior tendencies,[2] for thoughts as well as acts,[3] and for decisions to perform an act.[4]

In addition, a rationalization has been considered as a verbalization which purports to make the person's behavior more intelligible to others in terms of symbols currently employed by his group.[5] It follows from this kind of definition that the person may prepare his rationalization before he acts, or he may act first and rationalize afterward. In the cases of trust violation encountered significant rationalizations were always present *before* the criminal act took place, or at least at the time it took place, and, in fact, after the act had taken place the rationalization often was abandoned. If this observation were generalized to other behavior we would not say that an individual "buys an automobile and then rationalizes," as in the example above, but that he buys the car because he is able to rationalize. The rationalization is his motivation,[6] and it not only makes his behavior intelligible to others, but it makes it intelligible to *himself*.

Davis has used the term in this way in saying that "probably the simplest way of giving expression to unacceptable desires and of trying to avoid guilt feelings is to think up a good reason (*i.e.*, one sanctioned in the social group by a moral evaluation higher than the one which forbids the tabooed topic)."[7] He gives as an example the case of a student who thinks he "ought" to study for an examination but feels disinclined to do so. Such a student may tell himself that he needs exercise because exercise is essential to health, and health is more important than passing an examination. He then goes out to play golf. His rationalization, then, is *necessary* to the golf playing, not an excuse or an *ex post facto* justification for it. In this sense, a rationalization is an aspect of a logic which is an adjustive device, which serves the interests of contradictory ideas of "oughtness" or morality, and it is in this sense that we use the term.

On the present level of explanation, systematic causation, it is sufficient to indicate the presence or absence of a rationalization which, together with the knowledge that the position of trust can be violated, enables the person to perceive that the desired results may be produced by violation of the position of trust. The trusted person either uses such a rationalization or he does not. The essential point is that the person must perceive his position of trust as offering an opportunity for such violation, and that such perception, which involves the use of a rationalization, is a part of a process which begins with the structuring of a problem as non-shareable and ends with the criminal violation of financial trust. However, as indicated previously, a discussion of rationalizations used in trust violation is not entirely separable from discussion of the sources of those rationalizations.

In our hypothesis we have observed that one phase of the process which results in trust violation is the application, to the trusted person's own conduct, of language categories which enable him to adjust two rather conflicting sets of values and behavior patterns. But such verbalizations necessarily are impressed upon the person by other persons who have had prior experience with situations involving positions of trust and trust violation. Before they are internalized by the individual they exist as group definitions of situations in which crime is "appropriate." Contacts with such definitions obviously are necessary prior to their internalization as rationalizations. The following propositions, for example, are ideal-type definitions of situations in which trust violation is called for and which, hence, amount to ideologies which sanction the crime: "Some of our most respectable citizens got their start in life by using other people's money temporarily";[8] "In the real estate business there is nothing wrong about using deposits before the deal is closed"; "All people steal when they get in a tight spot."

The following propositions are the personalized versions of those definitions after they have been assimilated and internalized by an individual: "My intent is only to use this money temporarily so I am 'borrowing,' not 'stealing'"; "My immediate use of real estate deposits is 'ordinary business'"; "I have been trying to live an honest life but I have had nothing but troubles so 'to hell with it.'" The individual in a specific, present, situation uses such rationalizations in the

adjustment of personal conflicting values, but the use of the verbalization in this way is necessarily preceded by observation of rather general criminal ideologies.

◄o►

We see then that, having general information about trust violation
and about the conditions under which trust violation occurs, the trust
violator, upon the appearance of the non-shareable problem, applies
to his own situation a rationalization which the groups in which he
has had membership have applied to the behavior of others, and
which he himself has applied to the behavior of others. He perceives
that the general rule applies to his specific case. Such an application to
himself of the symbols held by the members of his groups has been
described by Mead as taking the rôle of the "generalized other."[9] Thus,
the imagination of how he appears to others, and of how he would appear if his non-shareable problem were revealed to others is a controlling "force" in the behavior of the trusted person.

In a "non-shareable-problem–position-of-trust" situation trusted
persons "objectify" their own actions to the extent that they place
themselves in the place of another person or group of persons with
the status of "trustee" and hypothesize their reactions. The hypothesized reactions to "borrowing" in order to solve a non-shareable problem, for example, are much different from hypothesized reactions to
"stealing," and the trusted person behaves accordingly. Similarly, the
hypothesized reactions to a conception of self as an "ill" person or as
a "pressed" person have different implications for behavior than hypothesized reactions to a conception of self as a "criminal."[10]

It is because of hypothesized reactions which do not consistently
and severely condemn his criminal behavior that the trusted person
takes the rôle of what *we* have called the "trust violator."[11] *He* often
does not think of himself as playing that rôle, but often thinks of himself as playing a rôle such as that of a special kind of "borrower,"
"businessman," or even "thief." In order to do so, he necessarily must
have come into contact with a culture which defined those rôles for
him. If the rôles were defined differently in his culture, or if he had
not come into contact with the group definitions, he would behave
differently.

The rationalizations used by trust violators, then, reflect contacts
with cultural ideologies which themselves are contradictory to the
theme that honesty is expected in all situations of trust.[12] When used
by the individual, such ideologies adjust contradictory personal values in regard to criminality on the one hand and integrity, honesty
and morality on the other.[13] Law-enforcement officials and judges do

not officially recognize such cultural contradictions, and in individual cases they hold that trust violation perpetrated according to a rationalization derived from such an ideology is not for that reason "excuseable." Trusted persons with non-shareable problems utilize rationalizations in order to select means, which otherwise would not be available to them, for solving those problems.[14] While the selection of means is recognized by the criminal law, most of the conditions under which such rationalizations are used do not constitute "necessity" according to the legal definitions, and hence they are not considered as sufficient for avoidance of legal liability.[15] The circumstances under which the selections are made are sufficient, however, to explain theoretically why an individual criminally violates his trust rather than behaving in some other manner, even if those circumstances do not "excuse" him from legal liability.

◄o►

Rather than "discovering" trust violation as a solution when non-shareable problems were present, the trust violators interviewed "rediscovered" culturally provided verbalizations which sanction violation and applied these verbalizations to their own conduct. But whether the process is called discovery or rediscovery, the existence of a culture which supplies the necessary sanctions is presupposed, as is contact with these aspects of culture by the trusted person.

◄o►

SUMMARY AND CONCLUSIONS

1.   The rationalizations which are used by trust violators are necessary and essential to criminal violation of trust. They are not merely *ex post facto* justifications for conduct which already has been enacted, but are pertinent and real "reasons" which the person has for acting. When the relationship between a personal non-shareable problem and the position of trust is perceived according to the bias induced by the presence of a rationalization which makes trust violation in some way justified, trust violation results.

2.   Each trusted person does not invent a new rationalization for his violation of trust, but instead he applies to his own situation a verbalization which has been made available to him by virtue of his having come into contact with a culture in which such verbalizations are present. Cultural ideologies which sanction trust violation are in basic contradiction to ideologies which hold non-violation as the norm, and

in trust violation the trusted person applies a general rule to his specific case.

3. The rationalizations used in trust violation are linked with the manner in which the trust is violated and to some extent with the social and economic position of the offender. A large majority of the independent businessmen and trusted employees who take funds over a period of time apply to a situation in which a non-shareable problem is present the rationalization that they are merely borrowing the funds. The application of this rationalization has obvious implications for the behavior of the person using it, since he considers that he is playing the rôle of the borrower rather than of the trust violator. When other rationalizations are used, the person behaves accordingly. Frequently it is necessary for an individual to abandon the rationalizations which he has been using, and when this occurs he looks upon himself as a criminal. Trusted persons who abscond with the funds or property entrusted to them have previously perceived the relationship between the position of trust and a non-shareable problem according to a rationalization which makes cultural ideals in regard to honesty and "responsibility" ineffective. This rationalization is of such a nature that the individual looks upon his rôle in violation as that of a criminal, but he thinks of himself as a special kind of "thief" rather than as a "borrower," "embezzler," or "trust violator."

NOTES

1. A. P. Noyes, *Modern Clinical Psychiatry* (Philadelphia: W. B. Saunders, 1940), p. 49. *Cf.* R. S. Woodworth, *Psychology* (New York: Henry Holt & Co., 1940), p. 537: "The question is what reason to assign for an act"; and F. L. Ruch, *Psychology and Life* (New York: Scott, Foresman & Co., 1941), p. 181: "The ascribing of false motives to one's behavior."

2. T. W. Richards, *Modern Clinical Psychology* (New York: McGraw-Hill, 1946), p. 84.

3. K. Young, *Personality and Problems of Adjustment* (New York: F. S. Crofts & Co., 1946), p. 122.

4. R. T. LaPiere and P. R. Farnsworth, *Social Psychology* (New York: McGraw-Hill, 1949), p. 13.

5. A. R. Lindesmith and A. L. Strauss, *Social Psychology* (New York: Dryden Press, 1949), p. 308.

6. *Cf.* C. Wright Mills, "Situated Actions and Vocabularies of Motive," *American Sociological Review,* 5 (December, 1940), 904–913.

7. Kingsley Davis, *Human Society* (New York: Macmillan, 1949), pp. 267–268. In his discussion of the specific things which are learned in

association with criminal and anti-criminal behavior patterns, Sutherland apparently uses the term rationalization in this same sense, to refer to an evaluation of criminal behavior. That is, a rationalization is considered as equivalent to an attitude about the "oughtness" of the behavior as conceived by the person. E. H. Sutherland, *Principles of Criminology* (New York: Lippincott, 1947), p. 6.

8. *Cf.* Alexander Dumas, *The Money Question,* an English translation of which appears in *Poet Lore,* 26 (March–April, 1915), pp. 129–227, especially Act II: "What is business? That's easy. It's other people's money, of course."

9. George H. Mead, "A Behavioristic Account of the Significant Symbol," *Journal of Philosophy,* 19 (March, 1922), 157–163. See also his *Mind, Self and Society* (Chicago: University of Chicago Press, 1934), pp. 135–226.

10. Although it was not in any way checked by her research, Redden offers the following hypothesis, based on Mead's distinction between the "I" and the "me," about the rôle-taking behavior of embezzlers. "In his rehearsal of consequences in the process of taking the rôle of another he [the embezzler] fails to integrate himself with the organized pattern of approved social behavior. He fails or refuses to try to devise a plan by reflective thinking which will increase his value to the organization and call forth recognition in terms of increased income. Thwarted in his attempt or impatient of the duration of time necessary to fulfill his wish on the socially desirable level, his mental activity is centered on a plan of borrowing, converting his employer's goods or money to his own use, to fulfill the wish for a margin above the equilibrium of income and cost of living to satisfy some latent desire in a minimum of time. He completes the act hypothetically, taking the rôle of another but contrary to the common organized pattern of social behavior in business relationships and in the social group. His hypothetical solution may be a new technique or method which if discovered by the employer would mean dismissal from his employ and community disapproval. His mental activity is in opposition to the organized sets of attitudes of the social group. The two aspects of the self of the embezzler are in conflict, the social or impersonal self integrates the hypothetical act with the organized social behavior of the group by naming the act resulting from the proposed plan borrowing, with intent to replace or repay; the other aspect of self, the personal or a-social, views his plan as opposed to organized social behavior, independent of the group and unknown to the group." Elizabeth Redden, *Embezzlement, A Study of One Kind of Criminal Behavior, With Prediction Tables Based on Fidelity Insurance Records,* Ph.D. Dissertation, University of Chicago, 1939, pp. 27–29.

11. In this connection, we shall see later that when the long-term violator who has convinced himself that he is a "borrower" decides that he is "in too deep" the attitudes of his group toward "embezzlement" and "crime" can no longer be avoided, and his behavior takes on the

characteristics of the rôle which he *then* conceives of himself as playing. Similarly, we shall see that while there exists in most groups in our culture a rather general condemnation of "trust violation" or "stealing" this condemnation is not as general when the "mitigating circumstances" are known. That is, some categories of criminal behavior are not as severely or consistently condemned as others. The trust violator behaves according to the cultural definitions of those categories.

12.   "When rationalizations are extensively developed and systematized as group doctrines and beliefs, they are known as ideologies. As such, they acquire unusual prestige and authority. The person who uses them has the sense of conforming to group expectations, of doing the 'right thing.'... Unscrupulous and sometimes criminal behavior in business and industry is justified in terms of an argument which begins and ends with the assertion that 'business is business.' ...The principal advantage of group rationalizations or ideologies, from the individual's standpoint, is that they give him a sense of support and sanction. They help him to view himself and his activities in a favorable light and to maintain his self-esteem and self-respect." A. R. Lindesmith and A. L. Strauss, *op. cit.*, pp. 309–310. Reproduced by permission of the publisher.

13.   In a letter to the author even an official of a bonding company differentiated between "embezzlers" and "crooks" by saying: "Actually the average embezzler is no more crook than you or I. As a result of circumstances, he finds himself in some position where, with no criminal intent, he 'borrows' from his employer. One circumstance leads to another and it is only a matter of time before he is discovered and discharged with or without prosecution."

14.   The fact that trust violators use rationalizations does not mean, of course, that they are more "rational" than other persons, or that they carefully weigh and consider the advantages and disadvantages of trust violation in an objective, careful, precise manner. The use of the rationalization makes this unnecessary, and once the trusted person has rationalized the violation of his trust it is impossible for him to be concerned with the question of whether the rationalization is a "good" one.

Probably it was the observation of this sort of thing which led Lottier to the formulation of that part of his theory which holds that in cases of embezzlement there is "no subjectively available alternative" to embezzlement. S. Lottier, "Tension Theory of Criminal Behavior," *American Sociological Review,* 7 (December, 1942), 840–848. Our analysis also can be considered as a detailed consideration of Riemer's general statement that the opportunities presented through occupancy of a position of trust form a "temptation" if the embezzler develops an "anti-social attitude" which makes possible the abandonment of the folk-ways of legitimate business behavior. Svend

Riemer, "Embezzlement: Pathological Basis," *Journal of Criminal Law and Criminology,* 32 (November–December, 1941), 411–423. As shall be shown later, however, most of the trust violators encountered did not so much abandon the folk-ways of legitimate business behavior as they did re-structure the situation in such a way that, from their point of view, they were *not* abandoning such folk-ways. Similarly, except for absconders, the attitudes of the men interviewed were not so much "anti-social" as they were "pro-social" in that the endeavor was to keep from considering themselves as criminals.

15. Jerome Hall, *Principles of Criminal Law* (Indianapolis: Bobbs-Merrill, 1947), pp. 415–426.

15 Techniques of Neutralization: A Theory of Delinquency
GRESHAM M. SYKES and DAVID MATZA

In attempting to uncover the roots of juvenile delinquency, the social scientist has long since ceased to search for devils in the mind or stigma of the body. It is now largely agreed that delinquent behavior, like most social behavior, is learned and that it is learned in the process of social interaction.

The classic statement of this position is found in Sutherland's theory of differential association, which asserts that criminal or delinquent behavior involves the learning of (a) techniques of committing crimes and (b) motives, drives, rationalizations, and attitudes favorable to the violation of law.[1] Unfortunately, the specific content of what is learned—as opposed to the process by which it is learned—has received relatively little attention in either theory or research. Perhaps the single strongest school of thought on the nature of this content has centered on the idea of a delinquent sub-culture. The basic characteristic of the delinquent sub-culture, it is argued, is a system of values that represents an inversion of the values held by respectable, law-abiding society. The world of the delinquent is the world of the law-abiding turned upside down and its norms constitute a countervailing force directed against the conforming social order. Cohen[2] sees the process of developing a delinquent sub-culture as a matter of building, maintaining, and reinforcing a code for behavior which exists by opposition, which stands in point by point contradiction to dominant values, particularly those of the middle class. Cohen's portrayal of delinquency is executed with a good deal of sophistication,

Reprinted from Gresham M. Sykes and David Matza, "Techniques of Neutralization: A Theory of Delinquency," *American Sociological Review,* vol. 22 (1957), pp. 664–670.

and he carefully avoids overly simple explanations such as those based on the principle of "follow the leader" or easy generalizations about "emotional disturbances." Furthermore, he does not accept the delinquent sub-culture as something given, but instead systematically examines the function of delinquent values as a viable solution to the lower-class, male child's problems in the area of social status. Yet in spite of its virtues, this image of juvenile delinquency as a form of behavior based on competing or countervailing values and norms appears to suffer from a number of serious defects. It is the nature of these defects and a possible alternative or modified explanation for a large portion of juvenile delinquency with which this paper is concerned.

The difficulties in viewing delinquent behavior as springing from a set of deviant values and norms—as arising, that is to say, from a situation in which the delinquent defines his delinquency as "right"— are both empirical and theoretical. In the first place, if there existed in fact a delinquent sub-culture such that the delinquent viewed his illegal behavior as morally correct, we could reasonably suppose that he would exhibit no feelings of guilt or shame at detection or confinement. Instead, the major reaction would tend in the direction of indignation or a sense of martyrdom.[3] It is true that some delinquents do react in the latter fashion, although the sense of martyrdom often seems to be based on the fact that others "get away with it" and indignation appears to be directed against the chance events or lack of skill that led to apprehension. More important, however, is the fact that there is a good deal of evidence suggesting that many delinquents *do* experience a sense of guilt or shame, and its outward expression is not to be dismissed as a purely manipulative gesture to appease those in authority. Much of this evidence is, to be sure, of a clinical nature or in the form of impressionistic judgments of those who must deal first hand with the youthful offender. Assigning a weight to such evidence calls for caution, but it cannot be ignored if we are to avoid the gross stereotype of the juvenile delinquent as a hardened gangster in miniature.

In the second place, observers have noted that the juvenile delinquent frequently accords admiration and respect to law-abiding persons. The "really honest" person is often revered, and if the delinquent is sometimes overly keen to detect hypocrisy in those who conform, unquestioned probity is likely to win his approval. A fierce attachment to a humble, pious mother or a forgiving, upright priest (the former, according to many observers, is often encountered in both juvenile delinquents and adult criminals) might be dismissed as rank sentimentality, but at least it is clear that the delinquent does not necessarily regard those who abide by the legal rules as immoral. In a similar vein, it can be noted that the juvenile delinquent may exhibit great resentment if illegal behavior is imputed to "significant others" in his immediate social environment or to heroes in the world of sport and entertainment. In other words, if the delinquent does hold to a set of values and norms that stand in complete opposition to those of respectable society, his norm-holding is of a peculiar sort. While supposedly thoroughly committed to the deviant system of the delinquent sub-culture, he would appear to recognize the moral validity of the dominant normative system in many instances.[4]

In the third place, there is much evidence that juvenile delinquents often draw a sharp line between those who can be victimized and those who cannot. Certain social groups are not to be viewed as "fair game" in the performance of supposedly approved delinquent acts while others warrant a variety of attacks. In general, the potentiality for victimization would seem to be a function of the social distance between the juvenile delinquent and others and thus we find implicit maxims in the world of the delinquent such as "don't steal from friends" or "don't commit vandalism against a church of your own faith."[5] This is all rather obvious, but the implications have not received sufficient attention. The fact that supposedly valued behavior tends to be directed against disvalued social groups hints that the "wrongfulness" of such delinquent behavior is more widely recognized by delinquents than the literature has indicated. When the pool of victims is limited by considerations of kinship, friendship, ethnic group, social class, age, sex, etc., we have reason to suspect that the virtue of delinquency is far from unquestioned.

In the fourth place, it is doubtful if many juvenile delinquents are totally immune from the demands for conformity made by the dominant social order. There is a strong likelihood that the family of the delinquent will agree with respectable society that delinquency is wrong, even though the family may be engaged in a variety of illegal activities. That is, the parental posture conducive to delinquency is not apt to be a positive prodding. Whatever may be the influence of parental example, what might be called the "Fagin" pattern of socialization into delinquency is probably rare. Furthermore, as Redl has indicated, the idea that certain neighborhoods are completely delinquent, offering the child a model for delinquent behavior without reservations, is simply not supported by the data.[6]

The fact that a child is punished by parents, school officials, and agencies of the legal system for his delinquency may, as a number of observers have cynically noted, suggest to the child that he should be more careful not to get caught. There is an equal or greater probability, however, that the child will internalize the demands for conformity. This is not to say that demands for conformity cannot be counteracted. In fact, as we shall see shortly, an understanding of how internal and external demands for conformity are neutralized may be crucial for understanding delinquent behavior. But it is to say that a complete denial of the validity of demands for conformity and the substitution of a new normative system is improbable, in light of the child's or adolescent's dependency on adults and encirclement by adults inherent in his status in the social structure. No matter how deeply enmeshed in patterns of delinquency he may be and no matter how much this involvement may outweigh his associations with the law-abiding, he cannot escape the condemnation of his deviance. Somehow the demands for conformity must be met and answered; they cannot be ignored as part of an alien system of values and norms.

In short, the theoretical viewpoint that sees juvenile delinquency as a form of behavior based on the values and norms of a deviant subculture in precisely the same way as law-abiding behavior is based on the values and norms of the larger society is open to serious doubt. The fact that the world of the delinquent is embedded in the larger world of those who conform cannot be overlooked nor can the delinquent be equated with an adult thoroughly socialized into an alternative way of life. Instead, the juvenile delinquent would appear to be at least partially committed to the dominant social order in that he frequently exhibits guilt or shame when he violates its proscriptions, accords approval to certain conforming figures, and distinguishes between appropriate and inappropriate targets for his deviance. It is to an explanation for the apparently paradoxical fact of his delinquency that we now turn.

As Morris Cohen once said, one of the most fascinating problems about human behavior is why men violate the laws in which they believe. This is the problem that confronts us when we attempt to explain why delinquency occurs despite a greater or lesser commitment to the usages of conformity. A basic clue is offered by the fact that social rules or norms calling for valued behavior seldom if ever take the form of categorical imperatives. Rather, values or norms appear as *qualified* guides for action, limited in their applicability in terms of time, place, persons, and social circumstances. The moral injunction against killing, for example, does not apply to the enemy during combat in time of war, although a captured enemy comes once again under the prohibition. Similarly, the taking and distributing of scarce goods in a time of acute social need is felt by many to be right, although under other circumstances private property is held inviolable. The normative system of a society, then, is marked by what Williams has termed *flexibility;* it does not consist of a body of rules held to be binding under all conditions.[7]

This flexibility is, in fact, an integral part of the criminal law in that measures for "defenses to crimes" are provided in pleas such as non-age, necessity, insanity, drunkenness, compulsion, self-defense, and so on. The individual can avoid moral culpability for his criminal action—and thus avoid the negative sanctions of society—if he can prove that criminal intent was lacking. *It is our argument that much delinquency is based on what is essentially an unrecognized extension of defenses to crimes, in the form of justifications for deviance that are seen as valid by the delinquent but not by the legal system or society at large.*

These justifications are commonly described as rationalizations. They are viewed as following deviant behavior and as protecting the individual from self-blame and the blame of others after the act. But there is also reason to believe that they precede deviant behavior and make deviant behavior possible. It is this possibility that Sutherland mentioned only in passing and that other writers have failed to exploit from the viewpoint of sociological theory. Disapproval flowing from internalized norms and conforming others in the social environment is neutralized, turned back, or deflected in advance. Social controls that serve to check or inhibit deviant motivational patterns are rendered inoperative, and the individual is freed to engage in delinquency without serious damage to his self image. In this sense, the delinquent both has his cake and eats it too, for he remains committed to the dominant normative system and yet so qualifies its imperatives that violations are "acceptable" if not "right." Thus the delinquent represents not a radical opposition to law-abiding society but something more like an apologetic failure, often more sinned against than sinning in his own eyes. We call these justifications of deviant behavior techniques of neutralization; and we believe these techniques make up a crucial component of Sutherland's "definitions favorable to the violation of law." It is by learning these techniques that the juvenile becomes delinquent, rather than by learning moral imperatives, values or attitudes standing in direct contradiction to those of the dominant society. In analyzing these techniques, we have found it convenient to divide them into five major types.

The Denial of Responsibility

In so far as the delinquent can define himself as lacking responsibility for his deviant actions, the disapproval of self or others is sharply reduced in effectiveness as a restraining influence. As Justice Holmes has said, even a dog distinguishes between being stumbled over and being kicked, and modern society is no less careful to draw a line between injuries that are unintentional, i.e., where responsibility is lacking, and those that are intentional. As a technique of neutralization, however, the denial of responsibility extends much further than the claim that deviant acts are an "accident" or some similar negation of personal accountability. It may also be asserted that delinquent acts are due to forces outside of the individual and beyond his control such as unloving parents, bad companions, or a slum neighborhood. In effect, the delinquent approaches a "billiard ball" conception of himself in which he sees himself as helplessly propelled into new situations. From a psychodynamic viewpoint, this orientation toward one's own actions may represent a profound alienation from self, but it is important to stress the fact that interpretations of responsibility are cultural constructs and not merely idiosyncratic beliefs. The similarity between this mode of justifying illegal behavior assumed by the delinquent and the implications of a "sociological" frame of reference or a "humane" jurisprudence is readily apparent.[8] It is not the validity of this orientation that concerns us here, but its function of deflecting blame attached to violations of social norms and its relative independence of a particular personality structure.[9] By learning to view himself as more acted upon than acting, the delinquent prepares the way for deviance from the dominant normative system without the necessity of a frontal assault on the norms themselves.

The Denial of Injury

A second major technique of neutralization centers on the injury or harm involved in the delinquent act. The criminal law has long made a distinction between crimes which are *mala in se* and *mala prohibita*—that is between acts that are wrong in themselves and acts that are illegal but not immoral—and the delinquent can make the same kind of distinction in evaluating the wrongfulness of his behavior. For the delinquent, however, wrongfulness may turn on the question of whether or not anyone has clearly been hurt by his deviance, and this matter is open to a variety of interpretations. Vandalism, for example, may be defined by the delinquent simply as "mischief"—after all, it may be claimed, the persons whose property has been destroyed can well afford it. Similarly, auto theft may be viewed as "borrowing," and gang fighting may be seen as a private quarrel, an agreed upon duel between two willing parties, and thus of no concern to the community at large. We are not suggesting that this technique of neutralization, labelled the denial of injury, involves an explicit dialectic. Rather, we are arguing that the delinquent frequently, and in a hazy fashion, feels that his behavior does not really cause any great harm despite the fact that it runs counter to law. Just as the link between the individual and his acts may be broken by the denial of responsibility, so may the link between acts and their consequences be broken by the denial of injury. Since society sometimes agrees with the delinquent, e.g., in matters such as truancy, "pranks," and so on, it merely reaffirms the idea that the delinquent's neutralization of social controls by means of qualifying the norms is an extension of common practice rather than a gesture of complete opposition.

The Denial of the Victim

Even if the delinquent accepts the responsibility for his deviant actions and is willing to admit that his deviant actions involve an injury or hurt, the moral indignation of self and others may be neutralized by an insistence that the injury is not wrong in light of the circumstances. The injury, it may be claimed, is not really an injury; rather, it is a form of rightful retaliation or punishment. By a subtle alchemy the delinquent moves himself into the position of an avenger and the victim is transformed into a wrong-doer. Assaults on homosexuals or suspected homosexuals, attacks on members of minority groups who are said to have gotten "out of place," vandalism as revenge on an unfair teacher or school official, thefts from a "crooked" store owner—all may be hurts inflicted on a transgressor, in the eyes of the delinquent. As Orwell has pointed out, the type of criminal admired by the general public has probably changed over the course of years and Raffles no longer serves as a hero;[10] but Robin Hood, and his latter day derivatives such as the tough detective seeking justice outside the law, still capture the popular imagination, and the delinquent may view his acts as part of a similar role.

To deny the existence of the victim, then, by transforming him into a person deserving of injury is an extreme form of a phenomenon we have mentioned before, namely, the delinquent's recognition of appropriate and inappropriate targets for his delinquent acts. In addition, however, the existence of the victim may be denied for the delinquent, in a somewhat different sense, by the circumstances of the delinquent act itself. Insofar as the victim is physically absent, unknown, or a vague abstraction (as is often the case in delinquent acts committed against property), the awareness of the victim's existence is weakened. Internalized norms and anticipations of the reactions of others must somehow be activated, if they are to serve as guides for behavior; and it is possible that a diminished awareness of the victim plays an important part in determining whether or not this process is set in motion.

The Condemnation of the Condemners

A fourth technique of neutralization would appear to involve a condemnation of the condemners or, as McCorkle and Korn have phrased it, a rejection of the rejectors.[11] The delinquent shifts the focus of attention from his own deviant acts to the motives and behavior of those who disapprove of his violations. His condemners, he may claim, are hypocrites, deviants in disguise, or impelled by personal spite. This orientation toward the conforming world may be of particular importance when it hardens into a bitter cynicism directed against those assigned the task of enforcing or expressing the norms of the dominant society. Police, it may be said, are corrupt, stupid, and brutal. Teachers always show favoritism and parents always "take it out" on their children. By a slight extension, the rewards of conformity—such as material success—become a matter of pull or luck, thus decreasing still further the stature of those who stand on the side of the law-abiding. The validity of this jaundiced viewpoint is not so important as its function in turning back or deflecting the negative sanctions attached to violations of the norms. The delinquent, in effect, has changed the subject of the conversation in the dialogue between his own deviant impulses and the reactions of others; and by attacking others, the wrongfulness of his own behavior is more easily repressed or lost to view.

The Appeal to Higher Loyalties

Fifth, and last, internal and external social controls may be neutralized by sacrificing the demands of the larger society for the demands of the smaller social groups to which the delinquent belongs such as the sibling pair, the gang, or the friendship clique. It is important to note that the delinquent does not necessarily repudiate the imperatives of the dominant normative system, despite his failure to follow them. Rather, the delinquent may see himself as caught up in a dilemma that must be resolved, unfortunately, at the cost of violating the law. One aspect of this situation has been studied by Stouffer and Toby in their research on the conflict between particularistic and universalistic demands, between the claims of friendship and general social obligations, and their results suggest that "it is possible to classify people according to a predisposition to select one or the other horn of a dilemma in a role conflict."[12] For our purposes, however, the most important point is that deviation from certain norms may occur not because the norms are rejected but because other norms, held to be more pressing or involving a higher loyalty, are accorded precedence. Indeed, it is the fact that both sets of norms are believed in that gives meaning to our concepts of dilemma and role conflict.

The conflict between the claims of friendship and the claims of law, or a similar dilemma, has of course long been recognized by the social scientist (and the novelist) as a common human problem. If the juvenile delinquent frequently resolves his dilemma by insisting that he must "always help a buddy" or "never squeal on a friend," even when it throws him into serious difficulties with the dominant social order, his choice remains familiar to the supposedly law-abiding. The delinquent is unusual, perhaps, in the extent to which he is able to see the fact that he acts in behalf of the smaller social groups to which he belongs as a justification for violations of society's norms, but it is a matter of degree rather than of kind.

"I didn't mean it." "I didn't really hurt anybody." "They had it coming to them." "Everybody's picking on me." "I didn't do it for myself." These slogans or their variants, we hypothesize, prepare the juvenile for delinquent acts. These "definitions of the situation" represent tangential or glancing blows at the dominant normative system rather than the creation of an opposing ideology; and they are extensions of patterns of thought prevalent in society rather than something created *de novo*.

Techniques of neutralization may not be powerful enough to fully shield the individual from the force of his own internalized values and the reactions of conforming others, for as we have pointed out, juvenile delinquents often appear to suffer from feelings of guilt and shame when called into account for their deviant behavior. And some delinquents may be so isolated from the world of conformity that techniques of neutralization need not be called into play. Nonetheless, we would argue that techniques of neutralization are critical in lessening the effectiveness of social controls and that they lie behind a large share of delinquent behavior. Empirical research in this area is scattered and fragmentary at the present time, but the work of Redl,[13] Cressey,[14] and others has supplied a body of significant data that has done much to clarify the theoretical issues and enlarge the fund of supporting evidence. Two lines of investigation seem to be critical at this stage. First, there is need for more knowledge concerning the differential distribution of techniques of neutralization, as operative patterns of thought, by age, sex, social class, ethnic group, etc. On *a priori* grounds it might be assumed that these justifications for deviance will be more readily seized by segments of society for whom a discrepancy between common social ideals and social practice is most apparent. It is also possible, however, that the habit of "bending" the dominant normative system—if not "breaking" it—cuts across our cruder social categories and is to be traced primarily to patterns of social interaction within the familial circle. Second, there is need for a greater understanding of the internal structure of techniques of neutralization, as a system of beliefs and attitudes, and its relationship to various types of delinquent behavior. Certain techniques of neutralization would appear to be better adapted to particular deviant acts than to others, as we have suggested, for example, in the case of offenses against property and the denial of the victim. But the issue remains far from clear and stands in need of more information.

In any case, techniques of neutralization appear to offer a promising line of research in enlarging and systematizing the theoretical grasp of juvenile delinquency. As more information is uncovered concerning techniques of neutralization, their origins, and their consequences, both juvenile delinquency in particular, and deviation from normative systems in general may be illuminated.

NOTES

1. E. H. Sutherland, *Principles of Criminology,* revised by D. R. Cressey, Chicago: Lippincott, 1955, pp. 77–80.
2. Albert K. Cohen, *Delinquent Boys,* Glencoe, Ill.: The Free Press, 1955.
3. This form of reaction among the adherents of a deviant subculture who fully believe in the "rightfulness" of their behavior and who are captured and punished by the agencies of the dominant social order can be illustrated, perhaps, by groups such as Jehovah's Witnesses, early Christian sects, nationalist movements in colonial areas, and conscientious objectors during World Wars I and II.
4. As Weber has pointed out, a thief may recognize the legitimacy of legal rules without accepting their moral validity. Cf. Max Weber, *The Theory of Social and Economic Organization* (translated by A. M. Henderson and Talcott Parsons), New York: Oxford University Press, 1947, p. 125. We are arguing here, however, that the juvenile delinquent frequently recognizes *both* the legitimacy of the dominant social order and its moral "rightness."
5. Thrasher's account of the "Itschkies"—a juvenile gang composed of Jewish boys—and the immunity from "rolling" enjoyed by Jewish drunkards is a good illustration. Cf. F. Thrasher, *The Gang,* Chicago: The University of Chicago Press, 1947, p. 315.
6. Cf. Solomon Kobrin, "The Conflict of Values in Delinquency Areas," *American Sociological Review,* 16 (October, 1951), pp. 653–661.
7. Cf. Robin Williams, Jr., *American Society,* New York: Knopf, 1951, p. 28.

8. A number of observers have wryly noted that many delinquents seem to show a surprising awareness of sociological and psychological explanations for their behavior and are quick to point out the causal role of their poor environment.

9. It is possible, of course, that certain personality structures can accept some techniques of neutralization more readily than others, but this question remains largely unexplored.

10. George Orwell, *Dickens, Dali, and Others*, New York: Reynal, 1946.

11. Lloyd W. McCorkle and Richard Korn, "Resocialization Within Walls," *The Annals of the American Academy of Political and Social Science,* 293, (May, 1954), pp. 88–98.

12. See Samuel A. Stouffer and Jackson Toby, "Role Conflict and Personality," in *Toward a General Theory of Action,* edited by Talcott Parsons and Edward A. Shils, Cambridge: Harvard University Press, 1951, p. 494.

13. See Fritz Redl and David Wineman, *Children Who Hate,* Glencoe: The Free Press, 1956.

14. See D. R. Cressey, *Other People's Money,* Glencoe: The Free Press, 1953.

Analysis and Critique

16 *Epidemiology and Individual Conduct:*
A Case from Criminology
DONALD R. CRESSEY

A principal thesis of this paper is that a theory explaining social be-havior in general, or any specific kind of social behavior, should have two distinct but consistent aspects. First, there must be a statement that explains the statistical distribution of the behavior in time and space (epidemiology), and from which predictive statements about unknown statistical distributions can be derived. Second, there must be a statement that identifies, at least by implication, the process by which individuals come to exhibit the behavior in question, and from which can be derived predictive statements about the behavior of indi-viduals. Concentration on either the epidemiological segment or the individual conduct segment of a theoretical problem is sometimes

Reprinted from Donald R. Cressey, "Epidemiology and Individual Conduct: A Case from Criminology," *Pacific Sociological Review,* vol. 3 (Fall 1960), pp. 47–58. Copyright JAI Press, Inc.

necessary, but it is erroneous and inefficient to ignore the second segment, to turn it over to another academic discipline, or to leave its solution to a specialized set of workers within a single discipline.

In some cases, data on both aspects of a problem are not available, so that a two-edged theory is impossible. For example, my work on trust violation was concerned almost exclusively with the process by which one becomes a criminal, but such concentration was necessary because reliable data on the distribution of this type of crime were not available.[1] Should data become available, then the generalization about trust *violators* should be integrated with a generalization about variations in trust *violation*. In other cases, concentration on one phase of an explanation may be merely a matter of interest or time. However, it might also be due to an undesirable informal or formal division of labor—such as that between sociologists and psychiatrists, or that indicated by the recent development of a special Section on Social Psychology within the American Sociological Association.

The need for integrated theories of epidemiology and individual conduct is demonstrated in the work done on Merton's theory of deviant behavior. Over twenty years ago, Merton presented a sociological statement purporting, among other things, to account for an excess of property crimes in the working class population. However, he left unanswered (and to some extent unasked) the question of why only a rather insignificant proportion of working class persons became property offenders.[2] While a few sociologists paid attention to this theory about the epidemiology of crime, psychiatric theory that is quite unrelated to Merton's theory has continued to dominate explanation of individual cases of working class (and other) criminality.[3] Only in the last five years has there been a significant attempt to identify the processes by which the blocking of legitimate means for achieving success, posed by Merton, might "work" to produce the criminality of individual working class persons. Even here, the most significant efforts have concentrated on variations in socially structured opportunities for deviation, rather than on the social psychological mechanisms involved in individual cases.[4]

In an even more significant case, a sociological theory of the epidemiology of crime has been neglected because it has been viewed as only an alternative to psychiatric theories about the process by which individuals become criminals. The implications of Sutherland's "theory of differential association" for explaining the high and low crime rates of various categories of persons have been all but ignored, just as the implications of Merton's theory for explanation of individual conduct have been neglected. Yet it is clear, as we will show later, that when Sutherland introduced the idea of differential association, in

1939, he was concerned with both phases of the general problem in criminology: explaining the distribution of crime rates, and identifying the process by which a person becomes a criminal.[5] His idea has had a profound effect on criminological and sociological thought, despite the fact that it has become a center of controversy. Significantly, the controversy has concentrated on the capacity of the statement to portray accurately the process by which individuals become criminals, and its capacity to explain the distribution of crime and delinquency has scarcely been studied or discussed. Yet we shall see that, in a very real sense, Sutherland was trying to do for criminology what Darwin did for biology. Although such an observation might seem pretentious when the range of phenomena included in the scope of Darwin's theory is compared with the range included in Sutherland's, each man did try to state a principle accounting for the presence or absence of "deviant" phenomena, and then also tried to specify the process by which "deviancy" comes to be present in individual cases.

We shall return to this comparison after examining the theory of differential association and some of the criticisms of one of its parts.

DIFFERENTIAL ASSOCIATION AND INDIVIDUAL CRIMINALITY

Sutherland's theory of differential association can best be understood if only that part of it which has become the center of attention and which purports to explain individual criminality is considered first. The essential ideas here are that "criminal behavior is learned in interaction with persons in a pattern of communication," and that the specific direction of motives, drives, rationalizations, and attitudes— whether in the direction of criminality or anti-criminality—is learned from persons who define the legal codes as rules to be observed and from persons whose attitudes are favorable to violation of legal codes. "A person becomes delinquent because of an excess of definitions favorable to violation of law over definitions unfavorable to violation of law."[6] In modern society, the two kinds of definitions of what is expected and desired in reference to legal codes exist side by side, and a person might present contradictory definitions to another person at different times and in different situations. Sutherland called the process of receiving these two kinds of definitions "differential association," because what is learned in association with criminal behavior patterns is in competition with what is learned in association with anti-criminal behavior patterns. "When persons become criminals, they do so because of contacts with criminal behavior patterns and

also because of isolation from anti-criminal patterns." The kind of social psychological process Sutherland seemed to have in mind will become clearer if we consider some of the details of his statement by reviewing both the principal interpretive errors apparently made by his
readers and the principal criticisms advanced by his criminological
colleagues.

SOME LITERARY ERRORS

The statement of the theory of differential association is not clear. In
two pages, Sutherland presented nine propositions, with little elaboration, that purport to explain both the epidemiology of crime and delinquency and the presence of criminality and delinquency in individual cases. It therefore is not surprising that his words do not always
convey the meaning he seemed to intend. Most significantly, as we
shall see later, the statement gives the impression that there is little
concern for explaining variations in crime and delinquency rates. This
is a serious error in communication on Sutherland's part. In reference
to the delinquent and criminal behavior of individuals, however, the
difficulty in communication seems to arise as much from readers' failure to study the words presented as from the words themselves. Five
principal errors, and a number of minor ones, have arisen because
readers do not always understand what Sutherland seemed to be trying to say.

First, it is common to believe, or (perhaps necessarily) to assume
momentarily, if only for purposes of research and discussion, that the
theory is concerned only with contacts or associations with criminal
and delinquent behavior patterns.[7] Vold, for example, says, "One of
the persistent problems that always has bedeviled the theory of differential association is the obvious fact that not everyone in contact with
criminality adopts or follows the criminal pattern."[8] At first glance, at
least, such statements seem to overlook or ignore the words "differential" and "excess" in Sutherland's presentation. After stating that a
person becomes delinquent because of an *excess* of definitions favorable to violation of law over definitions unfavorable to violation of law,
Sutherland continues by saying, "This is the principle of differential
association. It refers to both criminal and anti-criminal associations
and has to do with counter-acting forces." Thus, he does not say that
persons become criminals because of associations with criminal behavior patterns; he says that they become criminals because of an
overabundance of such associations, in comparison with associations
with anti-criminal behavior patterns. Accordingly, it is erroneous to
state or imply that the theory is invalid because a category of

persons—such as policemen, prison workers, or criminologists—have had extensive association with criminal behavior patterns but yet are not criminals.

Second, it is commonly believed that Sutherland says persons become criminals because of an excess of associations with *criminals*.[9] Because of the manner in which the theory is stated, and because of the popularity of the "bad companions" theory of criminality in our society, this error is easy to make. Sutherland's proposal is concerned with ratios of associations with *patterns of behavior,* no matter what the character of the person presenting them. Throughout his formal statement, Sutherland uses terms such as "definitions of legal codes as favorable or unfavorable," "definitions favorable to violation of law over definitions unfavorable to violation of law," and "association with criminal and anti-criminal patterns." Thus, if a mother teaches her son that "Honesty is the best policy" but also teaches him, perhaps inadvertently, that "It is all right to steal a loaf of bread when you are starving," she is presenting him with an anti-criminal behavior pattern and a criminal behavior pattern, even if she herself is honest, noncriminal, and even anti-criminal. One can learn criminal behavior patterns from persons who are not criminals, and one can learn anti-criminal behavior patterns from hoods, professional crooks, habitual offenders, and gangsters.

Third, in periods of time ranging from five to twelve years after publication of the formal statement with the word "systematic" omitted, at least five authors have erroneously believed that the theory pertains to "systematic" criminal behavior only.[10] This error is not important to the substance of Sutherland's current statement of the theory, but discussing it does tell something about the nature of the theory. The first formal statement was qualified so that it pertained only to "systematic" criminal behavior, rather than to the more general category "criminal behavior."[11] Sutherland deleted the word "systematic" from his second version of his theory, which first appeared in the Fourth Edition of his *Principles of Criminology,* in 1947. He explained that it was his belief that all but "the very trivial criminal acts" were "systematic," but he deleted the word because some research workers were unable to identify "systematic criminals," and other workers considered only an insignificant proportion of prisoners to be "systematic criminals."[12] The theory now refers to all criminal behavior. Limitation to "systematic" criminality was made for what seemed to be practical rather than logical reasons, and it was abandoned when it did not seem to have practical utility. Yet, one author (Caldwell) has recently been as critical of the word "systematic" as was an early article that attacked the original statement containing the word "systematic."[13]

Fourth, it is commonplace to say that the theory is defective because it does not explain why persons have the associations they have.[14] Although such expressions are valuable statements of what is needed in criminological research, they are erroneous when applied to differential association. Sutherland recognized that determining why persons have the associations they have is a desirable problem for research, and we shall later see that when his theory is viewed as a principle that attempts to account for variations in crime rates it does deal in a general way with differential opportunities for association with an excess of criminal behavior patterns. Nevertheless, the fact that the "individual conduct" part of the theory does not pretend to account for a person's associations cannot be considered a defect in it:

> It is not necessary, at this level of explanation, to explain why a person has the associations he has; this certainly involves a complex of things. In an area where the delinquency rate is high a boy who is sociable, gregarious, active, and athletic is very likely to come in contact with other boys in the neighborhood, learn delinquent behavior from them, and become a gangster; in the same neighborhood the psychopathic boy who is isolated, introvert, and inert may remain at home, not become acquainted with other boys in the neighborhood, and not become delinquent. In another situation, the sociable, athletic, aggressive boy may become a member of a scout troop and not become involved in delinquent behavior. The person's associations are determined in the general context of social organization.[15]

Fifth, other authors have erroneously taken "theory" to be synonymous with "bias" or "prejudice," and have condemned Sutherland's statement on this ground. For example, in connection with criticizing Sutherland for deleting "systematic" from the 1947 version of his theory, Caldwell has written that by 1947 "we had not acquired enough additional facts to enable [Sutherland] to explain all criminal behavior."[16] This statement does not clearly recognize that facts themselves do not explain anything, and that theory tries to account for the relationships between known facts, among other things. Confusion about the role of theory also is apparent in Clinard's statement that Sutherland's theory is "arbitrary," Glueck's statement that "social processes are dogmatically shaped to fit into the prejudices of the pre-existing theory of 'differential association'," and Jeffery's statement that "the theory does not differentiate between criminal and non-criminal behavior, since both types of behavior can be learned."[17] Such statements are not so much errors in interpretation of the differential association statement as they are errors regarding the role of theory, hypotheses, and facts in scientific research. Later, we will show that Sutherland's whole theory does organize and integrate known facts about crime. Here, we need only indicate that Merton, and many others, have dispelled the notion that sociological theory is arbitrarily imposed on the facts it seeks to explain.[18]

Additional errors stemming from the form of Sutherland's formal statement, from lack of careful reading of the statement, or from assumptions necessary to conducting research, have been made, but not with the frequency of the five listed above. Among these are confusion of the concept "definition of the situation" with the word "situation,"[19] confusion of the notion that persons associate with criminal and anti-criminal behavior patterns with the notion that it is groups that associate on a differential basis,[20] belief that the theory is concerned principally with learning the *techniques* for committing crimes,[21] belief that the theory refers to learning of behavior patterns that are neither criminal nor anti-criminal in nature,[22] belief that "differential association," when used in reference to professional thieves, means maintaining "a certain necessary aloofness from ordinary people,"[23] failure to recognize that the shorthand phrase "differential association" is equivalent to "differential association with criminal and anti-criminal behavior patterns," with the consequent assumption that the theory attempts to explain all behavior, not just criminal behavior,[24] and belief that the theory is concerned only with a raw ratio of associations between the two kinds of behavior patterns and does not contain the statement, explicitly made, that "differential association may vary in frequency, duration, priority, and intensity."[25]

SOME POPULAR CRITICISMS OF DIFFERENTIAL ASSOCIATION

Identification of some of the defects that various critics have found in Sutherland's statement also should make his theory clearer. Five principal types of criticism have been advanced in the literature. It would be incorrect to assume that a criticism advanced by many readers is more valid or important than one advanced by a single reader, but commenting on every criticism would take us too far afield. We can only mention, without elaboration, some of the criticisms advanced by only one or two authors. It has been stated or implied that the theory of differential association is defective because it omits consideration of free will,[26] is based on a psychology assuming rational deliberation,[27] ignores the role of the victim,[28] does not explain the origin of crime,[29] does not define terms such as "systematic" and "excess,"[30] does not take "biological factors" into account,[31] is of little or no value to "practical men,"[32] is not comprehensive enough because it is not interdisciplinary,[33] is not allied closely enough with more general sociological theory and research,[34] is too comprehensive because it applies to non-criminals,[35] and assumes that all persons have equal access to criminal and anti-criminal behavior patterns.[36] Some of these comments represent pairs of opposites, one criticism contradicting another, and others seem to be based on one or more of the errors described above. Still others are closely allied with the five principal types of criticism, and we shall return to them.

One popular form of "criticism" of differential association is not, strictly speaking, criticism at all. At least ten scholars have speculated that some kinds of criminal behavior are exceptional to the theory. Thus, it has been said that the theory does not apply to rural offenders,[37] to landlords who violated OPA regulations,[38] to criminal violators of financial trust,[39] to "naive check forgers,"[40] to white-collar criminals,[41] to perpetrators of "individual" and "personal" crimes,[42] to irrational and impulsive criminals,[43] to "adventitious" and/or "accidental" criminals,[44] to "occasional," "incidental," and "situational" offenders,[45] to murderers, non-professional shoplifters and non-career type of criminals,[46] to persons who commit crimes of passion,[47] and to men whose crimes were perpetrated under emotional stress.[48] It is significant that only the first five comments—those referring to rural offenders, landlords, trust violators, check forgers, and some white-collar criminals—are based on research. It also is significant that at least two authors have simply stated that the theory is subject to criticism because there are exceptions to it; the kind of behavior thought to be exceptional is not specified.[49]

The fact that most of the comments are not based on research means that the "criticisms" actually are proposals for research. Should a person conduct research on a particular type of offender and find that the theory does not hold, a revision is called for, providing the research actually tested the theory, or part of it. As indicated, this procedure has been used in five instances, and these instances need to be given careful attention. But in most cases, there is no evidence that the kind of behavior said to be exceptional is exceptional. For example, we do not know that "accidental" or "incidental" or "occasional" criminals have not gone through the process specified by Sutherland. Perhaps it is assumed that some types of criminal behavior are "obviously exceptional." However, a theoretical analysis indicated that one type of behavior that appears to be obviously exceptional—"compulsive criminality"—is not necessarily exceptional at all.[50]

A second principal kind of criticism attacks the theory because it does not adequately take into account the "personality traits," "personality factors," or "psychological variables" in criminal behavior. This is a real criticism, for it suggests that Sutherland's statement neglects an important determinant of criminality. Occasionally, the criticism is linked with the apparent assumption that some kinds of criminality are "obviously" exceptional. However, at least a dozen authors have proposed that Sutherland's statement is defective because it omits or overlooks the general role of personality traits in determining criminality.[51]

Sutherland took this kind of criticism seriously, and in an early period he stated that his theory probably would have to be revised to take account of personality traits.[52] Later he pointed out what he believed to be the fundamental weakness in his critics' argument: "Personality traits" and "personality" are words that merely specify a condition, like feeblemindedness, without showing the relationship between that condition and criminality. He posed three questions for advocates of "personality traits" as supplements to differential association: (1) What are the personality traits that should be regarded as significant? (2) Are there personal traits, to be used as supplements to differential association, which are not already included in the concept of differential association? (3) Can differential association, which is essentially a *process* of learning, be combined with personal traits, which are essentially the *product* of learning?[53]

Sutherland did not attempt to answer these questions, but the context of his discussion indicates his belief that differential association does explain why some persons with a trait like "aggressiveness" commit crimes, while other persons possessing the same trait do not. It also reveals his conviction that terms like "personality traits," "personality," and "psychogenic trait components" are (when used, with no further elaboration, to explain why a person becomes a criminal) synonyms for "unknown conditions."

Closely allied with the "personality trait" criticism is the assertion that Sutherland's statement does not adequately take into account the "response" patterns, "acceptance" patterns, and "receptivity" patterns of various individuals.[54] The essential notion here is that differential association emphasizes the social process of transmission but minimizes the individual process of reception. Stated in another way, the idea is that the theory of differential association deals only with external variables and does not take into account the meaning to the recipient of the various patterns of behavior presented to him in situations which are objectively quite similar but nevertheless variable, according to the recipient's perception of them. One variety of this type of criticism takes the form of asserting that criminals and non-criminals are sometimes reared in the "same environment"—criminal behavior patterns are presented to two persons, but only one of them becomes a criminal.

Sutherland was acutely aware of the social psychological problem posed by such concepts as "differential response patterns." Significantly, his proposed solution to the problem was his statement of the theory of differential association.[55] One of the principal objectives of the theory is to account for differences in individual responses to opportunities for crime and in individual responses to criminal behavior patterns presented. To illustrate, one person who walks by an unguarded and open cash register, or who is informed of the presence of such a condition in a nearby store, may perceive the situation as a "crime committing" one, while another person in the identical circumstances may perceive the situation as one in which the owner should be warned against carelessness. The difference in these two perceptions, Sutherland held, is due to differences in the prior associations with the two types of definition of situation, so that the alternatives in behavior are accounted for in terms of differential association. The differential in "response pattern," or the difference in "receptivity" to the criminal behavior pattern presented, then, is accounted for by differential association itself.[56] Elsewhere, we have insisted that one of the greatest defects in Sutherland's theory is its implication that receptivity to any behavior pattern presented is determined by the patterns presented earlier, that receptivity to those early presentations was determined by even earlier presentations, and so on back to birth.[57] But this is an assertion that the theory cannot be tested, not an assertion that it does not take into account the "differential response patterns" of individuals.

If "receptivity" is viewed in a different way, however, the critics appear to be on firm ground.[58] Sutherland did not identify what constitutes a definition "favorable to" or "unfavorable to" the violation of law, but he recognized that the same objective definition might be "favorable" or "unfavorable," depending on the relationship between the donor and the recipient. Consequently, he said that differential associations may vary in "intensity," which was not precisely defined but "has to do with such things as the prestige of the source of a criminal or anti-criminal pattern and with emotional reactions to the associations." This attempt at what is now called "reference group theory" merely begs the question; it tells us that some associations are to be given added *weight,* but it does not tell us how, or whether, early associations affect the *meaning* of later associations. If earlier associations determine whether a person will later identify specific behavior patterns as "favorable" or "unfavorable" to law violation, then these earlier associations determine the very meaning of the later ones, and do not merely give added weight to them. In other words, whether a person is prestigeful or not prestigeful to another may be determined by experiences that have nothing to do with criminality and anticriminality. Nevertheless, these experiences affect the meaning (whether "favorable" or "unfavorable") of patterns later presented to the person and, thus, they affect his "receptivity" to the behavior patterns.[59]

A fourth kind of criticism is more damaging than the first three, for it insists that the ratio of learned behavior patterns used by Sutherland to explain criminality cannot be determined with accuracy in specific cases. A minimum of eight authors have stated this criticism in seven different articles.[60] Short, for example, has pointed out the extreme difficulty of operationalizing terms such as "favorable to" and "unfavorable to"; nevertheless, he has devised various measures of differential association and has used them in a series of significant studies. Glaser has argued that "the phrase 'excess of definitions' itself lacks clear denotation in human experience," and Glueck has asked, "Has anybody actually counted the number of definitions favorable to violation of law and definitions unfavorable to violation of law, and demonstrated that in the pre-delinquency experience of the vast majority of delinquents and criminals, the former exceeds the latter?" In my work on trust violation, I was unable with the methods at my disposal to get embezzlers to identify specific persons or agencies from whom they learned behavior patterns favorable to trust violation. My general conclusion was, "It is doubtful that it can be shown empirically that the differential association theory applies or does not apply to crimes of financial trust violation or even to other kinds of criminal behavior."[61] I have been severely taken to task for not revising Sutherland's statement in light of this conclusion.[62] My reasons for not doing so have to do with the difference in the theory of differential association considered as a general principle which organizes and makes good sense of the data on crime rates, as compared to the theory considered only as a statement of the precise mechanism by which a person becomes a criminal. As we shall see below, a principle accounting for the distribution of deviancy, or any other phenomenon, can be valid even if a presumably coordinate theory specifying the process by which deviancy occurs in individual cases is *incorrect*, let alone untestable.

The fifth kind of criticism states in more general terms than the first four that the theory of differential association over-simplifies the process by which criminal behavior is learned. Such criticism ranges from simple assertions that the learning process is more complex than the theory states or implies,[63] to the idea that the theory does not adequately take into account some specific type of learning process, such as differential identification.[64] Between these two extremes are assertions that the theory is inadequate because it does not allow for a process in which criminality seems to be "independently invented" by the actor. I am one of the dozen authors who have advanced this kind of criticism,[65] and in this day of role theory, reference group theory, and complex learning theory, it would be foolhardy to assert that this type of general criticism is incorrect. But it is one thing to criticize the theory for failure to specify the learning process accurately and another to specify which aspects of the learning process should be included and in what way.[66] Clinard's and Glaser's attempts to utilize the process of identification, and Weinberg's, Sykes and Matza's, and my own efforts to utilize more general symbolic interactionist theory, seem to be the only published attempts that specifically substitute alternative learning processes for the mechanistic process specified by Sutherland. Even these attempts are, like Sutherland's statement, more in the nature of general indications of the kind of framework or orientation one should use in formulating a theory of criminality than they are statements of theory.

DIFFERENTIAL ASSOCIATION AND THE EPIDEMIOLOGY OF CRIME

We have already indicated that Sutherland's short, formal statement emphasizes the problem of explaining variations in the criminality of individuals but is designed to account for differences in crime rates as well. However, only a careful reader of the statement can discern that it is concerned with making sense of the gross facts about crime, rather than concentrating exclusively on individual criminality.[67] On the other hand, examination of Sutherland's writings clearly indicates that he was greatly, if not primarily, concerned with organizing and integrating the factual information about crime rates. In his account of how the theory of differential association developed, he made the following three points, which are sufficient to establish his concern for the epidemiology of crime.

> More significant for the development of the theory were certain questions which I raised in class discussions. One of these questions was, Negroes, young-adult males, and city dwellers all have relatively high crime rates: What do these three groups have in common that places them in this position? Another question was, Even if feeble-minded persons have a high crime rate, why do they commit crimes? It is not feeble-mindedness as such, for some feeble-minded persons do not commit crimes. Later I raised another question which became even more important in my search for generalizations. Crime rates have a high correlation with poverty if considered by areas of a city but a low correlation if considered chronologically in relation to the business cycle; this obviously means that poverty as such is not

an important cause of crime. How are the varying associations between crime and poverty explained?[68]

It was my conception that a general theory should take account of all the factual information regarding crime causation. It does this either by organizing the multiple factors in relation to each other or by abstracting them from certain common elements. It does not, or should not, neglect or eliminate any factors that are included in the multiple factor theory.[69]

The hypothesis of differential association seemed to me to be consistent with the principal gross findings in criminology. It explained why the Mollaccan children became progressively delinquent with length of residence in the deteriorated area of Los Angeles, why the city crime rate is higher than the rural crime rate, why males are more delinquent than females, why the crime rate remains consistently higher in deteriorated areas of cities, why the juvenile delinquency rate in a foreign nativity is high while the group lives in a deteriorated area and drops when the group moves out of the area, why second-generation Italians do not have the high murder rate their fathers had, why Japanese children in a deteriorated area of Seattle had a low delinquency rate even though in poverty, why crimes do not increase greatly in a period of depression. All of the general statistical facts seem to fit this hypothesis.[70]

It appears, then, that in writing about differential association Sutherland was trying to say, for example, that a high crime rate in urban areas can be considered the end product of social conditions that lead to a situation in which relatively large proportions of persons are presented with an excess of criminal behavior patterns. Similarly, the fact that the rate for all crimes is not higher in some urban areas than it is in some rural areas can be attributed to differences in conditions which affect the probabilities of exposure to criminal behavior patterns.[71] The important general point is that in a multi-group type of social organization, alternative and inconsistent standards of conduct are possessed by various groups, so that an individual who is a member of one group has a high probability of learning to use legal means for achieving success, or learning to deny the importance of success, while an individual in another group learns to accept the importance of success and to achieve it by illegal means. Stated in another way, there are alternative educational processes in operation, varying with groups, so that a person may be educated in either conventional or criminal means of achieving success. Sutherland sometimes called this situation "differential social organization" or "differential group organization," and he proposed that "Differential group organization should explain the crime rate, while differential association should explain the criminal behavior of a person. The two explanations must be consistent with each other."[72]

It should be noted that, in the quotations above, Sutherland referred to his statement as both a "theory" and a "hypothesis," and did not indicate any special concern for distinguishing between differential association as it applies to the epidemiology of crime and differential association as it applies to individual conduct. In order to avoid controversy about the essential characteristics of theories and hypotheses, we prefer to call differential association, as it is used in reference to crime rates, a "principle." Because sociology seems to be dominated by a logic and methodology derived from physics, through psychology, sociologists are reluctant to label a statement "theory" unless it is a generalization sufficiently detailed to permit derivation of predictive hypotheses that can be put to test by gathering *new* facts. Nevertheless, it might be argued that many "theories" in sociology are in fact principles that order *known* facts about rates—now called epidemiology—in some way, and that they only in very general ways specify directions for accumulation of new facts that might prove them wrong. Durkheim, for example, invented what may be termed a "principle of group integration" to account for, organize logically, and integrate systematically the data on variations in suicide rates. He did not invent a theory of suicide, derive hypotheses from it, and then collect data to determine whether the hypotheses were correct or incorrect. He tried to "make sense" of known facts about rates, and the principle he suggested remains the most valuable idea available to persons who would understand the differences in the rates of suicide between Protestants and Jews, urban dwellers and rural dwellers, etc.

We suggest, similarly, that Sutherland's statement is a "principle of normative conflict" which proposes that high crime rates occur in societies and groups characterized by conditions that lead to the development of extensive criminalistic subcultures. Sutherland made some attempt to account for the origins of these subcultures,[73] but he did not concentrate on this problem any more than Durkheim concentrated on attempting to account for the fact that Jewish families seem more closely integrated than non-Jewish families. He "made sense" of variations in crime rates by observing that modern societies are organized for crime as well as against it, and then observing further that crime rates are unequally distributed because of differences in the degree to which various categories of persons participate in this normative conflict.

DARWINISM AND SUTHERLANDISM

The value of general principles like "normative conflict" can be further established by returning to a comparison of Darwin and Sutherland. Although Darwin's contribution is called the "theory of evolution" and Sutherland's is called the "theory of differential association," both had two distinct parts. There is a remarkable similarity in the goals of the two "theories," the logic on which they are based, and the defects in them. Darwin invented the principle of natural selection, with its implication of evolution, to account for the strange distribution of "deviant" biological specimens and the forms of plant and animal life. Next, he tried to specify the process by which this principle of natural selection "works" in individual cases. Sutherland invented the principle of normative conflict to account for the strange distribution of high and low crime rates; he then tried to specify the mechanism by which this principle works to produce individual cases of criminality. The mechanism proposed is differential association:

> The second concept, differential association, is a statement of [normative] conflict from the point of view of the person who commits the crime. The two kinds of culture impinge on him or he has association with the two kinds of cultures and this is differential association.[74]

Darwin had three principal advantages over Sutherland. First, his emphasis was on the "epidemiological" part of his theory, rather than on the "individual conduct" part. His principle of natural selection ordered a wide range of facts that had been minutely detailed by thousands of careful observers. He knew quite precisely what facts his principle had to fit. For at least a century prior to *Origin of Species,* observation of the wonders of nature had been almost a national pastime in England. Great numbers of persons who, like Darwin, had little formal training in science were recording observations of biological and physical phenomena.[75] In the fifty years before *Origin,* at least a half dozen persons, including Darwin's grandfather, tried to put order into all these data by formulating something like a principle of natural selection. After publication of *Origin of Species,* the principle became a "hit" because it stirred up religious controversy, but also because thousands of amateur scientists could, like the professionals, check it against their own small world of observations and agree or disagree.

In contrast, Sutherland presented his theory to a world that knew little about crime and cared little about understanding it. Twenty-five years ago, the study of crime probably was more popular than it is at present, but detailed, precise observations were being made by only a handful of persons. As today, careful observations were being made largely by academic sociologists, and the amateurs in the field were more concerned with doing something about crime than they were in knowing about it. Moreover, much work in criminology was, and still is, sporadic and slipshod, so that we cannot be sure that the "facts" about crime are facts at all. Sutherland tried to induce order in what facts we have, sparse as they may be. His principle organized only a narrow range of observations which were not always valid, and which were known to only a handful of dedicated souls.

Moreover, Sutherland handicapped himself by presenting the principle as an appendage to a well-established textbook, and by not explicitly trying to show in a formal statement how the principle helped to integrate and organize the existing data on crime. He needed to confront the reader with an overwhelming number of valid observations that somehow seemed less likely to be mere happenstance occurrences after his principle was stated than they had seemed before it was stated. It seems likely that Sutherland did not try to promote his principle because of a characteristic he had in common with Darwin—extreme modesty. It is conceivable that he did not completely commit himself to his principle, in the form of a major publication like *Origin*, for the same reason that Darwin published four monographs on barnacles, none of them containing any reference to his principle, between the time he formulated the principle and the time he published it.[76] Sutherland was well aware of the failure of previous theories about crime, and he did not want to get too committed to his own formulation.[77]

Second, it was to Darwin's advantage that *Origin of Species* eventually attracted the attention of his professional colleagues; Sutherland's theoretical work is still so unknown even among sociologists that in at least two instances the words "differential association" have been invented as concepts describing phenomena quite unrelated to crime.[78] Publication in a textbook, as compared to a monograph, probably had some effect on this difference. Also, there is a tendency among sociologists to think of criminology as a distinct discipline, rather than observing that criminologists like Sutherland are interested in data on crime for the same theoretical reasons that other sociologists are interested in data on industry, family life, and politics. Sutherland's principle remains unknown to almost all psychiatrists, psychologists, and social workers.

The third, and by far the most important, advantage Darwin had over Sutherland was a set of research workers who appeared on the scene to correct him as well as criticize him. In simple fact, Sutherland's Mendel, Fisher, and Wright have not appeared. It turned out that Darwin was quite wrong after all. His principle of natural selection became one of the most important ideas in the history of man, but it was founded on an erroneous conception of the mechanisms by which heredity takes place in individual cases. Darwin adhered to the incorrect but popular "paint pot" theory that viewed heredity as a blending process, and because of this adherence he eventually had to joint the Lamarckian geneticists, holding that mysterious particles called "pangenes" are modified by environmental conditions and are then gathered together to form the hereditary elements of the sperm or egg.[79] Although Mendel "corrected" Darwin when he published his discovery in 1866, his work did not become known and understood until the turn of the century. Since then, research in genetics has given Darwin's principle what it most needed—mathematically precise statements of the process by which natural selection "works." What has remained of Darwin himself is his important first principle, the principle of natural selection, and not his ideas about genetics.

There are no known published accounts of research that would carefully quantify or in some other way induce exact precision in Sutherland's statement of the process by which normative conflict "works" to produce criminality in individual cases. The most significant work has been done by Daniel Glaser and James F. Short, Jr. Although critics agree, as we have indicated, that the differential association statement oversimplifies the process by which normative conflict "gets into" persons and produces criminality, an acceptable substitute that is consistent with the principle of normative conflict has not appeared.

THE VALUE OF DIFFERENTIAL ASSOCIATION

We have suggested that Sutherland, like Darwin, tried to formulate a principle that would organize available factual information on a type of deviation and then tried to specify the process by which that principle operates in individual cases of deviation. Sutherland's critics have argued that his specification of the latter process is incorrect, just as Darwin's specification of the hereditary process was incorrect. But inaccuracy in specifying the mechanism for becoming a criminal does not necessarily negate the value of the general principle, as the history of Darwinism has shown.

As an organizing principle, normative conflict makes understandable most of the variations in crime rates discovered by various researchers and observers, and it also focusses attention on crucial research areas.[80] In a publication to appear early next year, I have listed over thirty facts about the statistical distribution of crime by age, sex, race, nativity, size of community, and social class; and then examined the capacity of various criminological theories to integrate them logically.[81] The principle of normative conflict does not make good sense out of all the facts, but it seems to make better sense out of more of the facts than do any of the alternative theories. Probably we should not expect the principle to fit all the observations to which it might be applied. As the physicist-philosopher Phillipp Frank has said, "There is certainly no theory which is in complete agreement with all our observations. If we require complete agreement, we can certainly achieve it by merely recording the observations."[82]

On the other hand, it also seems safe to conclude that differential association is not a precise statement of the process by which one becomes a criminal. The idea that criminality is a consequence of an excess of intimate associations with criminal behavior patterns is valuable because, for example, it negates assertions that deviation from norms is simply a product of being emotionally insecure or living in a broken home, and then indicates in a general way why only some emotionally insecure persons and only some persons from broken homes commit crimes. Also, it directs attention to the idea that an efficient explanation of individual conduct is consistent with explanations of epidemiology. Yet the statement of the differential association process is not precise enough to stimulate rigorous empirical test, and it therefore has not been proved or disproved. This defect is shared with broader social psychological theory. As Schrag has pointed out, "The individual internalizes the norms of his group," and "Stimulus patterns that are active at the time of a response eventually acquire the capacity to elicit the response," are illustrations of assertions which cannot be confirmed or denied but which stand, at present, as substitutes for descriptions of the process by which persons learn social behavior.[83] Criminological theory can be no more precise than the general sociological theory and general social psychological theory of which it is a part.

It is important to observe, however, that the "individual conduct" part of Sutherland's statement does order data on individual criminality in a general way and, consequently, might be considered a principle itself. Thus, "differential association" may be viewed as a restatement of the principle of normative conflict, so that this one principle is used to account for the distribution of criminal and non-criminal behavior in both the life of the individual *and* in the statistics on collectivities. In this case, both individual behavior data and epidemiological rate data may be employed as indices of the variables in the principle, thus providing two types of hypotheses for testing it.[84] Glaser has recently shown that differential association makes sense of both the predictive efficiency of some parole prediction items and the lack of predictive efficiency of other items.[85] In effect, he tested the principle by determining whether parole prediction procedures which could have proven it false actually failed to prove it false. First, he shows that a majority of the most accurate predictors in criminological prediction research are deducible from differential association theory while the least accurate predictors are not deducible at all. Second, he shows that this degree of accuracy does not characterize alternative theories. Finally, he notes that two successful predictors of parole violation—type of offense and non-criminal employment opportunities—are not necessarily deducible from the theory, and he suggests a modification that would take this fact into account.

Future research on differential association might specify in more detail the mechanisms by which one becomes a criminal, but it probably will do so only if sociologists recognize the epidemiological principle with which the process is consistent. While it might be argued that Darwin's "theory of evolution" can only be illustrated, not tested, it is clear that genetics has been profoundly affected by Darwin's scientific desire to generalize broadly on his, and others' observations of the distribution of species.[86] Similarly, Sutherland's "theory of normative conflict" tends to be tautological and might not be testable. Nevertheless, it is a starting point for theory of criminal epidemiology, and its counterpart, differential association, indicates in a general way the process which should be closely studied as a first step to development of efficient theory of individual criminal conduct.

NOTES

1. Donald R. Cressey, *Other People's Money*, Glencoe: The Free Press, 1953.

2. Robert K. Merton, "Social Structure and Anomie," *American Sociological Review*, 3 (October, 1938), pp. 672–682.

3. Cf. Frank E. Hartung, "A Critique of the Sociological Approach to Crime and Correction," *Law and Contemporary Problems*, 23 (Autumn, 1958), pp. 703–734.

4. Richard A. Cloward, "Illegitimate Means, Anomie, and Deviant Behavior," *American Sociological Review*, 24 (April, 1959), pp. 164–176; and Richard A. Cloward and Lloyd E. Ohlin, "Types of Delinquent Subcultures," unpublished manuscript, December, 1958.

5. We do not mean to imply that this is the only general problem in criminology. In addition to the two phases of the general problem of etiology, criminologists are concerned with the sociology of criminal law and the sociology of punishment.

6. For a complete statement of Sutherland's theory, see Edwin H. Sutherland and Donald R. Cressey, *Principles of Criminology*, 5th edition, New York: Lippincott, 1955, pp. 74–81. Unless otherwise identified, all quotations of Sutherland are from these pages.

7. Robert G. Caldwell, *Criminology*, New York: Ronald Press, 1956, p. 182; Ruth S. Cavan, *Criminology*, 2nd edition, New York: Crowell, 1955, p. 701; Marshall B. Clinard, "The Process of Urbanization and Criminal Behavior," *American Journal of Sociology*, 48 (September, 1942), pp. 202–213; "Rural Criminal Offenders," *American Journal of Sociology*, 50 (July, 1944), pp. 38–45; "Criminological Theories of Violations of Wartime Regulations," *American Sociological Review*, 11 (June, 1946), pp. 258–270; "The Sociology of Delinquency and Crime," in Joseph Gittler, editor, *Review of Sociology*, New York: Wiley, 1957, p. 477; and *Sociology of Deviant Behavior*, New York: Rinehart, 1957, p. 240; H. Warren Dunham and Mary Knauer, "The Juvenile Court in Its Relationship to Adult Criminality," *Social Forces*, 32 (March, 1954), pp. 290–296; Mabel A. Elliott, *Crime in Modern Society*, New York: Harper & Bros., 1952, pp. 347–348; Sheldon Glueck, "Theory and Fact in Criminology," *British Journal of Delinquency*, 7 (October, 1956), pp. 92–109; Robert E. Lane, "Why Businessmen Violate the Law," *Journal of Criminal Law and Criminology*, 44 (July–August, 1953), pp. 151–165; Walter C. Reckless, *The Etiology of Delinquent and Criminal Behavior*, New York: Social Science Council, 1943, p. 60; James F. Short, Jr., "Differential Association and Delinquency," *Social Problems*, 4 (January, 1957), pp. 233–239; and "Differential Association with Delinquent Friends and Delinquent Behavior," *Pacific Sociological Review*, 1 (Spring, 1958), pp. 20–25; Harrison M. Trice, "Sociological Factors in Association with A.A.," *Journal of Criminal Law and Criminology*, 48 (November–December, 1957), pp. 374–386; George B. Vold, *Theoretical Criminology*, New York: Oxford University Press, 1958, pp. 194–195.

8. *Op. cit.*, p. 194.

9. Harry Elmer Barnes and Negley K. Teeters, *New Horizons in Criminology*, 3rd edition, Englewood Cliffs, New Jersey: Prentice-Hall, 1959, p. 159; Caldwell, *op. cit.*, pp. 182–183; Cavan, *op. cit.*, p. 701; Clinard, "The Process of Urbanization and Criminal Behavior," *op. cit.*; "Rural Criminal Offenders," *op. cit.*, and "Criminological Theories of Violations of Wartime Regulations," *op. cit.*; Elliott, *op. cit.*, p. 274; Daniel Glaser, "The Sociological Approach to Crime and Correction," *Law and Contemporary Problems*, 23 (Autumn, 1958), pp. 683–702; and "Differential Association and Criminological Prediction: Problems of Measurement," paper read at the annual meetings of the American Sociological Association, Chicago, September, 1959; Glueck, *op. cit.*; Lane, *op. cit.*; Reckless, *op. cit.*, p. 60; Harry M. Shulman, "The Family and Juvenile Delinquency," *Annals of the American Academy of Political and Social Science*, 261 (January, 1949), pp. 21–31; Donald R. Taft, *Criminology*, New York: Macmillan, 1956, p. 338.

10. Caldwell, *op. cit.*, pp. 182–184; Cavan, *op. cit.*, p. 701; Elliott, *op. cit.*, p. 274; Richard R. Korn and Lloyd W. McCorkle, *Criminology and Penology*, New York: Holt, 1959, pp. 297–298; Vold, *op. cit.*, pp. 197–198.

11. See Edwin H. Sutherland, *Principles of Criminology*, 3rd edition, New York: Lippincott, 1939, pp. 5–9. This statement proposed generally that systematic criminality is learned in a process of differential association but then went on to use "consistency" as one of the modes of affecting the impact of the various patterns presented in the process of association. Thus, "consistency" of the behavior patterns presented was used as a general explanation of criminality, but "consistency" also was used to describe the process by which differential association takes place. Like the word "systematic," "consistency" was deleted from the next version of the theory.

12. Edwin H. Sutherland, "Development of the Theory," in Albert K. Cohen, Alfred R. Lindesmith, and Karl F. Schuessler, editors, *The Sutherland Papers*, Bloomington: Indiana University Press, 1956, p. 21.

13. Arthur L. Leader, "A Differential Theory of Criminality," *Sociology and Social Research*, 26 (September, 1941), pp. 45–53.

14. Glueck, *op. cit.*; Clarence R. Jeffery, "An Integrated Theory of Crime and Criminal Behavior," *Journal of Criminal Law and Criminology*, 49 (March–April, 1959), pp. 533–552; Leader, *op. cit.*; Martin H. Neumeyer, *Juvenile Delinquency in Modern Society*, 2nd edition, New York: Van Nostrand, 1955, p. 152; James F. Short, Jr., "Differential Association as a Hypothesis: Problems of Empirical Testing," paper read at the annual meetings of the American Sociological Association, September, 1959; Trice, *op. cit.*; S. Kirson Weinberg, "Theories of Criminality and Problems of Prediction," *Journal of Criminal Law and Criminology*, 45 (November–December, 1954), pp. 412–429.

15. Sutherland and Cressey, *op. cit.*, p. 79.

16. *Op. cit.*, p. 182.

17. Clinard, *Sociology of Deviant Behavior, op. cit.*, p. 204; Glueck, *op. cit.*, p. 99; Jeffery, *op. cit.*, p. 537.

18. Robert K. Merton, *Social Theory and Social Structure*, rev. edition, Glencoe: The Free Press, 1957, pp. 85–117.

19. Milton L. Barron, *The Juvenile in Delinquent Society*, New York: Knopf, 1954, p. 101.

20. Elliott, *op. cit.*, p. 274.

21. Clinard, "Criminological Theories of Violations of Wartime Regulations," *op. cit.*

22. Taft writes of differential association "with others who have become relative failures or criminals," but Sutherland's theory has nothing to say about association with "failures," unless "failures" and "persons

representing criminal behavior patterns" are used synonymously. *Op. cit.;* p. 338.

23. Walter C. Reckless, *The Crime Problem,* 2nd edition, New York: Appleton-Century-Crofts, 1955, p. 169. This kind of error may stem from Sutherland himself, for in his work on the professional thief he used the term "differential association" to characterize the members of the behavior system, rather than to describe the process presented in the first statement of his theory, two years later. See Edwin H. Sutherland, *The Professional Thief,* Chicago: University of Chicago Press, 1937, pp. 206–207.

24. Howard B. Gill, "An Operational View of Criminology," *Archives of Criminal Psychodynamics,* October, 1957, p. 284; Jeffery, *op. cit.*

25. Clinard, "Criminological Theories of Violations of Wartime Regulations," *op. cit.* If these "modalities," as Sutherland called them, are ignored, then the theory would equate the impact of a behavior pattern presented once in a radio show with the impact of a pattern presented numerous times to a child who deeply loved and respected the donor. It does not so equate the patterns.

26. Caldwell, *op. cit.,* p. 182.

27. Weinberg, *op. cit.*

28. Clinard, "The Sociology of Delinquency and Crime, *op. cit.,* p. 479.

29. Jeffery, *op. cit.,* p. 537.

30. Leader, *op. cit.;* Caldwell, *op. cit.;* Marshall B. Clinard, "Criminological Research," in Robert K. Merton, Leonard Broom, and Leonard Cottrell, editors, *Sociology Today,* New York: Basic Books, 1959, pp. 510–513; Short, "Differential Association and Delinquency," *op. cit.*

31. Barnes and Teeters, *op. cit.,* p. 159; Caldwell, *op. cit.,* p. 182; Gill, *op. cit.,* pp. 289–291; Glueck, *op. cit.,* pp. 98–99; Olof Kinberg, "Kritiska reflexioner över den differentiella associationhypotesen," Chapter 24, in Ivar Agge, Gunnar Boalt, Bo Gerle, Maths Heuman, Carl-Gunnar Janson, Olof Kinberg, Sven Rengby, Torgny Segerstedt, and Thorsten Sellin, *Kriminologi,* Stockholm: Wahlstrom and Widstrand, 1955, pp. 415–429.

32. Barnes and Teeters, *op. cit.,* p. 210.

33. *Ibid.,* p. 162; Caldwell, *op. cit.,* p. 182; Gill, *op. cit.,* p. 284; Glueck, *op. cit.,* pp. 105, 108; Howard Jones, *Crime and the Penal System,* London: University Tutorial Press, 1956, p. 95.

34. Clarence Schrag, "Review of Principles of Criminology," *American Sociological Review,* 20 (August, 1955), pp. 500–501.

35. Gill, *op. cit.,* p. 284; Jeffery, *op. cit.,* p. 537.

36. Cloward, *op. cit.;* Short, "Differential Association as a Hypothesis," *op. cit.,* p. 3.

37. Clinard, "The Process of Urbanization and Criminal Behavior," and "Rural Criminal Offenders," *op. cit.*

38. Clinard, "Criminological Theories of Violations of Wartime Regulations," *op. cit.*

39. Donald R. Cressey, "Application and Verification of the Differential Association Theory," *Journal of Criminal Law and Criminology,* 43 (May-June, 1952), pp. 43-52.

40. Edwin M. Lemert, "Isolation and Closure Theory of Naive Check Forgery," *Journal of Criminal Law and Criminology,* 44 (September-October, 1953), pp. 293-307.

41. Clinard, *Sociology of Deviant Behavior, op. cit.*, p. 240; Korn and McCorkle, *op. cit.*, pp. 299-300.

42. Marshall B. Clinard, "Criminal Behavior Is Human Behavior," *Federal Probation,* 13 (March, 1949), pp. 21-27; "Research Frontiers in Criminology," *British Journal of Delinquency,* 7 (October, 1956), pp. 110-122; *Sociology of Deviant Behavior, op. cit.*, p. 229; and "Criminological Research," *op. cit.*, p. 512.

43. Elliot, *op. cit.*, p. 402; Vold, *op. cit.*, pp. 197-198.

44. Clinard, "Criminological Research," *op. cit.*, p. 511; Elliott, *op. cit.*, p. 402; Jeffery, *op. cit.*; Daniel Glaser, "Criminality Theories and Behavioral Images," *American Journal of Sociology,* 61 (March, 1956), p. 441.

45. Elliott, *op. cit.*, p. 402; Clinard, "Criminological Research," *op. cit.*, p. 512.

46. *Ibid.*

47. Jeffery, *op. cit.*

48. Elliot, *op. cit.*, pp. 347-348.

49. Barnes and Teeters, *op. cit.*, p. 159; Taft, *op. cit.*, p. 340.

50. Donald R. Cressey, "The Differential Association Theory and Compulsive Crimes," *Journal of Criminal Law and Criminology,* 45 (May-June, 1954), pp. 49-64.

51. Barnes and Teeters, *op. cit.*, p. 159; Barron, *op. cit.*, p. 147; Caldwell, *op. cit.*, pp. 179, 182, 184; Clinard, "Criminological Theories of Violations of Wartime Regulations," *op. cit.*; "Sociologists and American Criminology," *Journal of Criminal Law and Criminology,* 41 (January-February, 1951), pp. 549-577; "The Sociology of Delinquency and Crime," *op. cit.*; *Sociology of Deviant Behavior, op. cit.*, pp. 204-205, 229, 240 241; Gill, *op. cit.*, p. 286; Glueck, *op. cit.*, p. 97; Kinberg, *op. cit.*; Lane, *op. cit.*; Leader, *op. cit.*; S. F. Lottier, "Tension Theory of Criminal Behavior," *American Sociological Review,* 7 (December, 1942), pp. 840-848; Neumeyer, *op. cit.*, pp. 152-153; Short, "Differential Association as a Hypothesis," *op. cit.*, p. 4; Vold, *op. cit.*, p. 197.

52. Sutherland, "Development of the Theory" (1942), *op. cit.*, pp. 25-27.

53. Edwin H. Sutherland, *White Collar Crime,* New York: Dryden, 1949, p. 272.

54. John C. Ball, "Delinquent and Non-Delinquent Attitudes Toward the Prevalence of Stealing," *Journal of Criminal Law and Criminology,* 48 (September-October, 1957), pp. 259–274; Caldwell, *op. cit.,* p. 182; Clinard, "The Process of Urbanization and Criminal Behavior," *op. cit.;* "Sociologists and American Criminology," *op. cit.; Sociology of Deviant Behavior, op. cit.,* pp. 240–241; and "Criminological Research," *op. cit.;* Glueck, *op. cit.;* Jeffery, *op. cit.;* Korn and McCorkle, *op. cit.,* p. 298; Leader, *op. cit.;* Neumeyer, *op. cit.,* p. 152; Reckless, *The Crime Problem, op. cit.,* p. 109; and *The Etiology of Delinquent and Criminal Behavior, op. cit.,* p. 62; Trice, *op. cit.;* Vold, *op. cit.,* p. 196; Weinberg, *op. cit.*

55. See Edwin H. Sutherland, "Susceptibility and Differential Association," in Cohen, Lindesmith, and Schuessler, *op. cit.,* pp. 42–43. See also Solomon Kobrin, "The Conflict of Values in Delinquency Areas," *American Sociological Review,* 16 (October, 1951), pp. 653–661.

56. *Cf.* Ralph L. Beals, "Acculturation," in A. L. Kroeber, editor, *Anthropology Today,* Chicago: University of Chicago Press, 1953, pp. 621–641; and Richard Thurnwald, "The Psychology of Acculturation," *American Anthropologist,* 34 (October–December, 1932), pp. 557–569.

57. Cressey, "Application and Verification of the Differential Association Theory," *op. cit.*

58. I am indebted to Albert K. Cohen for assistance with this paragraph and with other points. Also, I am grateful to the following persons for suggested modifications of the original draft: Daniel Glaser, Sheldon Glueck, Michael Hakeem, Frank Hartung, C. Ray Jeffery, Richard T. Morris, Melvin Seeman, James F. Short, Jr., and George B. Vold.

59. This actually is the important point Vold was making in the quotation cited at footnote 8 above.

60. Ball, *op. cit.;* Clinard, "Criminological Research," *op. cit.;* Cressey, "Application and Verification of the Differential Association Theory," *op. cit.;* Glaser, "Criminality Theories and Behavioral Images," *op. cit.;* Glueck, *op. cit.,* p.96; Lane, *op. cit.;* Reckless, *The Etiology of Delinquent and Criminal Behavior, op. cit.,* p. 63; Schrag, *op. cit.;* Short, "Differential Association and Delinquency," *op. cit.;* "Differential Association as a Hypothesis," *op. cit.*

61. Cressey, "Application and Verification of the Differential Association Theory," *op. cit.,* p. 52.

62. Caldwell, *op. cit.,* p. 185.

63. See, for example, Ball, *op. cit.*

64. See, for example, Clinard, "The Process of Urbanization and Criminal Behavior," *op. cit.;* and Glaser, "Criminality Theories and Behavior Images," *op. cit.*

65. Caldwell, *op. cit.*, p. 183; Clinard, "The Sociology of Delinquency and Crime," *op. cit.*; and "Criminological Research," *op. cit.*; Cressey, "Application and Verification of the Differential Association Theory," *op. cit.*; and "The Differential Association Theory and Compulsive Crime," *op. cit.*; Daniel Glaser, "Review of *Principles of Criminology*," *Federal Probation*, 20 (December, 1956), pp. 66–67; "The Sociological Approach to Crime and Correction," *op. cit.*; and "Differential Association and Criminological Prediction," *op. cit.*; Glueck, *op. cit.*, pp. 93, 97; Korn and McCorkle, *op. cit.*, p. 299; Leader, *op. cit.*; Short, "Differential Association as a Hypothesis," *op. cit.*; Gresham Sykes and David Matza, "Techniques of Neutralization: A Theory of Delinquency," *American Sociological Review*, 22 (December, 1957), pp. 664–670; Weinberg, *op. cit.*

66. Despite the fact that Sutherland described a learning process, it should be noted that he protected himself by saying, "The process of learning criminal and anti-criminal patterns involves all the mechanisms that are involved in any other learning."

67. One of Sutherland's own students, colleagues, and editors has said, "Much that travels under the name of sociology of deviant behavior or of social disorganization is psychology—some of it very good psychology, but psychology. For example, Sutherland's theory of differential association, which is widely regarded as preeminently sociological, is not the less psychological because it makes much of the cultural milieu. It is psychological because it addresses itself to the question: How do people become the kind of individuals who commit criminal acts? A sociological question would be: What is it about the structure of social systems that determines the kinds of criminal acts that occur in these systems and the way in which such acts are distributed within these systems?" Albert K. Cohen, "The Study of Social Disorganization and Deviant Behavior," Chapter 21 in Robert K. Merton, Leonard Broom, and Leonard S. Cottrell, Jr., editors, *Sociology Today*, New York: Basic Books, 1959, p. 462.

68. Sutherland, "Development of the Theory," *op. cit.*, p. 15.

69. *Ibid.*, p. 18.

70. *Ibid.*, pp. 19 20.

71. *Cf.* Henry D. McKay, "Differential Association and Crime Prevention: Problems of Utilization," unpublished paper read at the annual meetings of the American Sociological Association, Chicago, September, 1959.

72. Sutherland, "Development of the Theory," *op. cit.*, p. 21.

73. See Sutherland and Cressey, *op. cit.*, pp. 82–92.

74. Sutherland, "Development of the Theory," *op. cit.*, pp. 20–21.

75. The popularity of scientific concern was a social movement growing out of Calvinism, which admonished its followers to observe God's laws by observing His works, the wonders of nature. Fashionable

English ladies carried pocket microscopes, which they would train on flowers and insects while strolling through the garden. See Gerald Dennis Meyer, *The Scientific Lady in England, 1650–1750*, Los Angeles: The University of California Press, 1955.

76. It is quite possible that Darwin never would have published his principle had it not been independently formulated by Alfred R. Wallace, who threatened to scoop him. See Garrett Hardin, *Nature and Man's Fate*, New York: Rinehart, 1959, pp. 42–45.

77. Sutherland, "Development of the Theory," *op. cit.*, p. 17.

78. Ronald Freedman, Amos H. Hawley, Werner S. Landecker, and Horace M. Miner, *Principles of Sociology*, 1st edition, New York: Holt, pp. 235–238; David Gold, "On Description of Differential Association," *American Sociological Review*, 22 (August, 1957), pp. 448–450.

79. Hardin, *op. cit.*, p. 118.

80. *Cf.* Llewellyn Gross, "Theory Construction in Sociology: A Methodological Inquiry," Chapter 17 in Llewellyn Gross, editor, *Symposium on Sociological Theory*, Evanston: Row, Peterson, 1959, pp. 548–555.

81. Donald R. Cressey, "Crime," Chapter 1 in Robert A. Nisbet, editor, *Social Problems and Social Disorganization*, New York: Harcourt, Brace (forthcoming). See also Donald R. Cressey, "The State of Criminal Statistics," *National Probation and Parole Association Journal*, 3 (July, 1957), pp. 230–241.

82. *Philosophy of Science*, Englewood Cliffs, New Jersey: Prentice-Hall, 1957, p. 353; quoted by Glaser, "Differential Association and Criminological Prediction," *op. cit.*

83. Clarence Schrag, "Some Foundations for a Theory of Correction," Chapter 8 in Donald R. Cressey, editor, *The Prison: Studies in Institutional Organization and Change*, New York: Holt (forthcoming), p. 8.

84. I am indebted to Daniel Glaser for calling this point to my attention.

85. "Differential Association and Criminological Prediction," *op. cit.* See also Daniel Glaser, "A Reconsideration of Some Parole Prediction Factors," *American Sociological Review*, 19 (June, 1954), pp. 335–341; and "The Efficiency of Alternative Approaches to Parole Prediction," *American Sociological Review*, 20 (June, 1955), pp. 283–287; and Daniel Glaser and Richard F. Hangren, "Predicting the Adjustment of Federal Probationers," *National Probation and Parole Association Journal*, 4 (July, 1958), pp. 258–267.

86. *Cf.* Garrett Hardin, "The Competitive Exclusion Principle," *Science*, 131 (April, 1960), pp. 1292–1298.

CHAPTER V

Control Theory

The readings presented in the preceding chapters were written by theorists who have sought to explain how deviance develops from structural conditions in society, interactional patterns, learning techniques, and rationalizations of behavior. In a very real sense, their major concern is accounting for deviant motivation and examining those factors that are assumed to be important reasons why people acquire such motivational aspirations. While the theorists considered in this chapter have a similar interest in motivation, the thrust of their argument is directed at explaining *conformity*, on the assumption that deviance will occur naturally unless people are motivated to conform.

Drawing upon the writings of 18th- and 19th-century social philosophers, control theorists assert that human beings are basically antisocial. They assume that deviance is part of the natural order in society; that is, norm violation is inherently attractive and exciting to most people, and therefore most people are motivated to deviate if they can get away with it. However, control theorists posit that deviant motivation alone does not adequately explain why people engage in norm-violating behavior; it is more important to understand why people do obey the rules of society. Control theory therefore focuses primarily on the forces that prevent people from deviating, not on those that encourage them to deviate.

The first reading in this chapter (Reading 17) is from *Family Relationships and Delinquent Behavior* by F. Ivan Nye. He suggests that parent-adolescent relationships are a significant factor in social control and the prevention of delinquency. After briefly examining the assumptions underlying a number of major theories of delinquency, Nye concludes that while they may be useful in accounting for the delinquent behavior of some individuals, they are relatively ineffective in explaining delinquency in general. He therefore proposes a "multi-causal" theory in which inadequate social control is regarded as the principal explanation for delinquency among youth. The crux of Nye's argument is summarized in the statement, "When controls internal and external are weak and alternative routes to goal achievement are restricted, delinquent behavior can be anticipated." Nye identifies four clusters of attitude and behavior patterns that elaborate his conception of social control—internal, indirect, and direct control, and needs satisfaction. He concludes that the family is "the single factor most important in exercising social control over adolescents" and thus in preventing delinquency.

Reading 18, excerpted from Travis Hirschi's *Causes of Delinquency*, extends the basic premises of control theory outlined by Nye, with special attention to the individual's bond to others. Hirschi's basic contention is that human beings are inherently antisocial and prone to deviate unless prevented from doing so by conformity-demanding commitments to others. Because most individuals do not engage in deviance most of the time, for Hirschi the central question in explaining deviance should be, "Why don't they do it?" In answering this question, he builds upon Durkheim's claim that the extent of a person's integration in groups is of paramount importance in explaining conformity and deviance. For Hirschi, internalization of accepted norms and sensitivity to the needs of others are the central elements fostering conformity in society. Thus, an individual who is insensitive to the expectations of others and does not feel bound by norms (i.e., the bond to society has been weakened) is free to form attachments and engage in relationships with others who may favor deviant activities and life-styles.

In Reading 19, Richard Gelles develops a theory of family violence that relies heavily on the insights of control theory. He begins by reviewing available theories of why people physically abuse members of their own families. His exchange/social control theory of family violence, which incorporates principles from these two theoretical traditions, is based on the central proposition that "people hit and abuse other family members because they can." The first principle is from exchange theory, which has to do with individuals' calculation of the relative costs and benefits of an intended action. This principle is that "people will use violence in the family if the costs of being violent do not outweigh the rewards." The other principle comes directly from social control theory: "family violence occurs in the absence of social controls which would bond people to the social order and negatively sanction family members for acts of violence." Thus, stronger family members will be physically violent toward those who are weaker when they see some benefit to it and when they can get away with it without substantial costs. The benefit is often dominance, and the costs may be the victim effectively striking back, arrest or imprisonment, or a loss in status such as embarrassment at being found out as an abuser by family or friends. Gelles also shows how his theoretical model can guide strategies for social policy to reduce the level of family violence and how it can be applied in the treatment of offenders.

In the Analysis and Critique section in this chapter (Reading 20), LaMar T. Empey focuses on Hirschi's control theory of delinquency. Empey points out that Hirschi's theory has sparked a great deal of interest and controversy, particularly in reaction to its assumptions regarding human nature and its empirical adequacy. Hirschi's own research findings that delinquent youths are less attached to conventional role models and norms than conforming youths are appear to be relatively consistent with his general theory and have been substantially confirmed in other research. Hirschi's research has, however, given rise to questions about "whether lack of attachment to school precedes or follows the possession of lower aspirations,"[1] the role intelligence plays in school failure, and the importance that attachment to peers plays in the development of delinquent behavior. Empey suggests that while control theory does appeal to common-sense assumptions regarding delinquency, there is a definite need for additional testing of its basic propositions.

According to Empey, the areas most in question with Hirschi's control theory are his assumptions regarding the antisocial character of human nature and the natural propensity to deviate. Empey asserts that this part of the theory is virtually impossible to test empirically and fails to consider how opportunity structures, peers, and the structural organization of modern industrial society impact on the emergence and continuation of deviance. Thus while control theory may be correct in indicating the importance of attachment, it does not adequately consider the impact of political, economic, and demographic forces on the social bond. Nor does it adequately analyze the consequences of being publicly labeled a deviant and the effect this may have on the individual's attachment to others and resulting role behavior.

Some of the theories presented in subsequent chapters deal with these issues and examine more fully the implications of social control. One of the new directions in deviance theory discussed in Chapter VIII is the trend to treat deviance as an illness, so individuals are not held responsible for their deviant acts. Peter Conrad and Joseph W. Schneider discuss medicine as an institution of social control in Reading 32.

NOTE

1. Lamar T. Empey, *American Delinquency* (Homewood, Ill.: Dorsey Press, 1982), p. 271.

17   *Family Relationships and Delinquent Behavior*
F. IVAN NYE

◄○►

"Social disorganization" implies lack of consensus on social norms, which may occur as cultural change presents an old and new pattern of behavior and where the conflicting norms of ethnic groups intermingle. Under these conditions, social control and even socialization may become quite ineffective. If the individual is personally involved in groups with conflicting norms, the conflict is likely to become internalized with resulting personality disorganization. It often occurs during the declining periods of institutions and societies when basic values and institutional norms come to be questioned. The reasons for this type of disorganization constitute a proper field of inquiry by the historical sociologist and are outside the scope of the present inquiry.

The "delinquency sub-culture" approach describes a way of life of locality groups or of a criminal "profession." Such locality groups in which the dominant means of achieving status are criminal can be delineated, and a criminal profession with its distinctive personnel, goals, norms, attitudes, and social control beyond doubt exists. Related to this conception of delinquency is the idea that criminal behavior results from a preponderance of contacts with criminal behavior and attitudes, whether or not the person exhibiting criminal behavior is identified as a criminal.

The principal postulate of the subcultural school of thought is that crime is and must be learned, the same as any other behavior. At least implied is the companion assumption that criminal and conforming behavior are equally quick and effective as means to ends. Exception must be taken to both of these ideas. While some criminal behavior requires special skills, much does not. Most boys of 16 and over know how to drive a car. When they find a car with the key in the lock, they can steal it without any new skills. Most criminal behavior is of this type, and adaptation of noncriminal skills can easily be accomplished. Likewise, the assumption that conforming and criminal behavior are equally quick and effective means to material ends will not bear close scrutiny. Theoretically, society provides both conforming and criminal means, but the bank teller who wants to sail the Mediterranean in his own yacht will find it difficult to save the money from his salary. Similarly, the 15-year-old boy will find it difficult to sell enough papers to buy a new sports car.

The "means-ends" theory requires further identification and can properly be associated with an early essay by Merton.[1] It postulates that criminal behavior results from extreme stress on material and other success, with little value placed on conforming behavior, as such. Most stress, presumably, would be felt by the lowest income groups who could not legitimately achieve high material goals. Recent research showing extensive criminal behavior in the middle and upper classes casts doubt upon this application; however, it may prove useful in explaining the relatively high crime rate throughout American compared to some other societies.

The "culture conflict" approach might well be combined with that of social disorganization since it is one of the principal sources of such disorganization. The principal assumption appears to be that the high delinquency in certain marginal groups is related to loss of social control, although, in some cases, personality disorganization occurs also. The high delinquency rates are particularly noticeable where groups are truly marginal and live in areas in which deinquency rates are high for nonmarginal groups also. Rates are low even in slum areas for groups which cling closely to the values, ideals, and norms of their ethnic groups. Such groups as the Japanese and Chinese have experienced little cultural conflict because they have maintained their cultures and societies relatively intact. Their delinquency rates are low.

The "personality maladjustment" theory shares one important assumption with the subculture and differential association theory: that is, that criminal behavior is caused by rather than a result of the lack of adequate controls to prevent it. At this point, however, the resemblance ends. Whereas the differential association theory sees criminal behavior as the expected result of criminal socialization, the personality maladjustment theory sees it as the incidental result of disturbed emotions. The kleptomaniac steals not because he wants the object but because he feels insecure or rejected. More extreme cases of mental derangement involve murder by paranoiacs who kill their imagined persecutors.

IS DELINQUENCY CAUSED OR PREVENTED?

The relationship of the present frame of reference to contemporary delinquency theories will be limited to two dimensions. Implicit in any study in delinquency is one or the other of two assumptions. One is the assumption that deviant behavior is "produced" by the variables under study; the other is the assumption that delinquent behavior occurs *in the absence of* controls or if controls are ineffective. Those who make the first assumption are oriented to the question: "What makes people commit delinquent acts?" Those who make the second assumption are oriented to the question: "What keeps people from committing delinquent acts?" The differential association and personality maladjustment theories stress the first assumption: that delinquent behavior is caused in a positive sense. Social disorganization, culture conflict, and the means-ends formulations are primarily attempts to explain ineffective controls which allow deviant behavior.

The position here taken is that the two factors are unequally involved in delinquent behavior. Some crimes, minor and serious, can be attributed to psychotic mental states or to less serious emotional and mental maladjustment. With equal certainty a number of adolescent delinquents and adult criminals can be shown to have learned deviant behavior patterns from parents, siblings, and peers by the same socialization processes that other children learn conforming behavior. Undoubtedly some delinquent behavior results from a *combination* of positive learning and weak and ineffective social control.

The present position is that such behavior is, however, comparatively rare and that most delinquent behavior is the result of insufficient social control, broadly defined. The laws of society protect the property and person of its individual members, but in the process society makes it impossible for most of its members to quickly and conveniently achieve their major goals. For example, the quickest way for a vice-president to become president would be to murder the president, but this is frowned upon. Society likewise forbids the appropriation of bank funds by bank employees. It forbids sexual intercourse between unmarried individuals. To children and young adolescents it even forbids most types of gainful employment.

Thus society effectively forbids the satisfaction of some goals and prescribes laborious routes involving lengthy postponement to others. When controls internal and external are weak and alternative routes to goal achievement are restricted, delinquent behavior can be anticipated. It might be maintained that the impact of criminal attitudes and behavior through socialization may weaken the several types of social control, as do severe personality disorders. This appears to us to be correct, but these etiological factors are believed best left as explanations of specific criminal phenomena rather than integrated into a single monolithic theory of social control.

SINGLE OR MULTIPLE CAUSATION

Past and present theories have generally sought to explain delinquent behavior in terms of single causation. The limitation of all single-cause theories is that they are unable to account for all cases. When this limitation becomes apparent there is some disposition to discard them as "disproved," while in fact they may be most useful in explaining some portion of the phenomena.

One alternative to single-cause explanations of criminal behavior is to subdivide it into smaller categories. Instead of criminal behavior considered as a whole, it may be subcategorized into "neurotic crime," "goal-directed crime," "socialized crime," and possibly others. If such subcategories are indeed more homogeneous than delinquent behavior as a whole, a single cause presumably would be more effective in explaining such sub-categories. This procedure may have considerable merit if these are, in fact, discrete categories, but a single individual in a single act may reveal the influence of a criminal environment, personal disorganization, and an intense desire for the object or experience in and for itself.

For these reasons the present frame of reference is multi-causal. It embraces a broad social control framework that sees most criminal behavior as a failure of controls, but does not deny the usefulness of delinquency sub-culture and personality disorganization approaches in the explanation of the behavior of some individuals, or that such "positive" factors sometimes combine with weak controls with delinquent behavior as the product.

SOCIAL CONTROL AND DELINQUENT BEHAVIOR

It is now generally agreed that instincts play a minor if not nonexistent role in human behavior. The human infant has no concept of "right" dress, safe driving speeds, moral sex behavior, private property, or any of the other norms of the society, whether custom or law. Conformity, not deviation, must be learned.

Older children and adults, of course, ordinarily do understand the prohibitions and duties fixed by society. Such knowledge does not, however, lessen biological or psychological needs, nor obscure perception that such needs can be met immediately provided law and custom are ignored or circumvented. It is our position, therefore, that in general behavior prescribed as delinquent or criminal need not be explained in any positive sense, since it usually results in quicker and easier achievement of goals than the normative behavior. The processes, agencies, and relationships which prevent it are the subject of social control as applied to delinquency. Social control is relevant also for non-utilitarian delinquent behavior, but the concept of personality disorganization is probably more useful for the explanation of non-utilitarian behavior.

Laws are generally negative in that they prescribe duties or prohibit behavior. They are, therefore, intrinsically difficult to enforce, even though deviation is rare in some societies.

The present conception of social control embraces four *not unrelated* clusters of attitude and behavior patterns: (1) direct control imposed from without by means of restriction and punishment, (2) internalized control exercised from within through conscience, (3) indirect control related to affectional identification with parents and other non-criminal persons, and (4) availability of alternative means to goals and values.[2]

INTERNAL CONTROL

Every society attempts to internalize its mores by integrating them into the developing conscience of the child. This control is both economical, since it is self-enforcing, and pervasive, since it is lost only when the person loses effective consciousness. If it were entirely effective, other types of control would be unnecessary. Since violation of the mores is found in every society, it can be assumed that such internalized control is never completely accomplished in any large group. Lack of effectiveness may be related to lack of agreement on the mores, frustration by the mores of the achievement of basic values, and limitations on guilt as a punishment factor. Related to lack of agreement on the mores and the frustration of values is the consistency with which adults provide conforming models for the child.

An additional factor in conscience formation may lie in the parent-child relationship itself. It is probable that few children accept the teachings of the parent unless they accept the "teacher" (parent).

INDIRECT CONTROL

Case studies in social control indicate affection for parents and other conforming individuals plays a major role in the control of deviant behavior. College students frequently state that they do not want to embarrass their parents by "getting into trouble," and even more often that they do not want parents to be hurt by and disappointed in their failure.[3] The same probably holds true also for some siblings, peers, and adult friends. This indirect control, however, can be exercised only when there is an affectional relationship to the conforming individual.

PARENTS AND INDIRECT CONTROL

Traditionally, in cases where rejection existed between parent and child, the attitude of the parent has been considered, and that of the child neglected. Thomas and Znaniecki, however, were aware of rejection of parents by children and described it in their study of second-generation Polish children in the United States.[4] The parents in that instance were the bearers of the Old World culture which was in conflict with American society at innumerable points. In that situation rejection of parents was frequent. Later, Bossard described a similar rejection of rural-reared parents by their city-bred children.[5] Upwardly mobile children likewise reject parents as bearers of the lower-class culture. Any parents obviously not competing successfully with other parents of their locality or occupational groups might similarly experience elements of rejection.

Parental rejection is considered to be a relative matter. The parent may be completely accepted, partially rejected, or completely rejected. Rejection in this instance does not refer to the normal change in the parent-child relationship which occurs as the adult role is substituted for that of the child. Usually the frequency with which the adolescent makes his own decisions increases, and gradually he shifts from a dependent position to one of equality. However, there are great differences in how the adolescent change is made and in the consequences of the change. For convenience, this developing relationship will be treated in three classes. In the first class, the relationship changes from a dependent one to an affectionate, more independent status with the adolescent seeing the parent in the role of a more experienced friend. In the second class, the adolescent frees himself from the parent and does not develop active dislike or hatred. Neither does he have affection or respect, or positive and negative feelings strike a rough balance, thus forming an indifferent or somewhat ambivalent relationship. In the third class, the adolescent develops an active dislike, disrespect, or both, for the parent. These attitudes vary along a continuum. Indirect control decreases as negative feelings toward parents increase.

DIRECT CONTROL

Important as are indirect controls, and important as the parent-child relationship is in forming and maintaining them, they cannot explain all conformity. No society depends on internal and indirect controls alone. Restraint of the individual may be exercised by police and other designated officials, or entirely by disapproval, ridicule, ostracism, banishment, the supernatural, and similar techniques used by informal groups or by society as a whole.

In American society, direct control is an important part of the total. Parents exercise it as they restrict their children concerning the time allowed away from home, their choice of companions, and type of activities. They accomplish direct control by keeping children within the home, allowing and forbidding behavior outside the home, and by promising and delivering punishment for infractions of parental or societal rules. Direct control is occasionally accomplished by a system of rewards for conformity.

That direct control can be quite effective in securing conformity can be shown by numerous examples. For instance, a small town established a reputation for being "tough" on speeders. A state highway goes through the town and is used by many who are not members of the community. The reputation of the town is such that all cars from the entire region conform very closely to the speed law.

A limitation on the effectiveness of direct control is that it is effective only when the child can expect to be detected in the delinquent act, is actually within the physical limits of the home, or is otherwise under the surveillance of adults. Since there are many times when the child is outside the sphere of direct control, it cannot be effective by itself.

NEED SATISFACTION

If all the needs of the individual could be met adequately and without delay, without violating laws, there would be no point in such violation, and a minimum of internal, indirect, and direct control would suffice to secure conformity. The objection may be made that many violations are committed for the excitement of the violation itself. However, other possibilities for excitement exist besides violating laws and regulations.

No complete and generally satisfactory list of needs, either of children or adults, has been compiled. There does seem to be essential consensus on the needs for affection, recognition, and security. With children, it is perhaps justifiable to add Thomas' fourth wish, that of new experience. Although these categories do not exhaust the needs of children, they are at least a beginning.

Only some of the child's needs, particularly those of the adolescent, can be satisfied within the family. The family does, however, also greatly affect the chances the adolescent will have in satisfying his needs in the school, in his peer group, and later, in his occupation. If he is able to satisfy his needs reasonably well outside the home, in socially approved ways, there is less pressure to achieve them through delinquent behavior.

As there are limitations upon what can be achieved by indirect and direct control, so also are there limitations as to need satisfactions. Adolescents have wants that must be deferred, at least, such as for foreign sport cars, sexual satisfactions, and adult income and status. Likewise, not everyone can be the captain of the football team, the campus queen or the winner of scholarship honors. At present, there is no way that adolescents can always be made to feel loved and secure and no assurance that there will always be something interesting to do. On the other side of the ledger, there is always some work to be done to obtain, in a legitimate manner, whatever recognition and privileges are possible.

Even though complete and immediate satisfaction of needs is not ordinarily possible, families can go far toward the legitimate satisfaction of needs within the family, and they can prepare and launch the adolescent in his interaction with school, peer group, and occupation, or they can fail almost totally in helping to meet needs in and outside the family through acceptable behavior.[6]

The family is considered to be the single factor most important in exercising social control over adolescents. This is not to maintain that it is the only significant group in this respect. Peer groups in neighborhoods, schools, churches, and other formal and informal groups are important, as are certain categories of adults such as teachers, police, ministers, adult friends, and national heroes. Thus, the present study does not encompass all variables related to delinquent behavior. It studies one believed to be significant for social control, that of parent-adolescent relationships, in some detail.

NOTES

1. Robert K. Merton, "Social Structure and Anomie," *American Sociological Review,* 3 (October 1938), pp. 672–82.
2. Reiss has suggested a dichotomy of personal and social control in which the person's ability to conform is contrasted with the ability of

social groups to make controls effective. We do not feel that a dichotomy is involved because we assume that all personal controls are the result of socialization and group membership, and as such, are a measure of the effectiveness of controls exercised by the relevant social groups. Albert J. Reiss, Jr., "Delinquency as a Failure of Personal and Social Controls," *American Sociological Review,* 16 (April 1951), pp. 196–207.

3. For a number of illustrations of the latter point, see Paul H. Landis, *Social Control,* New York, J. B. Lippincott Co., 1939, Chapters 20–21.

4. W. I. Thomas and Znaniecki, *The Polish Peasant in Europe and America,* Vol. 5, Boston, Gorham Press, 1920, Chapter 5.

5. J. H. S. Bossard, *The Sociology of Child Development,* New York, Harper and Brothers, 1954, Chapter 21.

6. Zucker has suggested that the affectional bond to parents is crucial. Herbert John Zucker, "Affectional Identification and Delinquency," *Archives of Psychology,* No. 286, New York, May 1943.

18 *A Control Theory of Delinquency*
TRAVIS HIRSCHI

"The more weakened the groups to which [the individual] belongs, the less he depends on them, the more he consequently depends only on himself and recognizes no other rules of conduct than what are founded on his private interests."[1]

Control theories assume that delinquent acts result when an individual's bond to society is weak or broken. Since these theories embrace two highly complex concepts, the *bond* of the individual to *society,* it is not surprising that they have at one time or another formed the basis of explanations of most forms of aberrant or unusual behavior. It is also not surprising that control theories have described the elements of the bond to society in many ways, and that they have focused on a variety of units as the point of control.

I begin with a classification and description of the elements of the bond to conventional society. I try to show how each of these elements is related to delinquent behavior and how they are related to each other. I then turn to the question of specifying the unit to which the person is presumably more or less tied, and to the question of the adequacy of the motivational force built into the explanation of delinquent behavior.

Reprinted from *Causes of Delinquency* by Travis Hirschi. Published by The University of California Press. Copyright © 1969 The Regents of the University of California Press.

ELEMENTS OF THE BOND

ATTACHMENT

In explaining conforming behavior, sociologists justly emphasize sensitivity to the opinion of others.[2] Unfortunately, ...they tend to suggest that man *is* sensitive to the opinion of others and thus exclude sensitivity from their explanations of deviant behavior. In explaining deviant behavior, psychologists, in contrast, emphasize insensitivity to the opinion of others.[3] Unfortunately, they too tend to ignore variation, and, in addition, they tend to tie sensitivity inextricably to other variables, to make it part of a syndrome or "type," and thus seriously to reduce its value as an explanatory concept. The psychopath is characterized only in part by "deficient attachment to or affection for others, a failure to respond to the ordinary motivations founded in respect or regard for one's fellows";[4] he is also characterized by such things as "excessive aggressiveness," "lack of superego control," and "an infantile level of response."[5] Unfortunately, too, the behavior that psychopathy is used to explain often becomes part of the *definition* of psychopathy. As a result, in Barbara Wootton's words: "[The psychopath] is...*par excellence*, and without shame or qualification, the model of the circular process by which mental abnormality is inferred from anti-social behavior while anti-social behavior is explained by mental abnormality."[6]

The problems of diagnosis, tautology, and name-calling are avoided if the dimensions of psychopathy are treated as causally and therefore problematically interrelated, rather than as logically and therefore necessarily bound to each other. In fact, it can be argued that all of the characteristics attributed to the psychopath follow from, are effects of, his lack of attachment to others. To say that to lack attachment to others is to be free from moral restraints is to use lack of attainment to explain the guiltlessness of the psychopath, the fact that he apparently has no conscience or superego. In his view, lack of attachment to others is not merely a symptom of psychopathy, it *is* psychopathy; lack of conscience is just another way of saying the same thing; and the violation of norms is (or may be) a consequence.

For that matter, given that man is an animal, "impulsivity" and "aggressiveness" can also be seen as natural consequences of freedom from moral restraints. However, since the view of man as endowed with natural propensities and capacities like other animals is peculiarly unpalatable to sociologists, we need not fall back on such a view to explain the amoral man's aggressiveness.[7] The process of becoming alienated from others often involves or is based on active interpersonal conflict. Such conflict could easily supply a reservoir of *socially derived* hostility sufficient to account for the aggressiveness of those whose attachments to others have been weakened.

Durkheim said it many years ago: "We are moral beings to the extent that we are social beings."[8] This may be interpreted to mean that we are moral beings to the extent that we have "internalized the norms" of society. But what does it mean to say that a person has internalized the norms of society? The norms of society are by definition shared by the members of society. To violate a norm is, therefore, to act contrary to the wishes and expectations of other people. If a person does not care about the wishes and expectations of other people—that is, if he is insensitive to the opinion of others—then he is to that extent not bound by the norms. He is free to deviate.

The essence of internalization of norms, conscience, or superego thus lies in the attachment of the individual to others.[9] This view has several advantages over the concept of internalization. For one, explanations of deviant behavior based on attachment do not beg the question, since the extent to which a person is attached to others can be measured independently of his deviant behavior. Furthermore, change or variation in behavior is explainable in a way that it is not when notions of internalization or superego are used. For example, the divorced man is more likely after divorce to commit a number of deviant acts, such as suicide or forgery. If we explain these acts by reference to the superego (or internal control), we are forced to say that the man "lost his conscience" when he got a divorce; and, of course, if he remarries, we have to conclude that he gets his conscience back.

This dimension of the bond to conventional society is encountered in most social control-oriented research and theory. F. Ivan Nye's "internal control" and "indirect control" refer to the same element, although we avoid the problem of explaining changes over time by locating the "conscience" in the bond to others rather than making it part of the personality.[10] Attachment to others is just one aspect of Albert J. Reiss's "personal controls"; we avoid his problems of tautological empirical *observations* by making the relationship between attachment and delinquency problematic rather than definitional.[11] Finally, Scott Briar and Irving Piliavin's "commitment" or "stake in conformity" subsumes attachment, as their discussion illustrates, although the terms they use are more closely associated with the next element to be discussed.[12]

COMMITMENT

"Of all passions, that which inclineth men least to break the laws, is fear. Nay, excepting some generous natures, it is the only thing, when there is the appearance of profit or pleasure by breaking the laws, that makes men keep them."[13] Few would deny that men on occasion obey the rules simply from fear of the consequences. This rational component in conformity we label commitment. What does it mean to say that a person is committed to conformity? In Howard S. Becker's formulation it means the following:

> First, the individual is in a position in which his decision with regard to some particular line of action has consequences for other interests and activities not necessarily [directly] related to it. Second, he has placed himself in that position by his own prior actions. A third element is present though so obvious as not to be apparent: the committed person must be aware [of these other interests] and must recognize that his decision in this case will have ramifications beyond it.[14]

The idea, then, is that the person invests time, energy, himself, in a certain line of activity—say, getting an education, building up a business, acquiring a reputation for virtue. When or whenever he considers deviant behavior, he must consider the costs of this deviant behavior, the risk he runs of losing the investment he has made in conventional behavior.

If attachment to others is the sociological counterpart of the superego or conscience, commitment is the counterpart of the ego or common sense. To the person committed to conventional lines of action, risking one to ten years in prison for a ten-dollar holdup is stupidity, because to the committed person the costs and risks obviously exceed ten dollars in value. (To the psychoanalyst, such an act exhibits failure to be governed by the "reality-principle.") In the sociological control theory, it can be and is generally assumed that the decision to commit a criminal act may well be rationally determined—that the actor's decision was not irrational given the risks and costs he faces. Of course, as Becker points out, if the actor is capable of in some sense calculating the costs of a line of action, he is also capable of calculational errors: ignorance and error return, in the control theory, as possible explanations of deviant behavior.

The concept of commitment assumes that the organization of society is such that the interests of most persons would be endangered if they were to engage in criminal acts. Most people, simply by the process of living in an organized society, acquire goods, reputations, prospects that they do not want to risk losing. These accumulations are society's insurance that they will abide by the rules. Many hypotheses about the antecedents of delinquent behavior are based on this premise. For example, Arthur L. Stinchcombe's hypothesis that "high school rebellion...occurs when future status is not clearly related to present performance"[15] suggests that one is committed to conformity not only by what one has but also by what one hopes to obtain. Thus "ambition" and/or "aspiration" play an important role in producing conformity. The person becomes committed to a conventional line of action, and he is therefore committed to conformity.

Most lines of action in a society are of course conventional. The clearest examples are educational and occupational careers. Actions thought to jeopardize one's chances in these areas are presumably avoided. Interestingly enough, even nonconventional commitments may operate to produce conventional conformity. We are told, at least, that boys aspiring to careers in the rackets or professional thievery are judged by their "honesty" and "reliability"—traits traditionally in demand among seekers of office boys.[16]

INVOLVEMENT

Many persons undoubtedly owe a life of virtue to a lack of opportunity to do otherwise. Time and energy are inherently limited: "Not that I would not, if I could, be both handsome and fat and well dressed, and a great athlete, and make a million a year, be a wit, a bon vivant, and a lady killer, as well as a philosopher, a philanthropist, a statesman, warrior, and African explorer, as well as a 'tone-poet' and saint. But the thing is simply impossible."[17] The things that William James here says he would like to be or do are all, I suppose, within the realm of conventionality, but if he were to include illicit actions he would still have to eliminate some of them as simply impossible.

Involvement or engrossment in conventional activities is thus often part of a control theory. The assumption, widely shared, is that a person may be simply too busy doing conventional things to find time to engage in deviant behavior. The person involved in conventional activities is tied to appointments, deadlines, working hours, plans, and the like, so the opportunity to commit deviant acts rarely arises. To the extent that he is engrossed in conventional activities, he cannot even think about deviant acts, let alone act out his inclinations.[18]

This line of reasoning is responsible for the stress placed on recreational facilities in many programs to reduce delinquency, for much of the concern with the high school dropout, and for the idea that boys should be drafted into the Army to keep them out of trouble. So obvious and persuasive is the idea that involvement in conventional activities is a major deterrent to delinquency that it was accepted even by Sutherland: "In the general area of juvenile delinquency it is probable that the most significant difference between juveniles who engage in delinquency and those who do not is that the latter are provided abundant opportunities of a conventional type for satisfying their recreational interests, while the former lack those opportunities or facilities."[19]

The view that "idle hands are the devil's workshop" has received more sophisticated treatment in recent sociological writings on delinquency. David Matza and Gresham M. Sykes, for example, suggest that delinquents have the values of a leisure class, the same values ascribed by Veblen to *the* leisure class: a search for kicks, disdain of work, a desire for the big score, and acceptance of aggressive toughness as proof of masculinity.[20] Matza and Sykes explain delinquency by reference to this system of values, but they note that adolescents at all class levels are "to some extent" members of a leisure class, that they "move in a limbo between earlier parental domination and future integration with the social structure through the bonds of work and marriage."[21] In the end, then, the leisure of the adolescent produces a set of values, which, in turn, leads to delinquency.

BELIEF

Unlike the cultural deviance theory, the control theory assumes the existence of a common value system within the society or group whose norms are being violated. If the deviant is committed to a value system different from that of conventional society, there is, within the context of the theory, nothing to explain. The question is, "Why does a man violate the rules in which he believes?" It is not, "Why do men differ in their beliefs about what constitutes good and desirable conduct?" The person is assumed to have been socialized (perhaps imperfectly) into the group whose rules he is violating; deviance is not a question of one group imposing its rules on the members of another group. In other words, we not only assume the deviant *has* believed the rules, we assume he believes the rules even as he violates them.

How can a person believe it is wrong to steal at the same time he is stealing? In the strain theory, this is not a difficult problem. (In fact, the strain theory was devised specifically to deal with this question.) The motivation to deviance adduced by the strain theorist is so strong that we can well understand the deviant act even assuming the deviator believes strongly that it is wrong.[22] However, given the control theory's assumptions about motivation, if both the deviant and the nondeviant believe the deviant act is wrong, how do we account for the fact that one commits it and the other does not?

Control theories have taken two approaches to this problem. In one approach, beliefs are treated as mere words that mean little or nothing if the other forms of control are missing. "Semantic dementia," the dissociation between rational faculties and emotional control which is said to be characteristic of the psychopath, illustrates this way of handling the problem.[23] In short, beliefs, at least insofar as they are expressed in words, drop out of the picture; since they do not differentiate between deviants and nondeviants, they are in the same class as "language" or any other characteristic common to all members of the group. Since they represent no real obstacle to the commission of delinquent acts, nothing need be said about how they are handled by those committing such acts. The control theories that do not mention beliefs (or values), and many do not, may be assumed to take this approach to the problem.

The second approach argues that the deviant rationalizes his behavior so that he can at once violate the rule and maintain his belief in it. Donald R. Cressey has advanced this argument with respect to embezzlement,[24] and Sykes and Matza have advanced it with respect to delinquency.[25] In both Cressey's and Sykes and Matza's treatments, these rationalizations (Cressey calls them "verbalizations," Sykes and Matza term them "techniques of neutralization") occur prior to the commission of the deviant act. If the neutralization is successful, the person is free to commit the act(s) in question. Both in Cressey and in Sykes and Matza, the strain that prompts the effort at neutralization also provides the motive force that results in the subsequent deviant act. Their theories are thus, in this sense, strain theories. Neutralization is difficult to handle within the context of a theory that adheres closely to control theory assumptions, because in the control theory there is no special motivational force to account for the neutralization. This difficulty is especially noticeable in Matza's later treatment of this topic, where the motivational component, the "will to delinquency" appears *after* the moral vacuum has been created by the techniques of neutralization.[26] The question thus becomes: Why neutralize?

In attempting to solve a strain theory problem with control theory tools, the control theorist is thus led into a trap. He cannot answer the crucial question. The concept of neutralization assumes the existence of moral obstacles to the commission of deviant acts. In order plausibly to account for a deviant act, it is necessary to generate motivation to deviance that is at least equivalent in force to the resistance provided by these moral obstacles. However, if the moral obstacles are removed, neutralization and special motivation are no longer required. We therefore follow the implicit logic of control theory and remove these moral obstacles by hypothesis. Many persons do not have an attitude of respect toward the rules of society; many persons feel no moral obligation to conform regardless of personal advantage. Insofar as the values and beliefs of these persons are consistent with their feelings, and there should be a tendency toward consistency, neutralization is unnecessary; it has already occurred.

Does this merely push the question back a step and at the same time produce conflict with the assumption of a common value system? I think not. In the first place, we do not assume, as does Cressey, that neutralization occurs in order to make a specific criminal act possible.[27] We do not assume, as do Sykes and Matza, that neutralization occurs to make many delinquent acts possible. We do not not assume, in other words, that the person constructs a system of rationalizations in order to justify commission of acts he *wants* to commit. We assume, in contrast, that the beliefs that free a man to commit deviant acts are *unmotivated* in the sense that he does not construct or adopt them in order to facilitate the attainment of illicit ends. In the second place, we do not assume, as does Matza, that "delinquents concur in the conventional assessment of delinquency."[28] We assume, in contrast, that there is *variation* in the extent to which people believe they should obey the rules of society, and, furthermore, that the less a person believes he should obey the rules, the more likely he is to violate them.[29]

In chronological order, then, a person's beliefs in the moral validity of norms are, for no teleological reason, weakened. The probability that he will commit delinquent acts is therefore increased. When and if he commits a delinquent act, we may justifiably use the weakness of his beliefs in explaining it, but no special motivation is required to explain either the weakness of his beliefs or, perhaps, his delinquency act.

The keystone of this argument is of course the assumption that there is variation in belief in the moral validity of social rules. This assumption is amenable to direct empirical test and can thus survive at least until its first confrontation with data. For the present, we must return to the idea of a common value system with which this section was begun.

The idea of a common (or, perhaps better, a single) value system is consistent with the fact, or presumption, of variation in the strength of moral beliefs. We have not suggested that delinquency is based on beliefs counter to conventional morality; we have not suggested that delinquents do not believe delinquent acts are wrong. They may well believe these acts are wrong, but the meaning and efficacy of such beliefs are contingent upon other beliefs and, indeed, on the strength of other ties to the conventional order.[30]

RELATIONS AMONG THE ELEMENTS

In general, the more closely a person is tied to conventional society in any of these ways, the more closely he is likely to be tied in the other ways. The person who is attached to conventional people is, for example, more likely to be involved in conventional activities and to accept conventional notions of desirable conduct. Of the six possible combinations of elements, three seem particularly important and will therefore be discussed in some detail.

ATTACHMENT AND COMMITMENT

It is frequently suggested that attachment and commitment (as the terms are used here) tend to vary inversely. Thus, according to delinquency research, one of the lower-class adolescent's "problems" is that he is unable to sever ties to parents and peers, ties that prevent him from devoting sufficient time and energy to educational and occupational aspirations. His attachments are thus seen as getting in the way of conventional commitments.[31] According to stratification research, the lower-class boy who breaks free from these attachments is more likely to be upwardly mobile.[32] Both research traditions thus suggest that those bound to *conformity* for instrumental reasons are less likely to be bound to conformity by emotional ties to conventional others. If the unattached compensate for lack of attachment by commitment to achievement, and if the uncommitted make up for their lack of commitment by becoming more attached to persons, we could conclude that neither attachment nor commitment will be related to delinquency.

Actually, despite the evidence apparently to the contrary, I think it safe to assume that attachment to conventional others and commitment to achievement tend to vary together. The common finding that middle-class boys are likely to choose instrumental values over those of family and friendship while the reverse is true of lower-class boys cannot, I think, be properly interpreted as meaning that middle-class boys are less attached than lower-class boys to their parents and peers. The zero-sum methodological model that produces such findings is highly likely to be misleading.[33] Also, although many of the characteristics of the upwardly mobile alluded to by Seymour M. Lipset and Reinhard Bendix could be accounted for as consequences rather than causes of mobility, a methodological critique of these studies is not necessary to conclude that we may expect to find a positive relation between attachment and commitment in the data to be presented here. The present study and the one study Lipset and Bendix cite as disagreeing with their general conclusion that the upwardly mobile come from homes in which interpersonal relations were unsatisfactory are both based on high school samples.[34] As Lipset and Bendix note, such studies necessarily focus on aspirations rather than actual mobility. For the present, it seems, we must choose between studies based on hopes for the occupational future and those based on construction or reconstruction of the familial past. Interestingly enough, the former are at least as likely to be valid as the latter.

COMMITMENT AND INVOLVEMENT

Delinquent acts are events. They occur at specific points in space and time. For a delinquent act to occur, it is necessary, as is true of all events, for a series of causal chains to converge at a given moment in time. Events are difficult to predict, and specification of some of the conditions necessary for them to occur often leaves a large residue of indeterminacy. For example, to say that a boy is free of bonds to conventional society is not to say that he will necessarily commit delinquent acts; he may and he may not. All we can say with certainty is that he is *more likely* to commit delinquent acts than the boy strongly tied to conventional society.

It is tempting to make a virtue of this defect and espouse "probabilistic theory," since it, and it alone, is consistent with "the facts."[35] Nevertheless, this temptation should be resisted. The primary virtue of control theory is not that it relies on conditions that make delinquency possible while other theories rely on conditions that make delinquency necessary. On the contrary, with respect to their logical framework, these theories are superior to control theory, and, if they were as adequate empirically as control theory, we should not hesitate to advocate their adoption in preference to control theory.

But they are not as adequate, and we must therefore seek to re duce the indeterminacy within control theory. One area of possible development is with respect to the link between elements of the bond affecting the probability that one will yield to temptation and those affecting the probability that one will be exposed to temptation.

The most obvious link in this connection is between educational and occupational aspirations (commitment) and involvement in conventional activities. We can attempt to show how commitment limits one's opportunities to commit delinquent acts and thus get away from the assumption implicit in many control theories that such opportunities are simply randomly distributed through the population in question.

ATTACHMENT AND BELIEF

That there is a more or less straightforward connection between attachment to others and belief in the moral validity of rules appears evident. The link we accept here and which we shall attempt to document is described by Jean Piaget:

It is not the obligatory character of the rule laid down by an individual that makes us respect this individual, it is the respect we feel for the individual that makes us regard as obligatory the rule he lays down. The appearance of the sense of duty in a child thus admits of the simplest explanation, namely that he receives commands from older children (in play) and from adults (in life), and that he respects older children and parents.[36]

In short, "respect is the source of law."[37] Insofar as the child respects (loves and fears) his parents, and adults in general, he will accept their rules. Conversely, insofar as this respect is undermined, the rules will tend to lose their obligatory character. It is assumed that belief in the obligatory character of rules will to some extent maintain its efficacy in producing conformity even if the respect which brought it into being no longer exists. It is also assumed that attachment may produce conformity even in the face of beliefs favorable to nonconformity. In short, these two sources of moral behavior, although highly and complexly related, are assumed to have an independent effect that justifies their separation.

THE BOND TO WHAT?

Control theorists sometimes suggest that attachment to any object outside one's self, whether it be the home town, the starry heavens, or the family dog, promotes moral behavior.[38] Although it seems obvious that some objects are more important than others and that the important objects must be identified if the elements of the bond are to produce the consequences suggested by the theory, a priori rankings of the objects of attachment have proved peculiarly unsatisfactory. Durkheim, for example, concludes that the three groups to whom attachment is most important in producing morality are the family, the nation, and humanity. He further concludes that, of these, the nation is most important.[39] All of which, given much contemporary thinking on the virtues of patriotism,[40] illustrates rather well the difficulty posed by such questions as: Which is more important in the control of delinquency, the father or the mother, the family or the school?

Although delinquency theory in general has taken a stand on many questions about the relative importance of institutions (for example, that the school is more important than the family), control theory has remained decidedly eclectic, partly because each element of the bond directs attention to different institutions. For these reasons, I shall treat specification of the units of attachment as a problem in the empirical interpretation of control theory, and not attempt at this point to say which should be more or less important.

WHERE IS THE MOTIVATION?

The most disconcerting question the control theorist faces goes something like this: "Yes, but *why* do they do it?" In the good old days, the control theorist could simply strip away the "veneer of civilization" and expose man's "animal impulses" for all to see. These impulses appeared to him (and apparently to his audience) to provide a plausible account of the motivation to crime and delinquency. His argument *was not* that delinquents and criminals alone are animals, but that we are all animals, and thus all naturally capable of committing criminal acts. It took no great study to reveal that children, chickens, and dogs occasionally assault and steal from their fellow creatures; that children, chickens, and dogs also behave for relatively long periods in a perfectly moral manner. Of course the acts of chickens and dogs are not "assault" or "theft," and such behavior is not "moral"; it is simply the behavior of a chicken or a dog. The chicken stealing corn from his neighbor knows nothing of the moral law; he does not *want* to violate rules; he wants merely to eat corn. The dog maliciously destroying a pillow or feloniously assaulting another dog is the moral equal of the chicken. No motivation to deviance is required to explain his acts. So, too, no special motivation to crime within the human animal was required to explain his criminal acts.

Times changed. It was no longer fashionable (within sociology, at least) to refer to animal impulses. The control theorist tended more and more to deemphasize the motivational component of his theory. He might refer in the beginning to "universal human needs," or some such, but the driving force behind crime and delinquency was rarely alluded to. At the same time, his explanations of crime and delinquency increasingly left the reader uneasy. What, the reader asked, is the control theorist assuming? Albert K. Cohen and James F. Short answer the question this way:

> ...it is important to point out one important limitation of both types of theory. They [culture conflict and social disorganization theories] are both *control* theories in the sense that they explain delinquency in terms of the *absence* of effective controls. They appear, therefore, to imply a model of motivation that assumes that the impulse to delinquency is an inherent characteristic of young people and does not itself need to be explained; it is something that erupts when the lid— i.e., internalized cultural restraints or external authority—is off.[41]

There are several possible and I think reasonable reactions to this criticism. One reaction is simply to acknowledge the assumption, to grant that one is assuming what control theorists have always assumed about the motivation to crime—that it is constant across persons (at least within the system in question): "There is no reason to assume that only those who finally commit a deviant act usually have the impulse to do so. It is much more likely that most people experience deviant impulses frequently. At least in fantasy, people are much more deviant than they appear."[42] There is certainly nothing wrong with *making* such an assumption. We are free to assume anything we wish to assume; the truth of our theory is presumably subject to empirical test.[43]

A second reaction, involving perhaps something of a quibble, is to defend the logic of control theory and to deny the alleged assumption. We can say the fact that control theory suggests the absence of something causes delinquency is not a proper criticism, since negative relations have as much claim to scientific acceptability as do positive relations.[44] We can also say that the present theory does not impute an inherent impulse *to delinquency* to anyone.[45] That, on the contrary, it denies the necessity of such an imputation: "The desires, and other passions of man, are in themselves no sin. No more are the actions, that proceed from those passions, till they know a law that forbids them."[46]

A third reaction is to accept the criticism as valid, to grant that a complete explanation of delinquency would provide the necessary impetus, and proceed to construct an explanation of motivation consistent with control theory. Briar and Piliavin provide situational motivation: "We assume these acts are prompted by short-term situationally induced desires experienced by all boys to obtain valued goods, to portray courage in the presence of, or be loyal to peers, to strike out at someone who is disliked, or simply to 'get kicks.'"[47] Matza, too, agrees that delinquency cannot be explained simply by removal of controls:

> Delinquency is only epiphenomenally action. . . . [It] is essentially infraction. It is rule-breaking behavior performed by juveniles aware that they are violating the law and of the nature of their deed, and made permissible by the neutralization of infractious [!] elements. Thus, Cohen and Short are fundamentally right when they insist that social control theory is incomplete unless it provides an impetus by which the potential for delinquency may be realized.[48]

The impetus Matza provides is a "feeling of desperation," brought on by the "mood of fatalism," "the experience of seeing one's self as effect" rather than cause. In a situation in which manliness is stressed, being pushed around leads to the mood of fatalism, which in turn produces a sense of desperation. In order to relieve his desperation, in order to cast off the mood of fatalism, the boy "makes things happen"—he commits delinquent acts.[49]

There are several additional accounts of "why they do it" that are to my mind persuasive and at the same time generally compatible with control theory.[50] But while all of these accounts may be compatible with control theory, they are by no means deducible from it. Furthermore, they rarely impute built-in unusual motivation to the delinquent: he is attempting to satisfy the same desires, he is reacting to the same pressures as other boys (as is clear, for example, in the previous quotation from Briar and Piliavin). In other words, if included, these accounts of motivation would serve the same function in the theory that "animal impulses" traditionally served: they might add to its persuasiveness and plausibility, but they would add little else, since they do not differentiate delinquents from nondelinquents.

In the end, then, control theory remains what it has always been: a theory in which deviation is not problematic. The question "Why do they do it?" is simply not the question the theory is designed to answer. The question is, "Why don't we do it?" There is much evidence that we would if we dared.

NOTES

1. Emile Durkheim, *Suicide,* trans. John A. Spaulding and George Simpson (New York: The Free Press, 1951), p. 209.

2. Books have been written on the increasing importance of interpersonal sensitivity in modern life. According to this view, controls from within have become less important than controls from without in *producing* conformity. Whether or not this observation is true as a description of historical trends, it is true that interpersonal sensitivity has become more important in *explaining* conformity. Although logically it should also have become more important in explaining nonconformity, the opposite has been the case, once again showing that Cohen's observation that an explanation of conformity should be an explanation of deviance cannot be translated as "an explanation of conformity has to be an explanation of deviance." For the view that interpersonal sensitivity currently plays a greater role than formerly in producing conformity, see William J. Goode, "Norm Commitment and Conformity to Role-Status Obligations," *American Journal of Sociology,* LXVI (1960), 246–258. And, of course, also see David Riesman, Nathan

Glazer, and Reuel Denney, *The Lonely Crowd* (Garden City, New York: Doubleday, 1950), especially Part I.

3. The literature on psychopathy is voluminous. See William McCord and Joan McCord, *The Psychopath* (Princeton: D. Van Nostrand, 1964).

4. John M. Martin and Joseph P. Fitzpatrick, *Delinquent Behavior* (New York: Random House, 1964), p. 130.

5. *Ibid.* For additional properties of the psychopath, see McCord and McCord, *The Psychopath*, pp. 1–22.

6. Barbara Wootton, *Social Science and Social Pathology* (New York: Macmillan, 1959), p. 250.

7. "The logical untenability [of the position that there are forces in man 'resistant to socialization'] was ably demonstrated by Parsons over 30 years ago, and it is widely recognized that the position is empirically unsound because it assumes [!] some universal biological drive system distinctly separate from socialization and social context—a basic and intransigent human nature" (Judith Blake and Kingsley Davis, "Norms, Values, and Sanctions," *Handbook of Modern Sociology,* ed. Robert E. L. Faris [Chicago: Rand McNally, 1964], p.471).

8. Emile Durkheim, *Moral Education,* trans. Everett K. Wilson and Herman Schnurer (New York: The Free Press, 1961), p. 64.

9. Although attachment alone does not exhaust the meaning of internalization, attachments and beliefs combined would appear to leave only a small residue of "internal control" not susceptible in principle to direct measurement.

10. F. Ivan Nye, *Family Relationships and Delinquent Behavior* (New York: Wiley, 1958), pp. 5–7.

11. Albert J. Reiss, Jr., "Delinquency as the Failure of Personal and Social Controls," *American Sociological Review,* XVI (1951), 196–207. For example, "Our observations show . . . that delinquent recidivists are less often persons with mature ego ideals or nondelinquent social roles" (p. 204).

12. Scott Briar and Irving Piliavin, "Delinquency, Situational Inducements, and Commitment to Conformity," *Social Problems,* XIII (1965), 41–42. The concept "stake in conformity" was introduced by Jackson Toby in his "Social Disorganization and Stake in Conformity: Complementary Factors in the Predatory Behavior of Hoodlums," *Journal of Criminal Law, Criminology and Police Science,* XLVIII (1957), 12–17. See also his "Hoodlum or Business Man: An American Dilemma," *The Jews,* ed. Marshall Sklare (New York: The Free Press, 1958), pp. 542–550. Throughout the text, I occasionally use "stake in conformity" in speaking in general of the strength of the bond to conventional society. So used, the concept is somewhat broader than is true for either Toby or Briar and Piliavin, where the concept is roughly equivalent to what is here called "commitment."

13. Thomas Hobbes, *Leviathan* (Oxford: Basil Blackwell, 1957), p. 195.

14. Howard S. Becker, "Notes on the Concept of Commitment," *American Journal of Sociology,* LXVI (1960), pp. 35–36.

15. Arthur L. Stinchcombe, *Rebellion in a High School* (Chicago: Quadrangle, 1964), p. 5.

16. Richard A. Cloward and Lloyd E. Ohlin, *Delinquency and Opportunity* (New York: The Free Press, 1960), p. 147, quoting Edwin H. Sutherland, ed., *The Professional Thief* (Chicago: University of Chicago Press, 1937), pp. 211–213.

17. William James, *Psychology* (Cleveland: World Publishng Co., 1948), p. 186.

18. Few activities appear to be so engrossing that they rule out contemplation of alternative lines of behavior, at least if estimates of the amount of time men spend plotting sexual deviations have any validity.

19. *The Sutherland Papers,* ed. Albert K. Cohen et al. (Bloomington, Indiana University Press, 1956), p. 37.

20. David Matza and Gresham M. Sykes, "Juvenile Delinquency and Subterranean Values," *American Sociological Review,* XXVI (1961), pp. 712–719.

21. *Ibid.,* p. 718.

22. The starving man stealing the loaf of bread is the image evoked by most strain theories. In this image, the starving man's belief in the wrongness of his act is clearly not something that must be explained away. It can be assumed to be present without causing embarrassment to the explanation.

23. McCord and McCord, *The Psychopath,* pp. 12–15.

24. Donald R. Cressey, *Other People's Money* (New York: The Free Press, 1953).

25. Gresham M. Sykes and David Matza, "Techniques of Neutralization: A Theory of Delinquency," *American Sociological Review,* XXII (1957), pp. 664–670.

26. David Matza, *Delinquency and Drift* (New York: Wiley, 1964), pp. 181–191.

27. In asserting that Cressey's assumption is invalid with respect to delinquency, I do not wish to suggest that it is invalid for the question of embezzlement, where the problem faced by the deviator is fairly specific and he can reasonably be assumed to be an upstanding citizen. (Although even here the fact that the embezzler's nonshareable financial problem often results from some sort of hanky-panky suggests that "verbalizations" may be less necessary than might otherwise be assumed.)

28. *Delinquency and Drift,* p. 43.

29. This assumption is not, I think, contradicted by the evidence presented by Matza against the existence of a delinquent subculture. In comparing the attitudes and actions of delinquents with the picture painted by delinquent subculture theorists, Matza emphasizes—and perhaps exaggerates—the extent to which delinquents are tied to the conventional order. In implicitly comparing delinquents with a supermoral man, I emphasize—and perhaps exaggerate—the extent to which they are not tied to the conventional order.

30. The position taken here is therefore somewhere between the "semantic dementia" and the "neutralization" positions. Assuming variation, the delinquent is, at the extremes, freer than the neutralization argument assumes. Although the possibility of wide discrepancy between what the delinquent professes and what he practices still exists, it is presumably much rarer than is suggested by studies of articulate "psychopaths."

31. The idea that the middle-class boy is less closely tied than the lower-class boy to his peers has been widely adopted in the literature on delinquency. The middle-class boy's "cold and rational" relations with his peers are in sharp contrast with the "spontaneous and warm" relations of the lower-class boy. See, for example, Albert K. Cohen, *Delinquent Boys* (New York: The Free Press, 1955), pp. 102–109.

32. The evidence in favor of this proposition is summarized in Seymour M. Lipset and Reinhard Bendix, *Social Mobility in Industrial Society* (Berkeley: University of California Press, 1959), especially pp. 249–259. For example: "These [business leaders] show strong traits of independence, they are characterized by an inability to form intimate relations and are consequently often socially isolated men" (p. 251).

33. Relations between measures of attachment and commitment are examined in Chapter VIII.

34. *Social Mobility*, p. 253.

35. Briar and Piliavin, "Situational Involvements," p. 45.

36. Jean Piaget, *The Moral Judgment of the Child*, trans. Marjorie Gabain (New York: The Free Press, n.d.), p. 101.

37. *Ibid.*, p. 379.

38. Durkheim, *Moral Education*, p. 83.

39. *Ibid.*, pp. 73–79.

40. In the end, Durkheim distinguishes between a patriotism that leads to concern for domestic problems and one that emphasizes foreign relations (especially that variety which puts "national sentiment in conflict with commitments of mankind").

41. See their "Juvenile Delinquency," in *Contemporary Social Problems*, ed. Robert K. Merton and Robert A. Nisbet (New York: Harcourt, Brace and World, 1961), p. 106.

42. Howard S. Becker, *Outsiders* (New York: The Free Press, 1963), p. 26. See also Kate Friedlander, *The Psycho-Analytic Approach to Juvenile Delinquency* (New York: International Universities Press, 1947), p. 7.

43. Cf. Albert K. Cohen, *Deviance and Control* (Englewood Cliffs, N.J.: Prentice-Hall, 1966), pp. 59–62.

44. I have frequently heard the statement "it's an absence of something explanation" used as an apparently damning criticism of a sociological theory. While the origins of this view are unknown to me, the fact that such a statement appears to have some claim to plausibility suggests one of the sources of uneasiness in the face of a control theory.

45. The popular "it's-an-id-argument" dismissal of explanations of deviant behavior assumes that the founding fathers of sociology somehow proved that the blood of man is neither warm nor red, but spiritual. The intellectual trap springs shut on the counterassumption that innate aggressive-destructive impulses course through the veins, as it should. The solution is not to accept both views, but to accept neither.

46. Thomas Hobbes, *Leviathan*, p. 83. Given the history of the sociological response to Hobbes, it is instructive to compare Hobbes' picture of the motivation behind the deviant act with that painted by Talcott Parsons. According to Parsons, the motive to deviate is a psychological trait or need that *the deviant* carries with him at all times. This need is itself deviant: *it cannot be satisfied by conformity*. Social controls enter merely as reality factors that determine the form and manner in which this need will be satisfied. If one path to deviant behavior is blocked, the deviant will continue searching until he finds a path that is open. Perhaps because this need arises from interpersonal conflict, and is thus socially derived, the image it presents of the deviant as fundamentally immoral, as doing evil *because* it is evil, has been largely ignored by those objecting to the control theorist's tendency to fall back on natural propensities as a source of the energy that results in the activities society defines as wrong. See Talcott Parsons, *The Social System* (New York: The Free Press, 1951), Chapter 7.

47. Briar and Piliavin, "Situational Inducements," p. 36.

48. *Delinquency and Drift*, p. 182.

49. Matza warns us that we cannot take the fatalistic mood out of context and hope to find important differences between delinquents and other boys: "That the subcultural delinquent is not significantly different from other boys is precisely the point" (*ibid.*, p. 89).

50. For example: Carl Werthman, "The Function of Social Definitions in the Development of Delinquent Careers," *Juvenile Delinquency and Youth Crime*, Report of the President's Commission on Law Enforcement and Administration of Justice (Washington: USGPO, 1967), pp. 155–170; Jackson Toby, "Affluence and Adolescent Crime," *ibid.*, pp. 132–144; James F. Short, Jr., and Fred L. Strodtbeck, *Group Process and Gang Delinquency* (Chicago: University of Chicago Press, 1965), pp. 248–264.

19 *An Exchange/Social Control Theory*
RICHARD J. GELLES

The study of child abuse, wife abuse, and other forms of domestic violence emerged as a publicly recognized problem and a scientific issue during the late 1960s and early '70s. Erin Pizzey, author of the first book-length treatment of battered wives, *Scream Quietly or the Neighbors Will Hear*, wrote in 1976 that those concerned with any form of social caring should empty their shelves and make space for a massive onslaught of literature on the subject of domestic violence. She was correct. In the next three years there was an exponential increase in the number of books and articles published on the various aspects of domestic violence.

A review of popular and professional literature reveals that social scientists and the public alike have asked questions and pursued knowledge along parallel lines. The first major question asked about domestic violence is, "How common is it?" A great deal of attention has been directed toward estimating incidence of child abuse, wife abuse, husband abuse, and even parent abuse—almost as if domestic violence could not be considered a legitimate social problem unless it had an incidence in the millions. The second major question asked was, "What causes people to be violent and abusive toward family members?" Answers from both the public and the research community tended toward myths, conventional wisdom, and simplistic theoretical models. With few exceptions (noted later), the answer to this question, as presented by social scientists, has tended to be a summary of factors found to be related to family violence. These associations and correlations, while illuminating, do not yet provide a corpus of knowledge that could be considered theoretical insight into the causes of domestic violence.

This chapter briefly reviews and summarizes the popular theoretical notions about domestic violence. The methodological dilemmas

Reprinted from Richard J. Gelles, "An Exchange/Social Control Theory," pp. 151–165 in David Finkelhor, Richard J. Gelles, Gerald T. Hotaling, and Murray A. Straus, *The Dark Side of Families: Current Family Violence Research* (Beverly Hills, CA: Sage Publications, 1983). By permission of Sage Publications, Inc.

This chapter is part of a program of research on family violence conducted at the University of Rhode Island. Funding for this research has been provided by NIMH Grant MH 227557 and OCD/NCCAN grants 90–425 and 90-C-1792. A revised version was presented at the annual meetings of the American Society of Criminology, Philadelphia, 1979.

that have inhibited the development of a knowledge base which could be used to test theoretical propositions about the causes of family violence are then reviewed. The existing theories of violence and aggression that can be brought to bear in explaining family violence are briefly reviewed. Finally, I advance the outline of an exchange/social control theory of intrafamily violence.

THEORETICAL NOTIONS ABOUT INTRAFAMILY VIOLENCE

PSYCHOPATHOLOGY: THE INTRAINDIVIDUAL LEVEL OF ANALYSIS

Public presentations on domestic violence frequently begin with graphic black and white or even color slides of battered and abused women and children. These slides produce, nearly without fail, gasps, groans, and exclamations of disbelief on the part of the audience (irrespective of its sophistication and experience). On a cognitive level, the reaction is also similar—that is, members of the audience tend to view the slides in disbelief and assume that people who inflict such injuries are psychologically deranged. The reaction of audiences is much the same as the response of clinicians who encounter cases of child and wife abuse—the offender must be psychologically ill. The early writing on both child abuse (e.g., Kempe et al., 1962; Steele & Pollock, 1974; Galdston, 1965) and wife abuse (e.g., Snell, Rosenwald, & Robey, 1964) portrayed the causes of domestic violence as arising from offenders' psychological problems. After ten years of continued research and administration of countless psychological tests, the summary evaluation of the psychopathological approach to domestic violence is that the proportion of individuals who batter their family members and suffer from psychological disorders is no greater than the proportion of the population in general with psychological disorders (Straus, 1980; Steele, 1978).

A unique aspect of the theoretical approach to wife-battering is the popular view (and a view alluded to in some of the professional literature—see Snell et al., 1964) that violence arises out of psychological problems of the victims. "Women like to be beaten," we are told. Or "battered women are crazy." There are, however, no scientific data to support either of these points of view, and if, indeed, battered women do behave strangely, it is probably as a consequence (not a cause) of being battered (Walker, 1979).

THE DETERMINING EFFECTS OF LEARNING AND STRESS

The earliest research on child abuse found that abusive adults were likely to have been raised in abusive homes (Steele & Pollock, 1974; Bennie & Sclare, 1969). The explanation for this finding was that being abused as a child produces a personality disorder which predisposes the individual to a life pattern of violence and aggression. The more contemporary interpretation of the relationship is that experience with, and exposure to, violence serves as a learning experience which teaches that violence can and should be used toward family members. Indeed, the research results have been so consistent that an aura of family determinism has begun to surround the data, such that many people expect that *all* victims of childhood violence will grow up to be violent adults. And it is expected that individuals who are not exposed to violence as children will grow up to be nonviolent. Such is not the case. Indeed, if it were, we would have one of the truly rare social scientific findings—a unicausal phenomenon.

While the relationship between exposure to and experience with violence as a child and violent behavior as an adult is consistent, and the time order clear, the relationship is not as strong as some reviews of the literature would argue (Potts & Herzberger, 1979). The relationship between experience with abuse as a child and later abusive behavior as an adult can be considered deterministic only under certain conditions (e.g., environmental stress) that would have to be specified by a larger theory.

The same can be said of the relationship between stress and family violence. Skolnick and Skolnick (1977) have stated that "family violence seems to be a product of psychological tensions and external stresses affecting all families at all social levels." While investigators find a consistent relationship between stress and violence, again there is the danger of accepting the relationship in its simplistic deterministic form.

Thus, while social learning and social psychological stress are found to be related to family violence, and probably are part of the causal flow of events which explains family violence, they have only been demonstrated as associations. Neither relationship is satisfactorily explained or empirically examined so as to constitute a theoretical explanation of family violence. While they may be necessary factors, they are not sufficient.

IDEOLOGY: SEXISM AND RACISM

A number of theoretical themes have emerged at the sociocultural level of analysis. Official statistics on child abuse and wife abuse indicate that women, blacks, minorities, and the poor are overrepresented victims of domestic violence. Research that is not limited to studying only officially labeled cases of domestic violence also finds relationships between income and family violence (an inverse relationship), race and violence, and minority status and violence (Straus, Gelles, & Steinmetz, 1980).

Some have argued that these data support the notion that the real cause of family violence is not psychological disorders or social learning; rather, it is oppressive sexism, racism, and a patriarchal social organization of capitalistic societies (see U.S. Commission on Civil Rights, 1978).

While it is easy for liberal-minded social scientists to sympathize with these conceptualizations, the jump from the relationship between income and violence to a theory of racism or sexism is large and not yet fully supported by the available empirical evidence.

The use of ideology in place of scientifically informed theory has become increasingly common in the emotion-charged field of domestic violence and has partially inhibited a serious scientific program of theory construction in this area.

FULLY DEVELOPED CAUSAL MODELS

Despite the fact that one of the earliest and most widely read studies of child abuse concluded that violence toward children was the product of a complex multidimensional process (Gil, 1970), the current state of the art in theory construction consists of profiles of abusers and abused (see for example Steinmetz, 1978) and simplistic, unicausal models. Fully developed causal models are rare. One exception is Garbarino's ecological model (1977); another is Justice and Justice's symbiosis model (1976). Interestingly, both of these theories have been applied only to child abuse. Straus's general system model of family violence (1973) is perhaps the only comprehensive theoretical model which attempts to explain all forms of family violence.

The next section reviews some of the methodological problems that have retarded the development of adequate multidimensional causal models of family violence.

METHODOLOGICAL DILEMMAS AND THEORY CONSTRUCTION

There are numerous reasons for the lack of sophisticated theoretical models in the study of domestic violence. First, most investigations concentrate on one aspect of family violence—either child abuse, wife abuse, or even husband or parent abuse. Only a minority of investigations conceptualize the problem of violence between family members at the family level of analysis. Thus, while theoretical models are applied to child abuse or wife abuse, few efforts attempt a general model of family violence.

DEFINING VIOLENCE AND ABUSE

One important difficulty is the problem of nominally defining violence and abuse. Both terms are perhaps more suited as political concepts than scientific ones—that is, they are pejorative, emotion-charged terms used to draw attention to behavior considered deviant. The terms "abuse" and "violence" have been applied to the narrow issue of physically striking a family member and causing injury (Kempe et al., 1962, Gil, 1970), to the act of striking a person with the intent of causing harm or injury—but not actually causing it (Gelles & Straus, 1979), to acts of violence where there is the high potential of causing injury (Straus et al., 1980), and to acts where there is no actual hitting at all—such as verbal abuse or psychological and emotional violence.

Because of the wide variation in nominal definitions of violence, there is a resulting lack of comparability among various investigations of types of domestic violence. A study that examines hitting children cannot be directly compared with another study of child abuse that defines abuse as sexual, psychological, emotional, and physical exploitation of children.

The lack of comparability means that a large base of knowledge of one uniform type of behavior has not been, and is not being, developed.

OPERATIONALIZATION OF ABUSE AND VIOLENCE

Perhaps the most difficult methodological problem facing those studying child abuse, wife abuse, and family violence has been to select an adequate sample of abusive and violent families to study. Social service providers and researchers tend to agree that it is extremely difficult for a family to admit to an interviewer that they are violent or abusive. Thus, nearly all investigations of child abuse and wife abuse operationalize "abuse" as those individuals or families who come to public attention and are publicly labeled as abusers. Child abuse cases are located in hospital and protective service agency records, while samples of abused women are drawn from residents of shelters for abused women.

Exceptions to this pattern are the studies of family violence conducted by Straus and Steinmetz (Steinmetz, 1974; Straus, 1974a, 1974b). They sampled college students and asked them to report on the level of violence in the students' home during the last year they lived at home. Steinmetz (1977) conducted one of the earliest studies based on a representative sample of families, but the sample was small (57 families) and the families were drawn from only one county in Delaware. More recently, a study of family violence using a nationally representative sample of 2143 families has been completed (Straus et al., 1980).

It is crucial to consider the problems of theory development in an area where the primary mode of operationalizing the dependent variable (abuse or violence) is to choose individuals and families who have been publicly labeled as abusers or violent. Simply stated, this method of operationalizing the dependent variable does not allow investigators to partial out the variables that make an individual or family vulnerable to being labeled "abusive" from the variable that led the individual or family to be abusive (Gelles, 1975).

The criticism that the family violence knowledge base suffers from the inadequate operationalization of the dependent variable and nonrepresentative sampling of subjects is similar to Polsky's critique of the knowledge base in the area of crime and delinquency. Polsky (1969) states that knowledge in this area is limited by the tendency of investigators to study only adjudicated or incarcerated criminals. Just as Polsky argues that criminologists know a great deal about people who are failures as criminals and delinquents (by virtue of getting caught), it appears that there is considerable information on which families are vulnerable to being labeled "abusers" and very little knowledge about which factors actually cause abuse.

AVAILABLE THEORETICAL MODELS

The methodological problems impinging on the study of intrafamily violence and the fact that the detailed scientific study of family violence really began at the beginning of this decade have combined to limit the amount of theory construction on the issue of family violence.

Even though there has been little in the way of theoretical work on the specific issue of family violence, theoretical frameworks and propositions have been developed from the study of violence and aggression that are applicable to the issue of family violence. Gelles and

Straus (1979) inventoried 15 theories which seemed to have relevance for understanding violence between family members.

The theories considered ranged from intrapsychic theories to macrosociological. The paper also attempted to develop an integrated theory of violence between family members. Unfortunately, simplicity was not possible, and a model which articulated the key elements of each theory of violence resulted in an integrated model long on heuristic value and equally long and complex to examine.

As a consequence of the large effort that was devoted to developing the integrated model, we learned that it would be wiser and more useful to work with a more "middle-range" theory and set of theoretical propositions. Exchange theory appeared to be the approach which best integrated the key elements of the diverse theories used to explain human violence. Moreover, exchange theory also has the virtue of providing a suitable perspective to explain and answer a variety of questions and issues in the study of family violence, such as "Why do women who are battered remain in violent marriages?" (Gelles, 1976).

AN EXCHANGE/SOCIAL CONTROL MODEL OF FAMILY VIOLENCE

An assumption of exchange theory which is relevant in explaining family violence is that human interaction is guided by the pursuit of rewards and the avoidance of punishment and costs (Gelles & Straus, 1979). In addition, an individual who supplies reward services to another obliges him to fulfill an obligation, and thus the second individual must furnish benefits to the first (Blau, 1964). If reciprocal exchange of rewards occurs, the interaction will continue. But if reciprocity is not received, the interaction will be broken off. However, intrafamilial relations are more complex than those studied by traditional exchange theorists. In some instances, it is not feasible or possible to break off interaction, even if there is no reciprocity. When the "principle of distributive justice" is violated, there can be increased anger, resentment, conflict, and violence.

Many students of family violence tend to view violence as the last resort to solving problems in the family (Goode, 1971). Nye (1979), however, notes that this need not be the case. Spanking, for instance, is frequently the first choice of action by many parents.

A central (and perhaps greatly oversimplified) proposition of an exchange/social control theory of family violence is that *people hit and abuse other family members because they can.* In applying the principles of general exchange theory we expect that people will use violence in the family if the costs of being violent do not outweigh the rewards. From social control theory we derive the proposition that family violence occurs in the absence of social controls which would bond people to the social order and negatively sanction family members for acts of violence.

The most difficult aspect of applying the propositions from the form of social control theory that has been used to explain juvenile delinquency (see Conger, 1980; Hirschi, 1969; Kornhauser, 1978) is that there are conflicting norms concerning the use of violence in families—and thus some confusion as to whether the normative social order in families is one of harmony and peace or conflict and violence. Publicly, at least, we think of the family as a loving, tranquil, peaceful social institution to which one flees *from* stress and danger. Privately, the family is perhaps society's most violent social institution (Straus et al., 1980). There exist mores and folkways which accept and even mandate the use of violence in families (such as the phrase "spare the rod and spoil the child" or the English law "rule of thumb" which gave husbands the right to strike their wives with sticks no larger than their thumbs). Thus, there is the dilemma as to whether social control is exerted to maintain a certain level of violence in families, or whether social control is designed to keep violence from occurring.

For purposes of the exchange/social control theory presented in this chapter, social control is assumed to be efforts to *prevent* intrafamilial violence. This assumption follows from exchange principles which we use to propose that while violence in families can be normative under some circumstances, there are *costs* for being violent. First, there could be the potential of the victim hitting back. Second, a violent assault could lead to an arrest and/or imprisonment. Finally, using violence could lead to a loss of status. Thus, there are significant costs involved in being violent (Goode, 1971).

INEQUALITY, PRIVACY, SOCIAL CONTROL, AND VIOLENCE

The first, overly simple proposition that people hit and abuse family members because they can may be expanded to the following:

1. Family members are more likely to use violence in the home when they expect that the costs of being violent are less than the rewards.
2. The absence of effective social controls over family relations decreases the costs of one family member being violent toward another.

3. Certain social and family structures serve to reduce social control in family relations, and therefore reduce the costs and/or increase the rewards of being violent.

The private nature of the modern family serves to reduce the degree of social control exercised over family relations (Laslett, 1973, 1978). Inequality in the home can reduce both social control and the costs of being violent. Finally, the image of the "real" man in society also reduces social control in the home and increases the rewards of being violent.

Inequality

The normative power structure in society and the family and the resulting sexual and generational inequality in the family serves to reduce the chances that victims of family violence can threaten or inflict harm on offenders.[1] Husbands are typically bigger than wives, have higher status positions, and earn more money. Because of this, they can use violence without fear of being struck back hard enough to be injured. Moreover, they do not risk having their wives take economic or social sanctions against them. Parents can use violence toward their children without fear that their children can strike back and injure them. The fact that the use of violence toward children by mothers decreases with the child's age (Gelles & Hargreaves, 1981) can be interpreted as a consequence of the greater risk of being hit back as the child grows older and larger.

Women and children may be the most frequent victims of family violence because they have no place to run and are not strong enough or do not possess sufficient resources to inflict costs on their attackers.

Privacy

Victims of family violence could turn to outside agencies to redress their grievances, but the private nature of the family reduces the accessibility of outside agencies of social control. Neighbors who report that they overhear incidents of family violence also say that they fear intervening in another person's home. Police, prosecutors, and courts are reluctant to pursue cases involving domestic violence. When these cases are followed up, the courts are faced with the no-win position of either doing nothing or separating the combatants. Thus, to protect a child, judges may view as their only alternative to remove the child from the home. To protect the woman, the solution may be a separation or divorce. Either situation puts the legal system in the position of breaking up a family to protect the individual members. Because courts typically view this as a drastic step, such court-ordered separations or removals are comparatively rare, unless there is stark evidence of repeated grievous injury.

Violence and the "Real Man"

One last cost of being violent is the loss of social status that goes along with being labeled a "child beater" or a "wife beater." However, there are subcultures where aggressive sexual and violent behavior is considered proof that someone is a "real man" (Toby, 1966). Thus, rather than risk status loss, the violent family members may actually realize a status gain. Moreover, that notion that "a man's home is his castle" reduces external social control over family life.

In situations where status can be lost by being violent, individuals employ accepted vocabularies of motive (Mills, 1940) or "accounts" (Lyman & Scott, 1970) to explain their untoward behavior. Thus, violent fathers or mothers might explain their actions by saying they were drunk or lost control. Parents who shared the same desire to batter their children might nod in agreement without realizing that a real loss of control would have produced a much more grievous injury or even death.

APPLYING EXCHANGE/SOCIAL CONTROL THEORY

An exchange/social control theory approach to family violence can be extremely helpful in explaining some of the patterns of family violence which have been uncovered in recent empirical investigations.

The child abuse literature notes that certain types of children are at greater risk for abuse. Ill, handicapped, premature, ugly, and demanding children are at greater risk of being abused by their parents (Friedrich & Boriskin, 1976). These children either make great demands on their parents (economically, socially, or psychologically), or, as in the case of deformed children or children seen as ugly by their parents, may be perceived as not providing sufficient gratification in return for the parents' investment of time and energy. In any case, when the parent perceives the costs of parenting to outweigh the rewards, the alternatives are limited. The relationship between parent and child is difficult to break—with the exception of giving the child up for adoption or foster care, or the death of the child or parent. Thus, with few alternatives and high dissatisfaction, the parent may resort to abusive violence.

A similar combination of lack of alternatives and violation of the principle of distributive justice is helpful in understanding conjugal violence. It should be noted that it is easier to explain why a spouse would remain with a violent partner (lack of alternatives) than it is to explain why the one partner adopted violence (see Gelles, 1976, for a discussion of why wives stay with battering husbands). Another facet of conjugal violence that can be seen through the exchange perspective is the use of violence to inflict "costs" on one's partner. Exchange theorists (for example, Homans, 1967) note that to inflict costs on someone who has injured you is rewarding. The idea of revenge being "sweet" can be used to examine why wives resort to extreme forms of violence in response to being punched or hit by their husbands and why husbands resort to violence to silence a wife.

Nye has applied exchange (what he calls choice) theory to family violence and developed a number of theoretical propositions. At the macrosocial level of analysis he states:

> Violence in the family is more frequent in societies that have no legal or other normative structure proscribing it. In societies that proscribe violence against some members (wives) but permit it against others (children), violence will be less frequent towards those members against whom it is proscribed than towards those against whom it is allowed. (Nye, 1979)

Nye goes on to propose that wife-beating and child-beating are less common in families that have relatives and/or friends nearby, while child-beating is more common in single-parent than in two-parent families. I would recast his propositions to read:

> Family violence is more common when nonnuclear family members (e.g., friends, relatives, bystanders) are unavailable, unable, or unwilling to be part of the daily system of family interaction, and thus unable to serve as agents of formal and informal social control.

In terms of the general pattern of relationships among family members, the greater the disparity between perceived investment in a family relationship such as parenting and the perceived returns on the investment, the greater the likelihood that there will be violence. The fact that children three to five years of age and children aged fifteen to seventeen were found to be the most likely victims of child abuse (Straus et al., 1980) could be the result of parents of younger children perceiving a rather large investment in their children while getting little in the way of actual return. Parents who abuse teenage children (and risk being hit back) may do so because they have evidence showing that their investment in rearing the children has yielded disappointing results.

These propositions, again, tend to view violence as a last resort or final alternative to a lack of reciprocity in the family. It is important to note that violence can be the first resort. Spanking children may be common because it is culturally approved and because it is immediately gratifying. Many parents justify the use of violence as a child training technique because it tends to bring with it the immediate emotional reward for the parent and the immediate cessation of the behavior of the child that led to the violence.

Exchange theory is also useful for explaining other findings in the study of family violence. The fact that pregnant women are at risk of physical abuse by their husbands may be due in part to the helplessness of these women and their inability to hit back. Parents who overestimate their children's ability and capabilities may abuse them because these parents expect more out of their relationship with their children than they receive (Nye, 1979).

IMPLICATIONS FOR TREATMENT

It is often difficult for social scientists who seek nomothetic explanations for human social behavior to apply their theories to the idiographic work of clinicians and practitioners who must deal with case-by-case problems of family violence. An exchange/social control theoretical orientation to family violence, however, is a perspective that is directly applicable to both treatment issues and social policy.

TREATMENT

Applying exchange/social control theory to clinical issues in the treatment of family violence results in the conclusion that if people abuse family members because they can, then a central goal of treatment is to make it so they *can't*. To do this, a clinician needs to increase the degree of social control exerted over family relations and to raise the costs of intrafamilial violence.

Increasing social control and raising the costs is not as easy as it would seem. A consistent finding in child abuse and family violence research is that perpetrators of domestic abuse typically have poor self-concepts. Thus, if we were to raise the costs of family violence by directing the offender to accept the pejorative label "abuser," one of the unanticipated consequences of this approach would be to further undermine the patient's self-concept and further exacerbate the factors causing the abuse.

Nevertheless, it is important to "cancel the hitting license" and move the patient to accept the responsibility for his or her violent and abusive behavior. This means that the clinician cannot accept accounts or rationalizations which attribute the violent behavior to drugs, alcohol, or an inability to control oneself. An example of how a counselor can "cancel the hitting license" by rejecting such accounts is the case of a husband who hit his wife on several occasions:

> Each time he felt he was wrong. He apologized—very genuinely. But still, he did it again. The husband explained that he and his wife got so worked up in their arguments that he "lost control." In his mind, it was almost involuntary, and certainly not something he did according to a rule or norm which gives one the right to hit his wife. But the marriage counselor in the case brought out the rules which permitted him to hit his wife. He asked the husband why, if he had "lost control," he didn't stab his wife! (Straus et al., 1980)

The norms that accept certain levels of permissible family violence are so pervasive that a counselor must be aware not to accept them in the course of therapy.

A variety of innovative treatment approaches to family violence, including EMERGE, the first men's counseling source for domestic violence, now advocate the "canceling of the hitting license" and the acceptance of responsibility for violence as a necessary part of treatment.

A second treatment approach implied by an exchange/social control theory is to reduce the social isolation experienced by violent families. Research finds that child abusers, wife abusers, and their families are more socially isolated than nonviolent families (Straus et al., 1980). Not only does isolation deprive families of social, psychological, and economic resources in times of stress, but it greatly reduces the possibility of external social control over family relations. Families with considerable stress and conflict could be well served by having community linkages on which they could draw for help or assistance in meeting stress and reducing conflict.

Third, research also finds that violence is more likely to occur in homes where the husband (and in some instances the wife) has *all* the power and makes *all* the decisions. Democratically run households with sharing of decision making are the least violent (Straus et al., 1980). This finding implies that if families were helped to change the power structure of their relations and reduce the inequity in decision making, this would reduce the risk of conflict and confrontation escalating into violence and abuse.

POLICY

Exchange/social control theory also speaks to necessary policy to reduce and prevent family violence. The following policy recommendations serve to raise the costs of being violent and establish firm, but not unnecessarily intrusive, social control in family relations:

1. *Elimination of the norms which legitimize and glorify violence in society and in the family.* A reduction of television and other media violence, and passing laws such as implemented by the Swedish Parliament which prohibit hitting children by teachers *and parents* are needed if violent behavior is truly to be considered inappropriate.
2. *Reducing economic and gender inequity.*
3. *Increasing the response capacity of the criminal justice system and child welfare system in cases of domestic abuse.* Police frequently are wary of getting involved in family disputes and courts often treat cases of wife abuse less seriously than other forms of assault. Child welfare systems do not have the resources to respond rapidly and effectively to all reports of child abuse. For the costs of family violence to be raised and for the social control to be effective, there must be a certainty of response by agents of social control.

NOTE

1. Earlier I dismissed the notion that sexism caused family violence as being not supported by the data. In this section, I draw on the same theory (sexual inequality causes violence) as that earlier dismissed. My concern in the earlier section was that the proposition about sexism and family violence was being advanced as a *single-factor explanation* of family violence (see for example Dobash & Dobash, 1979). What I reject is the ideological fervor used to advance the argument that sexism causes abuse, rather than the claim that gender inequality is part of a causal model.

REFERENCES

Bennie, E., & Sclare, A. The battered child syndrome. *American Journal of Psychiatry,* 1969, 125(7), 975–979.

Blau, P. M. *Exchange and power in social life.* New York: John Wiley, 1964.

Conger, R. D. Juvenile delinquency: Behavior restraint or behavior facilitation? In T. Hirschi & M. Gottfredson (Eds.), *Theory and fact in contemporary criminology.* Beverly Hills, CA: Sage, 1980.

Dobash, R. E., & Dobash, R. *Violence against wives.* New York: Free Press, 1979.

Friedrich, W. N., & Boriskin, J. A. The role of the child in abuse: A review of literature. *American Journal of Orthopsychiatry,* 1976, 46(4), 580–590.

Galdston, R. Observations of children who have been physically abused by their parents. *American Journal of Psychiatry,* 1965, 122(4), 440–443.

Garbarino, J. The human ecology of child maltreatment: A conceptual model for research. *Journal of Marriage and the Family,* 1977, 39(4), 721–735.

Gelles, R. J. The social construction of child abuse. *American Journal of Orthopsychiatry,* 1975, 45(3), 363–371.

Gelles, R. J. Abused wives: Why do they stay? *Journal of Marriage and the Family,* 1976, 38, 659–668.

Gelles, R. J., & Hargreaves, E. F. Maternal employment and violence toward children. *Journal of Family Issues,* 1981, 2(4), 509–530.

Gelles, R. J., & Straus, M. A. Determinants of violence in the family: Toward a theoretical integration. In W. Burr et al. (Eds.), *Contemporary theories about the family.* New York: Free Press, 1979.

Gil, D. *Violence against children: Physical child abuse in the United States.* Cambridge: Harvard University Press, 1970.

Goode, W. J. Force and violence in the family. *Journal of Marriage and the Family,* 1971, 33, 624–636.

Hirschi, T. *Causes of delinquency.* Berkeley: University of California Press, 1969.

Homans, G. C. Fundamental social processes. In N. Smelser (Ed.), *Sociology.* New York: John Wiley, 1967.

Justice, B., & Justice, R. *The abusing family.* New York: Human Sciences Press, 1976.

Kempe, C. et al. The battered child syndrome. *Journal of the American Medical Association,* July 7, 1962, 181, 17–24.

Kornhauser, R. R. *Social sources of delinquency: An appraisal of analytic models.* Cambridge, England: Cambridge University Press, 1978.

Lang, A. R. et al. Effects of alcohol on aggression in male social drinkers. *Journal of Abnormal Psychology,* 1975, 84, 508–518.

Laslett, B. The family as a public and private institution: A historical perspective. *Journal of Marriage and the Family,* 1973, 35(3), 480–492.

Laslett, B. Family membership, past and present. *Social Problems,* 1978, 25 (5), 476–490.

Lyman, S. M., & Scott, M. B. *A sociology of the absurd.* New York: Appleton-Century-Crofts, 1970.

Mills, C. W. Situated actions and vocabularies of motive. *American Sociological Review,* 1940, 5, 904–913.

Nye, F. I. Choice, exchange, and the family. In W. R. Burr et al. (Eds.), *Contemporary theories about the family* (Vol. 2). New York: Free Press, 1979.

Owens, D., & Straus, M. A. Childhood violence and adult approval of violence. *Aggressive Behavior,* 1975, 1(2), 193–211.

Pizzey, E. Review of *The violent home* by Richard J. Gelles. *Nursing Mirror,* 1976, January 29.

Polsky, N. *Hustlers, beats, and others.* Garden City, NY: Doubleday, 1969.

Potts, D., & Herzberger, S. *Child abuse: a cross generational pattern of child rearing?* Paper presented at the annual meetings of the Midwestern Psychological Association, Chicago, April 1979.

Schachter, S., & Singer, J. E. Cognitive, social, and physiological determinants of emotional states. *Psychological Review,* 1962, 69(5), 379–399.

Scheff, T. J. The role of the mentally ill and the dynamics of mental disorder: A research framework. *Sociometry,* 1963, 26, 436–453.

Skolnick, A., & Skolnick, J. H. (Eds.). *The family in transition* (2nd ed.). Boston: Little, Brown, 1977.

Snell, J. E., Rosenwald, R. J., & Robey, A. The wifebeater's wife: A study of family interaction. *Archives of General Psychiatry,* 1964, 11, 107–113.

Steele, B. F. The child abuser. In I. Kutash, S. Kutash, & L. Schlesinger (Eds.), *Violence: Perspectives on murder and aggression.* San Francisco: Jossey-Bass, 1978.

Steele, B. F., & Pollock, C. A psychiatric study of parents who abuse infants and small children. In R. Helfer & C. Kempe (Eds.), *The battered child* (2nd ed.). Chicago: University of Chicago Press, 1974.

Steinmetz, S. K. Occupational environment in relation to physical punishment and dogmatism. In S. Steinmetz & M. Straus (Eds.), *Violence in the family.* New York: Harper & Row, 1974.

Steinmetz, S. K. *The cycle of violence: Assertive, aggressive, and abusive family interaction.* New York: Praeger, 1977.

Steinmetz, S. K. Violence between family members. *Marriage and Family Review,* 1978, 1(3), 1–16.

Straus, M. A. A general systems theory approach to a theory of violence between family members. *Social Science Information,* 1973, 12, 105–125.

Straus, M. A. Cultural and social organization influences on violence between family members. In R. Prince & D. Barrier (Eds.), *Configurations: Biological and cultural factors in sexuality and family life.* Lexington, MA: D. C. Heath, 1974. (a)

Straus, M. A. Leveling, civility, and violence in the family. *Journal of Marriage and the Family,* 1974, 36, 13–30. (b)

Straus, M. A. A sociological perspective on the causes of family violence. In M. Green (Ed.), *Violence and the family.* Boulder, CO: Westview Press, 1980.

Straus, M. A., Gelles, R. J., & Steinmetz, S. K. *Behind closed doors: Violence in the American family.* Garden City, NY: Doubleday, 1980.

Toby, J. Violence and the masculine ideal: Some qualitative data. In M. Wolfgang (Ed.), *Patterns of violence. Annals of the American Academy of Political and Social Science,* 1966, 364.

U.S. Commission on Civil Rights. *Battered women: Issues of public policy.* Washington, DC: Government Printing Office, 1978.

Walker, L. E. *The battered woman.* New York: Harper & Row, 1979.

Washburn, C. *Primitive drinking: A study of the uses and functions of alcohol in preliterate societies.* New Haven, CT: College and University Press, 1961.

Analysis and Critique

20 Social Control Theory
LAMAR T. EMPEY

The publication of Hirschi's control theory in 1969 was valuable because it helped to rectify a striking anomaly in academic criminology: the tendency to downgrade the importance of intrafamily relationships. Although a host of social scientists in other disciplines had long felt that these relationships were vital in determining the course of child development, criminologists had argued, for almost half a century, that they were relatively unimportant when compared to socioeconomic, racial, and subcultural factors. They contended that delinquency results not from the way families are organized, but from the way society is structured. Indeed, when considering the most serious problem of all—lower-class male delinquency—intrafamily relationships are of little importance. Instead, no less than the delinquent boys who are members of them, families are but pawns in the larger scheme of human affairs.

Reprinted from LaMar T. Empey, *American Delinquency* (Homewood, Ill.: Dorsey Press, 1982), with the permission of Wadsworth Publishing Co., third edition copyright 1991.

Following the publication of Hirschi's theory, however, research on the family began to increase. Nonetheless, it sparked reactions that were negative as well as positive, ideological as well as scientific. It is a reconstruction of the delinquency problem that remains very much in contention today.

1. Assumptions about human nature and social order

This contention stems, in no little part, from Hirschi's resurrection of some old, very conservative points of view about human nature; namely that all people would be delinquent if given the chance. Without adequate socialization, or the presence of social control, delinquent conduct would be common. Rather than working for years to pay for a car, for example, people would simply steal one. What children must be taught, therefore, is not how to break the law but how to restrain their natural impulses and how to be law abiding.

Meanwhile, Hirschi, like other control theorists, also assumed that the social order is characterized by value consensus. People are not divided into subcultures according to differing values; rather, most people agree that crime is bad. Hence, it is only delinquents (and adult criminals) who defy convention and threaten social stability.

2. Logic and content of control theory

Social control theory is as much a theory of conformity as of delinquency. Since all of us are animals at birth who will prey upon others unless restrained, we must seek to explain what spells the difference between deviance and conformity.

The answer is the social bond. If the process of socialization is effective—if children are attached to others, committed to long-range goals, involved in conventional activities, and believe in the morality of law—the social bond will develop, a stake in conformity will be created, and conformist behavior will result. But if socialization is ineffective, natural human impulses will remain unrestrained, children will be free to deviate, and delinquent conduct will be the consequence. (See Figure 1.)

3. Policy implications

Hirschi's assumption about human nature aside, his version of control theory is the kind of explanation which makes sense to authorities and upon which they base many of their interventions. They can readily understand the need to reattach delinquents to some kind of fam-

FIGURE 1

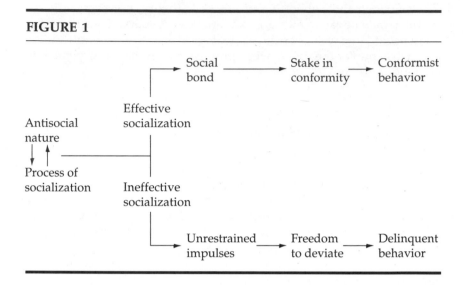

ily, recommit them to long-range goals, involve them in constructive activities, and cultivate their belief in the morality of law.

4. Logical and empirical adequacy

Hirschi contends that social control theory will predict delinquency across the lines of gender, class, and race. Relative to the concepts of attachment, this contention has held up rather well. Those elements of the theory which have best stood the test of logical and empirical scrutiny are those which (1) stress the idea that attachment to family and school is crucial in spelling the difference between conformity and deviance; (2) indicate that commitment to long-term educational and occupational goals is a barrier to, rather than a cause of, delinquent behavior; and (3) suggest that involvement in academic pursuits, if not other conventional activities, is useful in promoting conformity.

By contrast, the areas most in question are Hirschi's concepts of human nature and social order, and his view of the delinquent as a psychopath who lacks compassion and feeling for anyone. Just as cultural deviance, strain, and interactionist theories were extreme in painting delinquents as moral and gregarious people who violate the law only because they feel compelled to adhere to the expectations of others, social control theory probably goes too far in the opposite direction. When it indicates that delinquents are unsocialized predators, it underestimates the role of peers in generating support for delinquent conduct, overstates the importance of acquired beliefs as barriers to delinquent behavior, and leaves unaddressed the issues raised by the economic, political, and racial organization of society.

Although attachment, commitment, and involvement are barriers to delinquency, it cannot be said that all juveniles share an equal opportunity to experience these civilizing influences. Why, for example, is the prototypical perpetrator of violent crime synonymous with the prototypical victim—a young minority male who is a ghetto dweller?

Control theory is probably correct in suggesting that he is neither well attached to a stable home life, nor committed to conventional long-range goals, nor involved in academic pursuits. Furthermore, control theory is probably more realistic than cultural deviance, strain, or interactionist theories in painting the destructive consequences of a disrupted social bond. Life for the young urban street dweller is not a romantic odyssey, characterized by warm companionship and a carefree life. As Claude Brown put it so eloquently,

> I remember Johnny saying that the only thing in life a bad nigger was scared of was living too long. This just meant that if you were going to be respected in Harlem you had to be a bad nigger; and if you were going to be a bad nigger, you had to be ready to die. I wasn't ready to do any of that stuff. But I had to. I had to act crazy.
>
> Sometimes I used to get headaches thinking about it. I used to get sick. I couldn't get up. And sometimes I'd just jump out of bed and run out and say, "C'mon, man, let's go steal somethin'!" I'd get Turk, I'd get Tito, I'd get anybody who was around. I'd say, "C'mon, man, let's go pull a score." It seemed like the only way I could get away (1965:127).

Although Brown was, in fact, poorly attached to home and school, control theory is still unable to encompass the range of forces which contributed to his delinquent conduct. Being aware of his need for greater love and understanding from his parents, we also need to know that they were saddled with a legacy of racial discrimination, poverty, and injustice. Hence, if they were to do a better job of insulating him against the destructive influences that surrounded him, they had to somehow sublimate their own feelings of anger, demoralization, and inadequacy, arm him against the chaos that so often characterizes ghetto schools, and make algebra and social studies more attractive than life on the streets. Clearly, theirs was a herculean task for which better intrafamily relations were not the only answer. At the root of their problems were economic, political, and cultural forces that extended well beyond the limits of their immediate family—forces about which control theory does not provide us with adequate understanding.

In addition, research suggests that more privileged families also have problems of a more general type, generated by the impersonal character of modern society, the constant struggle for status and belonging, and the economic and ideological changes that can make the role of being a parent seem increasingly less rewarding.

In short, whether we seek to understand the delinquent behavior of either privileged or underprivileged youth, we must combine the insights provided by control theory with those provided by broader, more structural, theories. Beyond the study of intrafamily and school relationships, we must also explore the effects on these institutions by political, economic, and demographic forces. Childhood in American society is designed and organized by all of these social forces.

REFERENCE

Brown, Claude
1965 Manchild in the Promised Land. New York: Macmillan.

VI

Labeling and Deviance

The theorists considered in this chapter diverge sharply from the more traditional approaches to deviance we have considered to this point. Taking a more "relativist" position in which societal consensus and stability are not assumed, they focus on the changing and conflicting definitions of the norms in society and suggest that those of more powerful people may effect changes in individuals' status from nondeviant to deviant. Labeling theorists seek to understand three related issues:

1. What forms of behavior are defined as deviance in society?
2. Who, among the many who deviate, becomes defined as deviant?
3. What are the consequences of stigmatizing certain individuals or activities with a deviant label?

In focusing on these issues, this theory deals primarily with what happens to people *after* they have been singled out, identified, and defined as deviants. The thrust of the argument is that public condemnation may lock an individual into a deviant role, irrespective of interactional influences or society's structural conditions and controlling mechanisms.

Labeling theory thus concentrates on the consequences of identifying a person as deviant—a juvenile delinquent, a crook, a junkie, a homosexual, a troublemaker, and so on. One basic premise of this approach reaches back to Reading 1, in which Emile Durkheim notes that some people are criminals because a collective definition is attached to them, *not* because of any intrinsic quality of the acts they engage in. What happens to an individual who has been declared to be different or deviant by certain official "labelers" in a society (e.g., law enforcement officials, psychiatrists)? Just as important, how does such labeling alter the individual's self-concept? The answers to such questions incorporate the basic assumptions and research of the labeling approach.

No attempt is made in this approach to explain why individuals initially engage in certain actions that may be or have been defined as deviant in society. Rather, it stresses the important role of social definitions and negative social sanctions in pressuring individuals to engage in further deviant actions. It uses a "career development" model of deviant behavior in which deviance is the outcome of a process in which varying stages of initiation, acceptance, commitment, and imprisonment in a deviant role are primarily due to the actions of others. Deviance is therefore not viewed as an objective reality. The designation of deviance and the stigmatization of a person as a deviant is situational and contingent on the reactions of others toward that person's behavior or status.

The analysis in labeling theory centers on how others (the "definers") react to individuals or acts that these evaluators perceive in a negative way. It concentrates on the processes involved in making rules, on the context in which they are applied, and on their effects for those singled out as deviant. Thus, by its emphasis on subjective definitions of behavior and their consequences for those who are so labeled, labeling theorists further shift attention away from the individual's action and toward the ways in which institutionalized processes of social control and social definitions establish what (and who) is deviant. In short, it is the definition of an individual's behavior as deviant, rather than the behavior itself, that can cause a marked change in status which transforms a person's conception of self and initiates the process of locking that person into a "deviant career."

In a brief but eloquent statement from *Crime and the Community* (Reading 21), Frank Tannenbaum describes a process involving the subtle transference from a definition of *acts* committed by an individual as evil to the description of the *individual* as evil. As a result, most of the behavior of an individual who has been defined as evil comes to be looked on with suspicion. And, as the community's definition of a person changes from one who occasionally misbehaves to one who is a *delinquent*, so the person's self-definition changes. Tannenbaum sums up "the process of making the criminal" as "a process of tagging, defining, identifying, segregating, describing, emphasizing, making conscious and self-conscious; it becomes a way of stimulating, suggesting, emphasizing, and evoking the very traits that are complained of."

The selection from Edwin M. Lemert's *Social Pathology* (Reading 22) provides the main thrust and theoretical orientation of the labeling perspective. He describes a process, based on the effects of labeling, that transforms an individual's conception of self from one-who is "normal" into one who has become deviant.

According to Lemert, individuals may occasionally engage in behavior that has the potential of being defined as deviant or is so defined by others. At this stage, however, there is no severe societal reaction to the individuals themselves as being deviant. Such primary deviance, which may be the result of a variety of factors, does not affect the individuals' conception of self or their ability to perform social roles. However, if the societal reaction to their primary deviance becomes severe enough, they may be labeled by others and themselves as deviant persons. Then the opportunity for continuing to play "normal" social roles becomes disrupted, with adverse effects on both their social relationships and their self-conception. Because they have been publicly defined as abnormal, they may have no other alternative than to take on the deviant role as the basis for organizing their lives. At this point, their deviation has become secondary. Their conception of self changes, their opportunity to play conventional roles is limited, and they become more firmly entrenched in the role of the deviant.

For Lemert then, the central concern for labeling theory is not to account for deviance at the primary level. Rather, it is the processes resulting in societal reaction to primary deviance, which in turn produces secondary deviance, that require study and explanation. Lemert suggests an eight-step sequential model of interactions leading to secondary deviance which is helpful in demonstrating his conceptual scheme.

The selection from *Outsiders*, by Howard S. Becker (Reading 23), is titled "Career Deviance," but it also deals with sustained (secondary) rather than occasional (primary) deviance. The crux of Becker's argument is summarized in the statement, "One of the most crucial steps in the process of building a stable pattern of deviant behavior is likely to be the experience of being caught and publicly labeled as a deviant." The effect of this experience is a redefinition of both the person's public identity and private identity. The final step in stabilizing a deviant identity and the individual's own private identity is likely to be movement into an organized deviant group. Becker suggests that such groups are, in fact, an outgrowth of the labeling process. A person so labeled may turn to a group for moral support to provide a rationale for deviance, as well as technical support to provide instruction in how to carry on deviance with a minimum of trouble.

In Reading 24, Thomas J. Scheff applies the general principles of labeling theory to functional (nonorganically caused) mental disorders. The distinguishing feature of Scheff's approach is the idea that mental illness, as currently conceived, is a social role. Most forms of deviant behavior in society are clearly categorized. For instance, there are concisely delineated terms and categories for norm violations such as crime, prostitution, perversion, homosexuality, and so on. There are, however, other forms of norm violation—a residue of deviance— which do not fit neatly into any specific category. According to Scheff, much of the behavior that comes to be viewed and defined as mental illness falls into this "residual" category. Since the behaviors that constitute mental illness are so anomalous, there is little agreement among both lay people and professionals within the field about the criteria used in deciding what mental illness (and mental health for that matter) is or who is really mentally ill. Nevertheless, labels describing the behavior of "mad" people do exist, and when such a label is applied, especially by professionals in the mental health field, it may have the unintended consequence of firmly entrenching the individual in the role of a "mentally ill" person.

In the same way Lemert identifies the function of labeling in the processes leading from primary to secondary deviance and Becker argues that being publicly labeled as deviant is a crucial step in building a deviant identity, Scheff argues that because of labeling, mental illness (i.e., being viewed and playing the social role of a mentally ill person) becomes stabilized. In a series of nine propositions, Scheff draws attention to how various social processes operate to create stabilized residual deviance. His theory explicitly states, in Proposition 9, that "labeling is the single most important cause of careers of residual deviance"—that is, movement into a mentally ill role.

The Analysis and Critique section on labeling theory is a paper by Milton Mankoff (Reading 25) which takes as its focus of attack the very point made by Scheff and others concerning the significance of labeling as a cause of deviance. Mankoff raises a fundamental question concerning what types of deviance are best explained by labeling theory. His response to this question leads him to conclude that labeling theory does not apply to the great range of deviance that its proponents imply it should, nor is labeling the outstanding factor in deviant careers that they suggest. He cites numerous research findings from the literature on labeling—including the work of Donald Cressey (Reading 14), Lemert (Reading 22), and Becker (Reading 23)—to support these assertions.

Mankoff argues that a fascination with the dynamics of labeling has left some sociologists with an overly simplistic, restricted approach to deviance. He says the labeling model ignores the possibility of genuine commitment to deviance on the part of the rule-breaker, minimizes the importance of social and psychological factors other than labeling, and underestimates the successful deterrent effects of social control. A more fruitful line of inquiry, according to Mankoff, would be to broaden the analysis to include the institutional sources of career deviance. This is the direction taken by the theorists discussed in the next chapter, who concentrate their attention on the effects of conflict, politics, and power as causes of deviant behavior.

21 *The Dramatization of Evil*
FRANK TANNENBAUM

In the conflict between the young delinquent and the community there develop two opposing definitions of the situation. In the beginning the definition of the situation by the young delinquent may be in the form of play, adventure, excitement, interest, mischief, fun. Breaking windows, annoying people, running around porches, climbing over roofs, stealing from pushcarts, playing truant—all are items of play, adventure, excitement. To the community, however, these activities may and often do take on the form of a nuisance, evil, delinquency, with the demand for control, admonition, chastisement, punishment, police court, truant school. This conflict over the situation is one that arises out of a divergence of values. As the problem develops, the situation gradually becomes redefined. The attitude of the community hardens definitely into a demand for suppression. There is a gradual shift from the definition of the specific acts as evil to a definition of the individual as evil, so that all his acts come to be looked upon with suspicion. In the process of identification his companions, hang-outs, play, speech, income, all his conduct, the personality itself, become subject to scrutiny and question. From the community's point of view, the individual who used to do bad and mischievous things has now become a bad and unredeemable human being. From the individual's point of view there has taken place a similar change. He has gone slowly from a sense of grievance and injustice, of being unduly mistreated and punished, to a recognition that the definition of him as a human being is different from that of other boys in his neighborhood, his school, street, community. This recognition on his part becomes a process of self-identification and integration with the group which shares his activities. It becomes, in part, a process of rationalization; in part, a simple response to a specialized type of stimulus. The young delinquent becomes bad because he is defined as bad *and* because he is not believed if he is good. There is a persistent demand for consistency in character. The community cannot deal with people whom it cannot define. Reputation is this sort of public definition. Once it is established, then unconsciously all agencies combine to maintain this definition even when they apparently and consciously attempt to deny their own implicit judgment.

Early in his career, then, the incipient professional criminal develops an attitude of antagonism to the regulated orderly life that he is required to lead. This attitude is hardened and crystallized by opposition. The conflict becomes a clash of wills. And experience too often has proved that threats, punishments, beatings, commitments to institutions, abuse and defamation of one sort or another, are of no avail. Punishment breaks down against the child's stubbornness. What has happened is that the child has been defined as an "incorrigible" both by his contacts and by himself, and an attempt at a direct breaking down of will generally fails.

The child meets the situation in the only way he can, by defiance and escape—physical escape if possible, or emotional escape by derision, anger, contempt, hatred, disgust, tantrums, destructiveness, and physical violence. The response of the child is just as intelligent and intelligible as that of the schools, of the authorities. They have taken a simple problem, the lack of fitness of an institution to a particular child's needs, and have made a moral issue out of it with values outside the child's ken. It takes on the form of war between two wills, and the longer the war lasts, the more certainly does the child become incorrigible. The child will not yield because he cannot yield—his nature requires other channels for pleasant growth; the school system or society will not yield because it does not see the issues involved as between the incompatibility of an institution and a child's needs, sometimes physical needs, and will instead attempt to twist the child's nature to the institution with that consequent distortion of the child which makes an unsocial career inevitable. The verbalization of the conflict in terms of evil, delinquency, incorrigibility, badness, arrest, force, punishment, stupidity, lack of intelligence, truancy, criminality, gives the innocent divergence of the child from the straight road a meaning that it did not have in the beginning and makes its continuance in these same terms by so much the more inevitable.

The only important fact, when the issue arises of the boy's inability to acquire the specific habits which organized institutions attempt to impose upon him, is that this conflict becomes the occasion for him to acquire another series of habits, interests, and attitudes as a substitute. These habits become as effective in motivating and guiding conduct as would have been those which the orderly routine social institutions attempted to impose had they been acquired.

This conflict gives the gang its hold, because the gang provides escape, security, pleasure, and peace. The gang also gives room for the motor activity which plays a large role in a child's life. The attempt to break up the gang by force merely strengthens it. The arrest of the children has consequences undreamed-of, for several reasons.

First, only some of the children are caught though all may be equally guilty. There is a great deal more delinquency practiced and committed by the young groups than comes to the attention of the police. The boy arrested, therefore, is singled out in a specialized treatment. This boy, no more guilty than the other members of his group, discovers a world of which he knew little. His arrest suddenly precipitates a series of institutions, attitudes, and experiences which the other children do not share. For this boy there suddenly appear the police, the patrol wagon, the police station, the other delinquents and criminals found in the police lock-ups, the court with all its agencies such as bailiffs, clerks, bondsmen, lawyers, probation officers. There are bars, cells, handcuffs, criminals. He is questioned, examined, tested, investigated. His history is gone into, his family is brought into court. Witnesses make their appearance. The boy, no different from the rest of his gang, suddenly becomes the center of a major drama in which all sorts of unexpected characters play important roles. And what is it all about? about the accustomed things his gang has done and has been doing for a long time. In this entirely new world he is made conscious of himself as a different human being than he was before his arrest. He becomes classified as a thief, perhaps, and the entire world about him has suddenly become a different place for him and will remain different for the rest of his life.

THE DRAMATIZATION OF EVIL

The first dramatization of the "evil" which separates the child out of his group for specialized treatment plays a greater role in making the criminal than perhaps any other experience. It cannot be too often emphasized that for the child the whole situation has become different. He now lives in a different world. He has been tagged. A new and hitherto non-existent environment has been precipitated out for him.

The process of making the criminal, therefore, is a process of tagging, defining, identifying, segregating, describing, emphasizing, making conscious and self-conscious; it becomes a way of stimulating, suggesting, emphasizing, and evoking the very traits that are complained of. If the theory of relation of response to stimulus has any meaning, the entire process of dealing with the young delinquent is mischievous in so far as it identifies him to himself or to the environment as a delinquent person.

The person becomes the thing he is described as being. Nor does it seem to matter whether the valuation is made by those who would punish or by those who would reform. In either case the emphasis is upon the conduct that is disapproved of. The parents or the policeman, the older brother or the court, the probation officer or the juvenile institution, in so far as they rest upon the thing complained of, rest upon a false ground. Their very enthusiasm defeats their aim. The harder they work to reform the evil, the greater the evil grows under their hands. The persistent suggestion, with whatever good intentions, works mischief, because it leads to bringing out the bad behavior that it would suppress. The way out is through a refusal to dramatize the evil. The less said about it the better. The more said about something else, still better.

> The hard-drinker who keeps thinking of not drinking is doing what he can to initiate acts which lead to drinking. He is starting with the stimulus to his habit. To succeed he must find some positive interest or line of action which will inhibit the drinking series and which by instituting another course of action will bring him to his desired end.[1]

The dramatization of the evil therefore tends to precipitate the conflict situation which was first created through some innocent maladjustment. The child's isolation forces him into companionship with other children similarly defined, and the gang becomes his means of escape, his security. The life of the gang gives it special mores, and the attack by the community upon these mores merely overemphasizes the conflict already in existence, and makes it the source of a new series of experiences that lead directly to a criminal career.

In dealing with the delinquent, the criminal, therefore, the important thing to remember is that we are dealing with a human being who is responding normally to the demands, stimuli, approval, expectancy, of the group with whom he is associated. We are dealing not with an individual but with a group.

> In a study of 6,000 instances of stealing, with reference to the number of boys involved, it was found that in 90.4 per cent of the cases two or more boys were known to have been involved in the act and were consequently brought to court. Only 9.6 per cent of all the cases were acts of single individuals. Since this study was based upon the number of boys brought to court, and since in many cases not all of the boys involved were caught and brought to court, it is certain that

the percentage of group stealing is therefore even greater than 90.4 per cent. It cannot be doubted that delinquency, particularly stealing, almost invariably involves two or more persons.[2]

That group may be small gang, a gang of children just growing up, a gang of young "toughs" of nineteen or twenty, or a gang of older criminals of thirty. If we are not dealing with a gang we may be dealing with a family. And if we are not dealing with either of these especially we may be dealing with a community. In practice all these factors—the family, the gang, and the community—may be important in the development and maintenance of that attitude towards the world which makes a criminal career a normal, an accepted and approved way of life.

Direct attack upon the individual in these circumstances is a dubious undertaking. By the time the individual has become a criminal his habits have been so shaped that we have a fairly integrated character whose whole career is in tune with the peculiar bit of the environment for which he has developed the behavior and habits that cause him to be apprehended. In theory isolation from that group ought to provide occasion for change in the individual's habit structure. It might, if the individual were transplanted to a group whose values and activities had the approval of the wider community, and in which the newcomer might hope to gain full acceptance eventually. But until now isolation has meant the grouping in close confinement of persons whose strongest common bond has been their socially disapproved delinquent conduct. Thus the attack cannot be made without reference to group life.

The attack must be on the whole group; for only by changing its attitudes and ideals, interests and habits, can the stimuli which it exerts upon the individual be changed. Punishment as retribution has failed to reform, that is, to change character. If the individual can be made aware of a different set of values for which he may receive approval, then we may be on the road to a change in his character. But such a change of values involves a change in stimuli, which means that the criminal's social world must be changed before he can be changed.

NOTES

1. John Dewey, *Human Nature and Conduct* (New York: Henry Holt and Company, 1922), p. 35.
2. Clifford R. Shaw and Earl D. Myers, "The Juvenile Delinquent," *The Illinois Crime Survey*, pp. 662–663. Chicago, 1929.

22 *Primary and Secondary Deviation*
EDWIN M. LEMERT

SOCIOPATHIC INDIVIDUATION

The deviant person is a product of differentiating and isolating processes. Some persons are individually differentiated from others from the time of birth onward, as in the case of a child born with a congenital physical defect or repulsive appearance, and as in the case of a child born into minority racial or cultural group. Other persons grow to maturity in a family or in a social class where pauperism, begging, or crime are more or less institutionalized ways of life for the entire group. In these latter instances the person's sociopsychological growth may be normal in every way, his status as a deviant being entirely caused by his maturation within the framework of social organization and culture designated as "pathological" by the larger society. This is true of many delinquent children in our society.[1]

> It is a matter of great significance that the delinquent child, growing up in the delinquency areas of the city, has very little access to the cultural heritages of the larger conventional society. His infrequent contacts with this larger society are for the most part formal and external. Quite naturally his conception of moral values is shaped and molded by the moral code prevailing in his play groups and the local community in which he lives...the young delinquent has very little appreciation of the meaning of the traditions and formal laws of society.... Hence the conflict between the delinquent and the agencies of society is, in its broader aspects, a conflict of divergent cultures.

The same sort of gradual, unconscious process which operates in the socialization of the deviant child may also be recognized in the acquisition of socially unacceptable behavior by persons after having reached adulthood. However, with more verbal and sophisticated adults, step-by-step violations of societal norms tend to be progressively rationalized in the light of what is socially acceptable. Changes of this nature can take place at the level of either overt or covert behavior, but with a greater likelihood that adults will preface overt behavior changes with projective symbolic departures from society's norms. When the latter occur, the subsequent overt changes may appear to be "sudden" personality modifications. However, whether these changes are completely radical ones is to some extent a moot point. One writer

Reprinted from Edwin M. Lemert, *Social Pathology* (New York: McGraw-Hill Book Co., 1951).

holds strongly to the opinion that sudden and dramatic shifts in behavior from normal to abnormal are seldom the case, that a sequence of small preparatory transformations must be the prelude to such apparently sudden behavior changes. This writer is impressed by the day-by-day growth of "reserve potentialities" within personalities of all individuals, and he contends that many normal persons carry potentialities for abnormal behavior, which, given proper conditions, can easily be called into play.[2]

PERSONALITY CHANGES NOT ALWAYS GRADUAL

This argument is admittedly sound for most cases, but it must be taken into consideration that traumatic experiences often speed up changes in personality.[3] Nor can the "trauma" in these experiences universally be attributed to the unique way in which the person conceives of the experience subjectively. Cases exist to show that personality modifications can be telescoped or that there can be an acceleration of such changes caused largely by the intensity and variety of the social stimulation. Most soldiers undoubtedly have entirely different conceptions of their roles after intensive combat experience. Many admit to having "lived a lifetime" in a relatively short period of time after they have been under heavy fire in battle for the first time. Many generals have remarked that their men have to be a little "shooted" or "blooded" in order to become good soldiers. In the process of group formation, crises and interactional amplification are vital requisites to forging true, role-oriented group behavior out of individuated behavior.[4]

The importance of the person's conscious symbolic reactions to his or her own behavior cannot be overstressed in explaining the shift from normal to abnormal behavior or from one type of pathological behavior to another, particularly where behavior variations become systematized or structured into pathological roles. This is not to say that conscious choice is a determining factor in the differentiating process. Nor does it mean that the awareness of the self is a purely conscious perception. Much of the process of self-perception is doubtless marginal from the point of view of consciousness.[5] But however it may be perceived, the individual's self-definition is closely connected with such things as self-acceptance, the subordination of minor to major roles, and with the motivation involved in learning the skills, techniques, and values of a new role. *Self-definitions or self-realizations are likely to be the result of sudden perceptions and they are especially significant when they are followed immediately by overt demonstrations of the new role they symbolize.* The self-defining junctures are critical points of personality genesis and in the special case of the atypical person they mark a division between two different types of deviation.

PRIMARY AND SECONDARY DEVIATION

There has been an embarrassingly large number of theories, often without any relationship to a general theory, advanced to account for various specific pathologies in human behavior. For certain types of pathology, such as alcoholism, crime, or stuttering, there are almost as many theories as there are writers on these subjects. This has been occasioned in no small way by the preoccupation with the origins of pathological behavior and by the fallacy of confusing *original* causes with *effective* causes. All such theories have elements of truth, and the divergent viewpoints they contain can be reconciled with the general theory here if it is granted that original causes or antecedents of deviant behaviors are many and diversified. This holds especially for the psychological processes leading to similar pathological behavior, but it also holds for the situational concomitants of the initial aberrant conduct. A person may come to use excessive alcohol not only for a wide variety of subjective reasons but also because of diversified situational influences, such as the death of a loved one, business failure, or participating in some sort of organized group activity calling for heavy drinking of liquor. Whatever the original reasons for violating the norms of the community, they are important only for certain research purposes, such as assessing the extent of the "social problem" at a given time or determining the requirements for a rational program of social control. From a narrower sociological viewpoint the deviations are not significant until they are organized subjectively and transformed into active roles and become the social criteria for assigning status. The deviant individuals must react symbolically to their own behavior aberrations and fix them in their sociopsychological patterns. The deviations remain primary deviations or symptomatic and situational as long as they are rationalized or otherwise dealt with as functions of a socially acceptable role. Under such conditions normal and pathological behaviors remain strange and somewhat tensional bedfellows in the same person. Undeniably a vast amount of such segmental and partially integrated pathological behavior exists in our society and has impressed many writers in the field of social pathology.

Just how far and for how long a person may go in dissociating his sociopathic tendencies so that they are merely troublesome adjuncts of normally conceived roles is not known. Perhaps it depends upon the number of alternative definitions of the same overt behavior that he can develop; perhaps certain physiological factors (limits) are also involved. However, if the deviant acts are repetitive and have a high visibility, and if there is a severe societal reaction, which, through a process of identification is incorporated as part of the "me" of the individual, the probability is greatly increased that the integration of existing roles will be disrupted and that reorganization based upon a new role or roles will occur. (The "me" in this context is simply the subjective aspect of the societal reaction.) Reorganization may be the adoption of another normal role in which the tendencies previously defined as "pathological" are given a more acceptable social expression. The other general possibility is the assumption of a deviant role, if such exists; or, more rarely, the person may organize an aberrant sect or group in which he creates a special role of his own. *When a person begins to employ his deviant behavior or a role based upon it as a means of defense, attack, or adjustment to the overt and covert problems created by the consequent societal reaction to him, his deviation is secondary.* Objective evidences of this change will be found in the symbolic appurtenances of the new role, in clothes, speech, posture, and mannerisms, which in some cases heighten social visibility, and which in some cases serve as symbolic cues to professionalization.

ROLE CONCEPTIONS OF THE INDIVIDUAL MUST BE REINFORCED BY REACTIONS OF OTHERS

It is seldom that one deviant act will provoke a sufficiently strong societal reaction to bring about secondary deviation, unless in the process of introjection the individual imputes or projects meanings into the social situation which are not present. In this case anticipatory fears are involved. For example, in a culture where a child is taught sharp distinctions between "good" women and "bad" women, a single act of questionable morality might conceivably have a profound meaning for the girl so indulging. However, in the absence of reactions by the person's family, neighbors, or the larger community, reinforcing the tentative "bad-girl" self-definition, it is questionable whether a transition to secondary deviation would take place. It is also doubtful whether a temporary exposure to a severe punitive reaction by the community will lead a person to identify himself with a pathological role, unless, as we have said, the experience is highly traumatic. Most frequently there is a progressive reciprocal relationship between the deviation of the individual and the societal reaction, with a compounding of the societal reaction out of the minute accretions in the deviant behavior, until a point is reached where ingrouping and outgrouping between society and the deviant is manifest.[6] At this point a stigmatizing of the deviant occurs in the form of name calling, labeling, or stereotyping.

The sequence of interaction leading to secondary deviation is roughly as follows: (1) primary deviation; (2) social penalties; (3) further primary deviation; (4) stronger penalties and rejections; (5) further deviation, perhaps with hostilities and resentment beginning to focus upon those doing the penalizing; (6) crisis reached in the tolerance quotient, expressed in formal action by the community stigmatizing of the deviant; (7) strengthening of the deviant conduct as a reaction to the stigmatizing and penalties; (8) ultimate acceptance of deviant social status and efforts at adjustment on the basis of the associated role.

As an illustration of this sequence the behavior of an errant schoolboy can be cited. For one reason or another, let us say excessive energy, the schoolboy engages in a classroom prank. He is penalized for it by the teacher. Later, due to clumsiness, he creates another disturbance and again he is reprimanded. Then, as sometimes happens, the boy is blamed for something he did not do. When the teacher uses the tag "bad boy" or "mischief maker" or other invidious terms, hostility and resentment are excited in the boy, and he may feel that he is blocked in playing the role expected of him. Thereafter, there may be a strong temptation to assume his role in the class as defined by the teacher, particularly when he discovers that there are rewards as well as penalties deriving from such a role. There is, of course, no implication here that such boys go on to become delinquents or criminals, for the mischief-maker role may later become integrated with or retrospectively rationalized as part of a role more acceptable to school authorites.[7] If such a boy continues this unacceptable role and becomes delinquent, the process must be accounted for in the light of the general theory of this volume. There must be a spreading corroboration of a sociopathic self-conception and societal reinforcement at each step in the process.

The most significant personality changes are manifest when societal definitions and their subjective counterpart become generalized. When this happens, the range of major role choices becomes narrowed to one general class.[8] This was very obvious in the case of a young girl who was the daughter of a paroled convict and who was attending a small Middle Western college. She continually argued with herself and with the author, in whom she had confided, that in reality she belonged on the "other side of the railroad tracks" and that her life could be enormously simplified by acquiescing in this verdict and living accordingly. While in her case there was a tendency to dramatize her conflicts, nevertheless there was enough societal reinforcement of her self-conception by the treatment she received in her relationship with her father and on dates with college boys to lend it a painful reality. Once these boys took her home to the shoddy dwelling in a slum area where she lived with her father, who was often in a drunken condition, they abruptly stopped seeing her again or else became sexually presumptive.

NOTES

1. Shaw, C., *The Natural History of a Delinquent Career*, Chicago, 1941, pp. 75–76. Quoted by permission of the University of Chicago Press, Chicago.
2. Brown, L. Guy, *Social Pathology*, 1942, pp. 44–45.
3. Allport, G., *Personality, A Psychological Interpretation*, 1947, p. 57.
4. Slavson, S. R., *An Introduction to Group Psychotherapy*, 1943, pp. 10, 229*ff*.
5. Murphy, G., *Personality*, 1947, p. 482.
6. Mead, G., "The Psychology of Punitive Justice," *American Journal of Sociology*, 23 March, 1918, pp. 577–602.
7. Evidence for fixed or inevitable sequences from predelinquency to crime is absent. Sutherland, E. H., *Principles of Criminology*, 1939, 4th ed., p. 202.
8. Sutherland seems to say something of this sort in connection with the development of criminal behavior. *Ibid.*, p. 86.

23 *Career Deviance*
HOWARD S. BECKER

...[T]he normal development of people in our society (and probably in any society) can be seen as a series of progressively increasing commitments to conventional norms and institutions. The "normal" person, when he discovers a deviant impulse in himself, is able to check that impulse by thinking of the manifold consequences acting on it would produce for him. He has staked too much on continuing to be normal to allow himself to be swayed by unconventional impulses.

This suggests that in looking at cases of intended nonconformity we must ask how the person manages to avoid the impact of conventional commitments. He may do so in one of two ways. First of all, in the course of growing up the person may somehow have avoided entangling alliances with conventional society. He may, thus, be free to follow his impulses. The person who does not have a reputation to maintain or a conventional job he must keep may follow his impulses. He has nothing staked on continuing to appear conventional.

However, most people remain sensitive to conventional codes of conduct and must deal with their sensitivities in order to engage in a deviant act for the first time. Sykes and Matza have suggested that delinquents actually feel strong impulses to be law-abiding, and deal with them by techniques of neutralization: "justifications for deviance that are seen as valid by the delinquent but not by the legal system or society at large." They distinguish a number of techniques for neutralizing the force of law-abiding values.

◄○►

But we are not so much interested in the person who commits a deviant act once as in the person who sustains a pattern of deviance over a long period of time, who makes of deviance a way of life, who organizes his identity around a pattern of deviant behavior. It is not the casual experimenters with homosexuality (who turned up in such surprisingly large numbers in the Kinsey Report) that we want to find out about, but the man who follows a pattern of homosexual activity throughout his adult life.

One of the mechanisms that lead from casual experimentation to a more sustained pattern of deviant activity is the development of deviant motives and interests.... Here it is sufficient to say that many kinds of deviant activity spring from motives which are socially learned. Before engaging in the activity on a more or less regular basis, the person has no notion of the pleasures to be derived from it; he learns these in the course of interaction with more experienced deviants. He learns to be aware of new kinds of experiences and to think of them as pleasurable. What may well have been a random impulse to try something new becomes a settled taste for something already known and experienced. The vocabularies in which deviant motivations are phrased reveal that their users acquire them in interaction with other deviants. The individual *learns*, in short, to participate in a subculture organized around the particular deviant activity.

Deviant motivations have a social character even when most of the activity is carried on in a private, secret, and solitary fashion. In such cases, various media of communication may take the place of face-to-face interaction in inducting the individual into the culture....[P]ornographic pictures...were described to prospective buyers in a stylized language. Ordinary words were used in a technical shorthand designed to whet specific tastes. The word "bondage," for instance, was used repeatedly to refer to pictures of women restrained in handcuffs or straitjackets. One does not acquire a taste for "bondage photos" without having learned what they are and how they may be enjoyed.

One of the most crucial steps in the process of building a stable pattern of deviant behavior is likely to be the experience of being caught and publicly labeled as a deviant. Whether a person takes this step or not depends not so much on what he does as on what other people do, on whether or not they enforce the rule he has violated. Although I will consider the circumstances under which enforcement takes place in some detail later, two notes are in order here. First of all, even though no one else discovers the nonconformity or enforces the rules against it, the individual who has committed the impropriety may himself act as enforcer. He may brand himself as deviant because of what he has done and punish himself in one way or another for his behavior. This is not always or necessarily the case, but may occur. Second, there may be cases like those described by psychoanalysts in which the individual really wants to get caught and perpetrates his deviant act in such a way that it is almost sure he will be.

In any case, being caught and branded as deviant has important consequences for one's further social participation and self-image. The most important consequence is a drastic change in the individual's public identity. Committing the improper act and being publicly caught at it place him in a new status. He has been revealed as a different kind of person from the kind he was supposed to be. He is labeled a "fairy," "dope fiend," "nut" or "lunatic," and treated accordingly.

In analyzing the consequences of assuming a deviant identity let us make use of Hughes' distinction between master and auxiliary status traits.[1] Hughes notes that most statuses have one key trait which serves to distinguish those who belong from those who do not. Thus the doctor, whatever else he may be, is a person who has a certificate stating that he has fulfilled certain requirements and is licensed to practice medicine; this is the master trait. As Hughes points out, in our society a doctor is also informally expected to have a number of auxiliary traits: most people expect him to be upper middle class, white, male, and Protestant. When he is not there is a sense that he has in some way failed to fill the bill. Similarly, though skin color is the master status trait determining who is Negro and who is white, Negroes are informally expected to have certain status traits and not to have others; people are surprised and find it anomalous if a Negro turns out to be a doctor or a college professor. People often have the master status trait but lack some of the auxiliary, informally expected characteristics; for example, one may be a doctor but be female or Negro.

Hughes deals with this phenomenon in regard to statuses that are well thought of, desired and desirable (noting that one may have the formal qualifications for entry into a status but be denied full entry because of lack of the proper auxiliary traits), but the same process occurs in the case of deviant statuses. Possession of one deviant trait may have a generalized symbolic value, so that people automatically assume that its bearer possesses other undesirable traits allegedly associated with it.

To be labeled a criminal one need only commit a single criminal offense, and this is all the term formally refers to. Yet the word carries a number of connotations specifying auxiliary traits characteristic of anyone bearing the label. A man who has been convicted of housebreaking and thereby labeled criminal is presumed to be a person likely to break into other houses; the police, in rounding up known offenders for investigation after a crime has been committed, operate on this premise. Further, he is considered likely to commit other kinds of crimes as well, because he has shown himself to be a person without "respect for the law." Thus, apprehension for one deviant act exposes a person to the likelihood that he will be regarded as deviant or undesirable in other respects.

There is one other element in Hughes' analysis we can borrow with profit: the distinction between master and subordinate statuses.[2] Some statuses, in our society as in others, override all other statuses and have a certain priority. Race is one of these. Membership in the Negro race, as socially defined, will override most other status considerations in most other situations; the fact that one is a physician or middle-class or female will not protect one from being treated as a Negro first and any of these other things second. The status of deviant (depending on the kind of deviance) is this kind of master status. One receives the status as a result of breaking a rule, and the identification proves to be more important than most others. One will be identified as a deviant first, before other identifications are made. The question is raised: "What kind of person would break such an important rule?" And the answer is given: "One who is different from the rest of us, who cannot or will not act as a moral human being and therefore might break other important rules." The deviant identification becomes the controlling one.

Treating a person as though he were generally rather than specifically deviant produces a self-fulfilling prophecy. It sets in motion several mechanisms which conspire to shape the person in the image people have of him.[3] In the first place, one tends to be cut off, after being identified as deviant, from participation in more conventional groups, even though the specific consequences of the particular deviant activity might never of themselves have caused the isolation had there not also been the public knowledge and reaction to it. For example, being homosexual may not affect one's ability to do office work, but to be known as a homosexual in an office may make it impossible to continue working there. Similarly, though the effects of opiate drugs may not impair one's working ability, to be known as an addict will probably lead to losing one's job. In such cases, the individual finds it difficult to conform to other rules which he had no intention or desire to break, and perforce finds himself deviant in these areas as well. The homosexual who is deprived of a "respectable" job by the discovery of his deviance may drift into unconventional, marginal occupations where it does not make so much difference. The drug addict finds himself forced into other illegitimate kinds of activity, such as robbery and theft, by the refusal of respectable employers to have him around.

When the deviant is caught, he is treated in accordance with the popular diagnosis of why he is that way, and the treatment itself may likewise produce increasing deviance. The drug addict, popularly considered to be a weak-willed individual who cannot forego the indecent pleasures afforded him by opiates, is treated repressively. He is forbidden to use drugs. Since he cannot get drugs legally, he must get them illegally. This forces the market underground and pushes the price of drugs up far beyond the current legitimate market price into a bracket that few can afford on an ordinary salary. Hence the treatment of the addict's deviance places him in a position where it will probably be necessary to resort to deceit and crime in order to support his habit.[4] The behavior is a consequence of the public reaction to the deviance rather than a consequence of the inherent qualities of the deviant act.

Put more generally, the point is that the treatment of deviants denies them the ordinary means of carrying on the routines of everyday life open to most people. Because of this denial, the deviant must of necessity develop illegitimate routines. The influence of public reaction may be direct, as in the instances considered above, or indirect, a consequence of the integrated character of the society in which the deviant lives.

Societies are integrated in the sense that social arrangements in one sphere of activity mesh with other activities in other spheres in particular ways and depend on the existence of these other arrangements. Certain kinds of work lives presuppose a certain kind of family life. . . .

Many varieties of deviance create difficulties by failing to mesh with expectations in other areas of life. Homosexuality is a case in point. Homosexuals have difficulty in any area of social activity in which the assumption of normal sexual interests and propensities for marriage is made without question. In stable work organizations such as large business or industrial organizations there are often points at which the man who would be successful should marry; not to do so will make it difficult for him to do the things that are necessary for success in the organization and will thus thwart his ambitions. The necessity of marrying often creates difficult enough problems for the normal male, and places the homosexual in an almost impossible position. Similarly, in some male work groups where heterosexual prowess is required to retain esteem in the group, the homosexual has obvious difficulties. Failure to meet the expectations of others may force the individual to attempt deviant ways of achieving results automatic for the normal person.

Obviously, everyone caught in one deviant act and labeled a deviant does not move inevitably toward greater deviance in the way the preceding remarks might suggest. The prophecies do not always confirm themselves, the mechanisms do not always work. What factors tend to slow down or halt the movement toward increasing deviance? Under what circumstances do they come into play?

One suggestion as to how the person may be immunized against increasing deviance is found in a recent study of juvenile delinquents who "hustle" homosexuals.[5] These boys act as homosexual prostitutes to confirmed adult homosexuals. Yet they do not themselves become homosexual. Several things account for their failure to continue this kind of sexual deviancy. First, they are protected from police action by the fact that they are minors. If they are apprehended in a homosexual act, they will be treated as exploited children, although in fact they are the exploiters; the law makes the adult guilty. Second, they look on the homosexual acts they engage in simply as a means of making money that is safer and quicker than robbery or similar activities. Third, the standards of their peer group, while permitting homosexual prostitution, allow only one kind of activity, and forbid them to get any special pleasure out of it or to permit any expressions of endearment from the adult with whom they have relations. Infractions of these rules, or other deviations from normal heterosexual activity, are severely punished by the boy's fellows.

Apprehension may not lead to increasing deviance if the situation in which the individual is apprehended for the first time occurs at a point where he can still choose between alternate lines of action. Faced, for the first time, with the possible ultimate and drastic consequences of what he is doing, he may decide that he does not want to take the deviant road, and turn back. If he makes the right choice, he will be welcomed back into the conventional community; but if he makes the wrong move, he will be rejected and start a cycle of increasing deviance.

Ray has shown, in the case of drug addicts, how difficult it can be to reverse a deviant cycle.[6] He points out that drug addicts frequently attempt to cure themselves and that the motivation underlying their attempts is an effort to show nonaddicts whose opinions they respect that they are really not as bad as they are thought to be. On breaking their habit successfully, they find, to their dismay, that people still treat them as though they were addicts (on the premise, apparently, of "once a junkie, always a junkie").

A final step in the career of a deviant is movement into an organized deviant group. When a person makes a definite move into an organized group—or when he realizes and accepts the fact that he has already done so—it has a powerful impact on his conception of himself. A drug addict once told me that the moment she felt she was really "hooked" was when she realized she no longer had any friends who were not drug addicts.

Members of organized deviant groups of course have one thing in common: their deviance. It gives them a sense of common fate, of being in the same boat. From a sense of common fate, from having to face the same problems, grows a deviant subculture: a set of perspectives and understandings about what the world is like and how to deal with it, and a set of routine activities based on those perspectives. Membership in such a group solidifies a deviant identity.

Moving into an organized deviant group has several consequences for the career of the deviant. First of all, deviant groups tend, more than deviant individuals, to be pushed into rationalizing their position. At an extreme, they develop a very complicated historical, legal, and psychological justification for their deviant activity. The homosexual community is a good case. Magazines and books by homosexuals and for homosexuals include historical articles about famous homosexuals in history. They contain articles on the biology and physiology of sex, designed to show that homosexuality is a "normal" sexual response. They contain legal articles, pleading for civil liberties for homosexuals.[7] Taken together, this material provides a working philosophy for the active homosexual, explaining to him why he is the way he is, that other people have also been that way, and why it is all right for him to be that way.

Most deviant groups have a self-justifying rationale (or "ideology"), although seldom is it as well worked out as that of the homosexual. While such rationales do operate, as pointed out earlier, to neutralize the conventional attitudes that deviants may still find in themselves toward their own behavior, they also perform another function. They furnish the individual with reasons that appear sound for continuing the line of activity he has begun. A person who quiets his own doubts by adopting the rationale moves into a more princi-pled and consistent kind of deviance than was possible for him before adopting it.

The second thing that happens when one moves into a deviant group is that he learns how to carry on his deviant activity with a min-imum of trouble. All the problems he faces in evading enforcement of the rule he is breaking have been faced before by others. Solutions have been worked out. Thus, the young thief meets older thieves who, more experienced than he is, explain to him how to get rid of stolen merchandise without running the risk of being caught. Every deviant group has a great stock of lore on such subjects and the new recruit learns it quickly.

Thus, the deviant who enters an organized and institutionalized deviant group is more likely than ever before to continue his ways. He has learned, on the one hand, how to avoid trouble and, on the other hand, a rationale for continuing.

One further fact deserves mention. The rationales of deviant groups tend to contain a general repudiation of conventional moral rules, conventional institutions, and the entire conventional world.

NOTES

1. Everett C. Hughes, "Dilemmas and Contradictions of Status," *American Journal of Sociology,* L (March, 1945), 353–359
2. *Ibid.*
3. See Marsh Ray, "The Cycle of Abstinence and Relapse Among Heroin Addicts," *Social Problems,* 9 (Fall, 1961), 132–140.
4. See *Drug Addiction: Crime or Disease?* Interim and Final Reports of the Joint Committee of the American Bar Association and the American Medical Association on Narcotic Drugs (Bloomington, Indiana: Indiana University Press, 1961).
5. Albert J. Reiss, Jr., "The Social Integration of Queers and Peers," *Social Problems,* 9 (Fall, 1961), 102–120.
6. Ray, *op. cit.*
7. *One* and *The Mattachine Review* are magazines of this type that I have seen.

24 The Role of the Mentally Ill and the Dynamics of Mental Disorder: A Research Framework
THOMAS J. SCHEFF

Although the last two decades have seen a vast increase in the number of studies of functional mental disorder, there is as yet no substantial, verified body of knowledge in this area. A quotation from a recent symposium on schizophrenia summarizes the present situation:

> During the past decade, the problems of chronic schizophrenia have claimed the energy of workers in many fields. Despite significant contributions which reflect continuing progress, *we have yet to learn to ask ourselves the right questions.*[1]

Many investigators apparently agree; systematic studies have not only failed to provide answers to the problem of causation, but there is considerable feeling that the problem itself has not been formulated correctly.

One frequently noted deficiency in psychiatric formulations of the problem is the failure to incorporate social processes into the dynamics of mental disorder. Although the importance of these processes is increasingly recognized by psychiatrists, the conceptual models used in formulating research questions are basically concerned with individual rather than social systems. Genetic, biochemical, and psychological investigations seek different causal agents, but utilize similar models: dynamic systems which are located within the individual. In these investigations, social processes tend to be relegated to a subsidiary role, because the model focuses attention on individual differences, rather than on the social system in which the individuals are involved.

Recently a number of writers have sought to develop an approach which would give more emphasis to social processes. Lemert, Erikson, Goffman, and Szasz have notably contributed to this approach.[2] Lemert, particularly, by rejecting the more conventional concern with the origins of mental deviance, and stressing instead the potential importance of the societal reaction in stabilizing deviance, focuses primarily on mechanisms of social control. The work of all these authors suggests research avenues which are analytically sepa-

Reprinted from Thomas J. Scheff, "The Role of the Mentally Ill and the Dynamics of Mental Disorder," *Sociometry*, vol. 26, 1963, pp. 436–453.

This project was supported in part by the Graduate Research Committee of the University of Wisconsin. The help of many persons, too numerous to list here, who criticized earlier drafts is gratefully acknowledged.

rable from questions of individual systems and point, therefore, to a
theory which would incorporate social processes.

The purpose of the present paper is to contribute to the formulation of such a theory by stating a set of nine propositions which make
up basic assumptions for a social system model of mental disorder.
This set is largely derived from the work of the authors listed above,
all but two of the propositions (No. 4 and No. 5.) being suggested,
with varying degrees of explicitness, in the cited references. By stating
these propositions explicitly, this paper attempts to facilitate testing of
basic assumptions, all of which are empirically unverified, or only
partly verified. By stating these assumptions in terms of standard sociological concepts, this paper attempts to show the relevance to studies of mental disorder of findings from diverse areas of social science,
such as race relations and prestige suggestion. This paper also deline-
ates three problems which are crucial for a sociological theory of mental disorder: what are the conditions in a culture under which diverse
kinds of deviance become stable and uniform; to what extent, in different phases of careers of mental patients, are symptoms of mental
illness the result of conforming behavior; is there a general set of contingencies which lead to the definition of deviant behavior as a manifestation of mental illness? Finally, this paper attempts to formulate
special conceptual tools to deal with these problems, which are directly linked to sociological theory. The social institution of insanity,
residual deviance, the social role of the mentally ill, and the bifurca-
tion of the societal reaction into the alternative reactions of denial and
labeling are examples of such conceptual tools.

These conceptual tools are utilized to construct a theory of mental
disorder in which psychiatric symptoms are considered to be violations of social norms, and stable "mental illness" to be a social role.
The validity of this theory depends upon verification of the nine propositions listed below in future studies, and should, therefore, be applied with caution, and with appreciation for its limitations. One such
limitation is that the theory attempts to account for a much narrower
class of phenomena than is usually found under the rubric of mental
disorder; the discussion that follows will be focused exclusively on
stable or recurring mental disorder, and does not explain the causes of
single deviant episodes. A second major limitation is that the theory
probably distorts the phenomena under discussion. Just as the individual system models under-stress social processes, the model presented here probably exaggerates their importance. The social system
model "holds constant" individual differences, in order to articulate
the relationship between society and mental disorder. Ultimately, a
framework which encompassed both individual and social systems

would be desirable. Given the present state of knowledge, however, this framework may prove useful by providing an explicit contrast to the more conventional medical and psychological approaches, and thus assisting in the formulation of sociological studies of mental disorder.

THE SYMPTOMS OF "MENTAL ILLNESS" AS RESIDUALLY DEVIANT BEHAVIOR

One source of immediate embarrassment to any social theory of "mental illness" is that the terms used in referring to these phenomena in our society prejudge the issue. The medical metaphor "mental illness" suggests a determinate process which occurs within the individual: the unfolding and development of disease. It is convenient, therefore, to drop terms derived from the disease metaphor in favor of a standard sociological concept, deviant behavior, which signifies behavior that violates a social norm in a given society.

If the symptoms of mental illness are to be construed as violations of social norms, it is necessary to specify the type of norms involved. Most norm violations do not cause the violator to be labeled as mentally ill, but as ill-mannered, ignorant, sinful, criminal, or perhaps just harried, depending on the type of norm involved. There are innumerable norms, however, over which consensus is so complete that the members of a group appear to take them for granted. A host of such norms surround even the simplest conversation: a person engaged in conversation is expected to face toward his partner, rather than directly away from him; if his gaze is toward the partner, he is expected to look toward his eyes, rather than, say, toward his forehead; to stand at a proper conversational distance, neither one inch away nor across the room, and so on. A person who regularly violated these expectations probably would not be thought to be merely ill-bred, but as strange, bizarre, and frightening, because his behavior violates the assumptive world of the group, the world that is construed to be the only one that is natural, decent, and possible.

The culture of the group provides a vocabulary of terms for categorizing many norm violations: crime, perversion, drunkenness, and bad manners are familiar examples. Each of these terms is derived from the type of norm broken, and ultimately, from the type of behavior involved. After exhausting these categories, however, there is always a residue of the most diverse kinds of violations, for which the culture provides no explicit label. For example, although there is great cultural variation in what is defined as decent or real, each culture tends to reify its definition of decency and reality, and so provide no way of handling violations of its expectations in these areas. The typical norm governing decency or reality, therefore, literally "goes without saying" and its violation is unthinkable for most of its members. For the convenience of the society in construing those instances of unnamable deviance which are called to its attention, these violations may be lumped together into a residual category: witchcraft, spirit possession, or, in our own society, mental illness. In this paper, the diverse kinds of deviation for which our society provides no explicit label, and which, therefore, sometimes lead to the labeling of the violator as mentally ill, will be considered to be technically *residual deviance*.

THE ORIGINS, PREVALENCE AND COURSE OF RESIDUAL DEVIANCE

The first proposition concerns the origins of residual deviance. 1. *Residual deviance arises from fundamentally diverse sources.* It has been demonstrated that some types of mental disorder are the result of organic causes. It appears likely, therefore, that there are genetic, biochemical or physiological origins for residual deviance. It also appears that residual deviance can arise from individual psychological peculiarities and from differences in upbringing and training. Residual deviance can also probably be produced by various kinds of external stress: the sustained fear and hardship of combat, and deprivation of food, sleep, and even sensory experience.[3] Residual deviance, finally, can be a volitional act of innovation or defiance. The kinds of behavior deemed typical of mental illness, such as hallucinations, delusions, depression, and mania, can all arise from these diverse sources.

The second proposition concerns the prevalence of residual deviance which is analogous to the "total" or "true" prevalence of mental disorder (in contrast to the "treated" prevalence). 2. *Relative to the rate of treated mental illness, the rate of unrecorded residual deviance is extremely high.* There is evidence that grossly deviant behavior is often not noticed or, if it is noticed, it is rationalized as eccentricity. Apparently, many persons who are extremely withdrawn, or who "fly off the handle" for extended periods of time, who imagine fantastic events, or who hear voices or see visions are not labeled as insane either by themselves or others.[4] Their deviance, rather, is unrecognized, ignored, or rationalized. This pattern of inattention and rationalization will be called "denial."[5]

In addition to the kind of evidence cited above there are a number of epidemiological studies of total prevalence. There are numerous problems in interpreting the results of these studies; the major difficulty is that the definition of mental disorder is different in each study, as are the methods used to screen cases. These studies represent, however, the best available information and can be used to estimate total prevalence.

A convenient summary of findings is presented in Plunkett and Gordon.[6] This source compares the methods and populations used in eleven field studies, and lists rates of total prevalence (in percentages) as 1.7, 3.6, 4.5, 4.7, 5.3, 6.1, 10.9, 13.8, 23.3, 23.3, and 33.3.

How do these total rates compare with the rates of treated mental disorder? One of the studies cited by Plunkett and Gordon, the Baltimore study reported by Pasamanick, is useful in this regard since it includes both treated and untreated rates.[7] As compared with the untreated rate of 10.9 per cent, the rate of treatment in state, VA, and private hospitals of Baltimore residents was .5 per cent.[8] That is, for every mental patient there were approximately 20 untreated cases located by the survey. It is possible that the treated rate is too low, however, since patients treated by private physicians were not included. Judging from another study, the New Haven study of treated prevalence, the number of patients treated in private practice is small compared to those hospitalized: over 70 per cent of the patients located in that study were hospitalized even though extensive case-finding techniques were employed. The over-all treated prevalence in the New Haven study was reported as .8 per cent, which is in good agreement with my estimate of .7 per cent for the Baltimore study.[9] If we accept .8 per cent as an estimate of the upper limit of treated prevalence for the Pasamanick study, the ratio of treated to untreated cases is 1/14. That is, for every treated patient we should expect to find 14 untreated cases in the community.

One interpretation of this finding is that the untreated patients in the community represent those cases with less severe disorders, while those patients with severe impairments all fall into the treated group. Some of the findings in the Pasamanick study point in this direction. Of the untreated patients, about half are classified as suffering from minimal impairment. At least a fourth of the untreated group, then, involved very mild disorders.[10]

The evidence from the group diagnosed as psychotic does not support this interpretation, however. Almost all of the cases diagnosed as psychotic were judged to involve severe impairment, yet half of the diagnoses of psychosis occurred in the untreated group. In other words, according to this study there were as many untreated as treated cases of psychoses.[11]

On the basis of the high total prevalence rates cited above and other evidence, it seems plausible that residual deviant behavior is usually transitory, which is the substance of the third proposition.

3. *Most residual deviance is "denied" and is transitory.* The high rates of total prevalence suggest that most residual deviancy is unrecognized or rationalized away. For this type of deviance, which is amorphous and uncrystallized, Lemert uses the term "primary deviation."[12] Balint describes similar behavior as "the unorganized phase of illness."[13] Although Balint assumes that patients in this phase ultimately "settle down" to an "organized illness," other outcomes are possible. A person in this stage may "organize" his deviance in other than illness terms, e.g. as eccentricity or genius, or the deviant acts may terminate when situational stress is removed.

The experience of battlefield psychiatrists can be interpreted to support the hypothesis that residual deviance is usually transitory. Glass reports that combat neurosis is often self-terminating if the soldier is kept with his unit and given only the most superficial medical attention.[14] Descriptions of child behavior can be interpreted in the same way. According to these reports, most children go through periods in which at least several of the following kinds of deviance may occur: temper tantrums, head banging, scratching, pinching, biting, fantasy playmates or pets, illusory physical complaints, and fears of sounds, shapes, colors, persons, animals, darkness, weather, ghosts, and so on.[15] In the vast majority of instances, however, these behavior patterns do not become stable.

If residual deviance is highly prevalent among ostensibly "normal" persons and is usually transitory, as suggested by the last two propositions, what accounts for the small percentage of residual deviants who go on to deviant careers? To put the question another way, under what conditions is residual deviance stabilized? The conventional hypothesis is that the answer lies in the deviant himself. The hypothesis suggested here is that the most important single factor (but not the only factor) in the stabilization of residual deviance is the societal reaction. Residual deviance may be stabilized if it is defined to be evidence of mental illness, and/or the deviant is placed in a deviant status, and begins to play the role of the mentally ill. In order to avoid the implication that mental disorder is merely role-playing and pretence, it is first necessary to discuss the social institution of insanity.

SOCIAL CONTROL: INDIVIDUAL AND SOCIAL SYSTEMS OF BEHAVIOR

In *The Myth of Mental Illness*, Szasz proposes that mental disorder be viewed within the framework of "the game-playing model of human behavior." He then describes hysteria, schizophrenia, and other mental disorders as the "impersonation" of sick persons by those whose "real" problem concerns "problems of living." Although Szasz states that role-playing by mental patients may not be completely or even mostly voluntary, the implication is that mental disorder be viewed as a strategy chosen by the individual as a way of obtaining help from others. Thus, the term "impersonation" suggests calculated and deliberate shamming by the patient. In his comparisons of hysteria, malingering, and cheating, although he notes differences between these behavior patterns, he suggests that these differences may be mostly a matter of whose point of view is taken in describing the behavior.

The present paper also uses the role-playing model to analyze mental disorder, but places more emphasis on the involuntary aspects of role-playing than Szasz, who tends to treat role-playing as an individual system of behavior. In many social psychological discussions, however, role-playing is considered as a part of a social system. The individual plays his role by articulating his behavior with the cues and actions of other persons involved in the transaction. The proper performance of a role is dependent on having a cooperative audience. This proposition may also be reversed: having an audience which acts toward the individual in a uniform way may lead the actor to play the expected role even if he is not particularly interested in doing so. The "baby of the family" may come to find this role obnoxious, but the uniform pattern of cues and actions which confronts him in the family may lock in with his own vocabulary of responses so that it is inconvenient and difficult for him not to play the part expected of him. To the degree that alternative roles are closed off, the proffered role may come to be the only way the individual can cope with the situation.

One of Szasz's very apt formulations touches upon the social systemic aspects of role-playing. He draws an analogy between the role of the mentally ill and the "type-casting" of actors.[16] Some actors get a reputation for playing one type of role, and find it difficult to obtain other roles. Although they may be displeased, they may also come to incorporate aspects of the type-cast role into their self-conceptions, and ultimately into their behavior. Findings in several social psychological studies suggest that an individual's role behavior may be shaped by the kinds of "deference" that he regularly receives from others.[17]

One aspect of the voluntariness of role-playing is the extent to which the actor believes in the part he is playing. Although a role may be played cynically, with no belief, or completely sincerely, with whole-hearted belief, many roles are played on the basis of an intricate mixture of belief and disbelief. During the course of a study of a large public mental hospital, several patients told the author in confidence about their cynical use of their symptoms—to frighten new personnel, to escape from unpleasant work details, and so on. Yet these *same* patients, at other times, appear to have been sincere in their symptomatic behavior. Apparently it was sometimes difficult for them to tell whether they were playing the role or the role was playing them. Certain types of symptomatology are quite interesting in this connection. In simulation of previous psychotic states, and in the behavior pattern known to psychiatrists as the Ganser syndrome, it is apparently almost impossible for the observer to separate feigning of symptoms from involuntary acts with any degree of certainty.[18] In accordance with what has been said so far, the difficulty is probably that the patient is just as confused by his own behavior as is the observer.

This discussion suggests that a stable role performance may arise when the actor's role imagery locks in with the type of "deference" which he regularly receives. An extreme example of this process may be taken from anthropological and medical reports concerning the "dead role," as in deaths attributed to "bone-pointing." Death from bone-pointing appears to arise from the conjunction of two fundamental processes which characterize all social behavior. First, all individuals continually orient themselves by means of responses which are perceived in social interaction: the individual's identity and continuity of experience are dependent on these cues.[19] Secondly, the individual has his own vocabulary of expectations, which may in a particular situation either agree with or be in conflict with the sanctions to which he is exposed. Entry into a role may be complete when this role is part of the individual's expectations, and when these expectations are reaffirmed in social interaction. In the following pages this principle will be applied to the problem of the causation of mental disorder.

What are the beliefs and practices that constitute the social institution of insanity?[20] And how do they figure in the development of mental disorder? Two propositions concerning beliefs about mental disorder in the general public will now be considered.

4. *Stereotyped imagery of mental disorder is learned in early childhood.* Although there are no substantiating studies in this area, scattered observations lead the author to conclude that children learn a considerable amount of imagery concerning deviance very early, and that much of the imagery comes from their peers rather than from adults. The literal meaning of "crazy," a term now used in a wide variety of contexts, is probably grasped by children during the first years of elementary school. Since adults are often vague and evasive in their responses to questions in this area, an aura of mystery surrounds it. In this socialization the grossest stereotypes which are heir to childhood fears, e.g., of the "boogie man," survive. These conclusions are quite specu-

lative, of course, and need to be investigated systematically, possibly with techniques similar to those used in studies of the early learning of racial stereotypes.

Assuming, however, that this hypothesis is sound, what effect does early learning have on the shared conceptions of insanity held in the community? There is much fallacious material learned in early childhood which is later discarded when more adequate information replaces it. This question leads to hypothesis no. 5. 5. *The stereotypes of insanity are continually reaffirmed, inadvertently, in ordinary social interaction.*

Although many adults become acquainted with medical concepts of mental illness, the traditional stereotypes are not discarded, but continue to exist alongside the medical conceptions, because the stereotypes receive almost continual support from the mass media and in ordinary social discourse. In newspapers, it is a common practice to mention that a rapist or a murderer was once a mental patient. This negative information, however, is seldom offset by positive reports. An item like the following is almost conceivable:

> Mrs. Ralph Jones, an ex-mental patient, was elected president of the Fairview Home and Garden Society in their meetng last Thursday.

Because of highly biased reporting, the reader is free to make the unwarranted inference that murder and rape occur more frequently among ex-mental patients than among the population at large. Actually, it has been demonstrated that the incidence of crimes of violence, or of any crime, is much lower among ex-mental patients than among the general population.[21] Yet, this is not the picture presented to the public.

Reaffirmation of the stereotype of insanity occurs not only in the mass media, but also in ordinary conversation, in jokes, anecdotes, and even in conventional phrases. Such phrases as "Are you crazy?", or "It would be a madhouse," "It's driving me out of my mind," or "It's driving me distracted," and hundreds of others occur frequently in informal conversations. In this usage insanity itself is seldom the topic of conversation; the phrases are so much a part of ordinary language that only the person who considers each word carefully can eliminate them from his speech. Through verbal usages the stereotypes of insanity are a relatively permanent part of the social structure.

In a recent study Nunnally demonstrated that reaffirmation of stereotypes occurs in the mass media. In a systematic and extensive content analysis of television, radio, newspapers and magazines, including "confession" magazines, they found an image of mental disorder presented which was overwhelmingly stereotyped.

...media presentations emphasized the bizarre symptoms of the mentally ill. For example, information relating to Factor I (the conception that mentally ill persons look and act different from "normal" people) was recorded 89 times. Of these, 88 affirmed the factor, that is, indicated or suggested that people with mental-health problems "look and act different": only one item denied Factor I. In television dramas, for example, the afflicted person often enters the scene staring glassy-eyed, with his mouth widely ajar, mumbling incoherent phrases or laughing uncontrollably. Even in what would be considered the milder disorders, neurotic phobias and obsessions, the afflicted person is presented as having bizarre facial expressions and actions.[22]

DENIAL AND LABELING

According to the analysis presented here, the traditional stereotypes of mental disorder are solidly entrenched in the population because they are learned early in childhood and are continuously reaffirmed in the mass media and in everyday conversation. How do these beliefs function in the processes leading to mental disorder? This question will be considered by first referring to the earlier discussion of the societal reaction to residual deviance.

It was stated that the usual reaction to residual deviance is denial, and that in these cases most residual deviance is transitory. The societal reaction to deviance is not always denial, however. In a small proportion of cases the reaction goes the other way, exaggerating and at times distorting the extent and degree of deviation. This pattern of exaggeration, which we will call "labeling," has been noted by Garfinkel in his discussion of the "degradation" of officially recognized criminals.[23] Goffman makes a similar point in his description of the "discrediting" of mental patients.[24] Apparently under some conditions the societal reaction to deviance is to seek out signs of abnormality in the deviant's history to show that he was always essentially a deviant.

The contrasting social reactions of denial and labeling provide a means of answering two fundamental questions. If deviance arises from diverse sources—physical, psychological, and situational—how does the uniformity of behavior that is associated with insanity develop? Secondly, if deviance is usually transitory, how does it become stabilized in those patients who became chronically deviant? To summarize, what are the sources of uniformity and stability of deviant behavior?

In the approach taken here the answer to this question is based on hypotheses Nos. 4 and 5, that the role imagery of insanity is learned early in childhood, and is reaffirmed in social interaction. In a crisis, when the deviance of an individual becomes a public issue, the traditional stereotype of insanity becomes the guiding imagery for action, both for those reacting to the deviant and, at times, for the deviant himself. When societal agents and persons around the deviant react to him uniformly in terms of the traditional stereotypes of insanity, his amorphous and unstructured deviant behavior tends to crystallize in conformity to these expectations, thus becoming similar to the behavior of the other deviants classified as mentally ill, and stable over time. The process of becoming uniform and stable is completed when the traditional imagery becomes a part of the deviant's orientation for guiding his own behavior.

The idea that cultural stereotypes may stabilize primary deviance, and tend to produce uniformity in symptoms, is supported by cross-cultural studies of mental disorder. Although some observers insist there are underlying similarities, most agree that there are enormous differences in the manifest symptoms of stable mental disorder *between* societies, and great similarity *within* societies.[25]

These considerations suggest that the labeling process is a crucial contingency in most careers of residual deviance. Thus Glass, who observed that neuropsychiatric casualties may not become mentally ill if they are kept with their unit, goes on to say that military experience with psychotherapy has been disappointing. Soldiers who are removed from their unit to a hospital, he states, often go on to become chronically impaired.[26] That is, their deviance is stabilized by the labeling process, which is implicit in their removal and hospitalization. A similar interpretation can be made by comparing the observations of childhood disorders among Mexican-Americans with those of "Anglo" children. Childhood disorders such as *susto* (an illness believed to result from fright) sometimes have damaging outcomes in Mexican-American children.[27] Yet the deviant behavior involved is very similar to that which seems to have high incidence among Anglo children, with permanent impairment virtually never occurring. Apparently through cues from his elders the Mexican-American child, behaving initially much like his Anglo counterpart, learns to enter the sick role, at times with serious consequences.[28]

ACCEPTANCE OF THE DEVIANT ROLE

From this point of view, then, most mental disorder can be considered to be a social role. This social role complements and reflects the status of the insane in the social structure. It is through the social processes which maintain the status of the insane that the varied deviancies from which mental disorder arises are made uniform and stable. The stabilization and uniformization of residual deviance are completed when the deviant accepts the role of the insane as the framework within which he organizes his own behavior. Three hypotheses are stated below which suggest some of the processes which cause the deviant to accept such a stigmatized role.

6. *Labeled deviants may be rewarded for playing the stereotyped deviant role.* Ordinarily patients who display "insight" are rewarded by psychiatrists and other personnel. That is, patients who manage to find evidence of "their illness" in their past and present behavior, confirming the medical and societal diagnosis, receive benefits. This pattern of behavior is a special case of a more general pattern that has been called the "apostolic function" by Balint, in which the physician and others inadvertently cause the patient to display symptoms of the illness the physician thinks the patient has.[29] Not only physicians but other hospital personnel and even other patients reward the deviant for conforming to the stereotypes.[30]

7. *Labeled deviants are punished when they attempt the return to conventional roles.* The second process operative is the systematic blockage of entry to nondeviant roles once the label has been publicly applied. Thus the ex-mental patient, although he is urged to rehabilitate himself in the community, usually finds himself discriminated against in seeking to return to his old status, and on trying to find a new one in the occupational, marital, social, and other spheres.[31] Thus, to a degree, the labeled deviant is rewarded for deviating, and punished for attempting to conform.

8. *In the crisis occurring when a primary deviant is publicly labeled, the deviant is highly suggestible, and may accept the proffered role of the insane as the only alternative.* When gross deviancy is publicly recognized and made an issue, the primary deviant may be profoundly confused, anxious, and ashamed. In this crisis it seems reasonable to assume that the deviant will be suggestible to the cues that he gets from the reactions of others toward him.[32] But those around him are also in a crisis; the incomprehensible nature of the deviance, and the seeming need for immediate action lead them to take collective action against the deviant on the basis of the attitude which all share—the traditional stereotypes of insanity. The deviant is sensitive to the cues provided by these others and begins to think of himself in terms of the stereotyped role of insanity, which is part of his own role vocabulary also, since he, like those reacting to him, learned it early in childhood. In this situation his behavior may begin to follow the pattern suggested

by his own stereotypes and the reactions of others. That is, when a primary deviant organizes his behavior within the framework of mental disorder, and when his organization is validated by others, particularly prestigeful others such as physicians, he is "hooked" and will proceed on a career of chronic deviance.

The role of suggestion is noted by Warner in his description of bone-pointing magic:

> The effect of (the suggestion of the entire community on the victim) is obviously drastic. An analogous situation in our society is hard to imagine. If all a man's near kin, his father, mother, brothers and sisters, wife, children, business associates, friends and all the other members of society, should suddenly withdraw themselves because of some dramatic circumstance, refusing to take any attitude but one of taboo...and them perform over him a sacred ceremony...the enormous suggestive power of this movement...of the community after it has had its attitudes (toward the victim) crystallized can be somewhat understood by ourselves.[33]

If we substitute for black magic the taboo that usually accompanies mental disorder, and consider a commitment proceeding or even mental hospital admission as a sacred ceremony, the similarity between Warner's description and the typical events in the development of mental disorder is considerable.

The last three propositions suggest that once a person has been placed in a deviant status there are rewards for conforming to the deviant role, and punishments for not conforming to the deviant role. This is not to imply, however, that the symptomatic behavior of persons occupying a deviant status is always a manifestation of conforming behavior. To explain this point, some discussion of the process of self-control in "normals" is necessary.

In a recent discussion of the process of self-control, Shibutani notes that self-control is not automatic, but is an intricate and delicately balanced process, sustainable only under propitious circumstances.[34] He points out that fatigue, the reaction to narcotics, excessive excitement or tension (such as is generated in mobs), or a number of other conditions interfere with self-control; conversely, conditions which produce normal bodily states, and deliberative processes such as symbolization and imaginative rehearsal before action, facilitate it.

One might argue that a crucially important aspect of imaginative rehearsal is the image of himself that the actor projects into his future action. Certainly in American society, the cultural image of the "normal" adult is that of a person endowed with self-control ("willpower," "backbone," "strength of character," etc.). For the person who sees himself as endowed with the trait of self-control, self-control is facilitated, since he can imagine himself enduring stress during his imaginative rehearsal, and also while under actual stress.

For a person who has acquired an image of himself as lacking the ability to control his own actions, the process of self-control is likely to break down under stress. Such a person may feel that he has reached his "breaking-point" under circumstances which would be endured by a person with a "normal" self-conception. This is to say, a greater lack of self-control than can be explained by stress tends to appear in those roles for which the culture transmits imagery which emphasizes lack of self-control. In American society such imagery is transmitted for the roles of the very young and very old, drunkards and drug addicts, gamblers, and the mentally ill.

Thus, the social role of the mentally ill has a different significance at different phases of residual deviance. When labeling first occurs, it merely gives a name to primary deviation which has other roots. When (and if) the primary deviance becomes an issue, and is not ignored or rationalized away, labeling may create a social type, a pattern of "symptomatic" behavior in conformity with the stereotyped expectations of others. Finally, to the extent that the deviant role becomes a part of the deviant's self-conception, his ability to control his own behavior may be impaired under stress, resulting in episodes of compulsive behavior.

The preceding eight hypotheses form the basis for the final causal hypothesis. 9. *Among residual deviants, labeling is the single most important cause of careers of residual deviance.* This hypothesis assumes that most residual deviance, if it does not become the basis for entry into the sick role, will not lead to a deviant career. Most deviant careers, according to this point of view, arise out of career contingencies, and are therefore not directly connected with the origins of the initial deviance.[35] Although there is a wide variety of contingencies which lead to labeling rather than denial, these contingencies can be usefully classified in terms of the nature of the deviant behavior, the person who commits the deviant acts, and the community in which the deviance occurs. Other things being equal, the severity of the societal reaction to deviance is a function of, first, the degree, amount, and visibility of the deviant behavior; second, the power of the deviant, and the social distance between the deviant and the agents of social control; and finally, the tolerance level of the community, and the availability in the culture of the community of alternative nondeviant roles.[36] Particularly crucial for future research is the importance of the first two contingencies (the amount and degree of deviance), which are characteristics of the deviant, relative to the remaining five contingencies, which are characteristics of the social system.[37] To the extent that these five factors are found empirically to be independent determinants of labeling and denial, the status of the mental patient can be considered a partly ascribed rather than a completely achieved status. The dynamics of treated mental illness could then be profitably studied quite apart from the individual dynamics of mental disorder.

CONCLUSION

This paper has presented a sociological theory of the causation of stable mental disorder. Since the evidence advanced in support of the theory was scattered and fragmentary, it can only be suggested as a stimulus to further discussion and research. Among the areas pointed out for further investigation are field studies of the prevalence and duration of residual deviance; investigations of stereotypes of mental disorder in children, the mass media, and adult conversations; studies of the rewarding of stereotyped deviation, blockage of return to conventional roles, and of the suggestibility of primary deviants in crises. The final causal hypothesis suggests studies of the conditions under which denial and labeling of residual deviation occur. The variables which might effect the societal reaction concern the nature of the deviance, the deviant himself, and the community in which the deviation occurs. Although many of the hypotheses suggested are largely unverified, they suggest avenues for investigating mental disorder different than those that are usually followed, and the rudiments of a general theory of deviant behavior.

NOTES

1. Nathanial S. Apter, "Our Growing Restlessness with Problems of Chronic Schizophrenia," in Lawrence Appleby, *et al.*, *Chronic Schizophrenia*, Glencoe, Ill.: Free Press, 1958.

2. Edwin M. Lemert, *Social Pathology*, New York: McGraw-Hill, 1951; Kai T. Erikson, "Patient Role and Social Uncertainty—A Dilemma of the Mentally Ill," *Psychiatry*, 20 (August, 1957), pp. 263–274; Erving Goffman, *Asylums*, New York: Doubleday-Anchor, 1961; Thomas S. Szasz, *The Myth of Mental Illness*, New York: Hoeber-Harper, 1961.

3. Philip Solomon, *et al.* (eds.), *Sensory Deprivation*, Cambridge: Harvard, 1961; E. L. Bliss, *et al.*, "Studies of Sleep Deprivation—Relationship to Schizophrenia," *A.M.A. Archives of Neurology and Psychiatry*, 81 (March, 1959), pp. 348–359.

4. See, for example, John A. Clausen and Marian R. Yarrow, "Paths to the Mental Hospital," *Journal of Social Issues,* 11 (December, 1955), pp. 25–32; August B. Hollingshead and Frederick C. Redlich, *Social Class and Mental Illness,* New York: Wiley, 1958, pp. 172–176; and Elaine Cumming and John Cumming, *Closed Ranks,* Cambridge: Harvard, 1957, pp. 92–103.

5. The term "denial" is used in the same sense as in Cumming and Cumming, *ibid.,* Chap. VII.

6. Richard J. Plunkett and John E. Gordon, *Epidemiology and Mental Illness,* New York: Basic Books, 1960.

7. Benjamin Pasamanick, "A Survey of Mental Disease in an Urban Population, IV, An Approach to Total Prevalence Rates," *Archives of General Psychiatry,* 5 (August, 1961), pp. 151–155.

8. *Ibid.,* p. 153.

9. Hollingshead and Redlich, *op. cit.,* p. 199.

10. Pasamanick, *op. cit.,* pp. 153–154.

11. *Ibid.*

12. Lemert, *op. cit.,* Chap. 4.

13. Michael Balint, *The Doctor, His Patient, and the Illness,* New York: International Universities Press, 1957, p. 18.

14. Albert J. Glass, "Psychotherapy in the Combat Zone," in *Symposium on Stress,* Washington, D. C.: Army Medical Service Graduate School, 1953. Cf. Abraham Kardiner and H. Spiegel, *War Stress and Neurotic Illness,* New York: Hoeber, 1947, Chps. III–IV.

15. Frances L. Ilg and Louise B. Ames, *Child Behavior,* New York: Dell, 1960, pp. 138–188.

16. Szasz, *op. cit.,* p. 252. For discussion of type-casting see Orrin E. Klapp, *Heroes, Villains and Fools,* Englewood Cliffs, New Jersey: Prentice-Hall, 1962, pp. 5–8 and *passim.*

17. Cf. Zena S. Blau, "Changes in Status and Age Identification," *American Sociological Review,* 21 (April, 1956), pp. 198–203; James Benjamins, "Changes in Performance in Relation to Influences upon Self-Conceptualization *Journal of Abnormal and Social Psychology,* 45 (July, 1950), pp. 473–480; Albert Ellis, "The Sexual Psychology of Human Hermaphrodites," *Psychosomatic Medicine,* 7 (March, 1945), pp. 108–125; S. Liberman, "The Effect of Changes in Roles on the Attitudes of Role Occupants," *Human Relations,* 9 (1956), pp. 385–402. For a review of experimental evidence, see John H. Mann, "Experimental Evaluations of Role Playing," *Psychological Bulletin,* 53 (May, 1956), pp. 227–234. For an interesting demonstration of the inter-relations between the symptoms of patients on the same ward, see Sheppard G. Kellam and J. B. Chassan, "Social Context and Symptom Fluctuation," *Psychiatry,* 25 (November, 1962), pp. 370–381.

18. Leo Sadow and Alvin Suslick, "Simulation of a Previous Psychotic State," *A.M.A. Archives of General Psychiatry,* 4 (May, 1961), pp. 452–458.

19. Generalizing from experimental findings, Blake and Mouton make this statement about the processes of conformity, resistance to influence, and conversion to a new role:

> . . . an individual requires a stable framework, including salient and firm reference points, in order to orient himself and to regulate his interactions with others. This framework consists of external and internal anchorages available to the individual whether he is aware of them or not. With an acceptable framework he can resist giving or accepting information that is inconsistent with that framework or that requires him to relinquish it. In the absence of a stable framework he actively seeks to establish one through his own strivings by making use of significant and relevant information provided within the context of interaction. *By controlling the amount and kind of information available for orientation, he can be led to embrace conforming attitudes which are entirely foreign to his earlier ways of thinking.*

   Robert R. Blake and Jane S. Mouton, "Conformity, Resistance and Conversion," in *Conformity and Deviation,* Irwin A. Berg and Bernard M. Bass (eds.), New York: Harper, 1961, pp. 1–2. For a recent and striking demonstration of the effect on social communication in defining internal stimuli, see Stanley Schachter and Jerome E. Singer, "Cognitive, Social, and Physiological Determinants of Emotional State," *Psychological Review,* 69 (September, 1962), pp. 379–399.

20. The Cummings describe the social institution of insanity (the "patterned response" to deviance) in terms of denial, isolation, and insulation. Cumming and Cumming, *loc. cit.*

21. Henry Brill and Benjamin Malzberg, "Statistical Report Based on the Arrest Record of 5354 Male Ex-patients Released from New York State Mental Hospitals During the Period 1946–48," mimeographed document available from the authors; L. H. Cohen and H. Freeman, "How Dangerous to the Community Are State Hospital Patients?", *Connecticut State Medical Journal,* 9 (September, 1945), pp. 697–701.

22. Jum C. Nunnally, Jr., *Popular Conceptions of Mental Health,* New York: Holt, Rinehart and Winston, 1961, p. 74.

23. Harold Garfinkel, "Conditions of Successful Degradation Ceremonies," *American Journal of Sociology,* 61 (March, 1956), pp. 420–424.

24. Goffman, "The Moral Career of the Mental Patient," in *Asylums, op. cit.,* pp. 125–171.

25. P. M. Yap, "Mental Diseases Peculiar to Certain Cultures: A Survey of Comparative Psychiatry," *Journal of Mental Science,* 97 (April, 1951), pp.

313–327; Paul E. Benedict and Irving Jacks, "Mental Illness in Primitive Societies," *Psychiatry,* 17 (November, 1954), pp. 377–389.

26. Glass, *op. cit.*

27. Lyle Saunders, *Cultural Differences and Medical Care,* New York: Russell Sage, 1954, p. 142.

28. For discussion, with many illustrative cases, of the process in which persons play the "dead role" and subsequently die, see Charles C. Herbert, "Life-influencing Interactions," in *The Physiology of Emotions,* Alexander Simon, *et al.,* eds., New York: Charles C Thomas, 1961.

29. Balint, *op. cit.,* pp. 215–239. Cf. Thomas J. Scheff, "Decision Rules, Types of Error and Their Consequences in Medical Diagnosis," *Behavioral Science,* 8 (April, 1963), pp. 97–107.

30. William Caudill, F. C. Redlich, H. R. Gilmore, and E. B. Brody, "Social Structure and the Interaction Processes on a Psychiatric Ward," *American Journal of Orthopsychiatry,* 22 (April, 1952), pp. 314–334.

31. Lemert, *op. cit.,* provides an extensive discussion of this process under the heading of "Limitation of Participation," pp. 434–440.

32. This proposition receives support from Erikson's observations: Kai T. Erickson, *loc. cit.*

33. W. Lloyd Warner, *A Black Civilization,* rev. ed., New York: Harper, 1958, p. 242.

34. T. Shibutani, *Society and Personality,* Englewood Cliffs, N.J.: Prentice-Hall, 1961, Chapter 6, "Consciousness and Voluntary Conduct."

35. It should be noted, however, that these contingencies are causal only because they become part of a dynamic system: the reciprocal and cumulative interrelation between the deviant's behavior and the societal reaction. For example, the more the deviant enters the role of the mentally ill, the more he is defined by others as mentally ill, but the more he is defined as mentally ill, the more fully he enters the role, and so on. By representing this theory in the form of a flow chart, Walter Buckley pointed out that there are numerous such feedback loops implied here. For an explicit treatment of feedback, see Edwin M. Lemert, "Paranoia and the Dynamics of Exclusion," *Sociometry,* 25 (March, 1962), pp. 2–20.

36. *Cf.* Lemert, *op. cit.,* pp. 51–53, 55–68; Goffman, "The Moral Career of the Mental Patient," in *Asylums, op. cit.,* pp. 134–135; David Mechanic, "Some Factors in Indentifying and Defining Mental Illness," *Mental Hygiene,* 46 (January, 1962), pp. 66–74; for a list of similar factors in the reaction to physical illness, see Earl L. Koos, *The Health of Regionville,* New York: Columbia University Press, 1954, pp. 30–38.

37. *Cf.* Thomas J. Scheff, "Psychiatric and Social Contingencies in the Release of Mental Patients in a Midwestern State," forthcoming; Simon Dinitz, Mark Lefton, Shirley Angrist, and Benjamin Pasamanick,

"Psychiatric and Social Attributes as Predictors of Case Outcome in Mental Hospitalization," *Social Problems*, 8 (Spring, 1961), pp. 322–328.

Analysis and Critique

25 *Societal Reaction and Career Deviance: A Critical Analysis*
MILTON MANKOFF

INTRODUCTION

In recent years the societal reaction or labeling perspective of Tannen-baum (1938), as elaborated by Lemert (1951), Erikson (1962), Becker (1963), and Scheff (1966), has become well known and seemingly widely accepted in one form or another by sociologists studying social deviance. Whether Tannenbaum and others *intended* to expound a general theory of deviance (Gibbs, 1966b), particularly career devi-ance, is not nearly as important as the fact that the work of these soci-ologists has been perceived by many to form a fairly coherent body of thought on the subject. Accordingly, a great deal of research has been generated by using some central concepts associated with the labeling perspective (i.e., primary and secondary or career deviance and soci-etal reaction) to examine many forms of rule-breaking.

The bulk of the research growing out of this tradition has suc-ceeded in demonstrating that social labeling is not randomly applied throughout the population of rule-breakers (Cicourel, 1968; Piliavin and Briar, 1964). While not wishing to belittle the importance of such documentation and its implications for social theory (and social justice), one must point out that to date there has not been a system-atic examination of one of the labeling perspective's most profound derivative "theories"; that is, *rule-breakers become entrenched in deviant*

Reprinted from "Societal Reaction and Career Deviance: A Critical Analysis," Milton Mankoff, *The Sociological Quarterly*, 12:2 (Spring, 1971): pp. 204–217.

This is a revised version of a paper previously delivered at the 1969 meetings of the Pacific Sociological Association in Seattle, Washington. I am deeply indebted for both substantive and editorial assistance to William Chambliss, Marshall Clinard, Irving Horowitz, David Mechanic, Arnold Ross, Thomas Scheff, D. Lawrence Wieder, and several anonymous editorial referees.

roles because they are labeled "deviant" by others and are consequently excluded from resuming normal roles in the community (Lemert, 1951:75–79; Becker, 1963:31–36; Scheff, 1966). Much of the documentation of the discriminatory use of labeling is based on the belief that labeling is the primary determinant of career deviance. It is worthwhile, therefore, to examine the validity of this position. Without validation of this central notion, the research on the labeling process loses a great deal of its significance.

Among labeling theorists there are, of course, subtle disagreements concerning whether the labeling process is merely a necessary condition, or approaches a necessary and sufficient condition for the development of secondary or career deviance. Lemert (1967), for example, is extremely sensitive to the indeterminacy of the interaction between rule-breakers and other social actors and is even willing to exclude certain forms of rule-breaking from the general societal reaction model. Yet in focusing on the variety of paths rule-breakers travel he does not develop any explicit formulation of the conditions under which the societal reaction model is most applicable to the phenomena at hand.

The failure of those whose work falls within the boundaries of the labeling tradition to develop typologies that indicate which particular kinds of social deviance can be most fruitfully understood by using the concepts of labeling theory is a serious shortcoming which prevents evaluating the significance of their research. While labeling theorists may think they are only applying the principles of the labeling perspective to one form of deviation, their incidental endorsements of generalizability to other forms of deviant behavior make the critic wary of "straw men" arguments when he attempts to project the implications of specific research for general theory. Those who write about deviance from the labeling perspective, whether they feel they are being general theorists or not, should welcome an attempt to consider the limits of their model for explaining career deviance.

Given the above-mentioned confusion, it is the primary intention of this exploratory paper to examine critically some empirical studies bearing on the validity of labeling theory and to provide some tentative answers to the following queries:

1. Is societal reaction to rule-breaking a necessary and sufficient condition for career deviance?
2. Is societal reaction to rule-breaking equally significant in the determination of career deviance for all kinds of rule-breaking phenomena, or is it best applied to a limited number of rule-breaking phenomena?

3. What are the most serious obstacles to an adequate
assessment of the theory?

I shall consider two distinct types of rule-breaking phenomena,
ascriptive and achieved, which should illuminate the limitations of
the labeling perspective when it addresses itself to the source of career
deviance.[1] *Ascribed* rule-breaking occurs if the rule-breaker is characterized in terms of a particular physical or visible "impairment." He
does not necessarily have to act in order to be a rule-breaker; he ac-
quires that status regardless of his behavior or wishes. Thus, the very
beautiful and the very ugly can be considered ascriptive rule-breakers.
By contrast, *achieved* rule-breaking involves activity on the part of the
rule-breaker, regardless of his positive attachment to a deviant "way of
life." The embezzler who attempts to conceal his rule-breaking act, no
less than the regular marijuana user who freely admits his transgres-
sion, has had to achieve rule-breaking status, at least to some extent,
on the strength of his own actions.[2]

In evaluating the applicability of the labeling perspective on career
deviance to both types of rule-breaking phenomena, I shall employ
the logic of analytic induction, determining whether invidious societal
reaction to primary deviation represents a necessary and/or sufficient
condition for career deviance (Denzin, 1970:194–199).

Because the body of the paper shall attempt to demonstrate the
severe limitations of labeling theory as a general theory of career deviance and, more significantly, because at least some of the evidence for
my argument will come from the empirical research generated by *proponents* of the labeling perspective, I believe it is worthwhile considering the development and wide acceptance of labeling theory among
sociologists as a suitable topic for a study in the sociology of knowledge. Thus, in the last section of this paper, I shall present some heuristic remarks on the social sources of labeling theory as an intellectual
product and the implications of this analysis for the study of social deviance, the sociological profession, and public policy.

ASCRIPTIVE RULE-BREAKING

Labeling theorists, unlike most sociologists of deviant behavior, have
been particularly concerned with the effects of stigmatization on the
physically and visibly handicapped. Lemert's (1951: Chapters 5, 6) pi-
oneering text, *Social Pathology,* devoted two entire chapters to the blind
and persons with speech defects.

It seems quite evident that societal reaction is probably a *necessary* condition for deviant careers among certain kinds of physically or visibly handicapped persons, that is, those whose rule-breaking would not normally interfere with conventional role playing (e.g., dwarfs, the extremely ugly, women, blacks). One would be hard pressed to think of a group whose members become preoccupied with physical or visible traits they share that are not "labeled" by outsiders.

In considering whether societal reaction represents a sufficient condition for ascriptive career deviance, several problems arise. Labeling theorists have failed to specify which kinds of sanctions lead to career deviance and the degree of severity which is required to produce such an outcome. When considering necessary conditions, the above difficulty is not as severe if one can demonstrate the *absence* of societal reaction. . . it is a qualitative issue. When it comes to the role of labeling as a sufficient condition, however, one is dealing with a question which has a quantitative dimension (Turner, 1953).

Given the lack of clarity in conceptualizing and operationalizing societal reaction, any discussion of sufficient conditions must be exploratory. Gibbs' (1966a) recent attempt to develop a typology of social sanctions is suggestive of the many aspects which must be examined in an adequate treatment of this area.

For the purposes of this paper, I shall treat societal reaction as a qualitative phenomenon exclusively, involving the presence or absence of formal or informal sanctions (e.g., conviction and incarceration, prejudice and discrimination). In the case of ascribed rule-breaking, sanctions are almost always informal, exceptions being Jim Crow laws and physical requirements for certain occupations; achieved rule-breakers face both kinds of sanctions. It is debatable which are more severe, but we can assume that labeling theorists consider the typical sanctions meted out to rule-breakers—ostracism, economic discrimination, and incarceration—as sufficient conditions for career deviance as long as the labeling and punishment of rule-breakers is widely known and practiced by community members. It can always be argued, to be sure, that a more severe societal reaction would succeed in excluding the rule-breaker from normal roles and lead him inexorably to a deviant career. It is impossible to test such an assertion when the requisite degree of severity is left in doubt. Thus, it is possible that the labeling perspective is valid in the abstract, but its use in an historical context may be limited because of the concrete features of sanctions being used in a given society.

In any case, Goffman's (1963) work on stigma testifies to the powerful impact that labeling has on the social behavior of those stigmatized for physical and visible ascriptive rule-breaking. Davis' (1964) study of the attempts at "deviance disavowal" by handicapped persons indicates that deviant self-conceptions develop *even* when one is successful in minimizing stigmatization and discrimination. The "psychological" problems of black people in the United States are, of course, the most obvious examples of the operation of this process (Kardiner and Ovesey, 1951).

On the other hand, even among the severely stigmatized, variations in (*a*) power, (*b*) socio-economic status, (*c*) the acquisition of compensatory skills, and (*d*) defense mechanisms may enable some of the victims of labeling to assume a quasi-normal role in the community, while others must accept a deviant career.

Nevertheless, because ascribed rule-breaking is highly visible to community members and often the object of widespread prejudice, labeling may come close to being a sufficient condition for career deviance. Ascribed deviants such as dwarfs, women, the ugly, and blacks are not handicapped because their physical and/or visible traits prevent them from playing any particular roles but rather because of the invidious labeling process and the absence of factors which might tend to mitigate its effects. Ascribed deviance is based upon rule-breaking phenomena that fulfill all the requirements of the labeling paradigm: highly "visible" rule-breaking that is totally *dependent* upon the societal reaction of community members while being totally *independent* of the actions and intentions of rule-breakers.

The normal modes of social reintegration discussed by Parsons (1951:297–325) cannot operate because the interaction between rule-breakers and agents of social control is not based on true reciprocity. The deviant status of the ascriptive rule-breakers can ordinarily be terminated only by drastic cultural, structural, or aesthetic changes in the society in which they are members. Short of such societal transformation, the labeled ascriptive rule-breaker almost inevitably will be caught up in the mechanistic system which the proponents of the labeling perspective have discovered. The so-called black revolution and, on a smaller scale, the "hire the handicapped" campaigns, testify to the inability of ascribed rule-breakers to achieve social reintegration on the basis of individual adaptation as opposed to collective efforts to transform societal values, beliefs, and institutions.

ACHIEVED RULE-BREAKING

While ascribed rule-breaking can perhaps best be understood in terms of the labeling perspective, only a small proportion of the socially sanctioned rule-breaking that has preoccupied sociologists of deviant behavior involves ascribed phenomena. The normal concerns of students in this field, property and violent crime, "crimes without victims" (Schur, 1965), the various exotic sub-cultures often associated with certain occupational statuses (e.g., dance musicians, taxi-dancers, strippers), and "residual rule-breaking" (Scheff, 1966), involve the examination of achieved rule-breaking. Although the designation of these phenomena as rule-breaking necessarily involves the violation of normative standards and social labeling as does ascribed rule-breaking, unlike the ascribed case, achieved rule-breaking requires the commission of a norm-violating *act* by the rule-breaker. This act can be engaged in out of regrettable necessity or hedonism, consciously or unconsciously.

Several empirical studies, including, notably, the research of Lemert (1967:99–134) and Becker (1963:41–78), advocates of the labeling perspective, can be used to question whether societal reaction to achieved rule-breaking is a *necessary* condition for career deviance.

Lemert's (1967:99–134) detailed examination of systematic check forgers, for example, documents the way in which career deviance and deviant self-conceptions can develop prior to societal reaction. The career of the systematic check forger begins with a situation in which "closure" operates leading to the initial rule-breaking. The naive forger is involved in "dialectical" behavior, such as heavy gambling or living beyond his means, in which each expenditure forces him deeper in debt without permitting him to abandon his imprudent behavior. At some point he runs out of available cash and the pressures to continue his activities make forgery the only possible step. Among systematic check forgers Lemert finds that there is the thrill and excitement of living beyond one's means, as well as the challenging aspects of forgery itself, which accounts for the systematic nature of the offense. Societal reaction does not appear to be a significant cause of career deviance. In terms of self-conception systematic check forgers at first appear to accept their identity *after* arrest, often seeking capture in order to secure a stable self-image, according to Lemert. Yet, it seems that such offenders may merely feel the need for others to respond to them in the deviant role to which they have already become attached prior to experiencing social sanctions.

Perhaps a stronger case of the adoption of a deviant role without the experience of invidious societal reaction can be found in Cressey's (1953) study of violators of financial trust. Using the method of analytic induction, Cressey shows that a financial trust violation occurs among persons who have a problem that cannot be shared with others, become aware that financial trust violation can solve the problem, and are able to use contacts with criminal values to apply verbalizations to their behavior which act as rationalizations.

Cressey (1953:114–138) suggests that arrest often precedes the recognition of "criminality" on the part of trust violators. However, in other cases the rule-breaker accepts a deviant self-concept prior to any formal sanctions by employers or agents of social control. Chronic speculation is based primarily upon the desire and ability to "borrow" successfully without detection. Often a record of "borrowed" money is kept in the beginning with a clear intention of repayment. After the amount taken becomes too great to return, or perhaps they read about another case of trust violation in the newspaper, trust violators may recognize that they are "in too deep" and accept the fact that they are "criminals," not merely "borrowers." At this point, Cressey reports that trust violators may react in several ways: confess their crime, gamble wildly to restore funds, abscond, commit suicide, or increase defalcations with little discretion and no concern for repayment. In any case, it seems, from Cressey's discussion, that career deviance and deviant self-conceptions can arise without the actor experiencing societal reaction to initial rule-breaking.

An examination of Becker's (1963:41–78) classic study of the career development of regular marijuana users casts further doubt on the role of the labeling process in the generation of career deviance. According to Becker marijuana users go through three distinct career stages: (*a*) beginner, (*b*) occasional user, and (*c*) regular user. In terms of the labeling paradigm, the beginner is a primary deviant, and the regular user is a career deviant, with occasional use fitting somewhere in between. Becker was not particularly concerned with the reasons for beginning use of marijuana, but generally he accepted the position that initial use is based on curiosity. How, then, does the initiate go from the beginner stage to the stage of being a "head" or regular user? Becker did not see societal reaction entering into the picture in a traditional sense. Rather, the initiate learns:

1. To use the proper smoking technique in order to produce the proper subjective state.
2. To associate marijuana with the feeling state produced.
3. To interpret the feeling as pleasurable.

At no point in his narrative does Becker refer to invidious labeling as a factor in bringing about regular marijuana use.[3] At various stages in the career of the user, he is free to discontinue smoking. Regular use of marijuana seems to be depending upon finding the subjective effects of the drug pleasurable and solving certain problems of supply, discretion, and ethics. Thus, the case of marijuana smoking appears to be an excellent illustration of career deviance based primarily upon finding pleasure in a deviant manner.

Finally, an examination of the literature on homosexuality seems to indicate that a very similar career sequence may be operating as in the case of the marijuana user. Neither forced seduction by older homosexuals nor rejection by peers during childhood or adolescence seems to account for career deviation within this rule-breaking group (Schofield, 1965). Homosexual experimentation seems to be a prevalent feature of so-called normal socialization among adolescents. Some youths find that they enjoy such activity and, depending upon the opportunity structure and the importance of discretion, may choose to continue such activity. Many homosexuals are bisexual and even marry persons of the opposite sex. Career deviation occurs despite lack of visibility and social labeling.

In considering the question of whether societal reaction is a *sufficient* condition for career deviance among achieved rule-breakers, the same difficulties arise as in the earlier consideration of labeling as a sufficient condition for career deviance in the ascriptive case.

Unfortunately, much of the literature focuses on the effects of incarceration, ignoring the importance of informal societal reaction to rule-breaking. It is doubtless true that informal sanctions such as ostracism may be more damaging than legal penalties, but a prison sentence is certainly a severe form of punishment for transgressions.

If incarceration exacerbates attachment to deviant role-playing, one would predict that recidivism rates would be extremely high for ex-convicts. Such persons should be unable to find jobs because of discrimination when their criminal career and prison record become known to employers (Lemert, 1951:331–332). As a result of incarceration we would also expect convicts to harbor a great deal of resentment toward the "free" community and "reject the rejectors," thus facilitating a return to criminal associations and patterns (Lemert, 1951:77).

Data bearing upon the above hypotheses comes from Glaser's (1964) exhaustive research on the effectiveness of the federal prison and parole system. Lengthy reports were obtained from interviews and other modes of data collection pertaining to the experiences of several hundred federal prisoners in a modified panel design.

Using a cohort analysis, Glaser found that approximately one-third of parolees are recidivists between two and five years after parole is granted (Glaser, 1964:13–31).

In the area of post-release occupational adjustment Glaser finds that failure to achieve satisfactory employment is due primarily to unrealistic aspirations in view of the lack of skills held by ex-convicts. Stigma did not seem to play a significant role in occupational adjustment. Only four per cent of the job terminations of parolees were blamed (by the men themselves) on their previous criminal record. Similarly only nine per cent of the parolees who were unable to obtain a job within one week after parole attributed it to the stigma of their criminal past (Glaser, 1964:358–361).

Glaser's research can be dealt with critically, and it may well be that he under-represents by far the true recidivism rate and fails to consider the possibility that parolees were "putting on" the interviewers, attributing adjustment failures to their own limitations in order to show a "positive" attitude toward the rehabilitation process.[4] In any case his research suggests that the notion that prisons are criminogenic may require further study.

Cameron's (1964) study of professional and amateur shoplifters offers more evidence that the labeling process does not necessarily lead to career deviance. When amateur shoplifters ("snitches") were apprehended by department store detectives they were unable to accept themselves as "thieves" and ceased pilfering.

Finally, Chambliss (1969:360–378), in summarizing the literature on deterrence, has argued that rule-breakers who have a low commitment to criminal activity as a way of life and whose criminal behavior is instrumental rather than expressive (e.g., snitches, white collar criminals, gangland murders) may be deterred by punishment rather than become career deviants as a consequence of societal reaction.

Thus, the labeling perspective on career deviance does not appear to be very useful in understanding the dynamics of achieved rule-breaking. Societal reaction seems to be neither a necessary nor a sufficient condition for career-achieved deviance. The essential feature of achieved rule-breaking, the necessity for action on the part of the rule-breaker as well as social labeling by community members, makes it possible for rule-breakers to commit themselves to deviant careers without being "forced" by formal or informal agents of social control and to terminate rule-breaking despite the lack of social recognition for "rehabilitation." Moreover, such possibilities have been realized in the empirical world. Achieved rule-breaking permits individual adaptations to social labeling and social structures which are largely precluded in the case of ascribed rule-breaking.

PROBLEMS OF THEORY AND RESEARCH

In the previous section some evidence has been presented to suggest that societal reaction theory is not an adequate general theory of career deviant behavior. As a theoretical model it appears to be most applicable when rule-breaking is ascribed rather than achieved. Even in the ascribed case labeling probably serves only as a necessary rather than a necessary and sufficient condition for career deviance.

In examining some of the evidence pertaining to labeling theory, I have presented perhaps a stronger case for its shortcomings than is warranted. It is conceivable that some of the evidence cited which casts doubt on the "completeness" of labeling theory can be reinterpreted by proponents of the theory in such a manner as to justify its claim to be a general theory of career deviance. Moreover, as Hirschi and Selvin (1967:119-123) point out, it is a false criterion for causality to require "independent" variables to be related to "dependent" variables as necessary and/or sufficient conditions for their existence. Social labeling undoubtedly plays an important role in the generation of career deviation in many cases. Nevertheless, it is probably not as crucial in this process as some of its proponents would claim.

In order to aid in the development of a more complete theory of career deviance, I shall briefly discuss some of the shortcomings which limit the utility of the labeling perspective, particularly in considering achieved rule-breaking.

The most salient theoretical difficulty is in the conception of initial rule-breaking and the nature of the sources which bring it into being. There is a premise in the writings of the labeling theorists that whatever the causes of initial rule-breaking, they assume minimal importance or entirely cease operation after initial rule-breaking (Scheff, 1966:50-54; Lemert, 1967:40). Without such a premise, one might attribute career deviance and its consequences not to societal reaction but to the *continued* effects of social structural strains, psychological stress, or disease states which produced initial rule-breaking.

In this connection, the labeling model fails to seriously consider the possibility that deviant behavior may be persisted in even when the rule-breaker has every opportunity to return to the status of non-deviant (Becker, 1963:37), because of a positive attachment to rule-breaking. Given the fact that theorists within the labeling tradition often see their views as consistent with a conflict interpretation of deviance, as opposed to one involving consensus which attributes deviance to faulty socialization, one can find significant traces of consensual thinking implicit in their theorizing. The societal reaction paradigm implies that labelers really share the same *Weltanschauung* as rule-breakers. The only problem is that rule-breakers are imperfect creatures who stray from the fold on occasion. The logic of the labeling approach to career deviance precludes rule-breakers being credited (or discredited) with freely espousing career deviance as a positive alternative to career conformity. Labeling the rule-breaker will only serve to prevent his rapprochement with the non-rule-breaking elements of the community. Deviant conduct and attachment to a deviant role will strengthen when the community isolates and excludes the transgressor from normal social life. Implicit in the labeling model is the belief that rule-breakers really want to conform, even the most willful ones.

There are some labeling theorists who admit the possibility that initial rule-breaking behavior may be the product of a desire to reorganize the world or a particular segment of it. Scheff (1966:44–45), for example, illustrates this point by a discussion of the Dadaist movement in the arts, but unfortunately his defense of the innovative, willful rule-breaker is obviated by the fact that he traces the growth of the movement in terms of the enormous hostility toward it expressed by orthodox artists and critics. One might argue that it was the severity of the societal reaction which made the Dadaists more self-conscious of their "revolutionary" acts and more tenacious in their defense of those acts. Thus, Scheff (1966:44–45), even when defending the *Weltanschauung* of the rule-breaker undermines the defense by implying the possibility of involuntary career deviance.

Becker (1963) explicitly considers the possibility of "intended" rule-breaking. Often, in his ethnographic accounts, as in the case of the research on the dance musician (Becker, 1963:79–119) as well as the marijuana user (Becker, 1963:41–78), he seems to accept the existence of a self-sustaining counter-culture based on deviant identities. Nevertheless, a careful reading of Becker's "sequential model" for career deviance makes one conclude that given the chance to resume normal activities, the rule-breaker will invariably do so (Becker, 1963:36–39). His examples range from boys who engage in homosexual behavior without really believing in it to tortured heroin addicts. He talks of deviants forming subcultures which provide them with "rationalizations" for their deviance. The examples used and the terminology employed seem to betray the theorist's doubts about the legitimacy of deviant careers. Such doubts are necessarily linked to the labeling theory of career deviance which sees unfettered rule-breaking co-existing with the maintenance of social order. If rule-breakers truly represented subversive values such a co-existence would be untenable. The discrepancy between empirical research and theory construction is characteristic of labeling theory and shall be discussed shortly.

Another theoretical problem arises in regard to the issue of social sensitivity. After an actor engages in rule-breaking behavior he may feel shame, guilt, or fear of exposure. As Becker (1963:31) realizes, it is possible that this in itself may be sufficient to have the primary deviant label himself as "deviant," and he may then engage in all kinds of behaviors to cover up his initial rule-breaking and unwittingly exacerbate the problem (cf., Matza, 1969:150–152). Such "vicious cycles" apparently occur among stutterers and alcoholics (Lemert, 1967:56–57). Even granting that cultural standards are ultimately responsible for making the primary deviant self-conscious, simply focusing on labelers while ignoring the qualities of the rule-breaker can lead to a mistaken emphasis in understanding the dynamics of career deviance. It is important to determine the sources and salience of self-labeling in the development of career deviance.

A final theoretical dilemma involves the nature of the societal reaction itself. As mentioned earlier, labeling theorists have not clearly specified what sort of reaction on the part of community members—formal, informal, or both—is necessary and/or sufficient to produce career deviation. Lemert (1967:42) claims that to establish a totally deviant identity, stigmatization must be disseminated throughout the society. This is very unlikely to occur in advanced societies for almost *any* rule-breaking phenomenon. If we ignore Lemert's extreme statement we find that the lack of specification as to the type and severity of societal reaction makes the labeling theory impossible to refute. It can always be maintained that either a mild societal reaction is sufficient or that a different kind of reaction or more severe form of the same one would account for career deviance. In this manner one can explain all findings and predict none. Moreover, it can once again lead to a reductionist position in which it is the extreme sensitivity of the primary deviants (this time, to an *actual* societal reaction) which leads them to permanent entrenchment in deviant roles.

The major theoretical difficulties mentioned above generate related research dilemmas. One problem involves controlling the effects of the sources of initial rule-breaking; another involves controlling for the sensitivity of the rule-breaker to the possibility and actuality of societal reaction. Only by such a procedure can the impact of *actual* societal reaction be weighted.

Unfortunately, natural field settings make it impossible to adequately assess the theory because of the impossibility of controlling for either of the two variables which might confound the effects of actual societal reaction. Comparing experimental and control groups on these variables would require labeling both to see if they are equally "sensitive." To do this would obviously eliminate the usefulness of the control group since it would cease serving that function at the point when its members were influenced by a particular kind (mode and intensity) of societal reaction. An experimental design, as advocated by Scheff (1966:199), on the other hand, is objectionable principally on ethical grounds. Two groups (experimental and control) would have to be chosen from a population of primary deviants unaware that they are rule-breakers. Randomization could be used to control for the sources of primary deviation and social sensitivity. Unfortunately, even if it were possible to locate potential experimental subjects, the necessary invocation of societal reaction with the experimental group would be an obvious violation of professional ethics, particularly if one believed in the validity of labeling theory (since the researcher would suspect that he was possibly dooming his experimental group to career deviance).

LABELING THEORY AND THE SOCIOLOGY OF KNOWLEDGE

In the previous section I spoke about the seeming incongruity between empirical research and theory construction which characterizes much of the scholarship that falls within the labeling tradition. When "theory" ignores what research uncovers, one often finds a problem that is traceable to "ideology" rather than the competence of professionals. This issue must be squarely addressed if the study of social deviance is to attain scientific respectability and provide a guide to public policy.

Sociologists in general, and those who study deviant behavior in particular, are often beset by ambivalence in carrying out their life's work. On the one hand they are committed to value-neutrality and objectivity as part of their professional training; on the other hand, they frequently side with the perspective of the "underdog" and view themselves as liberal reformers in their role as citizens. Frequently, they try to combine both roles (Tumin, 1965; Becker, 1967).

Because of the operation of unique historical forces, American sociology was based upon the synthesis of liberal reformism and the social theories of European conservatives with their preoccupation with the problem of social order (Parsons, 1937, 1951; Nisbet, 1966; Nicolaus, 1969). As time went by the ideological roots of modern American sociology were forgotten, and the concerns of the field, while still retaining their conservative bias, were rephrased in the seemingly value-neutral language of contemporary sociological discourse (e.g., functions, dysfunctions, social disorganization). The continuing focus of sociological inquiry has, of course, been reinforced by the political context in which American sociologists seek research support (Nicolaus, 1969; Gouldner, 1968, 1970).

Given the intellectual and professional orientation of modern sociologists trained in and practicing their craft in the United States, it is understandable that a conflict should arise between the scientific and citizen roles of the professional sociologist. Thus, most sociologists, who wish "society" to be more tolerant of rule-breaking and solve various "social problems" while still retaining social cohesiveness and institutional continuity, must demonstrate that labeling and repression are inimical to the long-term stability of America's social institutions. Only in this way can they satisfy the requirements of their profession, freely express their political views, and develop cogent arguments acceptable to very conservative public policy decision-makers.

Unfortunately, the consequence of such a complex posture is to fail as a competent scientist, lose faith in the liberal political analysis, and meet rejection by "realistic" policy-makers, when the "data" fail to conform to expectations. Neither repression nor the lack of it seems to affect the propensity of youth to use psychedelic drugs; student activism grows whether the campuses are administered by "doves" or "hawks." Repression even seems to work better, at least in the short run, but at the expense of increasingly widespread alienation from authority.

The preoccupation with labeling as the source of chronic rule-breaking may blind sociologists to macro-sociological analysis which traces social instability and career deviance to the very institutional arrangements—economic, political, cultural—that are supposed to maintain order.[5] Unfortunately, returning to the neglected concerns of an institution—and conflict-oriented macro-sociology—may upset the symbiotic links between sociology as a profession and the sources of its material sustenance. Moreover, knowledge acquired through such an effort may destroy the strain of optimism that reformers have carefully nurtured despite attacks from the Left and Right. Liberal sociologists may not be able to have their cake and eat it: either certain "subversive" forms of rule-breaking may have to be suppressed via police state methods, or social life may have to be reorganized around values other than profit, productivity, and puritanism. In this regard, Erikson's (1966) macro-labeling perspective, emphasizing the functions of deviance and social control for the maintenance of social order, may demonstrate a willingness to face unpleasant choices not shared by micro-labeling theorists who focus on the functions of social control in the generation of deviant careers.

In order not to end on a somber note entirely, it might well be possible to eliminate negative sanctions against ascribed rule-breakers without endangering the social order. However, even this policy would have to be accompanied by a profound alteration in the minds of our citizens as well as the creation of new ways to deal with the economic problems associated with the incorporation of millions of persons into a labor market unable to provide employment, even demeaning employment, for many of its beautiful, healthy, white males.

CONCLUSION

This paper has been concerned with the empirical validation of one of the most significant "theories" derived from the labeling perspective, namely, rule-breakers become entrenched in deviant roles because they are labeled "deviant" by others and are consequently excluded from resuming normal societal roles. By dividing rule-breaking phenomena into two major types, ascribed and achieved rule-breaking distinguished by the necessity of rule-breaking *activity* on the part of the rule-breaker, the paper has attempted to demonstrate that the utility of this theory is severely limited.

Ascribed rule-breaking, because it involves a passive rule-breaker almost totally dependent upon the whims of social labelers, exemplifies the kind of rule-breaking phenomena for which the labeling model is most applicable. Even in this case, however, while social labeling may be a necessary condition for career deviance, it is probably not a sufficient condition for such a development. Variations in power, socio-economic status, the acquisition of compensatory skills, and defense mechanisms may permit some labeled ascribed rule-breakers to avoid career deviance. Nevertheless, collective attempts to change social values, beliefs, and institutions are probably necessary to end ascribed deviance in the face of the dependence of ascribed rule-breakers upon prevailing community ideology and behavior.

In the case of achieved rule-breaking, the labeling model is extremely inadequate in providing an explanation for the genesis of career deviance. Labeling theorists ignore the possibility of genuine commitment on the part of the rule-breaker to achieved career deviance. This failure of analysis stems from an underestimation of the importance of social and psychological factors other than labeling in generating deviant careers. Finally, labeling theory underestimates the possibilities for successful social control through labeling. The evidence suggests that while the labeling process may play a significant role in the development of career-achieved deviance it is neither a necessary nor sufficient condition for such an outcome.

Besides considering the particular strengths and weaknesses of the labeling model in regard to the generation of career ascribed and achieved deviance, the paper has also discussed some of the major dilemmas pertaining to theory and research which must be faced by those who may wish to assess labeling theory in the future. Among the theoretical problems are the previously stated failure to consider the *continuing* effects of the social structural and psychological sources of initial rule-breaking in the development of career deviance, the lack of concern with the vulnerability of certain rule-breakers to self-labeling processes which may reduce the significance of *objective* labeling practices in determining deviant careers, and the related omission of any serious analysis of the types and severity of actual social sanction which facilitate "successful" labeling. Ultimately, students of deviance will have to reconsider the mechanistic assumptions of labeling theory when applied to achieved and to a lesser degree ascribed rule-breaking. The implicit notions of human passivity, so characteristic of behaviorism, seem out of place in a sociological tradition that has been founded upon penetrating observations of the creative potential of human beings. Researchers will have to learn to control the effects of the sources of initial rule-breaking and sensitivity to self-labeling and particular types of societal reaction. Only in this way can they demonstrate the power of actual labeling processes by community members in determining career deviance.

Finally, because of the observation that the empirical research of labeling theorists has often provided evidence which contradicts the labeling model of career deviance the paper has briefly explored some of the ideological and social sources of this model. It has suggested that the model arises out of a tension between the reformist ideological orientations of most sociologists of deviance, the conservative bias of American sociology derived from European conservative social theory, and the pressures arising from the sources of political and financial support for the American sociological profession. These three factors have permitted some sociologists to become advocates of a theoretical perspective which resolves the tensions which are rooted in the conflict between ideology, professionalism, and political and financial pressure. Unfortunately, the inadequacy of the labeling perspective leads to ideological, scientific, and political bankruptcy. It is suggested that sociologists of social deviance concern themselves more with macro-sociological analysis in the future, focusing primarily on the institutional sources of career deviance. This focus may lead to greater understanding of the nature of career deviance, although it may result in shifting ideological, political and professional orientation for those who undertake this task.

In conclusion, this paper has left many problems unresolved, particularly the difficulties involved in the conceptualization and operationalization of "societal reaction" and the development of a viable research program designed to test the labeling model adequately. Nevertheless, directing attention toward some of the outstanding weaknesses of the model as it currently stands will hopefully lead to more productive attempts to grapple with the problems associated with the phenomenon of career deviance.

NOTES

1. For discussion of the utility of typological analysis with specific focus on typologies of criminal behavior, see Clinard and Quinney (1967:1–19), cf. McKinney (1966). The particular types under analysis in this paper were drawn from Parsons' (1951) consideration of role relationships. The element of reciprocity and the possibilities for active role-making rather than passive role-accepting implicit in achieved roles, as opposed to ascribed ones, were felt to be in contrast to the lack of autonomy characteristic of the ideal-typical rule-breaker in the labeling perspective. By exploring the implications of Parsons' distinction as it applies to types of rule-breaking, it is possible to see how the labeling perspective is dependent upon a passive actor whose rule-breaking is ascribed.

2. In the case of both ascribed and achieved rule-breaking, it is, of course, possible that persons are falsely accused of rule-breaking (Becker, 1963:20). Nevertheless, the above distinctions hold because the falsely accused ascribed rule-breaker is thought to *be* someone, whereas the falsely accused achieved rule-breaker is felt to have *done* something.

3. It would not be fair to fault Becker for not looking for a labeling process operating among the marijuana users he studied in the early 1950's. But since he has not revised in any essential manner his original thought on becoming a user and chose to reprint his classic study in a volume which includes his particular version of labeling theory (Becker, 1963:19–39;41–58) one would imagine that he would have reconsidered either his theoretical perspective on deviance or his marijuana study at the time.

4. Even if the true recidivism rate is extremely high, it does not follow that societal reaction is a sufficient condition for career criminality. An alternate explanation might be that the causes of initial rule-breaking are still operating after incarceration is over. For example, if a poor man steals and is sent to prison, he may continue to steal after release because he is still poor. Prison may provide temporary protection to the community since the rule-breaker is in no position to engage in certain criminal acts, but it is questionable whether it provides a long-term solution to the problem of "law and order."

    As for the issue of "putting on" the interviewer, it is also possible, of course, that the ex-convicts were exhibiting "false consciousness" and were not aware of the operation of discriminatory hiring policies.

If this is so it might well prevent recidivism, as ex-convicts may not become embittered and "reject the rejectors." They may simply become career "ritualists" in Merton's (1938) sense of the term.

5. Merton (1938), in the midst of the Great Depression, did attempt such an analysis of social deviance. The work, while provocative, had numerous flaws (Clinard, 1964) and seems to have gone out of favor in recent years.

REFERENCES

Becker, Howard S.
  1967   "Whose side are we on?" Social Problems 14 (Winter): 239–248.
  1963   Outsiders: Studies in the Sociology of Deviance. New York: The Free Press.

Cameron, Mary Owen
  1964   The Booster and the Snitch: Department Store Shoplifting. New York: The Free Press.

Chambliss, William J.
  1969   Crime and the Legal Process. New York: McGraw-Hill.

Cicourel, Aaron V.
  1968   The Social Organization of Juvenile Justice. New York: Wiley.

Clinard, Marshall
  1964   Anomie and Deviant Behavior: A Discussion and Critique. New York: The Free Press.

Clinard, Marshall and Richard Quinney
  1967   Criminal Behavior Systems: A Typology. New York: Holt, Rinehart, and Winston.

Cressey, Donald R.
  1953   Other People's Money. New York: The Free Press of Glencoe.

Davis, Fred
  1964   "Deviance disavowal: the management of strained interaction by the physically handicapped." Pp. 119–137 in Howard S. Becker (ed.), The Other Side: Perspectives on Deviance. New York: The Free Press.

Denzin, Norman K.
  1970   The Research Act: A Theoretical Introduction to Sociological Methods. Chicago: Aldine.

Erikson, Kai
  1966   Wayward Puritans: A Study in the Sociology of Deviance. New York: Wiley.

1962 "Notes on the sociology of deviance." Social Problems 9 (Spring):307–314.

Gibbs, J.
1966a "Sanctions." Social Problems 14 (Fall):147–159.
1966b "Conceptions of deviant behavior: the old and the new." Pacific Sociological Review 9 (Spring):9–14.

Glaser, Daniel
1964 The Effectiveness of a Prison and Parole System. New York: Bobbs-Merrill.

Goffman, Erving
1963 Stigma: Notes on the Management of Spoiled Identities. New Jersey: Prentice Hall.

Gouldner, Alvin
1970 The Coming Crisis of Western Sociology. New York: Basic Books.
1968 "The sociologist as partisan: sociology and the welfare state." American Sociologist 3 (May):103–116.

Hirschi, Travis and Hanan Selvin
1967 Delinquency Research: An Appraisal of Analytic Methods. New York: Free Press.

Kardiner, Abram and Lionel Ovesey
1951 The Mark of Oppression: Explorations in the Personality of the American Negro. Cleveland: World.

Lemert, Edwin
1967 Human Deviance, Social Problems, and Social Control. Englewood Cliffs, N.J.: Prentice-Hall.
1951 Social Pathology. New York: McGraw-Hill.

Matza, David
1969 Becoming Deviant. Englewood Cliffs, N.J.: Prentice-Hall.

McKinney, John C.
1966 Constructive Typology and Social Theory. New York: Appleton-Century-Crofts.

Merton, R.
1938 "Social structure and anomie." American Sociological Review (October):672–682.

Nicolaus, M.
1969 "The professional organization of sociology: a view from below." Antioch Review 29 (Fall):375–388.

Nisbet, Robert
1966 The Sociological Traditon. New York: Basic Books.

Parsons, Talcott
1951 The Social System. New York: Free Press.
1937 The Structure of Social Action. New York: McGraw-Hill.

Piliavin, L. and S. Briar
  1964 "Police encounters with juveniles." American Journal of Sociology
        69 (September):206–214.

Scheff, Thomas
  1966 Being Mentally Ill: A Sociological Theory. Chicago: Aldine.

Schofield, Michael
  1965 Sociological Aspects of Homosexuality. Boston: Little, Brown, and
        Company.

Schur, Edwin
  1965 Crimes Without Victims: Deviant Behavior and Public Policy. Engle-
        wood Cliffs, N.J.: Prentice-Hall.

Tannenbaum, Frank
  1938 Crime and the Community. Boston: Ginn and Co.

Tumin, M.
  1965 "The functionalist approach to social problems." Social Problems 12
        (Spring):379–388.

Turner, R.
  1953 "The quest for universals in sociological research." American Socio-
        logical Review 18 (December):604–611.

CHAPTER VII

Politics and Class in the Study of Deviance

To this point in *Theories of Deviance* we have presented the theoretical perspectives that we feel have had the greatest impact on the sociology of deviant behavior. The first three chapters, on the functional, social disorganization, and anomie theories, all stress study of the structural conditions in a complex society that are conducive to the emergence and continuation of deviant behavior. For the functionalists, deviance is perceived as a natural counterpart to social organization that may result in greater social solidarity among nondeviants. Social disorganization theorists recognize the relationship between deviance and social structure but view deviant behavior as fundamentally disruptive of the existing social order. Anomie theorists generally conceive of deviance as being endemic to a crisis-ridden or highly differentiated society.

Control theorists, discussed in Chapter V, take a different approach which emphasizes the deviance-inhibiting effects of being closely bound to others in the society. They conclude that deviance is apt to be greater in societies where interpersonal social bonds are weak or broken. Because control theorists start from the assumption that deviance is natural, they maintain that it is *conformity* that requires explanation. The control or containment of deviant impulses depends on the ties that bind a person to family, school, or other conventional institutions.

Chapter IV on differential association and neutralization and Chapter VI on labeling theory further shift attention from predominant concern for social structure to focus on the interactional processes that lead to and maintain patterns of deviant behavior. Differential association and neutralization theorists explain deviance as an out-

349

growth of socialization processes, maintaining that it is through social interaction with significant others that people learn the various motives, techniques, and rationalizations that involve them in norm-violating activity. Labeling theorists direct attention to those who define what and who is to be considered deviant and the effects of these evaluations on those who are labeled deviant.

For the theorists whose work is represented in this chapter on the effects of politics and class, the rules of a society grow out of political power struggles between different interest groups, and rule enforcement is largely dependent on whether it is in the interest of the most powerful individuals or groups to have the rules enforced. The ability to label another person's behavior as unacceptable—that is, as deviant—and to punish that person for it is a sign of privilege and status. To be labeled deviant and to become the object of informal sanctions as well as formal enforcement proceedings is symbolic of impotence and low status. Accordingly, deviance, conceived as publicly labeled wrongdoing, may be viewed as a product of power politics and class conflict in society. From this perspective, deviance is the result of a political process wherein the politically powerful rely on law to neutralize the actions of the less powerful.

For Joseph R. Gusfield (Reading 26), the "status politics" of the Temperance movement in the United States in the early part of the 20th century provides an example of an attempt by a powerful group to impose its rules on the society. In his opinion, the question of whether the production, sale, and consumption of alcoholic beverages should be legal is a matter not of morality but of the dominance of competing subcultural groups. Gusfield sees the passage of the 18th amendment in 1919 and the consequent establishment of Prohibition as a symbolic victory of middle-class, rural, Protestant nativists over urban, Catholic, recent immigrants. A social condition was created in which, Gusfield says, "Even if the law is not enforced or enforceable, the symbolic import of its passage is important to the reformer. It settles the controversies between those who represent clashing cultures. The public support of one conception of morality at the expense of another enhances the prestige and self-esteem of the victors and degrades the culture of the losers." In sum, the ability of a group to establish a rule which publicly labels certain behavior as deviant is one measure of that group's power and status.

An alternative to Gusfield's political theory of deviance, with its emphasis on conflicts among ethnic, religious, or cultural groups, is to explain it in terms of class conflict. This was the intent of "the new criminology" proposed by three English sociologists, Ian Taylor, Paul Walton, and Jock Young, in their book by that title published in 1973.

They set out to critique existing criminological theory and to propose guidelines for an alternative way of theorizing about crime and deviance. The central tenet of the critique is that the study of crime has too often been isolated from the more general study of society—a situation that frequently results in crime being treated as a pathological phenomenon which requires harsh measures of correction. As an alternative, Taylor, Walton, and Young call for "a social theory of deviance" based on the economic and political ideas of Karl Marx, as they have been interpreted by Marxist theorists:

> With Marx, we have been concerned with the social arrangements that have obstructed, and the social contradictions that enhance, man's chance of achieving full sociality—a state of freedom from material necessity, and (therefore) of material incentive, a release from the constraints of forced production, an abolition of the forced division of labour, and a set of social arrangements, therefore, in which there would be no politically, economically, and socially-induced need to criminalize deviance.[1]

Every sociologist who has been identified with the new criminology has not adopted Marx's terminology and approach to the extent that Steven Spitzer does in Reading 29. Richard Quinney, for example, presents in Reading 27 his theory of the social reality of crime in six precise propositions. This compact statement also pulls together many of the ideas that have been developed in the preceding chapters. For example, Quinney's statement that "Crime is not inherent in behavior, but is a judgment made by some about the actions and characteristics of others" was anticipated by Emile Durkheim in the chapter entitled "The Normal and the Pathological" in *The Rules of Sociological Method* (see Reading 1). Quinney emphasizes that criminal definitions are formulated and applied according to the interests of those groups in society that have the power to translate their interests into public policy or law—members of the highest social classes. Persons whose interests are not represented in the formulation and application of law—members of the lower social classes—are more likely to be defined as criminals.

Alexander Liazos elaborates on these points in his article "The Poverty of the Sociology of Deviance: Nuts, Sluts, and 'Preverts'" (Reading 28). Liazos would agree with Quinney about the role of class conflict in deviance designation. He contends, however, that the role of power in designating who and what are deviant has not been adequately explored, and writers on deviance have not related the phenomena they are studying to broader social issues. For the most part, then, the labeling perspective (see Chapter VI) has been oriented toward showing how the deviant is really no different from the rest of us. Liazos asserts that by focusing on the "dramatic" nature of the usual forms of deviance (prostitution, homosexuality, delinquency), and simply conceptualizing certain behaviors as deviant, labeling theorists actually perpetuate the popular conception of the deviant as being different from "normals." Furthermore, by concentrating on "those who have been successfully labeled as 'deviants,'" especially their identities and subcultural characteristics, this approach neglects an in-depth examination of other forms of deviance in American society. This is particularly evident with regard to what Liazos calls the "covert institutional violence" carried on by the politically powerful in the United States which leads to such social ills as poverty, war, racism, and sexism. The role of power in designations of deviance has been examined only in terms of middle-level officials such as the police, who do not have the power to make basic policy decisions. Liazos calls for a move away from the "exciting deviant" to an analysis of the deviance-producing activities of the politically powerful.

Liazos's appeal for more thorough exploration of the political economy of deviance is echoed in Steven Spitzer's "Toward a Marxian Theory of Deviance" (Reading 29). Spitzer shows how capitalist societies, by the nature of their economic system of production, generate "problem populations," especially the poor and the unemployed, that must somehow be controlled. He distinguishes between two broad types of deviant groups: "social junk," such as children, the dependent elderly, or the mentally ill, who represent a costly yet relatively harmless burden to society, and "social dynamite," such as alienated, unemployed youths, who can be dangerous and threatening. Social junk is usually controlled through the agencies of the therapeutic and welfare state, while social dynamite is normally processed through the legal system. He argues that modern welfare-state capitalism is presently faced with a growing crisis—the overproduction of deviant populations—and suggests several strategies, such as the decarceration movement, that may be used to alleviate it.

The Analysis and Critique section for this chapter is "The New Criminology: Continuity in Criminological Theory" (Reading 30), by Robert F. Meier. He examines the assumptions of the various theoretical approaches to theories of deviance and how they have shifted in emphasis over time and relates each to the ideas that have come to characterize the new criminology:

1. Society is dominated by a ruling elite.
2. The interests of the ruling class are formulated into criminal law.

3. The police power of the state protects the vested interests of elites.
4. Criminal sanctions are disproportionately applied against lower-class persons.
5. Crime is fundamentally the result of class conflict between those who wield power and the powerless.

According to Meier, this approach is not dramatically different from criminology's more established theoretical explanations of crime and criminal behavior, particularly those emanating from the social pathology perspective, the Chicago school, functionalism, and labeling theory. For Meier, the similarities of the new criminology and the more established theories are much greater than their differences. He argues that the main contribution of the new criminology may in fact amount to nothing more than rephrasing traditional ideas about crime and criminal behavior in political terms.

NOTE

1. Ian Taylor, Paul Walton and Jock Young, *The New Criminology: For a Social Theory of Deviance* (New York: Harper and Row, 1973), p. 270.

26 *Symbolic Crusade*
JOSEPH R. GUSFIELD

For many observers of American life the Temperance movement is evidence for an excessive moral perfectionism and an overly legalistic bent to American culture. It seems the action of devoted sectarians who are unable to compromise with human impulse. The legal measures taken to enforce abstinence display the reputed American faith in the power of Law to correct all evils. This moralism and utopianism bring smiles to the cynical and fear to the sinners. Such a movement seems at once naive, intolerant, saintly, and silly.

Although controversies of morality, religion, and culture have been recognized as endemic elements of American politics, they have generally been viewed as minor themes in the interplay of economic and class conflicts. Only in recent years have American historians and

Reprinted from *Symbolic Crusade* by Joseph R. Gusfield (Urbana-Champaign: University of Illinois Press, 1963). Second edition copyright 1986 by University of Illinois Press.

social scientists de-emphasized economic issues as the major points of dissension in American society.[1] We share this newer point of view, especially in its insistence on the significant role of cultural conflicts in American politics. Our social system has not experienced the sharp class organization and class conflict which have been so salient in European history. Under continuous conditions of relative affluence and without a feudal resistance to nineteenth-century commercialism and industry, American society has possessed a comparatively high degree of consensus on economic matters. In its bland attitude toward class issues, political controversy in the United States has given only a limited role to strong economic antagonisms. Controversies of personality, cultural difference, and the nuances of style and morality have occupied part of the political stage. Consensus about fundamentals of governmental form, free enterprise economy, and church power has left a political vacuum which moral issues have partially filled. Differences between ethnic groups, cultures, and religious organizations have been able to assume a greater importance than has been true of societies marked by deeper economic divisions. "...agreement on fundamentals will permit almost every kind of social conflict, tension and difference to find political expression."[2]

It is within an analytical context of concern with noneconomic issues that we have studied the Temperance movement. This is a study of moral reform as a political and social issue. We have chosen the Temperance movement because of its persistence and power in the history of the United States. Typical of moral reform efforts, Temperance has usually been the attempt of the moral people, in this case the abstainers, to correct the behavior of the immoral people, in this case the drinkers. The issue has appeared as a moral one, divorced from any direct economic interests in abstinence or indulgence. This quality of "disinterested reform" is the analytical focus of our study.

This book is an interpretation rather than a history because our interest is largely with the analysis of what is already known of the movement rather than with the presentation of new data. Some new field data will be presented and some new primary historical material has been gathered. A large number of already published materials has been utilized. Our interest is not in a definitive history of the movement. We have written within the methodological perspective of the sociologist interested in the general process of moral reform. Our concern is with the structural and cultural roots of the movement and with the consequences of Temperance activities and goals for its adherents, its "victims," and the relations between these two.

The sociologist picks up where the historian closes. Put in another way, he delves into the assumptions with which the historian begins. The amount written about Temperance is monumentally staggering to someone who tries to read it all. Claims, counterclaims, factual histories, and proceedings of organizations overwhelm us in their immensity. Despite the plethora of documents and analyses, we are left with either partisan writings, histories which preach, or analyses which fail to go beyond general remarks about moral perfectionism, rural-urban conflict, or the Protestant envy of the sinner.[3] It is here, in the analysis of the process, that the sociologist focuses his interest. He studies just that which is so often *ad hoc* to the interpretation of the historian.

In this book we will describe the relation between Temperance attitudes, the organized Temperance movement, and the conflicts between divergent subcultures in American society. Issues of moral reform are analyzed as one way through which a cultural group acts to preserve, defend, or enhance the dominance and prestige of its own style of living within the total society. In the set of religious, ethnic, and cultural communities that have made up American society, drinking (and abstinence) has been one of the significant consumption habits distinguishing one subculture from another. It has been one of the major characteristics through which Americans have defined their own cultural commitments. The "drunken bum," "the sophisticated gourmet," or the "blue-nosed teetotaler" are all terms by which we express our approval or disapproval of cultures by reference to the moral position they accord drinking. Horace Greeley recognized this cultural base to political loyalties and animosities in the 1844 elections in New York state: "Upon those Working Men who stick to their business, hope to improve their circumstances by honest industry and *go on Sundays to church rather than to the grogshop* [italics added] the appeals of Loco-Focoism fell comparatively harmless; while the opposite class were rallied with unprecedented unanimity against us."[4]

Precisely because drinking and nondrinking have been ways to identify the members of a subculture, drinking and abstinence became symbols of social status, identifying social levels of the society whose styles of life separated them culturally. They indicated to what culture the actor was committed and hence what social groups he took as his models of imitation and avoidance and his points of positive and negative reference for judging his behavior. The rural, native American Protestant of the nineteenth century respected Temperance ideals. He adhered to a culture in which self-control, industriousness, and impulse renunciation were both praised and made necessary. Any lapse was a serious threat to his system of respect. Sobriety was virtuous and, in a community dominated by middle-class Protestants, necessary to social acceptance and to self-esteem. In the twentieth century this is less often true. As Americans are less work-minded, more urban, and less theological, the same behavior which once brought rewards and self-assurance to the abstainer today more often brings contempt and rejection. The demands for self-control and individual industry count for less in an atmosphere of teamwork where tolerance, good interpersonal relations, and the ability to relax oneself and others are greatly prized. Abstinence has lost much of its utility to confer prestige and esteem.

Our attention to the significance of drink and abstinence as symbols of membership in status groups does not imply that religious and moral beliefs have not been important in the Temperance movement. We are not reducing moral reform to something else. Instead, we are adding something. Religious motives and moral fervor do not happen *in vacuo*, apart from a specific setting. We have examined the social conditions which made the facts of other people's drinking especially galling to the abstainer and the need for reformist action acutely pressing to him. These conditions are found in the development of threats to the socially dominant position of the Temperance adherent by those whose style of life differs from his. As his own claim to social respect and honor are diminished, the sober, abstaining citizen seeks for public acts through which he may reaffirm the dominance and prestige of his style of life. Converting the sinner to virtue is one way; law is another. Even if the law is not enforced or enforceable, the symbolic import of its passage is important to the reformer. It settles the controversies between those who represent clashing cultures. The public support of one conception of morality at the expense of another enhances the prestige and self-esteem of the victors and degrades the culture of the losers.

In its earliest development, Temperance[5] was one way in which a declining social elite tried to retain some of its social power and leadership. The New England Federalist "aristocracy" was alarmed by the political defeats of the early nineteenth century and by the decreased deference shown their clergy. The rural farmer, the evangelical Protestant, and the uneducated middle class appeared as a rising social group who rejected the social status, as well as political power, of the Federalist leadership. In the first quarter of the nineteenth century, the moral supremacy of the educated was under attack by the frontiersman, the artisan, and the independent farmer. The Federalist saw his own declining status in the increased power of the drinker, the ignorant, the secularist, and the religious revivalist. During the 1820's, the men who founded the Temperance movement sought to make Americans into a clean, sober, godly, and decorous people whose aspirations and style of living would reflect the moral leadership of New England Federalism. If they could not control the politics of the country, they reasoned that they might at least control its morals.

Spurred by religious revivalism, Temperance became more ultraist than its founders had intended. The settling of frontiers and the influx of non-Protestant cultures increased the symbolic importance of morality and religious behavior in distinguishing between the reputable and the disreputable. During the 1830's and 1840's, it became a large and influential movement, composed of several major organizations. Religious dedication and a sober life were becoming touchstones of middle-class respectability. Large numbers of men were attracted to Temperance organizations as a means of self-help. In the interests of social and economic mobility, they sought to preserve their abstinence or reform their own drinking habits. Abstinence was becoming a symbol of middle-class membership and a necessity for ambitious and aspiring young men. It was one of the ways society could distinguish the industrious from the ne'er-do-well; the steady worker from the unreliable drifter; the good credit risk from the bad gamble; the native American from the immigrant. In this process the movement lost its association with New England upper classes and became democratized.

The political role of Temperance emerged in the 1840's in its use as a symbol of native and immigrant, Protestant and Catholic tensions. The "disinterested reformer" of the 1840's was likely to see the curtailment of alcohol sales as a way of solving the problems presented by an immigrant, urban poor whose culture clashed with American Protestantism. He sensed the rising power of these strange, alien peoples and used Temperance legislation as one means of impressing upon the immigrant the central power and dominance of native American Protestant morality. Along with Abolition and Nativism, Temperance formed one of a trio of major movements during the 1840's and 1850's.

Throughout its history, Temperance has revealed two diverse types of disinterested reform. By the last quarter of the nineteenth century, these had become clear and somewhat distinct elements within the movement. One was an *assimilative reform*. Here the reformer was sympathetic to the plight of the urban poor and critical of the conditions produced by industry and the factory system. This urban, progressivist impulse in Temperance reflected the fears of an older, established social group at the sight of rising industrialism. While commercial and professional men saw America changing from a country of small towns to one of cities, they were still socially dominant. The norm of abstinence had become the public morality after the Civil War. In the doctrines of abstinence they could still offer the poor and the immigrants a way of living which had the sanction of respect and success attached to it. Through reform of the drinker, the middle-class professional and businessman coped with urban problems in a way which affirmed his sense of cultural dominance. He could feel his own social position affirmed by a Temperance argument that invited the drinker (whom he largely identified with the poor, the alien, and the downtrodden) to follow the reformer's habits and lift himself to middle-class respect and income. He was even able to denounce the rich for their sumptuary sophistication. He could do this because he felt secure that abstinence was still the public morality. It was not yet somebody else's America.

A more hostile attitude to reform is found when the object of the reformer's efforts is no longer someone he can pity or help. *Coercive reform* emerges when the object of reform is seen as an intractable defender of another culture, someone who rejects the reformer's values and really doesn't want to change. The champion of assimilative reform viewed the drinker as part of a social system in which the reformer's culture was dominant. On this assumption, his invitation to the drinker to reform made sense. The champion of coercive reform cannot make this assumption. He sees the object of reform as someone who rejects the social dominance of the reformer and denies the legitimacy of his life style. Since the dominance of his culture and the social status of his group are denied, the coercive reformer turns to law and force as ways to affirm it.

In the last quarter of the nineteenth century, coercive reform was most evident in the Populist wing of the Temperance movement. As a phase of the rural distrust of the city, it was allied to an agrarian radicalism which fought the power of industrial and urban political and economic forces. Already convinced that the old, rural middle class was losing out in the sweep of history, the Populist as Temperance adherent could not assume that his way of life was still dominant in America. He had to fight it out by political action which would coerce the public definition of what is moral and respectable. He had to shore up his waning self-esteem by inflicting his morality on everybody.

As America became more urban, more secular, and more Catholic, the sense of declining status intensified the coercive, Populist elements in the Temperance movement. The political defeat of Populism in both North and South heightened the decline, so evident in the drama of William Jennings Bryan. With the development of the Anti-Saloon League in 1896, the Temperance movement began to separate itself from a complex of economic and social reforms and concentrate on the cultural struggle of the traditional rural Protestant society against the developing urban and industrial social system. Coercive reform became the dominating theme of Temperance. It culminated in the drive for national Prohibition. The Eighteenth Amendment was the high point of the struggle to assert the public dominance of old middle-class values. It established the victory of Protestant over Catholic, rural over urban, tradition over modernity, the middle class over both the lower and the upper strata.

The significance of Prohibition is in the fact that it happened. The establishment of Prohibition laws was a battle in the struggle for status between two divergent styles of life. It marked the public affirmation of the abstemious, ascetic qualities of American Protestantism. In this sense, it was an act of ceremonial deference toward old middle-class culture. If the law was often disobeyed and not enforced, the respectability of its adherents was honored in the breach. After all, it was *their* law that drinkers had to avoid.

If Prohibition was the high point of old middle-class defense, Repeal was the nadir. As the Prohibition period lengthened and resistance solidified, Temperance forces grew more hostile, coercive, and nativist. The more assimilative, progressivist adherents were alienated from a movement of such soured Populism. In 1928, anti-Catholic and anti-urban forces led the movement with a "knockout punch" thrown at Al Smith in an open ring. By 1933, they had lost their power and their fight. In the Great Depression both the old order of nineteenth-century economics and the culture of the Temperance ethic were cruelly discredited.

The repeal of the Eighteenth Amendment gave the final push to the decline of old middle-class values in American culture. Since 1933, the Temperance movement has seen itself fighting a losing battle against old enemies and new ones. In contemporary American society, even in his own local communities, it is the total abstainer who is the despised nonconformist. The Protestant churches and the public schools are no longer his allies. The respectable, upper middle-class citizen can no longer be safely counted upon to support abstinence.

What underlies the tragic dilemmas of the Temperance movement are basic changes in the American social system and culture during the past half-century. As we have changed from a commercial society to an industrial one, we have developed a new set of values in which self-control, impulse renunciation, discipline, and sobriety are no longer such hallowed virtues. Thorstein Veblen, himself the epitome of the rural, middle-class Protestant, saw the new society of consumers coming into being. In his satirical fashion, he depicted a society in which leisure and consumption fixed men's status and took precedence over the work-mindedness and efficiency concerns of his own Swedish-American farm communities. More recently, David Riesman has brilliantly depicted the major outlines of this society by pointing to the intensity with which modern Americans are replacing an interest in work and morality with an interest in interpersonal relations and styles of consuming leisure.

For the "other-directed" man neither the intolerance nor the seriousness of the abstainer is acceptable. Nor is the intense rebelliousness and social isolation of the hard drinker acceptable. Analysis of American alcohol consumption is consistent with this. The contemporary American is less likely than his nineteenth-century ancestor to be either a total abstainer or a hard drinker. Moderation is his drinking watchword. One must get along with others and liquor has proven to be a necessary and effective facilitator to sociability. It relaxes reserve and permits fellowship at the same time that it displays the drinker's tolerance for some moral lapse in himself and others.

For those who have grown up to believe in the validity of the Temperance ethic, American culture today seems a strange system in which Truth is condemned as Falsehood and Vice as Virtue. The total abstainer finds himself the exponent of a point of view which is rejected in the centers of urban and national society and among their followers at all levels of American communities. Self-control and foresight made sense in a scarcity, production-minded economy. In an easygoing, affluent society, the credit mechanism has made the Ant a fool and the Grasshopper a hero of the counter-cyclical maintenance of consumer demand. In a consumption-centered society, people must learn to have fun and be good mixers if they are to achieve respect. Not Horatio Alger but *Playboy* magazine is the instructor of the college boy who wants to learn the skills of social ascent. Though they have their noses to the grindstone, their feet must tap to the sound of the dance.

It is at this point that the study of Temperance assumes significance for a general understanding of contemporary American politics and social tensions. Social systems and cultures die slowly, leaving their rear guards behind to fight delaying action. Even after they have ceased to be relevant economic groups, the old middle classes of America are still searching for some way to restore a sense of lost respect. The dishonoring of their values is a part of the process of cultural and social change. A heightened stress on the importance of tradition is a major response of such "doomed classes."

This fundamentalist defense is a primary motif in the current phase of Temperance. To different degrees and within different areas, the contemporary Temperance adherent is part of the rear guard with which small-town America and commercial capitalism fight their losing battle against a nationalized culture and an industrial economy of mass organizations. Increasingly, he fights alone. Churches, schools, and public officials are disdainful of "rigid" attitudes and doctrines. Within the American middle class, in almost all communities, there is a sharp split between two stylistic components. In one the abstainer can feel at home. Here the local community of neighbors and townsmen is the point of reference for behavior. In the other, the more cosmopolitan centers of urban institutions are mediated to the town through national institutions, communications media, and the two-way geographical mobility which brings in newcomers and sends out college students for training elsewhere. The clash between the drinker and the abstainer reflects these diverse references. The localistic culture clings to the traditional while the easier, relaxed, modern ways are the province of the national culture. It is this national culture which becomes the more prestigeful and powerful as America becomes more homogeneous.

The anger and bitterness of the "doomed class" is by no means an "irrational" reaction. There *has* been a decline in the social status of the old middle class and in the dominance of his values. This sense of anger at the loss of status and bitterness about lowered self-esteem pervades the entire Temperance movement today. It takes a number of forms. At one extreme and within certain Temperance elements, it is expressed as a general, diffuse criticism of modern political and social doctrines and a defense of tradition in almost all areas of American life. At the other extreme, within other parts of the Temperance movement, it is part of the intense nationalism, economic conservatism, and social stagnation of the radical right. (This latter is especially true of the Prohibition Party.)

The study of the American Temperance movement is a phase of the process by which, as Richard Hofstadter expressed it, "a large part of the Populist-Progressive tradition has turned sour, become illiberal and ill-tempered."[6] The values and the economic position of the native American Protestant, old middle class of individual enterprisers have been losing out in the shuffle of time and social change. The efforts of the old middle class and of those who have built their self-conceptions on their values to defend and restore their lost prestige have taken a number of forms. In fluoridation, domestic Communism, school curricula, and the United Nations, they have found issues which range tradition against modernity. Temperance has been one of the classic issues on which divergent cultures have faced each other in America. Such issues of style have been significant because they have been ways through which groups have tried to handle the problems which have been important to them.

NOTES

1. For manifestations of this viewpoint in American history see Lee Benson, *The Concept of Jacksonian Democracy* (Princeton, N.J.: Princeton University Press, 1961), and Louis Hartz, *The Liberal Tradition in America* (New York: Harcourt, Brace and Co., 1955). These trends in historiography are discussed in John Higham (ed.), *The Reconstruction of American History* (New York: Harper Torch Books, 1962).
2. Benson, *op. cit.*, p. 275.
3. A major exception to this is John A. Krout, *The Origins of Prohibition* (New York: A. A. Knopf, 1925). Even Peter Odegard's otherwise excellent work on *Pressure Politics* (New York: Columbia University Press, 1928) is marred by his utter lack of sympathy with Temperance goals. The same moralistic condemnation of moralism limits the utility of the very recent work of Andrew Sinclair, *Prohibition* (Boston: Little, Brown and Co., 1962).
4. Quoted in Benson, *op. cit.*, p. 199.
5. The term "Temperance" is an inadequate name for a movement which preaches total abstinence rather than "temperate" use of alcohol. The word was affixed to the movement in its early years (1820's) when its doctrine was not yet as extreme as it later came to be.
6. Richard Hofstadter, *The Age of Reform* (New York: A. A. Knopf, 1955), pp. 19–20.

27 *The Social Reality of Crime*
RICHARD QUINNEY

The theory contains six propositions and a number of statements within the propositions. With the first proposition I define crime. The next four are the explanatory units. In the final proposition the other five are collected to form a composite describing the social reality of crime. The propositions and their integration into a theory of crime

Reprinted from Richard Quinney, *The Social Reality of Crime* (Boston: Little, Brown and Company, 1970). Copyright © 1970 by Richard Quinney.

reflect the assumptions about explanation and about man and society outlined above.[1]

Proposition 1 (Definition of Crime): Crime is a definition of human conduct that is created by authorized agents in a politically organized society.

This is the essential starting point in the theory—a definition of crime—which itself is based on the concept of definition. Crime is a *definition* of behavior that is conferred on some persons by others. Agents of the law (legislators, police, prosecutors, and judges), representing segments of a politically organized society, are responsible for formulating and administering criminal law. Persons and behaviors, therefore, become criminal because of the *formulation* and *application* of criminal definitions. Thus, *crime is created.*

By viewing crime as a definition, we are able to avoid the commonly used "clinical perspective," which leads one to concentrate on the quality of the act and to assume that criminal behavior is an individual pathology.[2] Crime is not inherent in behavior, but is a judgment made by some about the actions and characteristics of others.[3] This proposition allows us to focus on the formulation and administration of the criminal law as it touches upon the behaviors that become defined as criminal. Crime is seen as a result of a process which culminates in the defining of persons and behaviors as criminal. It follows, then, that *the greater the number of criminal definitions formulated and applied, the greater the amount of crime.*

Proposition 2 (Formulation of Criminal Definitions): Criminal definitions describe behaviors that conflict with the interests of the segments of society that have the power to shape public policy.

Criminal definitions are formulated according to the interests of those *segments* (types of social groupings) of society which have the *power* to translate their interests into *public policy.* The interests—based on desires, values, and norms—which are ultimately incorporated into the criminal law are those which are treasured by the dominant interest groups in the society.[4] In other words, those who have the ability to have their interests represented in public policy regulate the formulation of criminal definitions.

That criminal definitions are formulated is one of the most obvious manifestations of *conflict* in society. By formulating criminal law (including legislative statutes, administrative rulings, and judicial decisions), some segments of society protect and perpetuate their own interests. Criminal definitions exist, therefore, because some segments of society are in conflict with others.[5] By formulating criminal definitions these segments are able to control the behavior of persons in other segments. It follows that *the greater the conflict in interests between the segments of a society, the greater the probability that the power segments will formulate criminal definitions.*

The interests of the power segments of society are reflected not only in the content of criminal definitions and the kinds of penal sanctions attached to them, but also in the *legal policies* stipulating how those who come to be defined as "criminal" are to be handled. Hence, procedural rules are created for enforcing and administering the criminal law. Policies are also established on programs for treating and punishing the criminally defined and for controlling and preventing crime. In the initial criminal definitions or the subsequent procedures, and in correctional and penal programs or policies of crime control and prevention, the segments of society that have power and interests to protect are instrumental in regulating the behavior of those who have conflicting interests and less power.[6] Finally, law changes with modifications in the interest structure. When the interests that underlie a criminal law are no longer relevant to groups in power, the law will be reinterpreted or altered to incorporate the dominant interests. Hence, *the probability that criminal definitions will be formulated is increased by such factors as (1) changing social conditions, (2) emerging interests, (3) increasing demands that political, economic, and religious interests be protected, and (4) changing conceptions of the public interest.* The social history of law reflects changes in the interest structure of society.

Proposition 3 (Application of Criminal Definitions): Criminal definitions are applied by the segments of society that have the power to shape the enforcement and administration of criminal law.

The powerful interests intervene in all stages in which criminal definitions are created. Since interests cannot be effectively protected by merely formulating criminal law, enforcement and administration of the law are required. The interests of the powerful, therefore, operate in *applying* criminal definitions. Consequently, crime is "political behavior and the criminal becomes in fact a member of a 'minority group' without sufficient public support to dominate the control of the police power of the state."[7] Those whose interests conflict with the interests represented in the law must either change their behavior or possibly find it defined as "criminal."

The probability that criminal definitions will be applied varies according to the extent to which the behaviors of the powerless conflict with the interests of the power segments. Law enforcement efforts and judicial activity are likely to be increased when the interests of the powerful are threatened by the opposition's behavior. Fluctuations and variations in the application of criminal definitions reflect shifts in the relations of the various segments in the power structure of society.

Obviously, the criminal law is not applied directly by the powerful segments. They delegate enforcement and administration of the law to authorized *legal agents,* who, nevertheless, represent their interests. In fact, the security in office of legal agents depends on their ability to represent the society's dominant interests.

Because the interest groups responsible for creating criminal definitions are physically separated from the groups to which the authority to enforce and administer law is delegated, local conditions affect the manner in which criminal definitions are applied.[8] In particular, communities vary in the law enforcement and administration of justice they expect. Application is also affected by the visibility of acts in a community and by its norms about reporting possible offenses. Especially important are the occupational organization and ideology of the legal agents.[9] Thus, the *probability that criminal definitions will be applied is influenced by such community and organizational factors as (1) community expectations of law enforcement and administration, (2) the visibility and public reporting of offenses, and (3) the occupational organization, ideology, and actions of the legal agents to whom the authority to enforce and administer criminal law is delegated.* Such factors determine how the dominant interests of society are implemented in the application of criminal definitions.

The probability that criminal definitions will be applied in *specific situations* depends on the actions of the legal agents. In the final analysis, a criminal definition is applied according to an *evaluation* by someone charged with the authority to enforce and administer the law. In the course of "criminalization," a criminal label may be affixed to a person because of real or fancied attributes: "Indeed, a person is evaluated, either favorably or unfavorably, not because he *does* something, or even because he *is* something, but because others react to their perceptions of him as offensive or inoffensive."[10] Evaluation by the definers is affected by the way in which the suspect handles the situation, but ultimately their evaluations and subsequent decisions determine the criminality of human acts. Hence, *the more legal agents evaluate behaviors and persons as worthy of criminal definition, the greater the probability that criminal definitions will be applied.*

Proposition 4 (Development of Behavior Patterns in Relation to Criminal Definitions): Behavior patterns are structured in segmentally organized society in relation to criminal definitions, and within this context persons engage in actions that have relative probabilities of being defined as criminal.

Although behavior varies, all behaviors are similar in that they represent the *behavior patterns* of segments of society. Therefore, all persons—whether they create criminal definitions or are the objects of criminal definitions—act according to *normative systems* learned in relative social and cultural settings.[11] Since it is not the equality of the behavior but the action taken against the behavior that makes it criminal, that which is defined as criminal in any society is relative to the behavior patterns of the segments of society that formulate and apply criminal definitions. Consequently, *persons in the segments of society whose behavior patterns are not represented in formulating and applying criminal definitions are more likely to act in ways that will be defined as criminal than those in the segments that formulate and apply criminal definitions.*

Once behavior patterns are established with some regularity within the respective segments of society, individuals are provided with a framework for developing *personal action patterns*. These patterns continually develop for each person as he moves from one experience to another. It is the development of these patterns that gives his behavior its own substance in relation to criminal definitions.

Man constructs his own patterns of action in participating with others. It follows, then, that *the probability that a person will develop action patterns that have a high potential of being defined as criminal depends on the relative substance of (1) structured opportunities, (2) learning experiences, (3) interpersonal associations and identifications, and (4) self-conceptions.* Throughout his experiences, each person creates a conception of himself as a social being. Thus prepared, he behaves according to the anticipated consequences of his actions.[12]

During experiences shared by the criminal definers and the criminally defined, personal action patterns develop among the criminally defined because they are so defined. After such persons have had continued experience in being criminally defined, they learn to manipulate the application of criminal definitions.[13]

Furthermore, those who have been defined as criminal begin to conceive of themselves as criminal; as they adjust to the definitions imposed upon them, they learn to play the role of the criminal.[14] Because of others' reactions, therefore, persons may develop personal action patterns that increase the likelihood of their being defined as criminal in the future. That is, *increased experience with criminal definitions increases the probability of developing actions that may be subsequently defined as criminal.*

Thus, both the criminal definers and the criminally defined are involved in reciprocal action patterns. The patterns of both the definers and the defined are shaped by their common, continued, and related experiences. The fate of each is bound to that of the other.

Proposition 5 (Construction of Criminal Conceptions): Conceptions of crime are constructed and diffused in the segments of society by various means of communication.

The "real world" is a social construction: man with the help of others creates the world in which he lives. Social reality is thus the world a group of people create and believe in as their own. This reality is constructed according to the kind of "knowledge" they develop, the ideas they are exposed to, the manner in which they select information to fit the world they are shaping, and the manner in which they interpret these conceptions.[15] Man behaves in reference to the *social meanings* he attaches to his experiences.

Among the constructions that develop in a society are those which determine what man regards as crime. Wherever we find the concept of crime, there we will find conceptions about the relevance of crime, the offender's characteristics, and the relation of crime to the social order.[16] These conceptions are constructed by communication. In fact, *the construction of criminal conceptions depends on the portrayal of crime in all personal and mass communications.* By such means, criminal conceptions are constructed and diffused in the segments of a society. The most critical conceptions are those held by the power segments of society. These are the conceptions that are certain of becoming incorporated into the social reality of crime. In general, then, *the more the power segments are concerned about crime, the greater the probability that criminal definitions will be created and that behavior patterns will develop in opposition to criminal definitions.* The formulation and application of criminal definitions and the development of behavior patterns related

FIGURE 1
MODEL OF THE SOCIAL REALITY OF CRIME

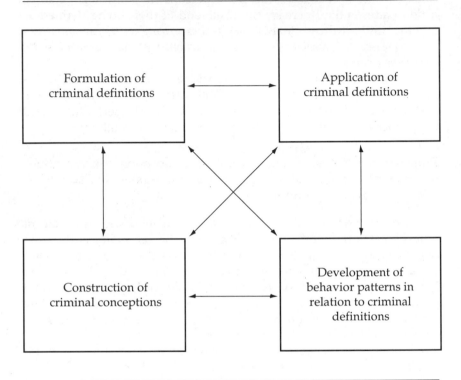

to criminal definitions are thus joined in full circle by the construction of criminal conceptions.

Proposition 6 (The Social Reality of Crime): The social reality of crime is constructed by the formulation and application of criminal definitions, the development of behavior patterns related to criminal definitions, and the construction of criminal conceptions.

These five propositions can be collected into a composite. The theory, accordingly, describes and explains phenomena that increase the probability of crime in society, resulting in the social reality of crime.

Since the first proposition is a definition and the sixth is a composite, the body of the theory consists of the four middle propositions. These form a model, as diagrammed in Figure 1, which relates the propositions into a theoretical system. Each proposition is related to the others forming a theoretical system of developmental propositions interacting with one another. The phenomena denoted in the propositions and their relationships culminate in what is regarded as the amount and character of crime in a society at any given time, that is, in the social reality of crime.

NOTES

1. For earlier background material, see Richard Quinney, "A Conception of Man and Society for Criminology," *Sociological Quarterly*, 6 (Spring, 1965), pp. 119–127; Quinney, "Crime in Political Perspective," *American Behavioral Scientist*, 8 (December, 1964), pp. 19–22; Quinney, "Is Criminal Behavior Deviant Behavior?" *British Journal of Criminology*, 5 (April, 1965), pp. 132–142.

2. See Jane R. Mercer, "Social System Perspective and Clinical Perspective: Frames of Reference for Understanding Career Patterns of Persons Labelled as Mentally Retarded," *Social Problems*, 13 (Summer, 1966), pp. 18–34.

3. This perspective in the study of social deviance has been developed in Becker, *Outsiders*; Kai T. Erikson, "Notes on the Sociology of Deviance," *Social Problems*, 9 (Spring, 1962), pp. 307–314; John I. Kitsuse, "Societal Reactions to Deviant Behavior: Problems of Theory and Method," *Social Problems*, 9 (Winter, 1962), pp. 247–256. Also see Ronald L. Akers, "Problems in the Sociology of Deviance: Social Definitions and Behavior," *Social Forces*, 46 (June, 1968), pp. 455–465; David J. Bordua, "Recent Trends: Deviant Behavior and Social Control," *Annals of the American Academy of Political and Social Science*, 369 (January, 1967), pp. 149–163; Jack P. Gibbs, "Conceptions of Deviant Behavior: The Old and the New," *Pacific Sociological Review*, 9 (Spring, 1966), pp. 9–14; Clarence R. Jeffery, "The Structure of American Criminological Thinking," *Journal of Criminal Law, Criminology and Police Science*, 46 (January-February, 1956), pp. 658–672; Austin T. Turk, "Prospects for Theories of Criminal Behavior," *Journal of Criminal Law, Criminology and Police Science*, 55 (December, 1964), pp. 454–461.

4. See Richard C. Fuller, "Morals and the Criminal Law," *Journal of Criminal Law, Criminology and Police Science*, 32 (March–April, 1942), pp. 624–630; Thorsten Sellin, *Culture Conflict and Crime* (New York: Social Science Research Council, 1938), pp. 21–25; Clarence R. Jeffery, "Crime, Law and Social Structure," *Journal of Criminal Law, Criminology and Police Science*, 47 (November–December, 1956), pp. 423–435; John J. Honigmann, "Value Conflict and Legislation," *Social Problems*, 7 (Summer, 1959), pp. 34–40; George Rusche and Otto Kirchheimer,

Punishment and Social Structure (New York: Columbia University Press, 1939); Roscoe Pound, *An Introduction to the Philosophy of Law* (New Haven: Yale University Press, 1922).

5. I am obviously indebted to the conflict formulation of George B. Vold, *Theoretical Criminology* (New York: Oxford University Press, 1958), especially pp. 203–242. A recent conflict approach to crime is found in Austin T. Turk, "Conflict and Criminality," *American Sociological Review,* 31 (June, 1966), pp. 338–352.

6. Considerable support for this proposition is found in the following studies: William J. Chambliss, "A Sociological Analysis of the Law of Vagrancy," *Social Problems,* 12 (Summer, 1964), pp. 66–77; Kai T. Erikson, *Wayward Puritans* (New York: John Wiley, 1966); Jerome Hall, *Theft, Law and Society,* 2nd ed. (Indianapolis: Bobbs-Merrill, 1952); Clarence R. Jeffery, "The Development of Crime in Early England," *Journal of Criminal Law, Criminology and Police Science,* 47 (March–April, 1957), pp. 647–666; Alfred R. Lindesmith, *The Addict and the Law* (Bloomington: Indiana University Press, 1965); Rusche and Kirchheimer, *Punishment and Social Structure;* Andrew Sinclair, *Era of Excess: A Social History of the Prohibition Movement* (New York: Harper & Row, 1964); Edwin H. Sutherland, "The Sexual Psychopath Law," *Journal of Criminal Law, Criminology and Police Science,* 40 (January– February, 1950), pp. 543–554.

7. Vold, *Theoretical Criminology,* p. 202. Also see Irving Louis Horowitz and Martin Liebowitz, "Social Deviance and Political Marginality: Toward a Redefinition of the Relation Between Sociology and Politics," *Social Problems,* 15 (Winter, 1968), pp. 280–296.

8. See Michael Banton, *The Policeman and the Community* (London: Tavistock, 1964); Egon Bittner, "The Police on Skid-Row: A Study of Peace Keeping," *American Sociological Review,* 32 (October, 1967), pp. 669–715; John P. Clark, "Isolation of the Police: A Comparison of the British and American Situations," *Journal of Criminal Law, Criminology and Police Science,* 56 (September, 1965), pp. 307–319; Nathan Goldman, *The Differential Selection of Juvenile Offenders for Court Appearance* (New York National Council on Crime and Delinquency, 1963); James Q. Wilson, *Varieties of Police Behavior* (Cambridge: Harvard University Press, 1968).

9. Abraham S. Blumberg, *Criminal Justice* (Chicago: Quadrangle Books, 1967); David J. Bordua and Albert J. Reiss, Jr., "Command, Control and Charisma: Reflections on Police Bureaucracy," *American Journal of Sociology,* 72 (July, 1966), pp. 68–76; Aaron V. Cicourel, *The Social Organization of Juvenile Justice* (New York: John Wiley, 1968); Arthur Niederhoffer, *Behind the Shield: The Police in Urban Society* (Garden City, N.Y.: Doubleday, 1967); Jerome H. Skolnick, *Justice Without Trial: Law Enforcement in Democratic Society* (New York: John Wiley, 1966); Arthur L. Stinchcombe, "Institutions of Privacy in the Determination of Police Administrative Practice," *American Journal of Sociology,* 69 (September,

1963), pp. 150–160; David Sudnow, "Normal Crimes: Sociological Features of the Penal Code in a Public Defender Office," *Social Problems*, 12 (Winter, 1965), pp. 255–276; William A. Westley, "Violence and the Police," *American Journal of Sociology*, 59 (July, 1953), pp. 34–41; Arthur Lewis Wood, *Criminal Lawyer* (New Haven: College & University Press, 1967).

10. Turk, "Conflict and Criminality," p. 340. For research on the evaluation of suspects by policemen, see Irving Piliavin and Scott Briar, "Police Encounters with Juveniles," *American Journal of Sociology*, 70 (September, 1964), pp. 206–214.

11. Assumed within the theory of the social reality of crime is Sutherland's theory of differential association. See Edwin H. Sutherland, *Principles of Criminology*, 4th ed. (Philadelphia: J. B. Lippincott, 1947). An analysis of the differential association theory is found in Melvin L. De Fleur and Richard Quinney, "A Reformulation of Sutherland's Differential Association Theory and a Strategy for Empirical Verification," *Journal of Research in Crime and Delinquency*, 3 (January, 1966), pp. 1–22.

12. On the operant nature of criminally defined behavior, see Robert L. Burgess and Ronald L. Akers, "A Differential Association-Reinforcement Theory of Criminal Behavior," *Social Problems*, 14 (Fall, 1966), pp. 128–147; C. R. Jeffery, "Criminal Behavior and Learning Theory," *Journal of Criminal Law, Criminology and Police Science*, 56 (September, 1965), pp. 294–300.

13. A discussion of the part the person plays in manipulating the deviant defining situation is found in Judith Lorber, "Deviance as Performance: The Case of Illness," *Social Problems*, 14 (Winter, 1967), pp. 302–310.

14. Edwin M. Lemert, *Human Deviance, Social Problems and Social Control* (Englewood Cliffs, N.J.: Prentice-Hall, 1964), pp. 40–64; Edwin M. Lemert, *Social Pathology* (New York: McGraw-Hill, 1951), pp. 3–98. A related and earlier discussion is in Frank Tannenbaum, *Crime and the Community* (New York: Columbia University Press, 1938), pp. 3–81.

15. See Berger and Luckmann, *The Social Construction of Reality*. Relevant research on the diffusion of information is discussed in Everett M. Rogers, *Diffusion of Innovations* (New York: The Free Press of Glencoe, 1962).

16. Research on public conceptions of crime is only beginning. See Alexander L. Clark and Jack P. Gibbs, "Social Control: A Reformulation," *Social Problems*, 12 (Spring, 1965), pp. 398–415; Thomas E. Dow, Jr., "The Role of Identification in Conditioning Public Attitude Toward the Offender," *Journal of Criminal Law, Criminology and Police Science*, 58 (March, 1967), pp. 75–79; William P. Lentz, "Social Status and Attitudes Toward Delinquency Control," *Journal of Research in Crime and Delinquency*, 3 (July, 1966), pp. 147–154; Jennie McIntyre,

"Public Attitudes Toward Crime and Law Enforcement," *Annals of the American Academy of Political and Social Science*, 374 (November, 1967), pp. 34–46; Anastassios D. Mylonas and Walter C. Reckless, "Prisoners' Attitudes Toward Law and Legal Institutions," *Journal of Criminal Law, Criminology and Police Science*, 54 (December, 1963), pp. 479–484; Elizabeth A. Rooney and Don C. Gibbons, "Social Reactions to 'Crimes Without Victims,'" *Social Problems*, 13 (Spring, 1966), pp. 400–410.

28   The Poverty of the Sociology of Deviance: Nuts, Sluts, and 'Preverts'*
ALEXANDER LIAZOS

C. Wright Mills left a rich legacy to sociology. One of his earliest, and best, contributions was "The Professional Ideology of Social Pathologists" (1943). In it, Mills argues that the small-town, middle-class background of writers of social problems textbooks blinded them to basic problems of social structure and power, and led them to emphasize melioristic, patchwork types of solutions to America's "problems." They assumed as natural and orderly the structure of small-town America; anything else was pathology and disorganization. Moreover, these "problems," "ranging from rape in rural districts to public housing," were not explored systematically and theoretically; they were not placed in some large political, historical, and social context. They were merely listed and decried.[1]

Since Mills wrote his paper, however, the field of social problems, social disorganization, and social pathology has undergone considerable changes. Beginning in the late 1940's and the 1950's, and culminating in the 1960's, the field of "deviance" has largely replaced the social problems orientation. This new field is characterized by a number of features which distinguish it from the older approach.[2]

Reprinted from Alexander Liazos, "The Poverty of the Sociology of Deviance: Nuts, Sluts, and 'Preverts,'" *Social Problems*, vol. 20, no. 1 (Summer 1972), pp. 103–120. Copyright © 1972 by the Society for the Study of Social Problems. By permission of the author and publisher.

*The subtitle of this paper came from two sources. (a) A Yale undergraduate once told me that the deviance course was known among Yale students as "nuts and sluts." (b) A former colleague of mine at Quinnipiac College, John Bancroft, often told me that the deviance course was "all about those 'preverts.'" When I came to write this paper, I discovered that these descriptions were correct, and concise summaries of my argument. I thank both of them. I also want to thank Gordon Fellman for a very careful reading of the first draft of the manuscript, and for discussing with me the general and specific issues I raise here.

First, there is some theoretical framework, even though it is often absent in edited collections (the Rubington and Weinberg (1968) edited book is an outstanding exception). Second, the small-town morality is largely gone. Writers claim they will examine the phenomena at hand—prostitution, juvenile delinquency, mental illness, crime, and others—objectively, not considering them as necessarily harmful and immoral. Third, the statements and theories of the field are based on much more extensive, detailed, and theoretically-oriented research than were those of the 1920's and 1930's. Fourth, writers attempt to fit their theories to some central theories, concerns, and problems found in the general field of sociology; they try to transcend mere moralizing.

The "deviant" has been humanized; the moralistic tone is no longer ever-present (although it still lurks underneath the explicit disavowals); and theoretical perspectives have been developed. Nevertheless, all is not well with the field of "deviance." Close examination reveals that writers of this field still do not try to relate the phenomena of "deviance" to larger social, historical, political, and economic contexts. The emphasis is still on the "deviant" and the "problems" *he* presents to himself and others, not on the society within which he emerges and operates.

I examined 16 textbooks in the field of "deviance," eight of them readers, to determine the state of the field. (They are preceded by an asterisk in the bibliography.) Theoretically, eight take the labelling-interactionist approach; three more tend to lean to that approach; four others argue for other orientations (anomie, structural-functional, etc.) or, among the readers, have an "eclectic" approach; and one (McCaghy, *et al.*, 1968) is a collection of biographical and other statements by "deviants" themselves, and thus may not be said to have a theoretical approach (although, as we shall see, the selection of the types of statements and "deviants" still implies an orientation and viewpoint). A careful examination of these textbooks revealed a number of ideological biases. These biases became apparent as much from what these books leave unsaid and unexamined, as from what they do say. The field of the sociology of deviance, as exemplified in these books, contains three important theoretical and political biases.

1. All writers, especially those of the labelling school, either state explicitly or imply that one of their main concerns is to *humanize* and *normalize* the "deviant," to show that he is essentially no different from us. But by the very emphasis on the "deviant" and his identity problems and sub-culture, the opposite effect may have been achieved. The persisting use of the label "deviant" to refer to the people we are considering is an indication of the feeling that these people are indeed different.

2. By the overwhelming emphasis on the "dramatic" nature of the usual types of "deviance"—prostitution, homosexuality, juvenile delinquency, and others—we have neglected to examine other, more serious and harmful forms of "deviance." I refer to *covert institutional violence* (defined and discussed below) which leads to such things as poverty and exploitation, the war in Vietnam, unjust tax laws, racism and sexism, and so on, which causes psychic and material suffering for many Americans, black and white, men and women.

3. Despite explicit statements by these authors of the importance of *power* in the designation of what is "deviant," in their substantive analyses they show a profound unconcern with power and its implications. The really powerful, the upper classes and the power elite, those Gouldner (1968) calls the "top dogs," are left essentially unexamined by these sociologists of deviance.

I

Always implicit, and frequently explicit, is the aim of the labelling school to humanize and normalize the "deviant." Two statements by Becker and Matza are representative of this sentiment.

> In the course of our work and for who knows what private reasons, we fall into deep sympathy with the people we are studying, so that while the rest of society views them as unfit in one or another respect for the deference ordinarily accorded a fellow citizen, we believe that they are at least as good as anyone else, more sinned against than sinning (Becker, 1967:100–101).

> The growth of the sociological view of deviant phenomena involved, as major phases, the replacement of a correctional stance by an *appreciation* of the deviant subject, the tacit purging of a conception of pathology by a new stress on human *diversity*, and the erosion of a simple distinction between deviant and conventional phenomena, resulting from intimate familiarity of the world as it is, which yielded a more sophisticated view stressing *complexity* (Matza, 1969:10).

For a number of reasons, however, the opposite effect may have been achieved; and "deviants" still seem different. I began to suspect this reverse effect from the many essays and papers I read while teaching the "deviance" course. The clearest example is the repeated use of the word "tolerate." Students would write that we must not persecute homosexuals, prostitutes, mental patients, and others, that we must be "tolerant" of them. But one tolerates only those one considers less than equal, morally inferior, and weak; those equal to oneself, one accepts and respects; one does not merely allow them to exist, one does not "tolerate" them.

The repeated assertion that "deviants" are "at least as good as anyone else" may raise doubts that this is in fact the case, or that we believe it. A young woman who grew up in the South in the 1940's and 1950's told Quinn (1954:146): "'You know, I think from the fact that I was told so often that I must treat colored people with consideration, I got the feeling that I could mistreat them if I wanted to.'" Thus with "deviants"; if in fact they are as good as we are, we would not need to remind everyone of this fact; we would take it for granted and proceed from there. But our assertions that "deviants" are not different may raise the very doubts we want to dispel. Moreover, why would we create a separate field of sociology for "deviants" if there were not something different about them? May it be that even we do not believe our statements and protestations?

The continued use of the word "deviant" (and its variants), despite its invidious distinctions and connotations, also belies our explicit statements on the equality of the people under consideration. To be sure, some of the authors express uneasiness over the term. For example, we are told,

> In our use of this term for the purpose of sociological investigation, we emphasize that we do not attach any value judgement, explicitly or implicitly, either to the word "deviance" or to those describing their behavior or beliefs in this book (McCaghy, *et al.*, 1968:v).

Lofland (1969:2, 9–10) expresses even stronger reservations about the use of the term, and sees clearly the sociological, ethical, and political problems raised by its continued use. Yet, the title of his book is *Deviance and Identity*.

Szasz (1970: xxv–xxvi) has urged that we abandon use of the term:

> Words have lives of their own. However much sociologists insist that the term "deviant" does not diminish the worth of the person or group so categorized, the implication of inferiority adheres to the word. Indeed, sociologists are not wholly exempt from blame: they describe addicts and homosexuals as deviants, but never Olympic champions or Nobel Prize winners. In fact, the term is rarely applied to people with admired characteristics, such as great wealth, superior skills, or fame—whereas it is often applied to those with despised characteristics, such as poverty, lack of marketable skills, or infamy.
>
> The term "social deviants"...does not make sufficiently explicit—as the terms "scapegoat" or "victim" do—that majorities usually categorize persons or groups as "deviant" in order to set them apart as inferior beings and to justify their social control, oppression, persecution, or even complete destruction.

Terms like victimization, persecution, and oppression are more accurate descriptions of what is really happening. But even Gouldner (1968), in a masterful critique of the labelling school, while describing social conflict, calls civil-rights and anti-war protesters "political deviants." He points out clearly that these protesters are resisting openly, not slyly, conditions they abhor. Gouldner is discussing political struggles; oppression and resistance to oppression; conflicts over values, morals, interests, and power; and victimization. Naming such protesters "deviants," even if *political* deviants, is an indication of the deep penetration within our minds of certain prejudices and orientations.

Given the use of the term, the definition and examples of "deviant" reveal underlying sentiments and views. Therefore, it is important that we redefine drastically the entire field, especially since it is a flourishing one: "Because younger sociologists have found deviance such a fertile and exciting field for their own work, and because students share these feelings, deviance promises to become an even more important area of sociological research and theory in the coming years." (Douglas, 1970a:3).

The lists and discussions of "deviant" acts and persons reveal the writers' biases and sentiments. These are acts which, "like robbery, burglary or rape [are] of a simple and dramatic predatory nature..." (The President's Commission on Law Enforcement and the Administration of Justice, in Dinitz, *et al.*, 1969:105). All 16 texts, without exception, concentrate on actions and persons of a "dramatic predatory nature," on "preverts." This is true of both the labelling and other schools. The following are examples from the latter:

> Ten different types of deviant behavior are considered: juvenile delinquency, adult crime, prison sub-cultures, homosexuality, prostitution, suicide, homicide, alcoholism, drug addiction and mental illness (Rushing, 1969: preface).

> Traditionally, in American sociology the study of deviance has focused on criminals, juvenile delinquents, prostitutes, suicides, the mentally ill, drug users and drug addicts, homosexuals, and political and religious radicals (Lefton, *et al.*, 1968:v).

> Deviant behavior is essentially violation of certain types of group norms; a deviant act is behavior which is proscribed in a certain way. [It must be] in a disapproved direction, and of sufficient degree to exceed the tolerance limit of the community....[such as] delinquency and crime, prostitution, homosexual behavior, drug addiction, alcoholism, mental disorders, suicide, marital and family maladjustment, discrimination against minority groups, and, to a lesser degree, role problems of old age (Clinard, 1968:28).

Finally, we are told that these are some examples of deviance every society must deal with: "...mental illness, violence, theft, and sexual misconduct, as well as...other similarly difficult behavior" (Dinitz, *et al.*, 1969:3).

The list stays unchanged with the authors of the labelling school.

> ...in Part I, "The Deviant Act," I draw rather heavily on certain studies of homicide, embezzlement, "naive" check forgery, suicide and a few other acts...in discussing the assumption of deviant identity (Part II) and the assumption of normal identity (Part III), there is heavy reference to certain studies of paranoia, "mental illness" more generally, and Alcoholics Anonymous and Synanon (Lofland, 1969:34).

> Homicide, suicide, alcoholism, mental illness, prostitution, and homosexuality are among the forms of behavior typically called deviant, and they are among the kinds of behavior that will be analyzed (Lofland, 1969:1). Included among my respondents were political radicals of the far left and the far right, homosexuals, militant blacks, convicts and mental hospital patients, mystics, narcotic addicts, LSD and Marijuana users, illicit drug dealers, delinquent boys, racially mixed couples, hippies, health-food users, and bohemian artists and village eccentrics (Simmons, 1969:10).

Simmons (1969:27, 29, 31) also informs us that in his study of stereotypes of "deviants" held by the public, these are the types he gave to people: homosexuals, beatniks, adulterers, marijuana smokers, political radicals, alcoholics, prostitutes, lesbians, ex-mental patients, atheists, ex-convicts, intellectuals, and gamblers. In Lemert (1967) we find that except for the three introductory (theoretical) chapters, the substantive chapters cover the following topics: alcohol drinking, four; check forgers, three; stuttering, two; and mental illness, two. Matza (1969) offers the following list of "deviants" and their actions that "must be appreciated if one adheres to a naturalistic perspective": paupers, robbers, motorcycle gangs, prostitutes, drug addicts, promiscuous homosexuals, thieving Gypsies, and "free love" Bohemians (1969:16). Finally, Douglas' collection (1970a) covers these forms of "deviance": abortion, nudism, topless barmaids, prostitutes, homosexuals, violence (motorcycle and juvenile gangs), shoplifting, and drugs.

The omissions from these lists are staggering. The covert, institutional forms of "deviance" (part II, below) are nowhere to be found. Reading these authors, one would not know that the most destructive use of violence in the last decade has been the war in Vietnam, in which the U.S. has heaped unprecedented suffering on the people and their land; more bombs have been dropped in Vietnam than in the entire World War II. Moreover, the robbery of the corporate world—through tax breaks, fixed prices, low wages, pollution of the environment, shoddy goods, etc.—is passed over in our fascination with "dramatic and predatory" actions. Therefore, we are told that "while they certainly are of no greater social importance to us than such subjects as banking and accounting [or military violence], subjects such as marijuana use and motorcycle gangs are of far greater interest to most of us. While it is only a coincidence that our scientific interests correspond with the emotional interest in deviants, it is a happy coincidence and, I believe, one that should be encouraged" (Douglas, 1970a:5). And Matza (1969:17), in commenting on the "appreciative sentiments" of the "naturalistic spirit," elaborates on the same theme: "We do not for a moment wish that we could rid ourselves of deviant phenomena. We are intrigued by them. They are an intrinsic, ineradicable, and vital part of human society."

An effort is made to transcend this limited view and substantive concern with dramatic and predatory forms of "deviance." Becker (1964:3) claims that the new (labelling) deviance no longer studies only "delinquents and drug addicts, though these classical kinds of deviance are still kept under observation." It increases its knowledge "of the processes of deviance by studying physicians, people with physical handicaps, the mentally deficient, and others whose doings were formerly not included in the area." The powerful "deviants" are still left untouched, however. This is still true with another aspect of the new deviance. Becker (1964:4) claims that in the labelling perspective "we focus attention on the other people involved in the process. We pay attention to the role of the non-deviant as well as that of the deviant." But we see that it is the ordinary non-deviants and the low-level agents of social control who receive attention, not the powerful ones (Gouldner, 1968).

In fact, the emphasis is more on the *subculture* and *identity* of the "deviants" themselves rather than on their oppressors and persecutors. To be sure, in varying degrees all authors discuss the agents of social control, but the fascination and emphasis are on the "deviant" himself. Studies of prisons and prisoners, for example, focus on prison subcultures and prisoner rehabilitation; there is little or no consideration of the social, political, economic, and power conditions which consign people to prisons. Only now are we beginning to realize that most prisoners are *political prisoners*—that their "criminal" actions (whether against individuals, such as robbery, or conscious political acts against the state) result largely from current social and political conditions, and are not the work of "disturbed" and "psychopathic" personalities. This realization came about largely because of the writings of political prisoners themselves: Malcolm X (1965), Eldridge Cleaver (1968), and George Jackson (1970), among others.[3]

In all these books, notably those of the labelling school, the concern is with the "deviant's" subculture and identity: his problems, motives, fellow victims, etc. The collection of memoirs and apologies of "deviants" in their own words (McCaghy, *et al.*, 1968) covers the lives and identities of "prevert deviants": prostitutes, nudists, abortionists, criminals, drug users, homosexuals, the mentally ill, alcoholics, and suicides. For good measure, some "militant deviants" are thrown in: Black Muslims, the SDS, and a conscientious objector. But one wonders about other types of "deviants": how do those who perpetrate the covert institutional violence in our society view themselves? Do they have identity problems? How do they justify their actions? How did the robber barons of the late 19th century steal, fix laws, and buy politicians six days of the week and go to church on Sunday? By what process can people speak of body counts and kill ratios with cool objectivity? On these and similar questions, this book (and all others)[4] provides no answers; indeed, the editors seem unaware that such questions should or could be raised.

Becker (1964), Rubington and Weinberg (1968), Matza (1969), and Bell (1971) also focus on the identity and subculture of "prevert deviants." Matza, in discussing the assumption of "deviant identity," uses as examples, and elaborates upon, thieves and marijuana users. In all these books, there are occasional references to and questions about the large social and political structure, but these are not explored in any depth; and the emphasis remains on the behavior, identity, and rehabilitation of the "deviant" himself. This bias continues in the latest book which, following the fashions of the times, has chapters on hippies and militant protesters (Bell, 1971).

Even the best of these books, Simmons' *Deviants* (1969), is not free of the overwhelming concentration of the "deviant" and his identity. It is the most sympathetic and balanced presentation of the lives of "deviants": their joys, sorrows, and problems with the straight world and fellow victims. Simmons demystifies the processes of becoming "deviant" and overcoming "deviance." He shows, as well as anyone does, that these victims *are* just like us; and the differences they possess and the suffering they endure are imposed upon them. Ultimately, however, Simmons too falls prey to the three biases shown in the work of others: *(a)* the "deviants" he considers are only of the "prevert" type; *(b)* he focuses mostly on the victim and his identity, not on the persecutors; and *(c)* the persecutors he does discuss are of the middle-level variety, the agents of more powerful others and institutions.

Because of these biases, there is an implicit, but very clear, acceptance by these authors of the current definitions of "deviance." It comes about because they concentrate their attention on those who have been *successfully labelled as "deviant,"* and not on those who break laws, fix laws, violate ethical and moral standards, harm individuals and groups, etc., but who either are able to hide their actions, or, when known, can deflect criticism, labelling, and punishment. The following are typical statements which reveal this bias.

"...no act committed by members of occupational groups [such as white-collar crimes], however unethical, should be considered as crime unless it is punishable by the state in some way" (Clinard, 1968:269). Thus, if some people can manipulate laws so that their unethical and destructive acts are not "crimes," we should cater to their power and agree that they are not criminals.

Furthermore, the essence of the labelling school encourages this bias, despite Becker's (1963:14) assertion that "...insofar as a scientist uses 'deviant' to refer to any rule-breaking behavior and takes as his subjects of study only those who have been *labelled* deviant, he will be hampered by the disparities between the two categories." But as the following statements from Becker and others show, this is in fact what the labelling school does do.

Deviance is "created by society...*social groups create deviance by making the rules whose infraction constitutes deviance,* and by applying those rules to particular people and labelling them as outsiders" (Becker, 1963:8–9). Clearly, according to this view, in cases where no group has labelled another, no matter what the other group or individuals have done, there is nothing for the sociologist to study and dissect.

> Rules are not made automatically. Even though a practice may be harmful in an objective sense to the group in which it occurs, the harm needs to be discovered and pointed out. People must be made to feel that something ought to be done about it (Becker, 1963:162).

> What is important for the social analyst is not what people are by his lights or by his standards, but what it is that people construe one another and themselves to be for what reasons and with what consequences (Lofland, 1969:35).

> ...deviance is in the eyes of the beholder. For deviance to become a social fact, somebody must perceive an act, person, situation, or event as a departure from social norms, must categorize the perception, must report the perception to others, must get them to accept this definition of the situation, and must obtain a response that conforms to this definition. Unless all these requirements are met, deviance as a social fact does not come into being (Rubington and Weinberg, 1968:v).

The implication of these statements is that the sociologist accepts current, successful definitions of what is "deviant" as the only ones worthy of his attention. To be sure, he may argue that those labelled "deviant" are not really different from the rest of us, or that there is no act intrinsically "deviant," etc. By concentrating on cases of successful labelling, however, he will not penetrate beneath the surface to look for other forms of "deviance"—undetected stealing, violence, and destruction. When people are not powerful enough to make the "deviant" label stick on others, we overlook these cases. But is it not as much a *social fact*, even though few of us pay much attention to it, that the corporate economy kills and maims more, is more violent, than any violence committed by the poor (the usual subject of studies of violence)? By what reasoning and necessity is the "violence" of the poor in the ghettoes more worthy of our attention than the military boot-camps which numb recruits from the horrors of killing the "enemy" ("Oriental human beings," as we learned during the Calley trial)? But because these acts are not labelled "deviant," because they are covert, institutional, and normal, their "deviant" qualities are overlooked and they do not become part of the province of the sociology of deviance. Despite their best liberal intentions, these sociologists seem to perpetuate the very notions they think they debunk, and others of which they are unaware.

II.

As a result of the fascination with "nuts, sluts, and preverts," and their identities and subcultures, little attention has been paid to the unethical, illegal, and destructive actions of powerful individuals, groups, and institutions in our society. Because these actions are carried out quietly in the normal course of events, the sociology of deviance does not consider them as part of its subject matter. This bias is rooted in the very conception and definition of the field. It is obvious when one examines the treatment, or, just as often, lack of it, of the issues of violence, crime, and white-collar crime.

Discussions of violence treat only one type: the "dramatic and predatory" violence committed by individuals (usually the poor and minorities) against persons and property. For example, we read, "crimes involving violence, such as criminal homicide, assault, and forcible rape, are concentrated in the slums" (Clinard, 1968:123). Wolfgang, an expert on violence, has developed a whole theory on the "subculture of violence" found among the lower classes (e.g., in Rushing, 1969:233–40). And Douglas (1970a:part 4, on violence) includes readings on street gangs and the Hell's Angels. Thompson (1966), in his book on the Hell's Angels, devotes many pages to an exploration of the Angels' social background. In addition, throughout the book, and especially in his concluding chapter, he places the Angels' violence in the perspective of a violent, raping, and destructive society, which refuses to confront the reality of the Angels by distorting, exaggerating, and romanticizing their actions. But Douglas reprints none of these pages; rather, he offers us the chapter where, during a July 4 weekend, the Angels were restricted by the police within a lakeside area, had a drunken weekend, and became a tourist sideshow and circus.

In short, violence is presented as the exclusive property of the poor in the slums, the minorities, street gangs, and motorcycle beasts. But if we take the concept *violence* seriously, we see that much of our political and economic system thrives on it. In violence, a person is *violated*—there is harm done to his person, his psyche, his body, his dignity, his ability to govern himself (Garver, in Rose, 1969:6). Seen in this way, a person can be violated in many ways; physical force is only one of them. As the readings in Rose (1969) show, a person can be violated by a system that denies him a decent job, or consigns him to a slum, or causes him brain damage by near-starvation during childhood, or manipulates him through the mass media, and so on endlessly.

Moreover, we must see that *covert institutional violence* is much more destructive than overt individual violence. We must recognize that people's lives are violated by the very normal and everyday workings of institutions. We do not see such events and situations as violent because they are not dramatic and predatory; they do not make for fascinating reading on the lives of preverts; but they kill, maim, and destroy many more lives than do violent individuals.

Here are some examples. Carmichael and Hamilton (1967:4), in distinguishing between *individual* and *institutional* racism, offer examples of each:

> When white terrorists bomb a black church and kill five black children, that is an act of individual racism, widely deplored by most segments of the society. But when in that same city—Birmingham, Alabama—five hundred black babies die each year because of lack of proper food, shelter, and medical facilities, and thousands more are destroyed and maimed physically, emotionally and intellectually because of conditions of poverty and discrimination in the black community, that is a function of institutional racism.

Surely this is violence; it is caused by the normal, quiet workings of institutions run by respectable members of the community. Many whites also suffer from the institutional workings of a profit-oriented society and economy; poor health, dead-end jobs, slum housing, hunger in rural areas, and so on, are daily realities in their lives. This is surely much worse violence than any committed by the Hell's Angels or street gangs. Only these groups get stigmatized and analyzed by sociologists of deviance, however, while those good people who live in luxurious homes (fixing tax laws for their benefit) off profits derived from an exploitative economic system—they are the pillars of their community.

Violence is committed daily by the government, very often by lack of action. The same system that enriches businessmen farmers with billions of dollars through farm subsidies cannot be bothered to appropriate a few millions to deal with lead poisoning in the slums. Young children

> ...get it by eating the sweet-tasting chips of peeling tenement walls, painted a generation ago with leaded paint.
>
> According to the Department of Health, Education and Welfare, 400,000 children are poisoned each year, about 30,000 in New York City alone. About 3,200 suffer permanent brain damage, 800 go blind or become so mentally retarded that they require hospitalization for the rest of their lives, and approximately 200 die.
>
> The tragedy is that lead poisoning is totally man-made and totally preventable. It is caused by slum housing. And there are now blood tests that can detect the disease, and medicines to cure it. Only a lack of purpose sentences 200 black children to die each year (Newfield, 1971).[5]

Newfield goes on to report that on May 20, 1971, a Senate-House conference eliminated $5 million from an appropriations budget. In fact, 200 children had been sentenced to death and thousands more to maiming and suffering.

Similar actions of violence are committed daily by the government and corporations; but in these days of misplaced emphasis, ignorance, and manipulation we do not see the destruction inherent in these actions. Instead, we get fascinated, angry, and misled by the violence of the poor and the powerless. We see the violence committed during political rebellions in the ghettoes (called "riots" in order to dismiss them), but all along we ignored the daily violence committed against the ghetto residents by the institutions of the society: schools, hospitals, corporations, the government. Check any of these books on deviance, and see how much of this type of violence is even mentioned, much less explored and described.

It may be argued that some of this violence is (implicitly) recognized in discussions of "white-collar" crime. This is not the case, however. Of the 16 books under consideration, only three pay some attention to white-collar crime (Cohen, 1966; Clinard, 1968; Dinitz, *et al.*, 1969); and of these, only the last covers the issue at some length. Even in these few discussions, however, the focus remains on the *individuals* who commit the actions (on their greediness, lack of morality, etc.), not on the economic and political institutions within which they operate. The selection in Dinitz, *et al.* (1969:99–109), from the President's Commission on Law Enforcement and the Administration of Justice, at least three times (pp. 101, 103, 108) argues that white-collar crime is "pervasive," causes "financial burdens" ("probably far greater than those produced by traditional common law theft offenses"), and is generally harmful. At least in these pages, however, there is no investigation of the social, political, and economic conditions which make the pervasiveness, and lenient treatment, of white-collar crime possible.

The bias against examining the structural conditions behind white-collar crime is further revealed in Clinard's suggestions on how to deal with it (in his chapter on "The Prevention of Deviant Behavior"). The only recommendation in three pages of discussion (704–7) is to teach everyone more "respect" for the law. This is a purely moralistic device; it pays no attention to the structural aspects of the problem, to the fact that even deeper than white-collar crime is ingrained a whole network of laws, especially tax laws, administrative policies, and institutions which systematically favor a small minority. More generally, discussions on the prevention of "deviance" and crime do not deal with institutional violence, and what we need to do to stop it.[6]

But there is an obvious explanation for this oversight. The people committing serious white-collar crimes and executing the policies of violent institutions are respectable and responsible individuals, not "deviants"; this is the view of the President's Commission on Law Enforcement and the Administration of Justice.

> Significantly, the Antitrust Division does not feel that lengthy prison sentences are ordinarily called for [for white-collar crimes]. It "rarely recommends jail sentences greater than 6 months—recommendations of 30-day imprisonment are most frequent." (Dinitz, *et al.*, 1969:105.)

> Persons who have standing and roots in a community, and are prepared for and engaged in legitimate occupations, can be expected to be particularly susceptible to the threat of criminal prosecution. Criminal proceedings and the imposition of sanctions have a much sharper impact upon those who have not been hardened by previous contact with the criminal justice system (in Dinitz, *et al.*, 1969:104).

At the same time, we are told elsewhere by the Commission that white-collar crime is pervasive and widespread; "criminal proceedings and the imposition of sanctions" do not appear to deter it much.

The executives convicted in the Electrical Equipment case were respectable citizens. "Several were deacons or vestrymen of their churches." The rest also held prestigious positions: president of the Chamber of Commerce, bank director, little-league organizer, and so on (Dinitz, *et al.*, 1969:107). Moreover, "generally...in cases of white-collar crime, neither the corporations as entities nor their responsible officers are invested with deviant characters..." (Cohen, 1966:30). Once more, there is quiet acquiescence to this state of affairs. There is no attempt to find out why those who steal millions and whose actions violate lives are not "invested with deviant characters." There is no consideration given to the possibility that, as responsible intellectuals, it is our duty to explore and expose the structural causes for corporate and other serious crimes, which make for much more suffering than does armed robbery. We seem satisfied merely to observe what is, and leave the causes unexamined.

In conclusion, let us look at another form of institutional "deviance." The partial publication of the Pentagon papers (June 1971) made public the conscious lying and manipulation by the government to quiet opposition to the Vietnam war. But lying pervades both government and economy. Deceptions and outright lies abound in advertising (see Henry, 1963). During the 1968 campaign, Presidential candidate Nixon blessed us with an ingenious form of deception. McGinniss (1969:149–50) is recording a discussion that took place before Nixon was to appear on live TV (to show spontaneity) the day before the election and answer, unrehearsed, questions phoned in by the viewing audience:

> "I understand Paul Keyes has been sitting up for two days writing questions," Roger Ailes said.
> "Well, not quite," Jack Rourke said. He seemed a little embarrassed.
> "What is going to happen?"
> "Oh..."
> "It's sort of semiforgery, isn't it?" Ailes said. "Keyes has a bunch of questions Nixon wants to answer. He's written them in advance to make sure they're properly worded. When someone calls in with something similar, they'll use Keyes' question and attribute it to the person who called. Isn't that it?"
> "More or less," Jack Rourke said.

In short, despite the supposedly central position of *social structure* in the sociological enterprise, there is general neglect of it in the field of "deviance." Larger questions, especially if they deal with political and economic issues, are either passed over briefly or overlooked completely. The focus on the actions of "nuts, sluts, and preverts" and the related slight of the criminal and destructive actions of the power-ful are instances of this avoidance.

III.

Most of the authors under discussion mention the importance of *power* in labelling people "deviant." They state that those who label (the victimizers) are more powerful than those they label (the victims). Writers of the labelling school make this point explicitly. According to Becker (1963:17), "who can...force others to accept their rules and what are the causes of their success? This is, of course, a question of political and economic power." Simmons (1969:131) comments that historically, "those in power have used their positions largely to per-petuate and enhance their own advantages through coercing and ma-nipulating the rest of the populace." And Lofland (1969:19) makes the same observation in his opening pages:

> It is in the situation of a very powerful party opposing a very weak one that the powerful party sponsors the *idea* that the weak party is breaking the rules of society. The very concepts of "society" and its "rules" are appropriated by powerful parties and made synonymous with their interests (and, of course, believed in by the naive, e.g., the undergraduate penchant for the phrases "society says...," "society expects...," "society does...").

But this insight is not developed. In none of the 16 books is there an extensive discussion of how power operates in the designation of de-viance. Instead of a study of power, of its concrete uses in modern, corporate America, we are offered rather fascinating explorations into the identities and subcultures of "deviants," and misplaced emphasis on the middle-level agents of social control. Only Szasz (1961, 1963, and notably 1970) has shown consistently the role of power in one area of "deviance," "mental illness." Through historical and contem-porary studies, he has shown that those labelled "mentally ill" (crazy, insane, mad, lunatic) and institutionalized have always been the pow-erless: women, the poor, peasants, the aged, and others. Moreover, he has exposed repeatedly the means used by powerful individuals and institutions in employing the "mental illness" label to discredit, perse-cute, and eliminate opponents. In short, he has shown the political el-ement in the "mental illness" game.

In addition, except for Szasz, none of the authors seems to realize that the stigma of prostitution, abortion, and other "deviant" acts unique to women comes about in large part from the powerlessness of women and their status in society. Moreover, to my knowledge, no one has bothered to ask why there have always been women prosti-tutes for men to satisfy their sexual desires, but very few men prostitutes for women to patronize. The very word *prostitute* we associate with women only, not men. Both men and women have been involved in this "immoral" act, but the stigma has been carried by the women alone.

All 16 books, some more extensively than others, discuss the ideology, modes of operation, and views of *agents of social control*, the people who designate what is to be "deviant" and those who handle the people so designated. As Gouldner (1968) has shown, however, these are the lower and middle level officials, not those who make basic policy and decisions. This bias becomes obvious when we look at the specific agents discussed.

For example, Simmons (1969:18) tells us that some of "those in charge at every level" are the following: "university administrators, patrolmen, schoolmasters, and similar public employees...." Do university administrators and teachers run the schools alone? Are they teaching and enforcing their own unique values? Do teachers alone create the horrible schools in the slums? Are the uniformity, punctuality, and conformity teachers inculcate their own psychological hang-ups, or do they represent the interests of an industrial-technological-corporate order? In another sphere, do the police enforce their own laws?

Becker (1963:14) has shown consistent interest in agents of social control. However, a close examination reveals limitations. He discusses "moral crusaders" like those who passed the laws against marijuana. The moral crusader, "the prototype of the rule creator," finds that "the existing rules do not satisfy him because there is some evil which profoundly disturbs him." But the only type of rule creator Becker discusses is the moral crusader, no other. The political manipulators who pass laws to defend their interests and persecute dissenters are not studied. The "unconventional sentimentality," the debunking motif Becker (1964:4–5) sees in the "new deviance," is directed toward the police, the prison officials, the mental hospital personnel, the "average" person and his prejudices. The basic social, political, and economic structure, and those commanding it who guide the labelling and persecution, are left untouched. We have become so accustomed to debunking these low-level agents that we do not even know how to begin to direct our attention to the ruling institutions and groups (for an attempt at such an analysis, see Liazos, 1970).

In a later paper, Becker (1967) poses an apparently insoluble dilemma. He argues that, in studying agents of social control, we are always forced to study subordinates. We can never really get to the top, to those who "really" run the show, for if we study X's superior Y, we find Z above him, and so on endlessly. Everyone has somebody over him, so there is no one at the top. But this is a clever point without substance. In this hierarchy some have more power than others and some are at the top; they may disclaim their position, of course, but it is our job to show otherwise. Some people in this society do have more power than others: parents over children, men over women; some have considerable power over others: top administrators of institutions, for one; and some have a great deal of power, those Domhoff (1967) and others have shown to be the ruling class. It should be our task to explore and describe this hierarchy, its bases of strength, its uses of the "deviant" label to discredit its opponents in order to silence them, and to find ways to eliminate this hierarchy.

Discussions of the police reveal the same misplaced emphasis on lower and middle level agents of social control. In three of the books (Matza, 1969:182–95; Rubington and Weinberg, 1968:ch. 7; Dinitz, *et al.*, 1969:40–47), we are presented with the biases and prejudices of policemen; their modes of operation in confronting delinquents and others; the pressures on them from various quarters; etc. In short, the focus is on the role and psychology of the policeman.

All these issues about the policeman's situation need to be discussed, of course; but there is an even more important issue which these authors avoid. We must ask, who passes the laws the police enforce? Whose agents are they? Why do the police exist? Three excellent papers (Cook, 1968; A. Silver, in Bordua, 1967; T. Hayden, in Rose, 1969) offer some answers to these questions. They show, through a historical description of the origins of police forces, that they have always been used to defend the status quo, the interests of the ruling powers. When the police force was created in England in the early 1800's, it was meant to defend the propertied classes from the "dangerous classes" and the "mob."[7] With the rise of capitalism and industrialism, there was much unrest from the suffering underclass; the professional police were meant to act as a buffer zone for the capitalist elite. Similarly, in America during the early part of this century, especially in the 1930's, police were used repeatedly to attack striking workers and break their strikes. During the Chicago "police riot" of 1968, the police were not merely acting out their aggressions and frustrations; as Hayden shows, they acted with the consent, direction, and blessing of Mayor Daley and the Democratic party (which party represents the "liberal" wing of the American upper class).

It must be stressed that the police, like all agents of social control, are doing someone else's work. Sometimes they enforce laws and prejudices of "society," the much maligned middle class (on sex, marijuana, etc.); but at other times it is not "society" which gives them their directives, but specific interested groups, even though, often, "society" is manipulated to express its approval of such actions. Above all, we must remember that *"in a fundamentally unjust society, even the most impartial, professional, efficient enforcement of the laws by the police cannot result in justice"* (Cook, 1968:2). More generally, in an unjust and exploitative society, no matter how "humane" agents of social control are, their actions necessarily result in repression.

Broad generalization is another device used by some of these authors to avoid concrete examination of the uses of power in the creation and labelling of "deviance." Clairborne (1971) has called such generalization *"schlock."* The following are some of the tactics he thinks are commonly used in writing popular *schlock* sociology (some sociologists of deviance use similar tactics, as we shall see).

> The Plausible Passive:
> "New scientific discoveries are being made every day. . . . These new ideas are being put to work more quickly. . ." [Toffler, in *Future Shock*, is] thereby rather neatly obscuring the fact that scientists and engineers (mostly paid by industry) are making the discoveries and industrialists (often with the aid of public funds) are putting them to work. An alternative to the Plausible Passive is the Elusive Impersonal: 'Buildings in New York literally disappear overnight.' What Toffler is trying to avoid saying is that contractors and real estate speculators *destroy* buildings overnight (Clairborne, 1971:118).

Rampant Reification, by which "conceptual abstractions are transformed into causal realities," also abounds. Toffler

> speaks of the "roaring current of change" as "an elemental force" and of "that great, growling engine of change—technology." Which of course completely begs the question of what fuels the engine and whose hand is on the throttle. One does not cross-examine an elemental force, let alone suggest that it may have been engendered by monopoly profits (especially in defense and aerospace) or accelerated by government incentives (e.g., open or concealed subsidies, low capital gains tax, accelerated depreciation—which Nixon is now seeking to reinstitute) (Clairborne, 1971:118).

There are parallels in the sociology of deviance. Clinard (1968:ch. 4) argues that urbanization and the slum are breeding grounds for "deviant behavior." But these conditions are reified, not examined concretely. He says about urbanization and social change:

> Rapid social and cultural change, disregard for the importance of stability of generations, and untempered loyalties also generally characterize urban life. New ideas are generally welcome, inventions and mechanical gadgets are encouraged, and new styles in such arts as painting, literature, and music are often approved (1968:90).

But the slum, urbanization, and change are not reified entities working out their independent wills. For example, competition, capitalism, and the profit motive—all encouraged by a government controlled by the upper classes—have had something to do with the rise of slums. There is a general process of urbanization, but at given points in history it is fed by, and gives profits to, specific groups. The following are a few historical examples: the land enclosure policies and practices of the English ruling classes in the 17th and 18th centuries; the building of cheap housing in the 19th century by the owners of factory towns; and the profits derived from "urban renewal" (which has destroyed neighborhoods, created even more crowded slums, etc.) by the building of highways, luxury apartments, and stores.

Another favorite theme of *schlock* sociology is that "All Men Are Guilty." That means nothing can be done to change things. There is a variation of this theme in the sociology of deviance when we are told that *(a)* all of us are deviant in some way, *(b)* all of us label some others deviant, and *(c)* "society" labels. Such statements preclude asking concrete questions: does the "deviance" of each of us have equal consequences for others? Does the labelling of each of us stick, and with what results?

For example, Simmons (1969:124) says:

> . . . I strongly suspect that officials now further alienate more culprits than they recruit back into conventional society, and I think they imprison at least as many people in deviance as they rehabilitate. We must remember that, with a sprinkling of exceptions, officials come from, are hired by, and belong to the dominant majority.

Who is that dominant majority? Are they always the numerical majority? Do they control the labelling and correctional process all by themselves? These questions are not raised.

Another case of *schlock* is found in Matza's discussion (lack of it, really) of "Leviathan" (1969, especially ch. 7). It is mentioned as a potent force in the labelling and handling of "deviance." But, vainly, one keeps looking for some exploration into the workings of "Leviathan." It remains a reified, aloof creature. What is it? Who controls it? How does it label? Why? Matza seems content to try to mesmerize us by mentioning it constantly (Leviathan is capitalized throughout); but we are never shown how it operates. It hovers in the background, it punishes, and its presence somehow cowers us into submission. But it remains a reified force whose presence is accepted without close examination.

The preceding examples typify much of what is wrong with the sociology of deviance: the lack of specific analysis of the role of power in the labelling process; the generalizations which, even when true, explain little; the fascination with "deviants"; the reluctance to study the "deviance" of the powerful.

IV.

I want to start my concluding comments with two disclaimers.

(a) I have tried to provide some balance and perspective in the field of "deviance," and in doing so I have argued against the exclusive emphasis on *nuts, sluts,* and *preverts* and their identities and subcultures. I do not mean, however, that the usually considered forms of "deviance" are unworthy of our attention. Suicide, prostitution, madness, juvenile delinquency, and others *are* with us; we cannot ignore them. People do suffer when labelled and treated as "deviant" (in *this* sense, "deviants" *are* different from conformists). Rather, I want to draw attention to phenomena which also belong to the field of "deviance."[8]

(b) It is because the sociology of deviance, especially the labelling approach, contains important, exciting, and revealing insights, because it tries to humanize the "deviant," and because it is popular, that it is easy to overlook some of the basic ideological biases still pervading the field. For this season, I have tried to explore and detail some of these biases. At the same time, however, I do not mean to dismiss the contributions of the field as totally negative and useless. In fact, in my teaching I have been using two of the books discussed here, Simmons (1969) and Rubington and Weinberg (1968).

The argument can be summarized briefly. (1) We should not study only, or predominantly, the popular and dramatic forms of "deviance." Indeed, we should banish the concept of "deviance" and speak of oppression, conflict, persecution, and suffering. By focusing on the dramatic forms, as we do now, we perpetuate most people's beliefs and impressions that such "deviance" is the basic cause of many of our troubles, that these people (criminals, drug addicts, political dissenters, and others) are the real "troublemakers"; and, necessarily, we neglect conditions of inequality, powerlessness, institutional violence, and so on, which lie at the bases of our tortured society. (2) Even when we do study the popular forms of "deviance," we do not avoid blaming the victim for his fate; the continued use of the term "deviant" is one clue to this blame. Nor have we succeeded in normalizing him, the focus on the "deviant" himself, on his identity and subculture, has tended to confirm the popular prejudice that he is different.

NOTES

1. Bend and Vogenfanger (1964) examined social problems textbooks of the early 1960's; they found there was little theory or emphasis on social structure in them.

2. What I say below applies to the "labelling-interactionist" school of deviance of Becker, Lemert, Erikson, Matza, and others: to a large degree, however, most of my comments also apply to the other schools.

3. The first draft of this paper was completed in July, 1971. The killing of George Jackson at San Quentin on August 21, 1971, which many people see as a political murder, and the Attica prisoner rebellion of early September, 1971, only strengthen the argument about political prisoners. Two things became clear: a) Not only a few "radicals," but many prisoners (if not a majority) see their fate as the outcome of political forces and decisions, and themselves as political prisoners (see Fraser, 1971). Robert Chrisman's argument (in Fraser, 1971) points to such a conclusion clearly: "To maintain that all black offenders are, by their actions, politically correct, is dangerous romanticism. Black antisocial behavior must be seen in and of its own terms and corrected for enhancement of the black community." But there is a political aspect, for black prisoners' condition "derives from the political inequity of black people in America. A black prisoner's crime may or may not have been a political action against the state, but the state's action against him is always political." I would stress that the same is true of most white prisoners, for they come mostly from the exploited poorer classes and groups. b) The state authorities, the political rulers, by their deeds if not their words, see such prisoners as political men and threats. The death of George Jackson, and the brutal crushing of the Attica rebellion, attest to the authorities' realization, and fear, that here were no mere riots with prisoners letting off steam, but authentic political actions, involving groups and individuals conscious of their social position and exploitation.

4. With the exception of E. C. Hughes, in Becker (1964).

5. As Gittlin and Hollander (1970) show, the children of poor whites also suffer from lead poisoning.

6. Investigation of the causes and prevention of institutional violence would probably be biting the hand that feeds the sociologist, for we read that the government and foundations (whose money comes from corporate profits) have supported research on "deviant behavior," especially its prevention. "This has meant particularly that the application of sociological theory to research has increased markedly in such areas as delinquency, crime, mental disorder, alcoholism, drug addiction, and discrimination" (Clinard, 1968:742). That's where the action is, not on white-collar crime, nor on the covert institutional violence of the government and economy.

7. See Rude (1966) on the role of mobs of poor workers and peasants in 18th and 19th century England and France.

8. The question of "what deviance is to the deviant" (Gordon Fellman, private communication), not what the labelling, anomie, and other schools, or the present radical viewpoint say *about* such a person, is not

dealt with here. I avoid this issue not because I think it unimportant, rather because I want to concentrate on the political, moral, and social issues raised by the biases of those presently writing about the "deviant."

REFERENCES

Becker, Howard S.
*1963   Outsiders. New York: Free Press.
*1964   (ed.) The Other Side. New York: Free Press.
1967   "Whose side are we on?" Social Problems 14:239–247 (reprinted in Douglas, 1970a, 99–111; references to this reprint).

Bell, Robert R.
*1971   Social Deviance: A Substantive Analysis. Homewood, Illinois: Dorsey.

Bend, Emil and Martin Vogenfanger
1964   "A new look at Mills' critique," in Mass Society in Crisis. Bernard Rosenberg, Israel Gerver, F. William Howton (eds.). New York: Macmillan, 1964, 111–122.

Bordua, David (ed.)
1967   The Police. New York: Wiley.

Carmichael, Stokeley and Charles V. Hamilton
1967   Black Power. New York: Random House.

Clairborne, Robert
1971   "Future schlock." The Nation, Jan. 25, 117–120.

Cleaver, Eldridge
1968   Soul on Ice. New York: McGraw-Hill.

Clinard, Marshall B.
*1968   Sociology of Deviant Behavior. (3rd ed.) New York: Holt, Rinehart, and Winston.

Cohen, Albert K.
*1966   Deviance and Control. Englewood Cliffs, N.J.: Prentice-Hall.

Cook, Robert M.
1968   "The police." The Bulletin of the American Independent Movement (New Haven, Conn.), 3:6, 1–6.

Dinitz, Simon, Russell R. Dynes, and Alfred C. Clarke (eds.)
*1969   Deviance. New York: Oxford University Press.

Domhoff, William G.
1967   Who Rules America? Englewood Cliffs, N.J.: Prentice-Hall.

*Textbooks in the field of deviance (Ed.'s note).

Douglas, Jack D.
*1970a   (ed.) Observations of Deviance. New York: Random House.
*1970b   (ed.) Deviance and Respectability: The Social Construction of Moral Meanings. New York: Basic Books.

Fraser, C. Gerald
1971   "Black prisoners finding new view of themselves as political prisoners." New York Times, Sept. 16.

Gittlin, Todd and Nanci Hollander
1970   Uptown: Poor Whites in Chicago. New York: Harper and Row.

Gouldner, Alvin W.
1968   "The sociologist as partisan: Sociology and the welfare state." American Sociologist 3:2, 103–116.

Henry, Jules
1963   Culture Against Man. New York: Random House.

Jackson, George
1970   Soledad Brother. New York: Bantam Books.

Lefton, Mark, J. K. Skipper, and C. H. McCaghy (eds.)
*1968   Approaches to Deviance. New York: Appleton-Century-Crofts.

Lemert, Edwin M.
*1967   Human Deviance, Social Problems, and Social Control. Englewood Cliffs, N.J.: Prentice-Hall.

Liazos, Alexander
1970   Processing for Unfitness: socialization of "emotionally disturbed" lower-class boys into the mass society. Ph.D. Dissertation, Brandeis University.

Lofland, John
*1969   Deviance and Identity. Englewood Cliffs, N.J.: Prentice-Hall.

McCaghy, Charles H., J. K. Skipper, and M. Lefton (eds.)
*1968   In Their Own Behalf: Voices from the Margin. New York: Appleton-Century-Crofts.

McGinniss, Joe
1969   The Selling of the President, 1968. New York: Trident.

Malcolm X
1965   The Autobiography of Malcolm X. New York: Grove.

Matza, David
*1969   Becoming Deviant. Englewood Cliffs, N.J.: Prentice-Hall.

Mills, C. Wright
1943   "The professional ideology of social pathologists." American Journal of Sociology 49:165–180.

Newfield, Jack
1971   "Let them eat lead." New York Times, June 16, p. 45.

Quinn, Olive W.
   1954   "The transmission of racial attitudes among white southerners."
           Social Forces 33:1, 41–47 (reprinted in E. Schuler, *et al.*, eds., Read-
           ings in Sociology, 2nd ed., New York: Crowell, 1960, 140–150).

Rose, Thomas (ed.)
   1969   Violence in America. New York: Random House.

Rubington, Earl and M. S. Weinberg (eds.)
  *1968   Deviance: The Interactionist Perspective. New York: Macmillan.

Rude, George
   1966   The Crowd in History. New York: Wiley.

Rushing, William A. (ed.)
  *1969   Deviant Behavior and Social Processes. Chicago: Rand McNally.

Simmons, J. L.
  *1969   Deviants. Berkeley, Cal.: Glendessary.

Szasz, Thomas S.
   1961   The Myth of Mental Illiness. New York: Harper and Row.
   1963   Law, Liberty, and Psychiatry. New York: Macmillan.
   1970   The Manufacture of Madness. New York: Harper and Row.

Thompson, Hunter S.
   1966   Hell's Angels. New York: Ballantine.

29 *Toward a Marxian Theory of Deviance*
STEVEN SPITZER

Within the last decade American sociologists have become increasingly reflective in their approach to deviance and social problems.
They have come to recognize that interpretations of deviance are often
ideological in their assumptions and implications, and that sociologists are frequently guilty of "providing the facts which make oppression more efficient and the theory which makes it legitimate to a larger
constituency" (Becker and Horowitz, 1972: 48). To combat this tendency students of deviance have invested more and more energy in
the search for a critical theory. This search has focused on three major
problems: (1) the definition of deviance, (2) the etiology of deviance,
and (3) the etiology of control.

Reprinted from Steven Spitzer, "Toward a Marxian Theory of Deviance." *Social
Problems*, vol. 22, no. 5 (June 1975), pp. 638–651. Copyright © 1975 by the Society for
the Study of Social Problems. By permission of the publisher.

    Revised version of a paper presented at the American Sociological Association
meetings, August, 1975. I would like to thank Cecile Sue Coren and Andrew T. Scull
for their criticisms and suggestions.

TRADITIONAL THEORIES AND THEIR PROBLEMS

Traditional theories approached the explanation of deviance with little equivocation about the phenomenon to be explained. Prior to the 1960s the subject matter of deviance theory was taken for granted and few were disturbed by its preoccupation with "dramatic and predatory" forms of social behavior (Liazos, 1972). Only in recent years have sociologists started to question the consequences of singling out "nuts," "sluts," "perverts," "lames," "crooks," "junkies," and "juicers" for special attention. Instead of adopting conventional wisdom about *who* and *what* is deviant, investigators have gradually made the definitional problem central to the sociological enterprise. They have begun to appreciate the consequences of studying the powerless (rather than the powerful)—both in terms of the relationship between *knowledge of* and *control over* a group, and the support for the "hierarchy of credibility" (Becker, 1967) that such a focus provides. Sociologists have discovered the significance of the definitional process in their own, as well as society's response to deviance, and this discovery has raised doubts about the direction and purpose of the field.

Even when the definitional issue can be resolved critics are faced with a second and equally troublesome problem. Traditional theories of deviance are essentially *non-structural* and *ahistorical* in their mode of analysis. By restricting investigation to factors which are manipulable within existing structural arrangements these theories embrace a "correctional perspective" (Matza, 1969) and divert attention from the impact of the political economy as a whole. From this point of view deviance is *in* but not *of* our contemporary social order. Theories that locate the source of deviance in factors as diverse as personality structure, family systems, cultural transmission, social disorganization and differential opportunity share a common flaw—they attempt to understand deviance apart from historically specific forms of political and economic organization. Because traditional theories proceed without any sense of historical development, deviance is normally viewed as an episodic and transitory phenomenon rather than an outgrowth of long-term structural change. Sensitive sociologists have come to realize that critical theory must establish, rather than obscure, the relationship between deviance, social structure and social change.

A final problem in the search for a critical theory of deviance is the absence of a coherent theory of control. More than ever before critics have come to argue that deviance cannot be understood apart from the dynamics of control. Earlier theories devoted scant attention to the control process precisely because control was interpreted as a natural response to behavior generally assumed to be problematic. Since theories of deviance viewed control as a desideratum, no theory of control was required. But as sociologists began to question conventional images of deviance they revised their impressions of social control. Rather than assuming that societal reaction was necessarily defensive and benign, skeptics announced that controls could actually cause deviance. The problem was no longer simply to explain the independent sources of deviance and control, but to understand the reciprocal relationship between the two.

In elevating control to the position of an independent variable a more critical orientation has evolved. Yet this orientation has created a number of problems of its own. If deviance is simply a *status*, representing the outcome of a series of control procedures, should our theory of deviance be reduced to a theory of control? In what sense, if any, is deviance an achieved rather than an ascribed status? How do we account for the historical and structural sources of deviance apart from those shaping the development of formal controls?

TOWARD A THEORY OF DEVIANCE PRODUCTION

A critical theory must be able to account for both *deviance* and *deviants*. It must be sensitive to the process through which deviance is subjectively constructed and deviants are objectively handled, as well as the structural bases of the behavior and characteristics which come to official attention. It should neither beg the explanation of deviant behavior and characteristics by depicting the deviant as a helpless victim of oppression, nor fail to realize that his identification as deviant, the dimensions of his threat, and the priorities of the control system are part of a broader social conflict. While acknowledging the fact that deviance is a *status* imputed to groups who share certain structural characteristics (e.g., powerlessness) we must not forget that these groups are defined by more than these characteristics alone.[1] We must not only ask why specific members of the underclass are selected for official processing, but also why they behave as they do. Deviant statuses, no matter how coercively applied, are in some sense achieved and we must understand this achievement in the context of political-economic conflict. We need to understand why capitalism produces both patterns of activity and types of people that are defined and managed as deviant.

In order to construct a general theory of deviance and control it is useful to conceive of a process of deviance production which can be understood in relationship to the development of class society. *Deviance production involves all aspects of the process through which populations are structurally generated, as well as shaped, channeled into, and manipulated within social categories defined as deviant.* This process includes the development of and changes in: (1) deviant definitions, (2) problem populations, and (3) control systems.

Most fundamentally, deviance production involves the development of and changes in deviant categories and images. A critical theory must examine where these images and definitions come from, what they reflect about the structure of and priorities in specific class societies, and how they are related to class conflict. If we are to explain, for example, how mental retardation becomes deviance and the feeble-minded deviant we need to examine the structural characteristics, economic and political dimensions of the society in which these definitions and images emerged. In the case of American society we must understand how certain correlates of capitalist development (proletarianization and nuclearization of the family) weakened traditional methods of assimilating these groups, how others (the emergence of scientific and meritocratic ideologies) sanctioned intellectual stratification and differential handling, and how still others (the attraction of unskilled labor and population concentrations) heightened concern over the "threat" that these groups were assumed to represent. In other words, the form and content of deviance definition must be assessed in terms of its relationship to both structural and ideological change.

A second aspect of deviance production is the development of and changes in problem behaviors and problem populations. If we assume that class societies are based on fundamental conflicts between groups, and that harmony is achieved through the dominance of a specific class, it makes sense to argue that deviants are culled from groups who create specific problems for those who rule. Although these groups may victimize or burden those outside of the dominant class, their problematic quality ultimately resides in their challenge to the basis and form of class rule. Because problem populations are not always "handled," they provide candidates for, but are in no sense equivalent to, official deviants. A sophisticated critical theory must investigate where these groups come from, why their behaviors and characteristics are problematic, and how they are transformed in a developing political economy. We must consider, for instance, why Chinese laborers in 19th century California and Chicanos in the Southwest during the 1930s became the object of official concern, and why drug laws evolved to address the "problems" that these groups came to represent (Helmer and Vietorisz, 1973; Musto, 1973).

The changing character of problem populations is related to deviance production in much the same way that variations in material resources affect manufacturing. Changes in the quantity and quality of raw materials influence the scope and priorities of production, but the characteristics of the final product depend as much on the methods of production as the source material. These methods comprise the third element in deviance production—the development and operation of the control system. The theory must explain why a system of control emerges under specific conditions and account for its size, focus and working assumptions. The effectiveness of the system in confronting problem populations and its internal structure must be understood in order to interpret changes in the form and content of control. Thus, in studying the production of the "mentally ill" we must not only consider why deviance has been "therapeutized," but also how this development reflects the subtleties of class control. Under capitalism, for example, formal control of the mad and the birth of the asylum may be examined as a response to the growing demands for order, responsibility and restraint (cf. Foucault, 1965).

THE PRODUCTION OF DEVIANCE IN CAPITALIST SOCIETY

The concept of deviance production offers a starting point for the analysis of both deviance and control. But for such a construct to serve as a critical tool it must be grounded in an historical and structural investigation of society. For Marx, the crucial unit of analysis is the mode of production that dominates a given historical period. If we are to have a Marxian theory of deviance, therefore, deviance production must be understood in relationship to specific forms of socio-economic organization. In our society, productive activity is organized capitalistically and it is ultimately defined by "the process that transforms on the one hand, the social means of subsistence and of production into capital, on the other hand the immediate producers into wage labourers" (Marx, 1967: 714).

There are two features of the capitalist mode of production important for purposes of this discussion. First, as a mode of production it forms the foundation or infrastructure of our society. This means that the starting point of our analysis must be an understanding of the economic organization of capitalist societies and the impact of that organization on all aspects of social life. But the capitalist mode of production is an important starting point in another sense. It contains contradictions which reflect the internal tendencies of capitalism. These contradictions are important because they explain the changing character of the capitalist system and the nature of its impact on social, political and intellectual activity. The formulation of a Marxist perspective on deviance requires the interpretation of the process through which the contradictions of capitalism are expressed. In particular, the theory must illustrate the relationship between specific contradictions, the problems of capitalist development and the production of a deviant class.

The superstructure of society emerges from and reflects the ongoing development of economic forces (the infrastructure). In class societies this superstructure preserves the hegemony of the ruling class through a system of class controls. These controls, which are institutionalized in the family, church, private associations, media, schools and the state, provide a mechanism for coping with the contradictions and achieving the aim of capitalist development.

Among the most important functions served by the superstructure in capitalist societies is the regulation and management of problem populations. Because deviance processing is only one of the methods available for social control, these groups supply raw material for deviance production, but are by no means synonymous with deviant populations. Problem populations tend to share a number of social characteristics, but most important among these is the fact that their behavior, personal qualities and/or position threaten the *social relations of production* in capitalist societies. In other words, populations become generally eligible for management as deviant when they disturb, hinder or call into question any of the following:

1. Capitalist modes of appropriating the product of human labor (e.g. when the poor "steal" from the rich).
2. The social conditions under which capitalist production takes place (e.g. those who refuse or are unable to perform wage labor).
3. Patterns of distribution and consumption in capitalist society (e.g. those who use drugs for escape and transcendence rather than sociability and adjustment).
4. The process of socialization for productive and non-productive roles (e.g. youth who refuse to be schooled or those who deny the validity of "family life").[2]
5. The ideology which supports the functioning of capitalist society (e.g. proponents of alternative forms of social organization).

Although problem populations are defined in terms of the threat and costs that they present to the social relations of production in capitalist societies, these populations are far from isomorphic with a revolutionary class. It is certainly true that some members of the problem population, may under specific circumstances possess revolutionary potential. But this potential can only be realized if the problematic group is located in a position of functional indispensability within the capitalist system. Historically, capitalist societies have been quite successful in transforming those who are problematic and indispensable (the proto-revolutionary class) into groups who are either problematic and dispensable (candidates for deviance processing), or indispensable but not problematic (supporters of the capitalist order). On the other hand, simply because a group is manageable does not mean that it ceases to be a problem for the capitalist class. Even though dispensable problem populations cannot overturn the capitalist system, they can represent a significant impediment to its maintenance and growth. It is in this sense that they become eligible for management as deviants.

Problem populations are created in two ways—either directly through the expression of fundamental contradictions in the capitalist mode of production or indirectly through disturbances in the system of class rule. An example of the first process is found in Marx's analysis of the "relative surplus-population."

Writing on the "General Law of Capitalist Accumulation" Marx explains how increased social redundance is inherent in the development of the capitalist mode of production:

> With the extension of the scale of production, and the mass of the labourers set in motion, with the greater breadth and fullness of all sources of wealth, there is also an extension of the scale on which greater attraction of labourers by capital is accompanied by their greater repulsion...The labouring population therefore produces, along with the accumulation of capital produced by it, the means by which itself is made relatively superfluous,...and it does this to an always increasing extent (Marx, 1967: 631).

In its most limited sense the production of a relative surplus-population involves the creation of a class which is economically redundant. But insofar as the conditions of economic existence determine social existence, this process helps explain the emergence of groups who become both threatening and vulnerable at the same time. The marginal status of these populations reduces their stake in the maintenance of the system while their powerlessness and dispensability renders them increasingly susceptible to the mechanisms of official control.

The paradox surrounding the production of the relative surplus-population is that this population is both useful and menacing to the accumulation of capital. Marx describes how the relative surplus-population "forms a disposable industrial army, that belongs to capital quite as absolutely as if the latter had bred it at its own cost," and how this army, "creates, for the changing needs of the self-expansion of capital, a mass of human material always ready for exploitation" (Marx, 1967: 632).

On the other hand, it is apparent that an excessive increase in what Marx called the "lowest sediment" of the relative surplus-population, might seriously impair the growth of capital. The harmony created by a large and economically stagnant surplus-population could jeopardize the preconditions for accumulation by undermining the ideology of equality so essential to the legitimation of production relations in bourgeois democracies, diverting revenues away from capital investment toward control and support operations, and providing a basis for political organization of the dispossessed.[3] To the extent that the relative surplus-population confronts the capitalist class as a threat to the social relations of production it reflects an important contradiction in modern capitalist societies: a surplus-population is a necessary product of and condition for the accumulation of wealth on a capitalist basis, but it also creates a form of social expense which must be neutralized or controlled if production relations and conditions for increased accumulation are to remain unimpaired.

Problem populations are also generated through contradictions which develop in the system of class rule. The institutions which make up the superstructure of capitalist society originate and are maintained to guarantee the interests of the capitalist class. Yet these institutions necessarily reproduce, rather than resolve, the contradictions of the capitalist order. In a dialectical fashion, arrangements which arise in order to buttress capitalism are transformed into their opposite—structures for the cultivation of internal threats. An instructive example of this process is found in the emergence and transformation of educational institutions in the United States.

The introduction of mass education in the United States can be traced to the developing needs of corporate capitalism (cf. Karier, 1973; Cohen and Lazerson, 1972; Bowles and Gintis, 1972; Spring, 1972). Compulsory education provided a means of training, testing and sorting, and assimilating wage-laborers, as well as withholding certain populations from the labor market. The system was also intended to preserve the values of bourgeois society and operate as an "inexpensive form of police" (Spring, 1973: 31). However, as Gintis (1973) and Bowles (1973) have suggested, the internal contradictions of schooling can lead to effects opposite of those intended. For the poor, early schooling can make explicit the oppressiveness and alienating character of capitalist institutions, while higher education can instill critical abilities which lead students to "bite the hand that feeds them." In both cases educational institutions create troublesome populations (i.e. drop outs and student radicals) and contribute to the very problems they were designed to solve.

After understanding how and why specific groups become generally bothersome in capitalist society, it is necessary to investigate the conditions under which these groups are transformed into proper objects for social control. In other words, we must ask what distinguishes the generally problematic from the specifically deviant. The rate at which problem populations are converted into deviants will reflect the relationship between these populations and the control system. This rate is likely to be influenced by the:

1. *Extensiveness and Intensity of State Controls.* Deviance processing (as opposed to other control measures) is more likely to occur when problem management is monopolized by the state. As state controls are applied more generally the proportion of official deviants will increase.

2. *Size and Level of Threat Presented by the Problem Population.* The larger and more threatening the problem population, the greater the likelihood that this population will have to be controlled through deviance processing rather than other methods. As the threat created by these populations exceeds the capacities of informal restraints, their management requires a broadening of the reaction system and an increasing centralization and coordination of control activities.

3. *Level of Organization of the Problem Population.* When and if problem populations are able to organize and develop limited amounts of political power, deviance processing becomes increasingly less effective as a tool for social control. The attribution of deviant status is most likely to occur when a group is relatively impotent and atomized.

4. *Effectiveness of Control Structures Organized through Civil Society.* The greater the effectiveness of the organs of civil society (i.e. the family, church, media, schools, sports) in solving the problems of class control, the less the likelihood that deviance processing (a more explicitly political process) will be employed.

5. *Availability and Effectiveness of Alternative Types of Official Processing.* In some cases the state will be able effectively to incorporate certain segments of the problem population into specially created "prosocial" roles. In the modern era, for example, conscription and public works projects (Piven and Cloward, 1971) helped neutralize the problems posed by troublesome populations without creating new or expanding old deviant categories.

6. *Availability and Effectiveness of Parallel Control Structures.* In many instances the state can transfer its costs of deviance production by supporting or at least tolerating the activities of independent control networks which operate in its interests. For example, when the state is denied or is reluctant to assert a monopoly over the use of force it is frequently willing to encourage vigilante organizations and private police in the suppression of problem populations. Similarly, the state is often benefited by the policies and practices of organized crime, insofar as these activities help pacify, contain and enforce order among potentially disruptive groups (Schelling, 1967).

7. *Utility of Problem Populations.* While problem populations are defined in terms of their threat and costs to capitalist relations of production, they are not threatening in every respect. They can be supportive economically (as part of a surplus labor pool or dual labor market), politically (as evidence of the need for state intervention) and ideologically (as scapegoats for rising discontent). In other words, under certain conditions capitalist societies derive benefits from maintaining a number of visible and uncontrolled "troublemakers" in their midst. Such populations are distinguished by the fact that while they remain generally bothersome, the costs that they inflict are most immediately absorbed by other members of the problem population. Policies evolve, not so much to eliminate or actively suppress these groups, but to deflect their threat away from targets which are sacred to the capitalist class. Victimization is permitted and even encouraged, as long as the victims are members of an expendable class.

Two more or less discrete groupings are established through the operations of official control. These groups are a product of different operating assumptions and administrative orientations toward the deviant population. On the one hand, there is *social junk* which, from the point of view of the dominant class, is a costly yet relatively harmless burden to society. The discreditability of social junk resides in the failure, inability or refusal of this group to participate in the roles supportive of capitalist society. Social junk is most likely to come to official attention when informal resources have been exhausted or when the magnitude of the problem becomes significant enough to create a basis for "public concern." Since the threat presented by social junk is passive, growing out of its inability to compete and its withdrawal from the prevailing social order, controls are usually designed to regulate and contain rather than eliminate and suppress the problem. Clear-cut examples of social junk in modern capitalist societies might include the officially administered aged, handicapped, mentally ill and mentally retarded.

In contrast to social junk, there is a category that can be roughly described as *social dynamite*. The essential quality of deviance manged as social dynamite is its potential actively to call into question established relationships, especially relations of production and domination. Generally, therefore, social dynamite tends to be more youthful, alienated and politically volatile than social junk. The control of social dynamite is usually premised on an assumption that the problem is acute in nature, requiring a rapid and focused expenditure of control resources. This is in contrast to the handling of social junk frequently based on a belief that the problem is chronic and best controlled through broad reactive, rather than intensive and selective measures. Correspondingly, social dynamite is normally processed through the legal system with its capacity for active intervention, while social junk is frequently (but not always)[4] administered by the agencies and agents of the therapeutic and welfare state.

Many varieties of deviant populations are alternatively or simultaneously dealt with as either social junk and/or social dynamite. The welfare poor, homosexuals, alcoholics and "problem children" are among the categories reflecting the equivocal nature of the control process and its dependence on the political, economic and ideological priorities of deviance production. The changing nature of these priorities and their implications for the future may be best understood by examining some of the tendencies of modern capitalist systems.

MONOPOLY CAPITAL AND DEVIANCE PRODUCTION

Marx viewed capitalism as a system constantly transforming itself. He explained these changes in terms of certain tendencies and contradictions immanent within the capitalist mode of production. One of the most important processes identified by Marx was the tendency for the organic composition of capital to rise. Simply stated, capitalism requires increased productivity to survive, and increased productivity is only made possible by raising the ratio of machines (dead labor) to men (living labor). This tendency is self-reinforcing since, "the further machine production advances, the higher becomes the organic composition of capital needed for an entrepreneur to secure the average profit" (Mandel, 1968: 163). This phenomenon helps us explain the course of capitalist development over the last century and the rise of monopoly capital (Baran and Sweezy, 1966).

For the purposes of this analysis there are at least two important consequences of this process. First, the growth of constant capital (machines and raw material) in the production process leads to an expansion in the overall size of the relative surplus-population. The reasons for this are obvious. The increasingly technological character of production removes more and more laborers from productive activity for longer periods of time. Thus, modern capitalist societies have been required progressively to reduce the number of productive years in a worker's life, defining both young and old as economically superfluous. Especially affected are the unskilled who become more and more expendable as capital expands.

In addition to affecting the general size of the relative surplus-population, the rise of the organic composition of capital leads to an increase in the relative stagnancy of that population. In Marx's original analysis he distinguished between forms of superfluous population that were floating and stagnant. The floating population consists of workers who are "sometimes repelled, sometimes attracted again in greater masses, the number of those employed increasing on the whole, although in a constantly decreasing proportion to the scale of production" (1967: 641). From the point of view of capitalist accumulation the floating population offers the greatest economic flexibility and the fewest problems of social control because they are most effectively tied to capital by the "natural laws of production." Unfortunately (for the capitalists at least), these groups come to comprise a smaller and smaller proportion of the relative surplus-population. The increasing specialization of productive activity raises the cost of reproducing labor and heightens the demand for highly skilled and "internally controlled" forms of wage labor (Gorz, 1970). The process through which unskilled workers are alternatively absorbed and expelled from the labor force is thereby impaired, and the relative surplus-population comes to be made up of increasing numbers of persons who are more or less permanently redundant. The boundaries between the "useful" and the "useless" are more clearly delineated, while standards for social disqualification are more liberally defined.

With the growth of monopoly capital, therefore, the relative surplus-population begins to take on the character of a population which is more and more absolute. At the same time, the market becomes a less reliable means of disciplining these populations and the "invisible hand" is more frequently replaced by the "visible fist." The implications for deviance production are twofold: (1) problem populations become gradually more problematic—both in terms of their size and their insensitivity to economic controls, and (2) the resources of the state need to be applied in greater proportion to protect capitalist relations of production and insure the accumulation of capital.

STATE CAPITALISM AND NEW FORMS OF CONTROL

The major problems faced by monopoly capitalism are surplus population and surplus production. Attempts to solve these problems have led to the creation of the welfare/warfare state (Baran and Sweezy, 1966; Marcuse, 1964; O'Connor, 1973; Gross, 1970). The warfare state attacks the problem of overconsumption by providing "wasteful" consumption and protection for the expansion of foreign markets. The welfare state helps absorb and deflect social expenses engendered by a redundant domestic population. Accordingly, the economic development of capitalist societies has come to depend increasingly on the support of the state.

The emergence of state capitalism and the growing interpenetration of the political and economic spheres have had a number of implications for the organization and administration of class rule. The most important effect of these trends is that control functions are increasingly transferred from the organs of civil society to the organs of political society (the state). As the maintenance of social harmony becomes more difficult and the contradictions of civil society intensify, the state is forced to take a more direct and extensive role in the management of problem populations. This is especially true to the extent that the primary socializing institutions in capitalist societies (e.g. the family and the church) can no longer be counted on to produce obedient and "productive" citizens.

Growing state intervention, especially intervention in the process of socialization, is likely to produce an emphasis on general-preventive (integrative), rather than selective-reactive (segregative) controls. Instead of waiting for troublemakers to surface and managing them through segregative techniques, the state is likely to focus more and more on generally applied incentives and assimilative controls. This shift is consistent with the growth of state capitalism because, on the one hand, it provides mechanisms and policies to nip disruptive influences "in the bud," and, on the other, it paves the way toward a more rational exploitation of human capital. Regarding the latter point, it is clear that effective social engineering depends more on social investment and anticipatory planning than coercive control, and societies may more profitably manage populations by viewing them as human capital, than as human waste. An investment orientation has long been popular in state socialist societies (Rimlinger, 1961, 1966), and its value, not surprisingly, has been increasingly acknowledged by many capitalist states.[5]

In addition to the advantages of integrative controls, segregative measures are likely to fall into disfavor for a more immediate reason— they are relatively costly to formulate and apply. Because of its fiscal problems the state must search for means of economizing control operations without jeopardizing capitalist expansion. Segregative handling, especially institutionalization, has been useful in manipulating and providing a receptacle for social junk and social dynamite. Nonetheless, the per capita cost of this type of management is typically quite high. Because of its continuing reliance on segregative controls the state is faced with a growing crisis—the overproduction of deviance. The magnitude of the problem and the inherent weaknesses of available approaches tend to limit the alternatives, but among those which are likely to be favored in the future are:

1. *Normalization.* Perhaps the most expedient response to the overproduction of deviance is the normalization of populations traditionally managed as deviant. Normalization occurs when deviance processing is reduced in scope without supplying specific alternatives, and certain segments of the problem population are "swept under the rug." To be successful this strategy requires the creation of invisible deviants who can be easily absorbed into society and disappear from view.

A current example of this approach is found in the decarceration movement which has reduced the number of inmates in prisons (BOP, 1972) and mental hospitals (NIMH, 1970) over the last fifteen years. By curtailing commitments and increasing turn-over rates the state is able to limit the scale and increase the efficiency of institutionalization. If, however, direct release is likely to focus too much attention on the shortcomings of the state a number of intermediate solutions can be adopted. These include subsidies for private control arrangements (e.g. foster homes, old age homes) and decentralized control facilities (e.g. community treatment centers, halfway houses). In both cases, the fiscal burden of the state is reduced while the dangers of complete normalization are avoided.

2. *Conversion.* To a certain extent the expenses generated by problem and deviant populations can be offset by encouraging their direct participation in the process of control. Potential troublemakers can be recruited as policemen, social workers and attendants, while confirmed deviants can be "rehabilitated" by becoming counselors, psychiatric aides and parole officers. In other words, if a large number of the controlled can be converted into a first line of defense, threats to the system of class rule can be transformed into resources for its support.[6]

3. *Containment.* One means of responding to threatening populations without individualized manipulation is through a policy of containment or compartmentalization. This policy involves the geographic segregation of large populations and the use of formal and informal sanctions to circumscribe the challenges that they present. Instead of classifying and handling problem populations in terms of the specific expenses that they create, these groups are loosely admin-

istered as a homogeneous class who can be ignored or managed passively as long as they remain in their place.

Strategies of containment have always flourished where social segregation exists, but they have become especially favored in modern capitalist societies. One reason for this is their compatibility with patterns of residential segregation, ghettoization, and internal colonialism (Blauner, 1969).

4. *Support of Criminal Enterprise.* Another way the overproduction of deviance may be eased is by granting greater power and influence to organized crime. Although predatory criminal enterprise is assumed to stand in opposition to the goals of the state and the capitalist class, it performs valuable and unique functions in the service of class rule (McIntosh, 1973). By creating a parallel opportunity structure, organized crime provides a means of support for groups who might otherwise become a burden on the state. The activities of organized crime are also important in the pacification of problem populations. Organized crime provides goods and services which ease the hardships and deflect the energies of the underclass. In this role the "crime industry" performs a cooling-out function and offers a control resource which might otherwise not exist. Moreover, insofar as criminal enterprise attempts to reduce uncertainty and risk in its operations, it aids the state in the maintenance of public order. This is particularly true to the extent that the rationalization of criminal activity reduces the collateral costs (i.e. violence) associated with predatory crime (Schelling, 1967).

CONCLUSION

A Marxian theory of deviance and control must overcome the weaknesses of both conventional interpretations and narrow critical models. It must offer a means of studying deviance which fully exploits the critical potential of Marxist scholarship. More than "demystifying" the analysis of deviance, such a theory must suggest directions and offer insights which can be utilized in the direct construction of critical theory. Although the discussion has been informed by concepts and evidence drawn from a range of Marxist studies, it has been more of a sensitizing essay than a substantive analysis. The further development of the theory must await the accumulation of evidence to refine our understanding of the relationships and tendencies explored. When this evidence is developed the contributions of Marxist thought can be more meaningfully applied to an understanding of deviance, class conflict and social control.

NOTES

1. For example, Turk (1969) defines deviance primarily in terms of the social position and relative power of various social groups.

2. To the extent that a group (e.g. homosexuals) blatantly and systematically challenges the validity of the bourgeois family it is likely to become part of the problem population. The family is essential to capitalist society as a unit for consumption, socialization and the reproduction of the socially necessary labor force (cf. Frankford and Snitow, 1972; Secombe, 1973; Zaretsky, 1973).

3. O'Connor (1973) discusses this problem in terms of the crisis faced by the capitalist state in maintaining conditions for profitable accumulation and social harmony.

4. It has been estimated, for instance, that $1/3$ of all arrests in America are for the offense of public drunkenness. Most of these apparently involve "sick" and destitute "skid row alcoholics" (Morris and Hawkins, 1969).

5. Despite the general tendencies of state capitalism, its internal ideological contradictions may actually frustrate the adoption of an investment approach. For example, in discussing social welfare policy Rimlinger (1966: 571) concludes that "in a country like the United States, which has a strong individualistic heritage, the idea is still alive that any kind of social protection has adverse productivity effects. A country like the Soviet Union, with a centrally planned economy and a collectivist ideology, is likely to make an earlier and more deliberate use of health and welfare programs for purposes of influencing productivity and developing manpower."

6. In his analysis of the lumpenproletariat Marx (1964) clearly recognized how the underclass could be manipulated as a "bribed tool of reactionary intrigue."

REFERENCES

Baran, Paul, and Paul M. Sweezy
    1966   Monopoly Capital. New York: Monthly Review Press.

Becker, Howard S.
    1967   "Whose side are we on?" Social Problems 14(Winter): 239–247.

Becker, Howard S., and Irving Louis Horowitz
    1972   "Radical politics and sociological research: observations on methodology and ideology." American Journal of Sociology 78(July): 48–66.

Blauner, Robert
    1969   "Internal colonialism and ghetto revolt." Social Problems 16 (Spring): 393–408.

Bowles, Samuel
1973   "Contradictions in United States higher education." Pp. 165–199 in
        James H. Weaver (ed.), Modern Political Economy: Radical Versus
        Orthodox Approaches. Boston: Allyn and Bacon.

Bowles, Samuel, and Herbert Gintis
1972   "I.Q. in the U.S. class structure." Social Policy 3(November/
        December): 65–96.

Bureau of Prisons
1972   National Prisoner Statistics. Prisoners in State and Federal Institu-
        tions for Adult Felons. Washington D.C.: Bureau of Prisons.

Cohen, David K., and Marvin Lazerson
1972   "Education and the corporate order." Socialist Revolution (March/
        April): 48–72.

Foucault, Michel
1965   Madness and Civilization. New York: Random House.

Frankford, Evelyn, and Ann Snitow
1972   "The trap of domesticity: notes on the family." Socialist Revolution
        (July/August): 83–94.

Gintis, Herbert
1973   "Alienation and power." Pp. 431–465 in James H. Weaver (ed.),
        Modern Political Economy: Radical Versus Orthodox Approaches.
        Boston: Allyn and Bacon.

Gorz, Andre
1970   "Capitalist relations of production and the socially necessary labor
        force." Pp. 155–171 in Arthur Lothstein (ed.), All We Are Saying...
        New York: G. P. Putnam.

Gross, Bertram M.
1970   "Friendly fascism: a model for America." Social Policy (November/
        December): 44–52.

Helmer, John, and Thomas Vietorisz
1973   "Drug use, the labor market and class conflict." Paper presented at
        Annual Meeting of the American Sociological Association.

Karier, Clarence J.
1973   "Business values and the educational state." Pp. 6–29 in Clarence J.
        Karier, Paul Violas, and Joel Spring (eds.), Roots of Crisis: Ameri
        can Education in the Twentieth Century. Chicago: Rand McNally.

Liazos, Alexander
1972   "The poverty of the sociology of deviance: nuts, sluts and 'pre-
        verts.'" Social Problems 20(Summer): 103–120.

Mandel, Ernest
1968   Marxist Economic Theory (Volume I). New York: Monthly Review
        Press.

Marcuse, Herbert
1964   One-Dimensional Man. Boston: Beacon Press.

Marx, Karl
1964   Class Struggles in France 1848–1850. New York: International Publishers.
1967   Capital (Volume I). New York: International Publishers.

Matza, David
1969   Becoming Deviant. Englewood Cliffs: Prentice Hall.

McIntosh, Mary
1973   "The growth of racketeering." Economy and Society (February): 35–69.

Morris, Norval, and Gordon Hawkins
1969   The Honest Politician's Guide to Crime Control. Chicago: University of Chicago Press.

Musto, David F.
1973   The American Disease: Origins of Narcotic Control. New Haven: Yale University Press.

National Institute of Mental Health
1970   Trends in Resident Patients—State and County Mental Hospitals, 1950–1968. Biometry Branch, Office of Program Planning and Evaluation. Rockville, Maryland: National Institute of Mental Health.

O'Connor, James
1975   The Fiscal Crisis of the State. New York: St. Martin's Press.

Piven, Frances, and Richard A. Cloward
1971   Regulating the Poor: The Functions of Public Welfare. New York: Random House.

Rimlinger, Gaston V.
1961   "Social security, incentives, and controls in the U.S. and U.S.S.R." Comparative Studies in Society and History 4 (November): 104–124.
1966   "Welfare policy and economic development: a comparative historical perspective." Journal of Economic History (December): 556–571.

Schelling, Thomas
1967   "Economics and criminal enterprise." Public Interest (Spring): 61–78.

Secombe, Wally
1973   "The housewife and her labour under capitalism." New Left Review (January-February): 3–24.

Spring, Joel
1972   Education and the Rise of the Corporate State. Boston: Beacon Press.

1973   "Education as a form of social control." Pp. 30–39 in Clarence J. Ka-
        rier, Paul Violas, and Joel Spring (eds.), Roots of Crisis: American
        Education in the Twentieth Century. Chicago: Rand McNally.

Turk, Austin T.
  1969   Criminality and Legal Order. Chicago: Rand McNally and Com-
          pany.

Zaretsky, Eli
  1973   "Capitalism, the family and personal life: parts 1 & 2." Socialist
          Revolution (January–April/May-June): 69–126, 19–70.

Analysis and Critique

30   The New Criminology: Continuity in Criminological Theory
ROBERT F. MEIER

In a recent essay, Francis Allen warned that "modern criminology is in danger of being enslaved by its own emancipation."[1] Professor Allen's despairing prognosis was occasioned by what he took to be unsatisfactory developments in the manner in which criminologists were selecting and approaching their work. The emancipation Allen referred to is that which had tied criminology to behavioral considerations; the enslavement is that which presently binds a new version of criminology to political considerations.

The search for political meanings and motives in the concept of crime and criminal behavior, which Professor Allen deplores, is thought by many to be a recent criminological development. Variously called "critical," "radical" or "the new criminology," the approach explicitly rejects more established paradigms, which are claimed to be incompatible with an acceptable social and humanistic view of crime and its control.[2] There is, however, more to the new criminology than the simple assertion that crime is a political phenomenon, for such a statement would merely be tautological. Laws obviously are passed by political bodies, and these bodies are largely committed to the prevailing social system. This is the case regardless of the economic system within which the law-passing body operates.[3]

Reprinted from Robert F. Meier, "The New Criminology: Continuity in Criminological Theory," *Journal of Criminal Law and Criminology*, vol. 67, no. 4 (1967), published by Northwestern University School of Law. By permission of the author.

The new criminology seems to be offering the discipline a distinctive conceptual framework within which to conduct its work. I will argue here, however, that rather than presenting criminology with a novel theoretical alternative, the new criminology has taken some of the discipline's more established notions and rephrased them in political terms. Specifically, one finds in the new criminology elements of a social pathological view, extensions of early University of Chicago criminology, an uneasy reliance on functionalism, and an abiding faith in labeling theory and its applications.

The new criminology came forward incrementally; there was never a time when there was not a new criminology, and then a time when there was. The gradual development of the new criminology has culminated in recent years in the establishment of a specialized journal, a cadre of identifiable members and relatively clear boundaries of study.

Gresham Sykes has claimed that the "radical" criminology does in fact warrant the label "new" since it is comprised of more than a series of ideas differing only in emphasis from conventional criminology. Sykes maintains that

> ...it does not appear that this new viewpoint in criminology simply grew out of existing ideas in the field in some...automatic process where pure logic breeds uncontaminated by the concerns and passions of the times. Nor does it appear that a flood of new data burst upon the field, requiring a new theoretical synthesis.[4]

Sykes believes that the advent of a new criminology can only be understood as the result of the sociohistorical forces which he believes were at work in the 1960's. These include: (1) an increased cynicism concerning the motives of those in power, the credibility of official pronouncements and the institution of government itself; (2) the growth of a counterculture which began to alter popular images of deviance and take more skeptical stances toward traditional bases of authority; and (3) an increasing politicalization of certain groups in American society which had accumulated enough power to dispute institutionalized discrimination and coercion.[5]

While this list may enumerate aspects of the external environment in which the new criminology arose, it does not account fully for its growth. Scientific paradigmatic shifts do not come about as a function of such mechanisms alone; they are also tied to internal intellectual developments in a discipline.[6] While the time must be "ripe" for the growth and eventual acceptance of intellectual alternatives, so too must be the intellectual climate in which practitioners of a discipline operate.

The new criminology's challenge to traditional perspectives is best understood by reference to the general development of competing theories. Although there is some dispute about the matter, sociologists of science generally have come to believe that the acceptance of a new perspective or theory is heavily dependent on older views being unable to deal with crucial problems, although this inability does not seem to depend on the availability of empirical evidence which runs counter to the older theory. In this sense, theoretical growth of science is not cumulative, but awaits the ascension of theoretical alternatives to replace the "damaged," unfinished theories. External forces (such as those described by Sykes) might under such conditions seem to play a determining role in the acceptance of the new alternative by certain members of the discipline. But this explanation overlooks the importance of internal, or discipline-specific, factors which are experienced by scholars in their scientific work. If, as Kuhn and Lakatos claim,[7] the eventual acceptance of a new theory occurs independent of empirical support, certain crisis situations present in a discipline portend the search for new theoretical views which will present practitioners with a different array of intellectual puzzles and justifications for their work, and which will point to the direction of subsequent research.

THE NEW CRIMINOLOGY

It is necessary to be cautious when writing about the new criminology. While the new criminologists ostensibly encourage open dialogues concerning the issues they raise,[8] they appear to be generally suspicious of evaluative statements of their work, and are apt to view such attempts as intellectual distractions. As one leading spokesman for the new criminology has put it:

> We should welcome debates which allow us to publicize and discuss our perspective, but at the same time, must avoid cooptation and concentrate on extending and systematizing an authentically radical criminology.[9]

Taking the risk, I will try to summarize some main ideas of the new criminology. Since the purpose of this essay is not essentially evaluative,[10] no attempt will be made to develop these ideas or to provide the kind of documentation offered by the new criminologists.[11]

Like Sykes,[12] I find the new criminology to be centered around a view of a society dominated by an elite which uses the criminal law as a means of meeting and controlling certain threats to the elite's power and position. By employing the legal apparatus to define acceptable standards of conduct and to repress that behavior (and those persons) who violate such standards, the powerful are able to maintain their privileged position.[13] The powerful are thus seen as a self-interested lot who manipulate the legal structure to their advantage.[14] The maximization of self-gain is the predominant motive guiding most, if not all, elite behavior in this system of social, political, and economic arrangements.

The meaning of crime in the new criminology is less to be found in the willful violation of legal statutes than in the conscious determination of standards which will serve the materialistic interests of those who are able to participate in the legal-definition process. Criminal behavior becomes defined as a function of social class position.[15] The law of theft, for example, is said to have been established by those in power who have more to lose from thievery. The law is almost invariably broken by persons in the more powerless lower classes who experience greater temptation toward theft.

The new criminology perceives crime as an immutable feature of capitalist society and its system of political arrangements which guarantee the position of an exploiting elite. "To locate the study of crime within a broader quest for social justice demands that one understand the relationship between crime and the *maintenance* of privilege."[16] The system of criminal justice is believed to be essentially coercive. The elite rule less on authority than on power. The powerless do not accept most criminal definitions on the basis of perceived legitimacy, but rather conform out of fear of force which the elite can bring to bear on deviance. This force, embodied by the police, courts, and correctional systems, serves the interests of the powerful by enforcing their rules.[17] Since system functionaries are recruited largely from the powerless classes, the elite must coopt them into their ideology through the inculcation of a "false consciousness."

The new criminology implies that if the elite did not control the criminal definition-process, a radical restructuring of the criminal code would result. This view is a misinterpretation, however, since the new criminologists do not call for the decriminalization of offenses such as homicide, robbery and rape, about which there is substantial consensus regarding their seriousness and the necessity for control. Nor do they claim that a socialist economic system would obviate these acts. The confusion that has been generated in this regard seems to stem from the new criminology's tendency to cite with approval research on the elite-supported origins of non-consensual crimes,[18] such as vagrancy, prostitution and the use of certain drugs.[19] It is implied that since all laws derive from similar political processes, the prime mover for *all* laws is some powerful elite. In the process the distinction is blurred between laws which seem to protect the interests of most persons (consensual crimes) and those laws which protect the interests of a smaller segment of society (non-consensual crimes).

In summary form, the tasks of the new criminology have been: (1) to "demystify" criminal law, both in its origins and applications, since to do so will uncover the interests of the powerful; (2) to conduct studies of social control agencies, bureaucracies, and mass media to expose their complicity with an elitist ideology; (3) to propose new criminal definitions which, correcting the imbalance created by the elite's influence on legislation, will include violations of certain inherent rights; and (4) to put the new criminology's theory into practice (termed "praxis") by attempting to alter the existing economic and political arrangements of capitalism, which are believed to give rise to the present situation.

To examine the genesis of these ideas, I will concentrate on the main perspectives in criminology, roughly in order of their historical emergence. The "social pathology view" was the first to be embraced by criminology in this country. It was followed by the "Chicago school of criminology," then by "functionalism." The "labeling perspective" is the most recent of the major criminological approaches. The new criminology has borrowed selectively from each of these positions in a synergistic manner.

SOCIAL PATHOLOGY

The social pathology approach to social problems was based on an analogy which likened society to the functioning of a biological organism. Social problems were those conditions which interfered with the "normal" (*i.e.*, "desirable") workings of society.[20] Problems such as poverty, mental illness, prostitution, and crime were condemned because "everyone knew" them to be wrong. The social pathological view, which came to prominence in the early years of this century, was congruent with the personal ideologies of its scholar-advocates.[21] The social pathologists were recruited largely from small midwestern communities and were imbued with a sense of the importance of religion, as well as a distrust of urban life. This "sacred provincialism" resulted in a moralistic approach which not only called attention to the existence of the "evil" of crime, but also provided the element of moral censure requisite to speed the correction of criminal behavior.

Though the new criminologists overtly reject the social pathological approach to crime, they have retained a number of its major features. The social pathologists were concerned with the *individual pathology of criminals;* the new criminologists deal with the *political pathology of capitalism.* In the new criminology, it is no longer the individual criminal who is considered pathological (nor is the criminal's illegal behavior necessarily considered pathological). It is rather the social and political system which is said to maintain the conditions which produce the criminal and his behavior. The concept of pathology is thus transferred from the actions of a powerless criminal to the behavior of a powerful elite. Consequently, the notion of pathology is aversive to the new criminologists not on principle, but on the basis of its misplaced application; simply put, the wrong sources have received the pathology label.

The theoretical problem that this class emphasis creates for the new criminology is often unrecognized but is nevertheless substantial. The location of "causes" of his behavior and the amount of influence ascribed to those causes have implications for the image of the deviant. If deviance is said to be produced by forces external to the individual, he is personally less responsible for his actions. In the new criminology, the word "powerless" represents not only a person's inability to participate effectively in political and economic decisions which might affect his life, but is also an appropriate adjective to describe his lack of responsibility for his own behavior. It is in this sense that the new criminologists seem to subscribe to what Hollander[22] has termed "selective determinism." While the actions of the mugger are deemed to be determined, those of the price fixer are not; while the actions of the murderer are the result of a repressive society,[23] the actions of the corrupt politician are not.

There is a related view, which might be termed "socialist utopian vision," which holds that once people have enough of the basics, such as the right kind of work and attractive opportunities for living and learning, there will be no materialism and hence no crime. While there may be some measure of truth in this claim, it is not self-evident and it has not been empirically demonstrated.

Declaring the actions of the powerless to be attributable to morality and those of the powerful attributable to materialism suggests a duality which can be resolved only by making materialism a function of power. If self-interest is defined in terms of power, then only the powerful can act from this motive. In this manner, the new criminologists invert the premise of the social pathologists. The pathologists claimed moral eminence only for the elite, whose forward vision and proficiency were necessary for a smoothly running, progressive society. The powerful were the moral, political, and economic leaders, while the powerless attempted to debase the lofty intents of the elite.

The selection of those persons, behaviors, and conditions considered pathological was made by the pathologists on moralistic grounds bolstered by elements of social Darwinism. The content of the new criminology is also ruled by moral, rather than scientific, bases. "Liberal" criminology has used the criminal law to define its boundaries: acts defined in the statutes have formed the basis for criminological inquiry. The new criminologists reject such a notion and call for the criminalization (or, at least, the study) of acts which are not presently criminal in a strict legalistic sense. Racism, sexism, imperialism and other forms of repression have been added to the new criminologists' agenda.[24] It is argued that the discipline of criminology should be humanistically oriented; that is, that criminology should serve the powerless by studying conditions which inhibit or destroy the free expression of uniquely human rights and values. New criminologists do not deny that the problems they choose to study are morally determined; indeed, they proclaim that problem selection based on any other criterion has never existed.[25] They maintain that they are merely being more candid about exposing their values than traditional criminologists, who often hide beneath a sea of liberal rhetoric. In this way the new criminology, rather than eschewing pathology, openly embraces it. What has changed are those conditions considered pathological, rather than the process by which such an identification is made.

CHICAGO CRIMINOLOGY

Chicago sociology[26] moved the concept of pathology from the individual to the group level; it was no longer *persons* who were *pathological* but *communities* (or, more precisely, "natural areas") that were *disorganized*. This disorganization was the result of a conflict of conduct norms among residents which produced ambiguous or contradictory standards of behavior. The concept of social disorganization further shed its pathological connotation in the work of Edwin H. Sutherland who talked of "differential social organization" in his general theory of crime.

Marx stressed the notion of political conflict. The fact that Marx had little to say about crime and law could mean either that he had scant interest in the subject, or that he had little insight into how this particular behavior related to the political conflict he described. The new criminology's use of the term "conflict" with respect to criminal behavior appears to derive from the Chicago tradition, rather than from Marx. That the proletariat and the bourgeoisie are in conflict over political power does not automatically lead to the conclusion that the powerful "create" crime, even though they may indeed control the means which produce definitions of crime. And even if that conclusion were demonstrated to be correct, it would not necessarily account for the powerless group behaving more criminally than the powerful unless crime were defined in terms of power, which would make this true by definition.

The Chicago theorists specified the relationship between crime and conflict, characterizing conflict in nonpolitical terms. Their theories, however, never reached the societal level of generalization.[27] What distinguishes the new criminology from previous structural theories is its emphasis on the relationship between political and economic factors on the one hand, and social and legal factors on the other. The roots of such a view can be traced to the work of Wilfem Bonger.[28] The new criminologists pay an intellectual debt to Bonger,[29] but find more contemporary meaning in the writings of prison inmates, revolutionaries, and other political dissidents such as George Jackson, Angela Davis, pre-1975 Eldridge Cleaver, Franz Fanon, Malcolm X and Bobby Seale.

Firsthand documentation of the repressive nature of the capitalist society has come to be empirically valued in the new criminology. But the use of such documentation is not singular to the new criminology; the Chicago theorists found substantial meaning for their work in similar kinds of reports.[30] Indeed, the utility of such accounts for both the Chicago theorists and the new criminologists is remarkably similar. Both are interested in the process whereby a person comes to commit a criminal act. What has changed is the location of the causes of behavior. One wonders whether the new criminologists would find a political meaning in Shaw's jackroller, and whether Sutherland would have been able to locate aspects of differential association in the life of Malcolm X.

The new criminology, as I have indicated, calls for a critical reappraisal of legalistic or state definitions of crime. Most of what is presently against the law, it is believed, probably should be outlawed, but there also is much that is neglected in these provisions. The most systematic statement of this issue is by the Schwendingers,[31] who call for a redefinition of the term "criminal" to include those conditions which violate basic human rights and potentials. This call for criminalizing certain acts of governments and corporations, however, does not derive directly from the new criminology, which has merely broadened and made more political one of the more enduring debates in criminology.

That the new criminology "discovered" the political nature of law is untrue, and may be an example of what Sorokin has called "intellectual amnesia."[32] In 1933, for instance, the Bureau of Social Hygiene, under the auspices of the Social Science Research Council, published a report dealing with the feasibility of establishing an institute of criminology. This document, known as the Michael and Adler Report,[33] set about to review what was then known about crime and to make recommendations concerning the possibility of an institute from which public policy planning might be made. The report noted that it was necessary for the law to keep pace with changing conditions: "It appears to be desirable that the behavior content of the criminal law should keep abreast of changes in behavior patterns or, at least, that it should not lag too far behind."[34] Michael and Adler also note that: "It is highly questionable that 'sociology' and what is called 'political science' are independent of each other."[35]

A few years later, Thorsten Sellin, under the auspices of the Social Science Research Council, set out to articulate some research directions for criminology.[36] Sellin called for a redefinition of the traditional parameters of criminological inquiry and maintained that focusing on the violations of conduct norms would provide theoretically better substance for criminology. Sutherland later entered this arena in defense of his then newly-minted concept of white-collar crime. Anticipating adverse reactions from those who believed that the criminal law was the only basis for the appellation "criminal," Sutherland defended his position against the legalist, Paul Tappan, in an exchange that anticipates much of the Schwendingers' work of a generation later.[37]

FUNCTIONALISM

That the new criminology should be "functionalist" is an outgrowth of the problems it deals with and the general approach taken toward their solution. Functional analysis, identified with persons whose ideas on crime are deemed to be theoretically and politically conservative, is a technique which explores the underlying dimensions of problems, looking for latent functions or features which have manifest dysfunctions. Merton's[38] analysis of political machines, Bell's[39] study of organized crime, and Davis's[40] investigation of prostitution all contain a similar theme: that while these problems are manifestly dysfunctional for society, they all exhibit latent functions which fuel and account for their existence. The new criminology, too, uses this style of research when examining the nature of crime and the functions of the criminal law. Its concentration on the society's elite foreshadows the conclusion that crime is manifestly functional for the elite, allowing them to use force to maintain their power, and latently dysfunctional in fomenting proletariat resentment and conflict.

Robert Merton is probably the most well-known functionalist. Merton and the new criminologists both stress social class position as a determinant of criminality. Merton notes that a denial of access to certain cultural goals and the ensuing frustration that this engenders is not randomly distributed, but is concentrated in the lower classes.[41] While Merton views the location of crime in the lower classes as problematic and in need of explanation, the new criminology sees it as natural and politically inevitable. This does not mean that official estimates are necessarily accurate indicators of criminal behavior (although such a position is not entirely incompatible with the new criminology), but rather that there is a lack of correspondence between the manifest and latent functions of the figures. Rather than informing us about the "correct" distribution of criminal behavior, official crime statistics covertly instruct us in the actions of agencies of social control, the class-based definition of crime, and the image of what is to be considered criminal. The political nature of criminal statistics is revealed only by understanding their latent functions.

If official records of crime are suspect, so too are the motivations of those who construct those records—the agents of social control.[42] On the manifest level their motivations are objective: to document violations of the normative demands of criminal law. On the latent level, however, we find that the criminal justice system operates against the best interests of the poor and powerless because it *intends* to do so.[43] This process of uncovering politically latent meanings is what is meant by "demystifying" the criminal law; that is, exposing the latent meanings and intentions in capitalist society. Once we are able to see below the powerful system of privilege maintenance, the new criminology maintains, we will uncover the real political plan.

The new criminology and Merton also share a common image of a criminal. Within Merton's perspective, the offender is one who has been unable to compete equitably with others who are better placed in society. But Merton's portrait of the criminal is only half drawn. We are able to glimpse something of the total picture in the "decision" of the criminal to "innovate" (as Merton defines it), but we are presented with the behavior rather than the person. Thus, we are told of the structural antecedents (culturally prescribed goals and unavailable means), the resulting personal frustration this generates, and the behavioral outcome (innovation); we are given nothing of the deviant himself, aside from his probable lower class status.

The new criminology presents a similarly incomplete picture of the offender. It locates a set of structural antecedents (capitalism), the resulting personal (*i.e.*, political) frustration this arouses, and the behavioral outcome (a political act, defined by the elite as crime). We are given little information about the deviant himself aside from his lower class position. If Merton gives us a glimmer of a frustrated person acting out of the same motivations for success as everyone else, the new criminology presents a more romantic, and at times heroic, image of the offender. In the new criminology, offenders seem like Robin Hoods. Merton and the new criminologists agree on one thing: Merton's materialistically frustrated innovators and the new criminology's politically defiant freedom fighters would act differently given a choice in the social structure. These criminals are driven to their crimes, not attracted by them.

POLITICS AND LABELING

In one of the most widely cited works in the sociology of deviance, Howard S. Becker[44] defines deviance relativistically: no behavior is inherently deviant since deviance is not a quality of an act, but the response of others to that act. "The deviant is one to whom the label has successfully been applied; deviant behavior is behavior that people so label."[45] The nature of the reaction is a function of social groups who created deviance by making rules whose infraction constitutes deviance, and who respond in terms of the rules they have created.[46] This reaction is not random, but rather is patterned and purposely given only to certain kinds of acts. This is why it is essential to return to the rule creation process to see whose rules are being broken. Becker informs us that

> ...people are in fact always *forcing* their rules on others, applying them more or less against the will and without the consent of those others....Differences in the ability to make rules and apply them to other people are essentially power differentials (either legal or extra-legal).[47]

Such rules are said to be the "object of conflict and disagreement, part of the political process of society."[48] Becker identifies certain groups which are particularly involved in creation of deviance, and calls the members "moral entrepreneurs."[49]

In addition to his emphasis on rule creation, Becker stresses the importance of the administration of those rules. Labeling theory shows that not only is rule-making concentrated in the hands of select groups, but that the application of criminal labels is not a random phenomenon. Since rules are not made to apply to all equally (they prohibit behavior that is largely indigenous to the lower classes), it is not surprising that the application of the law should follow social class lines.[50]

Richard Ericson,[51] writing on the English new criminologists, has observed that the new criminology has been defined in terms of what it is not, rather than what it is.[52] Ericson also notes the new criminology makes extensive use of labeling theory not only to orient members intellectually, but also to utilize the "blaming quality" labeling theory provides. This quality arises from the configuration of "causes" of deviance that labeling theory alleges. As Becker and Horowitz have stated:

> If sociology allows for a choice on the part of human actors, then it can blame, by the way it assigns causes, any of the people involved since they could have chosen not to do what they did. This has consequences for the political character of sociological analysis.[53]

The deviant in labeling theory is one whose behavior, at least in its secondary aspects, has been determined by the reactions of others. If he is not to blame for this condition, the audience which reacted to his behavior and thus perpetuated his deviance is much less innocent.

The political nature of the new criminology, summarized in the term "praxis" is, of course, inescapable. In the dual role of scholar and activist, the new criminologists have set for themselves an ideal of practicing what they preach. The new criminology offers not only a new theoretical alternative to traditional criminology, but also seeks to provide scientific legitimacy to socialist political activism. Critics of the new criminology have charged that it is little more than "rhetoric." This charge is sometimes dealt with by turning it back onto the critic: "The problem of 'rhetoric' is ...bothersome because the cry of 'too much rhetoric' itself can be a rhetorical device that obscures the real issues posed...."[54]

The rhetorical charge is a serious one, however, and cannot be dismissed in so cavalier a fashion. If the new criminology's claims to truth are based on nothing more than a particular set of values and moral positions, resolution of differences with opponents may not be possible. Acceptance of the new criminology can then take place only in like-minded persons, who do not perceive a general theoretical alternative. The new criminologists, not denying the rhetorical nature of their scholarship, indicate that this is the major reason why academic criminology has been unreceptive to their ideas and why some new criminologists have been denied university tenure. As one group of new criminologists points out: "To say that socialists are necessarily un-scientific is the form that red-baiting takes in the university."[55]

Thus, tenure problems encountered by two well-known criminologists have resulted, say the new criminologists, from their particular
political views rather than the quality of their scholarship.

Is this marriage of scholarship and political activism unique to the
new criminology? It would appear not. The issue was identified and
discussed prior to the present advent of the new criminology, particularly in the works of C. Wright Mills,[56] Robert Lynd,[57] Howard Becker,[58]
and Alvin Gouldner,[59] all of whom advocated vocationally relevant
scholarship. While these persons may be thought of as sympathetic
intellectually to the new criminology, their writings cannot be construed as being part of the new criminology.

The overlap with labeling theory can be summarized as follows: in
both the new criminology and labeling theory one sees concern with
(1) the creation and function of rules; (2) the enforcement of rules
(laws) for the benefit of the rule makers; (3) the effect of the application of rules in the form of social control for individuals; and (4) the
politicalization of deviants who see through the guise of the law to the
true nature of their own repression.

SUMMARY AND CONCLUSIONS

In addition to providing a valuable framework within which to study
rule making and rule application, labeling theory contributed to the
new criminology the idea that political considerations could be fused
to "scientific" information so that knowledge and politics constituted
two aspects of the same thing. The foundations of praxis and the concern with power and society lead inevitably to considerations of the
creation and application of rules. Because labeling theory, for one reason or another, concentrated on the consequences of the application
of rules, the way was cleared for the new criminology to focus on rule-
making as a substantive study area.

Criminology's interest in labeling theory also arises, in some measure, from the theory's ability to generate testable propositions which
are derived from an intuitively appealing but not self-evident irony:
social control efforts contain within them the basis for their own justification.

The new criminology also begins with an irony, but one derived
from functionalism. Functionalism's irony is that while problems have
manifest dysfunctions, they also have latent functions, and these latent functions help explain the persistence of those problems. The
new criminology extends this idea, but with a twist. The new criminology (1) performs the functional analysis not for society as a whole,

but only for the elite of that society, and (2) reverses the characterization of manifest and latent contributions. What is functional and dysfunctional largely depends on the amount of power one possesses. The new criminology pays little attention to the practical functions and dysfunctions of crime, especially for the powerless who have to bear the brunt of victimization and repressive measures.

The Chicago school was the first to legitimize (1) the explanatory concept of conflict (although it was defined slightly differently here), and (2) the use of first-person accounts of crime and empirical evidence in support of theoretical positions. Within the work of the Chicago school took place the beginnings of discussions about the criminal law and its content and scope.

The pathologists identified the genesis of social problems as stemming from personal and group inadequacies. The deviant was immoral and his behavior in need of correction. The new criminology, in its return to the pathological position, finds in the actions of the elite a different location for what is considered pathological. But if the pathologists' approach to crime was dictated by the sacred, the new criminologists employ secular (political) criteria for their determination. The pathological stance is maintained; it is only that new villains are identified.

The stuff of the new criminology is deeply rooted in criminological theory. This is neither praiseworthy, nor an indictment, since the utility of criminological theory is founded on other criteria. The developments in criminology and, indeed, in all other disciplines, are rarely wholly creative. The synergistic goal of the new criminology may be nothing more than a spirited eclecticism with fancy (and presently fashionable) political terms.

If much of the history of criminological theory in the United States can be seen as a reaction to pathology[60] (and that reaction has been increasing in recent years),[61] the new criminology is likely to draw sharp criticism. Francis Allen's fear, noted at the outset of this article, is neither a conservative lament nor misplaced antagonism. If criminology is indeed in danger of being enslaved by its own emancipation, it would appear its captive will be in the form of an old, rather than a new, jailer.

NOTES

1. F. Allen, *The Crimes of Politics* 13 (1974).
2. I. Taylor, P. Walton, and J. Young, *The New Criminology: For a Social Theory of Deviance* (1973).

3. E. Van den Haag, "No Excuses for Crime," 423 *Annals* 137 (1976).

4. G. Sykes, "The Rise of Critical Criminology," 65 *Journal of Criminal Law and Criminology* 206, 211 (1974).

5. See also Gibbons and Garabedian, "Conservative, Liberal and Radical Criminology: Some Trends and Observations," in *The Criminologist: Crime and the Criminal* 51 (C. Reasons, ed., 1974); Reasons, "The Politicizing of Crime, the Criminal and the Criminologist," 64 *Journal of Criminal Law and Criminology* 471 (1973).

6. T. Kuhn, *The Structure of Scientific Revolutions* (1962).

7. Kuhn, *supra* note 6, at 81; M. Polyani, *Personal Knowledge* 292 (1958); I. Lakatos, "Falsification and the Methodology of Scientific Research Programmes," *Criticism and the Growth of Knowledge* 100-101 (I. Lakatos and A. Musgrave, eds., 1970).

8. The editorial statement contained in the new criminology's journal follows the traditional format for such declarations: *"Crime and Social Justice welcomes contributions to all sections of the journal."* 4 *Crime and Social Justice* 72 (1975).

9. Platt, "Prospects for a Radical Criminology in the United States," 1 *Crime and Social Justice* 28 (1974). Note the similarity between the foregoing and the following exchange:

    "I *want* someone to tell me," Lieutenant Schiesskopf beseeched them all prayerfully. "If any of it is my fault, I *want* to be told."
    "He wants someone to tell him," Clevinger said.
    "He wants everyone to keep still, idiot," Yossarian answered.

    J. Heller, *Catch-22* at 68 (1961).

10. Some evaluative statements have begun to appear. See Allen, *supra* note 1; E. Thompson, *Whigs and Hunters: The Origins of the Black Act* (1975); E. van den Haag, *Punishing Criminals: Concerning a Very Old and Painful Question* (1975); J. Wilson, *Thinking about Crime* (1975); Carson, "Symbolic and Instrumental Dimensions of Early Factory Legislation," in *Crime, Criminology and Public Policy* 107 (R. Hood, ed., 1975); Carson, "The Sociology of Crime and the Emergence of Criminal Laws," in *Deviance and Social Control* 67 (P. Rock and M. McIntosh, eds., 1974); Gibbs and Erickson, "Major Developments in the Sociological Study of Deviance," in *Annual Review of Sociology* 21 (A. Inkeles, J. Coleman and N. Smelser, eds., 1975); Hirst, "Marx and Engels on Law, Crime, and Morality," in *Critical Criminology* 203 (I. Taylor, P. Walton, & J. Young, eds., 1975); Sykes, *supra* note 4; Turk, "Prospects and Pitfalls for Radical Criminology: A Critical Response to Platt," 4 *Crime and Social Justice* 41 (1975) (see note 9 *supra*); van den Haag, *supra* note 3: Walker, "Lost Causes in Criminology," in *Crime, Criminology and Public Policy* (R. Hood. ed., 1975).

11. That I have been somewhat selective in choosing which points I consider essential to the new criminology will be obvious; the selection has been guided by the nature of the argument presented here.

12. Sykes, *supra* note 4.

13. B. Kriseberg, *Crime and Privilege* (1975).

14. The term self-interest is most often used to denote selfishness, but there is a distinction: "Self-interest is the satisfaction of one's desires; selfishness is the satisfaction of one's desires at the expense of someone else." B. Dunham, *Man Against Myth* 41 (1947), quoted in H. Schwendinger and J. Schwendinger, *The Sociologists of the Chair* 190 (1974).

15. W. Chambliss, "Functional and Conflict Theories of Crime," 17 MSS Module 1 (1974). See also the revised version of this paper in *Whose Law? Whose Order?* 1 (W. Chambliss and M. Mankoff, eds., 1976).

16. Kriseberg, *supra* note 13 at 30. [Emphasis added.]

17. But see R. Quinney, *Critique of Legal Order: Crime Control in Capitalist Society* (1974).

18. J. Hall, *Theft, Law and Society* (2nd ed., 1952).

19. W. Chambliss, "A Sociological Analysis of the Law of Vagrancy," 12 *Social Problems* 67 (1964); Roby, "Politics and Criminal Law: Revision of the New York State Penal Law on Prostitution," 17 *Social Problems* 83 (1969); T. Duster, *The Legislation of Marality* (1970).

20. *The Solution of Social Problems* (E. Rubington and M. Weinberg, eds., 1971).

21. See Schwendinger and Schwendinger, *supra* note 14, who disagree with the well-known analysis of this issue contained in Mills, "The Professional Ideology of Social Pathologists," 49 *American Journal of Sociology* 165 (1943).

22. Hollander, "Sociology, Selective Determinism, and the Rise of Expectations," 8 *American Sociologist* 147 (1973).

23. A recent editorial in the new criminology's journal dedicated that issue to one of the former staff members of the journal, Mary Gay, who had been killed by her husband. The moral outrage such an act might otherwise generate was tempered: "Mary Gay was beaten to death by a man—her husband, who like her was a victim of a cruel system." 4 *Crime and Social Justice* 64 (1975) (dedication).

24. Schwendinger and Schwendinger, "Defenders of Order or Guardians of Human Rights?" 5 *Issues in Criminology* 123 (1970).

25. Krisberg, "Teaching Radical Criminology," 1 *Crime and Social Justice* 64, 65 (1974).

26. R. Faris, *Chicago Sociology* (1967).

27. This was accomplished by the functionalists; see text accompanying notes 38–42 *infra*.

28. W. Bonger, *Criminality and Economic Conditions* (1916).

29. The payment, however, is usually awkward since Bonger has been considered to have used a "totally un-Marxist" approach in his work.

Taylor, Walton and Young, *supra* note 2, at 298, quoted in Gibbs and Erickson, *supra* note 10, at 37–39.

30. C. Conwell, *The Professional Thief* (E. Sutherland, 1937); C. Shaw, *Brothers in Crime* (1938); Shaw, *The Jack-Roller* (1930). More recent examples from this tradition can be found in W. Chambliss, *Box Man: A Professional Thief's Journey* (1972); B. Jackson, *Outside the Law: A Thief's Primer* (1972).

31. Schwendinger and Schwendinger, *supra* note 24.

32. P. Sorokin, *Fads and Foibles in Modern Sociology* 3-20 (1956).

33. J. Michael and M. Adler, *Crime, Law and Social Science* (1933).

34. *Id.* at 26.

35. *Id.* at 83, n. 26.

36. T. Sellin, *Culture Conflict and Crime* (1938).

37. E. Sutherland, "Is 'White Collar Crime' Crime?" 10 *American Sociological Review* 132 (1945); P. Tappan, "Who Is the Criminal?" 12 *American Sociological Review* 96 (1947).

38. R. Merton, *Social Theory and Social Structure* 72 (1957).

39. D. Bell, *The End of Ideology* 115–58 (1960).

40. Davis, "Prostitution," in *Contemporary Social Problems* (R. Merton and R. Nisbet, eds., 1966).

41. Merton, *supra* note 39, at 131–94.

42. J. Young, *The Drugtakers* 174 (1971).

43. Sykes, *supra* note 4.

44. H. Becker, *Outsiders* (1963).

45. *Id.* at 9.

46. *Id.* at 9–10.

47. *Id.* at 17–18.

48. *Id.* at 18.

49. *Id.* at 147-63.

50. From the labeling tradition the uses of official criminal statistics have been most seriously questioned. These statistics point clearly to the conclusion that "street" crime is heavily concentrated in lower socio-economic groups. While this conclusion has been attenuated (but only mildly) by self-report and victimization studies which suggest a slightly more even distribution of this behavior throughout the class system, the claim is made that official statistics are relatively accurate estimates, not of criminal behavior, but of the actions of social control agencies. It is not evident whether there really is more crime in the lower classes, thus forcing the police to concentrate their efforts there, or whether the police concentrate their efforts there for other reasons. See Kitsuse and Cicourel, "A Note on the Uses of Official Statistics," 11 *Social Problems* 131 (1963).

51. R. Ericson, "British Criminology: A New Subject or Old Politics?" 16 *Canadian Journal of Criminology and Corrections* 352 (1974).

52. See also S. Cohen, *The Images of Deviance* 16 (1971); A. Gouldner, *The Coming Crisis in Sociology* 20 (1970).

53. Becker and Horowitz, "Radical Politics and Sociological Research," 78 *American Journal of Sociology* 58 (1972).

54. Krisberg, *supra* note 25, at 65.

55. Marzotto, Platt and Snare, "A Reply to Turk," 4 *Crime and Social Justice* 3, 44 (1975). See note 10 *supra*.

56. C. Mills, *The Sociological Imagination* (1959).

57. R. Lynd, *Knowledge for What?* (1939).

58. H. Becker, "Whose Side Are We On?" 20 *Social Problems* 239 (1967).

59. A. Gouldner, "The Sociologist as Partisan: Sociology and the Welfare State," 30 *American Sociologist* 103 (1968).

60. D. Matza, *Becoming Deviant* (1969).

61. A. Liazos, "The Poverty of the Sociology of Deviance: Nuts, Sluts and 'Preverts'," 20 *Social Problems* 103 (1972); Thio, "Class Bias in the Sociology of Deviance," 8 *American Sociologist* 1 (1973).

CHAPTER VIII

New Directions in
Deviance Theory

The thematic structure of this final chapter differs somewhat from that of the preceding chapters. Rather than focusing on a single explanation of deviance with a distinct theoretical frame of reference, these readings represent what we consider to be new developments in the field of deviance. We are not suggesting that the earlier approaches are no longer valid, nor do we believe that the current state of theorizing about deviance has resulted in "disorganized eclecticism." While no particular theory has dominated the field over the past ten years or so, it is clear that exciting new developments, questions, and methodologies are being employed in the study of deviance. Our objective is to introduce some of these recent trends, as well as to examine the relationships that exist between the more established theories and the new directions in the literature about deviance.

During the latter part of the 19th century and the beginning of the 20th, biological explanations predominated in most thought about the cause of crime. This perspective, influenced initially by the work of Cesare Lombroso, proposed that the deviant (e.g., the criminal) differs from the nondeviant in terms of significant anatomical or physiological traits or characteristics. Social scientists in general, and criminologists in particular, have been quick to point out the shortcomings of biological explanations of deviance. For the most part, criticisms of this approach have focused on either its inability to account for variations in *rates* of crime (in terms of such variables as geography, age, sex, ethnicity, race, and social class) or the threat to liberal ideology and the possibility of political abuse this approach represents. Modern "biological criminology" research takes into account the role of nonbiological factors in the genesis of deviant behavior or crime, as Diana H. Fishbein points out in the first selection in this chapter (Reading 31). She concludes, in fact, that a multidisciplinary approach which includes social, environmental, psychological, and biological factors holds the most promise in explaining deviance and developing strategies for predicting, preventing, and managing antisocial behavior.

In her extensive review of the research on the relevance of biology to the study of crime, Fishbein shows how the data on certain biological factors are related to a propensity to engage in antisocial behavior. Current biological perspectives on the study of crime do not propose that these factors cause crime, however. Rather, they maintain that genetic factors, together with social, environmental, structural, and psychological variables, interact in ways that may increase the probability that a person will engage in antisocial behavior. Fishbein also indicates some of the problems with research in this field and suggests that without more carefully designed empirical studies, findings on relationships between biology and antisocial behavior cannot be considered valid.

Concern with the possible political implications of biological explanations of deviance is most clearly directed at the trend to the "medicalization of deviance." Social scientists suggest that by concentrating too much attention on biological traits and characteristics and too little on social causes, deviance and the deviant person have been defined in medical terms, and they have been brought increasingly under the control of medical practitioners in psychiatry and public health. In Reading 32, Peter Conrad and Joseph W. Schneider point out that during the 20th century various forms of problematic behavior that previously had been conceptualized as sin, moral problems, or crimes have been redefined in terms of illness. This implies not only a shift in explanations of the cause of deviance to an illness analogy (e.g., behavior is the result of illness, not choice, so that deviants are not responsible for their actions), but also a change in public policy to the view that deviance is a disorder that can be "treated" in ways similar to medical illness. In this vein, a number of behavioral categories, such as alcoholism, childhood hyperactivity, transsexualism, child abuse and family violence, homosexuality, mental disorders, and learning disabilities have been medicalized.[1]

In reconceptualizing deviance as illness, this therapeutic view has given rise to a new control system comprised of a vast array of professions and professionals (e.g., physicians, psychologists, counselors, and specialists in child abuse). Conrad and Schneider define medical social control of deviant behavior as "a variant of medical intervention that seeks to eliminate, modify, isolate, or regulate behavior socially defined as deviant, with medical means and in the name of health." They assert that this new form of social control is replete with problems, not the least of which is that when society does not hold people accountable for their actions, it also does not deal with deviant behavior as a moral problem. If, in the perspective of medical social control, public debate about the social causes and moral issues involved in the designation and control of deviant behavior is cut off, deviance may become whatever medical professionals deem it to be; its control or prevention is then their responsibility.

Conrad and Schneider maintain that once deviant behavior has been medicalized, individuals' responsibility for their actions is assumed to be beyond their control. In this view, deviants are unable to make moral choices between right and wrong, so their behavior lacks motivation. Solutions for deviance therefore concentrate on the individual. The issues of personal responsibility and societal solutions for deviance advanced by critics of the medicalization perspective have a long history in sociological explanations of deviance and crime; they have been of paramount concern to sociologists and criminologists since at least the mid-18th century. These issues have their origin in classical theory, in which deviance and crime are viewed as a rational course of action. Modern variations of this view are taken up in the next two selections, which focus on rational choice and the routine activities of people.

Derek B. Cornish and Ronald V. Clarke (Reading 33) identify a "rational choice" perspective on crime in which it is assumed that "offenders seek to benefit themselves by their criminal behavior; that this involves the making of decisions and choices, however rudimentary on occasions these choices might be; and that these processes, constrained as they are by time, the offender's cognitive abilities, and by the availability of relevant information, exhibit limited rather than normative rationality." In the rational choice perspective, therefore, certain types of offenders choose to commit specific crimes for specific reasons, after considering the range of the proposed crime's choice-structuring properties.

Cornish and Clarke suggest that decisions about whether or not to violate the law are based on the potential offender's calculation of alternatives, opportunities, and potential payoffs (offender specificity), and of the characteristics of the situation, skills needed, and the relation of the offender's own needs and motives to the crime (offense specificity). The rational choice perspective is concerned not only with the decision-making process involved in committing a specific crime such as robbery, murder, or rape, however. It also has to do with factors associated with switching from one type of offense to another, involvement in crime as a career, the decision to halt criminal behavior, the ineffectiveness of rehabilitative policies, and the development of crime prevention strategies that focus on the situational character of specific offenses.

Another variation of classical theory is the "routine activity" model discussed by Lawrence E. Cohen and Marcus Felson in Reading 34. Like the rational choice perspective, this view posits that individuals who commit crimes are motivated to do so. Further, the motivation to commit a crime, specifically "direct-contact predatory violations" (violent crime against the person or direct-contact property crime), is mostly related to the "certainty, celerity and value of rewards to be gained from illegal predatory acts."

In Cohen and Felson's routine activity approach, crime and crime rate trends are seen as a function or reflection of people's daily activities. Rates of crime and their distribution thus are related not only to the motivation of offenders but also to the availability of suitable targets and the absence of capable guardians who can provide protection against victimization. Accordingly, predatory crime is more likely to occur when motivated offenders find themselves in close proximity to suitable targets that are not well protected (e.g., women jogging in sparsely populated public parks; easily transportable goods in homes that are left unguarded for significant periods). Cohen and Felson suggest that the rise in crime rates since the early 1960s may be related more to these factors than to those that are characteristic of more conventional theories of criminality, which emphasize lack of social control, disorganization, blockage of opportunity structures, and other structural characteristics of American society.

The Analysis and Critique section in this chapter, "Girls' Crime and Woman's Place: Toward a Feminist Model of Female Delinquency," by Meda Chesney-Lind (Reading 35), differs somewhat from the other perspectives. The author does not advance a particular theoretical viewpoint that attempts to explain deviance, such as rational choice or routine activity. Instead, her analysis is a general critique of the major theories of deviance and delinquency, including some of the contemporary explanations we have included under the heading of "New Directions."

One of the major points Chesney-Lind makes is that both commonsense notions and academic explanations of female deviance (and female delinquency in particular) are notoriously deficient. Most research has focused primarily on males, a pattern of neglect she finds "not all that unusual," since "All areas of social inquiry have been notoriously gender blind." Chesney-Lind points out that "theories developed to explain the misbehavior of working- or lower-class male youth fail to capture the full nature of delinquency in America; and, more to the point, are woefully inadequate when it comes to explaining female misbehavior and official reactions to girls' deviance." In her analysis, she finds that most theories of deviance fail to examine the full nature of delinquency in terms of who is involved and the sorts of offenses that are committed. In particular, they fail to consider whether explanations of deviance that focus on males can be extended to explain female deviance.

Neither academics, who have failed to pay much attention to female delinquency, nor the juvenile justice system, which has been obsessed with the presumed sexual nature of much female deviance, has carefully examined the relationship between sex roles and social structure. Theoretical models, justice policies, and research have generally failed to investigate how gender-specific socialization practices produce behavior patterns that operate differently on women and men. Chesney-Lind calls for more research that focuses specifically on the influence of the structure of modern society on the deviance of women. The feminist model of delinquency she proposes would focus on the effects of a patriarchal society, childhood abuse, poverty, and racism on both conforming and deviant behavior in females.

NOTE

1. Herb Haines, "Primum Non Nocere: Chemical Execution and the Limits Of Medical Social Control," *Social Problems*, 36, 5 (December 1989): 442–454.

31 *Biological Perspectives in Criminology*
DIANA H. FISHBEIN

Wilson and Herrnstein (1985) recently published a massive evaluation of the implications of biological data for topics of interest to criminolo-

Reprinted from Diana H. Fishbein, "Biological Perspectives in Criminology," *Criminology*, vol. 28, no. 1 (1990), pp. 27–72. By permission of the author and The American Society of Criminology.

I would like to express my appreciation for the editorial comments of Drs. C. Ray Jeffery, Derral Cheatwood, and Kathleen Block.

gists. Their message is that insufficient consideration has been given to biological and social interactions in criminological studies. Consistent observations that a small percentage of offenders are responsible for a preponderance of serious crime (Hamparin et al., 1978; Moffitt et al., 1989; Wolfgang, 1972) suggest that particular forces produce antisocial behavior in particular individuals. Further, much research shows that violent criminals have an early history of crime and aggression (Loeber and Dishion, 1983; Moffitt et al., 1989). The possibility that biological conditions may play a role in the development of antisocial and criminal behavior is accentuated by these reports and has spurred a search for biological markers in "vulnerable" subgroups (Mednick et al., 1987).

In the past, theories of the biological aspects of criminal behavior were marked by a general lack of knowledge regarding the human brain and by serious methodological shortcomings (see, e.g., Glueck and Glueck, 1956; Goddard, 1921; Hooten, 1939; Jacobs et al., 1965; Lombroso, 1918; Sheldon, 1949). Indeed, "biological criminology" was eventually discredited because its findings were largely unscientific, simplistic, and unicausal. Biological factors were globally rejected due to the inability of theorists to posit a rational explanation for the development of criminal behavior.

More recently, biological aspects of criminal behavior have been investigated by numerous behavioral scientists employing a multidisciplinary approach that promises to enhance substantially the rigor of the findings. Scientists in such fields as genetics, biochemistry, endocrinology, neuroscience, immunology, and psychophysiology have been intensively studying aspects of human behavior that are relevant to the criminologist and the criminal justice practitioner. Due to the highly technical and field-specific language of much of this research, findings generated from these works are not usually included in the literature reviews of criminologists. The relative lack of interdisciplinary communication has resulted in a lack of awareness of data pertinent to the study of crime and criminal behavior. This paper is a small step toward filling that gap.

The primary purpose of this paper is to present an overview of biological perspectives on the study of crime. Once acquainted with the parameters and findings of biological research, criminologists may begin to incorporate reliable biological aspects of criminal behavior into their theoretical and applied frameworks. Specific findings in biology are presented for criminologists to consider. Although the paper provides only an initial, condensed introduction to the vast amount of work accomplished in the behavioral sciences, it may help develop a sound, scientific, and pragmatic framework for future criminological research with a multidisciplinary orientation.

THEORETICAL AND METHODOLOGICAL PARAMETERS

Several critical issues must be addressed in order to (1) establish the relevancy of biology to the study of crime, (2) develop the groundwork for including biological data in criminological theories, (3) design research projects using compatible measurement instruments, data sets, and statistical techniques, and (4) determine the boundaries of practical applications of biological findings. These four requirements for multidisciplinary investigation in criminology are contingent on the assumptions and paradigm of the researcher, which have yet to be set forth adequately in the criminological literature. Pertinent issues include nature versus nurture, free will versus determinism, identifying relevant behavioral disorders and subject populations, assumptions and conceptual framework, and finally, methodological considerations. The discussion of these issues that follows may be opposed or modified by other criminologists with a biological orientation. This discussion is not intended as the last word, but rather as one of the first.

NATURE OR NURTURE?

The first issue that must be addressed before the parameters of biological research in criminology can be established is the age-old question of whether human behavior is a product of nature or nurture. Theoreticians of the past generally espoused one or the other viewpoint. Those who claim that nature contributes predominantly to an individual's behavior have been affiliated in the past with conservative political ideologies and were known as "hereditarians." In this circle, behavior was primarily attributed to inherited predispositions, and genetic influences were considered responsible for most of the variance in complex human behaviors.

The argument that nurture is the impetus for behavior was advocated by the "environmentalists," who were generally associated with a liberal ideology. Watson's (1925) interpretation of John Locke's *tabula rasa* (blank slate), for example, maintained that humans are born without predispositions to behave in any predetermined or predictable manner. Environmental inputs were considered primarily responsible for the final behavioral product, and manipulations of external inputs were thought to modify behavior.

These opposing views are reflected in past political and social movements, such as *radical behaviorism* and *social Darwinism,* many of which have had devastating social and scientific consequences. The concept of *predatory ethics,* couched in the possibility of the state's punitive sanctioning of "unacceptable" or merely predicted future behaviors, eventually contributed to a complete rejection of biological perspectives by many scientists and their sponsors. The threat of "control and oppression by science" was realized and feared.

Few behavioral scientists today adhere to either of these extreme views. A consensus has been emerging over the past 10 to 15 years that the "truth" lies somewhere in between—a "nature plus nurture" perspective (see Plomin, 1989). Although the nurture perspective has dominated fields such as criminology for the past few decades, substantial biological findings can no longer be ignored. Several studies on alcoholism, temperament, criminality, depression, and mental illness have established a solid role for genetic and biological influences (selected recent examples are detailed below). Even though behavioral scientists have yet to determine precisely the separate, relative contributions of biology and social learning to behavior, their findings are particularly relevant to the criminologist, who should play an instrumental role in their evaluation given the potential impact on policy.

Evidence for an interaction between nature and nurture comes from both animal and clinical studies, which demonstrates the strength and importance of the dynamic link between biological and acquired traits. One example of this interaction is that aggressive behavior in monkeys can be elicited by stimulating certain areas of the brain with implanted intracerebral electrodes (see Carlson, 1977:442–449). The final behavioral result depends on the hierarchical structure of the monkey colony. Dominant monkeys will exhibit aggressive behavior with electrical stimulation of the brain in the presence of a submissive monkey. The same monkeys will suppress aggressive behavior, on the other hand, if another dominant monkey is present. An example of this interaction in humans is illustrated by recent reports that gender differences in cognitive ability are decreasing (see Geary, 1989). Cognition, however, is fundamentally influenced by neural processes that operate during an individual's development (ontogeny). In an effort to explain changing trends in a seemingly immutable biological process, researchers are discovering that cultural and experiential conditions directly influence the developing pattern of cognitive abilities. For example, activity patterns (e.g., frequency of rough and tumble play) may alter cognitive ability (e.g., spatial skills) by modifying processes of brain development.

These illustrations remind us that as evidence for a substantial genetic influence grows we must be cautious not to replace environmental explanations with biological deterministic views. Instead, a more accommodating, balanced approach will carry more empirical weight.

FREE WILL OR DETERMINISM?

The acceptance of biological explanations for human behavior has been thought by many to preclude the possibility of free will. This fundamental fear has resulted in a pervasive rejection of biological contributions to behavior. Although some behavioral scientists are deterministic in their views, attributing behavior to everything from socioeconomic conditions to neurochemical events, most individuals prefer to credit their own free will for their behavior. A compromise reflecting a more accurate position on the forces behind human behavior is widely accepted, however—the theory of "conditional free will" (see Denno, 1988, for discussion of "degree determinism," a related view).

In probabilistic or stochastic theories, numerous causes or alternatives are presented to explain an effect. Each cause has a certain probability of resulting in that outcome, in some cases a measurable probability. Because it is rarely the case that an effect can be associated with only one cause, some dynamic interaction of causes, working in concert, is frequently responsible for the final result. In the assessment of human behavior, a most complex phenomenon, it is particularly difficult to separate those causes to assess their relative contributions.

In accordance with probability theory, social human behavior is contingent on a countless number of possible decisions from among which the individual may choose. Not all of those decisions are feasible, however, nor are the resources available that are required to act on them. Choosing a course of action, therefore, is limited by preset boundaries, which narrows the range of possibilities substantially. Decision-limiting factors include current circumstances and opportunities, learning experiences, physiological abilities, and genetic predispositions. Each one of these conditions collaborates internally (physically) and externally (environmentally) to produce a final action. The behavioral result is thus restricted to options available within these guidelines, yet it is "indeterminable" and cannot be precisely predicted. Stable individuals generally behave with some degree of expectability, however. In other words, certain patterns of behavior are a common individual characteristic, and some patterns are more probable than others in a given situation in a given individual.

The principle of conditional free will does not demand a deterministic view of human behavior. Rather, it postulates that individuals choose a course of action within a preset, yet to some degree changeable, range of possibilities and that, assuming the conditions are suitable for rational thought, we are accountable for our actions. Given "rational" thought processes, calculation of risks versus the benefits, and the ability to judge the realities that exist, the result is likely to be an adaptive response, that is, the behavior will be beneficial for the individual and the surrounding environment.

This theory of conditional free will predicts that if one or more conditions to which the individual is exposed are disturbed or irregular, the individual is more likely to choose a disturbed or irregular course of action. Thus, the risk of such a response increases as a function of the number of deleterious conditions. For example, a child with a learning disability may function well in society. With the addition of family instability, lack of appropriate educational programs, and a delinquent peer group, however, the learning-disabled child may be more prone to maladaptive behavior, which may, in turn, result in actions society has defined as criminal. The child's range of possible decisions has, in other words, been altered.

IDENTIFYING BEHAVIORS AND POPULATIONS FOR STUDY

Definitional issues are hotly debated among criminologists as a result of the growing recognition that not all "illegal" behaviors are dysfunctional or maladaptive and not all "legitimate" behaviors are moral, acceptable, or adaptive. In attempting to develop a framework for including biological perspectives in criminology, one must first identify behaviors of interest and appropriate subject populations.

The term *criminality* includes behaviors that do not necessarily offend all members of society, such as certain so-called victimless acts, and it excludes behaviors that may be antisocial or illegal but that are not detected by the criminal justice system. *Maladaptivity* includes antisocial behaviors that are costly to citizens and society overall. Such behaviors do not necessarily violate legal norms or come to official attention, however. Individuals who display maladaptive behavior do have a high probability of being labeled as delinquent or criminal, but being so labeled is not a sufficient criterion to be identified as maladaptive. For example, schizophrenics have abnormalities in brain structure and function that cause them to behave maladaptively; their behavior is poorly regulated, detrimental to their own well-being, and considered "deviant" by others. Nevertheless, they rarely manifest criminal tendencies. In the same vein, individuals who have been diagnosed as having antisocial personality disorder (American Psychiatric Association, 1987), a condition associated with several aberrant physiological traits (see Hare and Schalling, 1978; Howard, 1986; Yeudall et al., 1985), are more likely to violate legal norms given conducive social circumstances. Yet, there are numerous examples of individuals with antisocial personality disorder who find legal, albeit not always ethical, avenues for channeling their behavioral tendencies (e.g., some of those involved in competitive sports, high-risk activities, corporate life, and politics).

Criminal behavior is not exclusively maladaptive or dysfunctional behavior; thus, biological theories are differentially relevant to various forms of criminality. Biological findings in behavioral research are of particular interest for the study and management of maladaptive behaviors, both criminal and undetected behaviors that are detrimental to individuals so affected or their milieu. This paper focuses on maladaptive behaviors that may place an individual at risk for criminal stigmatization, in particular violent criminal behavior.

CONCEPTUAL FRAMEWORK

It is essential in this paper to provide a conceptual framework for eventually relating and integrating the concepts fundamental to criminology and behavioral biology. This task requires a model describing the underlying assumptions about human behavior generally, a theory of the etiological development of maladaptive behaviors specifically, and practical implications for the criminal justice system. Most important, this model of behavior must accommodate well-established theories in the social, psychological, and biological sciences. To this end, this section discusses the importance of the learning process, firmly entrenched in the theories of all three sciences, for the development of human behavior generally and maladaptive behavior specifically.

Individuals are not inherently criminal, nor do they suddenly become homicidal maniacs (except under unusual circumstances). Antisocial behavior has many precursors.[1] Manifestations of a problem are frequently observed in childhood when innate tendencies toward antisocial behavior or other risk factors are compounded by suboptimal environmental and social conditions (Denno, 1988; Lewis et al., 1979, 1985; Mednick et al., 1984). These early seeds of maladaptive behavior are commonly ignored, inappropriately treated, or not recognized as complications that warrant intervention. In such cases, the severity of the condition and resultant behaviors are well advanced by adolescence and adulthood. According to this "developmental course" model of human behavior, criminal behavior is virtually always secondary to an underlying problem(s), as illustrated in Figure 1.

One straightforward example of this process, which pervades the criminological literature, is the link between IQ or learning disabilities and delinquent/criminal behavior.[2] Children with conduct disorders tend to have lower IQ scores than nondeviant controls (Huesmann et al., 1984; Kellam et al., 1975; Lewis et al., 1981; Robins, 1966). Several investigators (Huesmann et al., 1984; Kellam et al., 1975; Olweus, 1979; Richman et al., 1982) have reported that an antecedent factor(s) contributes to both difficulties independently. Probable conditions that may antedate both low IQ and conduct disorder are parental psychopathology, temperamental disturbances, neurological problems, genetic susceptibilities, and disadvantageous environmental influences (Shonfeld et al., 1988). With a learning-disabled or conduct-disordered child, the existence of one or more of these deleterious conditions will increase the likelihood of further adjustment problems. Over time, behavioral difficulties become compounded and, to some extent, reinforced once the child has established mechanisms to protect himself or herself and cope with his or her liabilities. Thus, maladaptive behavior is a function of a cumulative, developmental process.

Although low IQ or a learning disability is not inherently criminogenic, in the absence of proper intervention the child may become frustrated attempting to pursue mainstream goals without the skills to achieve them. Kandel et al. (1988) demonstrated that juveniles with high IQ who were otherwise at high risk for criminal involvement due to their family environments resisted serious antisocial behavior. The researchers stated that their results could be interpreted according to Hirschi's (1969) social control theory. Specifically, students with a high IQ find school more rewarding and, consequently, bond more strongly to the conventional social order. Parents and school systems that are ill equipped to deal with a child suffering from a learning disability, on the other hand, may indirectly contribute to delinquency by removing the child from the classroom, thereby alienating him or her from friends and inculcating the belief that the child is "different," possibly even inadequate. Self-esteem is likely to decline dramatically, and the child may learn that there are rewards to be gained from interacting with others who experience similar frustrations. Thus, the child's behavior elicits a negative response from his or her environment, which leads to further reactions from the child (see Patterson et al., 1989). Consequently, the cycle of negatively interacting forces continues and the risk of becoming delinquent and eventually criminal is heightened.

FIGURE 1 Developmental Course Model (The Developmental Stages of Maladaptive Behavior)

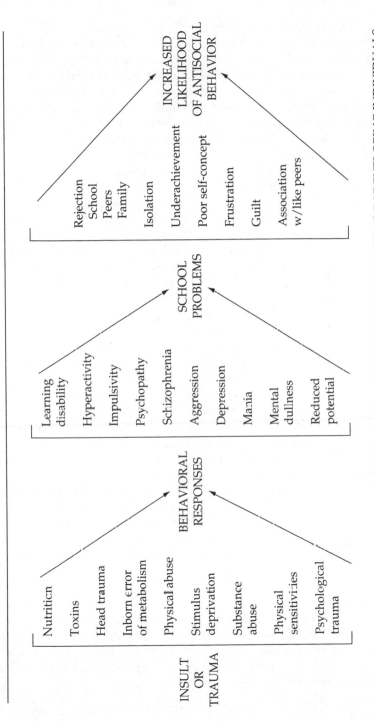

Once the individual attracts the attention of the criminal justice system, the problem is already significantly compounded and difficult to treat, and the costs to society are exorbitant. Evidence for the existence of a developmental phenomenon in antisocial behavior highlights the dire need for early detection and intervention. The earlier the intervention, the more favorable the outcome (Kadzin, 1987).

The learning process as it contributes to behavior cannot be underestimated in this model because, fundamentally, both biological and social behavior are learned. Biological traits and proclivities are not stationary characteristics; they are reinforced or, in some cases, altered through social learning processes. The tendency toward shyness or introversion, for example, is thought to be a stable biological and possibly heritable behavioral quality (see Kagan et al., 1988; Plomin and Daniels, 1986). Kagan et al. (1988) found that children who were extremely shy at the age of 1.5 to 2.5 years continued to be shy and restrained at the age of 7. The children who had moderate levels of shyness, however, did not necessarily retain that trait as they aged. Such temperamental traits may be reinforced by external rewards or expectations or may, on the other hand, be overcome by modeling. Thus, the actualization and longevity of this trait depend on environmental experiences or stressors, including hospitalization or family discord.

Humans are equipped with the innate biological capacity to learn as a product of their genetic blueprint, which is physically expressed in the structure of the brain. When an individual is exposed to a stimulus from the internal (biological) or external (social) environment, permanent changes occur in the neural structure and biochemical function of the brain. This process is referred to as "memory," experiences coded and stored for retrieval in the form of chemical transformations.

Bodily functions involved in memory are multifaceted. Sensation and perception are activities of stimuli reception. Attention and arousal prepare the individual to receive stimuli and react to them selectively. Motivational processes operate so that the individual attends to and later retrieves information. And motor systems permit a response to a memory or experience. When stimuli are received and remembered, all future behaviors are modified, and perception will be subsequently altered. Thus, humans interrelate current experiences with information previously learned, and the future response to an equivalent stimulus may be different. The integrity of each of the above activities determines whether the learning experience will result in accurately encoded memories to produce an appropriate behavioral response.

The learning process of comparing new information with memories to produce a response frequently results in "behavioral conditioning." There is an innate foundation for learning in our biological structure that sets contingencies for behavioral conditioning in an individual, consistent with the premise of conditional free will. Consequently, behavioral sequences are neither programmed nor innate; they are acquired. The two forms of behavioral conditioning, classical and instrumental, both directly involve biological mechanisms. Classical conditioning refers to the response elicited by a neutral stimulus that has been associated with the acquisition of a reward or the avoidance of harm; for example, a white laboratory coat is associated with food and elicits salivation or viewing drug paraphernalia elicits craving for a drug.

When an individual is instrumental in causing a stimulus to occur, operant or instrumental conditioning is at work. The stimulus being elicited either satiates a drive or permits one to avoid a noxious result. For example, if we learn that stealing results in a reward, the behavior will continue. On the other hand, if we are consistently punished for such behavior, we are unlikely to repeat the action. Thus, both forms of conditioning revolve around the same contingencies (biological dictates to avoid pain and seek pleasure, known as hedonism), which function to reinforce our behavior.

Certain behaviors are reinforced when the following conditions exist: (1) the behavior and the stimulus occur together in time and space (continuity), (2) repetition of the association strengthens the conditioned response, (3) the result either evokes pleasure or relieves pain, and (4) there is no interference, as in the form of new experiences, to weaken or extinguish the response. The concept of deterrence is founded on these principles.[3]

In general, the criminal justice system relies on the association made between specific, in this case illegal, behaviors and the application of a painful or punitive sanction, which generally involves the removal of certain freedoms and exposure to unpleasant living conditions. The painful stimulus must be temporally associated with the behavior, consistently applied, and intense enough to prevent further such behaviors. According to the fourth condition listed above, the individual must not learn that the intrinsic reward properties of the behavior are greater or more consistent than the punishment. And finally, opportunities for preferred modes of behavior must be available. Due to the prevalence of low clearance rates, trial delays, inconsistently applied dispositions, legal loopholes, the learning of improper reward and punishment contingencies, and a lack of available legitimate opportunities, the criminal justice system and society at large have been unable to meet the criteria set above for deterrence and prevention.

The experience of a painful consequence being associated with a behavior is encoded into memory, and when we calculate the consequences of performing that behavior in the future we are deterred by the possible negative response. The impetus for such behavioral change resides in our nervous system. We feel anxiety when the threat of a negative repercussion exists because of the learned association between the behavior and its likely consequence. Subjective feelings of anxiety are a result of autonomic nervous system responses (a portion of the nervous system that regulates functions not under our conscious control), such as increased heart rate, blood pressure, and hormone release. Thus, the brain initiates a release of hormones that stimulates a subjective feeling of stress whenever we contemplate a behavior that we have been effectively conditioned to avoid. Individuals with a properly functioning nervous system are quite effectively conditioned to avoid stressful situations given the learned contingencies discussed above. Most of us, for example, would experience psychological and physical discomfort at the thought of picking a pocket or burglarizing a convenience store. Thus, we make a rational choice based on a calculation of costs and benefits and, in this case, deterrence is most likely achieved.

The learning and conditioning of behavior occur differentially among individuals given their neurological status. For example, psychopaths are relatively unemotional, impulsive, immature, thrill-seeking, and "unconditionable" (Cleckley, 1964; Moffitt, 1983; Quay, 1965; Zuckerman, 1983). They have also been characterized as having low levels of perceptible anxiety and physiological responses during stressful events (Hare and Schalling, 1978; House and Milligan, 1976; Syndulko et al., 1975; Venables, 1987; Yeudall et al., 1985). Theoretically, psychopaths do not sufficiently experience the discomfort of anxiety associated with a proscribed behavior because they have a hypoaroused autonomic nervous system, and thus, they are not easily conditioned or deterred (Hare and Schalling, 1978; Lykken, 1957). They make a rational choice based on the calculation that the benefits of the act (e.g., monetary gain) outweigh the costs (e.g., anxiety and detection). Accordingly, one would expect that psychopaths encountered by the criminal justice system would be resistant to most deterrence programs.

Rewards and punishments influence behavior directly through brain mechanisms. Centers responsible for pain and pleasure are located in a section of the brain known as the limbic system. Not surprisingly, memories are encoded, stored, and retrieved in this same system. Direct electrical stimulation of certain areas within the limbic system (electrical stimulation of the brain, ESB) is inherently reinforcing, even in the absence of a biological or social drive (Olds and Milner, 1954). An animal quickly learns to perform for ESB due to its drive-inducing and intensely pleasurable effect. In humans, these areas are naturally stimulated when a behavior results in increases in specific neurotransmitters and peptides[4] responsible for either pleasure (i.e., dopamine) or the reduction of pain (i.e., serotonin or beta-endorphins). In large part, which chemicals are released and in which areas depend on both biological and social learning contingencies.[5]

This pain and pleasure mechanism is simply illustrated by the use of cocaine, which directly stimulates the release of dopamine in structures of the limbic system responsible for pleasure (Wise, 1984:15–33). The user quickly learns that cocaine is biologically rewarding, and, along with other reinforcing social circumstances associated with its use, he or she will be more likely to crave and reuse the drug. This is an example of both classical and instrumental conditioning. Other, more complicated, processes involving social learning or conditioning are also involved in the activation of pain and pleasure centers in the limbic system.

Imbalances of the limbic system may alter the proper stimulation of pain and pleasure centers. In schizophrenia, for example, the individual has disturbances in the ability to associate behaviors with a pleasurable outcome and behavior seemingly lacks purpose. It is believed that damage to neural reward structures has occurred (Stein and Wise, 1973). There is also evidence that some psychopaths experience intense pleasure from thrill-seeking or risk-taking activities and have a high pain threshold (Blackburn, 1978). Behaviors that involve an element of danger are not only exciting to these individuals, but they may be addictive in the conventional sense; they produce feelings of euphoria, and the participant may experience discomfort when unable to engage in such activities (Quay, 1965). The possibility that psychopaths have a disturbance in pain and pleasure centers is consistent with studies presented above showing that they have low levels of anxiety and are relatively "unconditionable." There is a large literature on the proneness of these individuals to become involved in delinquent and criminal activities (see Wilson and Herrnstein, 1985), again due to biological traits that are reinforced through social learning.

In sum, social behavior is learned through the principles of conditioning, which are founded on biological and genetic dictates in accord with stimulus-response relationships. Social rewards remain secondary to biological rewards; our desire for money is social, but it is secondary to being a means for obtaining food and shelter. Thus, social behavior satisfies biological needs and drives by providing adaptive mechanisms for reproduction, mating, rearing, defense, and numerous other biological functions. Even though these strategies are fundamentally biological, how we behave to satisfy them relies heavily on learning.

MEASUREMENT AND METHODOLOGICAL ISSUES

Research findings from various behavioral sciences that are relevant to the criminologist can be evaluated in the context of the parameters described above. The next section discusses selected studies that may have bearing on criminological research. A summary critique accompanies discussion of the studies. As a prelude to the discussion, this section examines some of the weaknesses common to such studies.

First, studies of incarcerated populations present obvious problems regarding the generalizability of findings in that any observed effect or correlation may be due to the effects of institutionalization rather than to the variable(s) of interest. Many studies that used institutionalized offenders as subjects did not attempt to measure or control for prison conditions and influences. Also, prisoners are a selective group, and thus their study does not include individuals outside that population with the trait of interest.

Second, many forms of bias in selecting subjects are evident in some studies. For example, several studies focus on criminal offenders and ignore pervasive illegal behaviors in undetected samples. There is a strong possibility that apprehended or incarcerated subjects differ from those who avoid detection in terms of their characteristics and the impact of criminal justice procedures.

Third, the use of control subjects is frequently neglected or inappropriate controls are examined. Unmatched controls or subjects with psychopathology (e.g., schizophrenics) are used all too often as comparison subjects.

Fourth, widely divergent conceptual and methodological principles are, at times, applied across studies, which makes it difficult to compare and replicate findings. Concepts such as psychopathy, antisocial personality, aggression, criminal behavior, and so on, are inconsistently defined and measured. Also, biological parameters are not uniformly identified, for example, electroencephalographic studies employ different measures of brain activity. Measurement instruments differ among studies and interpretations of findings are variable.

Fifth, several points of caution are particularly relevant to inter-pretation of studies of psychopathic subjects. The widespread use of self-report and retrospective data is problematic generally, but addi-tional problems arise when these data sources are used to examine of-fenders, a population notorious for falsifying records. Psychopaths, who are depicted as crafty deceivers, offer especially unreliable data. Yet, self-report measures are frequently used to select and categorize subjects. Not all criminals are psychopaths and vice versa. Moreover, psychological, behavioral, and physiological traits characterizing psy-chopathy occur along a continuum; psychopathy is not a binary phe-nomenon. Thus, both personality traits and actual behaviors must be carefully assessed before assigning subjects to groups. Last, the ter-minology used to describe individuals exhibiting psychopathic behav-ior is often inexact, confusing, and inconsistent (Blackburn, 1988). The literature suggests that psychopaths are not a homogeneous group (Eysenck, 1977; Hare and Schalling, 1978; Raine, 1988). At least two types of psychopaths have been identified that may be more or less prone to criminal activity: primary psychopaths, who are relatively unemotional, and secondary psychopaths, who have high levels of trait anxiety (Blackburn, 1986; Lykken, 1957). It is to be expected that psychopathy with and without anxiety will be characterized by quite distinct physiological generators and measurable features. Accord-ingly, reports of psychobiological differences between psychopaths and "normals" have disagreed depending on the definitions and se-lection criteria used (Devonshire et al., 1988).

Finally, of immediate importance, the majority of so-called multi-disciplinary studies have examined only a few variables in isolation, without accounting for interactive effects between biological and so-cioenvironmental conditions. A truly collaborative research project, examining an extensive data set and incorporating the sophisticated methodological and statistical techniques of sociologists, would hold the promise of yielding more informative results regarding the nature of bio-socio-environmental influences on antisocial behavior. (See Mednick et al., 1987, for detailed critiques of biological approaches to the study of criminal behavior.)

The discussion that follows concentrates on the biological aspects of this multifaceted relationship because the criminological literature has dealt almost exclusively with sociological and legal issues to the neglect of other interacting conditions. A variety of disciplines have examined maladaptive and psychopathological behaviors, and at least one example from each topical area (e.g., genetics and biology) is discussed.

SELECTED STUDIES OF THE BIOLOGY OF MALADAPTIVE BEHAVIOR

EVOLUTIONARY DICTATES

Human instinctual drives (e.g., eating, reproduction, and defensive behavior) ensure our survival and are essentially stable over time. The mechanisms for acting on these drives, however, especially the brain, continuously evolve to enhance our survival capabilities and have improved substantially. With the advent of human consciousness, psychological forces and cultural values interact and sometimes compete with biological drives dictated by evolutionary trends (Thiessen, 1976). Thus, human behavior is a product of the profound and complex interaction of biological and social conditions. Due to the intricacy of this interaction and the elusiveness of evolutionary directions, the nature and outcome of this process are difficult to identify and to study.

Most behaviors have some adaptive significance (i.e., they reflect an attempt to adapt to environmental conditions) and, thus, can be studied in an evolutionary context. Aggression is one form of behavior that has been extensively studied with respect to its adaptive significance. For example, "abnormal" environmental conditions have been associated with a display of extreme, overt aggression because they are perceived as threats to survival. The administration of an electrical shock or painful stimulus, loud noises, extreme heat, ESB, starvation, crowding, and other conditions elicit or exacerbate fighting behaviors in many primate species, including humans (Carlson, 1977; Thiessen, 1976; Valzelli, 1981). Abnormal environmental conditions characterize prisons and may contribute to the incidence of overt aggressive behavior among inmates; they may also partially explain the relationship between contacts with the criminal justice system (e.g., amount of time incarcerated) and recidivism rates. Also, the prevalence of abnormal environmental conditions has increased with the ever-increasing breakdown of the family structure, community disorganization, disparity between public policy and biological needs, crowding, learned helplessness, and other frequently cited characteristics of U.S. urbanization (Archer and Gartner, 1984:98–117; Larson, 1984:116–141). Investigation of how these deleterious conditions exacerbate maladaptive behavioral mechanisms may eventually lead to socioenvironmental programs to enhance, rather than detract from, adaptive capabilities.

Unfortunately, aggression has been inconsistently defined, and most studies of its evolution and adaptive significance have examined nonhuman animals, probably because of the complexity of human social systems that contribute to the manifestation of aggressive behavior. Due to space limitations and the relative lack of well-supported research in this area, a discussion of evolutionary dictates and aggressive behavior is not included here. The interested reader may refer to Thiessen (1976) and Valzelli (1981) for such discussion.

GENETIC CONTRIBUTIONS

Research on the genetic components of human behavior suffers in general from numerous methodological and interpretive flaws (Blehar et al., 1988; Clerget–Darpoux et al., 1986; DeFries and Plomin, 1978; Ghodsian–Carpey and Baker, 1987). It is difficult to isolate genetic factors from ontogenetic (developmental) events, cultural influences, early experiences, and housing conditions. As a result, most studies of human behavior have examined the transmission of socioenvironmental factors that can be more empirically observed and manipulated.

Genetic studies of criminal behavior specifically have been even more severely criticized (Mednick et al., 1987; Plomin et al., 1990; Rowe and Osgood, 1984; Walters and White, 1989; Wilson and Herrnstein, 1985). This research suffers from a high level of abstraction because "criminal behavior" is a legalistic label, not descriptive of actual behavior. This weakness is not unique to genetic research, however. Criminal behavior, as a single phenomenon, is far too variable and subject to individual and cultural judgments to be defined for reliable and valid investigation. Instead, research should be predicated on disaggregated behaviors that are reflective of actual acts that can be consistently and accurately measured and examined. Accordingly, genetic studies that focus on criminal behavior per se may be inherently flawed; as criminal behavior is heterogeneous, genetic effects may be more directly associated with particular traits that place individuals at risk for criminal labeling. Mednick et al. (1984) took a first step toward this goal by differentiating violent from property offenders. Concepts such as violent behavior, depression, alcoholism, and psychopathy more aptly reflect an actual behavioral pattern to which specific criteria for their identification can be applied (Plomin et al., 1990). Researchers need only agree on the criteria and measuring instruments.

As a rule, what is inherited is not a behavior; rather, it is the way in which an individual responds to the environment. It provides an orientation, predisposition, or tendency to behave in a certain fashion. Also, genetic influences on human behavior are polygenic—no single gene effect can be identified for most behaviors.

Intellectual deficits, which are closely tied to delinquent and criminal life-styles (Hirschi and Hindelang, 1977), are understood to be largely heritable (Bouchard and McGue, 1981; Cattell, 1982). Temperamental traits and personality types, possible precursors of maladaptive or criminal behavior, have also been shown to have heritable components in humans, for example, extraversion, depression, alcoholism, dominance, neuroticism, mania, impulsivity, hyperactivity, conduct disorder, sensation seeking, and hyperemotionality (Biederman et al., 1986; Cadoret et al., 1985; DeFries and Plomin, 1978; Ghodsian–Carpey and Baker, 1987; Plomin et al., 1990; Rushton et al., 1986). Individuals with such personality dispositions, compared with those without, have an increased familial incidence of similar behavioral problems and show differences, along with their family members, in certain biochemical, neuropsychological, and physiological parameters (Biederman et al., 1986; Cadoret et al., 1975; DeFries and Plomin, 1978; Hare and Schalling, 1978; Plomin et al., 1990; Rushton et al., 1986; Tarter et al., 1985; Zuckerman, 1983). The behavioral outcome is contingent on various stressors in the environment, life experiences, and current opportunities. A withdrawn and shy child, for instance, can alter his or her introverted temperament through the self-awareness and training required to become a more outgoing adult, given the availability of necessary personal and external resources.

Numerous studies have attempted to estimate the genetic contribution to the development of criminality, delinquency, aggression, and antisocial behavior. Each has used one of three methods designed to assess the relative contributions of environment and heredity to various aspects of human behavior: family, twin, and adoption studies. Overall, many of these behavioral genetic studies suffer from one or more of the methodological weaknesses discussed earlier. Genetic research designs and selected seminal studies are briefly described below. (Only a few researchers have comprehensively and critically reviewed the bulk of these studies; see Mednick et al., 1987; Plomin et al., 1990; Walters and White, 1989; Wilson and Herrnstein, 1985.)

Family Studies

The family study seeks to identify genetic influences on behavioral traits by evaluating similarities among family members. Cross-generational linkages have been reported for personality and behavioral attributes related to criminal behavior, including temper outbursts (Mattes and Fink, 1987), sociopathy (Cloninger et al., 1975, 1978; Guze et al., 1967), delinquency (Robins et al., 1975; Rowe, 1986), hyperactivity and attention deficit disorder (Cantwell, 1979), conduct disorder, aggression, violence, and psychopathy (Bach-y-Rita et al., 1971; Stewart et al., 1980; Stewart and DeBlois, 1983; Stewart and Leone, 1978; Twito and Stewart, 1982).

Despite conclusions from many of these studies that genetic effects are largely responsible for criminal behavior, this method of study does not directly assess genetic contributions. Environmental influences on measures of behavior may be common to parents and offspring, and thus, large environmental correlations among relatives cannot be accounted for. Diet, environmental toxins, neighborhood conditions, and television-viewing habits are only a few examples of environmental factors that similarly influence family members. Family studies also suffer from many of the weaknesses listed above. At this point, one may only conclude that the incidence of criminal and related behaviors appears to have a familial basis. The relative influences of genetics and environmental conditions cannot, however, be estimated.

Twin Studies

The classic twin design involves the testing of identical (monozygotic or MZ) and fraternal (dizygotic or DZ) twins. MZ twins share genetic material from the biologic parents and are thus considered genetically identical. DZ twins are approximately 50% genetically alike, as are regular siblings. The extent to which MZ resemblances with respect to a characteristic are greater than DZ resemblances provides evidence for a genetic influence on the variable. To the extent that there is still some degree of DZ resemblance after genetic influences have been accounted for, there is evidence for the influence of common family environment on the variable. For example, if a sample of MZ twins is 60% similar for IQ and a matched sample of DZ twins is 25% similar for IQ, one can conclude that IQ is largely a function of heredity.

Christiansen (1977b) reviewed nine twin studies on criminal behavior, including his own exemplary study (Christiansen, 1977a). Overall, the studies provide evidence for a genetics-environment interaction (see discussion in Wilson and Herrnstein, 1985). Dalgard and Kringler's (1976) findings were the exception. Although they found a trend, they did not find statistical significance for differences between MZ and DZ criminality. More current twin studies have found significant genetic effects for both self-report and official rates of delinquent or criminal behavior (Rowe, 1983; Rowe and Osgood, 1984) and personality or temperamental traits related to criminal behavior, for example, aggression (Ghodsian-Carpey and Baker, 1987;

Rowe, 1986; Rushton et al., 1986; Tellegen et al., 1988). Two additional studies did not find significant MZ–DZ differences in concordance rates for childhood aggression (Owen and Sines, 1970; Plomin et al., 1981). Plomin et al. (1990) examined numerous twin studies of criminal/delinquent behavior and aggression and noted that the results were highly inconsistent, possibly because no uniform measure of self-reported aggression and its constructs has been applied.

Twin studies commonly suffer from a number of unique methodological weaknesses (Plomin et al., 1980). First, MZ twins are selected more frequently due to their visibility, and study group sizes thus become disproportionate. Second, sampling techniques may favor the selection of MZ pairs that are similar in relevant behavioral traits, which biases the result. Third, MZ twins tend to share more similar environments than do DZ twins because of their similar appearance (DZ twins look no more alike than regular siblings). Because environmental assessments are not commonly conducted, such similarities cannot be estimated to determine their relative influence. In favor of the validity of the twin method, however, is evidence that physical and environmental similarities among MZ twins do not bias studies of personality (see DeFries and Plomin, 1978:480; Plomin and Daniels, 1987). Fourth, only recently have researchers employed biochemical tests to verify the zygosity of the twins. The bulk of genetic studies were performed prior to the ready availability of such tests, and thus, the genetic influence may have been underestimated. Fifth, measurement errors may further increase the tendency to underestimate genetic influences. On the other side of the coin, the twin method can only examine the level of genetic contribution over and above environmental influence. Thus, there is contamination from an unknown amount of environmental contribution and the influence of heredity may be overestimated.

No definitive conclusions can be drawn from twin studies of aggressiveness or criminal behavior because no consistent pattern of genetic influence emerges. Nevertheless, twin studies of criminal and related behaviors fairly consistently provide some intriguing evidence for a genetic effect, and genetic influences warrant continued, but more rigorous, study.

Adoption Studies

Adoption studies examine individuals who were raised from infancy by nonrelated adoptive parents rather than biological relatives. To the extent that subjects resemble the biological relatives and not the non-biologic relatives, heredity is thought to play a contributory role. The adoption study method promises to provide unambiguous evidence for the relative contribution of heredity as a cause for behavioral traits and for genetics-environment interactions. Nevertheless, the method has some weaknesses (see Walters and White, 1989, for examples). First, due to difficulties in locating subjects, sample sizes tend to be small, which reduces the power of the results. Second, selection bias may be introduced in the adoption process because assignment to adoptive parents may not be random with respect to biological parent characteristics. Third, a primary criticism of a majority of adoption studies on criminality is the inadequacy and inconsistency of the methods used to operationalize and measure the dependent variable (see Plomin et al., 1990; Walters and White, 1989). Fourth, researchers should ensure that the duration and type of biological parenting are similar among all subjects to avoid contamination. Ideally, infants should have been adopted within a few weeks of birth so that the age of adoption does not relate to subsequent criminal behavior (see Mednick, et al., 1984).

Several adoption studies indicate noteworthy genetic effects on criminal or delinquent behavior and related psychopathology (i.e., psychopathy).[6] For the most part, these studies suggest that biological relatives of criminal or antisocial probands have a greater history of criminal convictions or antisocial behavior than the biological relatives of noncriminal control adoptees. In general, family environment, including such indices as social class, rearing styles, and parental attitudes, played a smaller role than did purported genetic effects.

Bohman et al. (1982) further argue that genetic influences on criminality may differ from those who are also alcoholic. Specifically, when the biological parents are both criminal and alcoholic, crimes of adoptees tend to be more violent. There is no direct evidence, however, that criminality/antisocial personality and alcoholism are genetically linked to the same antecedent conditions. Nevertheless, the link between the two behaviors has been widely documented (see Cadoret et al., 1985).

Adoption studies highlight the importance of gene-environment interactional models (Rowe and Osgood, 1984). Mednick et al. (1984) proposed that having a criminal adoptive parent most profoundly affects those with a genetic propensity for criminality. In other words, those who inherited certain antisocial personality and temperamental traits are more likely to manifest criminal behaviors in the presence of deleterious environmental conditions (e.g., criminal parents). Even though these conditions interact to produce antisocial behavior, many researchers attest that environmental and genetic factors differentially influence behavior and that their relative contributions may be measurable (see Plomin et al., 1990).[7]

BIOLOGICAL CONTRIBUTIONS

Genetic foundations for behavioral disorders are manifested in a phenotype, which is the resulting, visible expression of a genetic trait. For example, one may have the genetic blueprint (or genotype) for brown and blue eyes, but the final, observable eye color (the phenotype) is brown. Although researchers can rarely trace a behavioral disorder to a specific gene, they can more aptly measure the manifestation of a genetic blueprint in nervous system features. Other biological traits associated with behavioral problems are not directly genetic in origin; they may be due to mutations in a genetic constitution, biochemical exposures, or a deleterious social environment. All of these conditions, from the genetic to the environmentally precipitated, exert their influence on the nervous system and, thus, can be measured and manipulated. The following correlates of behavioral disorders illustrate selected ways in which genetic and environmental factors impact on the nervous system to alter behavior.

Biochemical Correlates

A number of biochemical differences have been found between controls and individuals with psychopathy, antisocial personality, violent behavior, conduct disorder, and other behaviors associated with criminal behavior. These groups have been discriminated on the basis of levels of certain hormones, neurotransmitters, peptides, toxins, and metabolic processes (Brown et al., 1979; Davis et al., 1983; Eichelman and Thoa, 1972; Mednick et al., 1987; Rogeness et al., 1987; Roy et al., 1986; Valzelli, 1981; Virkkunen and Narvanen, 1987).

Current investigations of biochemical mechanisms of aggressiveness focus on the study of central neurotransmitter systems. Observations from animal and human studies, for example, indicate that serotonin, a neurotransmitter, globally inhibits behavioral responses to emotional stimuli and modulates aggression (Muhlbauer, 1985; Soubrie, 1986; van Praag et al., 1987). Several indicators of lower levels of serotonin activity in individuals characterized as violent or impulsive, in comparison with those who are not, have been reported (Brown et al., 1979; Fishbein et al., 1989; Linnoila et al., 1983; Virkkunen et al., 1987, 1989). These studies indicate that serotonin functioning is altered in some types of human aggressiveness and violent suicidal behavior. Thus, a decrease in serotonergic activity may produce disinhibition in both brain mechanisms and behavior and result in increased aggressiveness or impulsivity.

Findings of reduced serotonergic activity among individuals with impulsivity and aggressivity are well supported by behavioral and personality studies of animals and humans. Nevertheless, this research is relatively new to the area of antisocial behavior and frequently suffers from theoretical and methodological inadequacies (see Soubrie, 1986). First, categorizing subjects according to their behavioral attributes has been inconsistent across studies, and group assignment within studies is, in some cases, controversial. Second, because aggression is not a unitary phenomenon it is important to determine whether serotonergic activity levels are specific to types of aggression or whether they globally regulate aggression. Third, psychopathy or antisocial personality is frequently used to describe subjects without respect to the presence of trait anxiety (see above), which is known to involve serotonergic systems (Soubrie, 1986). This confusion may produce findings that are inconsistent and lack functional significance (van Praag et al., 1987). And fourth, serotonergic activity is all too often studied in isolation of other interacting biological systems. Thus, these studies have not been able to identify precisely the neural mechanisms for regulating aggression. They do, nevertheless, bring us closer to identifying neurobiological mechanisms for aggression, impulsivity, and antisocial behavior.

There is a noticeable absence of research on female criminality in general, and reports that do exist are largely sociological or anecdotal. Widom (1978) wrote that biological factors contributing to individual differences in temperament, arousal, or vulnerability to stress may be important in the etiology of female criminal behavior. Different socioenvironmental influences may differentially interact with biological sex differences to produce variations in male and female criminality (see, e.g., L. Ellis and Ames, 1987).

There is evidence that high levels of the male sex hormone testosterone may influence aggressive behavior in males (Kreuz and Rose, 1971; Olweus et al., 1988; Reda et al., 1983; Schiavi et al., 1984), although discrepant studies exist (Coe and Levine, 1983). It has been further suggested that sex hormones may also contribute to antisocial behavior in some women. The premenstrual period in particular has been associated with elevated levels of aggressivity and irritability. This phase of the hormonal cycle is marked by an imbalance in the estrogen-progesterone ratio, which may trigger both physical and psychological impairments in a subgroup of women. Sharp changes in mood, depression, irritability, aggression, difficulty in concentration,

and substance abuse are only a few behavioral disturbances that typify premenstruation in affected women (Haskett, 1987; Trunnell and
Turner, 1988).

A significant number of females imprisoned for aggressive criminal
acts were found to have committed their crimes during the premenstrual phase, and female offenders were found to be more irritable and
aggressive during this period (Cooke, 1945; Dalton, 1964, 1966; D. Ellis
and Austin, 1971; Morton et al., 1953; see D'Orban and Dalton, 1980,
and Epps, 1962, for negative findings). Overall, most of these studies
have been criticized for serious methodological shortcomings (see
Harry and Balcer, 1987). Nevertheless, there remains a general impression among investigators and clinicians that a small number of women
appear to be vulnerable to cyclical changes in hormonal levels, which
causes them to be more prone to increased levels of anxiety and hostility during the premenstrual phase (Carroll and Steiner, 1987; Clare,
1985). Ginsburg and Carter (1987) provide a thorough discussion of the
controversy about premenstrual syndrome, including evidence for its
existence, its association with behavioral disorders, and the legal, social, and biomedical implications. Because premenstrual syndrome is
difficult to diagnose and its etiology is still under investigation, an association between the menstrual cycle and female criminal behavior is too
remote and indirect to be conclusive at this time.

Exposure to toxic trace elements is yet another factor that has been
shown to interfere with brain function and behavior. Chronic or acute
exposure to lead, for example, has a deleterious effect on brain function by damaging organ systems, impairing intellectual development,
and subsequently interfering with the regulation of behavior. Sources
of lead include our diet and environment (e.g., paint chips and house
dust), and contamination among children may be serious and grossly
underestimated (Bryce-Smith and Waldron, 1974; Moore and Fleischman, 1975). Resulting impairments may be manifested as learning disabilities and cognitive deficits, particularly in measures of school
achievement, verbal and performance IQ, and mental dullness (see
Benignus et al., 1981; Lester and Fishbein, 1987; Pihl and Parkes,
1977). Because of the high correlation among school failure, learning
disabilities, and delinquency, lead intoxication is a relevant criminological issue.

A growing body of research has further demonstrated that lead
intoxication is significantly associated with hyperactivity and impulsivity (David et al., 1972; Needleman et al., 1979), putative precursors
to delinquency, and criminal behavior (Denno, 1988). Following chelation (removal) of lead from the body, David et al. (1976) found behav-

ioral improvements among hyperactive children. Pihl et al. (1982) reported that violent subjects had significantly elevated concentrations of lead compared with nonviolent criminals. They further suggest that subtoxic levels of lead have a potential effect on behavior and that lead detection can be an important diagnostic procedure. Children who are at risk for exposure to lead also tend to have poor diets, that is, diets low in calcium and iron, which help to protect the body from lead's effects. Many of these studies lack proper control groups and double blind procedures, yet accumulating evidence strongly suggests that, given other deleterious socioenvironmental conditions, an individual exposed to lead is more likely to manifest maladaptive behavior (see Rimland and Larson, 1983, for a review of studies).

Psychophysiological Correlates

Psychophysiological variables, for example, heart rate, blood pressure, attention and arousal levels, skin conductance, brain waves, and hormone levels, are quantifiable indices of nervous system function. These measurable conditions directly reflect emotional responses and can be experimentally manipulated in human populations.

Studies of criminal behavior, aggression, and psychopathy have repeatedly found psychophysiological evidence for mental abnormality and central nervous system disturbances as putative markers for criminal behavior. For example, psychopaths have been found to differ from nonpsychopathic controls in several physiological parameters. These indices include (a) electroencephalogram (EEG) differences, (b) cognitive and neuropsychological impairment, and (c) electrodermal, cardiovascular, and other nervous system measures.[8]

In particular, psychopathic individuals have been found to show relatively more slow wave activity in their spontaneous (that is, when resting with no provocation) EEG compared with controls, which may be related to differences in cognitive abilities (Hare, 1970; Howard, 1984; Pincus and Tucker, 1974; Syndulko, 1978). Some investigators have suggested that relatively high levels of EEG slowing in psychopathic subjects reflect a maturational lag in brain function (Kiloh et al., 1972; Pontius and Ruttiger, 1976). Thus, EEG slowing among individuals who also demonstrate immature behavior and an inability to learn from experience supports a maturational lag hypothesis. It may be suggested that EEG slowing among some psychopaths is consistent with findings of hypoaroused autonomic function (see above) and other differences in psychophysiologic parameters. Their need for external stimulation may be higher and more difficult to satisfy than in other populations due to a lower level of internal stimulation.

Psychopharmacological Inducements

Psychopharmacology is the study of the psychological and behavioral aspects of drug effects on brain metabolism and activity. Aggression, for example, can be elicited or extinguished by the administration of a pharmacologic agent. In fact, the pharmacologic treatment of aggressive and violent behavior has become increasingly popular and its efficacy in many cases has been demonstrated (Kuperman and Stewart, 1987; Lion, 1974, 1979; Yudofsky et al., 1987). Certain drugs, particularly many of the illicit drugs, are reported to increase aggressive responses, for example, amphetamines, cocaine, alcohol, and phencyclidine (PCP). The actual expression of aggressive behavior depends on the dose, route of administration, genetic factors, and type of aggression.

Several biological mechanisms have been proposed as explanations for alcohol-induced aggression: (1) pathological intoxication, sometimes involving psychomotor epilepsy or temporal lobe disturbance (Bach-y-Rita et al., 1970; Maletsky, 1976; Marinacci, 1963); (2) hypoglycemic reactions (low blood sugar; Cohen, 1980; Coid, 1979; Wallgren and Barry, 1970); and (3) alterations in neurotransmitter activity (Weingartner et al., 1983). These explanations do not completely account for the relationship, however, because most drinkers do not become aggressive. Indications are that alcohol either changes the psychological state or the psychological state has an effect on the behavioral outcome of alcohol consumption. In the second scenario, alcohol would stimulate an existing psychiatric condition or psychological predisposition to aggress or misbehave (Pihl and Ross, 1987). Hence, alcohol does not appear to "cause" aggression, but rather permits its expression under specific circumstances and biological conditions.

Chronic use of PCP, an illicit drug that is commonly used in combination with marijuana, has been repeatedly associated with extreme violence to self and others in individuals both with and without histories of violent behavior (Aronow et al., 1980; Fauman and Fauman, 1980; Linder et al., 1981; Schuckit and Morrissey, 1978; Seigal, 1978; Smith and Wesson, 1980). Violent reactions appear, according to some anecdotal reports, to be an extension of PCP toxic psychosis, which affects some users (Fauman and Fauman, 1980). Because only a subpopulation of users manifest violent behavior and some studies (e.g., Khajawall et al., 1982) did not find a relationship between PCP use and violence, additional research is needed to (1) determine whether PCP reliably elicits aggressive behavior among vulnerable users, (2) identify underlying mechanisms in PCP-induced aggression, and (3) determine the nature of the vulnerability that causes certain individuals to be particularly susceptible to that behavioral effect.

Investigators recognize that PCP effects result from a complex interaction among physical, psychological, and sociocultural variables (Smith and Wesson, 1980). PCP-related aggression may be due to influences on hormonal and neurotransmitter activity (Domino, 1978, 1980; Marrs-Simon et al., 1988). Also, neuropsychological impairments have been observed that minimally reflect a temporary organic brain syndrome (Cohen, 1977; Smith and Wesson, 1980). Additional studies of PCP users indicate that specific factors in the user's background, personality, and drug history are important determinants of the drug-related experience (Fauman and Fauman, 1980; McCardle and Fishbein, 1989). As a whole, these observations suggest that the consequences of PCP use, independent of the drug's purity and varying strengths, are determined by a number of factors, including pharmacological, psychological, and situational.

"Vulnerability" studies suggest that certain personality types may be more at risk for drug abuse than other types (Brook et al., 1985; Deykin et al., 1986; Kellam et al., 1980; McCardle and Fishbein, 1989). This does not mean, however, that these individuals will inevitably become drug abusers due to a natural predisposition. More recent studies provide evidence for the substantial contribution of family support systems in the final determination of whether an individual with a vulnerable personality type will, in fact, abuse drugs (Tarter et al., 1985:346–347). The dynamic interaction between natural and acquired traits in a given environment must always be considered inseparable in the evaluation of such complex phenomenon as human behavior.

IMPLICATIONS FOR CRIMINAL JUSTICE PRACTICES

In order to determine the relevance and significance of biological perspectives for criminology, researchers must estimate the incidence of biological disorders among maladaptive populations, identify etiologic mechanisms, assess the dynamic interaction among biological and socioenvironmental factors, and determine whether improvements in behavior follow large-scale therapeutic manipulations.

At this stage of scientific inquiry in the biological sciences, researchers have yet to determine the significance of biological disorders in criminal populations. Nor are they able to speak of a causal link between biological abnormalities and specific behavioral disorders. They are beginning to identify putative correlates or markers of antisocial behavior using biological tests (e.g., EEG slowing, body lead burden, neurotransmitter imbalance). Some of those correlations may prove to be spurious, but at present, which ones cannot be identified. Seen in this light, it would be premature to apply biological findings routinely to criminal justice procedures. Demands for evaluation of causal relationships are made in decisions regarding the granting of bail, release on personal recognizance, competency, guilty pleas, sentencing options, probation and parole, and proclivity to recidivate. Conclusions and prognoses regarding the role of biological factors in an offender's behavior, however, are not definitive at this time, regardless of the informational source.

To further establish the relevance of biology to criminology, researchers must demonstrate the ability to predict antisocial behavior reliably using a combination of biological and social variables. The central question thus becomes, can more of the variance in the incidence of antisocial behavior be explained with an integrated approach than with a unidisciplinary perspective? Many mental health professionals and researchers have reached a tentative consensus that predicting antisocial behavior with social or legal variables is inherently unreliable (Cocozza and Steadman, 1974; Gottfredson, 1986; Monahan, 1981; Wenk et al., 1972). Is it possible that prediction studies incorporating biological measures into sociological data bases will facilitate the isolation of significant predictors of antisocial behavior and enhance explanatory power?

In the introduction of Brizer and Crowner's recent text (1989) on the prediction of violence, Brizer aptly notes that the actual study of predictive ability suffers from methodological limitations, and thus, one cannot conclude that valid prediction is impossible. Studies reviewed in their text indicate that the inclusion of biological variables (e.g., integrity of central nervous system function) may, indeed, enhance predictive ability if dispositional (temperament and other features considered "innate") and situational factors are considered as interacting forces. In a separate study illustrative of this approach, Virkkunen et al. (1989) examined a selected set of behavioral and psychobiological variables to identify predictors of recidivism in a sample of violent offenders and arsonists. Their results suggested that recidivism is best predicted using a combination of behavioral and psychobiological variables, rather than with behavioral variables alone.

Denno (1988) conducted a fairly comprehensive study of the effects of numerous environmental and biological variables on criminal behavior, juvenile delinquency, and disciplinary problems. The model was able to predict 25% of future adult criminality among males and 19% of future adult criminality among females. Denno drew the following conclusions:

> Biological and environmental variables exert strong and independent influences on juvenile crime. . .[and] crime appears to be directly related to familial instability and, most important, a lack of behavioral control associated with neurological and central nervous system disorders (p. 659).

She cautions, however, that behavior should be predicted in terms of a series of probabilities of expected behavior, not in terms of cause and effect. Perhaps an approach that neither neglects nor places undue emphasis on socioenvironmental or biological features of behavior provides considerable promise as the direction of future research into practical problems in criminology.

The final stage of scientific inquiry requires that researchers be able to manipulate and control antisocial behavior, in this context with biological variables. Reliable behavioral changes attributable to biological treatments have yet to be demonstrated in this field, however. Biological intervention studies and programs render mixed and controvertible results, which indicate that the biology of antisocial behavior is under preliminary stages of investigation and requires further study before it can be applied to criminal justice practices. One particularly visible example of the controversial application of biological data is the pharmacologic treatment of sex offenders. Antiandrogen agents (e.g., Depo-Provera), which compete with male hormones believed to be responsible for sexual deviance, are administered in some clinics to suppress sex drive and, consequently, sex offending. Some research indicates that this approach has been moderately successful (Berlin, 1983; Berlin and Meinecke, 1981; Bradford, 1983; Cordoba and Chapel, 1983; Murray, 1987; Spodak et al., 1978). Others, however, criticize the approach because of (1) the equivocal findings that provide empirical support, (2) the fact that the behaviors resurface when the drug is discontinued, (3) its strictly experimental nature, (4) the issue of forced compliance, and (5) evidence that only nonviolent sex offenders respond to antiandrogen treatment (see Demsky, 1984). Such biological management techniques require further scientific support and, even more important, time for the legal system to become acquainted with their premises in order to establish appropriate guidelines.

It is perhaps unreasonable to expect dramatic behavioral improvements following a biological treatment, even when a disorder has been properly diagnosed. One of the central tenets of this paper is that behavior is a result of a dynamic interaction among many diverse social and biological conditions. The appropriate administration of a medication or other treatment may certainly be warranted for some individuals with identifiable pathology. However, this approach undermines the proposal that multiple factors are responsible for behavior. One cannot manipulate biological variables and expect behavior to change without attending to other interacting contributions. Once an individual has entered the criminal justice system, behavioral problems are substantially compounded and the treatment of only one condition does not yield adequate therapeutic results.

Findings of biological involvement in antisocial behavior have, in a few studies (e.g., Lewis et al., 1979, 1981, 1985, 1986, 1988), disclosed measurable abnormalities, but in a number of studies, measurements do not reach pathologic levels. In other words, many studies show group differences between violent and nonviolent subjects, but the biological values do not necessarily exceed normal limits and would not alarm a practicing physician. Findings of this type do not have intrinsic clinical significance, and they indicate that individual intervention programs should not be globally implemented based on current information.

Nevertheless, at the very least, the inclusion of biological measures holds promise of explaining individual variation within a social context. Why is it, for example, that not all children exposed to child abuse become violent as adults? Research into individual differences may be interpreted to suggest that whether child abuse contributes to violent behavior partially depends on the presence of brain damage or other central nervous system disorder (Lewis et al., 1979). Perhaps abused children without concomitant or resultant brain damage would be less aggressive and more in control of their impulses. Research yet to be conducted may also show that individuals with biological "disadvantages" respond with more violent or criminal behavior in a criminogenic environment than those equipped with biological "insulators," for example, high intelligence or adequate serotonergic activity.

Statistically significant findings generated to date show biological involvement in antisocial behavior only with respect to populations. Thus, society is closer to enacting prevention programs aimed at populations who are at risk for exposure to biological and socioenvironmental hazards that are known to increase the incidence of behavioral problems. Factors that may prove to be important contributors to relevant behavioral disorders (e.g., toxic element concentrations, child abuse/neglect, poor prenatal care, neurological impairments, substance abuse, and learning disabilities) could subsequently be manipulated on a wide scale to prevent the onset of behavioral or forensic disorders in the general population. Early detection programs could be implemented by school systems, and parents could be educated to recognize signs of an impairment. Screening clinics, regulating environmental toxins, school programs, prenatal care facilities, and public educational programs are only a few of the preventative measures possible. The number of "risk" factors could, in essence, be reduced or minimized.

An excellent example of this strategy was suggested by Moffitt et al. (1989) in their review of minor physical anomalies (MPAs), that is, observable minor malformations that result from a disturbance in fetal development. MPAs are thought to be indicators of other hidden anomalies, such as central nervous system impairment, that may result from some perinatal trauma (e.g., illness, poor diet, drug use, stress). Further, a relatively large number of MPAs have been observed among hyperactive and criminally violent populations. Obviously, there is no acceptable mode of individual remediation in such cases, particularly because of the remote association of MPAs with behavior. These consistent observations, however, emphasize the need for a global effort to provide proper prenatal care. Consequently, society can hope to reduce the incidence of developmental deficits related to the onset of behavioral disorders by recognizing their possible influence.

CLOSING COMMENTS

How biological variables interact with social and psychological factors to produce human behavior generally and antisocial behavior specifically is unknown. The bulk of biological studies, both those described herein and others not included, have examined only a few isolated variables and have generally failed to evaluate dynamic interrelationships among biological and socioenvironmental conditions (see Denno, 1988, and Wilson and Herrnstein, 1985, for detailed critiques). In order to evaluate the relative significance of biological contributions to antisocial behavior, sophisticated, statistical techniques (i.e., structural equation models) must be applied to multivariate designs that use rigorous measurement instruments. Studies of biological influence would benefit greatly from adopting the methodological and statistical techniques of sociologists to increase the rigor and relevance of the findings.

Caution against the premature application of biological findings is clearly called for. The weaknesses in design, sampling techniques, and statistical procedures delineated above preclude drawing definitive conclusions, and results are frequently contested and unreliable. Policies and programs based on equivocal and controversial findings waste time and money and potentially compromise individual rights and community safety. A number of legal, ethical, and political obstacles to the acceptance and application of biological and medical information by the criminal justice system are covered extensively elsewhere (Fishbein and Thatcher, in press; Jeffery, 1985; Marsh and Katz, 1985). At the very least, care must be taken not to stigmatize or otherwise traumatize individuals or groups that are, as yet, innocent of a criminal or civil violation. As researchers, we must avoid applying labels to behaviors we do not understand. In the event that biological measures are shown to be reliable and valid predictors of behavior and mental status, several serious civil rights and constitutional issues related to early identification and intervention in the absence of a proven violation of law would demand careful consideration. In cases in which a conviction is upheld, for example, forced compliance with a "therapeutic regimen" might result from findings that a biological abnormality played a role in an individual's antisocial behavior. One must recognize the numerous legal and ethical concerns generated by such a strategy. To avoid these transgressions, a collaborative, multidisciplinary approach might be forged strictly to identify the underlying sources of antisocial behaviors and minimize their occurrence in the population.

Overall, evidence to suggest that biological conditions have a profound impact on the adaptive, cognitive, and emotional abilities of the individual is compelling. Investigation of the discriminants for behavioral dysfunctions indicates that the impact of these factors is substantial. When a biological disadvantage is present due to genetic influences or when a physical trauma occurs during developmental stages of childhood, the resultant deficit may be compounded over time and drastically interfere with behavioral functions throughout life. Such conditions appear to place an individual at high risk for persistent problematic behavior. Disturbances associated with poor environmental and social conditions coupled with impaired brain function may eventually be amenable to intervention. The unfortunate reality for those who come into contact with the courts by virtue of their dysfunction, however, is that the underlying causes of their disorder are inaccurately evaluated or simply unattended. The capability to identify and predict the factors responsible for maladaptivity may eventually enable society to employ innovative methods of early detection, prevention, remediation, and evaluation.

Criminal justice policies must be based on well-founded theories and findings that survive scientific scrutiny. The application of scientific principles or findings to criminal justice programs that are well recognized and accepted by the discipline have more value than trial-and-error approaches in preventing or minimizing the onset of criminal behavior. Although biological techniques in the assessment of human behavior are still under the microscope and definitive answers have yet to surface, the foregoing description of biological foundations for behavior provides evidence of their applicability and value. The study of biological drives may also help to explain the development of specific social structures and control mechanisms (Jeffery, 1977; Pugh, 1977; Thiessen, 1976). Biological perspectives, for example, may enhance understanding of how certain control techniques employed throughout the criminal justice system, particularly in corrections, operate to further criminal activities through prisonization, crowding, dehumanization, and so forth. Use of this information in court or in policymaking can still be contested. Nevertheless, by undertaking a collaborative strategy, researchers can hope to develop more effective programs to reduce the incidence of antisocial behaviors (e.g., violence) and develop a legal system that reflects public consensus, meets human needs, and maintains an ethical and organized social structure.

NOTES

1. Antisocial children have a high incidence of adjustment problems, for example, low academic achievement, temper tantrums, conduct disorders, and negative attitudes (see Patterson et al., 1989, for a summary review).
2. See Critchley (1968), Hirschi and Hindelang (1977), McGee et al. (1986), McManus et al. (1985), Perlmutter (1987), Poremba (1975), Robins (1966), Shonfeld et al. (1988), Wolff et al. (1982).
3. Moffitt (1983) provides an excellent overview of the learning process in the suppression of punished behaviors as dictated by external and internal contingencies, e.g., cognitive abilities of the individual. Although Moffitt appropriately cautions against the uncritical application of the experimental model of punishment (procedures to manipulate behavior in a laboratory setting) to the process of punishing juvenile offenders, she discusses how the data may be used in constructing more effective deterrence programs.
4. Neurotransmitters and neuropeptides are chemical messengers in the brain that enable brain cells to communicate with each other and other structures.

5. See Gove and Wilmoth, in press, for a discussion of neurological processes that reinforce behavior. The authors suggest that risky and dangerous criminal behaviors stimulate neurological systems that act as positive reinforcers for continuing those forms of dangerous or criminal behaviors. A learning theory of behavior based on biological reward systems is presented.

6. For the former see Cloninger et al. (1982), Crowe (1972), Hutchings and Mednick (1975), Mednick et al. (1984), Sigvardsson et al. (1982); for the latter see Cadoret (1978), Cadoret et al. (1985), Crowe (1974), Schulsinger (1985).

7. Plomin and Daniels (1987) provide convincing evidence that genetic influences may explain within-family resemblances and that environmental influences more aptly explain within-family differences.

8. For (a), see Hill and Watterson (1942), Howard (1984), Mednick et al. (1981), Syndulko et al. (1975), Volavka (1987), Yeudall et al. (1985); for (b), see Bryant et al. (1984), Hurwitz et al. (1972), Jutai and Hare (1983), Lewis et al. (1985, 1986, 1988), Pontius and Yudowitz (1980), Raine and Venables (1987), Sutker and Allain (1987); and for (c), see Allen et al. (1971), Hare (1978), House and Milligan (1976), Lykken (1957), Mednick et al. (1982), Waid et al. (1979).

REFERENCES

Allen, H., L. Lewis, H. Goldman, and S. Dinitz
   1971   Hostile and simple sociopaths: An empirical typology. Criminology 9(1)27–47.

American Psychological Association
   1987   Diagnostic and Statistical Manual of Mental Disorders. 3rd ed., rev. (DSM-III-R). Washington, D.C.: American Psychological Association.

Archer, D. and R. Gartner
   1984   Violence and Crime in Cross-National Perspective. New Haven: Yale University Press.

Aronow, R., J.N. Miceli, and A.K. Done
   1980   A therapeutic approach to the acutely overdosed patient. Journal of Psychedelic Drugs 12:259–268.

Bach-y-Rita, G., J.R. Lion, and F.R. Ervin
   1970   Pathological intoxication. Clinical and electroencephalographic studies. American Journal of Psychiatry 127:698–703.

Bach-y-Rita, G., J.R. Lion, C.E. Climent, and F.R. Ervin
   1971   Episodic dyscontrol: A study of 130 violent patients. American Journal of Psychiatry 127:1473–1478.

Benignus, V.A., D.A. Otto, K.E. Muller, and K.J. Seiple
1981   Effects of age and body lead burden on CNS function in young
         children. II: EEG spectra. Electroencephalography and Clinical
         Neurophysiology 52:240–248.

Berlin, F.S.
1983   Sex offenders: A biomedical perspective and a status report on
         biomedical treatment. In J.G. Greer and I.R. Stuart (eds.), The
         Sexual Aggressor: Current Perspectives on Treatment. New York:
         Van Nostrand Reinhold.

Berlin, F.S. and C.F. Meinecke
1981   Treatment of sex offenders with antiandrogenic medication: Con-
         ceptualization, review of treatment modalities, and preliminary
         findings. American Journal of Psychiatry 138:601–607.

Biederman, J., K. Munir, D. Knee, W. Habelow, M. Armentano, S. Autor,
S.K. Hoge, and C. Waternaux
1986   A family study of patients with attention deficit disorder and
         normal controls. Journal of Psychiatric Research 20(4):263–274.

Blackburn, R.
1978   Psychopathy, arousal and the need for stimulation. In R.D. Hare
         and D. Schalling (eds.), Psychopathic Behaviour: Approaches to
         Research. Chichester, England: John Wiley & Sons.
1986   Patterns of personality deviation among violent offenders: Repli-
         cation and extension of an empirical taxonomy. British Journal of
         Criminology 26:254–269.
1988   On moral judgements and personality disorders: The myth of
         psychopathic personality revisited. British Journal of Psychiatry
         153:505–512.

Blehar, M.C., M.M. Weissman, E.S. Gershon, and R.M.A. Hirschfeld
1988   Family and genetic studies of affective disorders. Archives of
         General Psychiatry 45:289–292.

Bohman, M., C.R. Cloninger, S. Sigvardsson, and A.-L. von Knorring
1982   Predisposition to petty criminality in Swedish adoptees:
         I. Genetic and environmental heterogeneity. Archives of
         General Psychiatry 41:872–878.

Bouchard, T.J., Jr., and M. McGue
1981   Familial studies of intelligence: A review. Science 212:1055–1059.

Bradford, J.
1983   Research on sex offenders. Psychiatric Clinics of North America
         6:715–713.

Brizer, D.A. and M. Crowner
1989   Current Approaches to the Prediction of Violence. Washington,
         D.C.: American Psychiatric Press.

Brook, J.S., S. Gordon, and M. Whiteman
1985   Stability of personality during adolescence and its relationship

to stage of drug use. Genetic, Social and General Psychology Monographs 111(3):317–330.

Brown, G.L., F.K. Goodwin, J.C. Ballenger, P.F. Goyer, and L.F. Major
1979   Aggression in humans correlates with cerebrospinal fluid amine metabolites. Psychiatry Research 1(2):131–139.

Bryant, E.T., M.L. Scott, C.J. Golden, and D.C. Tori
1984   Neuropsychological deficits, learning disability, and violent behavior. Journal of Consulting and Clinical Psychology 52:323–324.

Bryce-Smith, D. and H.A. Waldron
1974   Lead, behavior, and criminality. The Ecologist 4:367–377.

Cadoret, R.J.
1978   Psychopathology in adopted away offspring of biologic parents with antisocial behavior. Archives of General Psychiatry 35:176–184.

Cadoret, R.J., L. Cunningham, R. Loftus, and J. Edwards
1975   Studies of adoptees from psychiatrically disturbed biologic parents. II. Temperament, hyperactive, antisocial and developmental variables. Journal of Pediatrics 87:301–306.

Cadoret, R.J., T.W. O'Gorman, E. Troughton, and E. Heywood
1985   Alcoholism and antisocial personality: Interrelationships, genetic and environmental factors. Archives of General Psychiatry 42:161–167.

Cantwell, D.P.
1979   Minimal brain dysfunction in adults: Evidence from studies of psychiatric illness in the families of hyperactive children. In L. Bellak (ed.), Psychiatric Aspects of Minimal Brain Dysfunction in Adults. New York: Grune and Stratton.

Carlson, N.R.
1977   Physiology of Behavior. Boston: Allyn & Bacon.

Carroll, B.J. and M. Steiner
1987   The psychobiology of premenstrual dysphoria: The role of prolactin. Psychoneuroendocrinology 3:171–180.

Cattell, R.B.
1982   The Inheritance of Personality and Ability: Research Methods and Findings. New York: Academic Press.

Christiansen, K.O.
1977a   A preliminary study of criminality among twins. In S.A. Mednick and K.O. Christiansen (eds.), Biosocial Bases of Criminal Behavior. New York: Gardner Press.

Clare, A.W.
1985   Hormones, behaviour and the menstrual cycle. Journal of Psychosomatic Research 29(3):225–233.

Cleckley, H.
1964   The Mask of Sanity. 4th ed. St. Louis: Mosby.

Clerget–Darpoux, F., L.R. Goldin, and E.S. Fershon
1986   Clinical methods in psychiatric genetics. III. Environmental strati-
        fication may simulate a genetic effect in adoption studies. Acta
        Psychiatric Scandinavia 74:305–311.

Cloninger, C.R., T. Reich, and S.B. Guze
1975   The multifactorial model of disease transmission: II. Sex differ-
        ences in the familial transmission of sociopathy (antisocial per-
        sonality). British Journal of Psychiatry 127:11–22.

Cloninger, C.R., K.O. Christiansen, R. Reich, and I.I. Gottesman
1978   Implications of sex differences in the prevalences of antisocial
        personality, alcoholism, and criminality for familial transmission.
        Archives of General Psychiatry 35:941–951.

Cloninger, C.R., S. Sigvardsson, M. Bohman, and A–L. von Knorring
1982   Predisposition to petty criminality in Swedish adoptees: II.
        Cross-fostering analysis of gene-environment interaction. Ar-
        chives of General Psychiatry 39:1242–1247.

Cocozza, J.J. and H.J. Steadman
1974   Some refinements in the measurement and prediction of danger-
        ous behavior. American Journal of Psychiatry 131:1012–1014.

Coe, C.L. and S. Levine
1983   Biology of aggression. Bulletin of the American Academy of
        Psychiatry Law 11:131–148.

Cohen, S.
1977   Angel dust. Journal of the American Medical Association
        238:515–516.
1980   Alcoholic hypoglycemia. Drug Abuse and Alcoholism Newsletter
        9(2):1–4.

Coid, J.
1979   Mania a potu: A critical review of pathological intoxication. Psy-
        chological Medicine 9:709–719.

Cooke, W.R.
1945   The differential psychology of the American woman. American
        Journal of Obstetrics and Gynecology 49:457–472.

Cordoba, O.A. and J.L. Chapel
1983   Medroxyprogesterone acetate antiandrogen treatment of hyper-
        sexuality in a pedophiliac sex offender. American Journal of Psy-
        chiatry 140:1036–1039.

Critchley, E.M.R.
1968   Reading retardation, dyslexia, and delinquency. British Journal of
        Psychiatry 115:1537–1547.

Crowe, R.R.
1972   The adopted offspring of women criminal offenders: A study of their arrest records. Archives of General Psychiatry 27:600–603.
1974   An adoption study of antisocial personality. Archives of General Psychiatry 31:785–791.

Dalgard, O.S. and E. Kringler
1976   A Norwegian twin study of criminality. British Journal of Criminology 16:213–232.

Dalton, K.
1964   The Premenstrual Syndrome. Springfield, Ill.: Charles C Thomas.
1966   The influence of mother's menstruation on her child. Proceedings of the Royal Society of Medicine 59:1014–1016.

David, O.J., J. Clark, and K. Voeller
1972   Lead and hyperactivity. Lancet 2:900.

David, O.J., S.P. Hoffman, J. Sverd, J. Clark, and K. Voeller
1976   Lead and hyperactivity: Behavioral response to chelation—A pilot study. American Journal of Psychiatry 133:1155.

Davis, B.A., P.H. Yu, A.A. Boulton, J.S. Wormith, and D. Addington
1983   Correlative relationship between biochemical activity and aggressive behavior. Progress in Neuro-Psychopharmacology and Biological Psychiatry 7:529–535.

DeFries, J.C. and R. Plomin
1978   Behavioral genetics. Annual Reviews in Psychology 29:473–515.

Demsky, L.S.
1984   The use of Depo-Provera in the treatment of sex offenders. The Journal of Legal Medicine 5:295–322.

Denno, D.W.
1988   Human biology and criminal responsibility: Free will or free ride? University of Pennsylvania Law Review 137(2):615–671.

Devonshire, P.A., R.C. Howard, and C. Sellars
1988   Frontal lobe functions and personality in mentally abnormal offenders. Personality and Individual Differences 9:339–344.

Deykin, E.Y., J.C. Levy, and V. Wells
1986   Adolescent depression, alcohol and drug abuse. American Journal of Public Health 76:178–182.

Domino, E.F.
1978   Neurobiology of phencyclidine—An update. In R.C. Peterson and R.C. Stillman (eds.), Phencyclidine (PCP) Abuse: An Appraisal. NIDA Research Monograph 21. Rockville, Md.: National Institute on Drug Abuse.
1980   History and pharmacology of PCP and PCP-related analogs. Journal of Psychedelic Drugs 12:223–227.

D'Orban, P.T. and J. Dalton
1980   Violent crime and the menstrual cycle. Psychological Medicine
10:353–359.

Eichelman, B.S. and N.B. Thoa
1972   The aggressive monoamines. Biological Psychiatry 6(2):143–163.

Ellis, L. and M.A. Ames
1987   Neurohormonal functioning and sexual orientation: A theory of
homosexuality-heterosexuality. Psychological Bulletin 101:233–
258.

Ellis, D. and P. Austin
1971   Menstruation and aggressive behavior in a correctional center for
women. Journal of Criminal Law, Criminology and Police Science
62:388–395.

Epps, P.
1962   Women shoplifters in Holloway Prison. In T.C.N. Gibbens and J.
Prince (eds.), Shoplifting. London: The Institute for the Study
and Treatment of Delinquency.

Eysenck, H.J.
1977   Crime and Personality. Rev. ed. London: Routledge & Kegan
Paul.

Fauman, M.A. and B.J. Fauman
1980   Chronic Phencyclidine (PCP) abuse: A psychiatric perspective.
Journal of Psychedelic Drugs 12:307–314.

Fishbein, D.H. and R. Thatcher
In press Legal applications of electrophysiological assessments. In J. Dy-
wan, R. Kaplan, F. Pirozzolo (eds.), Neuropsychology and the
Law. New York: Springer-Verlag.

Fishbein, D.H., D. Lozovsky, and J.H. Jaffe
1989   Impulsivity, aggression and neuroendocrine responses to serotonergic stimulation in substance abusers. Biological Psychiatry
25:1049–1066.

Geary, D.C.
1989   A model for representing gender differences in the pattern of
cognitive abilities. American Psychologist 44:1155–1156.

Ghodsian-Carpey, J. and L.A. Baker
1987   Genetic and environmental influences on aggression in 4 to 7
year old twins. Aggressive Behavior 13:173–186.

Ginsburg, B.E. and B.F. Carter
1987   Premenstrual Syndrome: Ethical and Legal Implications in a
Biomedical Perspective. New York: Plenum.

Glueck, S. and E.T. Glueck
1956   Physique and Delinquency. New York: Harper & Row.

Goddard, H.H.
1921   Juvenile Delinquency. New York: Dodd, Mead.

Gottfredson, S.
1986   Statistical and actual considerations. In F. Dutile and C. Foust (eds.), The Prediction of Criminal Violence. Springfield, Ill.: Charles C Thomas.

Gove, W.R. and C. Wilmoth
In press Risk, crime and physiological highs: A consideration of neurological processes which may act as positive reinforcers. In L. Ellis and H. Hoffman (eds.), Evolution, the Brain and Criminal Behavior: A Reader in Biosocial Criminology. New York: Praeger.

Guze, S.B., E.D. Wolfgram, J.K. McKinney, and D.P. Cantwell
1967   .Psychiatric illness in the families of convicted criminals: A study of 519 first-degree relatives. Diseases of the Nervous System 28:651–659.

Hamparin, D.M., R. Schuster, S. Dinitz, and J.P. Conrad
1978   The Violent Few: A Study of Dangerous Juvenile Offenders. Lexington, Mass.: Lexington Books.

Hare, R.D.
1970   Psychopathy: Theory and Research. New York: John Wiley & Sons.
1978   Electrodermal and cardiovascular correlates of psychopathy. In R.D. Hare and D. Schalling (eds.), Psychopathic Behavior. New York: John Wiley & Sons.

Hare, R.D. and D. Schalling
1978   Psychopathic Behavior. New York: John Wiley & Sons.

Harry, B. and C. Blacer
1987   Menstruation and crime: A critical review of the literature from the clinical criminology perspective. Behavioral Sciences and the Law 5(3):307–322.

Haskett, R.F.
1987   Premenstrual dysphoric disorder: Evaluation, pathophysiology and treatment. Progress in Neuro-Psychopharmacology and Biological Psychiatry 11:129–135.

Hill, D. and D. Watterson
1942   Electroencephalographic studies of the psychopathic personality. Journal of Neurological Psychiatry 5:47–64.

Hirschi, T.
1969   Causes of Delinquency. Berkeley: University of California Press.

Hirschi, T. and M.J. Hindelang
1977   Intelligence and delinquency: A revisionist review. Science 196:1393–1409.

Hooten, E.A.
1939   The American Criminal: An Anthropological Study. Cambridge,
        Mass.: Harvard University Press.

House, T.H. and W.L. Milligan
1976   Autonomic responses to modeled distress in prison psychopaths.
        Journal of Personality and Social Psychology 34:556–560.

Howard, R.C.
1984   The clinical EEG and personality in mentally abnormal offenders.
        Psychological Medicine 14:569–580.
1986   Psychopathy: A psychobiological perspective. Personality and
        Individual Differences 7(6):795–806.

Huesmann, L.R., L.D. Eron, M.M. Lefkowitz, and L.O. Walder
1984   Stability of aggression over time and generations. Developmental
        Psychology 20:1120–1134.

Hurwitz, I., R.M. Bibace, P.H. Wolff, and B.M. Rowbotham
1972   Neuropsychological function of normal boys, delinquent boys,
        and boys with learning problems. Perceptual and Motor Skills
        35(2):387–394.

Hutchings, B. and S.A. Mednick
1975   Registered criminality in the adoptive and biological parents of
        registered male criminal adoptees. In R.R. Fieve, D. Rosenthal,
        and H. Brill (eds.), Genetic Research in Psychiatry. Baltimore:
        Johns Hopkins University Press.

Jacobs, P.A., M. Brunton, M.M. Melville, R.P. Brittain, and W. McClemont
1965   Aggressive behaviour, mental sub-normality, and the XYY male.
        Nature 108:1351–1352.

Jeffery, C.R.
1977   Crime Prevention Through Environmental Design. Beverly Hills,
        Calif.: Sage.
1985   Attacks on the Insanity Defense: Biological Psychiatry and New
        Perspectives on Criminal Behavior. Springfield, Ill.: Charles C
        Thomas.

Jutai, J.W. and R.D. Hare
1983   Psychopathy and selective attention during performance of a
        complex perceptual-motor task. Psychophysiology 20:146–151.

Kadzin, A.E.
1987   Treatment of antisocial behavior in children: Current status and
        future directions. Psychological Bulletin 102:187–203.

Kagan, J., J.S. Reznick, and N. Snidman
1988   Biological bases of childhood shyness. Science 240: 167–171.

Kandel, E. and S.A. Mednick
1988   IQ as a protective factor for subjects at high risk for antisocial
        behavior. Journal of Consulting and Clinical Psychology 56:224–226.

Kellam, S.G., J.D. Branch, D.C. Agrawal, and M.E. Ensminger
1975   Mental Health and Going to School: The Woodlawn Program of
        Assessment, Early Intervention and Evaluation. Chicago: Univer-
        sity of Chicago Press.

Kellam, S.G., M.E. Ensminger, and M.B. Simon
1980   Mental health in first grade and teenage drug, alcohol, and ciga-
        rette use. Drug and Alcohol Dependence 5:273–304.

Khajawall, A.M., T.B. Erickson, and G.B. Simpson
1982   Chronic phencyclidine abuse and physical assault. American
        Journal of Psychiatry 139:1604–1606.

Kiloh, L.G., A.J. McComas, and J.W. Osselton
1972   Clinical Electroencephalography. 3rd ed. London: Butterworths.

Kreuz, L.E. and R.M. Rose
1971   Assessment of aggressive behavior and plasma testosterone in a
        young criminal population. Psychomatic Medicine 34:321–332.

Kuperman, S. and M. Stewart
1987   Use of propranolol to decrease aggressive outbursts in younger
        patients. Psychosomatics 28:315–319.

Larson, C.J.
1984   Crime, Justice and Society. New York: General Hall.

Lester, M.L. and D.H. Fishbein.
1987   Nutrition and Neuropsychological Development in Children. In
        R. Tarter, D.H. Van Thiel, and K. Edwards (eds.), Medical Neuro-
        psychology: The Impact of Disease on Behavior. New York:
        Plenum.

Lewis, D.O., S.S. Shanok, and D.A. Balla
1979   Perinatal difficulties, head and face trauma and child abuse in
        the medical histories of serious youthful offenders. American
        Journal of Psychiatry 136:419–423.

Lewis, D.O., S.S. Shanok, and J.N. Pincus
1981   The neuropsychiatric status of violent male delinquents. In D.O.
        Lewis (ed.), Vulnerabilities to Delinquency. New York: Spectrum.

Lewis, D.O., E. Moy, L.D. Jackson, R. Aaronson, N. Restifo, S. Serra, and
A. Simos
1985   Biopsychosocial characteristics of children who later murder: A
        prospective study. American Journal of Psychiatry 142:1161–1167.

Lewis, D.O., J.H. Pincus, M. Feldman, L. Jackson, and B. Bard
1986   Psychiatric, neurological, and psychoeducational characteristics
        of 15 death row inmates in the Unites States. American Journal
        of Psychiatry 143:838–845.

Lewis, D.O., J.H. Pincus, B. Bard, E. Richardson, L.S. Prichep, M. Feldman, C. Yeager
1988   Neuropsychiatric, psychoeducational, and family characteristics

of 14 juveniles condemned to death in the United States. American Journal of Psychiatry 145:584–589.

Linder, R.L., S.E. Lerner, and R.S. Burns
1981   The experience and effects of PCP abuse. In The Devil's Dust: Recognition, Management, and Prevention of Phencyclidine Abuse. Belmont, Calif.: Wadsworth.

Linnoila, M., M. Virkkunen, M. Scheinin, A. Nuutila, R. Rimon, and F.K. Goodwin
1983   Low cerebrospinal fluid 5-hydroxyindoleacetic acid concentration differentiates impulsive from nonimpulsive violent behavior. Life Sciences 33:2609–2614.

Lion, J.R.
1974   Diagnosis and treatment of personality disorders. In J.R. Lion (ed.), Personality Disorders: Diagnosis and Treatment. Baltimore: Williams and Wilkins.
1979   Benzodiazepines in the treatment of aggressive patients. Journal of Clinical Psychiatry 40:70–71.

Loeber, R. and T. Dishion
1983   Early predictors of male delinquency: A review. Psychological Bulletin 94:68–99.

Lombroso, C.
1918   Crime, Its Causes and Remedies. Boston: Little, Brown.

Lykken, D.T.
1957   A study of anxiety in the sociopathic personality. Journal of Abnormal and Social Psychology 55:6–10.

Maletsky, B.M.
1976   The diagnosis of pathological intoxication. Journal of Studies on Alcohol 37:1215–1228.

Marinacci, A.A.
1963   Special types of temporal lobe seizures following ingestion of alcohol. Bulletin of the Los Angeles Neurological Society 28:241–250.

Marrs–Simon, P.A., M. Weiler, M.C. Santangelo, M.T. Perry, and J.B. Leikin
1988   Analysis of sexual disparity of violent behavior in PCP intoxication. Veterinary and Human Toxicology 30(1):53–55.

Marsh, F.H. and J. Katz
1985   Biology, Crime and Ethics: A Study of Biological Explanations for Criminal Behavior. Cincinnati: Anderson Publishing.

Mattes, J.A. and M. Fink
1987   A family study of patients with temper outbursts. Journal of Psychiatric Research 21:249–255.

McCardle, L. and D.H. Fishbein
1989   The self-reported effects of PCP on human aggression. Addictive Behaviors 4(4):456–472.

McGee, R., S. Williams, D.L. Share, J. Anderson, and P.A. Silva
1986   The relationship between specific reading retardation, general reading backwardness and behavioural problems in a large sample of Dunedin boys: A longitudinal study from five to eleven years. Journal of Child Psychology and Psychiatry 27:597–610.

McManus, M., A. Brickman, N.E. Alessi, and W.L. Grapentine
1985   Neurological dysfunction in serious delinquents. Journal of the American Academy of Child Psychiatry 24:481–486.

Mednick, S.A., J. Volavka, W.F. Gabrielli, and T.M. Itil
1981   EEG predicts later delinquency. Criminology 19:219–229.

Mednick, S.A., V. Pollock, J. Volavka, W.F. Gabrielli, Jr.
1982   Biology and violence. In M.E. Wolfgang and N.A. Weiner (eds.), Criminal Violence. Beverly Hills, Calif.: Sage.

Mednick, S.A., W.F. Gabrielli, Jr., and B. Hutchings
1984   Genetic influences in criminal convictions: Evidence from an adoption cohort. Science 224:891–894.

Mednick, S.A., T.E. Moffitt, and S.A. Stack
1987   The Causes of Crime: New Biological Approaches. New York: Cambridge University Press.

Moffitt, T.E.
1983   The learning theory model of punishment: Implications for delinquency deterrence. Criminal Justice and Behavior 10:131–158.

Moffitt, T.E., S.A. Mednick, W.F. Gabrielli, Jr.
1989   Predicting careers of criminal violence: Descriptive data and predispositional factors. In D.A. Brizer and M. Crowner (eds.), Current Approaches to the Prediction of Violence. Washington, D.C.: American Psychiatric Press.

Monahan, J.
1981   The Clinical Prediction of Violent Behavior. Rockville, Md.: U.S. Department of Health and Human Services.

Moore, L.S. and A.I. Fleischman
1975   Subclinical lead toxicity. Orthomolecular Psychiatry 4:61–70.

Morton, J.H., H. Additon, and R.G. Addison
1953   A clinical study of premenstrual tension. American Journal of Obstetrics and Gynecology 65:1182–1191.

Muhlbauer, H.D.
1985   Human aggression and the role of central serotonin. Pharmacopsychiatry 18:218–221.

Murray, J.B.
1987   Psychopharmacological therapy of deviant sexual behavior. Journal of General Psychology 115:101–110.

Needleman, H.L., C. Gunnoe, A. Leviton, P. Reed, H. Peresie, C. Maher, and P. Barrett
1979   Deficits in psychologic and classroom performance of children with elevated dentine lead levels. New England Journal of Medicine 300:689-695.

Olds, J. and P. Milner
1954   Positive reinforcement produced by electrical stimulation of septal area and other regions of rat brain. Journal of Comparative and Physiological Psychology 47:419-427.

Olweus, D.
1979   Stability of aggressive reaction patterns in males: A review. Psychological Bulletin 86:852-875.

Olweus, D., A. Mattsson, D. Schalling, and H. Low
1988   Circulating testosterone levels and aggression in adolescent males: A causal analysis. Psychosomatic Medicine 50(3):261-272.

Owen, D. and J.O. Sines
1970   Heritability of personality in children. Behavior Genetics 1:235-248.

Patterson, G.R., B.D. DeBaryshe, and E. Ramsey
1989   A developmental perspective on antisocial behavior. American Psychologist 44:329-335.

Perlmutter, B.F.
1987   Delinquency and Learning Disabilities: Evidence for compensatory behaviors and adaptation. Journal of Youth and Adolescence 16:89-95.

Pihl, R.O. and M. Parkes
1977   Hair element content in learning disabled children. Science 198:204.

Pihl, R.O. and D. Ross
1987   Research on alcohol related aggression: A review and implications for understanding aggression. In S.W. Sadava (ed.), Drug Use and Psychological Theory. New York: Haworth Press.

Pihl, R.O., F. Ervin, G. Pelletier, W. Diekel, and W. Strain
1982   Hair element content of violent criminals. Canadian Journal of Psychiatry 27:533.

Pincus, J. and G. Tucker
1974   Behavioral Neurology. New York: Oxford University Press.

Plomin, R.
1989   Environment and Genes: Determinants of Behavior. American Psychologist 44:105-111.

Plomin, R. and D. Daniels
1986   Genetics and shyness. In W.H. Jones, J.M. Cheek, and S.R.

Briggs (eds.), Shyness: Perspectives on Research and Treatment. New York: Plenum.

1987   Why are children in the same family so different from one another? Behavioral and Brain Sciences 10:1–16.

Plomin, R., J.C. DeFries, and G.E. McClearn
1980   Behavioral Genetics: A Primer. San Francisco: W.H. Freeman.

Plomin, R., T.T. Foch, and D.C. Rowe
1981   Bobo clown aggression in childhood: Environment, not genes. Journal of Research in Personality 15:331–342.

Plomin, R., K. Nitz, and D.C. Rowe
1990   Behavioral genetics and aggressive behavior in childhood. In M. Lewis and S.M. Miller (eds.), Handbook of Developmental Psychopathology. New York: Plenum.

Pontius, A.A. and K.F. Ruttiger
1976   Frontal lobe system maturational lag in juvenile delinquents shown in narratives test. Adolescence XI(44):509–518.

Pontius, A.A. and B.S. Yudowitz
1980   Frontal lobe system dysfunction in some critical actions as shown in the narratives test. The Journal of Nervous and Mental Disease 168:111–117.

Poremba, C.
1975   Learning disabilities, youth and delinquency: Programs for intervention. In H.R. Myklebust (ed.), Progress in Learning Disabilities. Vol. III. New York: Grune & Stratton.

Pugh, G.E.
1977   The Biological Origin of Human Values. New York: Basic Books.

Quay, H.C.
1965   Psychopathic personality as pathological stimulation seeking. American Journal of Psychiatry 122:180–183.

Rada, R.T., D.R. Laws, R. Kellner, L. Stivastava, and G. Peake
1983   Plasma androgens in violent and nonviolent sex offenders. Bulletin of the American Academy of Psychiatry Law 11:149–158.

Raine, A.
1988   Psychopathy: A single or dual concept? Personality and Individual Differences 9(4):825–827.

Raine, A. and P.H. Venables
1987   Contingent negative variation, P3 evoked potentials and antisocial behavior. Psychophysiology 24(2):191–199.

Richman, N., J. Stevenson, and P.J. Graham
1982   Pre-school to School: A Behavioural Study. London: Academic Press.

Rimland, B. and G.E. Larson
1983   Hair mineral analysis and behavior: An analysis of 51 studies. Journal of Learning Disabilities 16:279–285.

Robins, L.N.
1966   Deviant Children Grown Up: A Sociological and Psychiatric Study of Sociopathic Personality. Baltimore: Williams & Wilkins.

Robins, L.N., P.A. West, and B.L. Herjanic
1975   Arrests and delinquency in two generations: A study of black urban families and their children. Journal of Child Psychology and Psychiatry 16:125–140.

Rogeness, G.A., M.A. Javors, J.W. Maas, C.A. Macedo, and C. Fischer
1987   Plasma dopamine-B-hydroxylase, HVA, MHPG, and conduct disorder in emotionally disturbed boys. Biological Psychiatry 22:1155–1158.

Rowe, D.C.
1983   Biometrical genetic models of self-reported delinquent behavior: A twin study. Behavior Genetics 13:473–489.
1986   Genetic and environmental components of antisocial behavior: A study of 265 twin pairs. Criminology 24(3):513–532.

Rowe, D.C. and D.W. Osgood
1984   Heredity and sociological theories of delinquency: A reconsideration. American Sociological Review 49:526–540.

Roy, A., M. Virkkunen, S. Guthrie, R. Poland, and M. Linnoila
1986   Monoamines, glucose metabolism, suicidal and aggressive behaviors. Psychopharmacology Bulletin 22(3):661–665.

Rushton, J.P., D.W. Fulker, M.C. Neale, D.K.B. Nias, and H.J. Eysenck
1986   Altruism and aggression: The heritability of individual differences. Journal of Personality and Social Psychology 50(6):1192–1198.

Schiavi, R.C., A. Theilgaard, D.R. Owen, and D. White
1984   Sex chromosome anomalies, hormones, and aggressivity. Archives of General Psychiatry 41:93–99.

Schuckit, M.A. and M.A. Morrissey
1978   Propoxyphene and phencyclidine (PCP) use in adolescents. Journal of Clinical Psychiatry 39:7–13.

Schulsinger, F.
1985   The experience from the adoption method in genetic research. Progress in Clinical and Biological Research 177:461–478.

Seigal, R.K.
1978   Phencyclidine, criminal behavior, and the defense of diminished capacity. In R.C. Peterson and R.C. Stillman (eds.), Phencyclidine (PCP) Abuse: An Appraisal. NIDA Research Monograph 21. Rockville, Md.: National Institute on Drug Abuse.

Sheldon, W.H.
1949   Varieties of Delinquent Youth. New York: Harper & Row.

Shonfeld, I.S., D. Shaffer, P. O'Connor, and S. Portnoy
1988   Conduct disorder and cognitive functioning: Testing three causal hypotheses. Child Development 59:993–1007.

Sigvardsson, S., C.R. Cloninger, M. Bohman, and A-L. von Knorring
1982   Predisposition to petty criminality in Swedish adoptees. III. Sex differences and validation of the male typology. Archives of General Psychiatry 39:1248–1253.

Smith, D.E. and D.R. Wesson
1980   PCP abuse: Diagnostic and pharmacological treatment approaches. Journal of Psychedelic Drugs 12:293–299.

Soubrie, P.
1986   Reconciling the role of central serotonin neurons in human and animal behavior. The Behavioral and Brain Sciences 9:319–364.

Spodak, M.K., Z.A. Falck, and J.R. Rappeport
1978   The hormonal treatment of paraphiliacs with Depo-Provera. Criminal Justice and Behavior 5:304–314.

Stein, L. and C.D. Wise
1973   Amphetamine and noradrenergic reward pathways. In E. Usdin, and S.H. Snyder (eds.), Frontiers in Catecholamine Research. New York: Pergamon.

Stewart, M.A. and C.S. de Blois
1983   Father-son resemblances in aggressive and antisocial behavior. British Journal of Psychiatry 142:78–84.

Stewart, M.A. and L. Leone
1978   A family study of unsocialized aggressive boys. Biological Psychiatry 13:107–117.

Stewart, M.A., C.S. de Blois, and C. Cummings
1980   Psychiatric disorder in the parents of hyperactive boys and those with conduct disorder. Journal of Child Psychology and Psychiatry 21:283–292.

Sutker, P.B. and A.N. Allain
1987   Cognitive abstraction, shifting, and control: Clinical sample comparisons of psychopaths and nonpsychopaths. Journal of Abnormal Psychology 96(1):73–75.

Syndulko, K.
1978   Electrocortical investigations of sociopathy. In R.D. Hare and D. Schalling (eds.), Psychopathic Behavior: Approaches to Research. Chichester, England: John Wiley & Sons.

Syndulko, K., D.A. Parker, R. Jens, I. Maltzman, and E. Ziskind
1975   Psychophysiology of sociopathy: Electrocortical measures. Biological Psychology 3:185–200.

Tarter, R.E., A.I. Alterman, and K.L. Edwards
1985   Vulnerability to alcoholism in men: A behavior-genetic perspective. Journal of Studies on Alcoholism 46(4):329–356.

Tellegen, A., D.T. Lykken, T.J. Bouchard, K. Wilcox, N. Segal, and S. Rich
1988   Personality similarity in twins reared apart and together. Journal of Personality and Social Psychology 54(6):1031–1039.

Thiessen, D.D.
1976   The Evolution and Chemistry of Aggression. Springfield, Ill.: Charles C Thomas.

Trunnell, E.P. and C.W. Turner
1988   A comparison of the psychological and hormonal factors in women with and without premenstrual syndrome. Journal of Abnormal Psychology 97:429–436.

Twito, T.J. and M.A. Stewart
1982   A half-sibling study of aggressive conduct disorder. Neuropsychobiology 8:144–150.

Valzelli, L.
1981   Psychobiology of Aggression and Violence. New York: Raven Press.

van Praag, H.M., R.S. Kahn, G.M. Asnis, S. Wetzler, S.L. Brown, A. Bleich, and M.L. Korn
1987   Denosologization of biological psychiatry or the specificity of 5-HT disturbances in psychiatric disorders. Journal of Affective Disorders 13:1–8.

Venables, P.H.
1987   Autonomic nervous system factors in criminal behavior. In S.A. Mednick, T.E. Moffitt, and S.A. Stack (eds.), The Causes of Crime: New Biological Approaches. New York: Cambridge University Press.

Virkkunen, M. and S. Narvanen
1987   Plasma insulin, tryptophan and serotonin levels during the glucose tolerance test among habitually violent and impulsive offenders. Neuropsychobiology 17:19–23.

Virkkunen, M., A. Nuutila, F.K. Goodwin, and M. Linnoila
1987   Cerebrospinal fluid monoamine metabolite levels in male arsonists. Archives of General Psychiatry 44:241–247.

Virkkunen, M., J. DeJong, J. Bartkko, F.K. Goodwin, and M. Linnoila
1989   Relationship of psychobiological variables to recidivism in violent offenders and impulsive fire setters. Archives of General Psychiatry 46:600–603.

Volavka, J.
1987   Electroencephalogram among criminals. In S.A. Mednick, T.E.

Moffitt, and S.A. Stack (eds.), The Causes of Crime: New Biological Approaches. New York: Cambridge University Press.

Waid, W.M., M.T. Orne, and S.K. Wilson
1979   Socialization, awareness and the electrodermal response to deception and self-disclosure. Journal of Abnormal Psychology 88:663–666.

Wallgren, H. and H. Barry
1970   Action of Alcohol. Vols. 1 and 2. New York: Elsevier.

Walters, G.D. and T.W. White
1989   Heredity and crime: Bad genes or bad research? Criminology 27:455–486.

Watson, J.B.
1925   Behaviorism. New York: W.W. Norton.

Weingartner, H., M.V. Rudorfer, M.S. Buchsbaum, and M. Linnoila
1983   Effects of serotonin on memory impairments produced by ethanol. Science 221:472–474.

Wenk, E.A., J.O. Robison, and G.W. Smith
1972   Can violence be predicted? Crime and Delinquency 18:393–402.

Widom, C.S.
1978   Toward an understanding of female criminality. Progress in Experimental Personality Research 8:245–308.

Wilson, J.Q. and R.J. Herrnstein
1985   Crime and Human Nature. New York: Simon & Schuster.

Wise, R.
1984   Neural Mechanisms of the Reinforcing Action of Cocaine. NIDA Research Monograph 50. Rockville, Md.: National Institute on Drug Abuse.

Wolff, P.H., D. Waber, M. Bauermeister, C. Cohen, and R. Ferber
1982   The neuropsychological status of adolescent delinquent boys. Journal of Child Psychology and Psychiatry 23:267–279.

Wolfgang, M.E., R.M. Figlio, and T. Sellin
1972   Delinquency in a Birth Cohort. Chicago: University of Chicago Press.

Yeudall, L.T., O. Fedora, and D. Fromm
1985   A Neuropsychological Theory of Persistent Criminality: Implications for Assessment and Treatment. Research Bulletin 97. Edmonton: Alberta Hospital.

Yudofsky, S.C., J.M. Silver, and S.E. Schneider
1987   Pharmacologic treatment of aggression. Psychiatric Annals 17:397–406.

Zuckerman, M.
1983   A biological theory of sensation seeking. In M. Zuckerman,

(ed.), Biological Basis of Sensation Seeking, Impulsivity and Anxiety. Hillsdale, N.J.: Lawrence Erlbaum Associates.

32 Medicine as an Institution of Social Control: Consequences for Society
PETER CONRAD and JOSEPH W. SCHNEIDER

◄○►

In our society we want to believe in medicine, as we want to believe in religion and our country; it wards off collective fears and reduces public anxieties (see Edelman, 1977). In significant ways medicine, especially psychiatry, has replaced religion as the most powerful extralegal institution of social control. Physicians have been endowed with some of the charisma of shamans. In the 20th century the medical model of deviance has ascended with the glitter of a rising star, expanding medicine's social control functions.... [We] focus directly on medicine as an agent of social control. First, we illustrate the range and varieties of medical social control. Next, we analyze the consequences of the medicalization of deviance and social control. Finally, we examine some significant social policy questions pertaining to medicine and medicalization in American society.

TYPES OF MEDICAL SOCIAL CONTROL

Medicine was first conceptualized as an agent of social control by Talcott Parsons (1951) in his seminal essay on the "sick role."... Eliot Freidson (1970) and Irving Zola (1972) have elucidated the jurisdictional mandate the medical profession has over anything that can be labeled an illness, regardless of its ability to deal with it effectively.

Reprinted from Peter Conrad and Joseph W. Schneider, "Medicine as an Institution of Social Control: Consequences for Society," pp. 241–260 in *Deviance and Medicalization: From Badness to Sickness* (Philadelphia, Temple Univ. Press, 1993).

Adapted, amended, and extended discussion from P. Conrad, "Types of Social Control," *Social Health & Illness*, 1979, 1, 1–12, by permission of Routledge & Kegan Paul Ltd.; and P. Conrad, "The Discovery of Hyperkinesis," *Social Problems*, 1975, 23, 12–21. Portions also taken from "Medicine" by P. Conrad and J. Schneider, in *Social Control for the 1980s: A Handbook for Order in a Democratic Society*, edited by Joseph S. Roucek, 1978, pp. 346–358, used with the permission of the publisher, Greenwood Press, Inc., Westport, Conn., and our forthcoming article in *Contemporary Crises*, reprinted by permission of Elsevier Scientific Publishing Co., Amsterdam.

The boundaries of medicine are elastic and increasingly expansive (Ehrenreich & Ehrenreich, 1975), and some analysts have expressed concern at the increasing medicalization of life (Illich, 1976). Although medical social control has been conceptualized in several ways, including professional control of colleagues (Freidson, 1975) and control of the micropolitics of physician-patient interaction (Waitzkin & Stoeckle, 1976), the focus here is narrower. Our concern...is with the medical control of deviant behavior, an aspect of the medicalization of deviance (Conrad, 1975; Pitts, 1968). Thus by medical social control we mean the ways in which medicine functions (wittingly or unwittingly) to secure adherence to social norms—specifically, by using medical means to minimize, eliminate, or normalize deviant behavior. This section illustrates and catalogues the broad range of medical controls of deviance and in so doing conceptualizes three major "ideal types" of medical social control.

On the most abstract level medical social control is the acceptance of a medical perspective as the dominant definition of certain phenomena. When medical perspectives of problems and their solutions become dominant, they diminish competing definitions. This is particularly true of problems related to bodily functioning and in areas where medical technology can demonstrate effectiveness (e.g., immunization, contraception, antibacterial drugs) and is increasingly the case for behavioral and social problems (Mechanic, 1973). This underlies the construction of medical norms (e.g., the definition of what is healthy) and the "enforcement" of both medical and social norms. Medical social control also includes medical advice, counsel, and information that are part of the general stock of knowledge: for example, a well-balanced diet is important, cigarette smoking causes cancer, being overweight increases health risks, exercising regularly is healthy, teeth should be brushed regularly. Such directives, even when unheeded, serve as road signs for desirable behavior. At a more concrete level, medical social control is enacted through professional medical intervention, qua medical treatment (although it may include some types of self-treatment such as self-medication or medically oriented self-help groups). This intervention aims at returning sick individuals to compliance with health norms and to their conventional social roles, adjusting them to new (e.g., impaired) roles, or, short of these, making individuals more comfortable with their condition (see Freidson, 1970; Parsons, 1951). Medical social control of deviant behavior is usually a variant of medical intervention that seeks to eliminate, modify, isolate, or regulate behavior socially defined as deviant, with medical means and in the name of health.

Traditionally, psychiatry and public health have served as the clearest examples of medical control. Psychiatry's social control functions with mental illness, especially in terms of institutionalization, have been described clearly (e.g., Miller, 1976; Szasz, 1970). Recently it has been argued that psychotherapy, because it reinforces dominant values and adjusts people to their life situations, is an agent of social control and a supporter of the status quo (Halleck, 1971; Hurvitz, 1973). Public health's mandate, the control and elimination of conditions and diseases that are deemed a threat to the health of the community, is more diffuse. It operates as a control agent by setting and enforcing certain "health" standards in the home, workplace, and community (e.g., food, water, sanitation) and by identifying, preventing, treating, and, if necessary, isolating persons with communicable diseases (Rosen, 1972). A clear example of the latter is the detection of venereal disease. Indeed, public health has exerted considerable coercive power in attempting to prevent the spread of infectious disease.

There are a number of types of medical control of deviance. The most common forms of medical social control include medicalizing deviant behavior—that is, defining the behavior as an illness or a symptom of an illness or underlying disease—and subsequent direct medical intervention. This medical social control takes three general forms: medical technology, medical collaboration, and medical ideology.

MEDICAL TECHNOLOGY

The growth of specialized medicine and the concomitant development of medical technology has produced an armamentarium of medical controls. Psychotechnologies, which include various forms of medical and behavioral technologies (Chorover, 1973), are the most common means of medical control of deviance. Since the emergence of phenothiazine medications in the early 1950s for the treatment and control of mental disorder, there has been a virtual explosion in the development and use of psychoactive medications to control behavioral deviance: tranquilizers such as chlordiazepoxide (Librium) and diazepam (Valium) for anxiety, nervousness, and general malaise; stimulant medications for hyperactive children; amphetamines for overeating and obesity; disulfiram (Antabuse) for alcoholism; methadone for heroin, and many others.[1] These pharmaceutical discoveries, aggressively promoted by a highly profitable and powerful drug industry (Goddard, 1973), often become the treatment of choice for deviant behavior. They are easily administered under professional medical control, quite potent in their effects (i.e., controlling, modifying, and even eliminating behavior), and are generally less expensive than other medical treatments and controls (e.g., hospitalization, altering environments, long-term psychotherapy).

Psychosurgery, surgical procedures meant to correct certain "brain dysfunctions" presumed to cause deviant behavior, was developed in the early 1930s as prefrontal lobotomy, and has been used as a treatment for mental illness. But psychosurgery fell into disrepute in the early 1950s because the "side effects" (general passivity, difficulty with abstract thinking) were deemed too undesirable, and many patients remained institutionalized in spite of such treatments. Furthermore, new psychoactive medications were becoming available to control the mentally ill. By the middle 1950s, however, approximately 40,000 to 50,000 such operations were performed in the United States (Freeman, 1959). In the late 1960s a new and technologically more sophisticated variant of psychosurgery (including laser technology and brain implants) emerged and was heralded by some as a treatment for uncontrollable violent outbursts (Delgado, 1969; Mark & Ervin, 1970). Although psychosurgery for violence has been criticized from both within as well as outside the medical profession (Chorover, 1974), and relatively few such operations have been performed, in 1976 a blue-ribbon national commission reporting to the Department of Health, Education and Welfare endorsed the use of psychosurgery as having "potential merit" and judged its risks "not excessive." This may encourage an increased use of this form of medical control.[2]

Behavior modification, a psychotechnology based on B.F. Skinner's and other behaviorists' learning theories, has been adopted by some medical professionals as a treatment modality. A variety of types and variations of behavior modification exist (e.g., token economies, tier systems, positive reinforcement schedules, aversive conditioning). While they are not medical technologies per se, they have been used by physicians for the treatment of mental illness, mental retardation, homosexuality, violence, hyperactive children, autism, phobias, alcoholism, drug addiction, eating problems, and other disorders. An irony of the medical use of behavior modification is that behaviorism explicitly denies the medical model (that behavior is a symptom of illness) and adopts an environmental, albeit still individual, solution to the problem. This has not, however, hindered its adoption by medical professionals.

Human genetics is one of the most exciting and rapidly expanding areas of medical knowledge. Genetic screening and genetic counseling are becoming more commonplace. Genetic causes are proposed for such a variety of human problems as alcoholism, hyperactivity, learning disabilities, schizophrenia, manic-depressive psychosis, homosexuality, and mental retardation. At this time, apart from specific genetic disorders such as phenylketonuria (PKU) and certain forms of retardation, genetic explanations tend to be general theories (i.e., at best positing "predispositions"), with only minimal empirical support, and are not at the level at which medical intervention occurs. The most well-publicized genetic theory of deviant behavior is that an XYY chromosome arrangement is a determinant factor in "criminal tendencies." Although this XYY research has been criticized severely (e.g., Fox, 1971), the controversy surrounding it may be a harbinger of things to come. Genetic anomalies may be discovered to have a correlation with deviant behavior and may become a causal explanation for this behavior. Medical control, in the form of genetic counseling (Sorenson, 1974), may discourage parents from having offspring with a high risk (e.g., 25%) of genetic impairment. Clearly the potentials for medical control go far beyond present use; one could imagine the possibility of licensing selected parents (with proper genes) to have children, and further manipulating gene arrangements to produce or eliminate certain traits.

MEDICAL COLLABORATION

Medicine acts not only as an independent agent of social control (as above), but frequently medical collaboration with other authorities serves social control functions. Such collaboration includes roles as information provider, gatekeeper, institutional agent, and technician. These interdependent medical control functions highlight the extent to which medicine is interwoven in the fabric of society. Historically, medical personnel have reported information on gunshot wounds and venereal disease to state authorities. More recently this has included reporting "child abuse" to child welfare or law enforcement agencies (Pfohl, 1977).

The medical profession is the official designator of the "sick role." This imbues the physician with authority to define particular kinds of deviance as illness and exempt the patient from certain role obligations. These are general gatekeeping and social control tasks. In some instances the physician functions as a specific gatekeeper for special exemptions from conventional norms; here the exemptions are authorized because of illness, disease, or disability. A classic example is the so-called insanity defense in certain crime cases. Other more commonplace examples include competency to stand trial, medical deferment from the draft or a medical discharge from the military; requiring physicians' notes to legitimize missing an examination or excessive absences in school, and, before abortion was legalized, obtaining two psychiatrists' letters testifying to the therapeutic necessity of the abortion. Halleck (1971) has called this "the power of medical excuse." In a slightly different vein, but still forms of gatekeeping and medical excuse, are medical examinations for disability or workman's compensation benefits. Medical reports required for insurance coverage and employment or medical certification of an epileptic as seizure free to obtain a driver's license are also gatekeeping activities.

Physicians in total institutions have one of two roles. In some institutions, such as schools for the retarded or mental hospitals, they are usually the administrative authority; in others, such as in the military or prisons, they are employees of the administration. In total institutions, medicine's role as an agent of social control (for the institution) is more apparent. In both the military and prisons, physicians have the power to confer the sick role and to offer medical excuse for deviance (see Daniels, 1969; Waitzkin & Waterman, 1974). For example, discharges and sick call are available medical designations for deviant behavior. Since physicians are both hired and paid by the institution, it is difficult for them to be fully an agent of the patient, engendering built-in role strains. An extreme example is in wartime when the physician's mandate is to return the soldier to combat duty as soon as possible. Under some circumstances physicians act as direct agents of control by prescribing medications to control unruly or disorderly inmates or to help a "neurotic" adjust to the conditions of a total institution. In such cases "captive professionals" (Daniels, 1969) are more likely to become the agent of the institution than the agent of the individual patient (Szasz, 1965; see also Menninger, 1967).

Under rather rare circumstances physicians may become "mere technicians," applying the sanctions of another authority who purchases their medical skills. An extreme example would be the behavior of the experimental and death physicians in Nazi Germany. A less heinous but nevertheless ominous example is provided by physicians who perform court-ordered sterilizations (Kittrie, 1971). Perhaps one could imagine sometime in the future, if the death penalty becomes commonplace again, physicians administering drugs as the "humanitarian" and painless executioners.[3]

MEDICAL IDEOLOGY

Medical ideology is a type of social control that involves defining a behavior or condition as an illness primarily because of the social and ideological benefits accrued by conceptualizing it in medical terms.

These effects of medical ideology may benefit the individual, the dominant interests in the society, or both. They exist independently of any organic basis for illness or any available treatment. Howard Waitzkin and Barbara Waterman (1974) call one latent function of medicalization "secondary gain," arguing that assumption of the sick role can fulfill personality and individual needs (e.g., gaining nurturance or attention) or legitimize personal failure (Shuval & Antonovsky, 1973).[4] One of the most important functions of the disease model of alcoholism and to a lesser extent drug addiction is the secondary gain of removing blame from, and constructing a shield against condemnation of, individuals for their deviant behavior. Alcoholics Anonymous, a nonmedical quasireligious self-help organization, adopted a variant of the medical model of alcoholism independent of the medical profession. One suspects the secondary gain serves their purposes well.

Disease designations can support dominant social interests and institutions. A poignant example is prominent 19th-century New Orleans physician S. W. Cartwright's antebellum conceptualization of the disease drapetomania, a condition that affected only slaves. Its major symptom was running away from their masters (Cartwright, S. W., 1851). Medical conceptions and controls often support dominant social values and morality: the 19th-century Victorian conceptualization of the illness of and addiction to masturbation and the medical treatments developed to control this disease make chilling reading in the 1970s (Comfort, 1967; Englehardt, 1974). The recent Soviet labeling of political dissidents as mentally ill is another example of the manipulation of illness designations to support dominant political and social institutions (Conrad, 1977). These examples highlight the sociopolitical nature of illness designations in general (Zola, 1975).

In sum, medicine as an institution of social control has a number of faces. The three types of medical social control discussed here do not necessarily exist as discrete entities but are found in combination with one another. For example, court-ordered sterilizations or medical prescribing of drugs to unruly nursing home patients combines both technological and collaborative aspects of medical control; legitimating disability status includes both ideological and collaborative aspects of medical control; and treating Soviet dissidents with drugs for their mental illness combines all three aspects of medical social control. It is clear that the enormous expansion of medicine in the past 50 years has increased the number of possible ways in which problems could be medicalized beyond those discussed in earlier chapters. In the next section we point out some of the consequences of this medicalization.

SOCIAL CONSEQUENCES OF
MEDICALIZING DEVIANCE

Jesse Pitts (1968), one of the first sociologists to give attention to the medicalization of deviance, suggests that "medicalization is one of the most effective means of social control and that it is destined to become the main mode of *formal* social control" (p. 391, emphasis in original).[5] Although his bold prediction is far-reaching (and, in light of recent developments, perhaps a bit premature), his analysis of a decade ago was curiously optimistic and uncritical of the effects and consequences of medicalization. Nonsociologists, especially psychiatric critic Thomas Szasz (1961, 1963, 1970, 1974) and legal scholar Nicholas Kittrie (1971), are much more critical in their evaluations of the ramifications of medicalization. Szasz's critiques are polemical and attack the medical, especially psychiatric, definitions and treatments for deviant behavior. Szasz's analyses, although path breaking, insightful, and suggestive, have not been presented in a particularly systematic form. Both he and Kittrie tend to focus on the effects of medicalization on individual civil liberties and judicial processes rather than on social consequences. Their writings, however, reveal that both are aware of sociological consequences.

In this section we discuss some of the more significant consequences and ramifications of defining deviant behavior as a medical problem. We must remind the reader that we are examining the *social* consequences of medicalizing deviance, which can be analyzed separately from the validity of medical definitions or diagnoses, the effectiveness of medical regimens, or their individual consequences. These variously "latent" consequences inhere in medicalization itself and occur *regardless* of how efficacious the particular medical treatment or social control mechanism. As will be apparent, our sociological analysis has left us skeptical of the social benefits of medical social control. We separate the consequences into the "brighter" and "darker" sides of medicalization. The "brighter" side will be presented first.

BRIGHTER SIDE

The brighter side of medicalization includes the positive or beneficial qualities that are attributed to medicalization. We review briefly the accepted socially progressive aspects of medicalizing deviance. They are separated more for clarity of presentation than for any intrinsic separation in consequence.

First, medicalization is related to a longtime *humanitarian* trend in the conception and control of deviance. For example, alcoholism is no longer considered a sin or even a moral weakness; it is now a disease. Alcoholics are no longer arrested in many places for "public drunkenness"; they are now somehow "treated," if only to be dried out for a time. Medical treatment for the alcoholic can be seen as a more humanitarian means of social control. It is not retributive or punitive, but at least ideally, therapeutic. Troy Duster (1970, p. 10) suggests that medical definitions increase tolerance and compassion for human problems and they "have now been reinterpreted in an almost nonmoral fashion." (We doubt this, but leave the morality issue for a later discussion.) Medicine and humanitarianism historically developed concurrently and, as some have observed, the use of medical language and evidence increases the prestige of human proposals and enhances their acceptance (Wootton, 1959; Zola, 1975). Medical definitions are imbued with the prestige of the medical profession and are considered the "scientific" and humane way of viewing a problem. . . .This is especially true if an apparently "successful" treatment for controlling the behavior is available, as with hyperkinesis.

Second, medicalization allows for the extension of the *sick role* to those labeled as deviants (see Chapter 2 [of *Deviance and Medicalization*] for our discussion of the sick role). Many of the perceived benefits of the medicalization of deviance stem from the assignment of the sick role. Some have suggested that this is the most significant element of adopting the medical model of deviant behavior (Sigler & Osmond, 1974). By defining deviant behavior as an illness or a result of illness, one is absolved of responsibility for one's behavior. It diminishes or *removes blame* from the individual for deviant actions. Alcoholics are no longer held responsible for their uncontrolled drinking, and perhaps hyperactive children are no longer the classroom's "bad boys" but children with a medical disorder. There is some clear secondary gain here for the individual. The label "sick" is free of the moral opprobrium and implied culpability of "criminal"or "sinner." The designation of sickness also may reduce guilt for drinkers and their families and for hyperactive children and their parents. Similarly, it may result in reduced stigma for the deviant. It allows for the development of more acceptable accounts of deviance: a recent film depicted a child witnessing her father's helpless drunken stupor; her mother remarked, "It's okay. Daddy's just sick."[6]

The sick role allows for the "confidential legitimation" of a certain amount of deviance, so long as the individual fulfills the obligations of the sick role.[7] As Renée Fox (1977) notes:

> The fact that the exemptions of sickness have been extended to people with a widening arc of attitudes, experiences and behaviors in American society means primarily that what is regarded as "condi-

> tionally legitimated deviance" has increased. . . . So long as [the devi-
> ant] does not abandon himself to illness or eagerly embrace it, but
> works actively on his own or with medical professionals to improve
> his condition, he is considered to be responding appropriately, even
> admirably, to an unfortunate occurrence. Under these conditions, ill-
> ness is accepted as legitimate deviance. (p. 15)[8]

The deviant, in essence, is medically excused for the deviation. But, as
Talcott Parsons (1972) has pointed out, "the conditional legitimation is
bought at a 'price,' namely, the recognition that illness itself is an undesirable state, to be recovered from as expeditiously as possible" (p.
108). Thus the medical excuse for deviance is only valid when the
patient-deviant accepts the medical perspective of the inherent undesirability of his or her sick behavior and submits to a subordinate relationship with an official agent of control (the physician) toward changing it. This, of course, negates any threat the deviant may pose to
society's normative structure, for such deviants do not challenge the
norm; by accepting deviance as sickness and social control as "treatment," the deviant underscores the validity of the violated norm.

Third, the medical model can be viewed as portraying an *optimistic* outcome for the deviant.[9] Pitts (1968) notes, "the possibility that a
patient may be exploited is somewhat minimized by therapeutic ideology, which creates an optimistic bias concerning the patient's fate" (p.
391).[10] The therapeutic ideology, accepted in some form by all
branches of medicine, suggests that a problem (e.g., deviant behavior)
can be changed or alleviated if only the proper treatment is discovered
and administered. Defining deviant behavior as an illness may also
mobilize hope in the individual patient that with proper treatment a
"cure" is possible (Frank, J., 1974). Clearly this could have beneficial
results and even become a self-fulfilling prophecy. Although the medical model is interpreted frequently as optimistic about individual
change, under some circumstances it may lend itself to pessimistic interpretations. The attribution of physiological cause coupled with the
lack of effective treatment engendered a somatic pessimism in the late
19th-century conception of madness. . . .

Fourth, medicalization lends the *prestige of the medical profession* to
deviance designations and treatments. The medical profession is the
most prestigious and dominant profession in American society (Freidson, 1970). As just noted, medical definitions of deviance become imbued with the prestige of the medical profession and are construed to
be the "scientific" way of viewing a problem. The medical mantle of
science may serve to deflect definitional challenges. This is especially
true if an apparently "successful" treatment for controlling the behav-

ior is available. Medicalization places the problem in the hands of healing physicians. "The therapeutic value of professional dominance, from the patient's point of view, is that it becomes the *doctor's problem*" (Ehrenreich & Ehrenreich, 1975, p. 156, emphasis in original). Physicians are assumed to be beneficent and honorable. "The medical and paramedical professions," Pitts (1968) contends, "especially in the United States, are probably more immune to corruption than are the judicial and parajudicial professions and relatively immune to political pressure" (p. 391).[11]

Fifth, medical social control is more *flexible* and often more *efficient* than judicial and legal controls. The impact of the flexibility of medicine is most profound on the "deviance of everyday life," since it allows "social pressures on deviance [to] increase without boxing the deviant into as rigid a category as 'criminal'" (Pitts, 1968, p. 391).[12] Medical controls are adjustable to fit the needs of the individual patient, rather than being a response to the deviant act itself. It may be more efficient (and less expensive) to control opiate addiction with methadone maintenance than with long prison terms or mental hospitalization. The behavior of disruptive hyperactive children, who have been immune to all parental and teacher sanctions, may dramatically improve after treatment with medications. Medical controls circumvent complicated legal and judicial procedures and may be applied more informally. This can have a considerable effect on social control structures. For example, it has been noted that defining alcoholism as a disease would reduce arrest rates in some areas up to 50%.

In sum, the social benefits of medicalization include the creation of humanitarian and non-punitive sanctions; the extension of the sick role to some deviants; a reduction of individual responsibility, blame, and possibly stigma for deviance; an optimistic therapeutic ideology; care and treatment rendered by a prestigious medical profession; and the availability of a more flexible and often more efficient means of social control.

DARKER SIDE

There is, however, another side to the medicalization of deviant behavior. Although it may often seem entirely humanitarian to conceptualize deviance as sickness as opposed to badness, it is not that simple. There is a "darker" side to the medicalization of deviance. In some senses these might be considered as the more clearly latent aspects of medicalization. In an earlier work Conrad (1975) elucidated four consequences of medicalizing deviance; building on that work, we expand our analysis to seven. Six are discussed here; the seventh is described separately in the next section.

Dislocation of Responsibility

As we have seen, defining behavior as a medical problem removes or profoundly diminishes responsibility from the individual. Although affixing responsibility is always complex, medicalization produces confusion and ambiguity about who is responsible. Responsibility is separated from social action; it is located in the nether world of bio-physiology or psyche. Although this takes the individual officially "off the hook," its excuse is only a partial one. The individual, the putative deviant, and the undesirable conduct are still associated. Aside from where such conduct is "seated," the sick deviant is the medium of its expression.

With the removal of responsibility also comes the lowering of status. A dual-class citizenship is created: those who are deemed responsible for their actions and those who are not. The not-completely-responsible sick are placed in a position of dependence on the fully responsible nonsick (Parsons, 1975, p. 108). Kittrie (1971, p. 347) notes in this regard that more than half the American population is no longer subject to the sanctions of criminal law. Such persons, among others, become true "second-class citizens."

Assumption of the Moral Neutrality of Medicine

Cloaked in the mantle of science, medicine and medical practice are assumed to be objective and value free. But this profoundly misrepresents reality. The very nature of medical practice involves value judgment. To call something a disease is to deem it undesirable. Medicine is influenced by the moral order of society—witness the diagnosis and treatment of masturbation as a disease in Victorian times—yet medical language of disease and treatment is assumed to be morally neutral. It is not, and the very technological-scientific vocabulary of medicine that defines disease obfuscates this fact.

Defining deviance as disease allows behavior to keep its negative judgment, but medical language veils the political and moral nature of this decision in the guise of scientific fact. There was little public clamor for moral definitions of homosexuality as long as it remained defined an illness, but soon after the disease designation was removed, moral crusaders (e.g., Anita Bryant) launched public campaigns condemning the immorality of homosexuality. One only needs to scratch the surface of medical designations for deviant behavior to find overtly moral judgments.

Thus, as Zola (1975) points out, defining a problem as within medical jurisdiction

> is not morally neutral precisely because in establishing its relevance as a key dimension for action, the moral issue is prevented from being squarely faced and occasionally from even being raised. By the acceptance of a specific behavior as an undesirable state the issue becomes not whether to treat an individual problem but how and when. (p. 86)[13]

Defining deviance as a medical phenomenon involves moral enterprise.

Domination of Expert Control

The medical profession is made up of experts; it has a monopoly on anything that can be conceptualized as an illness. Because of the way the medical profession is organized and the mandate it has from society, decisions related to medical diagnosis and treatment are controlled almost completely by medical professionals.

Conditions that enter the medical domain are not ipso facto medical problems, whether we speak of alcoholism, hyperactivity, or drug addiction. When a problem is defined as medical, it is removed from the public realm, where there can be discussion by ordinary people, and put on a plane where only medical people can discuss it. As Janice Reynolds (1973) succinctly states,

> The increasing acceptance, especially among the more educated segments of our populace, of technical solutions—solutions administered by disinterested and morally neutral experts—results in the withdrawal of more and more areas of human experience from the realm of public discussion. For when drunkenness, juvenile delinquency, sub par performance and extreme political beliefs are seen as symptoms of an underlying illness or biological defect the merits and drawbacks of such behavior or beliefs need not be evaluated. (pp. 220–221)[14]

The public may have their own conceptions of deviant behavior, but those of the experts are usually dominant. Medical definitions have a high likelihood for dominance and hegemony: they are often taken as the last scientific word. The language of medical experts increases mystification and decreases the accessibility of public debate.

Medical Social Control

Defining deviant behavior as a medical problem allows certain things to be done that could not otherwise be considered; for example, the body may be cut open or psychoactive medications given. As we elaborated above, this treatment can be a form of social control.

In regard to drug treatment, Henry Lennard (1971) observes: "Psychoactive drugs, especially those legally prescribed, tend to restrain individuals from behavior and experience that are not complementary with the requirements of the dominant value system" (p. 57). These forms of medical social control presume a prior definition of deviance as a medical problem. Psychosurgery on an individual prone to violent outbursts requires a diagnosis that something is wrong with his brain or nervous system. Similarly, prescribing drugs to restless, overactive, and disruptive schoolchildren requires a diagnosis of hyperkinesis. These forms of social control, what Stephan Chorover (1973) has called "psychotechnology," are powerful and often efficient means of controlling deviance. These relatively new and increasingly popular forms of medical control could not be used without the prior medicalization of deviant behavior. As is suggested from the discovery of hyperkinesis and to a lesser extent the development of methadone treatment of opiate addiction, if a mechanism of medical social control seems useful, then the deviant behavior it modifies will be given a medical label or diagnosis. We imply no overt malevolence on the part of the medical profession; rather, it is part of a larger process, of which the medical profession is only a part. The larger process might be called the individualization of social problems.

Individualization of Social Problems

The medicalization of deviance is part of a larger phenomenon that is prevalent in our society: the individualization of social problems. We tend to look for causes and solutions to complex social problems in the individual rather than in the social system. William Ryan (1971) has identified this process as "blaming the victim": seeing the causes of the problem in individuals (who are usually of low status) rather than as endemic to the society. We seek to change the "victim" rather than the society. The medical practice of diagnosing an illness in an individual lends itself to the individualization of social problems. Rather than seeing certain deviant behaviors as symptomatic of social conditions, the medical perspective focuses on the individual, diagnosing and treating the illness itself and generally ignoring the social situation.

Hyperkinesis serves as a good example of this. Both the school and parents are concerned with the child's behavior; the child is difficult at home and disruptive in school. No punishments or rewards seem consistently effective in modifying the behavior, and both parents and school are at their wits' end. A medical evaluation is suggested. The diagnosis of hyperkinetic behavior leads to prescribing stimulant medications. The child's behavior seems to become more socially acceptable, reducing problems in school and home. Treatment is considered a medical success.

But there is an alternative perspective. By focusing on the symptoms and defining them as hyperkinesis, we ignore the possibility that the behavior is not an illness but an adaptation to a social situation. It diverts our attention from the family or school and from seriously entertaining the idea that the "problem" could be in the structure of the social system. By giving medications, we are essentially supporting the existing social and political arrangements in that it becomes a "symptom" of an individual disease rather than a possible "comment" on the nature of the present situation. Although the individualization of social problems aligns well with the individualistic ethic of American culture, medical intervention against deviance makes medicine a de facto agent of dominant social and political interests.

Depoliticization of Deviant Behavior

Depoliticization of deviant behavior is a result of both the process of medicalization and the individualization of social problems. Probably one of the clearest recent examples of such depoliticization occurred when political dissidents in the Soviet Union were declared mentally ill and confined to mental hospitals (Conrad, 1977). This strategy served to neutralize the meaning of political protest and dissent, rendering it (officially, at least) symptomatic of mental illness.

The medicalization of deviant behavior depoliticizes deviance in the same manner. By defining the overactive, restless, and disruptive child as hyperkinetic, we ignore the meaning of the behavior in the context of the social system. If we focused our analysis on the school system, we might see the child's behavior as a protest against some aspect of the school or classroom situation, rather than symptomatic of an individual neurological disorder. Similar examples could be drawn of the opiate addict in the ghetto, the alcoholic in the workplace, and others. Medicalizing deviant behavior precludes us from recognizing it as a possible intentional repudiation of existing political arrangements.

There are other related consequences of the medicalization of deviance beyond the six discussed. The medical ideal of early intervention may lead to early labeling and secondary deviance (see Lemert, 1972). The "medical decision rule," which approximates "when in doubt, treat," is nearly the converse of the legal dictum "innocent until proven guilty" and may unnecessarily enlarge the population of deviants (Scheff, 1963). Certain constitutional safeguards of the judicial system that protect individuals' rights are neutralized or bypassed by medicalization (Kittrie, 1971). Social control in the name of benevolence is at once insidious and difficult to confront. Although these are all significant, we wish to expand on still another consequence of considerable social importance, the exclusion of evil.

EXCLUSION OF EVIL

Evil has been excluded from the imagery of modern human problems. We are uncomfortable with notions of evil; we regard them as primitive and nonhumanitarian, as residues from a theological era.[15] Medicalization contributes to the exclusion of concepts of evil in our society. Clearly medicalization is not the sole cause of the exclusion of evil, but it shrouds conditions, events, and people and prevents them from being confronted as evil. The roots of the exclusion of evil are in the Enlightenment, the diminution of religious imagery of sin, the rise of determinist theories of human behavior, and the doctrine of cultural relativity. Social scientists as well have excluded the concept of evil from their analytic discourses (Wolff, 1969; for exceptions, see Becker, 1975, and Lyman, 1978).

Although we cannot here presume to identify the forms of evil in modern times, we would like to sensitize the reader to how medical definitions of deviance serve to further exclude evil from our view. It can be argued that regardless of what we construe as evil (e.g., destruction, pain, alienation, exploitation, oppression), there are at least two general types of evil: evil intent and evil consequence. Evil intent is similar to the legal concept mens rea, literally, "evil mind." Some evil is intended by a specific line of action. Evil consequence is, on the other hand, the result of action. No intent or motive to do evil is necessary for evil consequence to prevail; on the contrary, it often resembles the platitude "the road to hell is paved with good intentions." In either case medicalization dilutes or obstructs us from seeing evil. Sickness gives us a vocabulary of motive (Mills, 1940) that obliterates evil intent. And although it does not automatically render evil consequences good, the allegation that they were products of a "sick" mind or body relegates them to a status similar to that of "accidents."

For example, Hitler orchestrated the greatest mass genocide in modern history, yet some have reduced his motivation for the destruction of the Jews (and others) to a personal pathological condition. To them and to many of us, Hitler was sick. But this portrays the horror of the Holocaust as a product of individual pathology; as Thomas

Szasz frequently points out, it prevents us from seeing and confronting man's inhumanity to man. Are Son of Sam, Charles Manson, the assassins of King and the Kennedys, the Richard Nixon of Watergate, Libya's Muammar Kaddafi, or the all-too-common child beater sick? Although many may well be troubled, we argue that there is little to be gained by deploying such a medical vocabulary of motives.[16] It only hinders us from comprehending the human element in the decisions we make, the social structures we create, and the actions we take. Hannah Arendt (1963), in her exemplary study of the banality of evil, contends that Nazi war criminal Adolph Eichmann, rather than being sick, was "terribly, terrifyingly normal."

Susan Sontag (1978) has suggested that on a cultural level, we use the metaphor of illness to speak of various kinds of evil. Cancer, in particular, provides such a metaphor: we depict slums and pornography shops as "cancers" in our cities; J. Edgar Hoover's favorite metaphor for communism was "a cancer in our midst"; and Nixon's administration was deemed "cancerous," rotting from within. In our secular culture, where powerful religious connotations of sin and evil have been obscured, cancer (and for that matter, illness in general) is one of the few available images of unmitigated evil and wickedness. As Sontag (1978) observes:

> But how to be...[moral] in the late twentieth century? How, when ...we have a sense of evil but no longer the religious or philosophical language to talk intelligently about evil. Trying to comprehend "radical" or "absolute" evil, we search for adequate metaphors. But the modern disease metaphors are all cheap shots...Only in the most limited sense is any historical event or problem like an illness. It is invariably an encouragement to simplify what is complex....(p. 85)

Thus we suggest that the medicalization of social problems detracts from our capability to see and confront the evils that face our world.

In sum, the "darker" side of the medicalization of deviance has profound consequences for the putative or alleged deviant and society. We now turn to some policy implications of medicalization.

MEDICALIZATION OF DEVIANCE AND SOCIAL POLICY

"Social policy" may be characterized as an institutionalized definition of a problem and its solutions. There are many routes for developing social policy in a complex society, but, as John McKnight (1977) contends, "There is no greater power than the right to define the question" (p. 85). The definition and designation of the problem itself may be the key to the development of social policy. Problem definitions often take on a life of their own; they tend to resist change and become the accepted manner of defining reality (see Caplan & Nelson, 1973). In a complex society, social policy is only rarely implemented as a direct and self-conscious master plan, as, for example, occurred with the development of community mental health centers.... It is far more common for social policies to evolve from the particular definitions and solutions that emerge from various political processes. Individual policies in diverse parts of society may conflict, impinge on, and modify one another. The overall social policy even may be residual to the political process. The medicalization of deviance never has been a formalized social policy; ... it has emerged from various combinations of turf battles, court decisions, scientific innovations, political expediences, medical entrepreneurship, and other influences. The medicalization of deviance has become in effect a de facto social policy.

In this discussion we explore briefly how some changes and trends in medicine and criminal justice as well as the recent "punitive backlash" may affect the future course of the medicalization of deviance.

CRIMINAL JUSTICE: DECRIMINALIZATION, DECARCERATION, AND THE THERAPEUTIC STATE

Over the past two decades the percent of officially defined deviants institutionalized in prisons or mental hospitals has decreased. There has been a parallel growth in "community-based" programs for social control. Although this "decarceration" has been most dramatic with the mentally ill, substantial deinstitutionalization has occurred in prison populations and with juvenile delinquents and opiate addicts as well (see Scull, 1977). Many deviants who until recently would have been institutionalized are being "treated" or maintained in community programs—for example, probation, work release, and community correctional programs for criminal offenders; counseling, vocational, or residential programs as diversion from juvenile court for delinquents; and methadone maintenance or therapeutic community programs in lieu of prison for opiate addicts.

This emerging social policy of decarceration has already affected medicalization. Assuming that the amount of deviance and number of deviants a society recognizes remains generally constant (see Erikson, 1966), a change in policy in one social control agency affects other social control agents. Thus decarceration of institutionalized deviants will lead to the deployment of other forms of social control. Because medical social control is one of the main types of social control deployed in the community, decarceration increases medicalization. Since the *Robinson* Supreme Court decision and the discovery of methadone maintenance the control of opiate addicts has shifted dramatically from the criminal justice system to the medical system. Control of some criminal offenders may be subtly transferred from the correctional system to the mental health system; one recent study found an increase in the number of males with prior police records admitted to psychiatric facilities and suggested this may be an indication of a medicalization of criminal behavior (Melick, Steadman, & Cocozza, 1979). There is also some evidence that probation officers, in their quest for professional status, adopt a medical model in their treatment of offenders (Chalfant, 1977). Although some observers have suggested that the apparent decarceration of mental patients from mental hospitals and the rise of community mental health facilities has at least partially demedicalized madness, . . . this is an inaccurate interpretation. Moreover, the extent of decarceration has been exaggerated; many of the former or would-be mental patients are located in other institutions, especially nursing homes (Redlich & Kellert, 1978). Here they remain under medical or quasimedical control. In short, decarceration appears to increase the medicalization of deviance.

Decriminalization also affects medicalization. Decriminalization means that a certain activity is no longer considered to be a criminal offense. But even when criminal sanctions are removed, the act may still maintain its definition as deviance. In this case, other noncriminal sanctions may emerge. . . . [T]he disease model of alcoholism did not begin its rise to prominence until after the repeal of Prohibition, that is, after alcohol use in general was decriminalized. More specifically, we can examine the response to the decriminalization of "public drunkenness" in the 1960s. A recent study has shown that although alcohol and drug psychoses comprised only 4.7% of the mental health population (inpatient and outpatient) in 1950, in 1975 "alcoholism accounted for 46 percent of state hospital patients" and became the largest diagnostic category in mental hospitals (Redlich & Kellert, 1978, p. 26). It is likely that the combination of the declining populations in state mental hospitals and the decriminalization of "public drunkenness" (e.g., police now bring drunks to the mental hospital instead of the drunk tank) is in part reflected in this enormous increase of alcoholics in the mental health system.

Medicalization allows for the decriminalization of certain activities (e.g., public drunkenness, some types of drug use) because (1) they remain defined as deviant (sick) and are not vindicated and (2) an alternative form of social control is available (medicine). If an act is decriminalized and also demedicalized (e.g., homosexuality), there may well be a backlash and a call for recriminalization or at least reaffirmation of its deviant status rather than a vindication. We postulate that if an act is decriminalized and yet not vindicated (i.e., still remains defined as deviant), its control may be transferred from the criminal justice to the medical system.[17]

In the 1960s and early 1970s considerable concern was voiced in some quarters concerning the "social policy" that was leading to the divestment of criminal justice and the rise of the therapeutic state (Kittrie, 1971; Leifer, 1969; Szasz, 1963). . . . [T]here has been some retreat from the "rehabilitative ideal" in criminal justice. On the other hand, both decarceration and decriminalization have increased medicalization. Thus we would conclude that although the "therapeutic state" is not becoming the dominant social policy as its earlier critics feared, neither is it showing signs of abating. We would suggest that to the extent that decarceration and decriminalization remain social policies, medicalization of deviance can be expected to increase.

TRENDS IN MEDICINE AND MEDICALIZATION

The medicalization of deviance has been influenced by changes in the medical profession and in social policy regarding medical care. The prestige of medicine has been growing since the turn of the century. Medical practice has become increasingly specialized; whereas only 20% of physicians were specialists in 1940, by the early 1970s nearly 80% considered themselves specialists (Twaddle & Hessler, 1977, p. 175). This is in part the result of the increasingly technological nature of medicine. The number of personnel employed in the medical sector has increased considerably since the Second World War. But the most spectacular growth has been in the cost and investment in medical care in the past three decades.

In 1950 the expenditures for medical care comprised 4.6% of the Gross National Product (GNP); by 1976 they accounted for 8.3%, for a total of over $130 billion spent on medical care. Since 1963 health expenditures have risen more than 10% yearly, while the rest of the economy has grown by 6% to 7%. In other words, medicine is the fastest expanding part of the service sector and one of the most expansive segments of our economy. In one sense we might see these increasing expenditures themselves as an index of increasing medicalization. But more likely, the increasing economic resources allocated to medical care create a substantial pool of money to draw from, thereby increasing the resources available for medical solutions to human problems. It should be noted, however, that the inflation of medical costs could ultimately become a factor in decreasing the medicalization of deviance, simply because medical solutions have become too costly.

Much of the rising cost of medical care has been attributed to the growth in third-party payments (i.e., when medical care is paid not by the patient or the provider of the care but by a third party). The major source of third-party payments has been Blue Cross and Blue Shield and the health insurance industry, and, since the enactment of Medicare and Medicaid in 1965, also the federal government. More than 51% of medical costs was paid directly by the patient in 1966; by 1975 this figure had dipped to less than 33% (Coe, 1978, p. 387). The largest increase in third-party payments has been the amount paid by the federal government; in 1975, 27.7% of medical costs was borne by the federal government, and this is expected to continue to increase. What this all means for the medicalization of deviance is that "third parties" are increasingly deciding what is appropriate medical care and what is not. For example, if medical insurance or Medicaid will pay for certain types of treatment, then the problem is more likely to be medicalized. Although the medical profession certainly has influence in this area, this removes the control of medicalization from medical hands and places it into the hands of the third-party payers. Although 90% of America's Blue Cross plans provide some hospital coverage for alcoholism, less than 10% of the cost of treatment is currently covered by private insurance and health-care protection programs (*Behavior Today,* June 21, 1976). Although many physicians consider obesity to be a bona fide medical condition, virtually no health insurers will pay for intestinal by-pass operations as a treatment for obesity. Clearly, changes in policies by third-party payers can drastically affect the types or amount of deviance medicalized.

Until about the past two decades, the dominant organization of medical practice was private, solo practice. There has been a growing bureaucratization of medical practice. The hospital rather than the private office is becoming the center for health care delivery. These large modern hospitals are both a result of, and an inducement for, the practice of highly specialized and technological medicine. Hospitals have their own organizational priorities of sustaining a smoothly running bureaucracy, maximizing profitable services, justifying technological equipment, and maintaining the patient-bed load at near full capacity. Although bureaucratic organizations reduce medical professional power, the institutional structure of the hospital is better suited to function as an agent of social control than the singular office practice. Hospital medicine can be practiced at a high biotechnological level, is less client dependent (because of third-party payments), has less personal involvement, and is more responsive to demands of other institutions, especially the state, on whom it is increasingly dependent for financial support.

For many years American medicine was considered to be suffering from a shortage of physicians. In the 1960s federal programs to expand medical schools increased greatly the number of physicians being trained. We have just begun to experience the effects of the rising number of physicians. Between 1970 and 1990 we can expect an 80% increase in the number of physicians—from about 325,000 to almost 600,000. And if present population and medical trends continue, as we expect they will, by 1990 there will be one physician for every 420 people in the United States and an even greater enlargement in the number of nurses and allied health workers (U.S. Department of Health, Education and Welfare, 1974).

One result of the growing number of medical personnel could be an increase in the number of problems that become defined as medical problems (after all, we have all these highly trained professionals to treat them). Although the greater number of physicians could result in better delivery of medical services, it could also increase medicalization as new physicians attempt to develop new areas of medical turf as old ones become saturated. David Mechanic (1974, p. 50) suggests, for instance, that for "family practice" to become a viable discipline in medicine, family practitioners would have to develop a "scientific and investigatory stance" toward common family practice problems such as "alcoholism, drug abuse, difficulties in sexual development, failure to conform to medical regimen and the like." The potential for the expansion of the medical domain here is great.

But there are also some countertrends in medicine. There is an emphasis on both self-care and individual responsibility for health (see Knowles, 1977). Health is becoming defined as more of a personal responsibility. As Zola (1972) observes, "At the same time the label 'illness' is being used to attribute 'diminished responsibility' to a whole host of phenomena, the issue of 'personal responsibility' seems to be re-emerging in medicine itself" (p. 491). Increased personal responsibility for sickness could cause the responsibility for the behavior to return to the individual. For instance, alcoholics would be deemed responsible for deviant drinking, obese people for their deviant bodies, and opiate addicts for their habits. This could ultimately spur some demedicalization.[18]

But the most important social policy affecting the future of medicalization hinges on the notion of a "right to adequate health care" and the development of a National Health Insurance (NHI) program. The proposal of an NHI program has become a significant political issue. In the past decade dozens of bills advocating different NHI plans have been submitted to various congressional committees. No specific NHI plan as yet has emerged as the most probable candidate for passage, but there is a high likelihood that some type of NHI plan will be enacted within the next decade. Because of the recent fiscal crunch and the strong lobbying of powerful vested interests (e.g., the health insurance industry, the medical profession, the hospital associations), it is unlikely that it will be an NHI program providing comprehensive coverage. More likely, NHI will not alter the present structure of the medical system and will resemble present insurance programs (although with increased public accountability); it will be at least partly federally financed and extend insurance coverage to all Americans. Regardless of which NHI bill is enacted, it will have an effect on medicalization. What the effect will be, however, is uncertain. There are at least three possible scenarios.

> *Scenario One:* Because the cost of paying for treatment is high and deemed prohibitive, fewer deviant behaviors are defined as medical problems. Perhaps alcoholism, marital problems, drug addiction, psychosurgery, and treatment for obesity will be excluded from NHI coverage.
>
> *Scenario Two:* Because NHI will pay for the treatment of anything defined as a medical problem, more deviance becomes medicalized. Gambling, divorce, boredom, narcissism, and lethargy will be defined as illnesses and treated medically.
>
> *Scenario Three:* Individuals are not considered responsible for their illnesses; so activities that are seen as leading to medical problems become defined as deviant. Smoking, eating poorly, getting insufficient exercise, or eschewing seat belts all will be defined as deviant. Certain medical problems could be excluded from NHI coverage because they are deemed to be willfully caused (i.e., "badness").

This final scenario takes us full circle, as we would develop the notion of "sickness as sin."[19] Scenarios two and three would further the convergence of illness and deviance. At this point, it is difficult to predict which, if any, of these scenarios might result from the enactment of NHI.

PUNITIVE BACKLASH

Since about 1970 there has been a "backlash" against the increasing "liberalization" of the treatment of deviance and the Supreme Court decisions that have granted criminal suspects and offenders greater "rights." This public reaction, coming mostly from the more conservative sectors of society, generally calls for more strict treatment of deviants and a return to more punitive sanctions.

This "punitive backlash" takes many forms. In 1973 New York passed a "get tough" law with mandatory prison sentences for drug dealers. Other legislative attempts have been made to impose mandatory minimum sentences on offenders. There is a considerable public clamor for the return of the death penalty. A current New York state law has allowed juveniles between ages 13 and 15 to be tried as adults for some offenses. The antiabortion crusade has made inroads into the availability of abortions and is aiming for the recriminalization of abortion. Recently antihomosexuality crusades have appeared from Florida to Oregon, defeating antidiscrimination referenda and limiting the rights of homosexuals.

This swell of public reaction may be in part a response to the therapeutic ideology and the perceived "coddling" of deviants. Should this backlash and other recent public reactions such as California's Proposition 13 taxpayer revolt continue to gather strength and grow in popularity, they well may force a retreat from the medicalization of deviance.

SOME SOCIAL POLICY RECOMMENDATIONS

Our examination of the medicalization of deviance in American society has led us to some conclusions related to social policy. In this discussion we briefly outline some social policy recommendations.

1. The medicalization of deviance needs to be recognized as a de facto social policy. Recognized as such, issues like those pointed to in this chapter could be raised and debated. It is important that public discussion by physicians, politicians, and lay persons alike be encouraged and facilitated. In recognition of the salience of medicalization and its consequences, perhaps "medicalization impact statements" should be required of social policy proposals affecting medicalization. For example, it is important to weigh the impact of NHI on medicalization.

2. Research is needed on the extent of medicalization, its benefits, and its costs. This includes research into the efficacy, the financial and social costs, and the extent of actual medicalization. We need continued research into the politics of medicalization and further investigation into the areas of medicalized deviance covered in [*Deviance and Medicalization*] as well as those not covered, such as the medicalization of suicide, old age and senility, obesity, abortion, and mental retardation. We need to compare these with uncontested medical problems that were at one time defined as deviance, such as epilepsy and leprosy. Close at-

tention needs to be given to the efficacy, costs, and benefits for each type of medicalization. Hopefully such knowledge and understanding will better guide social policy decisions concerning medicalization.

3. Medicalization removes the constitutional safeguards of the judicial process (see Kittrie, 1971). Because of this, it is important to create some type of medical due process or redress for putative deviants who are the objects of therapeutic interventions. Since this type of due process would probably be resisted by the medical profession and labeled antitherapeutic, we propose the development of some type of "counterpower" to medical social control. This could take the form of patient or deviant advocates, intervention review organizations, or even a Nader-type watchdog group. This would help ensure that individual rights were not circumvented in the name of health.

4. It is our belief that we need to develop social policies toward deviance that hold people *accountable* for their actions but do *not blame* them. This is a delicate but possible balance. One proposal is bypassing such slippery concepts as responsibility and guilt, substituting an assumption of human fallibility combined with accountability for human action. As Kittrie (1971) suggests,

> Every person who lives in a society is accountable to it for his antisocial behavior. Society, in return, may seek to curb his future misdeeds, not as a punishment for the improper exercise of free will but as a remedy for his human failings.

Although the notions of guilt, moral responsibility, and accountability are profound philosophical (and political) questions that cannot begin to be addressed here, we believe they must be directly discussed and reevaluated, since many people's lives are profoundly affected by them.

Presently our society's only "no blame" model for deviant behavior is the medical model. We need to develop new models of deviance that do not assume ultimate individual moral responsibility and yet do not define those who are not considered responsible as "sick." Presently the only alternative to the criminal-responsibility model is the medical-no-responsibility model. It is imperative that we free ourselves from the dichotomous crime or sickness models that create largely either-or situations, as well as from unworkable and contradictory crime-sickness hybrids, as with sex offenders.

New models of deviance need to be reconciled with social scientific knowledge about deviance. There is considerable evidence that economic, social, and family factors contribute to deviant behavior, and it is important to understand that the individual has only limited control over these factors. Yet it is also important, because of our understanding of human behavior, not to completely neglect its voluntary components. Thus we concur with Robert Veatch (1973) that rather than assuming that human behavior is caused by biophysiological elements ("sickness"), "it is preferable to make clear the missing categories—namely nonculpable deviancy caused psychologically, socially and culturally, for example, by lack of various forms of psychological, social, and cultural welfare" (p. 71). We need to create a "no blame" role for deviants that still holds the individual accountable for his or her action. We need to create a social role analogous to the sick role that does not assume sickness or remove responsibility and yet reconciles our understanding that there are "forces" beyond the scope of the individual that affect human behavior. For example, one can envision the conception of a "victim role"; the individual is viewed as a "victim" of life circumstances; these circumstances are known to increase the probability for certain types of "deviant" behavioral responses as well as attributions, yet because the behavior is not regarded as "determined" by the circumstances, the individual is accountable for deviant behavior. In other words, given the circumstances, the individual is accountable for the behavioral strategies chosen in a situation. Needless to say, this is a complex and sticky issue, replete with philosophical and pragmatic pitfalls. It provides an important challenge for social scientists and philosophers. We present this example only to suggest the possibility of alternatives to the medical-criminal model dichotomy. As Clarice Stoll (1968) observes, our "image of man" is central in determining our social response to deviance; we call for the development of an alternative image that reconciles societal response with the understandings of social and behavioral science.

Finally, because social control is necessary for the existence of society, we urge the development of alternative, noncriminal and nonmedical modes of social control appropriate to the new model of deviance.

MEDICALIZING DEVIANCE: A FINAL NOTE

The potential for medicalizing deviance has increased in the past few decades. The increasing dominance of the medical profession, the discovery of subtle physiological correlates of human behavior, and the creation of medical technologies (promoted by powerful pharmaceutical and medical technology industry interests) have advanced this trend. Although we remain skeptical of the overall social benefits of medicalization and are concerned about its "darker" side, it is much too simplistic to suggest a wholesale condemnation of medicalization. Offering alcoholics medical treatment in lieu of the drunk tank is undoubtedly a more humane response to deviance; methadone maintenance allows a select group of opiate addicts to make successful adaptations to society; some schoolchildren seem to benefit from stimulant medications for hyperkinesis; and the medical discovery of child abuse may well increase therapeutic intervention. Medicalization in general has reduced societal condemnation of deviants. But these benefits do not mean these conditions are in fact diseases or that the same results could not be achieved in another manner. And even in those instances of medical "success," the social consequences indicated... are still evident.

The most difficult consequence of medicalization for us to discuss is the exclusion of evil. In part this is because we are members of a culture that has largely eliminated evil from intellectual and public discourse. But our discomfort also stems from our ambivalence about what can meaningfully be construed as evil in our society. If we are excluding evil, what exactly are we excluding? We have no difficulty depicting such conditions as pain, violence, oppression, exploitation, and abject cruelty as evil. Social scientists of various stripes have been pointing to these evils and their consequences since the dawn of social science. It is also possible for us to conceive of "organizational evils" such as corporate price fixing, false advertising (or even all advertising), promoting life-threatening automobiles, or the wholesale drugging of nursing home patients to facilitate institutional management. We also have little trouble in seeing ideologies such as imperialism, chauvinism, and racial supremacy as evils. Our difficulty comes with seeing individuals as evil. While we would not adopt a Father-Flanagan-of-Boys-Town attitude of "there's no such thing as a bad boy," our own socialization and "liberal" assumptions as well as sociological perspective make it difficult for us to conceive of any individual as "evil." As sociologists we are more likely to see people as products of their psychological and social circumstances: there may be evil social structures, ideologies, or deeds, but not evil people. Yet when we confront a Hitler, an Idi Amin, or a Stalin of the forced labor camps, it is sometimes difficult to reach any other conclusion. We note this dilemma more as clarification of our stance than as a solution. There are both evils in society and people who are "victim" to those evils. Worthwhile social scientific goals include uncovering the evils, understanding and aiding the victims, and ultimately contributing to a more humane existence for all.

SUMMARY

In the 20th century, medicine has expanded as an institution of social control. On the most abstract level medical social control is the acceptance of a medical perspective as the dominant definition of certain phenomena. Medical social control of deviant behavior usually takes the form of medical intervention, attempting to modify deviant behavior with medical means and in the name of health. We identify three general forms of the medical social control of deviance: medical technology, medical collaboration, and medical ideology. Medical technology involves the use of pharmaceutical or surgical technologies as controls for deviance. Medical collaboration emphasizes the interwoven position of medicine in society and occurs when physicians collaborate with other authorities as information providers, gatekeepers, institutional agents, and technicians. Medical ideology as social control involves defining a behavior or condition as an illness primarily for the social and ideological benefits accrued by conceptualizing it in medical terms. Although these three "ideal types" are likely to be found in combination, they highlight the varied faces of medical social control.

There are important social consequences of medicalizing deviance. The "brighter" side of medicalization includes (1) a more humanitarian conception of deviance; (2) the extension of the sick role to deviants, minimizing blame and allowing for the conditional legitimation of a certain amount of deviance; (3) the more optimistic view of change presented by the medical model; (4) lending the prestigious mantle of the medical profession to deviance designations and treatments; and (5) the fact that medical social control is more flexible and sometimes more efficient than other controls. However, there is a "darker" side of medicalization, which includes (1) the dislocation of responsibility from the individual; (2) the assumption of the moral neutrality of medicine; (3) the problems engendered by the domination of expert control; (4) powerful medical techniques used for social control; (5) the individualization of complex social problems; (6) the depoliticization of deviant behavior; and (7) the exclusion of evil. It is this darker side that leaves us skeptical of the social benefits of medicalizing deviance.

The medicalization of deviance has become a de facto social policy. Changes in other "social policies" affect medicalization. Decarceration leads to the increasing deployment of medical social control, since it is one of the most effective social controls "in the community." Decriminalization may also increase medicalization because medicine provides an alternative social control mechanism. We postulate that if an act is decriminalized and not vindicated, its control may be transferred from the criminal justice system to the medical system. Although the therapeutic state has not become the dominant social policy, neither does it show any signs of withering away. Medicalization is also influenced by changes and trends in medicine. Medical practice is becoming increasingly specialized, technological, and bureaucratic. Society's economic investment (in terms of percentage of GNP) in medical care has nearly doubled in the past three decades. This is both an index of and incentive for medicalization. Bureaucratic medical practice removes some definitional power from the medical profession and places it in the hands of third-party payers (including the state) and hospital administrators. The number of physicians and other medical personnel will double by 1990; this may well cause further medicalization. On the other hand, the increased emphasis on self-care and individual responsibility for health, as well as the "fiscal crisis" of rapidly rising medical costs, may limit medicalization and spur demedicalization. The passage of a National Health Insurance program may have a profound effect on medicalization, although it is difficult to predict precisely what it will be. If the "punitive backlash" to perceived liberalized treatment of deviants gains strength, it may force some retreat from the medicalization of deviance.

We conclude with some brief social policy recommendations:

1. The medicalization of deviance needs to be recognized as a de facto social policy.
2. More research is needed on the extent, politics, benefits, and costs of medicalizing deviance.
3. Some form of "counterpower" to medical social control needs to be created.
4. A new model of deviance that holds people accountable for their actions but does not blame them needs to be developed, perhaps as a "victim" model. We need to be freed from the dichotomous crime or sickness models that create limiting either-or situations.

NOTES

1. Another pharmaceutical innovation, birth control pills, also functions as a medical control; in this case, the control of reproduction. There is little doubt that "the pill" has played a significant part in the sexual revolution since the 1960s and the redefinition of what constitutes sexual deviance.
2. A number of other surgical interventions for deviance have been developed in recent years. Surgery for "gender dysphoria" (transsexuality) and "intestinal by-pass" operations for obesity are both examples of surgical intervention for deviance. The legalization of abortions has also medicalized and legitimated an activity that was formerly deviant and brought it under medical-surgical control.

3. It is worth noting that in the recent Gary Gilmore execution a physician was involved; he designated the spot where the heartbeat was loudest and measured vital signs during the execution ceremony. A few states have actually passed death penalty legislation specifying injection of a lethal drug as the means of execution.

4. Although Waitzkin and Waterman suggest that such secondary gain functions are latent (i.e., unintended and unrecognized), the cases we have discussed here show that such "gains" are often intentionally pursued.

5. From Pitts, J. Social control: the concept. In D. Sills (Ed.), *International encyclopedia of social sciences* (Vol. 14). New York: Macmillan Publishing Co., Inc., 1968. Copyright 1968 by Crowell Collier and Macmillan, Inc.

6. It should be noted, however, that little empirical evidence exists for reduced stigmatization. Derek Phillips' (1963) research suggests that people seeking medical help for their personal problems are highly at risk for rejection and stigmatization. Certain illnesses carry their own stigma. Leprosy, epilepsy, and mental illness are all stigmatized illnesses (Gussow & Tracy, 1968); Susan Sontag (1978) proposes that cancer is highly stigmatized in American society. We need further research on the stigma-reducing properties of medical designations of deviance; it is by no means an automatic result of medicalization.

7. On the other hand, Paul Roman and Harrison Trice (1968, p. 248) contend that the sick role of alcoholic may actually reinforce deviant behavior by removing responsibility for deviant drinking behavior.

8. Reprinted by permission of *Daedalus,* Journal of the American Academy of Arts and Sciences, Boston, Mass. Spring 1977, *Doing better and feeling worse: health in the United States.*

9. For a contrasting viewpoint, see Rotenberg's (1978) work, discussed in [*Deviance and Medicalization: From Badness to Sickness*].

10. From Pitts, J. Social control: the concept. In D. Sills (Ed.), *International encyclopedia of social sciences* (Vol. 14). New York: Macmillan Publishing Co., Inc., 1968. Copyright 1968 by Crowell Collier and Macmillan, Inc.

11. Ibid.

12. Ibid.

13. Reprinted with permission from Pergamon Press, Ltd.

14. From "The medical institution: the death and disease-producing appendage" by Janice M. Reynolds, first published in *American society: a critical analysis* edited by Larry T. Reynolds and James M. Henslin. Copyright © 1973 by Longman Inc. Reprinted by permission of Longman.

15. Writing in the early 1970s, Kittrie (1971) noted, "Ours is increasingly becoming a society that views punishment as a primitive and vindictive tool and is therefore loath to punish" (p. 347). Some recent scholarship in penology and the controversy about the death penalty has slightly modified this trend.

16. We *do not* suggest that these individuals or any other deviants discussed in this book are or should be considered evil. We only wish to point out that medicalization on a societal level contributes to the exclusion of evil. To the extent that evil exists, we would argue that social structures and specific social conditions are the most significant cause of evil.

17. The decriminalization of abortion has led to its complete medicalization. It is interesting to speculate whether the decriminalization of marijuana, gambling, and prostitution would lead to medicalization. It is likely that with marijuana and gambling, "compulsive" and excessive indulgence would be defined as "sick"; with prostitution, medical certification might be required, as is presently the case in several European countries.

18. Reneé Fox (1977, pp. 19–21) contends that the recent trends of viewing patients as consumers, the emergence of physician extenders such as nurse practitioners and physicians' assistants, and "the increased insistence on patients' rights, self-therapy, mutual aid, community medical services and care by non-physician health professionals" constitute evidence for demedicalization. We think Fox is mistaken. *Demedicalization does not occur until a problem is no longer defined in medical terms and medical treatments are no longer seen as directly relevant to its solution.* Fox confuses deprofessionalization with demedicalization.

19. Paradoxically this could also encourage demedicalization, for the medical model then becomes less functional in removing the culpability for deviance.

REFERENCES

Arendt, H. *Eichmann in Jerusalem.* New York: Viking Press, 1963.

Becker, E. *Escape from evil.* New York: The Free Press, 1975.

Caplan, N., & Nelson, S. D. On being useful: the nature and consequences of psychological research on social problems. *Am. Psychologist,* 1973, *28,* 199–211.

Cartwright, S. W. Report on the diseases and physical peculiarities of the negro race. *N.O. Med. Surg. J.,* 1851, *7,* 691–715.

Chalfant, P. Professionalization and the medicalization of deviance: the case of probation officers. *Offender Rehabilitation,* 1977, *2,* 77–85.

Chorover, S. Big Brother and psychotechnology. *Psychol. Today,* 1973, *7,* 43–54 (Oct.).

Chorover, S.: Psychosurgery: a neuropsychological perspective. *Boston U. Law Rev.,* 1974, *74,* 231–248 (March).

Coe, R. M. *Sociology of medicine* (2nd ed.). New York: McGraw-Hill Book Co., 1978.

Comfort, A. *The anxiety makers.* London: Thomas Nelson & Sons, 1967.

Conrad, P. The discovery of hyperkinesis: notes on the medicalization of deviant behavior. *Social Prob.,* 1975, *23,* 12–21 (Oct.).

Conrad, P. Soviet dissidents, ideological deviance, and mental hospitalization. Presented at Midwest Sociological Society Meetings, Minneapolis, 1977.

Daniels, A. K. The captive professional: bureaucratic limitation in the practice of military psychiatry. *J. Health Soc. Behav.,* 1969, *10,* 255–265 (Dec.).

Delgado, J. M. R. *Physical control of the mind: toward a psychocivilized society.* New York: Harper and Row, Publishers, 1969.

Duster, T. *The legislation of morality.* New York: The Free Press, 1970.

Edelman, M. *Political language: words that succeed and policies that fail.* New York: Academic Press, Inc., 1977.

Ehrenreich, B., & Ehrenreich, J. Medicine and social control. In B. R. Mandell (Ed.), *Welfare in America: controlling the "dangerous" classes.* Englewood Cliffs, N.J.: Prentice-Hall, Inc., 1975.

Englehardt, H. T., Jr. The disease of masturbation: values and the concept of disease. *Bull. Hist. Med.,* 1974, *48,* 234–248 (Summer).

Erikson, K. T. *Wayward puritans.* New York: John Wiley & Sons, Inc., 1966.

Fox, Renée. The medicalization and demedicalization of American society. *Daedalus,* 1977, *106,* 9–22.

Fox, Richard G. The XYY offender: a modern myth? *J. Crimin. Law, Criminol., and Police Sci.,* 1971, *62* (1), 59–73.

Frank, J. *Persuasion and healing.* (Rev. ed.). New York: Schocken Books, Inc., 1974.

Freeman, W. Psychosurgery. In S. Arieti (Ed.), *American handbook of psychiatry* (Vol. 2). New York: Basic Books, Inc., 1959.

Freidson, E. *Profession of medicine.* New York: Harper & Row, Publishers Inc., 1970.

Freidson, E. *Doctoring together.* New York: Elsevier North-Holland, Inc., 1975.

Goddard, J. The medical business. *Sci. Am.,* 1973, *229,* 161–168 (Sept.).

Gussow, Z., & Tracy, G. S. Status, ideology and adaptation to stigmatized illness: a study of leprosy. *Hum. Organization,* 1968, *27,* 316–325.

Halleck, S. L. *The politics of therapy.* New York: Science House, 1971.

Hurvitz, N. Psychotherapy as a means of social control. *J. Consult. Clin. Psychol.,* 1973, *40,* 232–239.

Illich, I. *Medical nemesis*. New York: Pantheon Books, Inc., 1976.

Kittrie, N. *The right to be different: deviance and enforced therapy*. Baltimore: Johns Hopkins University Press, 1971. Copyright The Johns Hopkins Press, 1971.

Knowles, J. H. The responsibility of the individual. *Daedalus*, 1977, *106*, 57–80.

Leifer, R. *In the name of mental health*. New York: Science House, 1969.

Lemert, E. M. *Human deviance, social problems and social control* (2nd ed.). Englewood Cliffs, N.J.: Prentice-Hall, 1972.

Lennard, H. L., Epstein, L. J., Bernstein, A., & Ranson, D. C. *Mystification and drug misuse*. New York: Perennial Library, 1971.

Lyman, S. *The seven deadly sins: society and evil*. New York: St. Martin's Press, Inc., 1978.

Mark, V., & Ervin, F. *Violence and the brain*. New York: Harper & Row Publishers, Inc., 1970.

McKnight, J. Professionalized services and disabling help. In I. Illich et al., *Disabling professions*. London: Marion Boyars Publisher Ltd., 1977.

Mechanic, D. Health and illness in technological societies. *Hastings Center Stud.* 1973, *1*(3), 7–18.

Mechanic, D. *Politics, medicine and social science*. New York: John Wiley & Sons, Inc., 1974.

Melick, M. E., Steadman, H. J., & Cocozza, J. J. The medicalization of criminal behavior among mental patients. *J. Health Soc. Behav.*, 1979, *20*(3), 228–237.

Menninger, W. C. *A psychiatrist for a troubled world*. B. H. Hall (Ed.), New York: Viking Press, 1967.

Miller, K. S. *Managing madness*. New York: The Free Press, 1976.

Mills, C. W. Situated actions and vocabularies of motive. *Am. Sociol. Rev.*, 1940, *6*, 904–913.

Parsons, T. *The social system*. New York: The Free Press, 1951.

Parsons, T. Definitions of illness and health in light of American values and social structure. In E. G. Jaco (Ed.), *Patients, physicians and illness.* (2nd ed.). New York: The Free Press, 1972.

Parsons, T. The sick role and the role of the physician reconsidered. *Health Society*, 1975, *53*, 257–278 (Summer).

Pfohl, S. J. The 'discovery' of child abuse. *Social Prob.*, 1977, *24*, 310–323 (Feb.).

Phillips, D. L. Rejection: a possible consequence of seeking help for mental disorders. *Am. Soc. Rev.*, 1963, *28*, 963–972.

Pitts, J. Social control: the concept. In D. Sills (Ed.), *International encyclopedia of social sciences.* (Vol. 14). New York: Macmillan Publishing Co., Inc., 1968.

Redlich, F., & Kellert, S. R. Trends in American mental health. *Am. J. Psychiatry.* 1978, *135,* 22–28 (Jan.).

Reynolds, J. M. The medical institution: the death and disease-producing appendage. In L. T. Reynolds & J. M. Henslin (Eds.), *American society: a critical analysis.* New York: David McKay Co., Inc., 1973.

Roman, P. M. & Trice, H. M. The sick role, labelling theory and the deviant drinker. *Internat. J. Soc. Psychiatry,* 1968, *14,* 245–251.

Rosen, G. The evolution of social medicine. In H. E. Freeman, S. Levine, & L. Reeder (Eds.), *Handbook of medical sociology* (2nd ed.). Englewood Cliffs, N.J.: Prentice-Hall, Inc., 1972.

Rotenberg, M. *Damnation and deviance: the Protestant Ethic and the spirit of failure.* New York: The Free Press, 1978.

Ryan, W. *Blaming the victim.* New York: Vintage Books, 1971.

Scheff, T. J. Decision rules, types of errors, and their consequences in medical diagnosis. *Behav. Sci.,* 1963, *8,* 97–107.

Scull, A. *Decarceration.* Englewood Cliffs, N.J.: Prentice-Hall, Inc., 1977.

Shuval, J. T., & Antonovsky, A. Illness: a mechanism for coping with failure. *Soc. Sci. Med.,* 1973, *7,* 259–265.

Sigler, M., & Osmond, H. *Models of madness, models of medicine.* New York: Macmillan Publishing Co., Inc., 1974.

Sontag, S. *Illness as metaphor.* New York: Farrar, Straus & Giroux, 1978.

Sorenson, J. Biomedical innovation, uncertainty, and doctor-patient interaction. *J. Health Soc. Behav.,* 1974, *15,* 366–374 (Dec.).

Stoll, C. S. Images of man and social control. *Soc. Forces,* 1968, *47,* 119–127 (Dec.).

Szasz, T. *The myth of mental illness.* New York: Hoeber-Harper, 1961.

Szasz, T. *Law, liberty and psychiatry.* New York: Macmillan Publishing Co., Inc., 1963.

Szasz, T. Legal and moral aspects of homosexuality. In J. Marmor (Ed.), *Sexual inversion: the multiple roots of homosexuality.* New York: Basic Books, Inc., 1965.

Szasz, T. *The manufacture of madness,* New York: Harper & Row, Publishers, Inc., 1970.

Szasz, T. *Ceremonial chemistry.* New York: Anchor Books, 1974.

Twaddle, A. C., & Hessler, R. M. *A sociology of health.* St. Louis: The C. V. Mosby Co., 1977.

U.S. Department of Health, Education and Welfare. *The supply of health manpower* (Publication No. [HRA] 75–38). Washington, D.C.: U.S. Government Printing Office, 1974.

Veatch, R. M. The medical model: its nature and problems. *Hastings Center Stud.*, 1973, *1*(3), 59–76.

Waitzkin, H., & Stoeckle, J. Information control and the micropolitics of health care: summary of an ongoing project. *Soc. Sci. Med.*, 1976, *10*, 263–276 (June).

Waitzkin, H. K., & Waterman, B. *The exploitation of illness in capitalist society.* Indianapolis: The Bobbs-Merrill Co., Inc., 1974.

Wolff, K. For a sociology of evil. *J. Soc. Issues*, 1969, *25*, 111–125.

Wootton, B. *Social science and social pathology.* London: George Allen & Unwin, 1959.

Zola, I. K. Medicine as an institution of social control. *Sociological Rev.*, 1972, *20*, 487–504.

Zola, I. K. In the name of health and illness: on some socio-political consequences of medical influence. *Soc. Sci. Med.*, 1975, *9*, 83–87.

33   *Understanding Crime Displacement: An Application of Rational Choice Theory*
DEREK B. CORNISH and RONALD V. CLARKE

The model of the offender as a decision maker underlies much criminological work recently undertaken by psychologists, economists, and sociologists of deviance (Clarke and Cornish, 1985; Cornish and Clarke, 1986a). This "rational choice" perspective on crime assumes that offenders seek to benefit themselves by their criminal behavior; that this involves the making of decisions and choices, however rudimentary on occasions these choices might be; and that these processes, constrained as they are by time, the offender's cognitive abilities, and by the availability of relevant information, exhibit limited rather than normative rationality. Our own formulation of rational choice theory was founded on the additional premise that the decision processes and the factors taken into account are likely to vary greatly at the different stages of decision making and among different crimes. For this reason, we drew attention to the needs both to be crime-specific when analyzing criminal choices and to treat decisions

Reprinted from Derek B. Cornish and Ronald V. Clarke, "Understanding Criminal Displacement: An Application of Rational Choice Theory," *Criminology*, vol. 25, no. 4 (1987), pp. 933–947. By permission of The American Society of Criminology.

relating to the various stages of criminal involvement in particular crimes (initial involvement, continuation, desistance) separately from those, such as target selection, relating to the criminal event itself (Clarke and Cornish, 1985; Cornish and Clarke, 1986a).

A RATIONAL CHOICE PERSPECTIVE ON CRIME DISPLACEMENT

Our intention in developing an emphasis upon criminal decision making was to provide a general framework for thinking about the prevention and deterrence of crime, but our particular interest in rational choice theory arose out of work on "situational" crime prevention—a range of preventive measures, including defensible space architecture, target-hardening, and neighborhood watch, designed to reduce the opportunities for, and increase the risks of, committing specific kinds of crime (Clarke, 1983). Despite evidence of its utility, critics have seized upon one apparent weakness of the approach: that preventive measures which increase the difficulties of a particular crime will merely result in criminal activity being "displaced"—for example, to other targets, times, places, or types of crime (Reppetto, 1976; Gabor, 1981). Crucial to this objection is the belief that, to the offender, many if not most crimes are functionally equivalent—a view that derives from the traditional hydraulic view of offending as the product of enduring criminal drives or dispositions (Cornish and Clarke, 1986b).

Crucial to the viability of situational approaches, on the other hand, is the contrasting view that displacement is far from inevitable and occurs only under particular conditions. Rational choice theory assumes that offenders respond selectively to characteristics of particular offenses—in particular, to their opportunities, costs, and benefits—in deciding whether or not to displace their attentions elsewhere. Indeed, since the existence of criminal dispositions is questioned, so too is the corresponding notion of criminal "energies" which have to be displaced into alternative actions. If frustrated from committing a particular crime, the offender is not compelled to seek out another crime nor even a noncriminal solution. He may simply desist from any further action at all, rationalizing his loss of income (for example) in various ways: "It was good while it lasted"; "I would have ended up getting caught"; and so on. Such an analysis is consistent with the available empirical research, which is indicative of the contingent nature of displacement. For example, the fitting of steering column locks to *all* cars in West Germany in 1960 brought about a 60% reduction in car thefts, whereas their introduction only to new cars in

Great Britain displaced theft to the older, unprotected vehicles (Mayhew, Clarke, Sturman, and Hough, 1976). Again, while a variety of security measures dramatically reduced airliner hijackings in the early 1970s (Wilkinson, 1977), a police "crackdown" on subway robberies in New York City displaced robberies to the street (Chaiken, Lawless, and Stevenson, 1974).

Research of this kind, however, which merely analyzes crime patterns, is likely to yield only limited information about displacement. This is because, just as reductions in target crimes brought about by situational measures may be modest and difficult to detect, especially when crime as a whole is rising, so, too, evidence of displacement may lie concealed within the same overall crime statistics. Moreover, such research on its own fails to provide an adequate explanation for the occurrence or absence of displacement, although reasons may sometimes be inferred. Given these problems, additional ways of investigating displacement are needed and, in particular, studies which focus upon the offender's own explanations for his decisions and choices.

THE CONCEPT OF CHOICE-STRUCTURING PROPERTIES

A more promising approach to the study of displacement is suggested by rational choice theory's emphasis upon the need to adopt a crime-specific focus when attempting to explain or prevent criminal behavior. Rather than assuming that potential offenders are fueled by a general disposition to offend which makes them relatively indifferent to the nature of the offense they commit, the rational choice perspective asserts that specific crimes are chosen and committed for specific reasons. Decisions to offend, in other words, are influenced by the characteristics of both offenses and offenders, and are the product of interactions between the two. Thus, the final decision to become involved in a particular crime is the outcome of an appraisal process which (however cursory) evaluates the relative merits of a range of potential courses of action, comprising all those thought likely in the offender's view to achieve his or her current objective (for example, for money, sex, or excitement).

It follows that an understanding of the factors which the offender takes into account when performing this rudimentary cost-benefit analysis is necessary. These factors relate both to offense and offender characteristics but, for the present, can be usefully viewed as those *properties* of offenses (such as type and amount of payoff, perceived risk, skills needed, and so on) which are perceived by the offender as being especially salient to his or her goals, motives, experience, abilities, expertise, and preferences. Such properties provide a basis for selecting among alternative courses of action and, hence, effectively *structure* the offender's *choice*. The characteristics of offenses which render them differentially attractive to particular individuals or subgroups (or to the same individuals and groups at different times) have therefore been termed *choice-structuring properties*. It follows that the readiness with which the offender will be prepared to substitute one offense for another will depend upon the extent to which alternative offenses share characteristics which the offender considers salient to his or her goals and abilities. A recognition of the contingent, crime-specific nature of criminal decision making therefore has important implications for an understanding of displacement.

In the absence of information from offenders, some a priori selection of properties thought likely to be salient to offender decision making has to be made. For illustrative purposes, this is attempted later in the paper in relation to two broad groups of offenses—those of theft involving cash and of illegal substance abuse. The concept of choice-structuring properties was first employed, however, in the attempt to clarify policy issues relating to gambling and suicide (Cornish and Clarke, in press).

In the case of gambling (and following the work of Weinstein and Deitch, 1974), choice-structuring properties such as number and location of gambling outlets, frequency of events on which bets can be made, time elapsing before payment of winnings, range of odds and stakes, degree of personal involvement, skills needed or perceived, and "nerve" required, were employed to identify forms of gambling more or less designed to encourage high degrees of involvement and to attract the participation of particularly susceptible individuals (Cornish, 1978). In Britain, the widespread provision of "betting shops" in prime urban locations enables off-course gambling to take place throughout the afternoon. These premises offer a vast range of simple and complex betting strategies, a feeling of personal involvement and challenge fostered by the exercise of handicapping skills, and an atmosphere of "action" encouraged by the rapidity of events and payouts, presence of other gamblers laying bets and collecting winnings, and the use of live television commentary from the course—a combination of properties which provides an environment designed to encourage continuous gambling. The contrast with the choice-structuring properties of lotteries is significant: lotteries are held relatively infrequently, involve lengthy periods between staking and payout, offer the minimum of personal involvement, little scope for social interaction or the exercise of skill (real or perceived), a limited range of odds and bets, and very long odds against winning. The prime attraction to their adherents, therefore, is the possibility they offer of a big "windfall" for very little initial outlay. "Numbers," on the other hand, while ostensibly rather similar to the lottery, offers a wider variety of staking levels and odds, a larger number of events and swifter turnaround, greater perceived scope for the invocation of personal luck, and more social interaction—features which go some way to explaining why attempts to promote lotteries as legal alternatives to the numbers racket have proved unsuccessful (Kaplan and Maher, 1970).

It is in examples like these, where activities are examined in some detail, that the value of choice-structuring properties in clarifying the unique constellations of motives, opportunities, rewards, and costs offered by different forms of gambling becomes evident. Attention to these parameters also suggests a means of controlling participation in potentially dangerous forms of gambling through regulation of these properties. Indeed, this strategy appears to guide the efforts of regulatory bodies and legislators when monitoring and controlling certain forms of gambling such as betting and gaming, and those of promoters when trying to increase rates of participation and encourage escalation of involvement into more profitable forms. Manipulation of the choice-structuring properties of bingo, for example, in order to shorten the duration of individual games, the development of "linked bingo" to enable larger prizes to be offered, and the introduction, as "interval games," of gaming machines—whose choice-structuring properties, especially when deliberately manipulated by casino promoters (Hess and Diller, 1969), tend to encourage continuous gambling—all provide graphic examples of these strategies (Cornish, 1978).

In the case of suicide, properties of the various methods such as the degree of prior planning necessary, the courage required, likely pain, distastefulness of method, extent of disfigurement, time taken to die when conscious, scope for second thoughts, and chances of intervention, were used to explain why, when deprived of more acceptable methods, people do not always turn to other means of killing themselves. Domestic gas, for example, used to have particular advantages as a method of suicide: it was painless, very widely available, required little preparation, was highly lethal (death could take place in less than half an hour), was not bloody, and did not disfigure. These features help to explain how the detoxification of domestic gas—a method that had formerly accounted for over 50% of all suicides (Kreitman, 1976; Kreitman and Platt, 1984; Clarke and Mayhew, in press)—brought about a 35% decline in the national rate of suicide in

Britain during the 1960s. Some population subgroups such as the elderly and the less mobile may have found these advantages particularly compelling; there is evidence, for example, that suicidal women are more attracted by self-poisoning and more repulsed by violent and bloody methods (Marks, 1977). Since the needs and circumstances of particular subgroups may make certain methods uniquely attractive, then, it seems likely that reducing opportunities to use particular methods need not simply result in displacement to others, but can bring about genuine gains in the prevention of suicide deaths. Thus, an apparently obvious alternative to gassing, such as overdosing, which might appear to offer many of the same advantages, may nevertheless be subject to disadvantages which limit its viability as a substitute; for example, access to the most lethal drugs may require the cooperation of a doctor, or long-term planning and the faking of relevant symptoms, in order to build up sufficient quantities, while the range of more accessible nonprescription drugs may be either less lethal or, in the case of other alternatives such as domestic poisons, more painful to ingest (Clarke and Mayhew, in press).

CHOICE-STRUCTURING PROPERTIES OF CRIMES

Identifying an activity's unique blend of choice-structuring properties emphasizes its distinctive features and this, in turn, facilitates the making of comparisons between different activities. But, because crimes are such a heterogeneous group of behaviors, it is not immediately clear on what basis to group crimes for comparison. One possible criterion is suggested by the aim of the exercise, which is to enable the conditions under which displacement is more or less likely to occur to be specified. Since few would expect displacement across behaviors engaged in for widely differing purposes, the goals of offending could provide the primary criterion for selecting the crimes to be compared. Thus, crimes whose main purpose appears to be to obtain money might be analyzed together, while those whose goal is sexual outlet would need to be separately analyzed. Some a priori determination—later refined by empirical research—of the purposes being served by particular offenses will therefore need to be made before they are grouped together in order to analyze their choice-structuring properties. Although it may be the case that many crimes serve a mixture of goals, one of these will usually be dominant. This will provide the appropriate criterion for analysis, the remaining subsidiary purposes taking on the role of further choice-structuring properties for the particular offenses being compared.

For the sake of simplicity, it has so far been assumed that the individual chooses only from among criminal alternatives when seeking to achieve his goals. Given the wide range of noncriminal alternatives also available to the offender, however, confining comparisons of choice-structuring properties to those among *criminal* means alone may seem unduly restrictive. A crime such as drunken driving, for example, whose purpose is very specific and temporary (that is, the need to get home after drinking) and in relation to which alternative crimes are few or none, illustrates the point that for some crimes most, if not all, of the alternative means being compared will be noncriminal. In addition, displacement will usually be directed in such cases to legal behaviors: more likely alternatives to drunken driving may be to call a cab, use public transportation, or walk, rather than to persuade an equally drunk companion to drive the car instead. Notwithstanding this example, it seems intuitively more likely that criminal behavior will usually be contemplated only after legitimate means have been foreclosed or rejected. Drunken driving, it could be argued, is a special case since one of the effects of alcohol may be to short-circuit this usual sequence. Under these circumstances, the capacity of the otherwise law-abiding citizen to consider the long-range consequences of his actions may be temporarily impaired, and this may lead him to entertain criminal actions much sooner (Campbell and Gibbs, 1986: 126, 177). If criminal means are usually only considered at a later stage, this may suggest that they do in fact have something in common with each other and that these features provide some justification for limiting comparisons to crimes alone. But, while this meets the above objections, it also opens the door again to the very dispositional explanations of offending that the rational choice perspective was designed to challenge, since it suggests explanations in terms of offender characteristics, such as the tendency to select means which offer immediate gratification of needs, regardless of the consequences for others. Consequently, the preference at this stage is to defend confining comparison to crimes alone, not because criminal behavior is inherently different from other behaviors, but on pragmatic grounds alone: it is the possibility of displacement to other crimes which constitutes the major problem for crime-control policy.

Before embarking on a more detailed discussion of their application to the problem of crime displacement, it may be useful to provide hypothetical lists of the choice-structuring properties of two quite different offense groupings: those designed to yield cash (for example, burglary, theft with or without contact, shoplifting, mugging, bank robbery, fraud, tax evasion, and auto theft); and those concerned with the ingestion of illegal substances (such as marijuana, opiates, LSD, cocaine, "crack," amphetamines, barbiturates, and volatile substances).

As can be seen from Table 1, while specifying the dominant purpose and confining comparisons to criminal means takes one some way toward the goal of drawing up lists of choice-structuring properties, the resulting groupings of offenses will usually be rather broad. While it may be tempting to try for somewhat narrower arrays of offenses, such as those sharing a common modus operandi, this may be unhelpful when estimating the likelihood of displacement since it may result in the omission of important choice-structuring properties. In turn, their omission may make it difficult to explain, for example, why burglars who prey on distant affluent suburbs would never consider breaking into apartments in their neighborhood; why the shoplifter might be reluctant to contemplate mugging; or why the computer fraudster might give up crime entirely if it became too difficult to continue his frauds. In the course of his investigation of robbers' decision making, for example, Feeney (1986) notes the surprising fact that many of them thought burglary too unpredictable and risky.

Similar considerations apply to offenses of illegal substance abuse. An analysis of their choice-structuring properties indicates that different substances provide different experiences, and this—together with considerations of availability, cost, risk, expertise required, and social context of usage—suggests that a displacement and escalation among substances may be more limited than is usually thought. Information from opiate abusers, for example, suggests that a desire to join a specific drug culture of users may be an important determinant of initial involvement (Bennett, 1986); an alternative culture such as that represented by teenage glue sniffing may be seen to offer rather different, and less attractive, experiences in terms of social cachet, excitement, and alternative life-style. In addition, the specific psychological effects of the drugs themselves may restrict substitutability: today's energetic, acquisitive "yuppie" cocaine user may typically be of similar social background to the 1960s cannabis-using hippie, but the effects of cocaine may be more in tune with modern life-styles and aspirations than those produced by cannabis.

Choice-structuring properties may also highlight similarities between apparently different behaviors. For example, crimes such as burglary on a public housing project, in a middle-class suburb, or in a wealthy enclave may, *for some offenders*, have fewer attractive properties in common than apparently different offenses, such as burglary or mugging, committed in their own neighborhoods. While the latter offenses may involve different skills or risks, these may be counterbalanced by the advantages of offending within familiar territory. For

TABLE 1 CHOICE-STRUCTURING PROPERTIES OF TWO OFFENSE GROUPINGS

THEFT INVOLVING CASH

Availability (numbers of targets; accessibility)
Awareness of method (e.g., pickpocketing vs. insurance fraud)
Likely cash yield per crime
Expertise needed
Planning necessary (pickpocketing vs. bank robbery)
Resources required (transport; equipment)
Solo vs. associates required
Time required to commit
Cool nerves required (bank robbery vs. computer fraud)
Risks of apprehension
Severity of punishment
Physical danger
Instrumental violence required
Confrontation with victim (mugging vs. burglary)
Identifiable victim
Social cachet (safecracking vs. mugging)
"Fencing" necessary
Moral evaluation

ILLEGAL SUBSTANCE ABUSE

Availability (glue from hardware stores vs. prescription drug)
Awareness (special knowledge of doctors or pharmacists)
Social cachet (cocaine vs. heroin)
Solitary vs. social
Knowledge/skills required to administer (heroin vs. marijuana)
Technical equipment required (heroin)
Dangerousness of substance (crack vs. marijuana)
Primary method of administration (injecting vs. smoking)
Different forms substance can take
Nature of psychological effects
Number, type, and severity of side effects
Dependency
Length/intensity of "high" per dose
Financial costs
Legal penalties
Detectability
Interference with everyday tasks
Moral evaluation

these reasons, again, the most appropriate level of analysis for choice-structuring properties would seem to be at the most general level consistent with the likelihood of displacement.

Since the lists in Table 1 derive from a rational choice perspective on offending, they both concentrate upon the opportunities, costs, and benefits of the various alternatives being compared. Though no particular attempt has been made to reconcile differences between the two lists, some categories of choice-structuring properties (especially the more generally applicable ones such as "availability") are common to both, while others inevitably reflect unique features of each offense grouping. The properties listed are not necessarily those taken into account by the offender, who may not be fully aware either of the range of properties involved or of the part they play in his decisions. Rather, the properties listed have been selected on a priori grounds as being of most relevance to the task of comparing offenses and, hence, of establishing the likely limits of displacement within each offense grouping. Thus, there is likely to be more displacement between particular theft offenses where they share similar profiles of choice-structuring properties—for example, where the likely cash yield per crime is comparable, where similar skills and resources are required, and where the physical risks are the same. In contrast, where the profiles differ, this may clarify why displacement is unlikely to occur. Lastly, some choice-structuring properties may have a more pivotal role to play in decisions concerning displacement. It is generally accepted, for example, that some offenders will not contemplate crimes which involve the use of violence.

Little is known at present about offender decision making, and because of this the above lists may need modifying in the light of empirical research. But even at this stage such lists should provide a useful tool for those involved in crime prevention. By directing attention to those features of crimes which make them attractive to particular groups of offenders, such an approach will make it easier for policy makers to anticipate the direction and amount of any displacement to other forms of crime. In the past, for example, uncritical and often hidden assumptions that illegal substances are equivalent in their attractiveness and effects may have had damaging effects upon policy formation through their tendency to encourage preoccupation with the inevitability of displacement and escalation. Careful attention to choice-structuring properties of different activities, however, will enable the accuracy of assessments to be improved about the likely costs and benefits of undertaking new crime prevention initiatives in relation to specific forms of crimes. The lists will also alert policy makers to action that needs to be taken in order to forestall criminal displacement or even to facilitate displacement to noncriminal alternatives. Finally, lists of choice-structuring properties should assist in the evaluation of crime prevention initiatives by helping to orient the search for displacement.

CHOICE-STRUCTURING PROPERTIES AND OFFENDER PERCEPTIONS

The choice-structuring properties in Table 1 attempt to provide a comprehensive list of the salient ways in which crimes with similar goals differ from each other. Although policy makers require such comprehensive information in order to think constructively about displacement, it should not be assumed that offenders will utilize the data in a similar way. As mentioned above, they may lack information about the full range of offenses that could satisfy their goals, they may be unaware of the extent to which available opportunities have structured their choices, they may be ignorant of all the costs and benefits of the different offenses, and they may assign particular importance to certain choice-structuring properties (such as eschewing the use of violence, or restricting selection of victims to those of particular socioeconomic or ethnic groups), which then come to exert a disproportionate influence upon involvement and displacement decisions. Moreover, in practice, offenders may not always take account of the full range of properties. For example, the choice-structuring properties listed in Table 1 are mainly relevant to an individual's initial decision whether or not to get involved in a particular crime. They may have rather less application to more immediate decisions relating to the commission of a particular offense (or what may be termed the criminal "event"), although a similar comparison process—albeit using a different and more restricted range of properties—undoubtedly takes place when potential targets or victims are being compared. The present lists would become more salient again when, having committed the offense, the offender had to decide whether to continue with a particular form of crime or to desist. Last, as a result of the experience of committing the offense in question, further choice-structuring properties may become apparent to the offender and existing ones may assume a different value. Thus, the degree of steady nerves required may only become apparent once a mugging has been attempted.

As well as exemplifying one of the major premises of the rational choice perspective—that the offender's decision-making processes will tend to display limited rather than normative rationality—the above points also illustrate the dynamic nature of criminal decision making. Thus far it might well appear that a rather passive role has been assigned to choice-structuring properties in that it has been implied that offenders' needs lead them to search out suitable criminal opportunities in their environments. But, as the term implies, choice-structuring properties may often play a more active role in generating offending. Some of the opportunities may offer a constellation of properties sufficiently attractive to provide a temptation to crime, as is often argued to be the case with petty offenses such as shoplifting. These points underline the three-fold distinction made by Maguire (1980) and by Bennett and Wright (1984) among offenders who seize, search for, or create opportunities. It is also clear that, as well as specifying features of behaviors (kinds of gambling, methods of suicide, types of crime), choice-structuring properties implicitly specify salient characteristics of the actor, such as his or her needs, preferences, personal characteristics, and perceptions. In other words, the term "choice-structuring property" is a relational concept designed to provide an analytic tool for increasing an understanding of the interaction between person variables and arrays of behaviors—in the case of crime, to specify more closely offenders as well as the offenses they commit. Thus, where crime displacement occurs, a knowledge of the choice-structuring properties which the offenses share may permit more accurate identification of the subgroups of offenders involved; and this may well prove a more fruitful way of investigating the interface between offense and offender—and, in particular, issues relating to specialization and generalization (Cornish and Clarke, in press)—than the more static and rigid offender typologies of traditional criminology.

Greater knowledge about all these matters would undoubtedly improve policy makers' ability to predict the likelihood and direction of displacement. But, as well as requiring more information about the way offenders perceive and utilize the choice-structuring properties of crimes, more needs to be known about the criminal opportunity structure within which the offender operates if a complete picture of the determinants of displacement is to be given (Cook, 1986b). First, at a macro level, more ecological research is required in order to explore the changes in opportunities and, hence, in crime rates, brought about by changes in routine activities, life-styles, and commercial practices. As has been indicated above, the detoxification of domestic gas in Britain brought about a substantial decline in the national suicide rate during the 1960s. In the same way, participation in gambling rises whenever new facilities are created (Cornish, 1978). In relation to crime, Wilkins (1964) showed how rises in the rates of auto theft in

Britain parallel the increased rates of new car registrations, and Cohen and Felson (1979) showed how increases in burglary in the United States reflected the rise in "stealable" property and in numbers of women working outside the home. More recently, Tremblay's (1986) research on credit card bank frauds has indicated how the introduction of new commercial marketing strategies may also sometimes have unforeseen consequences. Thus, a move by certain Canadian banks to extend facilities for check cashing to nonregular customers able to guarantee the transaction by means of a credit card, offered existing credit card thieves a novel and lucrative way of preying directly upon the banking system itself instead of upon retailers alone.

The processes through which these changes in opportunities at the macro level take place also require elucidation. The escalation in deaths from car exhaust fumes in Britain from the beginning of the 1970s, for example, suggests that learning may have an important role to play in determining changes in suicide rates over time, as people gradually come to identify a novel and attractive method of suicide (Clarke and Lester, 1987). At the micro level, Tremblay's work provides some hints about the circumstances under which, for one particular form of crime, such diffusion of innovation might come about. Previous experience in committing similar forms of crime may sensitize offenders to new variations on their favorite themes; membership of criminal knowledge networks may speed up the diffusion of information among specialists, while the media may spread such information more widely among the noncriminal population. The more dramatic the event—such as hijacking, bank robbery, rape, murder, or suicide—the more vivid, detailed, and widespread the coverage, and the more often, at the time of the event and subsequently at committal and trial, the details are repeated. Under these circumstances, the likelihood of "copycat" offenses may be further enhanced.

RATIONAL CHOICE THEORY AND CRIME-CONTROL POLICY

The rational choice perspective was originally developed to provide policy makers with a useful framework to guide thinking about crime prevention and control. In line with this objective, the present paper has attempted to develop certain aspects of the theory in the interests of answering critics of situational crime prevention who have implicitly assumed that the outcome of such efforts is simply (and, seemingly, inevitably) to displace offending. A similar analysis, making use of the concept of choice-structuring properties, has also been attempted elsewhere to clarify aspects of the long-standing debate over whether offenders are generalists or specialists (Cornish and Clarke, in press). Rational choice approaches have also proved useful in suggesting reasons for the limited effectiveness of rehabilitative efforts (Cornish, 1987) in emphasizing the need of deterrent policies to pay greater attention to offenders' perceptions of opportunities, risks, costs, and benefits (Bennett and Wright, 1984), and in identifying potentially adverse side-effects of policies such as selective incapacitation (Cook, 1986a).

More generally, a rational choice perspective on offending can suggest, if not explanations, lines of enquiry to account for stability and change in criminal behavior. The importance of this for directing crime prevention policy and practice should not be underestimated. Taking Tremblay's study as an example once again, it is instructive to note that, even under the most apparently favorable of circumstances, displacement was by no means inevitable: only 10% of Tremblay's "checkmen" actually switched their attentions to credit card bank frauds. Before dismissing this discrepancy as a crude exemplification of Zipf's (1949) Principle of Least Effort, it should be recognized that this low take-up may well have resulted from the logistics of the situation—the limited period for which this particular "window of vulnerability" was left open by the banks and the fact that, even as knowledge grew about this novel form of crime, so were the risks and effort involved in its commission rapidly escalating. Critics of situational crime prevention might well take pause for thought from this example. For, whatever the value of longer-term social prevention strategies that attack the "root" causes of crime, the constant innovation in criminal methods in response to the changing criminal opportunity structure demands similar vigilance and continued investment of time and effort on the part of those engaged in crime control. It is hoped that the rational choice perspective can offer some assistance in this enterprise.

REFERENCES

Bennett, Trevor
  1986   A decision-making approach to opioid addiction. In Derek B. Cornish and Ronald V. Clarke (eds.), The Reasoning Criminal. New York: Springer-Verlag.

Bennett, Trevor and Richard Wright
  1984   Burglars on Burglary. Aldershot, Hants, England: Gower.

Campbell, Anne and John J. Gibbs
1986   Violent Transactions. Oxford: Basil Blackwell.

Chaiken, Jan M., Michael W. Lawless, and Keith Stevenson
1974   Impact of Police Activity on Crime: Robberies on the New York
        City Subway System. Report No. R–1424–N.Y.C. Santa Monica,
        CA: Rand Corporation.

Clarke, Ronald V.
1983   Situational crime prevention: Its theoretical basis and practical
        scope. In Michael Tonry and Norval Morris (eds.), Crime and
        Justice, Vol. 4. Chicago: University of Chicago Press.

Clarke, Ronald V. and Derek B. Cornish
1985   Modeling offenders' decisions: A framework for research and
        policy. In Michael Tonry and Norval Morris (eds.), Crime and
        Justice, Vol. 6. Chicago: University of Chicago Press.

Clarke, Ronald V. and David Lester
1987   Toxicity of car exhausts and opportunity for suicide: Comparison
        between Britain and the United States. Journal of Epidemiology
        and Community Health 41: 114–120.

Clarke, Ronald V. and Pat Mayhew
In Press The British gas suicide story and its criminological implications.
        In Michael Tonry and Norval Morris (eds.), Crime and Justice,
        Vol. 10. Chicago: University of Chicago Press.

Cohen, Lawrence E. and Marcus Felson
1979   Social change and crime rate trends: A routine activity approach.
        American Sociological Review 44: 588–608.

Cook, Philip J.
1986a   Criminal incapacitation effects considered in an adaptive choice
        framework. In Derek B. Cornish and Ronald V. Clarke (eds.),
        The Reasoning Criminal. New York: Springer-Verlag.
1986b   The demand and supply of criminal opportunities. In Michael
        Tonry and Norval Morris (eds.), Crime and Justice, Vol. 7. Chi-
        cago: University of Chicago Press.

Cornish, Derek B.
1978   Gambling: A review of the Literature. Home Office Research
        Study, No. 42. London: HMSO.
1987   Evaluating residential treatment for delinquents: A cautionary
        tale. In Klaus Hurrelmann and Franz-Xaver Kaufmann (eds.),
        Limits and Potentials of Social Intervention. Berlin/New York: de
        Gruyter/Aldine.

Cornish, Derek B. and Ronald V. Clarke
1986a   The Reasoning Criminal. New York: Springer-Verlag.
1986b   Situational prevention, displacement of crime and rational choice
        theory. In Kevin Heal and Gloria Laycock (eds.), Situational
        Crime Prevention: From Theory into Practice. London: HMSO.

In Press Crime specialisation, crime displacement and rational choice theory. In H. Wegener, F. Losel, and J. Haish (eds.), Criminal Behavior and the Justice System: Psychological Perspectives. New York: Springer-Verlag.

Feeney, Floyd
1986   Robbers as decision-makers. In Derek B. Cornish and Ronald V. Clarke (eds.), The Reasoning Criminal. New York: Springer-Verlag.

Gabor, Thomas
1981   The crime displacement hypothesis: An empirical examination. Crime and Delinquency 26: 390–404.

Hess, H.F. and J.V. Diller
1969   Motivation for gambling as revealed in the marketing methods of the legitimate gambling industry. Psychological Reports 25: 19–27.

Kaplan, L. and J. Maher
1970   The economics of the numbers game. American Journal of Economics and Sociology 29: 391–408.

Kreitman, Norman
1976   The coal gas story: United Kingdom suicide rates, 1960–71. British Journal of Preventive and Social Medicine 30: 86–93.

Kreitman, Norman and S. Platt
1984   Suicide, unemployment, and domestic gas detoxification in Britain. Journal of Epidemiology and Community Health 38: 1–6.

Maguire, Mike
1980   Burglary as Opportunity. Research Bulletin No. 10: 6–9. London: Home Office Research Unit.

Marks, Alan
1977   Sex differences and their effect upon cultural evaluations of methods of self-destruction. Omega 8: 65–70.

Mayhew, Patricia M., Ronald V. Clarke, Andrew Sturman, and J.M. Hough
1976   Crime as Opportunity. Home Office Research Study, No. 34. London: HMSO.

Reppetto, Thomas
1976   Crime prevention and the displacement phenomenon. Crime and Delinquency 22: 166–177.

Tremblay, Pierre
1986   Designing crime. British Journal of Criminology 26: 234–253.

Weinstein, D. and L. Deitch
1974   The impact of legalized gambling: The socio-economic consequences of lotteries and off-track betting. New York: Praeger.

Wilkins, Leslie T.
1964   Social Deviance. London: Tavistock.

Wilkinson, Paul
 1977   Terrorism and the Liberal State. London: Macmillan.

Zipf, George K.
 1949   Human Behavior and the Principle of Least Effort: An Introduction to Human Ecology. Cambridge, MA: Addison-Wesley.

34 *Social Change and Crime Rate Trends: A Routine Activity Approach*
LAWRENCE E. COHEN and MARCUS FELSON

INTRODUCTION

In its summary report the National Commission on the Causes and Prevention of Violence (1969: xxxvii) presents an important sociological paradox:

> Why, we must ask, have urban violent crime rates increased substantially during the past decade when the conditions that are supposed to cause violent crime have not worsened—have, indeed, generally improved?
>
> The Bureau of the Census, in its latest report on trends in social and economic conditions in metropolitan areas, states that most "indicators of well-being point toward progress in the cities since 1960." Thus, for example, the proportion of blacks in cities who completed high school rose from 43 percent in 1960 to 61 percent in 1968; unemployment rates dropped significantly between 1959 and 1967 and the median family income of blacks in cities increased from 61 percent to 68 percent of the median white family income during the same period. Also during the same period the number of persons living below the legally-defined poverty level in cities declined from 11.3 million to 8.3 million.

Despite the general continuation of these trends in social and economic conditions in the United States, the *Uniform Crime Report* (FBI, 1975:49) indicates that between 1960 and 1975 reported rates of rob-

Reprinted from Lawrence E. Cohen and Marcus Felson, "Social Change and Crime Rate Trends: A Routine Activity Approach," *American Sociological Review,* vol. 44 (1979), pp. 588–608. By permission of the American Sociological Association and the authors.

For their comments, we thank David J. Bordua, Ross M. Stolzenberg, Christopher S. Dunn, Kenneth C. Land, Robert Schoen, Amos Hawley, and an anonymous reviewer. Funding for this study was provided by these United States Government grants: National Institute for Mental Health 1-R01-MH31117-01; National Science Foundation, SOC-77-13261; and United States Army RI/DAHC 19-76-G-0016. The authors' name order is purely alphabetical.

bery, aggravated assault, forcible rape and homicide increased by 263%, 164%, 174%, and 188%, respectively. Similar property crime rate increases reported during this same period[1] (e.g., 200% for burglary rate) suggest that the paradox noted by the Violence Commission applies to nonviolent offenses as well.

In the present paper we consider these paradoxical trends in crime rates in terms of changes in the "routine activities" of everyday life. We believe the structure of such activities influences criminal opportunity and therefore affects trends in a class of crimes we refer to as *direct-contact predatory violations*. Predatory violations are defined here as illegal acts in which "someone definitely and intentionally takes or damages the person or property of another" (Glaser, 1971:4). Further, this analysis is confined to those predatory violations involving direct physical contact between at least one offender and at least one person or object which that offender attempts to take or damage.

We argue that structural changes in routine activity patterns can influence crime rates by affecting the convergence in space and time of the three minimal elements of direct-contact predatory violations: (1) motivated offenders, (2) suitable targets, and (3) the absence of capable guardians against a violation. We further argue that the lack of any one of these elements is sufficient to prevent the successful completion of a direct-contact predatory crime, and that the convergence in time and space of suitable targets and the absence of capable guardians may even lead to large increases in crime rates without necessarily requiring any increase in the structural conditions that motivate individuals to engage in crime. That is, if the proportion of motivated offenders or even suitable targets were to remain stable in a community, changes in routine activities could nonetheless alter the likelihood of their convergence in space and time, thereby creating more opportunities for crimes to occur. Control therefore becomes critical. If controls through routine activities were to decrease, illegal predatory activities could then be likely to increase. In the process of developing this explanation and evaluating its consistency with existing data, we relate our approach to classical human ecological concepts and to several earlier studies.

THE STRUCTURE OF CRIMINAL ACTIVITY

Sociological knowledge of how community structure generates illegal acts has made little progress since Shaw and McKay and their colleagues (1929) published their pathbreaking work, *Delinquency Areas*. Variations in crime rates over space long have been recognized (e.g., see Guerry, 1833; Quètelet, 1842), and current evidence indicates that the pattern of these relationships within metropolitan communities has persisted (Reiss, 1976). Although most spatial research is quite useful for describing crime rate patterns and providing post hoc explanations, these works seldom consider—conceptually or empirically—the fundamental human ecological character of illegal acts as *events* which occur at specific locations in *space* and *time,* involving specific persons and/or objects. These and related concepts can help us to develop an extension of the human ecological analysis to the problem of explaining changes in crime rates over time. Unlike many criminological inquiries, we do not examine why individuals or groups are inclined criminally, but rather we take criminal inclination as given and examine the manner in which the spatio-temporal organization of social activities helps people to translate their criminal inclinations into action. Criminal violations are treated here as routine activities which share many attributes of, and are interdependent with, other routine activities. This interdependence between the structure of illegal activities and the organization of everyday sustenance activities leads us to consider certain concepts from human ecological literature.

SELECTED CONCEPTS FROM HAWLEY'S HUMAN ECOLOGICAL THEORY

While criminologists traditionally have concentrated on the *spatial* analysis of crime rates within metropolitan communities, they seldom have considered the *temporal* interdependence of these acts. In his classic theory of human ecology, Amos Hawley (1950) treats the community not simply as a unit of territory but rather as an organization of symbiotic and commensalistic relationships as human activities are performed over both space and time.

Hawley identified three important temporal components of community structure: (1) *rhythm,* the regular periodicity with which events occur, as with the rhythm of travel activity; (2) *tempo,* the number of events per unit of time, such as the number of criminal violations per day on a given street; and (3) *timing,* the coordination among different activities which are more or less interdependent, such as the coordination of an offender's rhythms with those of a victim (Hawley, 1950:289; the examples are ours). These components of temporal organization, often neglected in criminological research, prove useful in analyzing how illegal tasks are performed—a utility which becomes more apparent after noting the spatio-temporal requirements of illegal activities.

THE MINIMAL ELEMENTS OF DIRECT-CONTACT PREDATORY VIOLATIONS

As we previously stated, despite their great diversity, direct-contact predatory violations share some important requirements which facilitate analysis of their structure. Each successfully completed violation minimally requires an *offender* with both criminal inclinations and the ability to carry out those inclinations, a person or object providing a *suitable target* for the offender, and *absence of guardians* capable of preventing violations. We emphasize that the lack of any one of these elements normally is sufficient to prevent such violations from occurring.[2] Though guardianship is implicit in everyday life, it usually is marked by the absence of violations; hence it is easy to overlook. While police action is analyzed widely, guardianship by ordinary citizens of one another and of property may be one of the most neglected elements in sociological research on crime, especially since it links seemingly unrelated social roles and relationships to the occurrence or absence of illegal acts.

The conjunction of these minimal elements can be used to assess how social structure may affect the tempo of each type of violation. That is, the probability that a violation will occur at any specific time and place might be taken as a function of the convergence of likely offenders and suitable targets in the absence of capable guardians. Through consideration of how trends and fluctuations in social conditions affect the frequency of this convergence of criminogenic circumstances, an explanation of temporal trends in crime rates can be constructed.

THE ECOLOGICAL NATURE OF ILLEGAL ACTS

This ecological analysis of direct-contact predatory violations is intended to be more than metaphorical. In the context of such violations, people, gaining and losing sustenance, struggle among themselves for property, safety, territorial hegemony, sexual outlet, physical control, and sometimes for survival itself. The interdependence between offenders and victims can be viewed as a predatory relationship between functionally dissimilar individuals or groups. Since predatory violations fail to yield any net gain in sustenance for the larger community, they can only be sustained by feeding upon other activities. As offenders cooperate to increase their efficiency at predatory violations and as potential victims organize their resistance to these violations, both groups apply the symbiotic principle to improve their sustenance position. On the other hand, potential victims of predatory crime may take evasive actions which encourage offenders to pursue targets other than their own. Since illegal activites must feed upon other activites, the spatial and temporal structure of routine legal activities should play an important role in determining the location, type and quantity of illegal acts occurring in a given community or society. Moreover, one can analyze how the structure of community organization as well as the level of technology in a society provide the circumstances under which crime can thrive. For example, technology and organization affect the capacity of persons with criminal inclinations to overcome their targets, as well as affecting the ability of guardians to contend with potential offenders by using whatever protective tools, weapons and skills they have at their disposal. Many technological advances designed for legitimate purposes—including the automobile, small power tools, hunting weapons, highways, telephones, etc.—may enable offenders to carry out their own work more effectively or may assist people in protecting their own or someone else's person or property.

Not only do routine legitimate activities often provide the wherewithal to commit offenses or to guard against others who do so, but they also provide offenders with suitable targets. Target suitability is likely to reflect such things as value (i.e., the material or symbolic desirability of a personal or property target for offenders), physical visibility, access, and the inertia of a target against illegal treatment by offenders (including the weight, size, and attached or locked features of property inhibiting its illegal removal and the physical capacity of personal victims to resist attackers with or without weapons). Routine production activities probably affect the suitability of consumer goods for illegal removal by determining their value and weight. Daily activities may affect the location of property and personal targets in visible and accessible places at particular times. These activities also may cause people to have on hand objects that can be used as weapons for criminal acts or self-protection or to be preoccupied with tasks which reduce their capacity to discourage or resist offenders.

While little is known about conditions that affect the convergence of potential offenders, targets and guardians, this is a potentially rich source of propositions about crime rates. For example, daily work activities separate many people from those they trust and the property they value. Routine activities also bring together at various times of day or night persons of different background, sometimes in the presence of facilities, tools or weapons which influence the commission or avoidance of illegal acts. Hence, the timing of work, schooling and leisure may be of central importance for explaining crime rates.

The ideas presented so far are not new, but they frequently are overlooked in the theoretical literature on crime. Although an investigation of the literature uncovers significant examples of descriptive and practical data related to the routine activities upon which illegal behavior feeds, these data seldom are treated within an analytical framework. The next section reviews some of this literature.

RELATION OF THE ROUTINE ACTIVITY APPROACH TO EXTANT STUDIES

A major advantage of the routine activity approach presented here is that it helps assemble some diverse and previously unconnected criminological analyses into a single substantive framework. This framework also serves to link illegal and legal activities, as illustrated by a few examples of descriptive accounts of criminal activity.

DESCRIPTIVE ANALYSES

There are several descriptive analyses of criminal acts in criminological literature. For example, Thomas Reppetto's (1974) study, *Residential Crime*, considers how residents supervise their neighborhoods and streets and limit access of possible offenders. He also considers how distance of households from the central city reduces risks of criminal victimization. Reppetto's evidence—consisting of criminal justice records, observations of comparative features of geographic areas, victimization survey data and offender interviews—indicates that offenders are very likely to use burglary tools and to have at least minimal technical skills, that physical characteristics of dwellings affect their victimization rates, that the rhythms of residential crime rate patterns are marked (often related to travel and work patterns of residents), and that visibility of potential sites of crime affects the risk that crimes will occur there. Similar findings are reported by Pope's (1977a; 1977b) study of burglary in California and by Scarr's (1972) study of burglary in and around the District of Columbia. In addition, many studies report that architectural and environmental design as well as community crime programs serve to decrease target suitability and increase capable guardianship (see, for example, Newman, 1973; Jeffery, 1971; Washnis, 1976), while many biographical or autobiographical descriptions of illegal activities note that lawbreakers take into account the nature of property and/or the structure of human activities as they go about their illegal work (see, e.g., Chambliss, 1972; Klockars, 1974;

Sutherland, 1937; Letkemann, 1973; Jackson, 1969; Martin, 1952; Maurer, 1964; Cameron, 1964; Williamson, 1968).

Evidence that the spatio-temporal organization of society affects patterns of crime can be found in several sources. Strong variations in specific predatory crime rates from hour to hour, day to day, and month to month are reported often (e.g., Wolfgang, 1958; Amir, 1971; Repetto, 1974; Scarr, 1972; FBI, 1975; 1976), and these variations appear to correspond to the various tempos of the related legitimate activities upon which they feed. Also at a microsociological level, Short and Strodtbeck (1965: chaps. 5 and 11) describe opportunities for violent confrontations of gang boys and other community residents which arise in the context of community leisure patterns, such as "quarter parties" in black communities, and the importance, in the calculus of decision making employed by participants in such episodes, of low probabilities of legal intervention. In addition, a wealth of empirical evidence indicates strong spatial variations over community areas in crime and delinquency rates[3] (for an excellent discussion and review of the literature on ecological studies of crimes, see Wilks, 1967). Recently, Albert Reiss (1976) has argued convincingly that these spatial variations (despite some claims to the contrary) have been supported consistently by both official and unofficial sources of data. Reiss further cites victimization studies which indicate that offenders are very likely to select targets not far from their own residence (see USDJ, 1974a; 1974b; 1974c).

MACROLEVEL ANALYSES OF CRIME TRENDS AND CYCLES

Although details about how crime occurs are intrinsically interesting, the important analytical task is to learn from these details how illegal activities carve their niche within the larger system of activities. This task is not an easy one. For example, attempts by Bonger (1916), Durkheim (1951; 1966), Henry and Short (1954), and Fleisher (1966) to link the rate of illegal activities to the economic condition of a society have not been completely successful. Empirical tests of the relationships postulated in the above studies have produced inconsistent results which some observers view as an indication that the level of crime is not related systematically to the economic conditions of a society (Mansfield et al., 1974: 463; Cohen and Felson, 1979).

It is possible that the wrong economic and social factors have been employed in these macro studies of crime. Other researchers have provided stimulating alternative descriptions of how social change affects the criminal opportunity structure, thereby influencing crime rates in particular societies. For example, at the beginning of the nineteenth century, Patrick Colquhoun (1800) presented a detailed, lucid description and analysis of crime in the London metropolitan area and suggestions for its control. He assembled substantial evidence that London was experiencing a massive crime wave attributable to a great increment in the assemblage and movement of valuable goods through its ports and terminals.

A similar examination of crime in the period of the English industrial expansion was carried out by a modern historian, J. J. Tobias (1967), whose work on the history of crime in nineteenth century England is perhaps the most comprehensive effort to isolate those elements of social change affecting crime in an expanding industrial nation. Tobias details how far-reaching changes in transportation, currency, technology, commerce, merchandising, poverty, housing, and the like, had tremendous repercussions on the amount and type of illegal activities committed in the nineteenth century. His thesis is that structural transformations either facilitated or impeded the opportunities to engage in illegal activities. In one of the few empirical studies of how recent social change affects the opportunity structure for crime in the United States, Leroy Gould (1969) demonstrated that the increase in the circulation of money and the availability of automobiles between 1921 and 1965 apparently led to an increase in the rate of bank robberies and auto thefts, respectively. Gould's data suggest that these relationships are due more to the abundance of opportunities to perpetrate the crimes than to short-term fluctuations in economic activities.

Although the sociological and historical studies cited in this section have provided some useful *empirical* generalizations and important insights into the incidence of crime, it is fair to say that they have not articulated systematically the *theoretical* linkages between routine legal activities and illegal endeavors. Thus, these studies cannot explain how changes in the larger social structure generate changes in the opportunity to engage in predatory crime and hence account for crime rate trends.[4] To do so requires a conceptual framework such as that sketched in the preceding section. Before attempting to demonstrate the feasibility of this approach with macrolevel data, we examine available microlevel data for its consistency with the major assumptions of this approach.

MICROLEVEL ASSUMPTIONS OF THE ROUTINE ACTIVITY APPROACH

The theoretical approach taken here specifies that crime rate trends in the post–World War II United States are related to patterns of what we have called routine activities. We define these as any recurrent and prevalent activities which provide for basic population and individual needs, whatever their biological or cultural origins. Thus routine activities would include formalized work, as well as the provision of standard food, shelter, sexual outlet, leisure, social interaction, learning and childrearing. These activities may go well beyond the minimal levels needed to prevent a population's extinction, so long as their prevalence and recurrence makes them a part of everyday life.

Routine activities may occur (1) at home, (2) in jobs away from home, and (3) in other activities away from home. The latter may involve primarily household members or others. We shall argue that, since World War II, the United States has experienced a major shift of routine activities away from the first category into the remaining ones, especially those nonhousehold activities involving nonhousehold members. In particular, we shall argue that this shift in the structure of routine activities increases the probability that motivated offenders will converge in space and time with suitable targets in the absence of capable guardians, hence contributing to significant increases in the direct-contact predatory crime rates over these years.

If the routine activity approach is valid, then we should expect to find evidence for a number of empirical relationships regarding the nature and distribution of predatory violations. For example, we would expect routine activities performed within or near the home and among family or other primary groups to entail lower risk of criminal victimization because they enhance guardianship capabilities. We should also expect that routine daily activities affect the location of property and personal targets in visible and accessible places at particular times, thereby influencing their risk of victimization. Furthermore, by determining their size and weight and in some cases their value, routine production activities should affect the suitability of consumer goods for illegal removal. Finally, if the routine activity approach is useful for explaining the paradox presented earlier, we should find that the circulation of people and property, the size and weight of consumer items etc., will parallel changes in crime rate trends for the post–World War II United States.

The veracity of the routine activity approach can be assessed by analyses of both microlevel and macrolevel interdependencies of human activities. While consistency at the former level may appear noncontroversial, or even obvious, one nonetheless needs to show that the approach does not contradict existing data before proceeding to investigate the latter level.

EMPIRICAL ASSESSMENT

CIRCUMSTANCES AND LOCATION OF OFFENSES

The routine activity approach specifies that household and family activities entail lower risk of criminal victimization than nonhousehold-nonfamily activities, despite the problems in measuring the former.[5]

National estimates from large-scale government victimization surveys in 1973 and 1974 support this generalization (see methodological information in Hindelang et al., 1976: Appendix 6). Table 1 presents several incident-victimization rates per 100,000 population ages 12 and older. Clearly, the rates in Panels A and B are far lower at or near home than elsewhere and far lower among relatives than others. The data indicate that risk of victimization varies directly with social distance between offender and victim. Panel C of this table indicates, furthermore, that risk of lone victimization far exceeds the risk of victimization for groups. These relationships are strengthened by considering time budget evidence that, on the average, Americans spend 16.26 hours per day at home, 1.38 hours on streets, in parks, etc., and 6.36 hours in other places (Szalai, 1972:795). Panel D of Table 1 presents our estimates of victimization per billion person-hours spent in such locations.[6] For example, personal larceny rates (with contact) are 350 times higher at the hands of strangers in streets than at the hands of nonstrangers at home. Separate computations from 1973 victimization data (USDJ, 1976: Table 48) indicate that there were two motor vehicle thefts per million vehicle-hours parked at or near home, 55 per million vehicle-hours in streets, parks, playgrounds, school grounds or parking lots, and 12 per million vehicle-hours elsewhere. While the direction of these relationships is not surprising, their magnitudes should be noted. It appears that risk of criminal victimization varies dramatically among the circumstances and locations in which people place themselves and their property.

TARGET SUITABILITY

Another assumption of the routine activity approach is that target suitability influences the occurrence of direct-contact predatory violations. Though we lack data to disaggregate all major components of target suitability (i.e., value, visibility, accessibility and inertia), together they imply that expensive and movable durables, such as vehicles and electronic appliances, have the highest risk of illegal removal.

TABLE 1 Incident-Specific Risk Rates for Rape, Robbery, Assault and Personal Larceny with Contact, United States, 1974

		Rape	Robbery	Assault	Personal Larceny with Contact	Total
A.	PLACE OF RESIDENCE[a]					
	In or near home	63	129	572	75	839
	Elsewhere	119	584	1,897	1,010	3,610
B.	VICTIM-OFFENDER RELATIONSHIP[a]					
	(lone offender)					
	Relative	7	13	158	5	183
	Well known	23	30	333	30	416
	Casual acquaintance	11	26	308	25	370
	Don't Know/Sight only	106	227	888	616	1,837
	(multiple offender)					
	Any known	10[c]	68	252	43	373
	All strangers	25[c]	349	530	366	1,270
C.	NUMBER OF VICTIMS[a]					
	One	179	647	2,116	1,062	4,004
	Two	3	47	257	19	326
	Three	0	13	53	3	09
	Four plus	0	6	43	1	50
D.	LOCATION AND RELATIONSHIP[b] (sole offender only)					
	Home, stranger	61	147	345	103	654
	Home, nonstranger	45	74	620	22	761
	Street, stranger	1,370	7,743	15,684	7,802	32,460
	Street, nonstranger	179	735	5,777	496	7,167
	Elsewhere, stranger	129	513	1,934	2,455	4,988
	Elsewhere, nonstranger	47	155	1,544	99	1,874

[a]Calculated from Hindelang et al., 1977: Tables 3.16, 3.18, 3.27, 3.28. Rates are per 100,000 persons ages 12 and over.
[b]See fn. 6 for source. Rates are per billion person-hours in stated locations.
[c]Based on white data only due to lack of suitable sample size for nonwhites as victims of rape with multiple offenders.

As a specific case in point, we compared the 1975 composition of stolen property reported in the Uniform Crime Report (FBI, 1976: Tables 26–7) with national data on personal consumer expenditures for goods (CEA, 1976: Tables 13–16) and to appliance industry estimates of the value of shipments the same year (*Merchandising Week*, 1976). We calculated that $26.44 in motor vehicles and parts were stolen for each $100 of these goods consumed in 1975, while $6.82 worth of electronic appliances were stolen per $100 consumed. Though these estimates are subject to error in citizen and police estimation, what is important here is their size relative to other rates. For example, only 8¢ worth of nondurables and 12¢ worth of furniture and nonelectronic household durables were stolen per $100 of each category consumed, the motor vehicle risk being, respectively, 330 and 220 times as great. Though we lack data on the "stocks" of goods subject to risk, these "flow" data clearly support our assumption that vehicles and electronic appliances are greatly overrepresented in thefts.

The 1976 Buying Guide issue of *Consumer Reports* (1975) indicates why electronic appliances are an excellent retail value for a thief. For example, a Panasonic car tape player is worth $30 per lb., and a Phillips phonograph cartridge is valued at over $5,000 per lb., while large appliances such as refrigerators and washing machines are only worth $1 to $3 per lb. Not surprisingly, burglary data for the District of Columbia in 1969 (Scarr, 1972: Table 9) indicate that home entertainment items alone constituted nearly four times as many stolen items as clothing, food, drugs, liquor, and tobacco combined and nearly eight times as many stolen items as office supplies and equipment. In addition, 69% of national thefts classified in 1975 (FBI, 1976: Tables 1, 26) involve automobiles, their parts or accessories, and thefts from automobiles or thefts of bicycles. Yet radio and television sets plus electronic components and accessories totaled only 0.10% of the total truckload tonnage terminated in 1973 by intercity motor carriers, while passenger cars, motor vehicle parts and accessories, motorcycles, bicycles, and their parts, totaled only 5.5% of the 410 million truckload tons terminated (ICC, 1974). Clearly, portable and movable durables are reported stolen in great disproportion to their share of the value and weight of goods circulating in the United States.

FAMILY ACTIVITIES AND CRIME RATES

One would expect that persons living in single-adult households and those employed outside the home are less obligated to confine their time to family activities within households. From a routine activity perspective, these persons and their households should have higher rates of predatory criminal victimization. We also expect that adolescents and young adults who are perhaps more likely to engage in peer group activities rather than family activities will have higher rates of criminal victimization. Finally, married persons should have lower rates than others. Tables 2 and 3 largely confirm these expectations (with the exception of personal larceny with contact). Examining these tables, we note that victimization rates appear to be related inversely to age and are lower for persons in "less active" statuses (e.g., keeping house, unable to work, retired) and persons in intact marriages. A notable exception is indicated in Table 2, where persons unable to work appear more likely to be victimized by rape, robbery and personal larceny with contact than are other "inactive persons." Unemployed persons also have unusually high rates of victimization. However, these rates are consistent with the routine activity approach offered here: the high rates of victimization suffered by the unemployed may reflect their residential proximity to high concentrations of potential offenders as well as their age and racial composition, while handicapped persons have high risk of personal victimization because they are less able to resist motivated offenders. Nonetheless, persons who keep house have noticeably lower rates of victimization than those who are employed, unemployed, in school or in the armed forces.

As Table 3 indicates, burglary and robbery victimization rates are about twice as high for persons living in single-adult households as for other persons in each age group examined. Other victimization data (USDJ, 1976: Table 21) indicate that, while household victimization rates tend to vary directly with household size, larger households have lower rates per person. For example, the total household victimization rates (including burglary, household larceny, and motor vehicle theft) per 1,000 households were 168 for single-person households and 326 for households containing six or more persons. Hence, six people distributed over six single-person households experience an average of 1,008 household victimizations, more than three times as many as one six-person household. Moreover, age of household head has a strong relationship to a household's victimization rate for these crimes. For households headed by persons under 20, the motor vehicle theft rate is nine times as high, and the burglary and household larceny rates four times as high as those for households headed by persons 65 and over (USDJ, 1976: Table 9).

While the data presented in this section were not collected originally for the purpose of testing the routine activity approach, our efforts to rework them for these purposes have proven fruitful. The routine activity approach is consistent with the data examined and,

TABLE 2 Selected Status-Specific Personal Victimization Rates for the United States (per 100,000 persons in each category)

Variables and Sources	Victim Category	Rape	Robbery	Assault	Personal Larceny with Contact	Personal Larceny without Contact
A. AGE (Source: Hindelang et al., 1977: Table 310, 1974 rates)	12–15	147	1,267	3,848	311	16,355
	16–19	248	1,127	5,411	370	15,606
	20–24	209	1,072	4,829	337	14,295
	25–34	135	703	3,023	263	10,354
	35–49	21	547	1,515	256	7,667
	50–64	33	411	731	347	4,588
	65+	20	388	492	344	1,845
B. MAJOR ACTIVITY OF VICTIM (Source: Hindelang et al., 1977: Table 313, 1974 rates)	(Male 16+)					
	Armed forces	—	1,388	4,153	118	16,274
	Employed	—	807	3,285	252	10,318
	Unemployed	—	2,179	7,984	594	15,905
	Keep house	—	0	2,475	463	3,998
	In school	—	1,362	5,984	493	17,133
	Unable to work	—	1,520	2,556	623	3,648
	Retired	—	578	662	205	2,080
	(Female 16+)					
	Keep house	116	271	978	285	4,433
	Employed	156	529	1,576	355	9,419
	Unemployed	798	772	5,065	461	12,338
	In school	417	430	2,035	298	12,810
	Unable to work	287	842	741	326	1,003
	Retired	120	172	438	831	1,571

TABLE 2 Continued

Variables and Sources / Victim Category	Rape	Robbery	Assault	Personal Larceny with Contact	Personal Larceny without Contact
C. MARITAL STATUS (Source: USDJ; 1977, Table 5, 1973 rates)					
(Male 12+)					
Never married	—	1,800	5,870	450	16,450
Married	—	550	2,170	170	7,660
Separated/Divorced	—	2,270	5,640	1,040	12,960
Widowed	—	1,150	1,500	—	4,120
(Female 12+)					
Never married	360	580	2,560	400	12,880
Married	70	270	910	220	6,570
Separated/Divorced	540	1,090	4,560	640	9,130
Widowed	—	450	590	480	2,460

Dash indicates too few offenses for accurate estimates of rate. However, rates in these cells are usually small.

TABLE 3   ROBBERY-BURGLARY VICTIMIZATION RATES BY AGES AND
NUMBER OF ADULTS IN HOUSEHOLD, 1974 AND 1976
GENERAL SOCIAL SURVEY

| AGE | NUMBER OF ADULTS IN HOUSEHOLD | | | | RATIO |
	ONE		TWO OR MORE		
18–35	0.200	(140)	0.095	(985)	2.11
36–55	0.161	(112)	0.079	(826)	2.04
56 and over	0.107	(262)	0.061	(640)	1.76
All ages	0.144	(514)	0.081	(2451)	1.78

(Numbers in parentheses are the base for computing risk rates.)
   Source: Calculated from 1974 and 1976 General Social Survey, National Opinion Research
Center, University of Chicago.

in addition, helps to accommodate within a rather simple and coherent analytical framework certain findings which, though not necessarily new, might otherwise be attributed only "descriptive" significance. In the next section, we examine macrosocial trends as they relate to trends in crime rates.

CHANGING TRENDS IN ROUTINE ACTIVITY STRUCTURE AND PARALLEL TRENDS IN CRIME RATES

The main thesis presented here is that the dramatic increase in the reported crime rates in the U.S. since 1960 is linked to changes in the routine activity structure of American society and to a corresponding increase in target suitability and decrease in guardian presence. If such a thesis has validity, then we should be able to identify these social trends and show how they relate to predatory criminal victimization rates.

TRENDS IN HUMAN ACTIVITY PATTERNS

The decade 1960–1970 experienced noteworthy trends in the activities of the American population. For example, the percent of the population consisting of female college students increased 118% (USBC, 1975: Table 225). Married female labor force participant rates increased

TABLE 4 PROPORTION OF HOUSEHOLDS UNATTENDED BY ANYONE 14
YEARS OLD OR OVER BY TIME OF DAY DURING FIRST VISIT BY
CENSUS BUREAU INTERVIEWER, 1960 AND 1971

TIME OF DAY	1960 CENSUS	NOVEMBER, 1971 CURRENT POPULATION SURVEY	PERCENT CHANGE
8:00– 8:59 a.m.	29%	43	+48.9%
9:00– 9:59 a.m.	29	44	+58
10:00–10:59 a.m.	31	42	+36
11:00–11:59 a.m.	32	41	+28
12:00–12:59 p.m.	32	41	+28
1:00– 1:59 p.m.	31	43	+39
2:00– 2:59 p.m.	33	43	+30
3:00– 3:59 p.m.	30	33	+10
4:00– 4:59 p.m.	28	30	+ 7
5:00– 5:59 p.m.	22	26	+18
6:00– 6:59 p.m.	22	25	+14
7:00– 7:50 p.m.	20	29	+45
8:00– 8:59 p.m.	24	22	– 8

Source: Calculated from USBC (1973b: Table A).

31% (USBC, 1975: Table 563), while the percent of the population living as primary individuals increased by 34% (USBC, 1975: Table 51;
see also Kobrin, 1976). We gain some further insight into changing
routine activity patterns by comparing hourly data for 1960 and 1971
on households *unattended* by persons ages 14 or over when U.S. census interviewers first called (see Table 4). These data suggest that the
proportion of households unattended at 8 A.M. increased by almost
half between 1960 and 1971. One also finds increases in rates of out-
of-town travel, which provides greater opportunity for both daytime
and nighttime burglary of residences. Between 1960 and 1970, there
was a 72% increase in state and national park visits per capita (USBC,
1975), an 144% increase in the percent of plant workers eligible for
three weeks vacation (BLS, 1975: Table 116), and an 184% increase in
overseas travellers per 100,00 population (USBC, 1975: Table 366). The
National Travel Survey, conducted as part of the U.S. Census Bureau's
Census of Transportation, confirms the general trends, tallying an
81% increase in the number of vacations taken by Americans from
1967 to 1972, a five-year period (USBC, 1973a: Introduction).

The dispersion of activities away from households appears to be a major recent social change. Although this decade also experienced an important 31% increase in the percent of the population ages 15–24, age structure change was only one of many social trends occurring during the period, especially trends in the circulation of people and property in American society.[7]

The importance of the changing activity structure is underscored by taking a brief look at demographic changes between the years 1970 and 1975, a period of continuing crime rate increments. Most of the recent changes in age structure relevant to crime rates already had occurred by 1970; indeed, the proportion of the population ages 15–24 increased by only 6% between 1970 and 1975, compared with a 15% increase during the five years 1965 to 1970. On the other hand, major changes in the structure of routine activities continued during these years. For example, in only five years, the estimated proportion of the population consisting of husband-present, married women in the labor force households increased by 11%, while the estimated number of non-husband-wife households per 100,000 population increased from 9,150 to 11,420, a 25% increase (USBC, 1976: Tables 50, 276; USBC, 1970–1975). At the same time, the percent of population enrolled in higher education increased 16% between 1970 and 1975.

RELATED PROPERTY TRENDS AND THEIR RELATION TO HUMAN ACTIVITY PATTERNS

Many of the activity trends mentioned above normally involve significant investments in durable goods. For example, the dispersion of population across relatively more households (especially non-husband-wife households) enlarges the market for durable goods such as television sets and automobiles. Women participating in the labor force and both men and women enrolled in college provide a market for automobiles. Both work and travel often involve the purchase of major movable or portable durables and their use away from home.

Considerable data are available which indicate that sales of consumer goods changed dramatically between 1960 and 1970 (as did their size and weight), hence providing more suitable property available for theft. For example, during this decade, constant-dollar personal consumer expenditures in the United States for motor vehicles and parts increased by 71%, while constant-dollar expenditures for other durables increased by 105% (calculated from CEA, 1976: Table B-16). In addition, electronic household appliances and small houseware shipments increased from 56.2 to 119.7 million units (*Electrical*

Merchandising Week, 1964; *Merchandising Week,* 1973). During the same decade, appliance imports increased in value by 681% (USBC, 1975: Table 1368).

This same period appears to have spawned a revolution in small durable product design which further feeds the opportunity for crime to occur. Relevant data from the 1960 and 1970 Sears catalogs on the weight of many consumer durable goods were examined. Sears is the nation's largest retailer and its policy of purchasing and relabeling standard manufactured goods makes its catalogs a good source of data on widely merchandised consumer goods. The lightest television listed for sale in 1960 weighed 38 lbs., compared with 15 lbs. for 1970. Thus, the lightest televisions were $2^{1}/_{2}$ times as heavy in 1960 as 1970. Similar trends are observed for dozens of other goods listed in the Sears catalog. Data from *Consumer Reports Buying Guide,* published in December of 1959 and 1969, show similar changes for radios, record players, slide projectors, tape recorders, televisions, toasters and many other goods. Hence, major declines in weight between 1960 and 1970 were quite significant for these and other goods, which suggests that the consumer goods market may be producing many more targets suitable for theft. In general, one finds rapid growth in property suitable for illegal removal and in household and individual exposure to attack during the years 1960–1975.

RELATED TRENDS IN BUSINESS ESTABLISHMENTS

Of course, as households and individuals increased their ownership of small durables, businesses also increased the value of the merchandise which they transport and sell as well as the money involved in these transactions. Yet the Census of Business conducted in 1958, 1963, 1967, and 1972 indicate that the number of wholesale, retail, service, and public warehouse establishments (including establishments owned by large organizations) was a nearly constant ratio of one for every 16 persons in the United States. Since more goods and money were distributed over a relatively fixed number of business establishments, the tempo of business activity per establishment apparently was increasing. At the same time, the percent of the population employed as sales clerks or salesmen in retail trade declined from 1.48% to 1.27%, between 1960 and 1970, a 14.7% decline (USBC, 1975: Table 589).

Though both business and personal property increased, the changing pace of activities appears to have exposed the latter to greater relative risk of attack, whether at home or elsewhere, due to the dispersion of goods among many more households, while concen-

trating goods in business establishments. However, merchandise in
retail establishments with heavy volume and few employees to guard
it probably is exposed to major increments in risk of illegal removal
than is most other business property.

COMPOSITION OF CRIME TRENDS

If these changes in the circulation of people and property are in fact
related to crime trends, the *composition* of the latter should reflect this.
We expect relatively greater increases in personal and household victimization as compared with most business victimizations, while
shoplifting should increase more rapidly than other types of thefts
from businesses. We expect personal offenses at the hands of strangers to manifest greater increases than such offenses at the hands of
nonstrangers. Finally, residential burglary rates should increase more
in daytime than nighttime.

The available time series on the composition of offenses confirm
these expectations. For example, Table 5 shows that commercial burglaries declined from 60% to 36% of the total, while daytime residential burglaries increased from 16% to 33%. Unlike the other crimes
against business, shoplifting increased its share. Though we lack
trend data on the circumstances of other violent offenses, murder data
confirm our expectations. Between 1963 and 1975, felon-type murders
increased from 17% to 32% of the total. Compared with a 47% increase
in the rate of relative killings in this period, we calculated a 294% increase in the murder rate at the hands of known or suspected felon
types.

Thus the trends in the composition of recorded crime rates appear
to be highly consistent with the activity structure trends noted earlier.
In the next section we apply the routine activity approach in order to
model crime rate trends and social change in the post–World War II
United States.

THE RELATIONSHIP OF THE HOUSEHOLD ACTIVITY RATIO TO FIVE ANNUAL OFFICIAL INDEX CRIME RATES IN THE UNITED STATES, 1947–1974

In this section, we test the hypothesis that aggregate official crime rate
trends in the United States vary directly over time with the dispersion
of activities away from family and household. The limitations of annual time series data do not allow construction of direct measures of
changes in hourly activity patterns, or quantities, qualities and move-

TABLE 5 OFFENSE ANALYSIS TRENDS FOR ROBBERY, BURGLARY, LARCENY AND MURDER; UNITED STATES, 1960–1975

A. ROBBERIES[a]	1960	1965	1970	
Highway robbery	52.6	57.0	59.8	
Residential robbery	8.0	10.1	13.1	
Commercial robbery	39.4	32.9	27.1	
Totals	100.0	100.0	100.0	
B. BURGLARIES	1960	1965	1970	1975
Residential	15.6	24.5	31.7	33.2
Residential nighttime	24.4	25.2	25.8	30.5
Commercial	60.0	50.2	42.5	36.3
Totals	100.0	99.9	100.0	100.0
C. LARCENIES	1960	1965	1970	1975
Shoplifting	6.0	7.8	9.2	11.3
Other	94.0	92.2	90.8	88.7
Totals	100.0	100.0	100.0	100.0
D. MURDERS	1963	1965	1970	1975
Relative killings	31.0	31.0	23.3	22.4
Romance, arguments[b]	51.0	48.0	47.9	45.2
Felon types[c]	17.0	21.0	28.8	32.4
Totals	100.0	100.0	100.0	100.0

Source: Offense analysis from UCR, various years.
[a]Excluding miscellaneous robberies. The 1975 distribution omitted due to apparent instability of post–1970 data.
[b]Includes romantic triangles, lovers' quarrels and arguments.
[c]Includes both known and suspected felon types.

ments of exact stocks of household durable goods, but the Current Population Survey does provide related time series on labor force and household structure. From these data, we calculate annually (beginning in 1947) a household activity ratio by adding the number of married, husband-present female labor force participants (source: BLS, 1975: Table 5) to the number of non-husband-wife households (source: USBC, 1947–1976), dividing this sum by the total number of households in the U.S. (source: USBC, 1947–1976). This calculation provides an estimate of the proportion of American households in year t expected to be most highly exposed to risk of personal and property victimization due to the dispersion of their activities away from family and household and/or their likelihood of owning extra sets of durables subject to high risk of attack. Hence, the household activity ratio should vary directly with official index crime rates.

Our empirical goal in this section is to test this relationship, with controls for those variables which other researchers have linked empirically to crime rate trends in the United States. Since various researchers have found such trends to increase with the proportion of the population in teen and young adult years (Fox, 1976; Land and Felson, 1976; Sagi and Wellford, 1968; Wellford, 1973), we include the population ages 15–24 per 100,000 resident population in year *t* as our first control variable (source: USBC, various years). Others (e.g., Brenner, 1976a; 1976b) have found unemployment rates to vary directly with official crime rates over time, although this relationship elsewhere has been shown to be empirically questionable (see Mansfield et al., 1974: 463; Cohen and Felson, 1979). Thus, as our second, control variable, we take the standard annual unemployment rate (per 100 persons ages 16 and over) as a measure of the business cycle (source: BLS, 1975).

Four of the five crime rates that we utilize here (forcible rape, aggravated assault, robbery and burglary) are taken from FBI estimates of offenses per 100,000 U.S. population (as revised and reported in OMB, 1973). We exclude larceny-theft due to a major definitional change in 1960 and auto theft due to excessive multicollinearity in the analysis.[8] For our homicide indicator we employ the homicide mortality rate taken from the vital statistics data collected by the Bureau of the Census (various years). The latter rate has the advantage of being collected separately from the standard crime reporting system and is thought to contain less measurement error (see Bowers and Pierce, 1975). Hence, this analysis of official index crime rates includes three violent offenses (homicide, forcible rape, and aggravated assault), one property offense (burglary), and one offense which involves both the removal of property and the threat of violence (robbery). The analysis thus includes one offense thought to have relatively low reporting reliability (forcible rape), one thought to have relatively high reliability (homicide), and three others having relatively intermediate levels of reporting quality (Ennis, 1967).

Since official crime rates in year *t* are likely to reflect some accumulation of criminal opportunity and inclinations over several years, one should not expect these rates to respond solely to the level of the independent variables for year *t*. A useful model of cumulative social change in circumstances such as this is the difference equation, which can be estimated in two forms (see Goldberg, 1958). One form takes the first difference $(Y_t - Y_{t-1})$ as the dependent variable—in this case, the change in the official crime rate per 100,000 population between year *t*–1 and year t. Alternatively, one can estimate the difference equation in autoregressive form by taking the official crime rate in year t as a function of the exogenous predictors plus the official crime rate in year t-1 on the right-hand side of the equation. (See Land, 1978, for a review of these and other methods and for references to related literature.) Both forms are estimable with ordinary least squares methods, which we employ for the years 1947 through 1974. The N is 28 years for all but the homicide rate, for which publication lags reduce our N to 26.

Even if a positive relationship between the household activity ratio and the official crime rates is observed, with controls for age and unemployment, we are open to the charge that this may be a spurious consequence of autocorrelation of disturbances, that is, the possibility that residuals are systematically related for nearby time points. While spurious relationships are a risk one also takes in cross-sectional regression analysis, time-series analysts have devised a variety of methods for monitoring and adjusting for spuriousness due to this autocorrelation, including the Durbin and Watson (1951) statistic, Durbin's h statistic (Durbin, 1970), the Griliches (1967) criterion, as well as Cochrane and Orcutt (1949) corrections. We employ (but do not report in detail) these methods to check for the likelihood that the observed relationship is spurious. (See Land, 1978, for a review of such tests and the related literature on their applicability and robustness; see Theil, 1971, for a methodological review.)

FINDINGS

Our time-series analysis for the years 1947–1974 consistently revealed positive and statistically significant relationships between the household activity ratio and each official crime rate change. Whichever official crime rate is employed, this finding occurs—whether we take the first difference for each crime rate as exogenous or estimate the equation in autoregressive form (with the lagged dependent variable on the right-hand side of the equation); whether we include or exclude the unemployment variable; whether we take the current scales of variables or convert them to natural log values; whether we employ the age structure variable as described or alter the ages examined (e.g., 14–24, 15–19, etc.). In short, the relationship is positive and significant in each case.

Before calculating the difference equations, we regressed each crime rate in year t on the three independent variables for year t. This ordinary structural equation also produced consistent positive and significant coefficients for the routine activity coefficient, the total variance explained ranges from 84% to 97%. However, the Durbin-Watson statistics for these equations indicated high risk of autocorrelation, which is hardly surprising since they ignore lagged effects. Reestimated equations taking first differences as endogenous reduced the risk of autocorrelation significantly (and also reduced variance explained to between 35% and 77%). These equations also consistently produce significant positive coefficients for the household activity variable. When unemployment is included in these equations, its coefficients are all negative and near zero.

The top panel of Table 6 presents regression estimates of first differences for five official crime rates, with the age structure and household activity variables in year t as the only predictors. Again, the household activity coefficients are consistently positive, with t ratios always significant with a one-tailed test. Except for the aggravated assault equation, the household activity variable has a t ratio and standardized coefficient greater than that of the age structure variable. The standardized coefficients for the household activity variable range from .42 to .72, while the age structure coefficients are consistently positive. In general, the household activity variable is a stronger predictor of official crime rate trends than the age structure.

The equations in the top panel of Table 6 generally have lower variance explained but also lower risk of autocorrelation of disturbances than those reported above. For all five equations, the Durbin-Watson statistic allows acceptance of the null hypothesis that autocorrelation is absent at the 1% level. A 5% level (which *increases* the likelihood of proving the statistic nonzero) allows us neither to accept nor reject the null hypothesis that autocorrelation is absent in the homicide and robbery equations.

Though autocorrelation has not been proven to exist in these five equations, its risk may be sufficient in two to motivate further efforts at equation estimation (see bottom panel of Table 6). We estimated the equations in autoregressive form to see if the risk abates. Since the Durbin-Watson statistic was not designed for evaluating autocorrelation in these equations, we calculated Durbin's h, a statistic specifically designed for equations estimated with a lagged dependent variable (Durbin, 1970), and recently found to be robust for small samples (Maddala and Rao, 1973). This statistic allows acceptance of the null hypothesis (at both 1% and 5% levels) that autocorrelation is absent for all five equations. Application of the Griliches (1967) criterion further allows acceptance of each equation as manifesting distributing lags rather than serial correlation. We also employed the Cochrane-Orcutt (1949) iterative procedure to calculate a correction estimate for any autocorrelation present. The resulting correction for the household activity coefficient proves minimal in all five cases. Finally, we

TABLE 6 Regression Equations for First Differences in Five Index Crime Rates and Sensitivity Analyses, United States, 1947–1974

	(1) Nonnegligent Homicide	(2) Forcible Rape	(3) Aggravated Assault	(4) Robbery	(5) Burglary
FIRST DIFFERENCE FORM					
Constant	-2.3632	-4.8591	-32.0507	-43.8838	-221.2303
t ratio	.3502	5.3679	7.6567	3.4497	3.7229
Proportion 15–24 (t;					
Standardized	.1667	.1425	.4941	.2320	.1952
Unstandardized	3.2190	6.4685	132.1072	116.7742	486.0806
t ratio	1.0695	.7505	3.3147	.9642	.8591
Household activity ratio (t)					
Standardized	.7162	.6713	.4377	.4242	.5106
Unstandardized	4.0676	8.9743	34.4658	62.8834	374.4746
t ratio	4.5959	3.5356	2.9364	1.7629	2.2474
Multiple R^2 adjusted	.6791	.5850	.7442	.3335	.4058
Degrees of freedom	23	25	25	25	25
Durbin-Watson value	2.5455	2.3388	2.3446	1.4548	1.7641
1% test	Accept	Accept	Accept	Accept	Accept
5% test	Uncertain	Accept	Accept	Uncertain	Accept
AUTOREGRESSIVE FORM					
Multiple R^2 adjusted	.9823	.9888	.9961	.9768	.9859
Durbin's h	-1.3751	-.7487	.9709	1.5490	1.1445
–1% test	Accept	Accept	Accept	Accept	Accept
–5% test	Accept	Accept	Accept	Accept	Accept
Grileches criterion	Accept	Accept	Accept	Accept	Accept
Cochrane-Orcutt correction					
Effect upon household activity	Minimal	Minimal	Minimal	Minimal	Minimal
Unemployment rate as control					
Effect upon household activity	Minimal	Minimal	Minimal	Minimal	Minimal

calculated each of the above equations for natural log values of the relevant variables, finding again that the household activity coefficient was consistently positive and statistically significant and the risk of autocorrelation reduced still further.

The positive and significant relationship between the household activity variable and the official crime rates is robust and appears to hold for both macro- and microlevel data; it explains five crime rate trends, as well as the changing composition of official crime rates reported in Table 5. These results suggest that routine activities may indeed provide the opportunity for many illegal activities to occur.

DISCUSSION

In our judgment many conventional theories of crime (the adequacy of which usually is evaluated by cross-sectional data, or no data at all) have difficulty accounting for the annual changes in crime rate trends in the post–World War II United States. These theories may prove useful in explaining crime trends during other periods, within specific communities, or in particular subgroups of the population. Longitudinal aggregate data for the United States, however, indicate that the trends for many of the presumed causal variables in these theoretical structures are in a direction opposite to those hypothesized to be the causes of crime. For example, during the decade 1960–1970, the percent of the population below the low-income level declined 44% and the unemployment rate declined 186%. Central city population as a share of the whole population declined slightly, while the percent of foreign stock declined 0.1%, etc. (see USBC, 1975: 654, 19, 39).

On the other hand, the convergence in time and space of three elements (motivated offenders, suitable targets, and the absence of capable guardians) appears useful for understanding crime rate trends. The lack of any of these elements is sufficient to prevent the occurrence of a successful direct-contact predatory crime. The convergence in time and space of suitable targets and the absence of capable guardians can lead to large increases in crime rates without any increase or change in the structural conditions that motivate individuals to engage in crime. Presumably, had the social indicators of the variables hypothesized to be the causes of crime in conventional theories changed in the direction of favoring increased crime in the post–World War II United States, the increases in crime rates likely would have been even more staggering than those which were observed. In any event, it is our belief that criminologists have underemphasized the importance of the convergence of suitable targets and the absence of capable guardians in explaining recent increases in the crime rate. Furthermore, the effects of the convergence in time and space of these elements may be multiplicative rather than additive. That is, their convergence by a fixed percentage may produce increases in crime rates far greater than that fixed percentage, demonstrating how some relatively modest social trends can contribute to some relatively large changes in crime rate trends. The fact that logged variables improved our equations (moving Durbin-Watson values closer to "ideal" levels) lends support to the argument that such an interaction occurs.

Those few investigations of cross-sectional data which include household indicators produce results similar to ours. For example, Roncek (1975) and Choldin and Roncek (1976) report on block-level data for San Diego, Cleveland and Peoria and indicate that the proportion of a block's households which are primary individual households consistently offers the best or nearly the best predictor of a block's crime rate. This relationship persisted after they controlled for numerous social variables, including race, density, age and poverty. Thus the association between household structure and risk of criminal victimization has been observed in individual-level and block-level cross-sectional data, as well as aggregate national time-series data.

Without denying the importance of factors motivating offenders to engage in crime, we have focused specific attention upon violations themselves and the prerequisites for their occurrence. However, the routine activity approach might in the future be applied to the analysis of offenders and their inclinations as well. For example, the structure of primary group activity may affect the likelihood that cultural transmission or social control of criminal inclinations will occur, while the structure of the community may affect the tempo of criminogenic peer group activity. We also may expect that circumstances favorable for carrying out violations contribute to criminal inclinations in the long run by rewarding these inclinations.

We further suggest that the routine activity framework may prove useful in explaining why the criminal justice system, the community and the family have appeared so ineffective in exerting social control since 1960. Substantial increases in the opportunity to carry out predatory violations may have undermined society's mechanisms for social control. For example, it may be difficult for institutions seeking to increase the certainty, celerity and severity of punishment to compete with structural changes resulting in vast increases in the certainty, celerity and value of rewards to be gained from illegal predatory acts.

It is ironic that the very factors which increase the opportunity to enjoy the benefits of life also may increase the opportunity for predatory violations. For example, automobiles provide freedom of movement to offenders as well as average citizens and offer vulnerable targets for theft. College enrollment, female labor force participation, urbanization, suburbanization, vacations and new electronic durables provide various opportunities to escape the confines of the household while they increase the risk of predatory victimization. Indeed, the opportunity for predatory crime appears to be enmeshed in the opportunity structure for legitimate activities to such an extent that it might be very difficult to root out substantial amounts of crime without modifying much of our way of life. Rather than assuming that predatory crime is simply an indicator of social breakdown, one might take it as a byproduct of freedom and prosperity as they manifest themselves in the routine activities of everyday life.

NOTES

1. Though official data severely underestimate crime, they at least provide a rough indicator of trends over time in the volume of several major felonies. The possibility that these data also reflect trends in rates at which offenses are reported to the police has motivated extensive victimology research (see Nettler, 1974; and Hindelang, 1976, for a review). This work consistently finds that seriousness of offense is the strongest determinant of citizen reporting to law enforcement officials (Skogan, 1976: 145; Hindelang, 1976: 401). Hence the upward trend in official crime rates since 1960 in the U.S. may reflect increases in *both* the volume and seriousness of offenses. Though disaggregating these two components may not be feasible, one may wish to interpret observed trends as generated largely by both.

2. The analytical distinction between target and guardian is not important in those cases where a personal target engages in self-protection from direct-contact predatory violations. We leave open for the present the question of whether a guardian is effective or ineffective in all situations. We also allow that various guardians may primarily supervise offenders, targets or both. These are questions for future examination.

3. One such ecological study by Sarah Boggs (1965) presents some similar ideas in distinguishing *familiarity* of offenders with their targets and *profitability* of targets as two elements of crime occurrence. Boggs's work stands apart from much research on the ecology of crime in its consideration of crime occurrence rates separately from offender rates. The former consist of the number of offenses committed in a given area per number of suitable targets within that area (as estimated by various indicators). The latter considers the residence of offenders in computing the number of offenders per unit of population. Boggs

examines the correlations between crime occurrence rates and offender rates for several offenses in St. Louis and shows that the two are often independent. It appears from her analysis that *both* target and offender characteristics play a central role in the location of illegal activity.

4. The concept of the opportunity for crime contained in the above research and in this study differs considerably from the traditional sociological usage of the *differential opportunity* concept. For example, Cloward and Ohlin (1960) employed this term in discussing how legitimate and illegitimate opportunities affect the resolution of adjustment problems leading to gang delinquency. From their viewpoint, this resolution depends upon the kind of social support for one or another type of illegitimate activity that is given at different points in the social structure (Cloward and Ohlin, 1960: 151). Rather than circumstantial determinants of crime, they use differential opportunity to emphasize structural features which motivate offenders to perpetrate certain types of crimes. Cloward and Ohlin are largely silent on the interaction of this motivation with target suitability and guardianship as this interaction influences crime rates.

5. Recent research indicates the existence of substantial quantities of family violence which remains outside of UCR data (see annotated bibliography of family violence in Lystad, 1974). While we cannot rule out the likelihood that much family violence is concealed from victimization surveys, the latter capture information absent from police data and still indicate that nonfamily members are usually much more dangerous than family members are to each other (see text). Also, when family violence leads to death, its suppression becomes quite difficult. The murder circumstances data indicate that about two-thirds of killings involve nonrelatives. Without denying the evidence that the level of family violence is far greater than police reports would indicate, available data also suggest that time spent in family activities within households incurs less risk of victimization than many alternative activities in other places. In addition, many of the most *common* offenses (such as robbery and burglary) always have been recognized as usually involving nonfamily members.

6. Billion person-hours can easily be conceptualized as 1,000,000 persons spending 1,000 hours each (or about 42 days) in a given location (Szalai, 1972:795). Fox obtained these data from a 1966 time budget study in 44 American cities. The study was carried out by the Survey Research Center, the University of Michigan. We combined four subsamples in computing our figures. We combined activities into three locations, as follows: (1) at or just outside home; (2) at another's home, restaurants or bars, or indoor leisure; (3) in streets, parks, or outdoor leisure. Our computing formula was
$$Q = [(R-10^5) \div (A \cdot 365)] \cdot 10.^9$$
where Q is the risk per billion person-hours; R is the victimization rate,

reported per 10^5 persons in Hindelang et al. (1976: Table 318); A is the hours spent per location calculated from Szalai (1972: 795); 365 is the multiplier to cover a year's exposure to risk, and 10^9 converts risk per person-hour to billion person-hours.

7. While the more sophisticated treatments of the topic have varied somewhat in their findings, most recent studies attempting to link crime rate increases to the changing age structure of the American population have found that the latter account for a relatively limited proportion of the general crime trend (see, for example, Sagi and Wellford, 1968; Ferdinand, 1970; and Wellford, 1973).

8. The auto theft rate lagged one year correlated quite strongly with the predictor variables. This multicollinearity impaired our difference equation analysis, although we again found consistently positive coefficients for the household activity ratio. We were able to remove autocorrelation by logging all variables and including the unemployment as a control, but do not report these equations.

REFERENCES

Amir, Menachem
1971   Patterns of Forcible Rape. Chicago: University of Chicago Press.

Boggs, Sarah
1965   "Urban crime patterns." American Sociological Review 30:899–905.

Bonger, W. A.
1916   Criminality and Economic Conditions. Boston: Little, Brown.

Bowers, W.J. and Glen L. Pierce
1975   "The illusion of deterrence of Isaac Ehrlich's research on capital punishment." Yale Law Journal 85:187–208.

Brenner, Harvey
1976a   Estimating the Social Costs of National Economic Policy: Implications for Mental and Physical Health and Criminal Aggression. Paper no. 5, Joint Economic Committee, Congress of the United States. Washington, D.C.: U.S. Government Printing Office.
1976b   Effects of the National Economy on Criminal Aggression II. Final Report to National Institute of Mental Health. Contract #282–76–0355FS.

Bureau of Labor Statistics (BLS)
1975   Handbook of Labor Statistics 1975—Reference Edition. Washington, D.C.: U.S. Government Printing Office.

Cameron, Mary Owen
1964   The Booster and the Snitch. New York: Free Press.

Chambliss, William J.
  1972   Boxman: A Professional Thief's Journey. New York: Harper and
          Row.

Choldin, Harvey M. and Dennis W. Roncek
  1976   "Density, population potential and pathology: a block-level
          analysis." Public Data Use 4:19–30.

Cloward, Richard and Lloyd Ohlin
  1960   Delinquency and Opportunity. New York: Free Press.

Cochrane, D., and G.H. Orcutt
  1949   "Application of least squares regression to relationships contain-
          ing autocorrelated error terms." Journal of the American Statisti-
          cal Association 44:32–61.

Cohen, Lawrence E. and Marcus Felson
  1979   "On estimating the social costs of national economic policy: a
          critical examination of the Brenner study." Social Indicatiors
          Research. In Press.

Colquhoun, Patrick
  1800   Treatise on the Police of the Metropolis. London: Baldwin.

Consumer Reports Buying Guide
  1959   Consumer Reports (December). Mt. Vernon: Consumers Union.
  1969   Consumer Reports (December). Mt. Vernon: Consumers Union.
  1975   Consumer Reports (December). Mt. Vernon: Consumers Union.

Council of Economic Advisors (CEA)
  1976   The Economic Report of the President. Washington, D.C.: U.S.
          Government Printing Office.

Durbin, J.
  1970   Testing for serial correlation when least squares regressors are
          lagged dependent variables." Econometrica 38:410–21.

Durbin, J., and G.S. Watson
  1951   "Testing for serial correlation in least squares regression, II."
          Biometrika 38:159–78.

Durkheim, Emile
  1951   Suicide: A Study in Sociology. New York: Free Press.

  1966   The Division of Labor in Society. New York: Free Press.

Electrical Merchandising Week
  1964   Statistical and Marketing Report (January). New York: Billboard
          Publications.

Ennis, Philip H.
  1967   "Criminal victimization in the U.S.: a report of a national sur-
          vey, field surveys II." The President's Commission on Law En-

forcement and the Administration of Justice. Washington, D.C.: U.S. Government Printing Office.

Federal Bureau of Investigation (FBI)
1975   Crime in the U.S.: Uniform Crime Report. Washington, D.C.: U.S. Government Printing Office.
1976   Crime in the U.S.: Uniform Crime Report. Washington, D.C.: U.S. Government Printing Office.

Ferdinand, Theodore N.
1970   "Demographic shifts and criminality." British Journal of Criminology 10:169-75.

Fleisher, Belton M.
1966   The Economics of Delinquency. Chicago: Quadrangle.

Fox, James A.
1976   An Econometric Analysis of Crime Data. Ph.D. dissertation, Department of Sociology, University of Pennsylvania. Ann Arbor: University Microfilms.

Glaser, Daniel
1971   Social Deviance. Chicago: Markham.

Goldberg, Samuel
1958   Introduction to Difference Equations. New York: Wiley.

Gould, Leroy
1969   "The changing structure of property crime in an affluent society." Social Forces 48:50-9.

Griliches, Z.
1967   "Distributed lags: a survey." Econometrica 35:16-49.

Guerry, A.M.
1833   "Essai sur la statistique morale de la France." Westminister Review 18:357.

Hawley, Amos
1950   Human Ecology: A Theory of Community Structure. New York: Ronald.

Henry, A.F. and J.F. Short
1954   Suicide and Homicide. New York: Free Press.

Hindelang, Michael J.
1976   Criminal Victimization in Eight American Cities: A Descriptive Analysis of Common Theft and Assault. Cambridge: Ballinger.

Hindelang, Michael J., Christopher S. Dunn, Paul Sutton and Alison L. Aumick
1976   Sourcebook of Criminal Justice Statistics—1975. U.S. Dept. of Justice, Law Enforcement Assistance Administration. Washington, D.C.: U.S. Government Printing Office.
1977   Sourcebook of Criminal Justice Statistics—1976. U.S. Dept. of

Justice, Law Enforcement Assistance Administration. Washington, D.C.: U.S. Government Printing Office.

Interstate Commerce Commission (ICC)
1974   Annual Report: Freight Commodity Statistics of Class I Motor Carriers of Property Operative in Intercity Service. Washington, D.C.: U.S. Government Printing Office.

Jackson, Bruce
1969   A Thief's Primer. New York: Macmillan.

Jeffery, C. R.
1971   Crime Prevention Through Environmental Design. Beverly Hills: Sage.

Klockars, Carl B.
1974   The Professional Fence. New York: Free Press.

Kobrin, Frances E.
1976   "The primary individual and the family: changes in living arrangements in the U.S. since 1940." Journal of Marriage and the Family 38:233-9.

Land, Kenneth C.
1978   "Modelling macro social change." Paper presented at annual meeting of the American Sociological Association, San Francisco.

Land, Kenneth C. and Marcus Felson
1976   "A general framework for building dynamic macro social indicator models: including an analysis of changes in crime rates and police expenditures." American Journal of Sociology 82:565-604.

Letkemann, Peter
1973   Crime as Work. Englewood Cliffs: Prentice-Hall.

Lystad, Mary
1974   An Annotated Bibliography: Violence at Home. DHEW Publication No. (ADM 75-136). Washington, D.C: U.S. Government Printing Office.

Maddala, G. S., and A. S. Rao
1973   "Tests for serial correlation in regression models with lagged dependent variables and serially correlated errors." Econometrica 41:761-74.

Mansfield, Roger, Leroy Gould, and J. Zvi Namenwirth
1974   "A Socioeconomic model for the prediction of societal rates of property theft." Social Forces 52:462-72.

Martin, John Bower
1952   My Life in Crime. New York: Harper.

Maurer, David W.
  1964   Whiz Mob. New Haven: College and University Press.

Merchandising Week
  1973   Statistical and Marketing Report (February). New York: Bill-
          board Publications.
  1976   Statistical and Marketing Report (March). New York: Billboard
          Publications.

National Commission on the Causes and Prevention of Violence
  1969   Crimes of Violence. Vol. 13. Washington, D.C.: U.S. Govern-
          ment Printing Office.

Nettler, Gwynn
  1974   Explaining Crime. New York: McGraw-Hill.

Newman, Oscar
  1973   Defensible Space: Crime Prevention Through Urban Design.
          New York: Macmillan.

Office of Management and the Budget (OMB)
  1973   Social Indicators 1973. Washington, D.C.: U.S. Government
          Printing Office.

Pope, Carl E.
  1977a   Crime-Specific Analysis: The Characteristics of Burglary Inci-
          dents. U.S. Dept. of Justice, Law Enforcement Assistance
          Administration. Analytic Report 10. Washington, D.C.: U.S.
          Government Printing Office.
  1977b   Crime-Specific Analysis: An Empirical Examination of Burglary
          Offense and Offender Characteristics. U.S. Dept. of Justice, Law
          Enforcement Assistance Administration. Analytical Report 12.
          Washington, D.C.: U.S. Government Printing Office.

Quètelet, Adolphe
  1842   A Treatise on Man. Edinburgh: Chambers.

Reiss, Albert J.
  1976   "Settling the frontiers of a pioneer in American criminology:
          Henry McKay." Pp. 64–88 in James F. Short, Jr. (ed.), Delin-
          quency, Crime, and Society. Chicago: University of Chicago
          Press.

Reppetto, Thomas J.
  1974   Residential Crime. Cambridge: Ballinger.

Roncek, Dennis
  1975   Crime Rates and Residential Densities in Two Large Cities.
          Ph.D. dissertation, Department of Sociology, University of
          Illinois, Urbana.

Sagi, Phillip C. and Charles E. Wellford
   1968   "Age composition and patterns of change in criminal statistics."
             Journal of Criminal Law, Criminology and Police Science
             59:29–36.

Scarr, Harry A.
   1972   Patterns of Burglary. U.S. Dept. of Justice, Law Enforcement
             Assistance Administration. Washington, D.C.: U.S. Government
             Printing Office.

Sears Catalogue
   1960   Chicago: Sears.
   1970   Chicago: Sears.

Shaw, Clifford R., Henry D. McKay, Frederick Zorbaugh and Leonard S.
Cottrell
   1929   Delinquency Areas. Chicago: University of Chicago Press.

Short, James F., and Fred Strodtbeck
   1965   Group Process and Gang Delinquency. Chicago: University of
             Chicago Press.

Skogan, Wesley G.
   1976   "The victims of crime: some material findings." Pp. 131–48 in
             Anthony L. Guenther (ed.), Criminal Behavior in Social
             Systems. Chicago: Rand McNally.

Sutherland, Edwin H.
   1937   The Professional Thief. Chicago: University of Chicago Press.

Szalai, Alexander (ed.)
   1972   The Use of Time: Daily Activities of Urban and Suburban Popu-
             lations in Twelve Countries. The Hague: Mouton.

Theil, Henri
   1971   Principles of Econometrics. New York: Wiley.

Tobias, J. J.
   1967   Crime and Industrial Society in the Nineteenth Century. New
             York: Schocken Books.

U.S. Bureau of the Census (USBC)
   1973a   Census of Transportation, 1972. U.S. Summary. Washington,
             D.C.: U.S. Government Printing Office.
   1973b   Who's Home When. Working Paper 37. Washington, D.C.: U.S.
             Government Printing Office.
   1975–   Statistical Abstract of the U.S. Washington, D.C.: U.S. Govern-
   1976   ment Printing Office.
   1947–   Current Population Studies. P–25 Series. Washington, D.C.:
   1976   U.S. Government Printing Office.

U.S. Department of Justice (USDJ)
   1974a   Preliminary Report of the Impact Cities, Crime Survey Results.

Washington, D.C.: Law Enforcement Assistance Administration (NCJISS).

1974b   Crime in the Nation's Five Largest Cities: Advance Report. Washington, D.C.: Law Enforcement Assistance Administration (NCJISS).

1974c   Crimes and Victims: A Report on the Dayton-San Jose Pilot Survey of Victimization. Washington, D.C.: Law Enforcement Assistance Administration.

1976   Criminal Victimizations in the U.S., 1973. Washington, D.C: Law Enforcement Assistance Administration (NCJISS).

1977   Criminal Victimizations in the U.S.: A Comparison of 1974 and 1975 Findings. Washington, D.C.: Law Enforcement Assistance Administration (NCJISS).

Washnis, George J.
1976   Citizen Involvement in Crime Prevention. Lexington: Heath.

Wellford, Charles F.
1973   "Age composition and the increase in recorded crime." Criminology 11:61–70.

Wilks, Judith A.
1967   "Ecological correlates of crime and delinquency." Pp. 138–56 in President's Commission on Law Enforcement and the Administration of Justice Task Force Report: Crime and Its Impact—An Assessment. Appendix A. Washington, D.C.: U.S. Government Printing Office.

Williamson, Henry
1968   Hustler! New York: Doubleday.

Wolfgang, Marvin E.
1958   Patterns of Criminal Homicide. Philadelphia: University of Pennsylvania Press.

Analysis and Critique

35   Girls' Crime and Woman's Place: Toward a Feminist Model of Female Delinquency
MEDA CHESNEY-LIND

I ran away so many times. I tried anything man, and they wouldn't

Source: Reprinted from Meda Chesney-Lind, "Girls' Crime and Woman's Place: Toward a Feminist Model of Female Delinquency," *Crime & Delinquency*, vol. 35, no. 1 (1989), pp. 5–29. Copyright © 1989, Sage Publications, Inc. By permission of the publisher.

believe me. . . . As far as they are concerned they think I'm the problem. You know, runaway, bad label. (Statement of a 16-year-old girl
who, after having been physically and sexually assaulted, started running away from home and was arrested as a "runaway" in Hawaii.)

You know, one of these days I'm going to have to kill myself before
you guys are gonna listen to me. I can't stay at home. (Statement of a
16-year-old Tucson runaway with a long history of physical abuse
[Davidson, 1982, p. 26].)

Who is the typical female delinquent? What causes her to get into
trouble? What happens to her if she is caught? These are questions
that few members of the general public could answer quickly. By contrast, almost every citizen can talk about "delinquency," by which they
generally mean male delinquency, and can even generate some fairly
specific complaints about, for example, the failure of the juvenile justice system to deal with such problems as "the alarming increase in
the rate of serious juvenile crime" and the fact that the juvenile courts
are too lenient on juveniles found guilty of these offenses (Opinion
Research Corporation, 1982).

This situation should come as no surprise since even the academic
study of delinquent behavior has, for all intents and purposes, been the
study of male delinquency. "The delinquent is a rogue male" declared
Albert Cohen (1955, p. 140) in his influential book on gang delinquency.
More than a decade later, Travis Hirschi, in his equally important book
entitled *The Causes of Delinquency*, relegated women to a footnote that
suggested, somewhat apologetically, that "in the analysis that follows,
the 'non-Negro' becomes 'white,' and the girls disappear."

This pattern of neglect is not all that unusual. All areas of social
inquiry have been notoriously gender blind. What is perhaps less well
understood is that theories developed to describe the misbehavior of
working- or lower-class male youth fail to capture the full nature of
delinquency in America; and, more to the point, are woefully inadequate when it comes to explaining female misbehavior and official reactions to girls' deviance.

To be specific, delinquent behavior involves a range of activities
far broader than those committed by the stereotypical street gang.
Moreover, many more young people than the small visible group of
"troublemakers" that exist on every intermediate and high school
campus commit some sort of juvenile offense and many of these
youth have brushes with the law. One study revealed, for example,
that 33% of all the boys and 14% of the girls born in 1958 had at least
one contact with the police before reaching their eighteenth birthday
(Tracy, Wolfgang, and Figlio, 1985, p. 5). Indeed, some forms of serious delinquent behavior, such as drug and alcohol abuse, are far more

frequent than the stereotypical delinquent behavior of gang fighting and vandalism and appear to cut across class and gender lines.

Studies that solicit from youth themselves the volume of their delinquent behavior consistently confirm that large numbers of adolescents engage in at least some form of misbehavior that could result in their arrest. As a consequence, it is largely trivial misconduct, rather than the commission of serious crime, that shapes the actual nature of juvenile delinquency. One national study of youth aged 15–21, for example, noted that only 5% reported involvement in a serious assault, and only 6% reported having participated in a gang fight. In contrast, 81% admitted to having used alcohol, 44% admitted to having used marijuana, 37% admitted to having been publicly drunk, 42% admitted to having skipped classes (truancy), 44% admitted having had sexual intercourse, and 15% admitted to having stolen from the family (McGarrell and Flanagan, 1985, p. 363). Clearly, not all of these activities are as serious as the others. It is important to remember that young people can be arrested for all of these behaviors.

Indeed, one of the most important points to understand about the nature of delinquency, and particularly female delinquency, is that youth can be taken into custody for both criminal acts and a wide variety of what are often called "status offenses." These offenses, in contrast to criminal violations, permit the arrest of youth for a wide range of behaviors that are violations of parental authority: "running away from home," "being a person in need of supervision," "minor in need of supervision," being "incorrigible," "beyond control," truant, in need of "care and protection," and so on. Juvenile delinquents, then, are youths arrested for either criminal or noncriminal status offenses; and, as this discussion will establish, the role played by uniquely juvenile offenses is by no means insignificant, particularly when considering the character of female delinquency.

Examining the types of offenses for which youth are actually arrested, it is clear that again most are arrested for the less serious criminal acts and status offenses. Of the one and a half million youth arrested in 1983, for example, only 4.5% of these arrests were for such serious violent offenses as murder, rape, robbery, or aggravated assault (McGarrell and Flanagan, 1985, p. 479). In contrast, 21% were arrested for a single offense (larceny theft) much of which, particularly for girls, is shoplifting (Shelden and Horvath, 1986).

Table 1 presents the five most frequent offenses for which male and female youth are arrested and from this it can be seen that while trivial offenses dominate both male and female delinquency, trivial offenses, particularly status offenses, are more significant in the case of girls' arrests; for example the five offenses listed in Table 1 account for nearly three-quarters of female offenses and only slightly more than half of male offenses.

More to the point, it is clear that, though routinely neglected in most delinquency research, status offenses play a significant role in girls' official delinquency. Status offenses accounted for about 25.2% of all girls' arrests in 1986 (as compared to 26.9% in 1977) and only about 8.3% of boys' arrests (compared to 8.8% in 1977). These figures are somewhat surprising since dramatic declines in arrests of youth for these offenses might have been expected as a result of the passage of the Juvenile Justice and Delinquency Prevention Act in 1974, which, among other things, encouraged jurisdictions to divert and deinstitutionalize youth charged with noncriminal offenses. While the figures in Table 1 do show a decline in these arrests, virtually all of this decline occurred in the 1970s. Between 1982 and 1986 girls' curfew arrests increased by 5.1% and runaway arrests increased by a striking 24.5%. And the upward trend continues; arrests of girls for running away increased by 3% between 1985 and 1986 and arrests of girls for curfew violations increased by 12.4% (Federal Bureau of Investigation, 1987, p. 171).

Looking at girls who find their way into juvenile court populations, it is apparent that status offenses continue to play an important role in the character of girls' official delinquency. In total, 34% of the girls, but only 12% of the boys, were referred to court in 1983 for these offenses (Snyder and Finnegan, 1987, pp. 6-20). Stating these figures differently, they mean that while males constituted about 81% of all delinquency referrals, females constituted 46% of all status offenders in courts (Snyder and Finnegan, 1987, p. 20). Similar figures were reported for 1977 by Black and Smith (1981). Fifteen years earlier, about half of the girls and about 20% of the boys were referred to court for these offenses (Children's Bureau, 1965). These data do seem to signal a drop in female status offense referrals, though not as dramatic a decline as might have been expected.

For many years statistics showing large numbers of girls arrested and referred for status offenses were taken to be representative of the different types of male and female delinquency. However, self-report studies of male and female delinquency do not reflect the dramatic differences in misbehavior found in official statistics. Specifically, it appears that girls charged with these noncriminal status offenses have been and continue to be significantly overrepresented in court populations.

Teilmann and Landry (1981) compared girls' contribution to arrests for runaway and incorrigibility with girls' self-reports of these two activities, and found a 10.4% overrepresentation of females

TABLE 1   RANK ORDER OF ADOLESCENT MALE AND FEMALE ARRESTS
FOR SPECIFIC OFFENSES, 1977 AND 1986

	MALE		
1977	**% OF TOTAL ARRESTS**	**1986**	**% OF TOTAL ARRESTS**
(1) Larceny-theft	18.4	(1) Larceny-theft	20.4
(2) Other offenses	14.5	(2) Other offenses	16.5
(3) Burglary	13.0	(3) Burglary	9.1
(4) Drug abuse violations	6.5	(4) Vandalism	7.0
(5) Vandalism	6.4	(5) Vandalism	6.3

	FEMALE		
1977	**% OF TOTAL ARRESTS**	**1986**	**% OF TOTAL ARRESTS**
(1) Larceny-theft	27.0	(1) Larceny-theft	25.7
(2) Runaway	22.9	(2) Runaway	20.5
(3) Other offenses	14.2	(3) Other offenses	14.8
(4) Liquor laws	5.5	(4) Liquor laws	8.4
(5) Curfew and loitering violations	4.0	(5) Curfew and loitering violations	4.7

	MALE		
	1977	**1986**	**% N CHANGE**
Arrests for serious violent offenses[a]	4.2%	4.7%	+2.3
Arrests for all violent offenses[b]	7.6%	9.6%	+10.3
Arrests for status offenses[c]	8.8%	8.3%	−17.8

	FEMALE		
	1977	**1986**	**% N CHANGE**
Arrests for serious violent offenses[a]	1.8%	2.0%	+1.7
Arrests for all violent offenses[b]	5.1%	7.1%	+26.0
Arrests for status offenses[c]	26.9%	25.2%	−14.7

Source: Compiled from Federal Bureau of Investigation (1987, p. 169).
  a. Arrests for murder and nonnegligent manslaughter, robbery, forcible rape, and
     aggravated assault.
  b. Also includes arrests for other assaults.
  c. Arrests for curfew and loitering law violation and runaway.

among those arrested for runaway and a 30.9% overrepresentation in arrests for incorrigibility. From these data they concluded that girls are "arrested for status offenses at a higher rate than boys, when contrasted to their self-reported delinquency rates" (Teilmann and Landry, 1981, pp. 74–75). These findings were confirmed in another recent self-report study. Figueira-McDonough (1985, p.277) analyzed the delinquent conduct of 2,000 youths and found "no evidence of greater involvement of females in status offenses." Similarly, Canter (1982) found in the National Youth Survey that there was no evidence of greater female involvement, compared to males, in any category of delinquent behavior. Indeed, in this sample, males were significantly more likely than females to report status offenses.

Utilizing Canter's national data on the extensiveness of girls' self-reported delinquency and comparing these figures to official arrests of girls (see Table 2) reveals that girls are underrepresented in every arrest category with the exception of status offenses and larceny theft. These figures strongly suggest that official practices tend to exaggerate the role played by status offenses in girls' delinquency.

Delinquency theory, because it has virtually ignored female delinquency, failed to pursue anomalies such as these found in the few early studies examining gender differences in delinquent behavior. Indeed, most delinquency theories have ignored status offenses. As a consequence, there is considerable question as to whether existing theories that were admittedly developed to explain male delinquency can adequately explain female delinquency. Clearly, these theories were much influenced by the notion that class and protest masculinity were at the core of delinquency. Will the "add women and stir approach" be sufficient? Are these really theories of delinquent behavior as some (Simons, Miller, and Aigner, 1980) have argued?

This article will suggest that they are not. The extensive focus on male delinquency and the inattention to the role played by patriarchal arrangements in the generation of adolescent delinquency and conformity has rendered the major delinquency theories fundamentally inadequate to the task of explaining female behavior. There is, in short, an urgent need to rethink current models in light of girls' situation in patriarchal society.

To understand why such work must occur, it is first necessary to explore briefly the dimensions of the androcentric bias found in the dominant and influential delinquency theories. Then the need for a feminist model of female delinquency will be explored by reviewing the available evidence on girls' offending. This discussion will also establish that the proposed overhaul of delinquency theory is not, as some might think, solely an academic exercise. Specifically, it is incor-

TABLE 2 COMPARISON OF SEX DIFFERENCES IN SELF-REPORTED AND OFFICIAL DELINQUENCY FOR SELECTED OFFENSES

	SELF-REPORT[a] M/F RATIOS	OFFICIAL STATISTICS[b] M/F ARREST RATIO	
	(1976)	1976	1986
Theft	3.5:1 (Felony theft) 3.4:1 (Minor theft)	2.5:1	2.7:1
Drug violation	1:1 (Hard drug use)	5.1:1	6.0:1 (Drug abuse violations)
Vandalism	5.1:1	12.3:1	10.0:1
Disorderly conduct	2.8:1	4.5:1	4.4:1
Serious assault	3.5:1 (Felony assault)	5.6:1	5.5:1 (Aggravated assault)
Minor assault	3.4:1	3.8:1	3.4:1
Status offenses	1.6:1	1.3:1	1.1:1 (Runaway, curfew)

a. Extracted from Rachelle Canter (1982, p. 383).
b. Compiled from Federal Bureau of Investigation (1986, p. 173).

rect to assume that because girls are charged with less serious offenses, they actually have few problems and are treated gently when they are drawn into the juvenile justice system. Indeed, the extensive focus on disadvantaged males in public settings has meant that girls' victimization and the relationship between that experience and girls' crime has been systematically ignored. Also missed has been the central role played by the juvenile justice system in the sexualization of girls' delinquency and the criminalization of girls' survival strategies. Finally, it will be suggested that the official actions of the juvenile justice system should be understood as major forces in girls' oppression as they have historically served to reinforce the obedience of all young women to demands of patriarchal authority no matter how abusive and arbitrary.

THE ROMANCE OF THE GANG OR THE *WEST SIDE STORY* SYNDROME

From the start, the field of delinquency research focused on visible lower-class male delinquency, often justifying the neglect of girls in the most cavalier of terms. Take, for example, the extremely important and influential work of Clifford R. Shaw and Henry D. McKay who, beginning in 1929, utilized an ecological approach to the study of juvenile delinquency. Their impressive work, particularly *Juvenile Delinquency in Urban Areas* (1942) and intensive biographical case studies such as Shaw's *Brothers in Crime* (1938) and *The Jackroller* (1930), set the stage for much of the subcultural research on gang delinquency. In their ecological work, however, Shaw and McKay analyzed only the official arrest data on male delinquents in Chicago and repeatedly referred to these rates as "delinquency rates" (though they occasionally made parenthetical reference to data on female delinquency) (see Shaw and McKay, 1942, p. 356). Similarly, their biographical work traced only male experiences with the law; in *Brothers in Crime,* for example, the delinquent and criminal careers of five brothers were followed for fifteen years. In none of these works was any justification given for the equation of male delinquency with delinquency.

Early fieldwork on delinquent gangs in Chicago set the stage for another style of delinquency research. Yet here too researchers were interested only in talking to and following the boys. Thrasher studied over a thousand juvenile gangs in Chicago during roughly the same period as Shaw and McKay's more quantitative work was being done. He spent approximately one page out of 600 on the five of six female gangs he encountered in the field observation of juvenile gangs. Thrasher (1927, p. 228) did mention, in passing, two factors he felt accounted for the lower number of girl gangs: "First, the social patterns for the behavior of girls, powerfully backed by the great weight of tradition and custom, are contrary to the gang and its activities; and secondly, girls, even in urban disorganized areas, are much more closely supervised and guarded than boys and usually well incorporated into the family groups or some other social structure."

Another major theoretical approach to delinquency focuses on the subculture of lower-class communities as a generating milieu for delinquent behavior. Here again, noted delinquency researchers concentrated either exclusively or nearly exclusively on male lower-class culture. For example, Cohen's work on the subculture of delinquent gangs, which was written nearly twenty years after Thrasher's, deliberately considers only boys' delinquency. His justification for the exclusion of the girls is quite illuminating:

> My skin has nothing of the quality of down or silk, there is nothing limpid or flute-like about my voice, I am a total loss with needle and thread, my posture and carriage are wholly lacking in grace. These imperfections cause me no distress—if anything, they are gratifying—because I conceive myself to be a man and want people to

recognize me as a full-fledged, unequivocal representative of my sex. My wife, on the other hand, is not greatly embarrassed by her inability to tinker with or talk about the internal organs of a car, by her modest attainments in arithmetic or by her inability to lift heavy objects. Indeed, I am reliably informed that many women—I do not suggest that my wife is among them—often affect ignorance, frailty and emotional instability because to do otherwise would be out of keeping with a reputation for indubitable femininity. In short, people do not simply want to excel; they want to excel as a man or as a woman [Cohen, 1955, p. 138].

From this Cohen (1955, p. 140) concludes that the delinquent response "however it may be condemned by others on moral grounds, has at least one virtue: it incontestably confirms, in the eyes of all concerned, his essential masculinity." Much the same line of argument appears in Miller's influential paper on the "focal concerns" of lower-class life with its emphasis on importance of trouble, toughness, excitement, and so on. These, the author concludes, predispose poor youth (particularly male youth) to criminal misconduct. However, Cohen's comments are notable in their candor and probably capture both the allure that male delinquency has had for at least some male theorists as well as the fact that sexism has rendered the female delinquent as irrelevant to their work.

Emphasis on blocked opportunities (sometimes the "strain" theories) emerged out of the work of Robert K. Merton (1938) who stressed the need to consider how some social structures exert a definite pressure upon certain persons in the society to engage in non-conformist rather than conformist conduct. His work influenced research largely through the efforts of Cloward and Ohlin who discussed access to "legitimate" and "illegitimate" opportunities for male youth. No mention of female delinquency can be found in their *Delinquency and Opportunity* except that women are blamed for male delinquency. Here, the familiar notion is that boys, "engulfed by a feminine world and uncertain of their own identification...tend to 'protest' against femininity" (Cloward and Ohlin, 1960, p.49). Early efforts by Ruth Morris to test this hypothesis utilizing different definitions of success based on the gender of respondents met with mixed success. Attempting to assess boys' perceptions about access to economic power status while for girls the variable concerned itself with the ability or inability of girls to maintain effective relationships, Morris was unable to find a clear relationship between "female" goals and delinquency (Morris, 1964).

The work of Edwin Sutherland emphasized the fact that criminal behavior was learned in intimate personal groups. His work, particularly the notion of differential association, which also influenced

Cloward and Ohlin's work, was similarly male oriented as much of his work was affected by case studies he conducted of male criminals. Indeed, in describing his notion of how differential association works, he utilized male examples (e.g., "In an area where the delinquency rate is high a boy who is sociable, gregarious, active, and athletic is very likely to come in contact with the other boys, in the neighborhood, learn delinquent behavior from them, and become a gangster" [Sutherland, 1978, p.131]). Finally, the work of Travis Hirschi on the social bonds that control delinquency ("social control theory") was, as was stated earlier, derived out of research on male delinquents (though he, at least, studied delinquent behavior as reported by youth themselves rather than studying only those who were arrested).

Such a persistent focus on social class and such an absence of interest in gender in delinquency is ironic for two reasons. As even the work of Hirschi demonstrated, and as later studies would validate, a clear relationship between social class position and delinquency is problematic, while it is clear that gender has a dramatic and consistent effect on delinquency causation (Hagan, Gillis, and Simpson, 1985). The second irony, and one that consistently eludes even contemporary delinquency theorists, is the fact that while the academics had little interest in female delinquents, the same could not be said for the juvenile justice system. Indeed, work on the early history of the separate system for youth reveals that concerns about girls' immoral conduct were really at the center of what some have called the "childsaving movement" (Platt, 1969) that set up the juvenile justice system.

"THE BEST PLACE TO CONQUER GIRLS"

The movement to establish separate institutions for youthful offenders was part of the larger Progressive movement, which among other things was keenly concerned about prostitution and other "social evils" (white slavery and the like) (Schlossman and Wallach, 1978; Rafter, 1985, p. 54). Childsaving was also a celebration of women's domesticity, though ironically women were influential in the movement (Platt, 1969; Rafter, 1985). In a sense, privileged women found, in the moral purity crusades and the establishment of family courts, a safe outlet for their energies. As the legitimate guardians of the moral sphere, women were seen as uniquely suited to patrol the normative boundaries of the social order. Embracing rather than challenging these stereotypes, women carved out for themselves a role in the policing of women and girls (Feinman, 1980; Freedman, 1981; Messerschmidt, 1987). Ultimately, many of the early childsavers' activities revolved around the monitoring of young girls', particularly immigrant girls', behavior to prevent their straying from the path.

This state of affairs was the direct consequence of a disturbing coalition between some feminists and the more conservative social purity movement. Concerned about female victimization and distrustful of male (and to some degree female) sexuality, notable women leaders, including Susan B. Anthony, found common cause with the social purists around such issues as opposing the regulation of prostitution and raising the age of consent (see Messerschmidt, 1987). The consequences of such a partnership are an important lesson for contemporary feminist movements that are, to some extent, faced with the same possible coalitions.

Girls were the clear losers in this reform effort. Studies of early family court activity reveal that virtually all the girls who appeared in these courts were charged for immorality or waywardness (Chesney-Lind, 1971; Schlossman and Wallach, 1978; Shelden, 1981). More to the point, the sanctions for such misbehavior were extremely severe. For example, in Chicago (where the first family court was founded), one-half of the girl delinquents, but only one-fifth of the boy delinquents, were sent to reformatories between 1899–1909. In Milwaukee, twice as many girls as boys were committed to training schools (Schlossman and Wallach, 1978, p. 72); and in Memphis females were twice as likely as males to be committed to training schools (Shelden, 1981, p. 70).

In Honolulu, during the period 1929–1930, over half of the girls referred to court were charged with "immorality," which meant evidence of sexual intercourse. In addition, another 30% were charged with "waywardness." Evidence of immorality was vigorously pursued by both arresting officers and social workers through lengthy questioning of the girl and, if possible, males with whom she was suspected of having sex. Other evidence of "exposure" was provided by gynecological examinations that were routinely ordered in virtually all girls' cases. Doctors, who understood the purpose of such examinations, would routinely note the condition of the hymen: "admits intercourse hymen rupture," "no laceration," "hymen ruptured" are typical of the notations on the forms. Girls during this period were also twice as likely as males to be detained where they spent five times as long on the average as their male counterparts. They were also nearly three times more likely to be sentenced to the training school (Chesney-Lind, 1971). Indeed, girls were half of those committed to training schools in Honolulu well into the 1950s (Chesney-Lind, 1973).

Not surprisingly, large numbers of girl's reformatories and training schools were established during this period as well as places of "rescue and reform." For example, Schlossman and Wallach note that 23 facilities for girls were opened during the 1910–1920 decade (in contrast to the 1850–1910 period where the average was 5 reformatories per decade [Schlossman and Wallach, 1985, p. 70]), and these institutions did much to set the tone of official response to female delinquency. Obsessed with precocious female sexuality, the institutions set about to isolate the females from all contact with males while housing them in bucolic settings. The intention was to hold the girls until marriageable age and to occupy them in domestic pursuits during their sometimes lengthy incarceration.

The links between these attitudes and those of juvenile courts some decades later are, of course, arguable; but an examination of the record of the court does not inspire confidence. A few examples of the persistence of what might be called a double standard of juvenile justice will suffice here.

A study conducted in the early 1970s in a Connecticut training school revealed large numbers of girls incarcerated "for their own protection." Explaining this pattern, one judge explained, "Why most of the girls I commit are for status offenses. I figure if a girl is about to get pregnant, we'll keep her until she's sixteen and then ADC (Aid to Dependent Children) will pick her up" (Rogers, 1972). For more evidence of official concern with adolescent sexual misconduct, consider Linda Hancock's (1981) content analysis of police referrals in Australia. She noted that 40% of the referrals of girls to court made specific mention of sexual and moral conduct compared to only 5% of the referrals of boys. These sorts of results suggest that all youthful female misbehavior has traditionally been subject to surveillance for evidence of sexual misconduct.

Gelsthorpe's (1986) field research on an English police station also revealed how everyday police decision making resulted in disregard of complaints about male problem behavior in contrast to active concern about the "problem behavior" of girls. Notable, here, was the concern about the girl's sexual behavior. In one case, she describes police persistence in pursuing a "moral danger" order for a 14-year-old picked up in a truancy run. Over the objections of both the girl's parents and the Social Services Department and in the face of a written confirmation from a surgeon that the girl was still premenstrual, the officers pursued the application because, in one officer's words, "I know her sort...free and easy. I'm still suspicious that she might be pregnant.

Anyway, if the doctor can't provide evidence we'll do her for being beyond the care and control of her parents, no one can dispute that. Running away is proof" (Gelsthorpe, 1986, p. 136). This sexualization of female deviance is highly significant and explains why criminal activities by girls (particularly in past years) were overlooked so long as they did not appear to signal defiance of parental control (see Smith, 1978).

In their historic obsession about precocious female sexuality, juvenile justice workers rarely reflected on the broader nature of female misbehavior or on the sources of this misbehavior. It was enough for them that girls' parents reported them out of control. Indeed, court personnel tended to "sexualize" virtually all female defiance that lent itself to that construction and ignore other misbehavior (Chesney-Lind, 1973, 1977; Smith, 1978). For their part, academic students of delinquency were so entranced with the notion of the delinquent as a romantic rogue male challenging a rigid and unequal class structure, that they spent little time on middle-class delinquency, trivial offenders, or status offenders. Yet it is clear that the vast bulk of delinquent behavior is of this type.

Some have argued that such an imbalance in theoretical work is appropriate as minor misconduct, while troublesome, is not a threat to the safety and well-being of the community. This argument might be persuasive if two additional points could be established. One, that some small number of youth "specialize" in serious criminal behavior while the rest commit only minor acts, and, two, that the juvenile court rapidly releases those youth that come into its purview for these minor offenses, thus reserving resources for the most serious youthful offenders.

The evidence is mixed on both of these points. Determined efforts to locate the "serious juvenile offender" have failed to locate a group of offenders who specialize only in serious violent offenses. For example, in a recent analysis of a national self-report data set, Elliott and his associates noted "there is little evidence for specialization in serious violent offending; to the contrary, serious violent offending appears to be embedded in a more general involvement in a wide range of serious and non-serious offenses" (Elliott, Huizinga, and Morse, 1987). Indeed, they went so far as to speculate that arrest histories that tend to highlight particular types of offenders reflect variations in police policy, practices, and processes of uncovering crime as well as underlying offending patterns.

More to the point, police and court personnel are, it turns out, far more interested in youth they charge with trivial or status offenses than anyone imagined. Efforts to deinstitutionalize "status offenders," for example, ran afoul of juvenile justice personnel who had little interest in releasing youth guilty of noncriminal offenses (Chesney-Lind, 1988). As has been established, much of this is a product of the system's history that encouraged court officers to involve themselves in the noncriminal behavior of youth in order to "save" them from a variety of social ills.

Indeed, parallels can be found between the earlier Progressive period and current national efforts to challenge the deinstitutionaliza-tion components of the Juvenile Justice and Delinquency Prevention Act of 1974. These come complete with their celebration of family val-ues and concerns about youthful independence. One of the argu-ments against the act has been that it allegedly gave children the "freedom to run away" (Office of Juvenile Justice and Delinquency Prevention, 1985) and that is has hampered "reunions" of "missing" children with their parents (Office of Juvenile Justice, 1986). Suspi-cions about teen sexuality are reflected in excessive concern about the control of teen prostitution and child pornography.

Opponents have also attempted to justify continued intervention into the lives of status offenders by suggesting that without such inter-vention, the youth would "escalate" to criminal behavior. Yet there is little evidence that status offenders escalate to criminal offenses, and the evidence is particularly weak when considering female delin-quents (particularly white female delinquents) (Datesman and Aickin, 1984). Finally, if escalation is occurring, it is likely the product of the justice system's insistence on enforcing status offense laws, thereby forcing youth in crisis to live lives of escaped criminals.

The most influential delinquency theories, however, have largely ducked the issue of status and trivial offenses and, as a consequence, neglected the role played by the agencies of official control (police, pro-bation officers, juvenile court judges, detention home workers, and training school personnel) in the shaping of the "delinquency prob-lem." When confronting the less than distinct picture that emerges from the actual distribution of delinquent behavior, however, the conclusion that agents of social control have considerable discretion in labeling or choosing not to label particular behavior as "delinquent" is inescap-able. This symbiotic relationship between delinquent behavior and the official response to that behavior is particularly critical when the ques-tion of female delinquency is considered.

TOWARD A FEMINIST THEORY OF DELINQUENCY

To sketch out completely a feminist theory of delinquency is a task be-yond the scope of this article. It may be sufficient, at this point, simply to identify a few of the most obvious problems with attempts to adapt male-oriented theory to explain female conformity and deviance. Most significant of these is the fact that all existing theories were developed with no concern about gender stratification.

Note that this is not simply an observation about the power of gender roles (though this power is undeniable). It is increasingly clear that gender stratification in patriarchal society is as powerful a system as is class. A feminist approach to delinquency means construction of explanations of female behavior that are sensitive to its patriarchal context. Feminist analysis of delinquency would also examine ways in which agencies of social control—the police, the courts, and the prisons—act in ways to reinforce woman's place in male society (Harris, 1977; Chesney-Lind, 1986). Efforts to construct a feminist model of delinquency must first and foremost be sensitive to the situations of girls. Failure to consider the existing empirical evidence on girls' lives and behavior can quickly lead to stereotypical thinking and theoretical dead ends.

An example of this sort of flawed theory building was the early fascination with the notion that the women's movement was causing an increase in women's crime; a notion that is now more or less discredited (Steffensmeier, 1980; Gora, 1982). A more recent example of the same sort of thinking can be found in recent work on the "power-control" model of delinquency (Hagan, Simpson, and Gillis, 1987). Here, the authors speculate that girls commit less delinquency in part because their behavior is more closely controlled by the patriarchal family. The authors' promising beginning quickly gets bogged down in a very limited definition of patriarchal control (focusing on parental supervision and variations in power within the family). Ultimately, the authors' narrow formulation of patriarchal control results in their arguing that mothers' work force participation (particularly in high status occupations) leads to increases in daughters' delinquency since these girls find themselves in more "egalitarian families."

This is essentially a not-too-subtle variation on the earlier "liberation" hypothesis. Now, mother's liberation causes daughter's crime. Aside from the methodological problems with the study (e.g., the authors argue that female-headed households are equivalent to upper-status "egalitarian" families where both parents work, and they measure delinquency using a six-item scale that contains no status offense items), there is a more fundamental problem with the hypothesis. There is no evidence to suggest that as women's labor force participation has increased, girls' delinquency has increased. Indeed, during the last decade when both women's labor force participation accelerated and the number of female-headed households soared, aggregate female delinquency measured both by self-report and official statistics either declined or remained stable (Ageton, 1983; Chilton and Datesman, 1987; Federal Bureau of Investigation, 1987).

By contrast, a feminist model of delinquency would focus more extensively on the few pieces of information about girls' actual lives and the role played by girls' problems, including those caused by racism and poverty, in their delinquency behavior. Fortunately, a considerable literature is now developing on girls' lives and much of it bears directly on girls' crime.

CRIMINALIZING GIRLS' SURVIVAL

It has long been understood that a major reason for girls' presence in juvenile courts was the fact that their parents insisted on their arrest. In the early years, conflicts with parents were by far the most significant referral source; in Honolulu 44% of the girls who appeared in court in 1929 through 1930 were referred by parents.

Recent national data, while slightly less explicit, also show that girls are more likely to be referred to court by "sources other than law enforcement agencies" (which would include parents). In 1983, nearly a quarter (23%) of all girls but only 16% of boys charged with delinquent offenses were referred to court by non–law enforcement agencies. The pattern among youth referred for status offenses (for which girls are overrepresented) was even more pronounced. Well over half (56%) of the girls charged with these offenses and 45% of the boys were referred by sources other than law enforcement (Snyder and Finnegan, 1987, p. 21; see also Pope and Feyerherm, 1982).

The fact that parents are often committed to two standards of adolescent behavior is one explanation for such a disparity—and one that should not be discounted as a major source of tension even in modern families. Despite expectations to the contrary, gender-specific socialization patterns have not changed very much and this is especially true for parents' relationships with their daughters (Katz, 1979). It appears that even parents who oppose sexism in general feel "uncomfortable tampering with existing traditions" and "do not want to risk their children becoming misfits" (Katz, 1979, p. 24). Clearly, parental attempts to adhere to and enforce these traditional notions will continue to be a source of conflict between girls and their elders. Another important explanation for girls' problems with their parents, which has received attention only in more recent years, is the problem of physical and sexual abuse. Looking specifically at the problem of childhood sexual abuse, it is increasingly clear that this form of abuse is a particular problem for girls.

Girls are, for example, much more likely to be the victims of child sexual abuse than are boys. Finkelhor and Baron estimate from a review of community studies that roughly 70% of the victims of sexual abuse are female (Finkelhor and Baron, 1986, p. 45). Girls' sexual abuse also tends to start earlier than boys' (Finkelhor and Baron, 1986, p.48); they are more likely than boys to be assaulted by a family member (often a stepfather) (DeJong, Hervada, and Emmett, 1983; Russell, 1986), and, as a consequence, their abuse tends to last longer than male sexual abuse (DeJong, Hervada, and Emmett, 1983). All of these factors are associated with more severe trauma—causing dramatic short- and long-term effects in victims (Adams-Tucker, 1982). The effects noted by researchers in this area move from the more well known "fear, anxiety, depression, anger and hostility, and inappropriate sexual behavior" (Browne and Finkelhor, 1986, p. 69) to behaviors of greater familiarity to criminologists, including running away from home, difficulties in school, truancy, and early marriage (Browne and Finkelhor, 1986).

Herman's study of incest survivors in therapy found that they were more likely to have run away from home than a matched sample of women whose fathers were "seductive" (33% compared to 5%). Another study of women patients found that 50% of the victims of child sexual abuse, but only 20% of the nonvictim group, had left home before the age of 18 (Meiselman, 1978).

Not surprisingly, then, studies of girls on the streets or in court populations are showing high rates of both physical and sexual abuse. Silbert and Pines (1981, p. 409) found, for example, that 60% of the street prostitutes they interviewed had been sexually abused as juveniles. Girls at an Arkansas diagnostic unit and school who had been adjudicated for either status or delinquent offenses reported similarly high levels of sexual abuse as well as high levels of physical abuse; 53% indicated they had been sexually abused, 255 recalled scars, 38% recalled bleeding from abuse, and 51% recalled bruises (Mouzakitas, 1981).

A sample survey of girls in the juvenile justice system in Wisconsin (Phelps et al., 1982) revealed that 79% had been subjected to physical abuse that resulted in some form of injury, and 32% had been sexually abused by parents or other persons who were closely connected to their families. Moreover, 50% had been sexually assaulted ("raped" or forced to participate in sexual acts) (Phelps et al., 1982, p. 66). Even higher figures were reported by McCormack and her associates (McCormack, Janus, and Burgess, 1986) in their study of youth in a runaway shelter in Toronto. They found that 73% of the females and 38% of the males had been sexually abused. Finally, a study of youth charged with running away, truancy, or listed as missing persons in Arizona found that 55% were incest victims (Reich and Gutierres, 1979).

Many young women, then, are running away from profound sexual victimization at home, and once on the streets they are forced further into crime in order to survive. Interviews with girls who have run away from home show, very clearly, that they do not have a lot of attachment to their delinquent activities. In fact, they are angry about being labeled as delinquent, yet all engaged in illegal acts (Koroki and Chesney-Lind, 1985). The Wisconsin study found that 54% of the girls who ran away found it necessary to steal money, food, and clothing in order to survive. A few exchanged sexual contact for money, food, and/or shelter (Phelps et al., 1982, p. 67). In their study of runaway youth, McCormack, Janus, and Burgess (1986, pp. 392-393) found that sexually abused female runaways were significantly more likely than their nonabused counterparts to engage in delinquent or criminal activities such as substance abuse, petty theft, and prostitution. No such pattern was found among male runaways.

Research (Chesney-Lind and Rodriguez, 1983) on the backgrounds of adult women in prison underscores the important links between women's childhood victimizations and their later criminal careers. The interviews revealed that virtually all of this sample were the victims of physical and/or sexual abuse as youngsters; over 60% had been sexually abused and about half had been raped as young women. This situation prompted these women to run away from home (three-quarters had been arrested for status offenses) where once on the streets they began engaging in prostitution and other forms of petty property crime. They also begin what becomes a lifetime problem with drugs. As adults, the women continue in these activities since they possess truncated educational backgrounds and virtually no marketable occupational skills (see also Miller, 1986).

Confirmation of the consequences of childhood sexual and physical abuse on adult female criminal behavior has also recently come from a large quantitative study of 908 individuals with substantiated and validated histories of these victimizations. Widom (1988) found that abused or neglected females were twice as likely as a matched group of controls to have an adult record (16% compared to 7.5). The difference was also found among men, but it was not as dramatic (42% compared to 33%). Men with abuse backgrounds were also more likely to contribute to the "cycle of violence" with more arrests for violent offenses as adult offenders than the control group. In contrast, when women with abuse backgrounds did become involved with the criminal justice system, their arrests tended to involve property and order offenses (such as disorderly conduct, curfew, and loitering violations) (Widom, 1988, p. 17).

Given this information, a brief example of how a feminist perspective on the causes of female delinquency might look seems appropriate. First, like young men, girls are frequently the recipients of violence and sexual abuse. But unlike boys, girls' victimization and their response to that victimization is specifically shaped by their status as young women. Perhaps because of the gender and sexual scripts found in patriarchal families, girls are much more likely than boys to be victims of family-related sexual abuse. Men, particularly men with traditional attitudes toward women, are likely to define their daughters or stepdaughters as their sexual property (Finkelhor, 1982). In a society that idealizes inequality in male/female relationships and venerates youth in women, girls are easily defined as sexually attractive by older men (Bell, 1984). In addition, girls' vulnerability to both physical and sexual abuse is heightened by norms that require that they stay at home where their victimizers have access to them.

Moreover, their victimizers (usually males) have the ability to invoke official agencies of social control in their efforts to keep young women at home and vulnerable. That is to say, abusers have traditionally been able to utilize the uncritical commitment of the juvenile justice system toward parental authority to force girls to obey them. Girls' complaints about abuse were, until recently, routinely ignored. For this reason, statutes that were originally placed in law to "protect" young people have, in the case of girls' delinquency, criminalized their survival strategies. As they run away from abusive homes, parents have been able to employ agencies to enforce their return. If they persisted in their refusal to stay in that home, however intolerable, they were incarcerated.

Young women, a large number of whom are on the run from homes characterized by sexual abuse and parental neglect, are forced by the very statutes designed to protect them into the lives of escaped convicts. Unable to enroll in school or take a job to support themselves because they fear detection, young female runaways are forced into the streets. Here they engage in panhandling, petty theft, and occasional prostitution in order to survive. Young women in conflict with their parents (often for very legitimate reasons) may actually be forced by present laws into petty criminal activity, prostitution, and drug use.

In addition, the fact that young girls (but not necessarily young boys) are defined as sexually desirable and, in fact, more desirable than their older sisters due to the double standard of aging means that their lives on the streets (and their survival strategies) take on unique shape—once again shaped by patriarchal values. It is no accident that girls on the run from abusive homes, or on the streets because of profound poverty, get involved in criminal activities that exploit their sexual object status. American society has defined as desirable youthful, physically perfect women. This means that girls on the streets, who have little else of value to trade, are encouraged to utilize this "resource" (Campagna and Poffenberger, 1988). It also means that the criminal subculture views them from this perspective (Miller, 1986).

FEMALE DELINQUENCY, PATRIARCHAL AUTHORITY, AND FAMILY COURTS

The early insights into male delinquency were largely gleaned by intensive field observation of delinquent boys. Very little of this sort of work has been done in the case of girls' delinquency, though it is vital to an understanding of girls' definitions of their own situations, choices, and behavior (for exceptions to this see Campbell, 1984; Peacock, 1981; Miller, 1986; Rosenberg and Zimmerman, 1977). Time must be spent listening to girls. Fuller research on the settings, such as families and schools, that girls find themselves in and the impact of variations in those settings should also be undertaken (see Figueira-McDonough, 1986). A more complete understanding of how poverty and racism shape girls' lives is also vital (see Messerschmidt, 1986; Campbell, 1984). Finally, current qualitative research on the reaction of official agencies to girls' delinquency must be conducted. This latter task, admittedly more difficult, is particularly critical to the development of delinquency theory that is as sensitive to gender as it is to race and class.

It is clear that throughout most of the court's history, virtually all female delinquency has been placed within the larger context of girls' sexual behavior. One explanation for this pattern is that familial control over girls' sexual capital has historically been central to the maintenance of patriarchy (Lerner, 1986). The fact that young women have relatively more of this capital has been one reason for the excessive concern that both families and official agencies of social control have expressed about youthful female defiance (otherwise much of the behavior of criminal justice personnel makes virtually no sense). Only if one considers the role of women's control over their sexuality at the point in their lives that their value to patriarchal society is so pronounced, does the historic pattern of jailing of huge numbers of girls guilty of minor misconduct make sense.

This framework also explains the enormous resistance that the movement to curb the juvenile justice system's authority over status offenders encountered. Supporters of the change were not really prepared for the political significance of giving youth the freedom to run. Horror stories told by the opponents of deinstitutionalization about victimized youth, youthful prostitution, and youthful involvement in pornography (Office of Juvenile Justice and Delinquency Prevention, 1985) all neglect the unpleasant reality that most of these behaviors were often in direct response to earlier victimization, frequently by parents, that officials had, for years, routinely ignored. What may be at stake in efforts to roll back deinstitutionalization efforts is not so much "protection" of youth as it is curbing the right of young women to defy patriarchy.

In sum, research in both the dynamics of girl's delinquency and official reactions to that behavior is essential to the development of theories of delinquency that are sensitive to its patriarchal as well as class and racial context.

REFERENCES

Adams-Tucker, Christine. 1982. "Proximate Effects of Sexual Abuse in Childhood." *American Journal of Psychiatry* 193:1252–1256.

Ageton, Suzanne S. 1983. "The Dynamics of Female Delinquency, 1976–1980." *Criminology* 21:555–584.

Bell, Inge Powell. 1984. "The Double Standard: Age." In *Women: A Feminist Perspective*, edited by Jo Freeman. Palo Alto, CA: Mayfield.

Black, T. Edwin and Charles P. Smith. 1981. *A Preliminary National Assessment of the Number and Characteristics of Juveniles Processed in the Juvenile Justice System*. Washington, DC: Government Printing Office.

Browne, Angela and David Finkelhor, 1986. "Impact of Child Sexual Abuse: A Review of Research." *Psychological Bulletin* 99:66–77.

Campagna, Daniel S. and Donald L. Poffenberger. 1988. *The Sexual Trafficking in Children*. Dover, DE: Auburn House.

Campbell, Ann. 1984. *The Girls in the Gang*. Oxford: Basil Blackwell.

Canter, Rachelle J. 1982. "Sex Differences in Self-Report Delinquency." *Criminology* 20:373–393.

Chesney-Lind, Meda. 1971. *Female Juvenile Delinquency in Hawaii*. Master's thesis, University of Hawaii.

_____ 1973. "Judicial Enforcement of the Female Sex Role." *Issues in Criminology* 3:51–71.

_____ 1978. "Young Women in the Arms of the Law." In *Women, Crime and the Criminal Justice System,* edited by Lee H. Bowker. Boston: Lexington.

_____ 1986. "Women and Crime: The Female Offender." *Signs* 12:78–96.

_____ 1988. "Girls and Deinstitutionalization: Is Juvenile Justice Still Sexist?" *Journal of Criminal Justice Abstracts* 20:144–165.

_____ and Noelie Rodriguez. 1983. "Women Under Lock and Key." *Prison Journal* 63:47–65.

Children's Bureau, Department of Health, Education and Welfare. 1965. *1964 Statistics on Public Institutions for Delinquent Children:* Washington, DC: Government Printing Office.

Chilton, Roland and Susan K. Datesman. 1987. "Gender, Race and Crime: An Analysis of Urban Arrest Trends, 1960-1980." *Gender and Society* 1:152–171.

Cloward, Richard A. and Lloyd E. Ohlin. 1960. *Delinquency and Opportunity.* New York: Free Press.

Cohen, Albert K. 1955. *Delinquent Boys: The Culture of the Gang.* New York: Free Press.

Datesman, Susan and Mikel Aickin. 1984. "Offense Specialization and Escalation Among Status Offenders." *Journal of Criminal Law and Criminology* 75:1246–1275.

Davidson, Sue, ed. 1982. *Justice for Young Women.* Tucson, AZ: New Directions for Young Women.

DeJong, Allan R., Arturo R. Hervada, and Gary A. Emmett. 1983. "Epidemiologic Variations in Childhood Sexual Abuse." *Child Abuse and Neglect* 7:155–162.

Elliott, Delbert, David Huizinga, and Barbara Morse. 1987. "A Career Analysis of Serious Violent Offenders." In *Violent Juvenile Crime: What Can We Do About It?* edited by Ira Schwartz. Minneapolis, MN: Hubert Humphrey Institute.

Federal Bureau of Investigation. 1987. *Crime in the United States 1986.* Washington, DC: Government Printing Office.

Feinman, Clarice. 1980. *Women in the Criminal Justice System.* New York: Praeger.

Figueira-McDonogh, Josefina. 1985. "Are Girls Different? Gender Discrepancies Between Delinquent Behavior and Control." *Child Welfare* 64:273–289.

_____ 1986. "School Context, Gender, and Delinquency." *Journal of Youth and Adolescence* 15:79–98.

Finkelhor, David. 1982. "Sexual Abuse: A Sociological Perspective." *Child Abuse and Neglect* 6:95–102.

_____ and Larry Baron. 1986. "Risk Factors for Child Sexual Abuse." *Journal of Interpersonal Violence* 1:43–71.

Freedman, Estelle. 1981. *Their Sisters' Keepers*. Ann Arbor: University of Michigan Press.

Gelsthorpe, Loraine. 1986. "Towards a Sceptical Look at Sexism." *International Journal of the Sociology of Law* 14:125–152.

Gora, JoAnn. 1982. *The New Female Criminal: Empirical Reality or Social Myth*. New York: Praeger.

Hagan, John, A. R. Gillis, and John Simpson. 1985. "The Class Structure of Gender and Delinquency: Toward a Power-Control Theory of Common Delinquent Behavior." *American Journal of Sociology* 90:1151–1178.

Hagan, John, John Simpson, and A. R. Gillis. 1987. "Class in the Household: A Power-Control Theory of Gender and Delinquency." *American Journal of Sociology* 92:788–816.

Hancock, Linda. 1981. "The Myth That Females Are Treated More Leniently than Males in the Juvenile Justice System." *Australian and New Zealand Journal of Criminology* 16:4–14.

Harris, Anthony. 1977. "Sex and Theories of Deviance." *American Sociological Review* 42:3–16.

Herman, Julia L. 1981. *Father-Daughter Incest*. Cambridge, MA: Harvard University Press.

Katz, Phyllis A. 1979. "The Development of Female Identity." In *Becoming Female: Perspectives on Development*, edited by Claire B. Kopp. New York: Plenum.

Koroki, Jan and Meda Chesney-Lind. 1985. *Everything Just Going Down the Drain*. Hawaii: Youth Development and Research Center.

Lerner, Gerda. 1986. *The Creation of Patriarchy*. New York: Oxford.

McCormack, Arlene, Mark-David Janus, and Ann Wolbert Burgess. 1986. "Runaway Youths and Sexual Victimization: Gender Differences in an Adolescent Runaway Population." *Child Abuse and Neglect* 10:387–395.

McGarrell, Edmund F. and Timothy J. Flanagan, eds. 1985. *Sourcebook of Criminal Justice Statistics—1984*. Washington, DC: Government Printing Office.

Meiselman, Karen. 1978. *Incest*. San Francisco: Jossey-Bass.

Merton, Robert K. 1938. "Social Structure and Anomie." *American Sociological Review* 3 (October):672–682.

Messerschmidt, James. 1986. *Capitalism, Patriarchy, and Crime: Toward a Socialist Feminist Criminology*. Totowa, NJ: Rowman & Littlefield.

_____ 1987. "Feminism, Criminology, and the Rise of the Female Sex Delinquent, 1880-1930." *Contemporary Crises* 11:243-263.

Miller, Eleanor. 1986. *Street Woman*. Philadelphia: Temple University Press.

Miller, Walter B. 1958. "Lower Class Culture as the Generating Milieu of Gang Delinquency." *Journal of Social Issues* 14:5-19.

Morris, Ruth. 1964. "Female Delinquency and Relational Problems." *Social Forces* 43:82-89.

Mouzakitas, C. M. 1981. "An Inquiry into the Problem of Child Abuse and Juvenile Delinquency." In *Exploring the Relationship Between Child Abuse and Delinquency*, edited by R. J. Hunner and Y. E. Walkers. Montclair, NJ: Allanheld, Osmun.

National Female Advocacy Project. 1981. *Young Women and the Justice System: Basic Facts and Issues*. Tucson, AZ: New Directions for Young Women.

Office of Juvenile Justice and Delinquency Prevention. 1985. *Runaway Children and the Juvenile Justice and Delinquency Prevention Act: What is the Impact?* Washington, DC: Government Printing Office.

_____ 1986. *America's Missing and Exploited Children. Report and Recommendations of the U.S. Attorney General's Advisory Board on Missing Children*. Washington, D.C.: Government Printing Office.

Opinion Research Corporation. 1982. "Public Attitudes Toward Youth Crime: National Public Opinion Poll." Mimeographed. Minnesota: Hubert Humphrey Institute of Public Affairs, University of Minnesota.

Peacock, Carol. 1981. *Hand Me Down Dreams*. New York: Schocken.

Phelps, R.J. et al. 1982. *Wisconsin Female Juvenile Offender Study Project Summary Report*. Wisconsin: Youth Policy and Law Center, Wisconsin Council on Juvenile Justice.

Platt, Anthony M. 1969. *The Childsavers*. Chicago: University of Chicago Press.

Pope, Carl and William H. Feyerherm. 1982. "Gender Bias in Juvenile Court Dispositions." *Social Service Review* 6:1-17.

Rafter, Nicole Hahn. 1985. *Partial Justice*. Boston: Northeastern University Press.

Reich, J. W. and S. E. Gutierres. 1979. "Escape/Aggression Incidence in Sexually Abused Juvenile Delinquents." *Criminal Justice and Behavior* 6:239-243.

Rogers, Kristine. 1972. "'For Her Own Protection...': Conditions of Incarceration for Female Juvenile Offenders in the State of Connecticut." *Law and Society Review* (Winter):223-246.

Rosenberg, Debby and Carol Zimmerman. 1977. *Are My Dreams Too Much to Ask For?* Tucson, AZ: New Directions for Young Women.

Russell, Diana E. 1986. *The Secret Trauma: Incest in the Lives of Girls and Women.* New York: Basic Books.

Schlossman, Steven and Stephanie Wallach. 1978. "The Crime of Precocious Sexuality: Female Juvenile Delinquency in the Progressive Era." *Harvard Educational Review* 48:65–94.

Shaw, Clifford R. 1930. *The Jack-Roller.* Chicago: University of Chicago Press.

_____ 1938. *Brothers in Crime.* Chicago: University of Chicago Press.

_____ and Henry D. McKay. 1942. *Juvenile Delinquency in Urban Areas.* Chicago: University of Chicago Press.

Shelden, Randall. 1981. "Sex Discrimination in the Juvenile Justice System: Memphis, Tennessee, 1900-1917." In *Comparing Female and Male Offenders,* edited by Marguerite Q. Warren. Beverly Hills, CA: Sage.

_____ and John Horvath. 1986. "Processing Offenders in a Juvenile Court: A Comparison of Males and Females." Paper presented at the annual meeting of the Western Society of Criminology, Newport Beach, CA, February 27–March 2.

Silbert, Mimi and Ayala M. Pines. 1981. "Sexual Child Abuse as an Antecedent to Prostitution." *Child Abuse and Neglect* 5:407–411.

Simons, Ronald L., Martin G. Miller, and Stephen M. Aigner. 1980. "Contemporary Theories of Deviance and Female Delinquency: An Empirical Test." *Journal of Research in Crime and Delinquency* 17:42–57.

Smith, Lesley Shacklady. 1978. "Sexist Assumptions and Female Delinquency." In *Women, Sexuality and Social Control,* edited by Carol Smart and Barry Smart. London: Routledge & Kegan Paul.

Snyder, Howard N. and Terrence A. Finnegan. 1987. *Delinquency in the United States.* Washington, DC: Department of Justice.

Steffensmeier, Darrell J. 1980. "Sex Differences in Patterns of Adult Crime, 1965-1977." *Social Forces* 58:1080–1109.

Sutherland, Edwin. 1978. "Differential Association." In *Children of Ishmael: Critical Perspectives on Juvenile Justice,* edited by Barry Krisberg and James Austin. Palo Alto, CA: Mayfield.

Teilmann, Katherine S. and Pierre H. Landry, Jr. 1981. "Gender Bias in Juvenile Justice." *Journal of Research in Crime and Delinquency* 18:47–80.

Thrasher, Frederic M. 1927. *The Gang.* Chicago: University of Chicago Press.

Tracy, Paul E., Marvin E. Wolfgang, and Robert M. Figlio. 1985. *Delinquency in Two Birth Cohorts: Executive Summary.* Washington, DC: Department of Justice.

Widom, Cathy Spatz. 1988. "Child Abuse, Neglect, and Violent Criminal Behavior." Unpublished manuscript.

Name Index

Subject Index

THEORIES OF DEVIANCE, 4TH EDITION

Edited by Gloria Reardon, Belvidere, Illinois
Production supervision by Kim Vander Steen, Palatine, Illinois
Internal design by Lesiak/Crampton Design, Inc., Chicago, Illinois
Cover design by Jeanne Calabrese, Berwyn, Illinois
Composition by Point West, Inc., Carol Stream, Illinois
Printed and bound by Braun-Brumfield, Inc., Ann Arbor, Michigan
Paper, Restorecote
The text is set in Palatino